CONSUMER CREDIT PROTECTION ACT

UNITED STATES CODE

TITLE 15
COMMERCE AND TRADE

CHAPTER 41
CONSUMER CREDIT PROTECTION

15 U.S.C. §§ 1601-1693r,
as amended

Revised
January 2024

CONTENTS

DETAILED CONTENTS

SUBCHAPTER I - Consumer Credit Cost Disclosure (Truth In Lending Act)

SUBCHAPTER II - Restrictions on Garnishment

SUBCHAPTER II-A - Credit Repair Organizations

SUBCHAPTER III - Credit Reporting Agencies (Fair Credit Reporting Act)

SUBCHAPTER IV - Equal Credit Opportunity
(Equal Credit Opportunity Act)

SUBCHAPTER V - Debt Collection Practices
(Fair Debt Collection Practices Act)

SUBCHAPTER VI - Electronic Fund Transfers (Electronic Fund Transfer Act)

TRUTH IN LENDING ACT

15 U.S.C. §§ 1601-1667f, as amended

This Act (Title I of the Consumer Credit Protection Act) authorizes the Commission to enforce compliance by most non-depository entities with a variety of statutory provisions. Among other requirements, the Act requires creditors who deal with consumers to make certain written disclosures concerning finance charges and related aspects of credit transactions (including disclosing an annual percentage rate) and comply with other mandates, and requires advertisements to include certain disclosures. The Act has been amended on numerous occasions, adding requirements for credit cards and open-end credit; for mortgage credit such as ability to repay standards, loan origination, anti-steering, appraisal independence, and mortgage servicing; and others. A number of laws amending and enforced under this Act are listed separately.

Subchapter I, Consumer Credit Cost Disclosure

SUBCHAPTER I—CONSUMER CREDIT COST DISCLOSURE

PART A—GENERAL PROVISIONS

§1601. Congressional findings and declaration of purpose

(a) Informed use of credit

The Congress finds that economic stabilization would be enhanced and the competition among the various financial institutions and other firms engaged in the extension of consumer credit would be strengthened by the informed use of credit. The informed use of credit results from an awareness of the cost thereof by consumers. It is the purpose of this subchapter to assure a meaningful disclosure of credit terms so that the consumer will be able to compare more readily the various credit terms available to him and avoid the uninformed use of credit, and to protect the consumer against inaccurate and unfair credit billing and credit card practices.

(b) Terms of personal property leases

The Congress also finds that there has been a recent trend toward leasing automobiles and other durable goods for consumer use as an alternative to installment credit sales and that these leases have been offered without adequate cost disclosures. It is the purpose of this subchapter to assure a meaningful disclosure of the terms of leases of personal property for personal, family, or household purposes so as to enable the lessee to compare more readily the various lease terms available to him, limit balloon payments in consumer leasing, enable comparison of lease terms with credit terms where appropriate, and to assure meaningful and accurate disclosures of lease terms in advertisements.

(Pub. L. 90–321, title I, §102, May 29, 1968, 82 Stat. 146; Pub. L. 93–495, title III, §302, Oct. 28, 1974, 88 Stat. 1511; Pub. L. 94–240, §2, Mar. 23, 1976, 90 Stat. 257.)

EDITORIAL NOTES

AMENDMENTS

1976—Pub. L. 94–240 designated existing provisions as subsec. (a) and added subsec. (b).
1974—Pub. L. 93–495 inserted provisions expanding purposes of subchapter to include protection of consumer against inaccurate and unfair credit billing and credit card practices.

STATUTORY NOTES AND RELATED SUBSIDIARIES

EFFECTIVE DATE OF 2010 AMENDMENT

Pub. L. 111–203, title XIV, §1400(c), July 21, 2010, 124 Stat. 2136, provided that:
"(1) REGULATIONS.—The regulations required to be prescribed under this title [see Tables for classification] or the amendments made by this title shall—
"(A) be prescribed in final form before the end of the 18-month period beginning on the designated transfer date; and
"(B) take effect not later than 12 months after the date of issuance of the regulations in final form.
"(2) EFFECTIVE DATE ESTABLISHED BY RULE.—Except as provided in paragraph (3), a section, or provision thereof, of this title shall take effect on the date on which the final regulations implementing such section, or provision, take effect.
"(3) EFFECTIVE DATE.—A section of this title for which regulations have not been issued on the date that is 18 months after the designated transfer date shall take effect on such date."

EFFECTIVE DATE OF 1976 AMENDMENT

Amendment by Pub. L. 94–240 effective on expiration of one year after Mar. 23, 1976, see section 6 of Pub. L. 94–240, set out as an Effective Date note under section 1667 of this title.

EFFECTIVE DATE OF 1974 AMENDMENT

For effective date of amendment by Pub. L. 93–495, see section 308 of Pub. L. 93–495, set out as an Effective Date note under section 1666 of this title.

EFFECTIVE DATE

Pub. L. 90–321, title V, §504(a), May 29, 1968, 82 Stat. 167, provided that: "Except as otherwise specified, the provisions of this Act [see Short Title note set out below] take effect upon enactment [May 29, 1968]."

SHORT TITLE OF 2018 AMENDMENT

Pub. L. 115–174, §1(a), May 24, 2018, 132 Stat. 1296, provided that: "This Act [see Tables for classification] may be cited as the 'Economic Growth, Regulatory Relief, and Consumer Protection Act'."

SHORT TITLE OF 2015 AMENDMENT

Pub. L. 114–94, div. G, title LXXXIX, §89001, Dec. 4, 2015, 129 Stat. 1799, provided that: "This title [amending sections 1639c and 1639d of this title and enacting provisions set out as a note under section 5512 of Title 12, Banks and Banking] may be cited as the 'Helping Expand Lending Practices in Rural Communities Act of 2015' or the 'HELP Rural Communities Act of 2015'."

SHORT TITLE OF 2010 AMENDMENT

Pub. L. 111–319, §1, Dec. 18, 2010, 124 Stat. 3457, provided that: "This Act [amending section 1681m of this title and enacting provisions set out as a note under section 1681m of this title] may be cited as the 'Red Flag Program Clarification Act of 2010'."

Pub. L. 111–203, title XIV, §1400(a), July 21, 2010, 124 Stat. 2136, provided that: "This title [see Tables for classification] may be cited as the 'Mortgage Reform and Anti-Predatory Lending Act'."

SHORT TITLE OF 2009 AMENDMENT

Pub. L. 111–93, §1, Nov. 6, 2009, 123 Stat. 2998, provided that: "This Act [amending section 1666b of this title] may be cited as the 'Credit CARD Technical Corrections Act of 2009'."

Pub. L. 111–24, §1(a), May 22, 2009, 123 Stat. 1734, provided that: "This Act [enacting sections 1616, 1651, 1665c to 1665e, 1666i–1, 1666i–2, and 1693l–1 of this title and section 1a–7b of Title 16, Conservation, amending sections 1602, 1632, 1637, 1640, 1650, 1666b, 1666c, 1666j, 1681b, 1681j, and 1693m to 1693r of this title, enacting provisions set out as notes under sections 1602, 1637, 1638, 1666b, 1681j, and 1693l–1 of this title and section 5311 of Title 31, Money and Finance, and amending provisions set out as notes under sections 1638 and 1693 of this title] may be cited as the 'Credit Card Accountability Responsibility and Disclosure Act of 2009' or the 'Credit CARD Act of 2009'."

SHORT TITLE OF 2008 AMENDMENT

Pub. L. 110–315, title X, §1001, Aug. 14, 2008, 122 Stat. 3478, provided that: "This title [enacting section 1650 of this title and sections 1019d and 9709 of Title 20, Education, amending sections 1602, 1603, 1638, and 1640 of this title, section 2903 of Title 12, Banks and Banking, and section 1092 of Title 20, and enacting provisions set out as notes under sections 1638 and 1640 of this title, section 2903 of Title 12, and section 9709 of Title 20] may be cited as the 'Private Student Loan Transparency and Improvement Act of 2008'."

Pub. L. 110–289, div. B, title V, §2501, July 30, 2008, 122 Stat. 2855, provided that: "This title [amending sections 1638 and 1640 of this title and sections 24 and 338a of Title 12, Banks and Banking, and enacting provisions set out as a note under section 1638 of this title] may be cited as the 'Mortgage Disclosure Improvement Act of 2008'."

Pub. L. 110–241, §1, June 3, 2008, 122 Stat. 1565, provided that: "This Act [amending section 1681n of this title and enacting provisions set out as notes under section 1681n of this title] may be cited as the 'Credit and Debit Card Receipt Clarification Act of 2007'."

SHORT TITLE OF 2003 AMENDMENT

Pub. L. 108–159, §1(a), Dec. 4, 2003, 117 Stat. 1952, provided that: "This Act [enacting sections 1681c–1, 1681c–2, 1681s–3, 1681w, and 1681x of this title and sections 9701 to 9708 of Title 20, Education, amending sections 1681a, 1681b, 1681c, 1681g, 1681i, 1681j, 1681m, 1681o, 1681p, 1681s, 1681s–2, 1681t, 1681u, and 1681v of this title and section 5318 of Title 31, Money and Finance, enacting provisions set out as notes under this section, sections 1681, 1681a, 1681b, 1681c, 1681c–1, 1681i, 1681j, 1681m, 1681n, 1681s–2, 1681s–3 of this title, and section 9701 of Title 20, and amending provisions set out as a note under this section] may be cited as the 'Fair and Accurate Credit Transactions Act of 2003'."

SHORT TITLE OF 1999 AMENDMENT

Pub. L. 106–102, title VII, §701, Nov. 12, 1999, 113 Stat. 1463, provided that: "This subtitle [subtitle A (§§701–705) of title VII of Pub. L. 106–102, amending sections 1693b, 1693c, and 1693h of this title] may be cited as the 'ATM Fee Reform Act of 1999'."

SHORT TITLE OF 1998 AMENDMENT

Pub. L. 105–347, §1, Nov. 2, 1998, 112 Stat. 3208, provided that: "This Act [amending sections 1681a to 1681c, 1681g, 1681i, 1681k, and 1681s of this title and enacting provisions set out as a note under section 1681a of this title] may be cited as the 'Consumer Reporting Employment Clarification Act of 1998'."

SHORT TITLE OF 1996 AMENDMENT

Pub. L. 104–208, div. A, title II, §2401, Sept. 30, 1996, 110 Stat. 3009–426, provided that: "This chapter [chapter 1 (§§2401–2422) of subtitle D of title II of div. A of Pub. L. 104–208, enacting section 1681s–2 of this title, amending sections 1681a to 1681e, 1681g to 1681j, 1681m to 1681o, 1681q to 1681s, and 1681t of this title, and enacting provisions set out as notes under sections 1681a, 1681b, and 1681g of this title] may be cited as the 'Consumer Credit Reporting Reform Act of 1996'."

SHORT TITLE OF 1995 AMENDMENTS

Pub. L. 104–29, §1, Sept. 30, 1995, 109 Stat. 271, provided that: "This Act [enacting section 1649 of this title, amending sections 1605, 1631, 1635, 1640, and 1641 of this title, and enacting provisions set out as notes under section 1605 of this title] may be cited as the 'Truth in Lending Act Amendments of 1995'."

Pub. L. 104–12, §1, May 18, 1995, 109 Stat. 161, provided that: "This Act [amending section 1640 of this title] may be cited as the 'Truth in Lending Class Action Relief Act of 1995'."

SHORT TITLE OF 1994 AMENDMENT

Pub. L. 103–325, title I, §151, Sept. 23, 1994, 108 Stat. 2190, provided that: "This subtitle [subtitle B (§§151–158) of title I of Pub. L. 103–325, enacting sections 1639 and 1648 of this title, amending sections 1602, 1604, 1610, 1640, 1641, and 1647 of this title, and enacting provisions set out as notes under this section and section 1602 of this title] may be cited as the 'Home Ownership and Equity Protection Act of 1994'."

SHORT TITLE OF 1992 AMENDMENT

Pub. L. 102–537, §1, Oct. 27, 1992, 106 Stat. 3531, provided that: "This Act [enacting section 1681s–1 of this title, amending section 1681a of this title, and enacting provisions set out as a note under section 1681a of this title] may be cited as the 'Ted Weiss Child Support Enforcement Act of 1992'."

SHORT TITLE OF 1988 AMENDMENTS

Pub. L. 100–709, §1, Nov. 23, 1988, 102 Stat. 4725, provided that: "This Act [enacting sections 1637a, 1647, and 1665b of this title, amending sections 1632 and 1637 of this title, and enacting provisions set out as notes under section 1637a of this title] may be cited as the 'Home Equity Loan Consumer Protection Act of 1988'."

Pub. L. 100–583, §1, Nov. 3, 1988, 102 Stat. 2960, provided that: "This Act [amending sections 1610, 1632, 1637, 1640, and 1646 of this title and enacting provisions set out as a note under section 1637 of this title] may be cited as the 'Fair Credit and Charge Card Disclosure Act of 1988'."

SHORT TITLE OF 1981 AMENDMENT

Pub. L. 97–25, §1, July 27, 1981, 95 Stat. 144, provided: "That this Act [amending sections 1602 and 1666f of this title, section 29 of Title 12, Banks and Banking, and sections 205 and 212 of Title 42, The Public Health and Welfare; enacting provisions set out as notes under this section and sections 1602 and 1666f of this title; and amending provisions set out as notes under sections 1602 and 1666f of this title] may be cited as the 'Cash Discount Act'."

SHORT TITLE OF 1980 AMENDMENT

Pub. L. 96–221, title VI, §601, Mar. 31, 1980, 94 Stat. 168, provided that: "This title [enacting section 1646 of this title, amending sections 57a, 1602 to 1607, 1610, 1612, 1613, 1631, 1632, 1635, 1637, 1638, 1640, 1641, 1643, 1663, 1664, 1665a, 1666, 1666d, 1667d, and 1691f of this title, repealing sections 1614, 1636, and 1639 of this title, and enacting provisions set out as notes under sections 1602 and 1607 of this title] may be cited as the 'Truth in Lending Simplification and Reform Act'."

SHORT TITLE OF 1976 AMENDMENTS

Pub. L. 94–240, §1, Mar. 23, 1976, 90 Stat. 257, provided that: "This Act [enacting sections 1667 to 1667e of this title, amending this section and section 1640 of this title, and enacting provisions set out as a note under section 1667 of this title] may be cited as the 'Consumer Leasing Act of 1976'."

Pub. L. 94–239, §1(a), Mar. 23, 1976, 90 Stat. 251, provided that: "This Act [enacting section 1691f of this title, amending this section and sections 1691b, 1691c, 1691d, 1691e of this title, repealing section 1609 of this title, enacting provisions set out as notes under this section, and repealing provision set out as a note under this section] may be cited as the 'Equal Credit Opportunity Act Amendments of 1976'."

SHORT TITLE OF 1974 AMENDMENT

Pub. L. 93–495, title III, §301, Oct. 28, 1974, 88 Stat. 1511, provided that: "This title [enacting sections 1666 to 1666j of this title, amending this section and sections 1602, 1610, 1631, 1632, and 1637 of this title, and enacting provision set out as a note under section 1666 of this title] may be cited as the 'Fair Credit Billing Act'."

Pub. L. 93–495, title V, §501, Oct. 28, 1974, 88 Stat. 1521, which provided that title V of Pub. L. 93–495 (enacting subchapter IV of this chapter and notes set out under section 1691 of this title) could be cited as the "Equal Credit Opportunity Act", was repealed by Pub. L. 94–239, §1(c), Mar. 23, 1976, 90 Stat. 251.

SHORT TITLE

Pub. L. 90–321, §1, May 29, 1968, 82 Stat. 146, provided that: "This Act [enacting this chapter, sections 891 to 896 of Title 18, Crimes and Criminal Procedure, and provisions set out as notes under this section, sections 1631 and 1671 of this title, and section 891 of Title 18] may be cited as the 'Consumer Credit Protection Act'."

Pub. L. 90–321, title I, §101, May 29, 1968, 82 Stat. 146, provided that: "This title [enacting this subchapter] may be cited as the 'Truth in Lending Act'."

Pub. L. 90–321, title IV, §401, as added by Pub. L. 104–208, div. A, title II, §2451, Sept. 30, 1996, 110 Stat. 3009–454, provided that: "This title [enacting subchapter II–A of this chapter] may be cited as the 'Credit Repair Organizations Act'."

Pub. L. 90–321, title VI, §601, as added by Pub. L. 91–508, title VI, §601, Oct. 26, 1970, 84 Stat. 1128, as amended by Pub. L. 108–159, title VIII, §811(a), Dec. 4, 2003, 117 Stat. 2011, provided that: "This title [enacting subchapter III of this chapter] may be cited as the 'Fair Credit Reporting Act'."

Pub. L. 90–321, title VII, §709, as added by Pub. L. 94–239, §1(b), Mar. 23, 1976, 90 Stat. 251, provided that: "This title [enacting subchapter IV of this chapter and notes set out under section 1691 of this title] may be cited as the 'Equal Credit Opportunity Act'."

Pub. L. 90–321, title VIII, §801, as added by Pub. L. 95–109, Sept. 20, 1977, 91 Stat. 874, provided that: "This title [enacting subchapter V of this chapter] may be cited as the 'Fair Debt Collection Practices Act'."

Pub. L. 90–321, title IX, §901, as added by Pub. L. 95–630, title XX, §2001, Nov. 10, 1978, 92 Stat. 3728, provided that: "This title [enacting subchapter VI of this chapter] may be cited as the 'Electronic Fund Transfer Act'."

SEVERABILITY

Pub. L. 90–321, title V, §501, May 29, 1968, 82 Stat. 167, provided that: "If a provision enacted by this Act [see Short Title note above], is held invalid, all valid provisions that are severable from the invalid provision remain in effect. If a provision enacted by this Act is held invalid in one or more of its applications, the provision remains in effect in all valid applications that are severable from the invalid application or applications."

EXEMPTION OR MODIFICATION OF MORTGAGE DISCLOSURE REQUIREMENTS

Pub. L. 111–203, title XIV, §1405(b), July 21, 2010, 124 Stat. 2142, provided that: "Notwithstanding any other provision of this title [see Tables for classification], in order to improve consumer awareness and understanding of transactions involving residential mortgage loans through the use of disclosures, the Board may, by rule, exempt from or modify disclosure requirements, in whole or in part, for any class of residential mortgage loans if the Board determines that such exemption or modification is in the interest of consumers and in the public interest."

ANALYSIS OF FURTHER RESTRICTIONS ON OFFERS OF CREDIT OR INSURANCE

Pub. L. 108–159, title II, §213(e), Dec. 4, 2003, 117 Stat. 1979, provided that:

"(1) IN GENERAL.—The Board shall conduct a study of—

"(A) the ability of consumers to avoid receiving written offers of credit or insurance in connection with transactions not initiated by the consumer; and

"(B) the potential impact that any further restrictions on providing consumers with such written offers of credit or insurance would have on consumers.

"(2) REPORT.—The Board shall submit a report summarizing the results of the study required under paragraph (1) to the Congress not later than 12 months after the date of enactment of this Act [Dec. 4, 2003], together with such recommendations for legislative or administrative action as the Board may determine to be appropriate.

"(3) CONTENT OF REPORT.—The report described in paragraph (2) shall address the following issues:

"(A) The current statutory or voluntary mechanisms that are available to a consumer to notify lenders and insurance providers that the consumer does not wish to receive written offers of credit or insurance.

"(B) The extent to which consumers are currently utilizing existing statutory and voluntary mechanisms to avoid receiving offers of credit or insurance.

"(C) The benefits provided to consumers as a result of receiving written offers of credit or insurance.

"(D) Whether consumers incur significant costs or are otherwise adversely affected by the receipt of written offers of credit or insurance.

"(E) Whether further restricting the ability of lenders and insurers to provide written offers of credit or insurance to consumers would affect—

"(i) the cost consumers pay to obtain credit or insurance;

"(ii) the availability of credit or insurance;

"(iii) consumers' knowledge about new or alternative products and services;

"(iv) the ability of lenders or insurers to compete with one another; and

"(v) the ability to offer credit or insurance products to consumers who have been traditionally underserved."

[For definitions of terms used in section 213(e) of Pub. L. 108–159, set out above, see section 2 of Pub. L. 108–159, set out as a Definitions note under section 1681 of this title.]

FEDERAL RESERVE STUDY OF HOME EQUITY LENDING AND APPROPRIATE INTEREST RATE INDEX

Pub. L. 103–325, title I, §157, Sept. 23, 1994, 108 Stat. 2197, provided that during the period beginning 180 days after Sept. 23, 1994, and ending 2 years after that date, the Board of Governors of the Federal Reserve System was to conduct a study and submit to the Congress a report, including recommendations for any appropriate legislation, regarding whether consumers engaging in open end credit transactions as defined in section 1602 of this title secured by principal dwellings have adequate Federal protection and whether a more appropriate interest rate index existed for purposes of section 1602(bb)(1)(A) of this title than the yield on Treasury securities.

HEARINGS ON HOME EQUITY LENDING

Pub. L. 103–325, title I, §158, Sept. 23, 1994, 108 Stat. 2197, as amended by Pub. L. 111–203, title X, §1096, July 21, 2010, 124 Stat. 2102, provided that:

"(a) HEARINGS.—Not less than once during the 3-year period beginning on the date of enactment of this Act [Sept. 23, 1994], and regularly thereafter, the Bureau, in consultation with the Advisory Board to the Bureau, shall conduct a public hearing to examine the home equity loan market and the adequacy of existing regulatory and legislative provisions and the provisions of this subtitle [see Short Title of 1994 Amendment note above] in protecting the interests of consumers, and low-income consumers in particular.

"(b) PARTICIPATION.—In conducting hearings required by subsection (a), the Bureau shall solicit participation from consumers, representatives of consumers, lenders, and other interested parties."

STUDY BY FEDERAL RESERVE BOARD OF GOVERNORS COVERING EFFECT OF CHARGE CARD TRANSACTIONS UPON CARD ISSUERS, MERCHANTS, AND CONSUMERS

Pub. L. 97–25, title II, §202, July 27, 1981, 95 Stat. 145, directed Board of Governors of Federal Reserve System, not later than 2 years after July 27, 1981, to prepare a study and submit its findings to Congress on the effect of charge card transactions upon card issuers, merchants, and consumers.

INFERENCE OF LEGISLATIVE INTENT IN SECTION CAPTIONS AND CATCHLINES

Pub. L. 90–321, title V, §502, May 29, 1968, 82 Stat. 167, provided that: "Captions and catchlines are intended solely as aids to convenient reference, and no inference as to the legislative intent with respect to any provision enacted by this Act [enacting this chapter, section 891 to 896 of Title 18, Crimes and

Criminal Procedure, and provisions set out as notes under this section, sections 1631 and 1671 of this title, and section 891 of Title 18] may be drawn from them."

GRAMMATICAL USAGES

Pub. L. 90–321, title V, §503, May 30, 1968, 82 Stat. 167, provided that: "In this Act [enacting this chapter, sections 891 to 896 of Title 18, Crimes and Criminal Procedure, and provisions set out as notes under this section, sections 1631 and 1671 of this title, and section 891 of Title 18]:

"(1) The word 'may' is used to indicate that an action either is authorized or is permitted.
"(2) The word 'shall' is used to indicate that an action is both authorized and required.
"(3) The phrase 'may not' is used to indicate that an action is both unauthorized and forbidden.
"(4) Rules of law are stated in the indicative mood."

DEFINITION

Pub. L. 111–203, title XIV, §1495, July 21, 2010, 124 Stat. 2207, provided that: "For purposes of this title [see Tables for classification], the term 'designated transfer date' means the date established under section 1062 of this Act [12 U.S.C. 5582]."

§1602. Definitions and rules of construction

(a) The definitions and rules of construction set forth in this section are applicable for the purposes of this subchapter.

(b) BUREAU.—The term "Bureau" means the Bureau of Consumer Financial Protection.

(c) The term "Board" refers to the Board of Governors of the Federal Reserve System.

(d) The term "organization" means a corporation, government or governmental subdivision or agency, trust, estate, partnership, cooperative, or association.

(e) The term "person" means a natural person or an organization.

(f) The term "credit" means the right granted by a creditor to a debtor to defer payment of debt or to incur debt and defer its payment.

(g) The term "creditor" refers only to a person who both (1) regularly extends, whether in connection with loans, sales of property or services, or otherwise, consumer credit which is payable by agreement in more than four installments or for which the payment of a finance charge is or may be required, and (2) is the person to whom the debt arising from the consumer credit transaction is initially payable on the face of the evidence of indebtedness or, if there is no such evidence of indebtedness, by agreement. Notwithstanding the preceding sentence, in the case of an open-end credit plan involving a credit card, the card issuer and any person who honors the credit card and offers a discount which is a finance charge are creditors. For the purpose of the requirements imposed under part D of this subchapter and sections 1637(a)(5), 1637(a)(6), 1637(a)(7), 1637(b)(1), 1637(b)(2), 1637(b)(3), 1637(b)(8), and 1637(b)(10) of this title, the term "creditor" shall also include card issuers whether or not the amount due is payable by agreement in more than four installments or the payment of a finance charge is or may be required, and the Bureau shall, by regulation, apply these requirements to such card issuers, to the extent appropriate, even though the requirements are by their terms applicable only to creditors offering open-end credit plans. Any person who originates 2 or more mortgages referred to in subsection (aa) in any 12-month period or any person who originates 1 or more such mortgages through a mortgage broker shall be considered to be a creditor for purposes of this subchapter. The term "creditor" includes a private educational lender (as that term is defined in section 1650 of this title) for purposes of this subchapter.

(h) The term "credit sale" refers to any sale in which the seller is a creditor. The term includes any contract in the form of a bailment or lease if the bailee or lessee contracts to pay as compensation for use a sum substantially equivalent to or in excess of the aggregate value of the property and services involved and it is agreed that the bailee or lessee will become, or for no other or a nominal consideration has the option to become, the owner of the property upon full compliance with his obligations under the contract.

(i) The adjective "consumer", used with reference to a credit transaction, characterizes the transaction as one in which the party to whom credit is offered or extended is a natural person, and the money, property, or services which are the subject of the transaction are primarily for personal, family, or household purposes.

(j) The terms "open end credit plan" and "open end consumer credit plan" mean a plan under which the creditor reasonably contemplates repeated transactions, which prescribes the terms of such transactions, and which provides for a finance charge which may be computed from time to time on the outstanding unpaid balance. A credit plan or open end consumer credit plan which is an open end credit plan or open end consumer credit plan within the meaning of the preceding sentence is an open end credit plan or open end consumer credit plan even if credit information is verified from time to time.

(k) The term "adequate notice," as used in section 1643 of this title, means a printed notice to a cardholder which sets forth the pertinent facts clearly and conspicuously so that a person against whom it is to operate could reasonably be expected to have noticed it and understood its meaning. Such notice may be given to a cardholder by printing the notice on any credit card, or on each periodic statement of account, issued to the cardholder, or by any other means reasonably assuring the receipt thereof by the cardholder.

(l) The term "credit card" means any card, plate, coupon book or other credit device existing for the purpose of obtaining money, property, labor, or services on credit.

(m) The term "accepted credit card" means any credit card which the cardholder has requested and received or has signed or has used, or authorized another to use, for the purpose of obtaining money, property, labor, or services on credit.

(n) The term "cardholder" means any person to whom a credit card is issued or any person who has agreed with the card issuer to pay obligations arising from the issuance of a credit card to another person.

(o) The term "card issuer" means any person who issues a credit card, or the agent of such person with respect to such card.

(p) The term "unauthorized use," as used in section 1643 of this title, means a use of a credit card by a person other than the cardholder who does not have actual, implied, or apparent authority for such use and from which the cardholder receives no benefit.

(q) The term "discount" as used in section 1666f of this title means a reduction made from the regular price. The term "discount" as used in section 1666f of this title shall not mean a surcharge.

(r) The term "surcharge" as used in this section and section 1666f of this title means any means of increasing the regular price to a cardholder which is not imposed upon customers paying by cash, check, or similar means."

(s) The term "State" refers to any State, the Commonwealth of Puerto Rico, the District of Columbia, and any territory or possession of the United States.

(t) The term "agricultural purposes" includes the production, harvest, exhibition, marketing, transportation, processing, or manufacture of agricultural products by a natural person who cultivates, plants, propagates, or nurtures those agricultural products, including but not limited to the acquisition of farmland, real property with a farm residence, and personal property and services used primarily in farming.

(u) The term "agricultural products" includes agricultural, horticultural, viticultural, and dairy products, livestock, wildlife, poultry, bees, forest products, fish and shellfish, and any products thereof, including processed and manufactured products, and any and all products raised or produced on farms and any processed or manufactured products thereof.

(v) The term "material disclosures" means the disclosure, as required by this subchapter, of the annual percentage rate, the method of determining the finance charge and the balance upon which a finance charge will be imposed, the amount of the finance charge, the amount to be financed, the total of payments, the number and amount of payments, the due dates or periods of payments scheduled to repay the indebtedness, and the disclosures required by section 1639(a) of this title.

(w) The term "dwelling" means a residential structure or mobile home which contains one to four family housing units, or individual units of condominiums or cooperatives.

(x) The term "residential mortgage transaction" means a transaction in which a mortgage, deed of trust, purchase money security interest arising under an installment sales contract, or equivalent consensual security interest is created or retained against the consumer's dwelling to finance the acquisition or initial construction of such dwelling.

(y) As used in this section and section 1666f of this title, the term "regular price" means the tag or posted price charged for the property or service if a single price is tagged or posted, or the price charged for the property or service when payment is made by use of an open-end credit plan or a credit card if either (1) no price is tagged or posted, or (2) two prices are tagged or posted, one of which is charged when payment is made by use of an open-end credit plan or a credit card and the other when payment is made by use of cash, check, or similar means. For purposes of this definition, payment by check, draft, or other negotiable instrument which may result in the debiting of an open-end credit plan or a credit cardholder's open-end account shall not be considered payment made by use of the plan or the account.

(z) Any reference to any requirement imposed under this subchapter or any provision thereof includes reference to the regulations of the Bureau under this subchapter or the provision thereof in question.

(aa) The disclosure of an amount or percentage which is greater than the amount or percentage required to be disclosed under this subchapter does not in itself constitute a violation of this subchapter.

(bb) HIGH-COST MORTGAGE.—

(1) DEFINITION.—

(A) IN GENERAL.—The term "high-cost mortgage", and a mortgage referred to in this subsection, means a consumer credit transaction that is secured by the consumer's principal dwelling, other than a reverse mortgage transaction, if—

(i) in the case of a credit transaction secured—

(I) by a first mortgage on the consumer's principal dwelling, the annual percentage rate at consummation of the transaction will exceed by more than 6.5 percentage points (8.5 percentage points, if the dwelling is personal property and the transaction is for less than $50,000) the average prime offer rate, as defined in section 1639c(b)(2)(B) of this title, for a comparable transaction; or

(II) by a subordinate or junior mortgage on the consumer's principal dwelling, the annual percentage rate at consummation of the transaction will exceed by more than 8.5 percentage points the average prime offer rate, as defined in section 1639c(b)(2)(B) of this title, for a comparable transaction;

(ii) the total points and fees payable in connection with the transaction, other than bona fide third party charges not retained by the mortgage originator, creditor, or an affiliate of the creditor or mortgage originator, exceed—

(I) in the case of a transaction for $20,000 or more, 5 percent of the total transaction amount; or
(II) in the case of a transaction for less than $20,000, the lesser of 8 percent of the total transaction amount or $1,000 (or such other dollar amount as the Board shall prescribe by regulation); or

(iii) the credit transaction documents permit the creditor to charge or collect prepayment fees or penalties more than 36 months after the transaction closing or such fees or penalties exceed, in the aggregate, more than 2 percent of the amount prepaid.

(B) INTRODUCTORY RATES TAKEN INTO ACCOUNT.—For purposes of subparagraph (A)(i), the annual percentage rate of interest shall be determined based on the following interest rate:
(i) In the case of a fixed-rate transaction in which the annual percentage rate will not vary during the term of the loan, the interest rate in effect on the date of consummation of the transaction.
(ii) In the case of a transaction in which the rate of interest varies solely in accordance with an index, the interest rate determined by adding the index rate in effect on the date of consummation of the transaction to the maximum margin permitted at any time during the loan agreement.
(iii) In the case of any other transaction in which the rate may vary at any time during the term of the loan for any reason, the interest charged on the transaction at the maximum rate that may be charged during the term of the loan.

(C) MORTGAGE INSURANCE.—For the purposes of computing the total points and fees under paragraph (4), the total points and fees shall exclude—
(i) any premium provided by an agency of the Federal Government or an agency of a State;
(ii) any amount that is not in excess of the amount payable under policies in effect at the time of origination under section 203(c)(2)(A) of the National Housing Act (12 U.S.C. 1709(c)(2)(A)), provided that the premium, charge, or fee is required to be refundable on a pro-rated basis and the refund is automatically issued upon notification of the satisfaction of the underlying mortgage loan; and
(iii) any premium paid by the consumer after closing.

(2)(A) After the 2-year period beginning on the effective date of the regulations promulgated under section 155 of the Riegle Community Development and Regulatory Improvement Act of 1994, and no more frequently than biennially after the first increase or decrease under this subparagraph, the Bureau may by regulation increase or decrease the number of percentage points specified in paragraph (1)(A), if the Bureau determines that the increase or decrease is—
(i) consistent with the consumer protections against abusive lending provided by the amendments made by subtitle B of title I of the Riegle Community Development and Regulatory Improvement Act of 1994; and
(ii) warranted by the need for credit.

(B) An increase or decrease under subparagraph (A)—
(i) may not result in the number of percentage points referred to in paragraph (1)(A)(i)(I) being less than 6 percentage points or greater than 10 percentage points; and
(ii) may not result in the number of percentage points referred to in paragraph (1)(A)(i)(II) being less than 8 percentage points or greater than 12 percentage points.

(C) In determining whether to increase or decrease the number of percentage points referred to in subparagraph (A), the Bureau shall consult with representatives of consumers, including low-income consumers, and lenders.
(3) The amount specified in paragraph (1)(B)(ii) shall be adjusted annually on January 1 by the annual percentage change in the Consumer Price Index, as reported on June 1 of the year preceding such adjustment.
(4) For purposes of paragraph (1)(B), points and fees shall include—
(A) all items included in the finance charge, except interest or the time-price differential;
(B) all compensation paid directly or indirectly by a consumer or creditor to a mortgage originator from any source, including a mortgage originator that is also the creditor in a table-funded transaction;
(C) each of the charges listed in section 1605(e) of this title (except an escrow for future payment of taxes), unless—
(i) the charge is reasonable;
(ii) the creditor receives no direct or indirect compensation; and
(iii) the charge is paid to a third party unaffiliated with the creditor; and

(D) premiums or other charges payable at or before closing for any credit life, credit disability, credit unemployment, or credit property insurance, or any other accident, loss-of-income, life or health insurance, or any payments directly or indirectly for any debt cancellation or suspension agreement or contract, except that insurance premiums or debt cancellation or suspension fees calculated and paid in full on a monthly basis shall not be considered financed by the creditor;
(E) the maximum prepayment fees and penalties which may be charged or collected under the terms of the credit transaction;

(F) all prepayment fees or penalties that are incurred by the consumer if the loan refinances a previous loan made or currently held by the same creditor or an affiliate of the creditor; and

(G) such other charges as the Bureau determines to be appropriate.

(5) CALCULATION OF POINTS AND FEES FOR OPEN-END CONSUMER CREDIT PLANS.—In the case of open-end consumer credit plans, points and fees shall be calculated, for purposes of this section and section 1639 of this title, by adding the total points and fees known at or before closing, including the maximum prepayment penalties which may be charged or collected under the terms of the credit transaction, plus the minimum additional fees the consumer would be required to pay to draw down an amount equal to the total credit line.

(6) This subsection shall not be construed to limit the rate of interest or the finance charge that a person may charge a consumer for any extension of credit.

(cc) The term "reverse mortgage transaction" means a nonrecourse transaction in which a mortgage, deed of trust, or equivalent consensual security interest is created against the consumer's principal dwelling—

(1) securing one or more advances; and

(2) with respect to which the payment of any principal, interest, and shared appreciation or equity is due and payable (other than in the case of default) only after—

(A) the transfer of the dwelling;

(B) the consumer ceases to occupy the dwelling as a principal dwelling; or

(C) the death of the consumer.

(dd) DEFINITIONS RELATING TO MORTGAGE ORIGINATION AND RESIDENTIAL MORTGAGE LOANS.—

(1) COMMISSION.—Unless otherwise specified, the term "Commission" means the Federal Trade Commission.

(2) MORTGAGE ORIGINATOR.—The term "mortgage originator"—

(A) means any person who, for direct or indirect compensation or gain, or in the expectation of direct or indirect compensation or gain—

(i) takes a residential mortgage loan application;

(ii) assists a consumer in obtaining or applying to obtain a residential mortgage loan; or

(iii) offers or negotiates terms of a residential mortgage loan;

(B) includes any person who represents to the public, through advertising or other means of communicating or providing information (including the use of business cards, stationery, brochures, signs, rate lists, or other promotional items), that such person can or will provide any of the services or perform any of the activities described in subparagraph (A);

(C) does not include any person who is—

(i) not otherwise described in subparagraph (A) or (B) and who performs purely administrative or clerical tasks on behalf of a person who is described in any such subparagraph; or

(ii) a retailer of manufactured or modular homes or an employee of the retailer if the retailer or employee, as applicable—

(I) does not receive compensation or gain for engaging in activities described in subparagraph (A) that is in excess of any compensation or gain received in a comparable cash transaction;

(II) discloses to the consumer—

(aa) in writing any corporate affiliation with any creditor; and

(bb) if the retailer has a corporate affiliation with any creditor, at least 1 unaffiliated creditor; and

(III) does not directly negotiate with the consumer or lender on loan terms (including rates, fees, and other costs).

(D) does not include a person or entity that only performs real estate brokerage activities and is licensed or registered in accordance with applicable State law, unless such person or entity is compensated by a lender, a mortgage broker, or other mortgage originator or by any agent of such lender, mortgage broker, or other mortgage originator;

(E) does not include, with respect to a residential mortgage loan, a person, estate, or trust that provides mortgage financing for the sale of 3 properties in any 12-month period to purchasers of such properties, each of which is owned by such person, estate, or trust and serves as security for the loan, provided that such loan—

(i) is not made by a person, estate, or trust that has constructed, or acted as a contractor for the construction of, a residence on the property in the ordinary course of business of such person, estate, or trust;

(ii) is fully amortizing;

(iii) is with respect to a sale for which the seller determines in good faith and documents that the buyer has a reasonable ability to repay the loan;

(iv) has a fixed rate or an adjustable rate that is adjustable after 5 or more years, subject to reasonable annual and lifetime limitations on interest rate increases; and

(v) meets any other criteria the Board may prescribe;

(F) does not include the creditor (except the creditor in a table-funded transaction) under paragraph (1), (2), or (4) of section 1639b(c) of this title; and

(G) does not include a servicer or servicer employees, agents and contractors, including but not limited to those who offer or negotiate terms of a residential mortgage loan for purposes of renegotiating, modifying, replacing and subordinating principal of existing mortgages where borrowers are behind in their payments, in default or have a reasonable likelihood of being in default or falling behind.

(3) NATIONWIDE MORTGAGE LICENSING SYSTEM AND REGISTRY.—The term "Nationwide Mortgage Licensing System and Registry" has the same meaning as in the Secure and Fair Enforcement for Mortgage Licensing Act of 2008 [12 U.S.C. 5101 et seq.].

(4) OTHER DEFINITIONS RELATING TO MORTGAGE ORIGINATOR.—For purposes of this subsection, a person "assists a consumer in obtaining or applying to obtain a residential mortgage loan" by, among other things, advising on residential mortgage loan terms (including rates, fees, and other costs), preparing residential mortgage loan packages, or collecting information on behalf of the consumer with regard to a residential mortgage loan.

(5) RESIDENTIAL MORTGAGE LOAN.—The term "residential mortgage loan" means any consumer credit transaction that is secured by a mortgage, deed of trust, or other equivalent consensual security interest on a dwelling or on residential real property that includes a dwelling, other than a consumer credit transaction under an open end credit plan or, for purposes of sections 1639b and 1639c of this title and section 1638(a) (16), (17), (18), and (19) of this title, and sections 1638(f) and 1640(k) of this title, and any regulations promulgated thereunder, an extension of credit relating to a plan described in section 101(53D) of title 11.

(6) SECRETARY.—The term "Secretary", when used in connection with any transaction or person involved with a residential mortgage loan, means the Secretary of Housing and Urban Development.

(7) SERVICER.—The term "servicer" has the same meaning as in section 2605(i)(2) of title 12.

(ee) BONA FIDE DISCOUNT POINTS AND PREPAYMENT PENALTIES.—For the purposes of determining the amount of points and fees for purposes of subsection (aa), either the amounts described in paragraph (1) or (2) of the following paragraphs, but not both, shall be excluded:

(1) Up to and including 2 bona fide discount points payable by the consumer in connection with the mortgage, but only if the interest rate from which the mortgage's interest rate will be discounted does not exceed by more than 1 percentage point—

(A) the average prime offer rate, as defined in section 1639c of this title; or

(B) if secured by a personal property loan, the average rate on a loan in connection with which insurance is provided under title I of the National Housing Act (12 U.S.C. 1702 et seq.).

(2) Unless 2 bona fide discount points have been excluded under paragraph (1), up to and including 1 bona fide discount point payable by the consumer in connection with the mortgage, but only if the interest rate from which the mortgage's interest rate will be discounted does not exceed by more than 2 percentage points—

(A) the average prime offer rate, as defined in section 1639c of this title; or

(B) if secured by a personal property loan, the average rate on a loan in connection with which insurance is provided under title I of the National Housing Act (12 U.S.C. 1702 et seq.).

(3) For purposes of paragraph (1), the term "bona fide discount points" means loan discount points which are knowingly paid by the consumer for the purpose of reducing, and which in fact result in a bona fide reduction of, the interest rate or time-price differential applicable to the mortgage.

(4) Paragraphs (1) and (2) shall not apply to discount points used to purchase an interest rate reduction unless the amount of the interest rate reduction purchased is reasonably consistent with established industry norms and practices for secondary mortgage market transactions.

(Pub. L. 90–321, title I, §103, May 29, 1968, 82 Stat. 147; Pub. L. 91–508, title V, §501, Oct. 26, 1970, 84 Stat. 1126; Pub. L. 93–495, title III, §303, Oct. 28, 1974, 88 Stat. 1511; Pub. L. 94–222, §3(a), Feb. 27, 1976, 90 Stat. 197; Pub. L. 96–221, title VI, §§602, 603(a), (b), 604, 612(a)(2), (b), Mar. 31, 1980, 94 Stat. 168, 169, 175, 176; Pub. L. 97–25, title I, §102, July 27, 1981, 95 Stat. 144; Pub. L. 97–320, title VII, §702(a), Oct. 15, 1982, 96 Stat. 1538; Pub. L. 103–325, title I, §§152(a)–(c), 154(a), Sept. 23, 1994, 108 Stat. 2190, 2191, 2196; Pub. L. 110–315, title X, §1011(b), Aug. 14, 2008, 122 Stat. 3481; Pub. L. 111–24, title I, §108, May 22, 2009, 123 Stat. 1743; Pub. L. 111–203, title X, §1100A(1), (2), title XIV, §§1401, 1431, July 21, 2010, 124 Stat. 2107, 2137, 2157; Pub. L. 115–174, title I, §107, May 24, 2018, 132 Stat. 1304.)

EDITORIAL NOTES

REFERENCES IN TEXT

The Riegle Community Development and Regulatory Improvement Act of 1994, referred to in subsec. (bb)(2)(A)(i), is Pub. L. 103–325, Sept. 23, 1994, 108 Stat. 2160. Section 155 of the Act is set out below. For classification of subtitle B of title I of the Act, known as the "Home Ownership and Equity Protection Act of

1994", see Short Title of 1994 Amendment note set out under section 1601 of this title. For complete classification of this Act to the Code, see Short Title note set out under section 4701 of Title 12, Banks and Banking, and Tables.

The Secure and Fair Enforcement for Mortgage Licensing Act of 2008, referred to in subsec. (dd)(3), is title V of div. A of Pub. L. 110–289, July 30, 2008, 122 Stat. 2810, also known as the S.A.F.E. Mortgage Licensing Act of 2008, which is classified generally to chapter 51 (§5101 et seq.) of Title 12, Banks and Banking. For complete classification of this Act to the Code, see Short Title note set out under section 5101 of Title 12 and Tables.

The National Housing Act, referred to in subsec. (ee)(1)(B), (2)(B), is act June 27, 1934, ch. 847, 48 Stat. 1246. Title I of the Act is classified generally to subchapter II (§1702 et seq.) of chapter 13 of Title 12, Banks and Banking. For complete classification of this Act to the Code, see section 1701 of Title 12 and Tables.

AMENDMENTS

2018—Subsecs. (cc), (dd). Pub. L. 115–174, §107(1), redesignated subsec. (cc), relating to definitions relating to mortgage origination and residential mortgage loans, as (dd). Former subsec. (dd) redesignated (ee).

Subsec. (dd)(2)(C). Pub. L. 115–174, §107(2), added subpar. (C) and struck out former subpar. (C) which read as follows: "does not include any person who is (i) not otherwise described in subparagraph (A) or (B) and who performs purely administrative or clerical tasks on behalf of a person who is described in any such subparagraph, or (ii) an employee of a retailer of manufactured homes who is not described in clause (i) or (iii) of subparagraph (A) and who does not advise a consumer on loan terms (including rates, fees, and other costs);".

Subsec. (ee). Pub. L. 115–174, §107(1), redesignated subsec. (dd) as (ee).

2010—Pub. L. 111–203, §1100A(2), which directed substitution of "Bureau" for "Board" wherever appearing, was executed by making the substitution wherever appearing in subsecs. (g), (z), and (bb)(2) (A), (C), (4)(D), but not in subsec. (c), to reflect the probable intent of Congress.

Subsecs. (b) to (z). Pub. L. 111–203, §1100(A)(1), added subsec. (b) and redesignated former subsecs. (b) to (z) as (c) to (aa), respectively.

Subsec. (bb). Pub. L. 111–203, §1431(a), which directed amendment of subsec. (aa) by inserting subsec. heading, adding par. (1), and striking out former par. (1), was executed by making the amendment to subsec. (bb) to reflect the probable intent of Congress and the redesignation of subsec. (aa) as (bb) by Pub. L. 111–203, §1100(A)(1). See below. Text of former par. (1) read as follows: "A mortgage referred to in this subsection means a consumer credit transaction that is secured by the consumer's principal dwelling, other than a residential mortgage transaction, a reverse mortgage transaction, or a transaction under an open end credit plan, if—

"(A) the annual percentage rate at consummation of the transaction will exceed by more than 10 percentage points the yield on Treasury securities having comparable periods of maturity on the fifteenth day of the month immediately preceding the month in which the application for the extension of credit is received by the creditor; or

"(B) the total points and fees payable by the consumer at or before closing will exceed the greater of—

"(i) 8 percent of the total loan amount; or
"(ii) $400."

Pub. L. 111–203, §1100(A)(1), redesignated subsec. (aa) as (bb). Former subsec. (bb) redesignated (cc).

Subsec. (bb)(2)(B). Pub. L. 111–203, §1431(b), which directed amendment of subsec. (aa)(2) by adding subpar. (B) and striking out former subpar. (B), was executed by making the amendment to subsec. (bb) (2) to reflect the probable intent of Congress and the redesignation of subsec. (aa) as (bb) by Pub. L. 111–203, §1100(A)(1). See above. Text of former subpar. (B) read as follows: "An increase or decrease under subparagraph (A) may not result in the number of percentage points referred to in subparagraph (A) being—

"(i) less that 8 percentage points; or
"(ii) greater than 12 percentage points."

Subsec. (bb)(4)(B). Pub. L. 111–203, §1431(c)(1)(A), which directed amendment of subsec. (aa)(4) by adding subpar. (B) and struck out former subpar. (B), was executed by making the amendment to subsec. (bb)(4) to reflect the probable intent of Congress and the redesignation of subsec. (aa) as (bb) by Pub. L. 111–203, §1100(A)(1). See above. Text of former subpar. (B) read as follows: "all compensation paid to mortgage brokers;".

Subsec. (bb)(4)(D) to (G). Pub. L. 111–203, §1431(c)(1)(B), (C), which directed amendment of subsec. (aa)(4) by adding subpars. (D) to (F) and redesignating former subpar. (D) as (G), was executed by making the amendment to subsec. (bb)(4) to reflect the probable intent of Congress and the redesignation of subsec. (aa) as (bb) by Pub. L. 111–203, §1100(A)(1). See above.

Subsec. (bb)(5), (6). Pub. L. 111–203, §1431(c)(2), which directed amendment of subsec. (aa) by adding par. (5) and redesignating former par. (5) as (6), was executed by making the amendment to subsec. (bb) to reflect the probable intent of Congress and the redesignation of subsec. (aa) as (bb) by Pub. L. 111–203, §1100(A)(1). See above.

Subsec. (cc). Pub. L. 111–203, §1401, added subsec. (cc) relating to definitions relating to mortgage origination and residential mortgage loans.

Pub. L. 111–203, §1100(A)(1), redesignated subsec. (bb) as (cc) defining the term "reverse mortgage transaction".

Subsec. (dd). Pub. L. 111–203, §1431(d), added subsec. (dd).

2009—Subsec. (i). Pub. L. 111–24 substituted "terms 'open end credit plan' and 'open end consumer credit plan' mean" for "term 'open end credit plan' means" in first sentence and inserted "or open end consumer credit plan" after "credit plan" wherever appearing in second sentence.

2008—Subsec. (f). Pub. L. 110–315 inserted at end "The term 'creditor' includes a private educational lender (as that term is defined in section 1650 of this title) for purposes of this subchapter."

1994—Subsec. (f). Pub. L. 103–325, §152(c), inserted at end "Any person who originates 2 or more mortgages referred to in subsection (aa) in any 12-month period or any person who originates 1 or more such mortgages through a mortgage broker shall be considered to be a creditor for purposes of this subchapter."

Subsec. (u). Pub. L. 103–325, §152(b), substituted "the due dates" for "and the due dates" and inserted before period at end ", and the disclosures required by section 1639(a) of this title".

Subsec. (aa). Pub. L. 103–325, §152(a), added subsec. (aa).

Subsec. (bb). Pub. L. 103–325, §154(a), added subsec. (bb).

1982—Subsec. (f). Pub. L. 97–320 struck out provision that a person who regularly arranged for the extension of consumer credit payable in more than four installments or for which the payment of a finance charge was or might have been required from persons not creditors was a creditor, and provision that this subchapter applied to any creditor, irrespective of his or its status as a natural person or any type of organization, who was a card issuer.

1981—Subsecs. (x) to (z). Pub. L. 97–25 added subsec. (z) and, effective Apr. 10, 1982, redesignated subsecs. (x), (y), and (z) as (y), (z), and (x), respectively.

1980—Subsec. (f). Pub. L. 96–221, §602(a), substituted provisions defining term "creditor" as referring only to a person who both regularly extends consumer credit, subject to specified conditions, and is the person to whom the debt arising is initially payable on the face of the indebtedness or by agreement, and notwithstanding such provisions, also refers to a person regularly arranging for the extension of consumer credit, and a card issuer and any person honoring the credit card, subject to specified conditions, for provisions defining term "creditor" as referring only to creditors who regularly extend, or arrange for the extension of credit payable in more than four installments or where a finance charge is or may be required, and substituted "(a)(5)" for "(a)(6)", "(a)(6)" for "(a)(7)", "(a)(7)" for "(a)(8)", "(b)(8)" for "(b)(9)", and "(b)(10)" for "(b)(11)".

Subsec. (g). Pub. L. 96–221, §602(b), substituted "in which the seller is a creditor" for "with respect to which credit is extended or arranged by the seller".

Subsec. (h). Pub. L. 96–221, §603(a), struck out applicability to agricultural purposes.

Subsec. (i). Pub. L. 96–221, §604, inserted provisions respecting the reasonable contemplations of the creditor, and verification of credit information from time to time.

Subsecs. (s), (t). Pub. L. 96–221, §603(b), added subsecs. (s) and (t). Former subsecs. (s) and (t) redesignated (x) and (y), respectively.

Subsec. (u). Pub. L. 96–221, §612(a)(2), added subsec. (u).

Subsecs. (v), (w). Pub. L. 96–221, §612(b), added subsecs. (v) and (w).

Subsecs. (x), (y). Pub. L. 96–221, §603(b), redesignated former subsecs. (s) and (t) as (x) and (y), respectively.

1976—Subsecs. (p) to (t). Pub. L. 94–222 added subsecs. (p) and (q) and redesignated former subsecs. (p) to (r) as (r) to (t), respectively.

1974—Subsec. (f). Pub. L. 93–495 inserted provision requiring the credit to be payable by agreement in more than four installments and defining term "creditor" for the purposes of the requirements imposed under the enumerated sections of this chapter.

1970—Subsecs. (j) to (r). Pub. L. 91–508 added subsecs. (j) to (o) and redesignated former subsecs. (j) to (l) as (p) to (r), respectively.

STATUTORY NOTES AND RELATED SUBSIDIARIES

EFFECTIVE DATE OF 2010 AMENDMENT

Amendment by section 1100A(1), (2) of Pub. L. 111–203 effective on the designated transfer date, see section 1100H of Pub. L. 111–203, set out as a note under section 552a of Title 5, Government Organization and Employees.

Amendment by sections 1401 and 1431 of Pub. L. 111–203 effective on the date on which final regulations implementing that amendment take effect, or on the date that is 18 months after the designated transfer date if such regulations have not been issued by that date, see section 1400(c) of Pub. L. 111–203, set out as a note under section 1601 of this title.

EFFECTIVE DATE OF 2009 AMENDMENT

Pub. L. 111–24, §3, May 22, 2009, 123 Stat. 1735, provided that: "This Act [enacting sections 1616, 1651, 1665c to 1665e, 1666i–1, 1666i–2, and 1693l–1 of this title and section 1a–7b of Title 16, Conservation, amending this section and sections 1632, 1637, 1640, 1650, 1666b, 1666c, 1666j, 1681b, 1681j, and 1693m to 1693r of this title, enacting provisions set out as notes under this section and sections 1637, 1638, 1666b, 1681j, and 1693l–1 of this title and section 5311 of Title 31, Money and Finance, and amending provisions set out as notes under sections 1638 and 1693 of this title] and the amendments made by this Act shall become effective 9 months after the date of enactment of this Act [May 22, 2009], except as otherwise specifically provided in this Act."

EFFECTIVE DATE OF 1982 AMENDMENT

Pub. L. 97–320, title VII, §702(b), Oct. 15, 1982, 96 Stat. 1538, provided that: "The amendment made by subsection (a) [amending this section] shall take effect on the effective date of title VI of the Depository Institutions Deregulation and Monetary Control Act of 1980 [two years and six months after Mar. 31, 1980, see Effective Date of 1980 Amendment note below]."

EFFECTIVE DATE OF 1981 AMENDMENT

Section 102(b) of Pub. L. 97–25 provided that the amendment made by that section is effective Apr. 10, 1982.

EFFECTIVE DATE OF 1980 AMENDMENT

Pub. L. 96–221, title VI, §625, Mar. 31, 1980, 94 Stat. 185, as amended by Pub. L. 97–25, title III, §301, July 27, 1981, 95 Stat. 145; Pub. L. 97–110, title III, §301, Dec. 26, 1981, 95 Stat. 1515, provided that:

"(a) Except as provided in section 608(b) [set out as an Effective Date of 1980 Amendment note under section 1607 of this title], the amendments made by this title [enacting section 1646 of this title, amending sections 57a, 1602 to 1606, 1610, 1612, 1613, 1631, 1632, 1635, 1637, 1638, 1640, 1641, 1643, 1663, 1664, 1665a, 1666, 1666d, 1667d, and 1691f of this title, repealing sections 1614, 1636, and 1639 of this title, and enacting provisions set out as a note under section 1601 of this title] shall take effect upon the expiration of two years and six months after the date of enactment of this title [Mar. 31, 1980].

"(b) All regulations, forms, and clauses required to be prescribed under the amendments made by this title shall be promulgated at least one year prior to such effective date.

"(c) Notwithstanding subsections (a) and (b), any creditor may comply with the amendments made by this title, in accordance with the regulations, forms, and clauses prescribed by the Board, prior to such effective date. Any creditor who elects to comply with such amendments and any assignee of such a creditor shall be subject to the provisions of sections 130 and 131 of the Truth in Lending Act, as amended by sections 615 and 616, respectively, of this title [sections 1640 and 1641 of this title]."

EFFECTIVE DATE OF 1974 AMENDMENT

For effective date of amendment by Pub. L. 93–495, see section 308 of Pub. L. 93–495, set out as an Effective Date note under section 1666 of this title.

REGULATIONS

Pub. L. 111–24, §2, May 22, 2009, 123 Stat. 1735, provided that: "The Board of Governors of the Federal Reserve System (in this Act [see Short Title of 2009 Amendment note set out under section 1601 of this title] referred to as the 'Board') may issue such rules and publish such model forms as it considers necessary to carry out this Act and the amendments made by this Act."

Pub. L. 103–325, title I, §155, Sept. 23, 1994, 108 Stat. 2197, provided that: "Not later than 180 days after the date of enactment of this Act [Sept. 23, 1994], the Board of Governors of the Federal Reserve System shall issue such regulations as may be necessary to carry out this subtitle [subtitle B (§§151–158) of title I of Pub. L. 103–325, see Short Title of 1994 Amendment note set out under section 1601 of this title], and such regulations shall become effective on the date on which disclosure regulations are required to become effective under section 105(d) of the Truth in Lending Act [15 U.S.C. §1604(d)]."

APPLICABILITY OF 1994 AMENDMENTS AND REGULATIONS TO SUBSECTION (AA) MORTGAGES

Pub. L. 103–325, title I, §156, Sept. 23, 1994, 108 Stat. 2197, provided that: "This subtitle [subtitle B (§§151–158) of title I of Pub. L. 103–325, see Short Title of 1994 Amendment note set out under section 1601 of this title], and the amendments made by this subtitle, shall apply to every mortgage referred to in section 103(aa) of the Truth in Lending Act [now 15 U.S.C. 1602(bb)] (as added by section 152(a) of this Act) consummated on or after the date on which regulations issued under section 155 [set out above] become effective."

§1603. Exempted transactions

This subchapter does not apply to the following:

(1) Credit transactions involving extensions of credit primarily for business, commercial, or agricultural purposes, or to government or governmental agencies or instrumentalities, or to organizations.

(2) Transactions in securities or commodities accounts by a broker-dealer registered with the Securities and Exchange Commission.

(3) Credit transactions, other than those in which a security interest is or will be acquired in real property, or in personal property used or expected to be used as the principal dwelling of the consumer and other than private education loans (as that term is defined in section 1650(a) of this title), in which the total amount financed exceeds $50,000.[1]

(4) Transactions under public utility tariffs, if the Bureau determines that a State regulatory body regulates the charges for the public utility services involved, the charges for delayed payment, and any discount allowed for early payment.

(5) Transactions for which the Bureau, by rule, determines that coverage under this subchapter is not necessary to carry out the purposes of this subchapter.

(6) Repealed. Pub. L. 96–221, title VI, §603(c)(3), Mar. 31, 1980, 94 Stat. 169.

(7) Loans made, insured, or guaranteed pursuant to a program authorized by title IV of the Higher Education Act of 1965 [20 U.S.C. 1070 et seq.].

(Pub. L. 90–321, title I, §104, May 29, 1968, 82 Stat. 147; Pub. L. 93–495, title IV, §402, Oct. 28, 1974, 88 Stat. 1517; Pub. L. 96–221, title VI, §603(c), Mar. 31, 1980, 94 Stat. 169; Pub. L. 97–320, title VII, §701(a), Oct. 15, 1982, 96 Stat. 1538; Pub. L. 104–208, div. A, title II, §2102(a), Sept. 30, 1996, 110 Stat. 3009–398; Pub. L. 110–315, title X, §1022, Aug. 14, 2008, 122 Stat. 3488; Pub. L. 111–203, title X, §§1100A(2), 1100E(a)(1), July 21, 2010, 124 Stat. 2107, 2111.)

EDITORIAL NOTES

REFERENCES IN TEXT

The Higher Education Act of 1965, referred to in par. (7), is Pub. L. 89–329, Nov. 8, 1965, 79 Stat. 1219. Title IV of the Act is classified generally to subchapter IV (§1070 et seq.) of chapter 28 of Title 20, Education. For complete classification of this Act to the Code, see Short Title note set out under section 1001 of Title 20 and Tables.

AMENDMENTS

2010—Par. (3). Pub. L. 111–203, §1100E(a)(1), substituted "$50,000" for "$25,000".

Pars. (4), (5). Pub. L. 111–203, §1100A(2), substituted "Bureau" for "Board".

2008—Par. (3). Pub. L. 110–315 inserted "and other than private education loans (as that term is defined in section 1650(a) of this title)" after "consumer".

1996—Pars. (5) to (7). Pub. L. 104–208 added par. (5) and redesignated former pars. (5) and (6) as (6) and (7), respectively.

1982—Par. (6). Pub. L. 97–320 added par. (6).

1980—Par. (1). Pub. L. 96–221, §603(c)(1), inserted provision relating to applicability to agricultural purposes.

Par. (3). Pub. L. 96–221, §603(c)(2), substituted provision excepting security interest in real property, or in personal property used as the consumer's principal dwelling, for provisions excepting real property transactions.

Par. (5). Pub. L. 96–221, §603(c)(3), struck out par. (5) which related to credit transactions primarily for agricultural purposes where the amount financed exceeds $25,000.

1974—Par. (5). Pub. L. 93–495 added par. (5).

STATUTORY NOTES AND RELATED SUBSIDIARIES

EFFECTIVE DATE OF 2010 AMENDMENT

Amendment by Pub. L. 111–203 effective on the designated transfer date, see section 1100H of Pub. L. 111–203, set out as a note under section 552a of Title 5, Government Organization and Employees.

EFFECTIVE DATE OF 1982 AMENDMENT

Section 701(c) of Pub. L. 97–320, as amended by Pub. L. 97–457, §31, Jan. 12, 1983, 96 Stat. 2511, provided that: "The amendment made by subsection (a) [amending this section] and subsection (b) [enacting section 1099 of Title 20, Education] shall be effective with respect to loans made prior to, on, and after the date of the enactment of this Act [Oct. 15, 1982]."

EFFECTIVE DATE OF 1980 AMENDMENT

Amendment by Pub. L. 96–221 effective on expiration of two years and six months after Mar. 31, 1980, with all regulations, forms, and clauses required to be prescribed to be promulgated at least one year prior to such effective date, and allowing any creditor to comply with any amendments, in accordance with the regulations, forms, and clauses prescribed by the Board prior to such effective date, see section 625 of Pub. L. 96–221, set out as a note under section 1602 of this title.

EFFECTIVE DATE OF 1974 AMENDMENT

Amendment by Pub. L. 93–495 effective Oct. 28, 1974, see section 416 of Pub. L. 93–495, set out as an Effective Date note under section 1665a of this title.

EXCEPTIONS IN AREAS WHERE MAJOR DISASTER EXISTS

Board of Governors of Federal Reserve System authorized to make exceptions to requirements of this subchapter for transactions within an area in which the President has determined that a major disaster exists, if Board determines that exception can reasonably be expected to alleviate hardships to the public that outweigh possible adverse effects, see section 50002 of Pub. L. 105–18, set out as a note under section 4008 of Title 12, Banks and Banking, and similar provisions listed thereunder.

ADJUSTMENTS FOR INFLATION

Pub. L. 111–203, title X, §1100E(b), July 21, 2010, 124 Stat. 2111, provided that: "On and after December 31, 2011, the Bureau [of Consumer Financial Protection] shall adjust annually the dollar amounts described in sections 104(3) and 181(1) of the Truth in Lending Act [15 U.S.C. 1603(3), 1667(1)] (as amended by this section), by the annual percentage increase in the Consumer Price Index for Urban Wage Earners and Clerical Workers, as published by the Bureau of Labor Statistics, rounded to the nearest multiple of $100, or $1,000, as applicable." Threshold amounts in effect during particular periods of time can be found in Code of Federal Regulations, Title 12, Supplement I to Part 1013, under Section 1013.2—Definitions, under 2(e)—Consumer Lease, paragraph 11.

[1] *See Adjustments for Inflation note below.*

§1604. Disclosure guidelines

(a) Promulgation, contents, etc., of regulations

The Bureau shall prescribe regulations to carry out the purposes of this subchapter. Except with respect to the provisions of section 1639 of this title that apply to a mortgage referred to in section 1602(aa) [1] of this title, such regulations may contain such additional requirements, classifications, differentiations, or other provisions, and may provide for such adjustments and exceptions for all or any class of transactions, as in the judgment of the Bureau are necessary or proper to effectuate the purposes of this subchapter, to prevent circumvention or evasion thereof, or to facilitate compliance therewith.

(b) Model disclosure forms and clauses; publication, criteria, compliance, etc.

The Bureau shall publish a single, integrated disclosure for mortgage loan transactions (including real estate settlement cost statements) which includes the disclosure requirements of this subchapter in conjunction with the disclosure requirements of the Real Estate Settlement Procedures Act of 1974 [12 U.S.C. 2601 et seq.] that, taken together, may apply to a transaction that is subject to both or either provisions of law. The purpose of such model disclosure shall be to facilitate compliance with the disclosure requirements of this subchapter and the Real Estate Settlement Procedures Act of 1974, and to aid the borrower or lessee in understanding the transaction by utilizing readily understandable language to simplify the technical nature of the disclosures. In devising such forms, the Bureau shall consider the use by creditors or lessors of data processing or similar automated equipment. Nothing in this subchapter may be construed to require a creditor or lessor to use any such model form or clause prescribed by the Bureau under this section. A creditor or lessor shall be deemed to be in compliance with the disclosure provisions of this subchapter with respect to other than numerical disclosures if the creditor or lessor (1) uses any appropriate model form or clause as published by the Bureau, or (2) uses any such model form or clause and changes it by (A) deleting any information which is not required by this subchapter, or (B) rearranging the format, if in making such deletion or rearranging the format, the creditor or lessor does not affect the substance, clarity, or meaningful sequence of the disclosure.

(c) Procedures applicable for adoption of model forms and clauses

Model disclosure forms and clauses shall be adopted by the Bureau after notice duly given in the Federal Register and an opportunity for public comment in accordance with section 553 of title 5.

(d) Effective dates of regulations containing new disclosure requirements

Any regulation of the Bureau, or any amendment or interpretation thereof, requiring any disclosure which differs from the disclosures previously required by this part, part D, or part E or by any regulation of the Bureau promulgated thereunder shall have an effective date of that October 1 which follows by at least six months the date of promulgation, except that the Bureau may at its discretion take interim action by regulation, amendment, or interpretation to lengthen the period of time permitted for creditors or lessors to adjust their forms to accommodate new requirements or shorten the length of time for creditors or lessors to make such adjustments when it makes a specific finding that such action is necessary to comply with the findings of a court or to prevent unfair or deceptive disclosure practices. Notwithstanding the previous sentence, any creditor or lessor may comply with any such newly promulgated disclosure requirements prior to the effective date of the requirements.

(e) Disclosure for charitable mortgage loan transactions

With respect to a mortgage loan transaction involving a residential mortgage loan offered at 0 percent interest with only bonafide and reasonable fees and that is primarily for charitable purposes by an organization described in section 501(c)(3) of title 26 and exempt from taxation under section 501(a) of such title, forms HUD–1 and GFE (as defined under section 1024.2(b) of title 12, Code of Federal Regulations) together with a disclosure substantially in the form of the Loan Model Form H–2 (as depicted in Appendix H to part 1026 of title 12, Code of Federal Regulations) shall, collectively, be an appropriate model form for purposes of subsection (b) of this section.

(f) Exemption authority

(1) In general

The Bureau may exempt, by regulation, from all or part of this subchapter all or any class of transactions, other than transactions involving any mortgage described in section 1602(aa) [1] of this title, for which, in the determination of the Bureau, coverage under all or part of this subchapter does not provide a meaningful benefit to consumers in the form of useful information or protection.

(2) Factors for consideration

In determining which classes of transactions to exempt in whole or in part under paragraph (1), the Bureau shall consider the following factors and publish its rationale at the time a proposed exemption is published for comment:

(A) The amount of the loan and whether the disclosures, right of rescission, and other provisions provide a benefit to the consumers who are parties to such transactions, as determined by the Bureau.

(B) The extent to which the requirements of this subchapter complicate, hinder, or make more expensive the credit process for the class of transactions.

(C) The status of the borrower, including—

(i) any related financial arrangements of the borrower, as determined by the Bureau;

(ii) the financial sophistication of the borrower relative to the type of transaction; and

(iii) the importance to the borrower of the credit, related supporting property, and coverage under this subchapter, as determined by the Bureau;

(D) whether the loan is secured by the principal residence of the consumer; and

(E) whether the goal of consumer protection would be undermined by such an exemption.

(g) Waiver for certain borrowers

(1) In general

The Bureau, by regulation, may exempt from the requirements of this subchapter certain credit transactions if—

(A) the transaction involves a consumer—

(i) with an annual earned income of more than $200,000; or

(ii) having net assets in excess of $1,000,000 at the time of the transaction; and

(B) a waiver that is handwritten, signed, and dated by the consumer is first obtained from the consumer.

(2) Adjustments by the Bureau

The Bureau, at its discretion, may adjust the annual earned income and net asset requirements of paragraph (1) for inflation.

(h) Deference

Notwithstanding any power granted to any Federal agency under this subchapter, the deference that a court affords to the Bureau with respect to a determination made by the Bureau relating to the meaning or interpretation of any provision of this subchapter, other than section 1639e or 1639h of this title, shall be applied as if the Bureau were the only agency authorized to apply, enforce, interpret, or administer the provisions of this subchapter.

(i) Authority of the Board to prescribe rules

Notwithstanding subsection (a), the Board shall have authority to prescribe rules under this subchapter with respect to a person described in section 5519(a) of title 12. Regulations prescribed under this subsection may contain such classifications, differentiations, or other provisions, as in the judgment of the Board are necessary or proper to effectuate the purposes of this subchapter, to prevent circumvention or evasion thereof, or to facilitate compliance therewith.

(Pub. L. 90–321, title I, §105, May 29, 1968, 82 Stat. 148; Pub. L. 96–221, title VI, §605, Mar. 31, 1980, 94 Stat. 170; Pub. L. 103–325, title I, §152(e)(2)(A), Sept. 23, 1994, 108 Stat. 2194; Pub. L. 104–208, div. A, title II, §§2102(b), 2104, Sept. 30, 1996, 110 Stat. 3009–399, 3009-401; Pub. L. 111–203, title X, §1100A(2), (4)–(7), title XIV, §1472(c), July 21, 2010, 124 Stat. 2107, 2108, 2190; Pub. L. 116–342, §2(a), Jan. 13, 2021, 134 Stat. 5134.)

EDITORIAL NOTES

REFERENCES IN TEXT

Section 1602(aa) of this title, referred to in subsecs. (a) and (f)(1), was redesignated section 1602(bb) of this title by Pub. L. 111–203, title X, §1100A(1)(A), July 21, 2010, 124 Stat. 2107.

The Real Estate Settlement Procedures Act of 1974, referred to in subsec. (b), is Pub. L. 93–533, Dec. 22, 1974, 88 Stat. 1724, which is classified principally to chapter 27 (§2601 et seq.) of Title 12, Banks and Banking. For complete classification of this Act to the Code, see Short Title note set out under section 2601 of Title 12 and Tables.

AMENDMENTS

2021—Subsec. (e). Pub. L. 116–342 added subsec. (e).

2010—Subsec. (a). Pub. L. 111–203, §1100A(2), (4), substituted "Bureau" for "Board" in two places, substituted "Except with respect to the provisions of section 1639 of this title that apply to a mortgage referred to in section 1602(aa) of this title, such regulations may contain such additional requirements,"for "Except in the case of a mortgage referred to in section 1602(aa) of this title, these regulations may contain such", and inserted "all or" after "exceptions for".

Subsec. (b). Pub. L. 111–203, §1100A(2), (5), substituted "Bureau" for "Board" wherever appearing in last three sentences and substituted first two sentences for former first sentence which read as follows: "The Board shall publish model disclosure forms and clauses for common transactions to facilitate compliance with the disclosure requirements of this subchapter and to aid the borrower or lessee in understanding the transaction by utilizing readily understandable language to simplify the technical nature of the disclosures."

Subsecs. (c), (d). Pub. L. 111–203, §1100A(2), substituted "Bureau" for "Board" wherever appearing.

Subsec. (f). Pub. L. 111–203, §1100A(2), (6), substituted "Bureau" for "Board" wherever appearing and inserted "all or" after "from all or part of this subchapter" in par. (1).

Subsec. (g). Pub. L. 111–203, §1100A(2), substituted "Bureau" for "Board" in pars. (1) and (2).

Subsec. (h). Pub. L. 111–203, §1472(c), which directed addition of subsec. (h) at end of section, was executed by adding subsec. (h) before subsec. (i), to reflect the probable intent of Congress and prior amendment by Pub. L. 111–203, §1100A(7). See below.

Subsec. (i). Pub. L. 111–203, §1100A(7), added subsec. (i).

1996—Subsec. (f). Pub. L. 104–208, §2102(b), added subsec. (f).

Subsec. (g). Pub. L. 104–208, §2104, added subsec. (g).

1994—Subsec. (a). Pub. L. 103–325 substituted "Except in the case of a mortgage referred to in section 1602(aa) of this title, these" for "These" in second sentence.

1980—Pub. L. 96–221 designated existing provisions as subsec. (a) and added subsecs. (b) to (d).

STATUTORY NOTES AND RELATED SUBSIDIARIES

Amendment by section 1100A(2), (4)–(7) of Pub. L. 111–203 effective on the designated transfer date, see section 1100H of Pub. L. 111–203, set out as a note under section 552a of Title 5, Government Organization and Employees.

Amendment by section 1472(c) of Pub. L. 111–203 effective on the date on which final regulations implementing that amendment take effect, or on the date that is 18 months after the designated transfer date if such regulations have not been issued by that date, see section 1400(c) of Pub. L. 111–203, set out as a note under section 1601 of this title.

EFFECTIVE DATE OF 1980 AMENDMENT

Amendment by Pub. L. 96–221 effective on expiration of two years and six months after Mar. 31, 1980, with all regulations, forms, and clauses required to be prescribed to be promulgated at least one year prior to such effective date, and allowing any creditor to comply with any amendments, in accordance with the regulations, forms, and clauses prescribed by the Board prior to such effective date, see section 625 of Pub. L. 96–221, set out as a note under section 1602 of this title.

1 See References in Text note below.

§1605. Determination of finance charge

(a) "Finance charge" defined

Except as otherwise provided in this section, the amount of the finance charge in connection with any consumer credit transaction shall be determined as the sum of all charges, payable directly or indirectly by the person to whom the credit is extended, and imposed directly or indirectly by the creditor as an incident to the extension of credit. The finance charge does not include charges of a type payable in a comparable cash transaction. The finance charge shall not include fees and amounts imposed by third party closing agents (including settlement agents, attorneys, and escrow and title companies) if the creditor does not require the imposition of the charges or the services provided and does not retain the charges. Examples of charges which are included in the finance charge include any of the following types of charges which are applicable:

(1) Interest, time price differential, and any amount payable under a point, discount, or other system or additional charges.

(2) Service or carrying charge.

(3) Loan fee, finder's fee, or similar charge.

(4) Fee for an investigation or credit report.

(5) Premium or other charge for any guarantee or insurance protecting the creditor against the obligor's default or other credit loss.

(6) Borrower-paid mortgage broker fees, including fees paid directly to the broker or the lender (for delivery to the broker) whether such fees are paid in cash or financed.

(b) Life, accident, or health insurance premiums included in finance charge

Charges or premiums for credit life, accident, or health insurance written in connection with any consumer credit transaction shall be included in the finance charges unless

(1) the coverage of the debtor by the insurance is not a factor in the approval by the creditor of the extension of credit, and this fact is clearly disclosed in writing to the person applying for or obtaining the extension of credit; and

(2) in order to obtain the insurance in connection with the extension of credit, the person to whom the credit is extended must give specific affirmative written indication of his desire to do so after written disclosure to him of the cost thereof.

(c) Property damage and liability insurance premiums included in finance charge

Charges or premiums for insurance, written in connection with any consumer credit transaction, against loss of or damage to property or against liability arising out of the ownership or use of property, shall be included in the finance charge unless a clear and specific statement in writing is furnished by the creditor to the person to whom the credit is extended, setting forth the cost of the insurance if obtained from or through the creditor, and stating that the person to whom the credit is extended may choose the person through which the insurance is to be obtained.

(d) Items exempted from computation of finance charge in all credit transactions

If any of the following items is itemized and disclosed in accordance with the regulations of the Bureau in connection with any transaction, then the creditor need not include that item in the computation of the finance charge with respect to that transaction:

(1) Fees and charges prescribed by law which actually are or will be paid to public officials for determining the existence of or for perfecting or releasing or satisfying any security related to the credit transaction.

(2) The premium payable for any insurance in lieu of perfecting any security interest otherwise required by the creditor in connection with the transaction, if the premium does not exceed the fees and charges described in paragraph (1) which would otherwise be payable.

(3) Any tax levied on security instruments or on documents evidencing indebtedness if the payment of such taxes is a precondition for recording the instrument securing the evidence of indebtedness.

(e) Items exempted from computation of finance charge in extensions of credit secured by an interest in real property

The following items, when charged in connection with any extension of credit secured by an interest in real property, shall not be included in the computation of the finance charge with respect to that transaction:

(1) Fees or premiums for title examination, title insurance, or similar purposes.

(2) Fees for preparation of loan-related documents.

(3) Escrows for future payments of taxes and insurance.

(4) Fees for notarizing deeds and other documents.

(5) Appraisal fees, including fees related to any pest infestation or flood hazard inspections conducted prior to closing.

(6) Credit reports.

(f) Tolerances for accuracy

In connection with credit transactions not under an open end credit plan that are secured by real property or a dwelling, the disclosure of the finance charge and other disclosures affected by any finance charge—

(1) shall be treated as being accurate for purposes of this subchapter if the amount disclosed as the finance charge—

(A) does not vary from the actual finance charge by more than $100; or

(B) is greater than the amount required to be disclosed under this subchapter; and

(2) shall be treated as being accurate for purposes of section 1635 of this title if—

(A) except as provided in subparagraph (B), the amount disclosed as the finance charge does not vary from the actual finance charge by more than an amount equal to one-half of one percent of the total amount of credit extended; or

(B) in the case of a transaction, other than a mortgage referred to in section 1602(aa) [1] of this title, which—

(i) is a refinancing of the principal balance then due and any accrued and unpaid finance charges of a residential mortgage transaction as defined in section 1602(w) [1] of this title, or is any subsequent refinancing of such a transaction; and

(ii) does not provide any new consolidation or new advance;

if the amount disclosed as the finance charge does not vary from the actual finance charge by more than an amount equal to one percent of the total amount of credit extended.

(Pub. L. 90–321, title I, §106, May 29, 1968, 82 Stat. 148; Pub. L. 96–221, title VI §606, Mar. 31, 1980, 94 Stat. 170; Pub. L. 104–29, §§2(a), (b)(1), (c)–(e), 3(a), Sept. 30, 1995, 109 Stat. 271, 272; Pub. L. 111–203, title X, §1100A(2), July 21, 2010, 124 Stat. 2107.)

EDITORIAL NOTES

REFERENCES IN TEXT

Subsecs. (aa) and (w) of section 1602 of this title, referred to in subsec. (f)(2)(B), were redesignated subsecs. (bb) and (x), respectively, of section 1602 of this title by Pub. L. 111–203, title X, §1100A(1)(A), July 21, 2010, 124 Stat. 2107.

AMENDMENTS

2010—Subsec. (d). Pub. L. 111–203 substituted "Bureau" for "Board" in introductory provisions.

1995—Subsec. (a). Pub. L. 104–29, §2(a), in introductory provisions inserted after second sentence "The finance charge shall not include fees and amounts imposed by third party closing agents (including settlement agents, attorneys, and escrow and title companies) if the creditor does not require the imposition of the charges or the services provided and does not retain the charges."

Subsec. (a)(6). Pub. L. 104–29, §2(b)(1), added par. (6).

Subsec. (d)(3). Pub. L. 104–29, §2(c), added par. (3).

Subsec. (e)(2). Pub. L. 104–29, §2(d), amended par. (2) generally, substituting "loan-related" for "a deed, settlement statement, or other".

Subsec. (e)(5). Pub. L. 104–29, §2(e), inserted before period ", including fees related to any pest infestation or flood hazard inspections conducted prior to closing".

Subsec. (f). Pub. L. 104–29, §3(a), added subsec. (f).

1980—Subsec. (a). Pub. L. 96–221, §606(a), inserted provisions excluding charges of a type payable in comparable cash transactions and indicated that pars. (1) to (5) are examples of charges.

Subsec. (d). Pub. L. 96–221, §606(b), struck out pars. (3) and (4) setting forth applicability to taxes and any other type of charge, respectively.

STATUTORY NOTES AND RELATED SUBSIDIARIES

EFFECTIVE DATE OF 2010 AMENDMENT

Amendment by Pub. L. 111–203 effective on the designated transfer date, see section 1100H of Pub. L. 111–203, set out as a note under section 552a of Title 5, Government Organization and Employees.

EFFECTIVE DATE OF 1995 AMENDMENT

Pub. L. 104–29, §2(b)(2), Sept. 30, 1995, 109 Stat. 271, provided that: "The amendment made by paragraph (1) [amending this section] shall take effect on the earlier of—

"(A) 60 days after the date on which the Board of Governors of the Federal Reserve System issues final regulations under paragraph (3) [set out below]; or

"(B) the date that is 12 months after the date of the enactment of this Act [Sept. 30, 1995]."

EFFECTIVE DATE OF 1980 AMENDMENT

Amendment by Pub. L. 96–221 effective on expiration of two years and six months after Mar. 31, 1980, with all regulations, forms, and clauses required to be prescribed to be promulgated at least one year prior to such effective date, and allowing any creditor to comply with any amendments, in accordance with the regulations, forms, and clauses prescribed by the Board prior to such effective date, see section 625 of Pub. L. 96–221, set out as a note under section 1602 of this title.

REGULATIONS

Pub. L. 104–29, §2(b)(3), Sept. 30, 1995, 109 Stat. 271, provided that: "The Board of Governors of the Federal Reserve System shall promulgate regulations implementing the amendment made by paragraph (1) [amending this section] by no later than 6 months after the date of the enactment of this Act [Sept. 30, 1995]."

ENSURING THAT FINANCE CHARGES REFLECT COST OF CREDIT

Pub. L. 104–29, §2(f), Sept. 30, 1995, 109 Stat. 272, provided that:

"(1) REPORT.—

"(A) IN GENERAL.—Not later than 6 months after the date of the enactment of this Act [Sept. 30, 1995], the Board of Governors of the Federal Reserve System shall submit to the Congress a report containing recommendations on any regulatory or statutory changes necessary—

"(i) to ensure that finance charges imposed in connection with consumer credit transactions more accurately reflect the cost of providing credit; and

"(ii) to address abusive refinancing practices engaged in for the purpose of avoiding rescission.

"(B) REPORT REQUIREMENTS.—In preparing the report under this paragraph, the Board shall—

"(i) consider the extent to which it is feasible to include in finance charges all charges payable directly or indirectly by the consumer to whom credit is extended, and imposed directly or indirectly by the creditor as an incident to the extension of credit (especially those charges excluded from finance charges under section 106 of the Truth in Lending Act [15 U.S.C. 1605] as of the date of the enactment of this Act), excepting only those charges which are payable in a comparable cash transaction; and

"(ii) consult with and consider the views of affected industries and consumer groups.

"(2) REGULATIONS.—The Board of Governors of the Federal Reserve System shall prescribe any appropriate regulation in order to effect any change included in the report under paragraph (1), and shall publish the regulation in the Federal Register before the end of the 1-year period beginning on the date of enactment of this Act."

1 See References in Text note below.

§1606. Determination of annual percentage rate

(a) "Annual percentage rate" defined

The annual percentage rate applicable to any extension of consumer credit shall be determined, in accordance with the regulations of the Bureau,

(1) in the case of any extension of credit other than under an open end credit plan, as

(A) that nominal annual percentage rate which will yield a sum equal to the amount of the finance charge when it is applied to the unpaid balances of the amount financed, calculated according to the actuarial method of allocating payments made on a debt between the amount financed and the amount of the finance charge, pursuant to which a payment is applied first to the accumulated finance charge and the balance is applied to the unpaid amount financed; or

(B) the rate determined by any method prescribed by the Bureau as a method which materially simplifies computation while retaining reasonable accuracy as compared with the rate determined under subparagraph (A).[1]

(2) in the case of any extension of credit under an open end credit plan, as the quotient (expressed as a percentage) of the total finance charge for the period to which it relates divided by the amount upon which the finance charge for that period is based, multiplied by the number of such periods in a year.

(b) Computation of rate of finance charges for balances within a specified range

Where a creditor imposes the same finance charge for balances within a specified range, the annual percentage rate shall be computed on the median balance within the range, except that if the Bureau determines that a rate so computed would not be meaningful, or would be materially misleading, the annual percentage rate shall be computed on such other basis as the Bureau may be regulation require.

(c) Allowable tolerances for purposes of compliance with disclosure requirements

The disclosure of an annual percentage rate is accurate for the purpose of this subchapter if the rate disclosed is within a tolerance not greater than one-eighth of 1 per centum more or less than the actual rate or rounded to the nearest one-fourth of 1 per centum. The Bureau may allow a greater tolerance to simplify compliance where irregular payments are involved.

(d) Use of rate tables or charts having allowable variance from determined rates

The Bureau may authorize the use of rate tables or charts which may provide for the disclosure of annual percentage rates which vary from the rate determined in accordance with subsection (a)(1)(A) by not more than such tolerances as the Bureau may allow. The Bureau may not allow a tolerance greater than 8 per centum of that rate except to simplify compliance where irregular payments are involved.

(e) Authorization of tolerances in determining annual percentage rates

In the case of creditors determining the annual percentage rate in a manner other than as described in subsection (d), the Bureau may authorize other reasonable tolerances.

(Pub. L. 90–321, title I, §107, May 29, 1968, 82 Stat. 149; Pub. L. 96–221, title VI, §607, Mar. 31, 1980, 94 Stat. 170; Pub. L. 111–203, title X, §1100A(2), July 21, 2010, 124 Stat. 2107.)

EDITORIAL NOTES

AMENDMENTS

2010—Pub. L. 111–203 substituted "Bureau" for "Board" wherever appearing.

1980—Subsec. (c). Pub. L. 96–221, §607(a), substituted provisions relating to allowable tolerances for purposes of compliance with disclosure requirements, for provisions relating to rounding off of annual percentage rates which are converted from single add-on or other rates.

Subsec. (e). Pub. L. 96–221, §607(b), struck out reference to subsection (c) of this section.

Subsec. (f). Pub. L. 96–221, §607(c), struck out subsec. (f) setting forth requirements for form of expressing percentage rates prior to Jan. 1, 1971.

STATUTORY NOTES AND RELATED SUBSIDIARIES

EFFECTIVE DATE OF 2010 AMENDMENT

Amendment by Pub. L. 111–203 effective on the designated transfer date, see section 1100H of Pub. L. 111–203, set out as a note under section 552a of Title 5, Government Organization and Employees.

EFFECTIVE DATE OF 1980 AMENDMENT

Amendment by Pub. L. 96–221 effective on expiration of two years and six months after Mar. 31, 1980, with all regulations, forms, and clauses required to be prescribed to be promulgated at least one year prior to such effective date, and allowing any creditor to comply with any amendments, in accordance with the regulations, forms, and clauses prescribed by the Board prior to such effective date, see section 625 of Pub. L. 96–221, set out as a note under section 1602 of this title.

§1607. Administrative enforcement

(a) Enforcing agencies

Subject to subtitle B of the Consumer Financial Protection Act of 2010 [12 U.S.C. 5511 et seq.], compliance with the requirements imposed under this subchapter shall be enforced under—

(1) section 8 of the Federal Deposit Insurance Act [12 U.S.C. 1818], by the appropriate Federal banking agency, as defined in section 3(q) of the Federal Deposit Insurance Act (12 U.S.C. 1813(q)), with respect to—

(A) national banks, Federal savings associations, and Federal branches and Federal agencies of foreign banks;

(B) member banks of the Federal Reserve System (other than national banks), branches and agencies of foreign banks (other than Federal branches, Federal agencies, and insured State branches of foreign banks), commercial lending companies owned or controlled by foreign banks, and organizations operating under section 25 or 25A of the Federal Reserve Act [12 U.S.C. 601 et seq., 611 et seq.]; and

(C) banks and State savings associations insured by the Federal Deposit Insurance Corporation (other than members of the Federal Reserve System), and insured State branches of foreign banks;

(2) the Federal Credit Union Act [12 U.S.C. 1751 et seq.], by the Director of the National Credit Union Administration, with respect to any Federal credit union;

(3) part A of subtitle VII of title 49, by the Secretary of Transportation, with respect to any air carrier or foreign air carrier subject to that part;

(4) the Packers and Stockyards Act, 1921 [7 U.S.C. 181 et seq.] (except as provided in section 406 of that Act [7 U.S.C. 226, 227]), by the Secretary of Agriculture, with respect to any activities subject to that Act;

(5) the Farm Credit Act of 1971 [12 U.S.C. 2001 et seq.], by the Farm Credit Administration with respect to any Federal land bank, Federal land bank association, Federal intermediate credit bank, or production credit association; and

(6) subtitle E of the Consumer Financial Protection Act of 2010 [12 U.S.C. 5561 et seq.], by the Bureau, with respect to any person subject to this subchapter.

(7) sections 21B and 21C of the Securities Exchange Act of 1934 [15 U.S.C. 78u–2, 78u–3], in the case of a broker or dealer, other than a depository institution, by the Securities and Exchange Commission.

(b) Violations of this subchapter deemed violations of pre-existing statutory requirements; additional agency powers

For the purpose of the exercise by any agency referred to in subsection (a) of its powers under any Act referred to in that subsection, a violation of any requirement imposed under this subchapter shall be deemed to be a violation of a requirement imposed under that Act. In addition to its powers under any provision of law specifically referred to in subsection (a), each of the agencies referred to in that subsection may exercise, for the purpose of enforcing compliance with any requirement imposed under this subchapter, any other authority conferred on it by law.

(c) Overall enforcement authority of the Federal Trade Commission

Except to the extent that enforcement of the requirements imposed under this subchapter is specifically committed to some other Government agency under any of paragraphs (1) through (5) of subsection (a), and subject to subtitle B of the Consumer Financial Protection Act of 2010 [12 U.S.C. 5511 et seq.], the Federal Trade Commission shall be authorized to enforce such requirements. For the purpose of the exercise by the Federal Trade Commission of its functions and powers under the Federal Trade Commission Act [15 U.S.C. 41 et seq.], a violation of any requirement imposed under this subchapter shall be deemed a violation of a requirement imposed under that Act. All of the functions and powers of the Federal Trade Commission under the Federal Trade Commission Act are available to the Federal Trade Commission to enforce compliance by any person with the requirements under this subchapter, irrespective of whether that person is engaged in commerce or meets any other jurisdictional tests under the Federal Trade Commission Act.

(d) Rules and regulations

The authority of the Bureau to issue regulations under this subchapter does not impair the authority of any other agency designated in this section to make rules respecting its own procedures in enforcing compliance with requirements imposed under this subchapter.

(e) Adjustment of finance charges; procedures applicable, coverage, criteria, etc.

(1) In carrying out its enforcement activities under this section, each agency referred to in subsection (a) or (c), in cases where an annual percentage rate or finance charge was inaccurately disclosed, shall notify the creditor of such disclosure error and is authorized in accordance with the provisions of this subsection to require the creditor to make an adjustment to the account of the person to whom credit was extended, to assure that such person will not be

required to pay a finance charge in excess of the finance charge actually disclosed or the dollar equivalent of the annual percentage rate actually disclosed, whichever is lower. For the purposes of this subsection, except where such disclosure error resulted from a willful violation which was intended to mislead the person to whom credit was extended, in determining whether a disclosure error has occurred and in calculating any adjustment, (A) each agency shall apply (i) with respect to the annual percentage rate, a tolerance of one-quarter of 1 percent more or less than the actual rate, determined without regard to section 1606(c) of this title, and (ii) with respect to the finance charge, a corresponding numerical tolerance as generated by the tolerance provided under this subsection for the annual percentage rate; except that (B) with respect to transactions consummated after two years following March 31, 1980, each agency shall apply (i) for transactions that have a scheduled amortization of ten years or less, with respect to the annual percentage rate, a tolerance not to exceed one-quarter of 1 percent more or less than the actual rate, determined without regard to section 1606(c) of this title, but in no event a tolerance of less than the tolerances allowed under section 1606(c) of this title, (ii) for transactions that have a scheduled amortization of more than ten years, with respect to the annual percentage rate, only such tolerances as are allowed under section 1606(c) of this title, and (iii) for all transactions, with respect to the finance charge, a corresponding numerical tolerance as generated by the tolerances provided under this subsection for the annual percentage rate.

(2) Each agency shall require such an adjustment when it determines that such disclosure error resulted from (A) a clear and consistent pattern or practice of violations, (B) gross negligence, or (C) a willful violation which was intended to mislead the person to whom the credit was extended. Notwithstanding the preceding sentence, except where such disclosure error resulted from a willful violation which was intended to mislead the person to whom credit was extended, an agency need not require such an adjustment if it determines that such disclosure error—

(A) resulted from an error involving the disclosure of a fee or charge that would otherwise be excludable in computing the finance charge, including but not limited to violations involving the disclosures described in sections 1605(b), (c) and (d) of this title, in which event the agency may require such remedial action as it determines to be equitable, except that for transactions consummated after two years after March 31, 1980, such an adjustment shall be ordered for violations of section 1605(b) of this title;

(B) involved a disclosed amount which was 10 per centum or less of the amount that should have been disclosed and (i) in cases where the error involved a disclosed finance charge, the annual percentage rate was disclosed correctly, and (ii) in cases where the error involved a disclosed annual percentage rate, the finance charge was disclosed correctly; in which event the agency may require such adjustment as it determines to be equitable;

(C) involved a total failure to disclose either the annual percentage rate or the finance charge, in which event the agency may require such adjustment as it determines to be equitable; or

(D) resulted from any other unique circumstance involving clearly technical and nonsubstantive disclosure violations that do not adversely affect information provided to the consumer and that have not misled or otherwise deceived the consumer.

In the case of other such disclosure errors, each agency may require such an adjustment.
(3) Notwithstanding paragraph (2), no adjustment shall be ordered—

(A) if it would have a significantly adverse impact upon the safety or soundness of the creditor, but in any such case, the agency may—

(i) require a partial adjustment in an amount which does not have such an impact; or

(ii) require the full adjustment, but permit the creditor to make the required adjustment in partial payments over an extended period of time which the agency considers to be reasonable, if (in the case of an agency referred to in paragraph (1), (2), or (3) of subsection (a)), the agency determines that a partial adjustment or making partial payments over an extended period is necessary to avoid causing the creditor to become undercapitalized pursuant to section 38 of the Federal Deposit Insurance Act [12 U.S.C. 1831o];

(B) the [1] amount of the adjustment would be less than $1, except that if more than one year has elapsed since the date of the violation, the agency may require that such amount be paid into the Treasury of the United States, or

(C) except where such disclosure error resulted from a willful violation which was intended to mislead the person to whom credit was extended, in the case of an open-end credit plan, more than two years after the violation, or in the case of any other extension of credit, as follows:

(i) with respect to creditors that are subject to examination by the agencies referred to in paragraphs (1) through (3) of subsection (a) of this section, except in connection with violations arising from practices identified in the current examination and only in connection with transactions that are consummated after the date of the immediately preceding examination, except that where practices giving rise to violations identified in earlier examinations have not been corrected, adjustments for those violations shall be required in connection with transactions consummated after the date of examination in which such practices were first identified;

(ii) with respect to creditors that are not subject to examination by such agencies, except in connection with transactions that are consummated after May 10, 1978; and

(iii) in no event after the later of (I) the expiration of the life of the credit extension, or (II) two years after the agreement to extend credit was consummated.

(4)(A) Notwithstanding any other provision of this section, an adjustment under this subsection may be required by an agency referred to in subsection (a) or (c) only by an order issued in accordance with cease and desist procedures provided by the provision of law referred to in such subsections.

(B) In case of an agency which is not authorized to conduct cease and desist proceedings, such an order may be issued after an agency hearing on the record conducted at least thirty but not more than sixty days after notice of the alleged violation is served on the creditor. Such a hearing shall be deemed to be a hearing which is subject to the provisions of section 8(h) of the Federal Deposit Insurance Act [12 U.S.C. 1818(h)] and shall be subject to judicial review as provided therein.

(5) Except as otherwise specifically provided in this subsection and notwithstanding any provision of law referred to in subsection (a) or (c), no agency referred to in subsection (a) or (c) may require a creditor to make dollar adjustments for errors in any requirements under this subchapter, except with regard to the requirements of section 1666d of this title.

(6) A creditor shall not be subject to an order to make an adjustment, if within sixty days after discovering a disclosure error, whether pursuant to a final written examination report or through the creditor's own procedures, the creditor notifies the person concerned of the error and adjusts the account so as to assure that such person will not be required to pay a finance charge in excess of the finance charge actually disclosed or the dollar equivalent of the annual percentage rate actually disclosed, whichever is lower.

(7) Notwithstanding the second sentence of subsection (e)(1), subsection (e)(3)(C)(i), and subsection (e)(3)(C)(ii), each agency referred to in subsection (a) or (c) shall require an adjustment for an annual percentage rate disclosure error that exceeds a tolerance of one quarter of one percent less than the actual rate, determined without regard to section 1606(c) of this title, with respect to any transaction consummated between January 1, 1977, and March 31, 1980.

(Pub. L. 90–321, title I, §108, May 29, 1968, 82 Stat. 150; Pub. L. 91–206, §3, Mar. 10, 1970, 84 Stat. 49; Pub. L. 93–495, title IV, §403, Oct. 28, 1974, 88 Stat. 1517; Pub. L. 95–630, title V, §501, Nov. 10, 1978, 92 Stat. 3680; Pub. L. 96–221, title VI, §608(a), (c), Mar. 21, 1980, 94 Stat. 171, 173; Pub. L. 98–443, §9(n), Oct. 4, 1984, 98 Stat. 1708; Pub. L. 101–73, title VII, §744(k), Aug. 9, 1989, 103 Stat. 439; Pub. L. 102–242, title II, §212(b), Dec. 19, 1991, 105 Stat. 2299; Pub. L. 102–550, title XVI, §1604(a)(5), Oct. 28, 1992, 106 Stat. 4082; Pub. L. 104–208, div. A, title II, §2106, Sept. 30, 1996, 110 Stat. 3009–402; Pub. L. 111–203, title X, §1100A(2), (8), title XIV, §1414(b), July 21, 2010, 124 Stat. 2107, 2108, 2152.)

EDITORIAL NOTES

REFERENCES IN TEXT

The Consumer Financial Protection Act of 2010, referred to in subsecs. (a) and (c), is title X of Pub. L. 111–203, July 21, 2010, 124 Stat. 1955. Subtitles B (§§1021–1029A) and E (§§1051–1058) of the Act are classified generally to parts B (§5511 et seq.) and E (§5561 et seq.), respectively, of subchapter V of chapter 53 of Title 12, Banks and Banking. For complete classification of this Act to the Code, see Short Title note set out under section 5301 of Title 12 and Tables.

Sections 25 and 25A of the Federal Reserve Act, referred to in subsec. (a)(1)(B), are classified to subchapters I (§601 et seq.) and II (§611 et seq.), respectively, of chapter 6 of Title 12, Banks and Banking.

The Federal Credit Union Act, referred to in subsec. (a)(2), is act June 26, 1934, ch. 750, 48 Stat. 1216, which is classified generally to chapter 14 (§1751 et seq.) of Title 12. For complete classification of this Act to the Code, see section 1751 of Title 12 and Tables.

The Packers and Stockyards Act, 1921, referred to in subsec. (a)(4), is act Aug. 15, 1921, ch. 64, 42 Stat. 159, which is classified generally to chapter 9 (§181 et seq.) of Title 7, Agriculture. For complete classification of this Act to the Code, see section 181 of Title 7 and Tables.

The Farm Credit Act of 1971, referred to in subsec. (a)(5), is Pub. L. 92–181, Dec. 10, 1971, 85 Stat. 583, which is classified generally to chapter 23 (§2001 et seq.) of Title 12, Banks and Banking. For complete classification of this Act to the Code, see Short Title note set out under section 2001 of Title 12 and Tables.

The Federal Trade Commission Act, referred to in subsec. (c), is act Sept. 26, 1914, ch. 311, 38 Stat. 717, which is classified generally to subchapter I (§41 et seq.) of chapter 2 of this title. For complete classification of this Act to the Code, see section 58 of this title and Tables.

CODIFICATION

In subsec. (a)(3), "part A of subtitle VII of title 49" substituted for "the Federal Aviation Act of 1958" and "that part" substituted for "that Act" on authority of Pub. L. 103–272, §6(b), July 5, 1994, 108 Stat. 1378, the first section of which enacted subtitles II, III, and V to X of Title 49, Transportation.

AMENDMENTS

2010—Subsec. (a). Pub. L. 111–203, §1100A(8)(A), added subsec. (a) and struck out former subsec. (a) which listed agencies under which compliance with subchapter requirements would be enforced.

Subsec. (a)(7). Pub. L. 111–203, §1414(b), added par. (7).

Subsec. (c). Pub. L. 111–203, §1100A(8)(B), added subsec. (c) and struck out former subsec. (c). Prior to amendment, text read as follows: "Except to the extent that enforcement of the requirements imposed under this subchapter is specifically committed to some other Government agency under subsection (a) of this section, the Federal Trade Commission shall enforce such requirements. For the purpose of the exercise by the Federal Trade Commission of its functions and powers under the Federal Trade Commission Act, a violation of any requirement imposed under this subchapter shall be deemed a violation of a requirement imposed under that Act. All of the functions and powers of the Federal Trade Commission under the Federal Trade Commission Act are available to the Commission to enforce compliance by any person with the requirements imposed under this subchapter, irrespective of whether that person is engaged in commerce or meets any other jurisdictional tests in the Federal Trade Commission Act."

Subsec. (d). Pub. L. 111–203, §1100A(2), substituted "Bureau" for "Board".

1996—Subsec. (e)(3). Pub. L. 104–208 struck out "ordered (A) if" and inserted "ordered—
   "(A) if";
struck out "may require a partial" and inserted "may—
   "(i) require a partial";
struck out ", except that with respect to any transaction consumated after March 31, 1980, the agency shall require" and inserted "; or
   "(ii) require";
directed the substitution of "reasonable, if (in the case of an agency referred to in paragraph (1), (2), or (3) of subsection (a)), the agency determines that a partial adjustment or making partial payments over an extended period is necessary to avoid causing the creditor to become undercapitalized pursuant to section 38 of the Federal Deposit Insurance Act;
   "(B) the";
for "reasonable, (B) the", which was executed by making the substitution for "reasonable, (B) if the"; and struck out "(C) except" and inserted
   "(C) except".

1992—Subsec. (a)(1)(C). Pub. L. 102–550 substituted semicolon for period at end.

1991—Subsec. (a). Pub. L. 102–242, §212(b)(2), inserted at end "The terms used in paragraph (1) that are not defined in this subchapter or otherwise defined in section 3(s) of the Federal Deposit Insurance Act (12 U.S.C. 1813(s)) shall have the meaning given to them in section 1(b) of the International Banking Act of 1978 (12 U.S.C. 3101)."

Pub. L. 102–242, §212(b)(1), added par. (1) and struck out former par. (1) which read as follows: "section 8 of the Federal Deposit Insurance Act, in the case of
   "(A) national banks, by the Comptroller of the Currency.
   "(B) member banks of the Federal Reserve System (other than national banks), by the Board.
   "(C) banks insured by the Federal Deposit Insurance Corporation (other than members of the Federal Reserve System), by the Board of Directors of the Federal Deposit Insurance Corporation."

1989—Subsec. (a)(2). Pub. L. 101–73 amended par. (2) generally. Prior to amendment, par. (2) read as follows: "section 5(d) of the Home Owner's Loan Act of 1933, section 407 of the National Housing Act, and sections 6(i) and 17 of the Federal Home Loan Bank Act, by the Federal Home Loan Bank Board (acting directly or through the Federal Savings and Loan Insurance Corporation), in the case of any institution subject to any of those provisions."

1984—Subsec. (a)(4). Pub. L. 98–443 substituted "Secretary of Transportation" for "Civil Aeronautics Board".

1980—Subsec. (e). Pub. L. 96–221, §608(a), added subsec. (e).

Pub. L. 96–221, §608(c), struck out in pars. (1)(A)(i) and (7) ", except in the case of an irregular mortgage lending transaction" after "section 1606(c) of this title". See Effective Date of 1980 Amendment note below.

1974—Subsec. (a)(4) to (6). Pub. L. 93–495 redesignated pars. (5) and (6) as (4) and (5), respectively. Former par. (4), which related to enforcement by the Interstate Commerce Commission, was struck out.

STATUTORY NOTES AND RELATED SUBSIDIARIES

EFFECTIVE DATE OF 2010 AMENDMENT

Amendment by section 1100A(2), (8) of Pub. L. 111–203 effective on the designated transfer date, see section 1100H of Pub. L. 111–203, set out as a note under section 552a of Title 5, Government Organization and Employees.

Amendment by section 1414(b) of Pub. L. 111–203 effective on the date on which final regulations implementing that amendment take effect, or on the date that is 18 months after the designated transfer
38

date if such regulations have not been issued by that date, see section 1400(c) of Pub. L. 111–203, set out as a note under section 1601 of this title.

EFFECTIVE DATE OF 1992 AMENDMENT

Amendment by Pub. L. 102–550 effective as if included in the Federal Deposit Insurance Corporation Improvement Act of 1991, Pub. L. 102–242, as of Dec. 19, 1991, see section 1609(a) of Pub. L. 102–550, set out as a note under section 191 of Title 12, Banks and Banking.

EFFECTIVE DATE OF 1984 AMENDMENT

Amendment by Pub. L. 98–443 effective Jan. 1, 1985, see section 9(v) of Pub. L. 98–443, set out as a note under section 5314 of Title 5, Government Organization and Employees.

EFFECTIVE DATE OF 1980 AMENDMENT

Pub. L. 96–221, title VI, §608(b), Mar. 31, 1980, 94 Stat. 173, provided that: "This section [amending this section] shall take effect on the date of enactment of the Truth in Lending Simplification and Reform Act [Mar. 31, 1980]."

Pub. L. 96–221, title VI, §608(c), Mar. 31, 1980, 94 Stat. 173, provided that the amendment made by that section is effective one year after Mar. 31, 1980.

EFFECTIVE DATE OF 1974 AMENDMENT

Amendment by Pub. L. 93–495 effective Oct. 28, 1974, see section 416 of Pub. L. 93–495, set out as an Effective Date note under section 1665a of this title.

TRANSFER OF FUNCTIONS

"National Credit Union Administration Board" substituted for "Director of the Bureau of Federal Credit Unions" in subsec. (a)(3) pursuant to section 3 of Pub. L. 91–206 and section 501 of Pub. L. 95–630 [12 U.S.C. 1752a] which transferred functions of Bureau of Federal Credit Unions, and Director thereof, to National Credit Union Administration and vested authority for management of Administration in National Credit Union Administration Board.

[1] So in original. Probably should be preceded by "if".

§1608. Views of other agencies

In the exercise of its functions under this subchapter, the Bureau may obtain upon requests the views of any other Federal agency which, in the judgment of the Bureau, exercises regulatory or supervisory functions with respect to any class of creditors subject to this subchapter.

(Pub. L. 90–321, title I, §109, May 29, 1968, 82 Stat. 150; Pub. L. 111–203, title X, §1100A(2), July 21, 2010, 124 Stat. 2107.)

EDITORIAL NOTES

AMENDMENTS

2010—Pub. L. 111–203 substituted "Bureau" for "Board" in two places.

STATUTORY NOTES AND RELATED SUBSIDIARIES

EFFECTIVE DATE OF 2010 AMENDMENT

Amendment by Pub. L. 111–203 effective on the designated transfer date, see section 1100H of Pub. L. 111–203, set out as a note under section 552a of Title 5, Government Organization and Employees.

§1609. Repealed. Pub. L. 94–239, §3(b)(1), Mar. 23, 1976, 90 Stat. 253

Section, Pub. L. 90–321, title I, §110, May 29, 1968, 82 Stat. 151, provided for establishment of an advisory committee authorized to seek to achieve a fair representation of interests of sellers of merchandise on credit, lenders, and the public.

EFFECTIVE DATE OF REPEAL

Repeal effective Mar. 23, 1976, see section 708 of Pub. L. 90–321, set out as an Effective Date note under section 1691 of this title.

§1610. Effect on other laws

(a) Inconsistent provisions; procedures applicable for determination

(1) Except as provided in subsection (e), this part and parts B and C, do not annul, alter, or affect the laws of any State relating to the disclosure of information in connection with credit transactions, except to the extent that those laws are inconsistent with the provisions of this subchapter, and then only to the extent of the inconsistency. Upon its own motion or upon the request of any creditor, State, or other interested party which is submitted in accordance with procedures prescribed in regulations of the Bureau, the Bureau shall determine whether any such inconsistency exists. If the Bureau determines that a State-required disclosure is inconsistent, creditors located in that State may not make disclosures using the inconsistent term or form, and shall incur no liability under the law of that State for failure to use such term or form, notwithstanding that such determination is subsequently amended, rescinded, or determined by judicial or other authority to be invalid for any reason.

(2) Upon its own motion or upon the request of any creditor, State, or other interested party which is submitted in accordance with procedures prescribed in regulations of the Bureau, the Bureau shall determine whether any disclosure required under the law of any State is substantially the same in meaning as a disclosure required under this subchapter. If the Bureau determines that a State-required disclosure is substantially the same in meaning as a disclosure required by this subchapter, then creditors located in that State may make such disclosure in compliance with such State law in lieu of the disclosure required by this subchapter, except that the annual percentage rate and finance charge shall be disclosed as required by section 1632 of this title, and such State-required disclosure may not be made in lieu of the disclosures applicable to certain mortgages under section 1639 of this title.

(b) State credit charge statutes

Except as provided in section 1639 of this title, this subchapter does not otherwise annul, alter or affect in any manner the meaning, scope or applicability of the laws of any State, including, but not limited to, laws relating to the types, amounts or rates of charges, or any element or elements of charges, permissible under such laws in connection with the extension or use of credit, nor does this subchapter extend the applicability of those laws to any class of persons or transactions to which they would not otherwise apply. The provisions of section 1639 of this title do not annul, alter, or affect the applicability of the laws of any State or exempt any person subject to the provisions of section 1639 of this title from complying with the laws of any State, with respect to the requirements for mortgages referred to in section 1602(aa) [1] of this title, except to the extent that those State laws are inconsistent with any provisions of section 1639 of this title, and then only to the extent of the inconsistency.

(c) Disclosure as evidence

In any action or proceeding in any court involving a consumer credit sale, the disclosure of the annual percentage rate as required under this subchapter in connection with that sale may not be received as evidence that the sale was a loan or any type of transaction other than a credit sale.

(d) Contract or other obligations under State or Federal law

Except as specified in sections 1635, 1640, and 1666e of this title, this subchapter and the regulations issued thereunder do not affect the validity or enforceability of any contract or obligation under State or Federal law.

(e) Certain credit and charge card application and solicitation disclosure provisions

The provisions of subsection (c) of section 1632 of this title and subsections (c), (d), (e), and (f) of section 1637 of this title shall supersede any provision of the law of any State relating to the disclosure of information in any credit or charge card application or solicitation which is subject to the requirements of section 1637(c) of this title or any renewal notice which is subject to the requirements of section 1637(d) of this title, except that any State may employ or establish State laws for the purpose of enforcing the requirements of such sections.

(Pub. L. 90–321, title I, §111, May 29, 1968, 82 Stat. 151; Pub. L. 93–495, title III, §307(b), Oct. 28, 1974, 88 Stat. 1516; Pub. L. 96–221, title VI, §609, Mar. 31, 1980, 94 Stat. 173; Pub. L. 100–583, §4, Nov. 3, 1988, 102 Stat. 2967; Pub. L. 103–325, title I, §152(e)(2)(B), (C), Sept. 23, 1994, 108 Stat. 2194; Pub. L. 111–203, title X, §1100A(2), July 21, 2010, 124 Stat. 2107.)

EDITORIAL NOTES

REFERENCES IN TEXT

Section 1602(aa) of this title, referred to in subsec. (b), was redesignated section 1602(bb) of this title by Pub. L. 111–203, title X, §1100A(1)(A), July 21, 2010, 124 Stat. 2107.

AMENDMENTS

2010—Subsec. (a). Pub. L. 111–203 substituted "Bureau" for "Board" wherever appearing.

1994—Subsec. (a)(2). Pub. L. 103–325, §152(e)(2)(B), which directed the amendment of par. (2) by inserting ", and such State-required disclosure may not be made in lieu of the disclosures applicable to certain mortgages under section 1639 of this title" before period, was executed by making the insertion before period at end of par. (2), to reflect the probable intent of Congress.

Subsec. (b). Pub. L. 103–325, §152(e)(2)(C), substituted "Except as provided in section 1639 of this title, this subchapter" for "This subchapter" and inserted at end "The provisions of section 1639 of this title do not annul, alter, or affect the applicability of the laws of any State or exempt any person subject to the provisions of section 1639 of this title from complying with the laws of any State, with respect to the requirements for mortgages referred to in section 1602(aa) of this title, except to the extent that those State laws are inconsistent with any provisions of section 1639 of this title, and then only to the extent of the inconsistency."

1988—Subsec. (a)(1). Pub. L. 100–583, §4(1), substituted "Except as provided in subsection (e), this part" for "This part".

Subsec. (e). Pub. L. 100–583, §4(2), added subsec. (e).

1980—Subsec. (a). Pub. L. 96–221 designated existing provisions as par. (1), substituted provisions respecting the effect of this part and parts B and C of this subchapter, and procedures applicable for determination, for provisions respecting the effect of this subchapter, and added par. (2).

1974—Subsec. (d). Pub. L. 93–495 inserted reference to section 1666e of this title.

STATUTORY NOTES AND RELATED SUBSIDIARIES

EFFECTIVE DATE OF 2010 AMENDMENT

Amendment by Pub. L. 111–203 effective on the designated transfer date, see section 1100H of Pub. L. 111–203, set out as a note under section 552a of Title 5, Government Organization and Employees.

EFFECTIVE DATE OF 1980 AMENDMENT

Amendment by Pub. L. 96–221 effective on expiration of two years and six months after Mar. 31, 1980, with all regulations, forms, and clauses required to be prescribed to be promulgated at least one year prior to such effective date, and allowing any creditor to comply with any amendments, in accordance with the regulations, forms, and clauses prescribed by the Board prior to such effective date, see section 625 of Pub. L. 96–221, set out as a note under section 1602 of this title.

EFFECTIVE DATE OF 1974 AMENDMENT

For effective date of amendment by Pub. L. 93–495, see section 308 of Pub. L. 93–495, set out as an Effective Date note under section 1666 of this title.

---

[1] See References in Text note below.

§1611. Criminal liability for willful and knowing violation

Whoever willfully and knowingly

(1) gives false or inaccurate information or fails to provide information which he is required to disclose under the provisions of this subchapter or any regulation issued thereunder,

(2) uses any chart or table authorized by the Bureau under section 1606 of this title in such a manner as to consistently understate the annual percentage rate determined under section 1606(a)(1)(A) of this title, or

(3) otherwise fails to comply with any requirement imposed under this subchapter,

shall be fined not more than $5,000 or imprisoned not more than one year, or both.

(Pub. L. 90–321, title I, §112, May 29, 1968, 82 Stat. 151; Pub. L. 111–203, title X, §1100A(2), July 21, 2010, 124 Stat. 2107.)

EDITORIAL NOTES

AMENDMENTS

2010—Par. (2). Pub. L. 111–203 substituted "Bureau" for "Board".

STATUTORY NOTES AND RELATED SUBSIDIARIES

EFFECTIVE DATE OF 2010 AMENDMENT

Amendment by Pub. L. 111–203 effective on the designated transfer date, see section 1100H of Pub. L. 111–203, set out as a note under section 552a of Title 5, Government Organization and Employees.

§1612. Effect on government agencies

(a) Consultation requirements respecting compliance of credit instruments issued to participating creditor

Any department or agency of the United States which administers a credit program in which it extends, insures, or guarantees consumer credit and in which it provides instruments to a creditor which contain any disclosures required by this subchapter shall, prior to the issuance or continued use of such instruments, consult with the Bureau to assure that such instruments comply with this subchapter.

(b) Inapplicability of Federal civil or criminal penalties to Federal, State, and local agencies

No civil or criminal penalty provided under this subchapter for any violation thereof may be imposed upon the United States or any department or agency thereof, or upon any State or political subdivision thereof, or any agency of any State or political subdivision.

(c) Inapplicability of Federal civil or criminal penalties to participating creditor where violating instrument issued by United States

A creditor participating in a credit program administered, insured, or guaranteed by any department or agency or the United States shall not be held liable for a civil or criminal penalty under this subchapter in any case in which the violation results from the use of an instrument required by any such department or agency.

(d) Applicability of State penalties to violations by participating creditor

A creditor participating in a credit program administered, insured, or guaranteed by any department or agency of the United States shall not be held liable for a civil or criminal penalty under the laws of any State (other than laws determined under section 1610 of this title to be inconsistent with this subchapter) for any technical or procedural failure, such as a failure to use a specific form, to make information available at a specific place on an instrument, or to use a specific typeface, as required by State law, which is caused by the use of an instrument required to be used by such department or agency.

(Pub. L. 90–321, title I, §113, May 29, 1968, 82 Stat. 151; Pub. L. 96–221, title VI, §622(a), Mar. 31, 1980, 94 Stat. 184; Pub. L. 111–203, title X, §1100A(2), July 21, 2010, 124 Stat. 2107.)

EDITORIAL NOTES

AMENDMENTS

2010—Subsec. (a). Pub. L. 111–203 substituted "Bureau" for "Board".
1980—Pub. L. 96–221 amended section generally, designating existing provisions as subsec. (b) and adding subsecs. (a), (c), and (d).

STATUTORY NOTES AND RELATED SUBSIDIARIES

EFFECTIVE DATE OF 2010 AMENDMENT

Amendment by Pub. L. 111–203 effective on the designated transfer date, see section 1100H of Pub. L. 111–203, set out as a note under section 552a of Title 5, Government Organization and Employees.

EFFECTIVE DATE OF 1980 AMENDMENT

Amendment by Pub. L. 96–221 effective on expiration of two years and six months after Mar. 31, 1980, with all regulations, forms, and clauses required to be prescribed to be promulgated at least one year prior to such effective date, and allowing any creditor to comply with any amendments, in accordance with the regulations, forms, and clauses prescribed by the Board prior to such effective date, see section 625 of Pub. L. 96–221, set out as a note under section 1602 of this title.

§1613. Annual reports to Congress by Bureau

Each year the Bureau shall make a report to the Congress concerning the administration of its functions under this subchapter, including such recommendations as the Bureau deems necessary or appropriate. In addition, each report of the Bureau shall include its assessment of the extent to which compliance with the requirements imposed under this subchapter is being achieved.

(Pub. L. 90–321, title I, §114, May 29, 1968, 82 Stat. 151; Pub. L. 96–221, title VI, §610(a), Mar. 31, 1980, 94 Stat. 174; Pub. L. 97–375, title II, §209(b), Dec. 21, 1982, 96 Stat. 1825; Pub. L. 111–203, title X, §1100A(2), July 21, 2010, 124 Stat. 2107.)

EDITORIAL NOTES

AMENDMENTS

2010—Pub. L. 111–203 substituted "Bureau" for "Board" wherever appearing.

1982—Pub. L. 97–375 struck out requirement that the Attorney General make a report on the same terms as the Board.

1980—Pub. L. 96–221 substituted "Each year" for "Not later than January 3 of each year after 1969,".

STATUTORY NOTES AND RELATED SUBSIDIARIES

EFFECTIVE DATE OF 2010 AMENDMENT

Amendment by Pub. L. 111–203 effective on the designated transfer date, see section 1100H of Pub. L. 111–203, set out as a note under section 552a of Title 5, Government Organization and Employees.

EFFECTIVE DATE OF 1980 AMENDMENT

Amendment by Pub. L. 96–221 effective on expiration of two years and six months after Mar. 31, 1980, with all regulations, forms, and clauses required to be prescribed to be promulgated at least one year prior to such effective date, and allowing any creditor to comply with any amendments, in accordance with the regulations, forms, and clauses prescribed by the Board prior to such effective date, see section 625 of Pub. L. 96–221, set out as a note under section 1602 of this title.

§1614. Repealed. Pub. L. 96–221, title VI, §616(b), Mar. 31, 1980, 94 Stat. 182

Section, Pub. L. 90–321, title I, §115, as added Pub. L. 93–495, title IV, §413(a), Oct. 28, 1974, 88 Stat. 1520, related to liability of assignees. See section 1641 of this title.

STATUTORY NOTES AND RELATED SUBSIDIARIES

EFFECTIVE DATE OF REPEAL

Repeal effective on expiration of two years and six months after Mar. 31, 1980, with all regulations, forms, and clauses required to be prescribed to be promulgated at least one year prior to such effective date, and allowing any creditor to comply with any amendments, in accordance with the regulations, forms, and clauses prescribed by the Board prior to such effective date, see section 625 of Pub. L. 96–221, set out as an Effective Date of 1980 Amendment note under section 1602 of this title.

§1615. Prohibition on use of "Rule of 78's" in connection with mortgage refinancings and other consumer loans

(a) Prompt refund of unearned interest required

(1) In general

If a consumer prepays in full the financed amount under any consumer credit transaction, the creditor shall promptly refund any unearned portion of the interest charge to the consumer.

(2) Exception for refund of de minimus [1] amount

No refund shall be required under paragraph (1) with respect to the prepayment of any consumer credit transaction if the total amount of the refund would be less than $1.

(3) Applicability to refinanced transactions and acceleration by the creditor

This subsection shall apply with respect to any prepayment of a consumer credit transaction described in paragraph (1) without regard to the manner or the reason for the prepayment, including—

(A) any prepayment made in connection with the refinancing, consolidation, or restructuring of the transaction; and

(B) any prepayment made as a result of the acceleration of the obligation to repay the amount due with respect to the transaction.

(b) Use of "Rule of 78's" prohibited

For the purpose of calculating any refund of interest required under subsection (a) for any precomputed consumer credit transaction of a term exceeding 61 months which is consummated after September 30, 1993, the creditor shall compute the refund based on a method which is at least as favorable to the consumer as the actuarial method.

(c) Statement of prepayment amount

(1) In general

Before the end of the 5-day period beginning on the date an oral or written request is received by a creditor from a consumer for the disclosure of the amount due on any precomputed consumer credit account, the creditor or assignee shall provide the consumer with a statement of—

(A) the amount necessary to prepay the account in full; and

(B) if the amount disclosed pursuant to subparagraph (A) includes an amount which is required to be refunded under this section with respect to such prepayment, the amount of such refund.

(2) Written statement required if request is in writing

If the customer's request is in writing, the statement under paragraph (1) shall be in writing.

(3) 1 free annual statement

A consumer shall be entitled to obtain 1 statement under paragraph (1) each year without charge.

(4) Additional statements subject to reasonable fees

Any creditor may impose a reasonable fee to cover the cost of providing any statement under paragraph (1) to any consumer in addition to the 1 free annual statement required under paragraph (3) if the amount of the charge for such additional statement is disclosed to the consumer before furnishing such statement.

(d) Definitions

For the purpose of this section—

(1) Actuarial method

The term "actuarial method" means the method of allocating payments made on a debt between the amount financed and the finance charge pursuant to which a payment is applied first to the accumulated finance charge and any remainder is subtracted from, or any deficiency is added to, the unpaid balance of the amount financed.

(2) Consumer, credit

The terms "consumer" and "creditor" have the meanings given to such terms in section 1602 of this title.

(3) Creditor

The term "creditor"—

(A) has the meaning given to such term in section 1602 of this title; and

(B) includes any assignee of any creditor with respect to credit extended in connection with any consumer credit transaction and any subsequent assignee with respect to such credit.

(Pub. L. 102–550, title IX, §933, Oct. 28, 1992, 106 Stat. 3891.)

EDITORIAL NOTES

CODIFICATION

Section was enacted as part of the Housing and Community Development Act of 1992, and not as part of the Consumer Credit Protection Act which comprises this chapter.

1 So in original. Probably should be "de minimis".

§1616. Board review of consumer credit plans and regulations

(a) Required review

Not later than 2 years after the effective date of this Act and every 2 years thereafter, except as provided in subsection (c)(2), the Board shall conduct a review, within the limits of its existing resources available for reporting purposes, of the consumer credit card market, including—

(1) the terms of credit card agreements and the practices of credit card issuers;

(2) the effectiveness of disclosure of terms, fees, and other expenses of credit card plans;

(3) the adequacy of protections against unfair or deceptive acts or practices relating to credit card plans; and

(4) whether or not, and to what extent, the implementation of this Act and the amendments made by this Act has affected—

(A) cost and availability of credit, particularly with respect to non-prime borrowers;

(B) the safety and soundness of credit card issuers;

(C) the use of risk-based pricing; or

(D) credit card product innovation.

(b) Solicitation of public comment

In connection with conducting the review required by subsection (a), the Board shall solicit comment from consumers, credit card issuers, and other interested parties, such as through hearings or written comments.

(c) Regulations

(1) Notice

Following the review required by subsection (a), the Board shall publish a notice in the Federal Register that—

(A) summarizes the review, the comments received from the public solicitation, and other evidence gathered by the Board, such as through consumer testing or other research; and

(B) either—

(i) proposes new or revised regulations or interpretations to update or revise disclosures and protections for consumer credit cards, as appropriate; or

(ii) states the reason for the determination of the Board that new or revised regulations are not necessary.

(2) Revision of review period following material revision of regulations

In the event that the Board materially revises regulations on consumer credit card plans, a review need not be conducted until 2 years after the effective date of the revised regulations, which thereafter shall be treated as the new date for the biennial review required by subsection (a).

(d) Board report to the Congress

The Board shall report to Congress not less frequently than every 2 years, except as provided in subsection (c)(2), on the status of its most recent review, its efforts to address any issues identified from the review, and any recommendations for legislation.

(e) Additional reporting

The Federal banking agencies (as that term is defined in section 1813 of title 12) and the Federal Trade Commission shall provide annually to the Board, and the Board shall include in its annual report to Congress under section 247 of title 12, information about the supervisory and enforcement activities of the agencies with respect to compliance by credit card issuers with applicable Federal consumer protection statutes and regulations, including—

(1) this Act, the amendments made by this Act, and regulations prescribed under this Act and such amendments; and

(2) section 5 of the Federal Trade Commission Act [15 U.S.C. 45], and regulations prescribed under the Federal Trade Commission Act [15 U.S.C. 41 et seq.], including part 227 of title 12 of the Code of Federal Regulations, as prescribed by the Board (referred to as "Regulation AA").

(Pub. L. 111–24, title V, §502, May 22, 2009, 123 Stat. 1755.)

EDITORIAL NOTES

REFERENCES IN TEXT

The effective date of this Act, referred to in subsec. (a), is 9 months after May 22, 2009, except as otherwise specifically provided in Pub. L. 111–24, see section 3 of Pub. L. 111–24, set out as an Effective Date of 2009 Amendment note under section 1602 of this title.

This Act, referred to in subsecs. (a)(4) and (e)(1), is Pub. L. 111–24, May 22, 2009, 123 Stat. 1734, known as the Credit Card Accountability Responsibility and Disclosure Act of 2009, and also as the Credit CARD Act of 2009, which enacted this section and sections 1651, 1665c to 1665e, 1666i–1, 1666i–2, and 1693l–1 of this title and section 1a–7b of Title 16, Conservation, amended sections 1602, 1632, 1637, 1640, 1650, 1666b, 1666c, 1666j, 1681b, 1681j, and 1693m to 1693r of this title, enacted provisions set out as notes under sections 1602, 1637, 1638, 1666b, 1681j, and 1693l–1 of this title and section 5311 of Title 31, Money and Finance, and amended provisions set out as notes under sections 1638 and 1693 of this title. For complete classification of this Act to the Code, see Short Title of 2009 Amendment note set out under section 1601 of this title and Tables.

The Federal Trade Commission Act, referred to in subsec. (e)(2), is act Sept. 26, 1914, ch. 311, 38 Stat. 717, which is classified generally to subchapter I (§41 et seq.) of chapter 2 of this title. For complete classification of this Act to the Code, see section 58 of this title and Tables.

CODIFICATION

Section was enacted as part of the Credit Card Accountability Responsibility and Disclosure Act of 2009, also known as the Credit CARD Act of 2009, and not as part of the Consumer Credit Protection Act which comprises this chapter.

STATUTORY NOTES AND RELATED SUBSIDIARIES

EFFECTIVE DATE

Section effective 9 months after May 22, 2009, except as otherwise specifically provided, see section 3 of Pub. L. 111–24, set out as an Effective Date of 2009 Amendment note under section 1602 of this title.

DEFINITION

For definition of "Board", see section 2 of Pub. L. 111–24, set out as a Regulations note under section 1602 of this title.

PART B—CREDIT TRANSACTIONS

§1631. Disclosure requirements

(a) Duty of creditor or lessor respecting one or more than one obligor

Subject to subsection (b), a creditor or lessor shall disclose to the person who is obligated on a consumer lease or a consumer credit transaction the information required under this subchapter. In a transaction involving more than one obligor, a creditor or lessor, except in a transaction under section 1635 of this title, need not disclose to more than one of such obligors if the obligor given disclosure is a primary obligor.

(b) Creditor or lessor required to make disclosure

If a transaction involves one creditor as defined in section 1602(f) [1] of this title, or one lessor as defined in section 1667(3) of this title, such creditor or lessor shall make the disclosures. If a transaction involves more than one creditor or lessor, only one creditor or lessor shall by required to make the disclosures. The Bureau shall by regulation specify which creditor or lessor shall make the disclosures.

(c) Estimates as satisfying statutory requirements; basis of disclosure for per diem interest

The Bureau may provide by regulation that any portion of the information required to be disclosed by this subchapter may be given in the form of estimates where the provider of such information is not in a position to know exact information. In the case of any consumer credit transaction a portion of the interest on which is determined on a per diem basis and is to be collected upon the consummation of such transaction, any disclosure with respect to such portion of interest shall be deemed to be accurate for purposes of this subchapter if the disclosure is based on information actually known to the creditor at the time that the disclosure documents are being prepared for the consummation of the transaction.

(d) Tolerances for numerical disclosures

The Bureau shall determine whether tolerances for numerical disclosures other than the annual percentage rate are necessary to facilitate compliance with this subchapter, and if it determines that such tolerances are necessary to facilitate compliance, it shall by regulation permit disclosures within such tolerances. The Bureau shall exercise its authority to permit tolerances for numerical disclosures other than the annual percentage rate so that such tolerances are narrow enough to prevent such tolerances from resulting in misleading disclosures or disclosures that circumvent the purposes of this subchapter.

(Pub. L. 90–321, title I, §121, May 29, 1968, 82 Stat. 152; Pub. L. 93–495, title III, §307(c), (d), title IV, §409, Oct. 28, 1974, 88 Stat. 1516, 1519; Pub. L. 94–205, §11, Jan. 2, 1976, 89 Stat. 1159; Pub. L. 96–221, title VI, §611, Mar. 31, 1980, 94 Stat. 174; Pub. L. 104–29, §3(b), Sept. 30, 1995, 109 Stat. 273; Pub. L. 111–203, title X, §1100A(2), July 21, 2010, 124 Stat. 2107.)

REFERENCES IN TEXT

Section 1602(f) of this title, referred to in subsec. (b), was redesignated section 1602(g) of this title by Pub. L. 111–203, title X, §1100A(1)(A), July 21, 2010, 124 Stat. 2107.

AMENDMENTS

2010—Subsecs. (b) to (d). Pub. L. 111–203 substituted "Bureau" for "Board" wherever appearing.

1995—Subsec. (c). Pub. L. 104–29 inserted at end "In the case of any consumer credit transaction a portion of the interest on which is determined on a per diem basis and is to be collected upon the consummation of such transaction, any disclosure with respect to such portion of interest shall be deemed to be accurate for purposes of this subchapter if the disclosure is based on information actually known to the creditor at the time that the disclosure documents are being prepared for the consummation of the transaction."

1980—Subsec. (a). Pub. L. 96–221 substituted provisions respecting to which obligor duty of creditor or lessor, where one or more than one obligor is involved, is owed, for provisions setting forth clear and conspicuous disclosure requirements for creditors to persons extended consumer credit.

Subsec. (b). Pub. L. 96–221 substituted provisions relating to disclosure requirements of creditor or lessor, for provisions relating to statement of information where more than one obligor is involved.

Subsecs. (c), (d). Pub. L. 96–221 added subsecs. (c) and (d).

1976—Subsec. (c). Pub. L. 94–205 struck out subsec. (c) which related to disclosure including a full statement of closing costs incurred and permitted estimates of such information where the lender was not in a position to know exact information.

1974—Subsec. (a). Pub. L. 93–495, §307(c), inserted reference to part D of this subchapter and struck out "and upon whom a finance charge is or may be imposed" after "extended".

Subsec. (b). Pub. L. 93–495, §307(d), inserted reference to part D of this subchapter.

Subsec. (c). Pub. L. 93–495, §409, added subsec (c).

STATUTORY NOTES AND RELATED SUBSIDIARIES

EFFECTIVE DATE OF 2010 AMENDMENT

Amendment by Pub. L. 111–203 effective on the designated transfer date, see section 1100H of Pub. L. 111–203, set out as a note under section 552a of Title 5, Government Organization and Employees.

EFFECTIVE DATE OF 1980 AMENDMENT

Amendment by Pub. L. 96–221 effective on expiration of two years and six months after Mar. 31, 1980, with all regulations, forms, and clauses required to be prescribed to be promulgated at least one year prior to such effective date, and allowing any creditor to comply with any amendments, in accordance with the regulations, forms, and clauses prescribed by the Board prior to such effective date, see section 625 of Pub. L. 96–221, set out as a note under section 1602 of this title.

EFFECTIVE DATE OF 1976 AMENDMENT

Amendment by Pub. L. 94–205 effective Jan. 2, 1976, see section 12 of Pub. L. 94–205, set out as a note under section 2602 of Title 12, Banks and Banking.

EFFECTIVE DATE OF 1974 AMENDMENT

For effective date of amendment by section 307(c), (d) of Pub. L. 93–495, see section 308 of Pub. L. 93–495, set out as an Effective Date note under section 1666 of this title.

For effective date of amendment by section 409 of Pub. L. 93–495, see section 416 of Pub. L. 93–495, set out as an Effective Date note under section 1665a of this title.

EFFECTIVE DATE

Pub. L. 90–321, title V, §504(b), May 29, 1968, 82 Stat. 167, provided in part that chapter 2 of title I, which enacted sections 1631 to 1641 of this title, is effective July 1, 1969.

REAL ESTATE SETTLEMENT PROCEDURES

Provisions of Real Estate Settlement Procedures Act of 1974, as superseding provisions of subsec. (c) of this section insofar as applying to federally related mortgage loans, see section 2605 of Title 12, Banks and Banking.

§1632. Form of disclosure; additional information

(a) Information clearly and conspicuously disclosed; "annual percentage rate" and "finance charge"; order of disclosures and use of different terminology

Information required by this subchapter shall be disclosed clearly and conspicuously, in accordance with regulations of the Bureau. The terms "annual percentage rate" and "finance charge" shall be disclosed more conspicuously than other terms, data, or information provided in connection with a transaction, except information relating to the identify of the creditor. Except as provided in subsection (c), regulations of the Bureau need not require that disclosures pursuant to this subchapter be made in the order set forth in this subchapter and, except as otherwise provided, may permit the use of terminology different from that employed in this subchapter if it conveys substantially the same meaning.

(b) Optional information by creditor or lessor

Any creditor or lessor may supply additional information or explanation with any disclosures required under parts D and E and, except as provided in sections 1637a(b)(3) and 1638(b)(1) of this title, under this part.

(c) Tabular format required for certain disclosures under section 1637(c)

(1) In general

The information described in paragraphs (1)(A), (3)(B)(i)(I), (4)(A), and (4)(C)(i)(I) of section 1637(c) of this title shall be—

(A) disclosed in the form and manner which the Bureau shall prescribe by regulations; and

(B) placed in a conspicuous and prominent location on or with any written application, solicitation, or other document or paper with respect to which such disclosure is required.

(2) Tabular format

(A) Form of table to be prescribed

In the regulations prescribed under paragraph (1)(A) of this subsection, the Bureau shall require that the disclosure of such information shall, to the extent the Bureau determines to be practicable and appropriate, be in the form of a table which—

(i) contains clear and concise headings for each item of such information; and

(ii) provides a clear and concise form for stating each item of information required to be disclosed under each such heading.

(B) Bureau discretion in prescribing order and wording of table

In prescribing the form of the table under subparagraph (A), the Bureau may—

(i) list the items required to be included in the table in a different order than the order in which such items are set forth in paragraph (1)(A) or (4)(A) of section 1637(c) of this title; and

(ii) subject to subparagraph (C), employ terminology which is different than the terminology which is employed in section 1637(c) of this title if such terminology conveys substantially the same meaning.

(C) Grace period

Either the heading or the statement under the heading which relates to the time period referred to in section 1637(c)(1)(A)(iii) of this title shall contain the term "grace period".

(d) Additional electronic disclosures

(1) Posting agreements

Each creditor shall establish and maintain an Internet site on which the creditor shall post the written agreement between the creditor and the consumer for each credit card account under an open-end consumer credit plan.

(2) Creditor to provide contracts to the Bureau

Each creditor shall provide to the Bureau, in electronic format, the consumer credit card agreements that it publishes on its Internet site.

(3) Record repository

The Bureau shall establish and maintain on its publicly available Internet site a central repository of the consumer credit card agreements received from creditors pursuant to this subsection, and such agreements shall be easily accessible and retrievable by the public.

(4) Exception

This subsection shall not apply to individually negotiated changes to contractual terms, such as individually modified workouts or renegotiations of amounts owed by a consumer under an open end consumer credit plan.

(5) Regulations

The Bureau, in consultation with the other Federal banking agencies (as that term is defined in section 1681a of this title) and the Bureau,[1] may promulgate regulations to implement this subsection, including specifying the format for posting the agreements on the Internet sites of creditors and establishing exceptions to paragraphs (1) and (2), in any case in which the administrative burden outweighs the benefit of increased transparency, such as where a credit card plan has a de minimis number of consumer account holders.

(Pub. L. 90–321, title I, §122, May 29, 1968, 82 Stat. 152; Pub. L. 93–495, title III, §307(e), (f), Oct. 28, 1974, 88 Stat. 1516, 1517; Pub. L. 96–221, title VI, §611, Mar. 31, 1980, 94 Stat. 175; Pub. L. 100–583, §2(b), Nov. 3, 1988, 102 Stat. 2966; Pub. L. 100–709, §2(d), Nov. 23, 1988, 102 Stat. 4731; Pub. L. 111–24, title II, §204, May 22, 2009, 123 Stat. 1746; Pub. L. 111–203, title X, §1100A(2), (3), July 21, 2010, 124 Stat. 2107.)

EDITORIAL NOTES

AMENDMENTS

2010—Subsecs. (a), (c). Pub. L. 111–203, §1100A(2), substituted "Bureau" for "Board" wherever appearing.

Subsec. (d)(2), (3). Pub. L. 111–203, §1100A(2), substituted "Bureau" for "Board" wherever appearing.

Subsec. (d)(5). Pub. L. 111–203 substituted "The Bureau, in" for "The Board, in" and "and the Bureau, may" for "and the Federal Trade Commission, may".

2009—Subsec. (d). Pub. L. 111–24 added subsec. (d).

1988—Subsec. (a). Pub. L. 100–583, §2(b)(1), substituted "Except as provided in subsection (c), regulations" for "Regulations".

Subsec. (b). Pub. L. 100–709 substituted "sections 1637a(b)(3) and 1638(b)(1)" for "section 1638(b)(1)".

Subsec. (c). Pub. L. 100–583, §2(b)(2), added subsec. (c).

1980—Subsec. (a). Pub. L. 96–221 substituted provisions setting forth form of disclosure to meet requirements of this subchapter, for provisions setting forth form of disclosure authorized under this part or part D of this subchapter.

Subsec. (b). Pub. L. 96–221 substituted provisions setting forth disclosure requirements for additional information by creditors or lessors, for provisions setting forth disclosure requirements for additional information by creditors.

1974—Subsecs. (a), (b). Pub. L. 93–495 inserted references to part D of this subchapter.

STATUTORY NOTES AND RELATED SUBSIDIARIES

EFFECTIVE DATE OF 2010 AMENDMENT

Amendment by Pub. L. 111–203 effective on the designated transfer date, see section 1100H of Pub. L. 111–203, set out as a note under section 552a of Title 5, Government Organization and Employees.

EFFECTIVE DATE OF 2009 AMENDMENT

Amendment by Pub. L. 111–24 effective 9 months after May 22, 2009, except as otherwise specifically provided, see section 3 of Pub. L. 111–24, set out as a note under section 1602 of this title.

EFFECTIVE DATE OF 1988 AMENDMENT

For effective date of amendments by Pub. L. 100–709, see Regulations; Effective Date note below.

EFFECTIVE DATE OF 1980 AMENDMENT

Amendment by Pub. L. 96–221 effective on expiration of two years and six months after Mar. 31, 1980, with all regulations, forms, and clauses required to be prescribed to be promulgated at least one year prior to such effective date, and allowing any creditor to comply with any amendments, in accordance with the regulations, forms, and clauses prescribed by the Board prior to such effective date, see section 625 of Pub. L. 96–221, set out as a note under section 1602 of this title.

EFFECTIVE DATE OF 1974 AMENDMENT

For effective date of amendment by Pub. L. 93–495, see section 308 of Pub. L. 93–495, set out as an Effective Date note under section 1666 of this title.

REGULATIONS; EFFECTIVE DATE

For provisions relating to promulgation of regulations to implement amendment by Pub. L. 100–709, and effective date of such amendment in connection with those regulations, see section 7 of Pub. L. 100–709, set out as a note under section 1637a of this title.

For provisions relating to promulgation of regulations to implement amendment by Pub. L. 100–583, and effective date of such amendment in connection with those regulations, see section 7 of Pub. L. 100–583, set out as a note under section 1637 of this title.

¹ *So in original.*

§1633. Exemption for State-regulated transactions

The Bureau shall by regulation exempt from the requirements of this part any class of credit transactions within any State if it determines that under the law of that State that class of transactions is subject to requirements substantially similar to those imposed under this part, and that there is adequate provision for enforcement.

(Pub. L. 90–321, title I, §123, May 29, 1968, 82 Stat. 152; Pub. L. 111–203, title X, §1100A(2), July 21, 2010, 124 Stat. 2107.)

EDITORIAL NOTES

AMENDMENTS

2010—Pub. L. 111–203 substituted "Bureau" for "Board".

STATUTORY NOTES AND RELATED SUBSIDIARIES

EFFECTIVE DATE OF 2010 AMENDMENT

Amendment by Pub. L. 111–203 effective on the designated transfer date, see section 1100H of Pub. L. 111–203, set out as a note under section 552a of Title 5, Government Organization and Employees.

§1634. Effect of subsequent occurrence

If information disclosed in accordance with this part is subsequently rendered inaccurate as the result of any act, occurrence, or agreement subsequent to the delivery of the required disclosures, the inaccuracy resulting therefrom does not constitute a violation of this part.

(Pub. L. 90–321, title I, §124, May 29, 1968, 82 Stat. 152.)

§1635. Right of rescission as to certain transactions

(a) Disclosure of obligor's right to rescind

Except as otherwise provided in this section, in the case of any consumer credit transaction (including opening or increasing the credit limit for an open end credit plan) in which a security interest, including any such interest arising by operation of law, is or will be retained or acquired in any property which is used as the principal dwelling of the person to whom credit is extended, the obligor shall have the right to rescind the transaction until midnight of the third business day following the consummation of the transaction or the delivery of the information and rescission forms required under this section together with a statement containing the material disclosures required under this subchapter, whichever is later, by notifying the creditor, in accordance with regulations of the Bureau, of his intention to do so. The creditor shall clearly and conspicuously disclose, in accordance with regulations of the Bureau, to any obligor in a transaction subject to this section the rights of the obligor under this section. The creditor shall also provide, in accordance with regulations of the Bureau, appropriate forms for the obligor to exercise his right to rescind any transaction subject to this section.

(b) Return of money or property following rescission

When an obligor exercises his right to rescind under subsection (a), he is not liable for any finance or other charge, and any security interest given by the obligor, including any such interest arising by operation of law, becomes void upon such a rescission. Within 20 days after receipt of a notice of rescission, the creditor shall return to the obligor any money or property given as earnest money, downpayment, or otherwise, and shall take any action necessary or appropriate to reflect the termination of any security interest created under the transaction. If the creditor has delivered any property to the obligor, the obligor may retain possession of it. Upon the performance of the creditor's obligations under this section, the obligor shall tender the property to the creditor, except that if return of the property in kind would be impracticable or inequitable, the obligor shall tender its reasonable value. Tender shall be made at the location of the property or at the residence of the obligor, at the option of the obligor. If the creditor does not take possession of the property within 20 days after tender by the obligor, ownership of the property vests in the obligor without obligation on his part to pay for it. The procedures prescribed by this subsection shall apply except when otherwise ordered by a court.

(c) Rebuttable presumption of delivery of required disclosures

Notwithstanding any rule of evidence, written acknowledgment of receipt of any disclosures required under this subchapter by a person to whom information, forms, and a statement is required to be given pursuant to this section does no more than create a rebuttable presumption of delivery thereof.

(d) Modification and waiver of rights

The Bureau may, if it finds that such action is necessary in order to permit homeowners to meet bona fide personal financial emergencies, prescribe regulations authorizing the modification or waiver of any rights created under this section to the extent and under the circumstances set forth in those regulations.

(e) Exempted transactions; reapplication of provisions

This section does not apply to—

(1) a residential mortgage transaction as defined in section 1602(w) [1] of this title;
(2) a transaction which constitutes a refinancing or consolidation (with no new advances) of the principal balance then due and any accrued and unpaid finance charges of an existing extension of credit by the same creditor secured by an interest in the same property;
(3) a transaction in which an agency of a State is the creditor; or
(4) advances under a preexisting open end credit plan if a security interest has already been retained or acquired and such advances are in accordance with a previously established credit limit for such plan.

(f) Time limit for exercise of right

An obligor's right of rescission shall expire three years after the date of consummation of the transaction or upon the sale of the property, whichever occurs first, notwithstanding the fact that the information and forms required under this section or any other disclosures required under this part have not been delivered to the obligor, except that if (1) any agency empowered to enforce the provisions of this subchapter institutes a proceeding to enforce the provisions of this section within three years after the date of consummation of the transaction, (2) such agency finds a violation of this section, and (3) the obligor's right to rescind is based in whole or in part on any matter involved in such proceeding, then the obligor's right of rescission shall expire three years after the date of consummation of the transaction or upon the earlier sale of the property, or upon the expiration of one year following the conclusion of the proceeding, or any judicial review or period for judicial review thereof, whichever is later.

(g) Additional relief

In any action in which it is determined that a creditor has violated this section, in addition to rescission the court may award relief under section 1640 of this title for violations of this subchapter not relating to the right to rescind.

(h) Limitation on rescission

An obligor shall have no rescission rights arising solely from the form of written notice used by the creditor to inform the obligor of the rights of the obligor under this section, if the creditor provided the obligor the appropriate form of written notice published and adopted by the Bureau, or a comparable written notice of the rights of the obligor, that was properly completed by the creditor, and otherwise complied with all other requirements of this section regarding notice.

(i) Rescission rights in foreclosure

(1) In general

Notwithstanding section 1649 of this title, and subject to the time period provided in subsection (f), in addition to any other right of rescission available under this section for a transaction, after the initiation of any judicial or nonjudicial foreclosure process on the primary dwelling of an obligor securing an extension of credit, the obligor shall have a right to rescind the transaction equivalent to other rescission rights provided by this section, if—

(A) a mortgage broker fee is not included in the finance charge in accordance with the laws and regulations in effect at the time the consumer credit transaction was consummated; or
(B) the form of notice of rescission for the transaction is not the appropriate form of written notice published and adopted by the Bureau or a comparable written notice, and otherwise complied with all the requirements of this section regarding notice.

(2) Tolerance for disclosures

Notwithstanding section 1605(f) of this title, and subject to the time period provided in subsection (f), for the purposes of exercising any rescission rights after the initiation of any judicial or nonjudicial foreclosure process on the principal dwelling of the obligor securing an extension of credit, the disclosure of the finance charge and other disclosures affected by any finance charge shall be treated as being accurate for purposes of this section if the amount disclosed as the finance charge does not vary from the actual finance charge by more than $35 or is greater than the amount required to be disclosed under this subchapter.

(3) Right of recoupment under State law

Nothing in this subsection affects a consumer's right of rescission in recoupment under State law.

(4) Applicability

This subsection shall apply to all consumer credit transactions in existence or consummated on or after September 30, 1995.

(Pub. L. 90–321, title I, §125, May 29, 1968, 82 Stat. 153; Pub. L. 93–495, title IV, §§404, 405, 412, Oct. 28, 1974, 88 Stat. 1517, 1519; Pub. L. 96–221, title VI, §612(a)(1), (3)–(6), Mar. 31, 1980, 94 Stat. 175, 176; Pub. L. 98–479, title II, §205, Oct. 17, 1984, 98 Stat. 2234; Pub. L. 104–29, §§5, 8, Sept. 30, 1995, 109 Stat. 274, 275; Pub. L. 111–203, title X, §1100A(2), July 21, 2010, 124 Stat. 2107.)

EDITORIAL NOTES

REFERENCES IN TEXT

Section 1602(w) of this title, referred to in subsec. (e)(1), was redesignated section 1602(x) of this title by Pub. L. 111–203, title X, §1100A(1)(A), July 21, 2010, 124 Stat. 2107.

AMENDMENTS

2010—Subsecs. (a), (d), (h), (i)(1)(B). Pub. L. 111–203 substituted "Bureau" for "Board" wherever appearing.

1995—Subsec. (h). Pub. L. 104–29, §5, added subsec. (h).

Subsec. (i). Pub. L. 104–29, §8, added subsec. (i).

1984—Subsec. (e). Pub. L. 98–479 redesignated par. (1) as subsec. (e), redesignated subpars. (A), (B), (C), and (D) of par. (1) as pars. (1), (2), (3), and (4), respectively, and struck out par. (2) which read as follows: "The provisions of paragraph (1)(D) shall cease to be effective 3 years after the effective date of the Truth in Lending Simplification Reform Act."

1980—Subsec. (a). Pub. L. 96–221, §612(a)(1), substituted provisions relating to the right of rescission until midnight of the third business day following the consummation of the transaction or the delivery of the information and rescission forms required together with the statement containing the material disclosures required under this subchapter, whichever is later, for provisions relating to right of rescission until midnight of the third business day following the consummation of the transaction or the delivery of the required disclosures and all other material disclosures required under this part, whichever is later.

Subsec. (b). Pub. L. 96–221, §612(a)(3), (4), inserted provisions setting forth applicability of procedures prescribed by this subsection, and substituted "20" for "ten" in two places.

Subsec. (c). Pub. L. 96–221, §612(a)(5), inserted "information, forms, and" after "whom".

Subsec. (e). Pub. L. 96–221, §612(a)(6), substituted provisions relating to nonapplicability to residential mortgage transactions, refinancing or consolidation transactions, etc., for provisions relating to nonapplicability to creation or retention of first liens.

Subsec. (f). Pub. L. 96–221, §612(a)(6), substituted provisions setting forth duration of right of rescission where the required information and forms or other disclosures required under this part have not been delivered to the obligor, and exceptions to such term, for provisions setting forth duration of right of rescission where the required disclosures or any other material disclosures required under this part have not been delivered to the obligor.

Subsec. (g). Pub. L. 96–221, §612(a)(6), added subsec. (g).

1974—Subsecs. (a), (b). Pub. L. 93–495, §404, inserted provisions relating to security interest arising by operation of law.

Subsec. (e). Pub. L. 93–495, §412, inserted exemption for consumer credit transactions where a State agency is the creditor.

Subsec. (f). Pub. L. 93–495, §405, added subsec. (f).

STATUTORY NOTES AND RELATED SUBSIDIARIES

EFFECTIVE DATE OF 2010 AMENDMENT

Amendment by Pub. L. 111–203 effective on the designated transfer date, see section 1100H of Pub. L. 111–203, set out as a note under section 552a of Title 5, Government Organization and Employees.

EFFECTIVE DATE OF 1980 AMENDMENT

Amendment by Pub. L. 96–221 effective on expiration of two years and six months after Mar. 31, 1980, with all regulations, forms, and clauses required to be prescribed to be promulgated at least one year prior to such effective date, and allowing any creditor to comply with any amendments, in accordance with the regulations, forms, and clauses prescribed by the Board prior to such effective date, see section 625 of Pub. L. 96–221, set out as a note under section 1602 of this title.

EFFECTIVE DATE OF 1974 AMENDMENT

Amendment by Pub. L. 93–495 effective Oct. 28, 1974, see section 416 of Pub. L. 93–495, set out as an Effective Date note under section 1665a of this title.

¹ See References in Text note below.

§1636. Repealed. Pub. L. 96–221, title VI, §614(e)(1), Mar. 31, 1980, 94 Stat. 180

Section, Pub. L. 90–321, title I, §126, May 29, 1968, 82 Stat. 153, related to contents of periodic statements.

EFFECTIVE DATE OF REPEAL

Repeal effective on expiration of two years and six months after Mar. 31, 1980, with all regulations, forms, and clauses required to be prescribed to be promulgated at least one year prior to such effective date, and allowing any creditor to comply with any amendments, in accordance with the regulations, forms, and clauses prescribed by the Board prior to such effective date, see section 625 of Pub. L. 96–221, set out as an Effective Date of 1980 Amendment note under section 1602 of this title.

§1637. Open end consumer credit plans

(a) Required disclosures by creditor

Before opening any account under an open end consumer credit plan, the creditor shall disclose to the person to whom credit is to be extended each of the following items, to the extent applicable:

(1) The conditions under which a finance charge may be imposed, including the time period (if any) within which any credit extended may be repaid without incurring a finance charge, except that the creditor may, at his election and without disclosure, impose no such finance charge if payment is received after the termination of such time period. If no such time period is provided, the creditor shall disclose such fact.

(2) The method of determining the balance upon which a finance charge will be imposed.

(3) The method of determining the amount of the finance charge, including any minimum or fixed amount imposed as a finance charge.

(4) Where one or more periodic rates may be used to compute the finance charge, each such rate, the range of balances to which it is applicable, and the corresponding nominal annual percentage rate determined by multiplying the periodic rate by the number of periods in a year.

(5) Identification of other charges which may be imposed as part of the plan, and their method of computation, in accordance with regulations of the Bureau.

(6) In cases where the credit is or will be secured, a statement that a security interest has been or will be taken in (A) the property purchased as part of the credit transaction, or (B) property not purchased as part of the credit transaction identified by item or type.

(7) A statement, in a form prescribed by regulations of the Bureau of the protection provided by sections 1666 and 1666i of this title to an obligor and the creditor's responsibilities under sections 1666a and 1666i of this title. With respect to one billing cycle per calendar year, at intervals of not less than six months or more than eighteen months, the creditor shall transmit such statement to each obligor to whom the creditor is required to transmit a statement pursuant to subsection (b) for such billing cycle.

(8) In the case of any account under an open end consumer credit plan which provides for any extension of credit which is secured by the consumer's principal dwelling, any information which—

(A) is required to be disclosed under section 1637a(a) of this title; and

(B) the Bureau determines is not described in any other paragraph of this subsection.

(b) Statement required with each billing cycle

The creditor of any account under an open end consumer credit plan shall transmit to the obligor, for each billing cycle at the end of which there is an outstanding balance in that account or with respect to which a finance charge is imposed, a statement setting forth each of the following items to the extent applicable:

(1) The outstanding balance in the account at the beginning of the statement period.

(2) The amount and date of each extension of credit during the period, and a brief identification, on or accompanying the statement of each extension of credit in a form prescribed by the Bureau sufficient to enable the obligor either to identify the transaction or to relate it to copies of sales vouchers or similar instruments previously furnished, except that a creditor's failure to disclose such information in accordance with this paragraph shall not be deemed a failure to comply with this part or this subchapter if (A) the creditor maintains procedures reasonably

adapted to procure and provide such information, and (B) the creditor responds to and treats any inquiry for clarification or documentation as a billing error and an erroneously billed amount under section 1666 of this title. In lieu of complying with the requirements of the previous sentence, in the case of any transaction in which the creditor and seller are the same person, as defined by the Bureau, and such person's open end credit plan has fewer than 15,000 accounts, the creditor may elect to provide only the amount and date of each extension of credit during the period and the seller's name and location where the transaction took place if (A) a brief identification of the transaction has been previously furnished, and (B) the creditor responds to and treats any inquiry for clarification or documentation as a billing error and an erroneously billed amount under section 1666 of this title.

(3) The total amount credited to the account during the period.

(4) The amount of any finance charge added to the account during the period, itemized to show the amounts, if any, due to the application of percentage rates and the amount, if any, imposed as a minimum or fixed charge.

(5) Where one or more periodic rates may be used to compute the finance charge, each such rate, the range of balances to which it is applicable, and, unless the annual percentage rate (determined under section 1606(a)(2) of this title) is required to be disclosed pursuant to paragraph (6), the corresponding nominal annual percentage rate determined by multiplying the periodic rate by the number of periods in a year.

(6) Where the total finance charge exceeds 50 cents for a monthly or longer billing cycle, or the pro rata part of 50 cents for a billing cycle shorter than monthly, the total finance charge expressed as an annual percentage rate (determined under section 1606(a)(2) of this title), except that if the finance charge is the sum of two or more products of a rate times a portion of the balance, the creditor may, in lieu of disclosing a single rate for the total charge, disclose each such rate expressed as an annual percentage rate, and the part of the balance to which it is applicable.

(7) The balance on which the finance charge was computed and a statement of how the balance was determined. If the balance is determined without first deducting all credits during the period, that fact and the amount of such payments shall also be disclosed.

(8) The outstanding balance in the account at the end of the period.

(9) The date by which or the period (if any) within which, payment must be made to avoid additional finance charges, except that the creditor may, at his election and without disclosure, impose no such additional finance charge if payment is received after such date or the termination of such period.

(10) The address to be used by the creditor for the purpose of receiving billing inquiries from the obligor.

(11)(A) A written statement in the following form: "Minimum Payment Warning: Making only the minimum payment will increase the amount of interest you pay and the time it takes to repay your balance.", or such similar statement as is established by the Bureau pursuant to consumer testing.

(B) Repayment information that would apply to the outstanding balance of the consumer under the credit plan, including—

(i) the number of months (rounded to the nearest month) that it would take to pay the entire amount of that balance, if the consumer pays only the required minimum monthly payments and if no further advances are made;

(ii) the total cost to the consumer, including interest and principal payments, of paying that balance in full, if the consumer pays only the required minimum monthly payments and if no further advances are made;

(iii) the monthly payment amount that would be required for the consumer to eliminate the outstanding balance in 36 months, if no further advances are made, and the total cost to the consumer, including interest and principal payments, of paying that balance in full if the consumer pays the balance over 36 months; and

(iv) a toll-free telephone number at which the consumer may receive information about accessing credit counseling and debt management services.

(C)(i) Subject to clause (ii), in making the disclosures under subparagraph (B), the creditor shall apply the interest rate or rates in effect on the date on which the disclosure is made until the date on which the balance would be paid in full.

(ii) If the interest rate in effect on the date on which the disclosure is made is a temporary rate that will change under a contractual provision applying an index or formula for subsequent interest rate adjustment, the creditor shall apply the interest rate in effect on the date on which the disclosure is made for as long as that interest rate will apply under that contractual provision, and then apply an interest rate based on the index or formula in effect on the applicable billing date.

(D) All of the information described in subparagraph (B) shall—

(i) be disclosed in the form and manner which the Bureau shall prescribe, by regulation, and in a manner that avoids duplication; and

(ii) be placed in a conspicuous and prominent location on the billing statement.

(E) In the regulations prescribed under subparagraph (D), the Bureau shall require that the disclosure of such information shall be in the form of a table that—

(i) contains clear and concise headings for each item of such information; and

(ii) provides a clear and concise form stating each item of information required to be disclosed under each such heading.

(F) In prescribing the form of the table under subparagraph (E), the Bureau shall require that—

(i) all of the information in the table, and not just a reference to the table, be placed on the billing statement, as required by this paragraph; and

(ii) the items required to be included in the table shall be listed in the order in which such items are set forth in subparagraph (B).

(G) In prescribing the form of the table under subparagraph (D), the Bureau shall employ terminology which is different than the terminology which is employed in subparagraph (B), if such terminology is more easily understood and conveys substantially the same meaning.

(12) REQUIREMENTS RELATING TO LATE PAYMENT DEADLINES AND PENALTIES.—

(A) LATE PAYMENT DEADLINE REQUIRED TO BE DISCLOSED.—In the case of a credit card account under an open end consumer credit plan under which a late fee or charge may be imposed due to the failure of the obligor to make payment on or before the due date for such payment, the periodic statement required under subsection (b) with respect to the account shall include, in a conspicuous location on the billing statement, the date on which the payment is due or, if different, the date on which a late payment fee will be charged, together with the amount of the fee or charge to be imposed if payment is made after that date.

(B) DISCLOSURE OF INCREASE IN INTEREST RATES FOR LATE PAYMENTS.—If 1 or more late payments under an open end consumer credit plan may result in an increase in the annual percentage rate applicable to the account, the statement required under subsection (b) with respect to the account shall include conspicuous notice of such fact, together with the applicable penalty annual percentage rate, in close proximity to the disclosure required under subparagraph (A) of the date on which payment is due under the terms of the account.

(C) PAYMENTS AT LOCAL BRANCHES.—If the creditor, in the case of a credit card account referred to in subparagraph (A), is a financial institution which maintains branches or offices at which payments on any such account are accepted from the obligor in person, the date on which the obligor makes a payment on the account at such branch or office shall be considered to be the date on which the payment is made for purposes of determining whether a late fee or charge may be imposed due to the failure of the obligor to make payment on or before the due date for such payment.

(c) Disclosure in credit and charge card applications and solicitations

(1) Direct mail applications and solicitations

(A) Information in tabular format

Any application to open a credit card account for any person under an open end consumer credit plan, or a solicitation to open such an account without requiring an application, that is mailed to consumers shall disclose the following information, subject to subsection (e) and section 1632(c) of this title:

(i) Annual percentage rates

(I) Each annual percentage rate applicable to extensions of credit under such credit plan.

(II) Where an extension of credit is subject to a variable rate, the fact that the rate is variable, the annual percentage rate in effect at the time of the mailing, and how the rate is determined.

(III) Where more than one rate applies, the range of balances to which each rate applies.

(ii) Annual and other fees

(I) Any annual fee, other periodic fee, or membership fee imposed for the issuance or availability of a credit card, including any account maintenance fee or other charge imposed based on activity or inactivity for the account during the billing cycle.

(II) Any minimum finance charge imposed for each period during which any extension of credit which is subject to a finance charge is outstanding.

(III) Any transaction charge imposed in connection with use of the card to purchase goods or services.

(iii) Grace period

(I) The date by which or the period within which any credit extended under such credit plan for purchases of goods or services must be repaid to avoid incurring a finance charge, and, if no such period is offered, such fact shall be clearly stated.

(II) If the length of such "grace period" varies, the card issuer may disclose the range of days in the grace period, the minimum number of days in the grace period, or the average number of days in the grace period, if the disclosure is identified as such.

(iv) Balance calculation method

(I) The name of the balance calculation method used in determining the balance on which the finance charge is computed if the method used has been defined by the Bureau, or a detailed explanation of the balance calculation method used if the method has not been so defined.

(II) In prescribing regulations to carry out this clause, the Bureau shall define and name not more than the 5 balance calculation methods determined by the Bureau to be the most commonly used methods.

(B) Other information

In addition to the information required to be disclosed under subparagraph (A), each application or solicitation to which such subparagraph applies shall disclose clearly and conspicuously the following information, subject to subsections (e) and (f):

(i) Cash advance fee

Any fee imposed for an extension of credit in the form of cash.

(ii) Late fee

Any fee imposed for a late payment.

(iii) Over-the-limit fee

Any fee imposed in connection with an extension of credit in excess of the amount of credit authorized to be extended with respect to such account.

(2) Telephone solicitations

(A) In general

In any telephone solicitation to open a credit card account for any person under an open end consumer credit plan, the person making the solicitation shall orally disclose the information described in paragraph (1)(A).

(B) Exception

Subparagraph (A) shall not apply to any telephone solicitation if—
(i) the credit card issuer—
(I) does not impose any fee described in paragraph (1)(A)(ii)(I); or
(II) does not impose any fee in connection with telephone solicitations unless the consumer signifies acceptance by using the card;

(ii) the card issuer discloses clearly and conspicuously in writing the information described in paragraph (1) within 30 days after the consumer requests the card, but in no event later than the date of delivery of the card; and
(iii) the card issuer discloses clearly and conspicuously that the consumer is not obligated to accept the card or account and the consumer will not be obligated to pay any of the fees or charges disclosed unless the consumer elects to accept the card or account by using the card.

(3) Applications and solicitations by other means

(A) In general

Any application to open a credit card account for any person under an open end consumer credit plan, and any solicitation to open such an account without requiring an application, that is made available to the public or contained in catalogs, magazines, or other publications shall meet the disclosure requirements of subparagraph (B), (C), or (D).

(B) Specific information

An application or solicitation described in subparagraph (A) meets the requirement of this subparagraph if such application or solicitation contains—
(i) the information—
(I) described in paragraph (1)(A) in the form required under section 1632(c) of this title, subject to subsection (e), and
(II) described in paragraph (1)(B) in a clear and conspicuous form, subject to subsections (e) and (f);

(ii) a statement, in a conspicuous and prominent location on the application or solicitation, that—
(I) the information is accurate as of the date the application or solicitation was printed;
(II) the information contained in the application or solicitation is subject to change after such date; and
(III) the applicant should contact the creditor for information on any change in the information contained in the application or solicitation since it was printed;

(iii) a clear and conspicuous disclosure of the date the application or solicitation was printed; and
(iv) a disclosure, in a conspicuous and prominent location on the application or solicitation, of a toll free telephone number or a mailing address at which the applicant may contact the creditor to obtain any change in the information provided in the application or solicitation since it was printed.

(C) General information without any specific term

An application or solicitation described in subparagraph (A) meets the requirement of this subparagraph if such application or solicitation—
(i) contains a statement, in a conspicuous and prominent location on the application or solicitation, that—
(I) there are costs associated with the use of credit cards; and
(II) the applicant may contact the creditor to request disclosure of specific information of such costs by calling a toll free telephone number or by writing to an address, specified in the application;

(ii) contains a disclosure, in a conspicuous and prominent location on the application or solicitation, of a toll free telephone number and a mailing address at which the applicant may contact the creditor to obtain such information; and

(iii) does not contain any of the items described in paragraph (1).

(D) Applications or solicitations containing subsection (a) disclosures

An application or solicitation meets the requirement of this subparagraph if it contains, or is accompanied by—

(i) the disclosures required by paragraphs (1) through (6) of subsection (a);

(ii) the disclosures required by subparagraphs (A) and (B) of paragraph (1) of this subsection included clearly and conspiciously [1] (except that the provisions of section 1632(c) of this title shall not apply); and

(iii) a toll free telephone number or a mailing address at which the applicant may contact the creditor to obtain any change in the information provided.

(E) Prompt response to information requests

Upon receipt of a request for any of the information referred to in subparagraph (B), (C), or (D), the card issuer or the agent of such issuer shall promptly disclose all of the information described in paragraph (1).

(4) Charge card applications and solicitations

(A) In general

Any application or solicitation to open a charge card account shall disclose clearly and conspicuously the following information in the form required by section 1632(c) of this title, subject to subsection (e):

(i) Any annual fee, other periodic fee, or membership fee imposed for the issuance or availability of the charge card, including any account maintenance fee or other charge imposed based on activity or inactivity for the account during the billing cycle.

(ii) Any transaction charge imposed in connection with use of the card to purchase goods or services.

(iii) A statement that charges incurred by use of the charge card are due and payable upon receipt of a periodic statement rendered for such charge card account.

(B) Other information

In addition to the information required to be disclosed under subparagraph (A), each written application or solicitation to which such subparagraph applies shall disclose clearly and conspicuously the following information, subject to subsections (e) and (f):

(i) Cash advance fee

Any fee imposed for an extension of credit in the form of cash.

(ii) Late fee

Any fee imposed for a late payment.

(iii) Over-the-limit fee

Any fee imposed in connection with an extension of credit in excess of the amount of credit authorized to be extended with respect to such account.

(C) Applications and solicitations by other means

Any application to open a charge card account, and any solicitation to open such an account without requiring an application, that is made available to the public or contained in catalogs, magazines, or other publications shall contain—

(i) the information—

(I) described in subparagraph (A) in the form required under section 1632(c) of this title, subject to subsection (e), and

(II) described in subparagraph (B) in a clear and conspicuous form, subject to subsections (e) and (f);

(ii) a statement, in a conspicuous and prominent location on the application or solicitation, that—

(I) the information is accurate as of the date the application or solicitation was printed;

(II) the information contained in the application or solicitation is subject to change after such date; and

(III) the applicant should contact the creditor for information on any change in the information contained in the application or solicitation since it was printed;

(iii) a clear and conspicuous disclosure of the date the application or solicitation was printed; and

(iv) a disclosure, in a conspicuous and prominent location on the application or solicitation, of a toll free telephone number or a mailing address at which the applicant may contact the creditor to obtain any change in the information provided in the application or solicitation since it was printed.

(D) Issuers of charge cards which provide access to open end consumer credit plans

If a charge card permits the card holder to receive an extension of credit under an open end consumer credit plan, which is not maintained by the charge card issuer, the charge card issuer may provide the information described in subparagraphs (A) and (B) in the form required by such subparagraphs in lieu of the information required to be provided under paragraph (1), (2), or (3) with respect to any credit extended under such plan, if the charge card issuer discloses clearly and conspicuously to the consumer in the application or solicitation that—

(i) the charge card issuer will make an independent decision as to whether to issue the card;

(ii) the charge card may arrive before the decision is made with respect to an extension of credit under an open end consumer credit plan; and

(iii) approval by the charge card issuer does not constitute approval by the issuer of the extension of credit.

The information required to be disclosed under paragraph (1) shall be provided to the charge card holder by the creditor which maintains such open end consumer credit plan before the first extension of credit under such plan.

(E) Charge card defined

For the purposes of this subsection, the term "charge card" means a card, plate, or other single credit device that may be used from time to time to obtain credit which is not subject to a finance charge.

(5) Regulatory authority of the Bureau

The Bureau may, by regulation, require the disclosure of information in addition to that otherwise required by this subsection or subsection (d), and modify any disclosure of information required by this subsection or subsection (d), in any application to open a credit card account for any person under an open end consumer credit plan or any application to open a charge card account for any person, or a solicitation to open any such account without requiring an application, if the Bureau determines that such action is necessary to carry out the purposes of, or prevent evasions of, any paragraph of this subsection.

(6) Additional notice concerning "introductory rates"

(A) In general

Except as provided in subparagraph (B), an application or solicitation to open a credit card account and all promotional materials accompanying such application or solicitation for which a disclosure is required under paragraph (1), and that offers a temporary annual percentage rate of interest, shall—

(i) use the term "introductory" in immediate proximity to each listing of the temporary annual percentage rate applicable to such account, which term shall appear clearly and conspicuously;

(ii) if the annual percentage rate of interest that will apply after the end of the temporary rate period will be a fixed rate, state in a clear and conspicuous manner in a prominent location closely proximate to the first listing of the temporary annual percentage rate (other than a listing of the temporary annual percentage rate in the tabular format described in section 1632(c) of this title), the time period in which the introductory period will end and the annual percentage rate that will apply after the end of the introductory period; and

(iii) if the annual percentage rate that will apply after the end of the temporary rate period will vary in accordance with an index, state in a clear and conspicuous manner in a prominent location closely proximate to the first listing of the temporary annual percentage rate (other than a listing in the tabular format prescribed by section 1632(c) of this title), the time period in which the introductory period will end and the rate that will apply after that, based on an annual percentage rate that was in effect within 60 days before the date of mailing the application or solicitation.

(B) Exception

Clauses (ii) and (iii) of subparagraph (A) do not apply with respect to any listing of a temporary annual percentage rate on an envelope or other enclosure in which an application or solicitation to open a credit card account is mailed.

(C) Conditions for introductory rates

An application or solicitation to open a credit card account for which a disclosure is required under paragraph (1), and that offers a temporary annual percentage rate of interest shall, if that rate of interest is revocable under any circumstance or upon any event, clearly and conspicuously disclose, in a prominent manner on or with such application or solicitation—

(i) a general description of the circumstances that may result in the revocation of the temporary annual percentage rate; and

(ii) if the annual percentage rate that will apply upon the revocation of the temporary annual percentage rate—

(I) will be a fixed rate, the annual percentage rate that will apply upon the revocation of the temporary annual percentage rate; or

(II) will vary in accordance with an index, the rate that will apply after the temporary rate, based on an annual percentage rate that was in effect within 60 days before the date of mailing the application or solicitation.

(D) Definitions

In this paragraph—

(i) the terms "temporary annual percentage rate of interest" and "temporary annual percentage rate" mean any rate of interest applicable to a credit card account for an introductory period of less than 1 year, if that rate is less than an annual percentage rate that was in effect within 60 days before the date of mailing the application or solicitation; and

(ii) the term "introductory period" means the maximum time period for which the temporary annual percentage rate may be applicable.

(E) Relation to other disclosure requirements

Nothing in this paragraph may be construed to supersede subsection (a) of section 1632 of this title, or any disclosure required by paragraph (1) or any other provision of this subsection.

(7) Internet-based solicitations

(A) In general

In any solicitation to open a credit card account for any person under an open end consumer credit plan using the Internet or other interactive computer service, the person making the solicitation shall clearly and conspicuously disclose—

(i) the information described in subparagraphs (A) and (B) of paragraph (1); and

(ii) the information described in paragraph (6).

(B) Form of disclosure

The disclosures required by subparagraph (A) shall be—

(i) readily accessible to consumers in close proximity to the solicitation to open a credit card account; and

(ii) updated regularly to reflect the current policies, terms, and fee amounts applicable to the credit card account.

(C) Definitions

For purposes of this paragraph—

(i) the term "Internet" means the international computer network of both Federal and non-Federal interoperable packet switched data networks; and

(ii) the term "interactive computer service" means any information service, system, or access software provider that provides or enables computer access by multiple users to a computer server, including specifically a service or system that provides access to the Internet and such systems operated or services offered by libraries or educational institutions.

(8) Applications from underage consumers

(A) Prohibition on issuance

No credit card may be issued to, or open end consumer credit plan established by or on behalf of, a consumer who has not attained the age of 21, unless the consumer has submitted a written application to the card issuer that meets the requirements of subparagraph (B).

(B) Application requirements

An application to open a credit card account by a consumer who has not attained the age of 21 as of the date of submission of the application shall require—

(i) the signature of a cosigner, including the parent, legal guardian, spouse, or any other individual who has attained the age of 21 having a means to repay debts incurred by the consumer in connection with the account, indicating joint liability for debts incurred by the consumer in connection with the account before the consumer has attained the age of 21; or

(ii) submission by the consumer of financial information, including through an application, indicating an independent means of repaying any obligation arising from the proposed extension of credit in connection with the account.

(C) Safe harbor

The Bureau shall promulgate regulations providing standards that, if met, would satisfy the requirements of subparagraph (B)(ii).

(d) Disclosure prior to renewal

(1) In general

A card issuer that has changed or amended any term of the account since the last renewal that has not been previously disclosed or that imposes any fee described in subsection (c)(1)(A)(ii)(I) or (c)(4)(A)(i) shall transmit to a consumer at least 30 days prior to the scheduled renewal date of the consumer's credit or charge card account a clear and conspicuous disclosure of—

(A) the date by which, the month by which, or the billing period at the close of which, the account will expire if not renewed;

(B) the information described in subsection (c)(1)(A) or (c)(4)(A) that would apply if the account were renewed, subject to subsection (e); and

(C) the method by which the consumer may terminate continued credit availability under the account.

(2) Short-term renewals

The Bureau may by regulation provide for fewer disclosures than are required by paragraph (1) in the case of an account which is renewable for a period of less than 6 months.

(e) Other rules for disclosures under subsections (c) and (d)

(1) Fees determined on the basis of a percentage

If the amount of any fee required to be disclosed under subsection (c) or (d) is determined on the basis of a percentage of another amount, the percentage used in making such determination and the identification of the amount against which such percentage is applied shall be disclosed in lieu of the amount of such fee.

(2) Disclosure only of fees actually imposed

If a credit or charge card issuer does not impose any fee required to be disclosed under any provision of subsection (c) or (d), such provision shall not apply with respect to such issuer.

(f) Disclosure of range of certain fees which vary by State allowed

If the amount of any fee required to be disclosed by a credit or charge card issuer under paragraph (1)(B), (3)(B)(i) (II), (4)(B), or (4)(C)(i)(II) of subsection (c) varies from State to State, the card issuer may disclose the range of such fees for purposes of subsection (c) in lieu of the amount for each applicable State, if such disclosure includes a statement that the amount of such fee varies from State to State.

(g) Insurance in connection with certain open end credit card plans

(1) Change in insurance carrier

Whenever a card issuer that offers any guarantee or insurance for repayment of all or part of the outstanding balance of an open end credit card plan proposes to change the person providing that guarantee or insurance, the card issuer shall send each insured consumer written notice of the proposed change not less than 30 days prior to the change, including notice of any increase in the rate or substantial decrease in coverage or service which will result from such change. Such notice may be included on or with the monthly statement provided to the consumer prior to the month in which the proposed change would take effect.

(2) Notice of new insurance coverage

In any case in which a proposed change described in paragraph (1) occurs, the insured consumer shall be given the name and address of the new guarantor or insurer and a copy of the policy or group certificate containing the basic terms and conditions, including the premium rate to be charged.

(3) Right to discontinue guarantee or insurance

The notices required under paragraphs (1) and (2) shall each include a statement that the consumer has the option to discontinue the insurance or guarantee.

(4) No preemption of State law

No provision of this subsection shall be construed as superseding any provision of State law which is applicable to the regulation of insurance.

(5) Bureau definition of substantial decrease in coverage or service

The Bureau shall define, in regulations, what constitutes a "substantial decrease in coverage or service" for purposes of paragraph (1).

(h) Prohibition on certain actions for failure to incur finance charges

A creditor of an account under an open end consumer credit plan may not terminate an account prior to its expiration date solely because the consumer has not incurred finance charges on the account. Nothing in this subsection shall prohibit a creditor from terminating an account for inactivity in 3 or more consecutive months.

(i) Advance notice of rate increase and other changes required

(1) Advance notice of increase in interest rate required

In the case of any credit card account under an open end consumer credit plan, a creditor shall provide a written notice of an increase in an annual percentage rate (except in the case of an increase described in paragraph (1), (2), or (3) of section 1666i–1(b) of this title) not later than 45 days prior to the effective date of the increase.

(2) Advance notice of other significant changes required

In the case of any credit card account under an open end consumer credit plan, a creditor shall provide a written notice of any significant change, as determined by rule of the Bureau, in the terms (including an increase in any fee or finance charge, other than as provided in paragraph (1)) of the cardholder agreement between the creditor and the obligor, not later than 45 days prior to the effective date of the change.

(3) Notice of right to cancel

Each notice required by paragraph (1) or (2) shall be made in a clear and conspicuous manner, and shall contain a brief statement of the right of the obligor to cancel the account pursuant to rules established by the Bureau before the effective date of the subject rate increase or other change.

(4) Rule of construction

Closure or cancellation of an account by the obligor shall not constitute a default under an existing cardholder agreement, and shall not trigger an obligation to immediately repay the obligation in full or through a method that is less beneficial to the obligor than one of the methods described in section 1666i–1(c)(2) of this title, or the imposition of any other penalty or fee.

(j) Prohibition on penalties for on-time payments

(1) Prohibition on double-cycle billing and penalties for on-time payments

Except as provided in paragraph (2), a creditor may not impose any finance charge on a credit card account under an open end consumer credit plan as a result of the loss of any time period provided by the creditor within which the obligor may repay any portion of the credit extended without incurring a finance charge, with respect to—

(A) any balances for days in billing cycles that precede the most recent billing cycle; or

(B) any balances or portions thereof in the current billing cycle that were repaid within such time period.

(2) Exceptions

Paragraph (1) does not apply to—

(A) any adjustment to a finance charge as a result of the resolution of a dispute; or

(B) any adjustment to a finance charge as a result of the return of a payment for insufficient funds.

(k) Opt-in required for over-the-limit transactions if fees are imposed

(1) In general

In the case of any credit card account under an open end consumer credit plan under which an over-the-limit fee may be imposed by the creditor for any extension of credit in excess of the amount of credit authorized to be extended under such account, no such fee shall be charged, unless the consumer has expressly elected to permit the creditor, with respect to such account, to complete transactions involving the extension of credit under such account in excess of the amount of credit authorized.

(2) Disclosure by creditor

No election by a consumer under paragraph (1) shall take effect unless the consumer, before making such election, received a notice from the creditor of any over-the-limit fee in the form and manner, and at the time, determined by the Bureau. If the consumer makes the election referred to in paragraph (1), the creditor shall provide notice to the consumer of the right to revoke the election, in the form prescribed by the Bureau, in any periodic statement that includes notice of the imposition of an over-the-limit fee during the period covered by the statement.

(3) Form of election

A consumer may make or revoke the election referred to in paragraph (1) orally, electronically, or in writing, pursuant to regulations prescribed by the Bureau. The Bureau shall prescribe regulations to ensure that the same options are available for both making and revoking such election.

(4) Time of election

A consumer may make the election referred to in paragraph (1) at any time, and such election shall be effective until the election is revoked in the manner prescribed under paragraph (3).

(5) Regulations

The Bureau shall prescribe regulations—

(A) governing disclosures under this subsection; and

(B) that prevent unfair or deceptive acts or practices in connection with the manipulation of credit limits designed to increase over-the-limit fees or other penalty fees.

(6) Rule of construction

Nothing in this subsection shall be construed to prohibit a creditor from completing an over-the-limit transaction, provided that a consumer who has not made a valid election under paragraph (1) is not charged an over-the-limit fee for such transaction.

(7) Restriction on fees charged for an over-the-limit transaction

With respect to a credit card account under an open end consumer credit plan, an over-the-limit fee may be imposed only once during a billing cycle if the credit limit on the account is exceeded, and an over-the-limit fee, with respect to such excess credit, may be imposed only once in each of the 2 subsequent billing cycles, unless the consumer has obtained an additional extension of credit in excess of such credit limit during any such subsequent cycle or the consumer reduces the outstanding balance below the credit limit as of the end of such billing cycle.

(l) Limit on fees related to method of payment

With respect to a credit card account under an open end consumer credit plan, the creditor may not impose a separate fee to allow the obligor to repay an extension of credit or finance charge, whether such repayment is made by mail, electronic transfer, telephone authorization, or other means, unless such payment involves an expedited service by a service representative of the creditor.

(m) Use of term "fixed rate"

With respect to the terms of any credit card account under an open end consumer credit plan, the term "fixed", when appearing in conjunction with a reference to the annual percentage rate or interest rate applicable with respect to such account, may only be used to refer to an annual percentage rate or interest rate that will not change or vary for any reason over the period specified clearly and conspicuously in the terms of the account.

(n) Standards applicable to initial issuance of subprime or "fee harvester" cards

(1) In general

If the terms of a credit card account under an open end consumer credit plan require the payment of any fees (other than any late fee, over-the-limit fee, or fee for a payment returned for insufficient funds) by the consumer in the first year during which the account is opened in an aggregate amount in excess of 25 percent of the total amount of credit authorized under the account when the account is opened, no payment of any fees (other than any late fee, over-the-limit fee, or fee for a payment returned for insufficient funds) may be made from the credit made available under the terms of the account.

(2) Rule of construction

No provision of this subsection may be construed as authorizing any imposition or payment of advance fees otherwise prohibited by any provision of law.

(o) Due dates for credit card accounts

(1) In general

The payment due date for a credit card account under an open end consumer credit plan shall be the same day each month.

(2) Weekend or holiday due dates

If the payment due date for a credit card account under an open end consumer credit plan is a day on which the creditor does not receive or accept payments by mail (including weekends and holidays), the creditor may not treat a payment received on the next business day as late for any purpose.

(p) Parental approval required to increase credit lines for accounts for which parent is jointly liable

No increase may be made in the amount of credit authorized to be extended under a credit card account for which a parent, legal guardian, or spouse of the consumer, or any other individual has assumed joint liability for debts incurred by the consumer in connection with the account before the consumer attains the age of 21, unless that parent, guardian, or spouse approves in writing, and assumes joint liability for, such increase.

(r) [2] College card agreements

(1) Definitions

For purposes of this subsection, the following definitions shall apply:

(A) College affinity card

The term "college affinity card" means a credit card issued by a credit card issuer under an open end consumer credit plan in conjunction with an agreement between the issuer and an institution of higher education, or an alumni organization or foundation affiliated with or related to such institution, under which such cards are issued to college students who have an affinity with such institution, organization and—

(i) the creditor has agreed to donate a portion of the proceeds of the credit card to the institution, organization, or foundation (including a lump sum or 1-time payment of money for access);

(ii) the creditor has agreed to offer discounted terms to the consumer; or

(iii) the credit card bears the name, emblem, mascot, or logo of such institution, organization, or foundation, or other words, pictures, or symbols readily identified with such institution, organization, or foundation.

(B) College student credit card account

The term "college student credit card account" means a credit card account under an open end consumer credit plan established or maintained for or on behalf of any college student.

(C) College student

The term "college student" means an individual who is a full-time or a part-time student attending an institution of higher education.

(D) Institution of higher education

The term "institution of higher education" has the same meaning as in section [3] 1001 and 1002 of title 20.

(2) Reports by creditors

(A) In general

Each creditor shall submit an annual report to the Bureau containing the terms and conditions of all business, marketing, and promotional agreements and college affinity card agreements with an institution of higher education, or an alumni organization or foundation affiliated with or related to such institution, with respect to any college student credit card issued to a college student at such institution.

(B) Details of report

The information required to be reported under subparagraph (A) includes—

(i) any memorandum of understanding between or among a creditor, an institution of higher education, an alumni association, or foundation that directly or indirectly relates to any aspect of any agreement referred to in such subparagraph or controls or directs any obligations or distribution of benefits between or among any such entities;

(ii) the amount of any payments from the creditor to the institution, organization, or foundation during the period covered by the report, and the precise terms of any agreement under which such amounts are determined; and

(iii) the number of credit card accounts covered by any such agreement that were opened during the period covered by the report, and the total number of credit card accounts covered by the agreement that were outstanding at the end of such period.

(C) Aggregation by institution

The information required to be reported under subparagraph (A) shall be aggregated with respect to each institution of higher education or alumni organization or foundation affiliated with or related to such institution.

(D) Initial report

The initial report required under subparagraph (A) shall be submitted to the Bureau before the end of the 9-month period beginning on May 22, 2009.

(3) Reports by Bureau

The Bureau shall submit to the Congress, and make available to the public, an annual report that lists the information concerning credit card agreements submitted to the Bureau under paragraph (2) by each institution of higher education, alumni organization, or foundation.

(Pub. L. 90–321, title I, §127, May 29, 1968, 82 Stat. 153; Pub. L. 93–495, title III, §§304, 305, title IV, §§411, 415, Oct. 28, 1974, 88 Stat. 1511, 1519, 1521; Pub. L. 96–221, title VI, §613(a)–(e), Mar. 31, 1980, 94 Stat. 176, 177; Pub. L. 100–583, §§2(a), 6, Nov. 3, 1988, 102 Stat. 2960, 2968; Pub. L. 100–709, §2(b), Nov. 23, 1988, 102 Stat. 4729; Pub. L. 109–8, title XIII, §§1301(a), 1303(a), 1304(a), 1305(a), 1306(a), Apr. 20, 2005, 119 Stat. 204, 209, 211, 212; Pub. L. 111–24, title I, §§101(a)(1), 102(a), 103, 105, 106(a), title II, §§201(a), 202, 203, title III, §§301, 303, 305(a), May 22, 2009, 123 Stat. 1735, 1738, 1741-1743, 1745-1749; Pub. L. 111–203, title X, §1100A(2), July 21, 2010, 124 Stat. 2107.)

EDITORIAL NOTES

AMENDMENTS

2010—Pub. L. 111–203 substituted "Bureau" for "Board" wherever appearing.

2009—Subsec. (b)(11). Pub. L. 111–24, §201(a), amended par. (11) generally, revising the minimum payment disclosures required from creditors.

Subsec. (b)(12). Pub. L. 111–24, §202, amended par. (12) generally. Prior to amendment, par. (12) read as follows: "If a late payment fee is to be imposed due to the failure of the obligor to make payment on or before a required payment due date, the following shall be stated clearly and conspicuously on the billing statement:

"(A) The date on which that payment is due or, if different, the earliest date on which a late payment fee may be charged.

"(B) The amount of the late payment fee to be imposed if payment is made after such date."

Subsec. (c)(8). Pub. L. 111–24, §301, added par. (8).

Subsec. (d)(1). Pub. L. 111–24, §203(3), substituted "A card issuer that has changed or amended any term of the account since the last renewal that has not been previously disclosed or" for "Except as provided in paragraph (2), a card issuer" in introductory provisions.

Subsec. (d)(2), (3). Pub. L. 111–24, §203(1), (2), redesignated par. (3) as (2) and struck out former par. (2) which provided a special rule for certain disclosures.

Subsec. (i). Pub. L. 111–24, §101(a)(1), added subsec. (i).

Subsecs. (j) to (l). Pub. L. 111–24, §102(a), added subsecs. (j) to (l).

Subsec. (m). Pub. L. 111–24, §103, added subsec. (m).

Subsec. (n). Pub. L. 111–24, §105, added subsec. (n).

Subsec. (o). Pub. L. 111–24, §106(a), added subsec. (o).

Subsec. (p). Pub. L. 111–24, §303, added subsec. (p).

Subsec. (r). Pub. L. 111–24, §305(a), added subsec. (r).

2005—Subsec. (b)(11). Pub. L. 109–8, §1301(a), added par. (11).

Subsec. (b)(12). Pub. L. 109–8, §1305(a), added par. (12).

Subsec. (c)(6). Pub. L. 109–8, §1303(a), added par. (6).

Subsec. (c)(7). Pub. L. 109–8, §1304(a), added par. (7).

Subsec. (h). Pub. L. 109–8, §1306(a), added subsec. (h).

1988—Subsec. (a)(8). Pub. L. 100–709 added par. (8).

Subsecs. (c) to (f). Pub. L. 100–583, §2(a), added subsecs. (c) to (f).

Subsec. (g). Pub. L. 100–583, §6, added subsec. (g).

1980—Subsec. (a)(1). Pub. L. 96–221, §613(a)(1), inserted provisions requiring the creditor to disclose that no time period is provided.

Subsec. (a)(5). Pub. L. 96–221, §613(a)(2), (3), redesignated par. (6) as (5) and inserted provisions relating to identification of other charges, and regulations by the Board. Former par. (5), relating to elective rights of the creditor, was struck out.

Subsec. (a)(6). Pub. L. 96–221, §613(a)(2), (3), redesignated par. (7) as (6) and revised nomenclature and expanded statement requirements. Former par. (6) redesignated (5).

Subsec. (a)(7), (8). Pub. L. 96–221, §613(a)(2), (d), redesignated par. (8) as (7) and substituted provisions relating to one billing cycle per calendar year, for provisions relating to each of two billing cycles per year. Former par. (7) redesignated (6).

Subsec. (b)(2). Pub. L. 96–221, §613(b), inserted provisions relating to failure of the creditor to disclose information in accordance with this paragraph, and made minor changes in phraseology.

Subsec. (b)(7) to (11). Pub. L. 96–221, §613(c), struck out par. (7) which related to elective rights of the creditor, and redesignated pars. (8) to (11) as (7) to (10), respectively.

Subsec. (c). Pub. L. 96–221, §613(e), struck out subsec. (c) which related to the time for making disclosures with respect to open end consumer credit plans having an outstanding balance of more than $1 at or after the close of the first full billing cycle.

1974—Subsec. (a)(1). Pub. L. 93–495, §415(1), inserted exception relating to nonimposition of a finance charge at the election of the creditor and without disclosure.

Subsec. (a)(8). Pub. L. 93–495, §304(a), added par. (8).

Subsec. (b)(2). Pub. L. 93–495, §411, substituted provisions requiring a brief identification on or accompanying the statement of credit extension sufficient to enable the obligor to identify the transaction or relate it to copies of sales vouchers or similar instruments previously furnished, for provisions requiring for purchases a brief identification, unless previously furnished, of the goods or services purchased.

Subsec. (b)(10). Pub. L. 93–495, §415(2), inserted exception relating to nonimposition of additional finance charge at the election of the creditor and without disclosure.

Subsec. (b)(11). Pub. L. 93–495, §305, added par. (11).

Subsec. (c). Pub. L. 93–495, §304(b), substituted provisions relating to disclosure requirements in a notice mailed or delivered to the obligor not later than the time of mailing the next statement required by subsec. (b) of this section, for provisions relating to disclosure requirements in a notice mailed or delivered to the obligor not later than thirty days after July 1, 1969.

STATUTORY NOTES AND RELATED SUBSIDIARIES

EFFECTIVE DATE OF 2010 AMENDMENT

Amendment by Pub. L. 111–203 effective on the designated transfer date, see section 1100H of Pub. L. 111–203, set out as a note under section 552a of Title 5, Government Organization and Employees.

EFFECTIVE DATE OF 2009 AMENDMENT

Amendment by Pub. L. 111–24 effective 9 months after May 22, 2009, except as otherwise specifically provided, see section 3 of Pub. L. 111–24, set out as a note under section 1602 of this title.

Pub. L. 111–24, title I, §101(a)(2), May 22, 2009, 123 Stat. 1736, provided that: "Notwithstanding section 3 [see Effective Date of 2009 Amendment note set out under section 1602 of this title], section 127(i) of the Truth in Lending Act [15 U.S.C. 1637(i)], as added by this subsection, shall become effective 90 days after the date of enactment of this Act [May 22, 2009]."

EFFECTIVE DATE OF 2005 AMENDMENT

Pub. L. 109–8, title XIII, §1301(b)(2), Apr. 20, 2005, 119 Stat. 207, provided that: "Section 127(b)(11) of the Truth in Lending Act [subsec. (b)(11) of this section], as added by subsection (a) of this section, and the regulations issued under paragraph (1) of this subsection [set out as a note under this section] shall not take effect until the later of—

"(A) 18 months after the date of enactment of this Act [Apr. 20, 2005]; or

"(B) 12 months after the publication of such final regulations by the Board [of Governors of the Federal Reserve System] [Jan. 29, 2009, see 74 F.R. 5244]."

Pub. L. 109–8, title XIII, §1303(b)(2), Apr. 20, 2005, 119 Stat. 211, provided that: "Section 127(c)(6) of the Truth in Lending Act [subsec. (c)(6) of this section], as added by this section, and regulations issued under paragraph (1) of this subsection [set out as a note under this section] shall not take effect until the later of—

"(A) 12 months after the date of enactment of this Act [Apr. 20, 2005]; or

"(B) 12 months after the date of publication of such final regulations by the Board [of Governors of the Federal Reserve System] [Jan. 29, 2009, see 74 F.R. 5244]."

Pub. L. 109–8, title XIII, §1304(b)(2), Apr. 20, 2005, 119 Stat. 212, provided that: "The amendment made by subsection (a) [amending this section] and the regulations issued under paragraph (1) of this subsection [set out as a note under this section] shall not take effect until the later of—

"(A) 12 months after the date of enactment of this Act [Apr. 20, 2005]; or

"(B) 12 months after the date of publication of such final regulations by the Board [of Governors of the Federal Reserve System] [Jan. 29, 2009, see 74 F.R. 5244]."

Pub. L. 109–8, title XIII, §1305(b)(2), Apr. 20, 2005, 119 Stat. 212, provided that: "The amendment made by subsection (a) [amending this section] and regulations issued under paragraph (1) of this subsection [set out as a note under this section] shall not take effect until the later of—

"(A) 12 months after the date of enactment of this Act [Apr. 20, 2005]; or

"(B) 12 months after the date of publication of such final regulations by the Board [of Governors of the Federal Reserve System] [Jan. 29, 2009, see 74 F.R. 5244]."

Pub. L. 109–8, title XIII, §1306(b)(2), Apr. 20, 2005, 119 Stat. 212, provided that: "The amendment made by subsection (a) [amending this section] and regulations issued under paragraph (1) of this subsection [set out as a note under this section] shall not take effect until the later of—

"(A) 12 months after the date of enactment of this Act [Apr. 20, 2005]; or

"(B) 12 months after the date of publication of such final regulations by the Board [of Governors of the Federal Reserve System] [Jan. 29, 2009, see 74 F.R. 5244]."

EFFECTIVE DATE OF 1988 AMENDMENT

For effective date of amendments by Pub. L. 100–709, see Regulations; Effective Date note below.

EFFECTIVE DATE OF 1980 AMENDMENT

Amendment by Pub. L. 96–221 effective on expiration of two years and six months after Mar. 31, 1980, with all regulations, forms, and clauses required to be prescribed to be promulgated at least one year prior to such effective date, and allowing any creditor to comply with any amendments, in accordance with the regulations, forms, and clauses prescribed by the Board prior to such effective date, see section 625 of Pub. L. 96–221, set out as a note under section 1602 of this title.

EFFECTIVE DATE OF 1974 AMENDMENT

For effective date of amendment by sections 304 and 305 of Pub. L. 93–495, see section 308 of Pub. L. 93–495, set out as an Effective Date note under section 1666 of this title.

For effective date of amendment by section 411 of Pub. L. 93–495, see section 416 of Pub. L. 93–495, set out as an Effective Date note under section 1665a of this title.

Amendment by section 415 of Pub. L. 93–495 effective Oct. 28, 1974, see section 416 of Pub. L. 93–495, set out as an Effective Date note under section 1665a of this title.

REGULATIONS

Pub. L. 111–24, title II, §201(c), May 22, 2009, 123 Stat. 1745, provided that:

"(1) IN GENERAL.—Not later than 6 months after the date of enactment of this Act [May 22, 2009], the Board [of Governors of the Federal Reserve System] shall issue guidelines, by rule, in consultation with the Secretary of the Treasury, for the establishment and maintenance by creditors of a toll-free telephone number for purposes of providing information about accessing credit counseling and debt management services, as required under section 127(b)(11)(B)(iv) of the Truth in Lending Act [15 U.S.C. 1637(b)(11)(B)(iv)], as added by this section.

"(2) APPROVED AGENCIES.—Guidelines issued under this subsection shall ensure that referrals provided by the toll-free number referred to in paragraph (1) include only those nonprofit budget and credit counseling agencies approved by a United States bankruptcy trustee pursuant to section 111(a) of title 11, United States Code."

Pub. L. 109–8, title XIII, §1301(b)(1), Apr. 20, 2005, 119 Stat. 207, provided that: "The Board of Governors of the Federal Reserve System (hereafter in this title [amending this section and sections 1637a, 1638, 1664, and 1665b of this title and enacting provisions set out as notes under this section and section 1637a of this title] referred to as the 'Board') shall promulgate regulations implementing the requirements of section 127(b)(11) of the Truth in Lending Act [subsec. (b)(11) of this section], as added by subsection (a) of this section."

Pub. L. 109–8, title XIII, §1303(b)(1), Apr. 20, 2005, 119 Stat. 211, provided that: "The Board [of Governors of the Federal Reserve System] shall promulgate regulations implementing the requirements of section 127(c)(6) of the Truth in Lending Act [subsec. (c)(6) of this section], as added by this section."

Pub. L. 109–8, title XIII, §1304(b)(1), Apr. 20, 2005, 119 Stat. 211, provided that: "The Board [of Governors of the Federal Reserve System] shall promulgate regulations implementing the requirements of section 127(c)(7) of the Truth in Lending Act [subsec. (c)(7) of this section], as added by this section."

Pub. L. 109–8, title XIII, §1305(b)(1), Apr. 20, 2005, 119 Stat. 212, provided that: "The Board [of Governors of the Federal Reserve System] shall promulgate regulations implementing the requirements of section 127(b)(12) of the Truth in Lending Act [subsec. (b)(12) of this section], as added by this section."

Pub. L. 109–8, title XIII, §1306(b)(1), Apr. 20, 2005, 119 Stat. 212, provided that: "The Board [of Governors of the Federal Reserve System] shall promulgate regulations implementing the requirements of section 127(h) of the Truth in Lending Act [subsec. (h) of this section], as added by this section."

Pub. L. 109–8, title XIII, §1309, Apr. 20, 2005, 119 Stat. 213, provided that:

"(a) REGULATIONS.—Not later than 6 months after the date of enactment of this Act [Apr. 20, 2005], the Board [of Governors of the Federal Reserve System], in consultation with the other Federal banking agencies (as defined in section 3 of the Federal Deposit Insurance Act [12 U.S.C. 1813]), the National Credit Union Administration Board, and the Federal Trade Commission, shall promulgate regulations to provide guidance regarding the meaning of the term 'clear and conspicuous', as used in subparagraphs (A), (B), and (C) of section 127(b)(11) and clauses (ii) and (iii) of section 127(c)(6)(A) of the Truth in Lending Act [subsecs. (b)(11) and (c)(6)(A) of this section].

"(b) EXAMPLES.—Regulations promulgated under subsection (a) shall include examples of clear and conspicuous model disclosures for the purposes of disclosures required by the provisions of the Truth in Lending Act [15 U.S.C. 1601 et seq.] referred to in subsection (a).

"(c) STANDARDS.—In promulgating regulations under this section, the Board [of Governors of the Federal Reserve System] shall ensure that the clear and conspicuous standard required for disclosures made under the provisions of the Truth in Lending Act referred to in subsection (a) can be implemented in a manner which results in disclosures which are reasonably understandable and designed to call attention to the nature and significance of the information in the notice."

REGULATIONS; EFFECTIVE DATE

For provisions relating to promulgation of regulations to implement amendment by Pub. L. 100–709, and effective date of such amendment in connection with those regulations, see section 7 of Pub. L. 100–709, set out as a note under section 1637a of this title.

Pub. L. 100–583, §7, Nov. 3, 1988, 102 Stat. 2968, provided that: "Any regulation required to be prescribed by the Board under the amendments made by section 2 [amending this section and section 1632 of this title] shall—

"(1) take effect not later than the end of the 150-day period beginning on the date of the enactment of this Act [Nov. 3, 1988]; and

"(2) apply only with respect to applications, solicitations, and other material distributed after the end of the 150-day period beginning after the end of the period referred to in paragraph (1), except that —

"(A) in the case of applications and solicitations subject to paragraph (3) or (4)(C) of section 127(c) of the Truth in Lending Act [15 U.S.C. 1637(c)(3), (4)(C)] (as added by section 2), such period shall be 240 days; and

"(B) any card issuer may, at its option, comply with the requirements of the amendments made by this Act [see Short Title of 1988 Amendment note under section 1601 of this title] prior to the applicable effective date, in which case the amendments made by this Act shall be fully applicable to such card issuer."

REPORTS TO CONGRESS

Pub. L. 111–24, title III, §305(b), May 22, 2009, 123 Stat. 1750, provided that:

"(1) STUDY.—The Comptroller General of the United States shall, from time to time, review the reports submitted by creditors under section 127(r) of the Truth in Lending Act [15 U.S.C. 1637(r)], as added by this section, and the marketing practices of creditors to determine the impact that college affinity card agreements and college student card agreements have on credit card debt.

"(2) REPORT.—Upon completion of any study under paragraph (1), the Comptroller General shall periodically submit a report to the Congress on the findings and conclusions of the study, together with such recommendations for administrative or legislative action as the Comptroller General determines to be appropriate."

Pub. L. 100–583, §8, Nov. 3, 1988, 102 Stat. 2969, provided that: "Not later than 1 year after the regulations prescribed under section 7 of this Act [set out as a note above] become effective and annually thereafter, the Board of Governors of the Federal Reserve System shall transmit to the Congress a report containing an assessment by the Board of the profitability of credit card operations of depository institutions, including an analysis of any impact of the amendments made by this Act [see Short Title of 1988 Amendment note under section 1601 of this title] on such profitability."

[1] *So in original. Probably should be "conspicuously".*

[2] *So in original. No subsec. (q) has been enacted.*

[3] *So in original. Probably should be "sections".*

§1637a. Disclosure requirements for open end consumer credit plans secured by consumer's principal dwelling

(a) Application disclosures

In the case of any open end consumer credit plan which provides for any extension of credit which is secured by the consumer's principal dwelling, the creditor shall make the following disclosures in accordance with subsection (b):

(1) Fixed annual percentage rate

Each annual percentage rate imposed in connection with extensions of credit under the plan and a statement that such rate does not include costs other than interest.

(2) Variable percentage rate

In the case of a plan which provides for variable rates of interest on credit extended under the plan—
(A) a description of the manner in which such rate will be computed and a statement that such rate does not include costs other than interest;
(B) a description of the manner in which any changes in the annual percentage rate will be made, including—
(i) any negative amortization and interest rate carryover;
(ii) the timing of any such changes;
(iii) any index or margin to which such changes in the rate are related; and
(iv) a source of information about any such index;

(C) if an initial annual percentage rate is offered which is not based on an index—
(i) a statement of such rate and the period of time such initial rate will be in effect; and
(ii) a statement that such rate does not include costs other than interest;

(D) a statement that the consumer should ask about the current index value and interest rate;
(E) a statement of the maximum amount by which the annual percentage rate may change in any 1-year period or a statement that no such limit exists;
(F) a statement of the maximum annual percentage rate that may be imposed at any time under the plan;
(G) subject to subsection (b)(3), a table, based on a $10,000 extension of credit, showing how the annual percentage rate and the minimum periodic payment amount under each repayment option of the plan would have been affected during the preceding 15-year period by changes in any index used to compute such rate;
(H) a statement of—
(i) the maximum annual percentage rate which may be imposed under each repayment option of the plan;
(ii) the minimum amount of any periodic payment which may be required, based on a $10,000 outstanding balance, under each such option when such maximum annual percentage rate is in effect; and
(iii) the earliest date by which such maximum annual interest rate may be imposed; and

(I) a statement that interest rate information will be provided on or with each periodic statement.

(3) Other fees imposed by the creditor

An itemization of any fees imposed by the creditor in connection with the availability or use of credit under such plan, including annual fees, application fees, transaction fees, and closing costs (including costs commonly described as "points"), and the time when such fees are payable.

(4) Estimates of fees which may be imposed by third parties

(A) Aggregate amount

An estimate, based on the creditor's experience with such plans and stated as a single amount or as a reasonable range, of the aggregate amount of additional fees that may be imposed by third parties (such as governmental authorities, appraisers, and attorneys) in connection with opening an account under the plan.

(B) Statement of availability

A statement that the consumer may ask the creditor for a good faith estimate by the creditor of the fees that may be imposed by third parties.

(5) Statement of risk of loss of dwelling

A statement that—

(A) any extension of credit under the plan is secured by the consumer's dwelling; and

(B) in the event of any default, the consumer risks the loss of the dwelling.

(6) Conditions to which disclosed terms are subject

(A) Period during which such terms are available

A clear and conspicuous statement—

(i) of the time by which an application must be submitted to obtain the terms disclosed; or

(ii) if applicable, that the terms are subject to change.

(B) Right of refusal if certain terms change

A statement that—

(i) the consumer may elect not to enter into an agreement to open an account under the plan if any term changes (other than a change contemplated by a variable feature of the plan) before any such agreement is final; and

(ii) if the consumer makes an election described in clause (i), the consumer is entitled to a refund of all fees paid in connection with the application.

(C) Retention of information

A statement that the consumer should make or otherwise retain a copy of information disclosed under this subparagraph.

(7) Rights of creditor with respect to extensions of credit

A statement that—

(A) under certain conditions, the creditor may terminate any account under the plan and require immediate repayment of any outstanding balance, prohibit any additional extension of credit to the account, or reduce the credit limit applicable to the account; and

(B) the consumer may receive, upon request, more specific information about the conditions under which the creditor may take any action described in subparagraph (A).

(8) Repayment options and minimum periodic payments

The repayment options under the plan, including—

(A) if applicable, any differences in repayment options with regard to—

(i) any period during which additional extensions of credit may be obtained; and

(ii) any period during which repayment is required to be made and no additional extensions of credit may be obtained;

(B) the length of any repayment period, including any differences in the length of any repayment period with regard to the periods described in clauses (i) and (ii) of subparagraph (A); and

(C) an explanation of how the amount of any minimum monthly or periodic payment will be determined under each such option, including any differences in the determination of any such amount with regard to the periods described in clauses (i) and (ii) of subparagraph (A).

(9) Example of minimum payments and maximum repayment period

An example, based on a $10,000 outstanding balance and the interest rate (other than a rate not based on the index under the plan) which is, or was recently, in effect under such plan, showing the minimum monthly or periodic payment, and the time it would take to repay the entire $10,000 if the consumer paid only the minimum periodic payments and obtained no additional extensions of credit.

(10) Statement concerning balloon payments

If, under any repayment option of the plan, the payment of not more than the minimum periodic payments required under such option over the length of the repayment period—

(A) would not repay any of the principal balance; or

(B) would repay less than the outstanding balance by the end of such period,

as the case may be, a statement of such fact, including an explicit statement that at the end of such repayment period a balloon payment (as defined in section 1665b(f) of this title) would result which would be required to be paid in full at that time.

(11) Negative amortization

If applicable, a statement that—

(A) any limitation in the plan on the amount of any increase in the minimum payments may result in negative amortization;

(B) negative amortization increases the outstanding principal balance of the account; and

(C) negative amortization reduces the consumer's equity in the consumer's dwelling.

(12) Limitations and minimum amount requirements on extensions of credit

(A) Number and dollar amount limitations

Any limitation contained in the plan on the number of extensions of credit and the amount of credit which may be obtained during any month or other defined time period.

(B) Minimum balance and other transaction amount requirements

Any requirement which establishes a minimum amount for—

    (i) the initial extension of credit to an account under the plan;

    (ii) any subsequent extension of credit to an account under the plan; or

    (iii) any outstanding balance of an account under the plan.

(13) Statement regarding tax deductibility

A statement that—

(A) the consumer should consult a tax advisor regarding the deductibility of interest and charges under the plan; and

(B) in any case in which the extension of credit exceeds the fair market value (as defined under title 26) of the dwelling, the interest on the portion of the credit extension that is greater than the fair market value of the dwelling is not tax deductible for Federal income tax purposes.

(14) Disclosure requirements established by Bureau

Any other term which the Bureau requires, in regulations, to be disclosed.

(b) Time and form of disclosures

(1) Time of disclosure

(A) In general

The disclosures required under subsection (a) with respect to any open end consumer credit plan which provides for any extension of credit which is secured by the consumer's principal dwelling and the pamphlet required under subsection (e) shall be provided to any consumer at the time the creditor distributes an application to establish an account under such plan to such consumer.

(B) Telephone, publications, and third party applications

In the case of telephone applications, applications contained in magazines or other publications, or applications provided by a third party, the disclosures required under subsection (a) and the pamphlet required under subsection (e) shall be provided by the creditor before the end of the 3-day period beginning on the date the creditor receives a completed application from a consumer.

(2) Form

(A) In general

Except as provided in paragraph (1)(B), the disclosures required under subsection (a) shall be provided on or with any application to establish an account under an open end consumer credit plan which provides for any extension of credit which is secured by the consumer's principal dwelling.

(B) Segregation of required disclosures from other information

The disclosures required under subsection (a) shall be conspicuously segregated from all other terms, data, or additional information provided in connection with the application, either by grouping the disclosures separately on the application form or by providing the disclosures on a separate form, in accordance with regulations of the Bureau.

(C) Precedence of certain information

The disclosures required by paragraphs (5), (6), and (7) of subsection (a) shall precede all of the other required disclosures.

(D) Special provision relating to variable interest rate information

Whether or not the disclosures required under subsection (a) are provided on the application form, the variable rate information described in subsection (a)(2) may be provided separately from the other information required to be disclosed.

(3) Requirement for historical table

In preparing the table required under subsection (a)(2)(G), the creditor shall consistently select one rate of interest for each year and the manner of selecting the rate from year to year shall be consistent with the plan.

(c) Third party applications

In the case of an application to open an account under any open end consumer credit plan described in subsection (a) which is provided to a consumer by any person other than the creditor—

(1) such person shall provide such consumer with—

　(A) the disclosures required under subsection (a) with respect to such plan, in accordance with subsection (b); and

　(B) the pamphlet required under subsection (e); or

(2) if such person cannot provide specific terms about the plan because specific information about the plan terms is not available, no nonrefundable fee may be imposed in connection with such application before the end of the 3-day period beginning on the date the consumer receives the disclosures required under subsection (a) with respect to the application.

(d) "Principal dwelling" defined

For purposes of this section and sections 1647 and 1665b of this title, the term "principal dwelling" includes any second or vacation home of the consumer.

(e) Pamphlet

In addition to the disclosures required under subsection (a) with respect to an application to open an account under any open end consumer credit plan described in such subsection, the creditor or other person providing such disclosures to the consumer shall provide—

　(1) a pamphlet published by the Bureau pursuant to section 4 of the Home Equity [1] Consumer Protection Act of 1988; or

　(2) any pamphlet which provides substantially similar information to the information described in such section, as determined by the Bureau.

(Pub. L. 90–321, title I, §127A, as added Pub. L. 100–709, §2(a), Nov. 23, 1988, 102 Stat. 4725; amended Pub. L. 109–8, title XIII, §1302(a)(1), Apr. 20, 2005, 119 Stat. 208; Pub. L. 111–203, title X, §1100A(2), July 21, 2010, 124 Stat. 2107.)

EDITORIAL NOTES

REFERENCES IN TEXT

Section 4 of the Home Equity Loan Consumer Protection Act of 1988, referred to in subsec. (e)(1), is section 4 of Pub. L. 100–709, which is set out as a note below.

AMENDMENTS

2010—Subsecs. (a)(14), (b)(2)(B), (e). Pub. L. 111–203 substituted "Bureau" for "Board" wherever appearing.

2005—Subsec. (a)(13). Pub. L. 109–8 substituted "tax deductibility" for "consultation of tax advisor" in heading, designated existing provisions as introductory provisions and subpar. (A), inserted dash, substituted "; and" for period at end of subpar. (A), and added subpar. (B).

STATUTORY NOTES AND RELATED SUBSIDIARIES

EFFECTIVE DATE OF 2010 AMENDMENT

Amendment by Pub. L. 111–203 effective on the designated transfer date, see section 1100H of Pub. L. 111–203, set out as a note under section 552a of Title 5, Government Organization and Employees.

EFFECTIVE DATE OF 2005 AMENDMENT

Amendment by Pub. L. 109–8 effective 180 days after Apr. 20, 2005, and not applicable with respect to cases commenced under Title 11, Bankruptcy, before such effective date, except as otherwise provided, see section 1501 of Pub. L. 109–8, set out as a note under section 101 of Title 11.

EFFECTIVE DATE

For effective date of section, see Regulations; Effective Date note below.

REGULATIONS

Pub. L. 109–8, title XIII, §1302(c), Apr. 20, 2005, 119 Stat. 209, provided that:

"(1) IN GENERAL.—The Board [of Governors of the Federal Reserve System] shall promulgate regulations implementing the amendments made by this section [amending this section and sections 1638, 1664, and 1665b of this title].

"(2) EFFECTIVE DATE.—Regulations issued under paragraph (1) shall not take effect until the later of—

　"(A) 12 months after the date of enactment of this Act [Apr. 20, 2005]; or

REGULATIONS; EFFECTIVE DATE

Pub. L. 100–709, §7, Nov. 23, 1988, 102 Stat. 4734, provided that:

"(a) REGULATIONS.—Before the end of the 60-day period beginning on the date of the enactment of this Act [Nov. 23, 1988], the Board of Governors of the Federal Reserve System shall prescribe such regulations as may be necessary to carry out the proposes [sic] of the amendments made by this Act [enacting this section and sections 1647 and 1665b of this title, amending sections 1632 and 1637 of this title, and enacting provisions set out as notes under this section and section 1601 of this title].

"(b) EFFECTIVE DATE.—The amendments made by this Act, and the regulations prescribed pursuant to subsection (a) with respect to such amendments, shall apply to—

"(1) any agreement to open an account under an open end consumer credit plan under which extensions of credit are secured by a consumer's principal dwelling which is entered into after the end of the 5-month period beginning on the date on which the regulations prescribed under subsection (a) become final; and

"(2) any application to open such an account which is distributed by, or received by a creditor, after the end of such 5-month period.

"(c) VOLUNTARY COMPLIANCE.—Notwithstanding subsection (b), any creditor may comply with the amendments made by this Act, in accordance with the regulations prescribed by the Board, before the effective date established under such subsection."

CONSUMER EDUCATION

Pub. L. 100–709, §4, Nov. 23, 1988, 102 Stat. 4733, provided that: "The Board of Governors of the Federal Reserve System shall develop and prepare a pamphlet for distribution to consumers which contains—

"(1) a general description of open end consumer credit plans secured by the consumer's principal dwelling and the terms and conditions under which such loans are generally extended; and

"(2) a discussion of the potential advantages and disadvantages of such plans, including how to compare among home equity plans and between home equity and closed end credit plans."

---

[1] *So in original. Probably should be followed by "Loan".*

---

§1638. Transactions other than under an open end credit plan

(a) Required disclosures by creditor

For each consumer credit transaction other than under an open end credit plan, the creditor shall disclose each of the following items, to the extent applicable:

(1) The identity of the creditor required to make disclosure.

(2)(A) The "amount financed", using that term, which shall be the amount of credit of which the consumer has actual use. This amount shall be computed as follows, but the computations need not be disclosed and shall not be disclosed with the disclosures conspicuously segregated in accordance with subsection (b)(1):

(i) take the principal amount of the loan or the cash price less downpayment and trade-in;

(ii) add any charges which are not part of the finance charge or of the principal amount of the loan and which are financed by the consumer, including the cost of any items excluded from the finance charge pursuant to section 1605 of this title; and

(iii) subtract any charges which are part of the finance charge but which will be paid by the consumer before or at the time of the consummation of the transaction, or have been withheld from the proceeds of the credit.

(B) In conjunction with the disclosure of the amount financed, a creditor shall provide a statement of the consumer's right to obtain, upon a written request, a written itemization of the amount financed. The statement shall include spaces for a "yes" and "no" indication to be initialed by the consumer to indicate whether the consumer wants a written itemization of the amount financed. Upon receiving an affirmative indication, the creditor shall provide, at the time other disclosures are required to be furnished, a written itemization of the amount financed. For the purposes of this subparagraph, "itemization of the amount financed" means a disclosure of the following items, to the extent applicable:

(i) the amount that is or will be paid directly to the consumer;

(ii) the amount that is or will be credited to the consumer's account to discharge obligations owed to the creditor;

(iii) each amount that is or will be paid to third persons by the creditor on the consumer's behalf, together with an identification of or reference to the third person; and

(iv) the total amount of any charges described in the preceding subparagraph (A)(iii).

(3) The "finance charge", not itemized, using that term.

(4) The finance charge expressed as an "annual percentage rate", using that term. This shall not be required if the amount financed does not exceed $75 and the finance charge does not exceed $5, or if the amount financed exceeds $75 and the finance charge does not exceed $7.50.

(5) The sum of the amount financed and the finance charge, which shall be termed the "total of payments".

(6) The number, amount, and due dates or period of payments scheduled to repay the total of payments.

(7) In a sale of property or services in which the seller is the creditor required to disclose pursuant to section 1631(b) of this title, the "total sale price", using that term, which shall be the total of the cash price of the property or services, additional charges, and the finance charge.

(8) Descriptive explanations of the terms "amount financed", "finance charge", "annual percentage rate", "total of payments", and "total sale price" as specified by the Bureau. The descriptive explanation of "total sale price" shall include reference to the amount of the downpayment.

(9) Where the credit is secured, a statement that a security interest has been taken in (A) the property which is purchased as part of the credit transaction, or (B) property not purchased as part of the credit transaction identified by item or type.

(10) Any dollar charge or percentage amount which may be imposed by a creditor solely on account of a late payment, other than a deferral or extension charge.

(11) A statement indicating whether or not the consumer is entitled to a rebate of any finance charge upon refinancing or prepayment in full pursuant to acceleration or otherwise, if the obligation involves a precomputed finance charge. A statement indicating whether or not a penalty will be imposed in those same circumstances if the obligation involves a finance charge computed from time to time by application of a rate to the unpaid principal balance.

(12) A statement that the consumer should refer to the appropriate contract document for any information such document provides about nonpayment, default, the right to accelerate the maturity of the debt, and prepayment rebates and penalties.

(13) In any residential mortgage transaction, a statement indicating whether a subsequent purchaser or assignee of the consumer may assume the debt obligation on its original terms and conditions.

(14) In the case of any variable interest rate residential mortgage transaction, in disclosures provided at application as prescribed by the Bureau for a variable rate transaction secured by the consumer's principal dwelling, at the option of the creditor, a statement that the periodic payments may increase or decrease substantially, and the maximum interest rate and payment for a $10,000 loan originated at a recent interest rate, as determined by the Bureau, assuming the maximum periodic increases in rates and payments under the program, or a historical example illustrating the effects of interest rate changes implemented according to the loan program.

(15) In the case of a consumer credit transaction that is secured by the principal dwelling of the consumer, in which the extension of credit may exceed the fair market value of the dwelling, a clear and conspicuous statement that—

(A) the interest on the portion of the credit extension that is greater than the fair market value of the dwelling is not tax deductible for Federal income tax purposes; and

(B) the consumer should consult a tax adviser for further information regarding the deductibility of interest and charges.

(16) In the case of a variable rate residential mortgage loan for which an escrow or impound account will be established for the payment of all applicable taxes, insurance, and assessments—

(A) the amount of initial monthly payment due under the loan for the payment of principal and interest, and the amount of such initial monthly payment including the monthly payment deposited in the account for the payment of all applicable taxes, insurance, and assessments; and

(B) the amount of the fully indexed monthly payment due under the loan for the payment of principal and interest, and the amount of such fully indexed monthly payment including the monthly payment deposited in the account for the payment of all applicable taxes, insurance, and assessments.

(17) In the case of a residential mortgage loan, the aggregate amount of settlement charges for all settlement services provided in connection with the loan, the amount of charges that are included in the loan and the amount of such charges the borrower must pay at closing, the approximate amount of the wholesale rate of funds in connection with the loan, and the aggregate amount of other fees or required payments in connection with the loan.

(18) In the case of a residential mortgage loan, the aggregate amount of fees paid to the mortgage originator in connection with the loan, the amount of such fees paid directly by the consumer, and any additional amount received by the originator from the creditor.

(19) In the case of a residential mortgage loan, the total amount of interest that the consumer will pay over the life of the loan as a percentage of the principal of the loan. Such amount shall be computed assuming the consumer makes each monthly payment in full and on-time, and does not make any over-payments.

(b) Form and timing of disclosures; residential mortgage transaction requirements

(1) Except as otherwise provided in this part, the disclosures required under subsection (a) shall be made before the credit is extended. Except for the disclosures required by subsection (a)(1) of this section, all disclosures required under subsection (a) and any disclosure provided for in subsection (b), (c), or (d) of section 1605 of this title shall be

conspicuously segregated from all other terms, data, or information provided in connection with a transaction, including any computations or itemization.

(2)(A) Except as provided in subparagraph (G), in the case of any extension of credit that is secured by the dwelling of a consumer, which is also subject to the Real Estate Settlement Procedures Act [12 U.S.C. 2601 et seq.], good faith estimates of the disclosures required under subsection (a) shall be made in accordance with regulations of the Bureau under section 1631(c) of this title and shall be delivered or placed in the mail not later than three business days after the creditor receives the consumer's written application, which shall be at least 7 business days before consummation of the transaction.

(B) In the case of an extension of credit that is secured by the dwelling of a consumer, the disclosures provided under subparagraph (A),[1] shall be in addition to the other disclosures required by subsection (a), and shall—

(i) state in conspicuous type size and format, the following: "You are not required to complete this agreement merely because you have received these disclosures or signed a loan application."; and

(ii) be provided in the form of final disclosures at the time of consummation of the transaction, in the form and manner prescribed by this section.

(C) In the case of an extension of credit that is secured by the dwelling of a consumer, under which the annual rate of interest is variable, or with respect to which the regular payments may otherwise be variable, in addition to the other disclosures required by subsection (a), the disclosures provided under this subsection shall do the following:

(i) Label the payment schedule as follows: "Payment Schedule: Payments Will Vary Based on Interest Rate Changes".

(ii) State in conspicuous type size and format examples of adjustments to the regular required payment on the extension of credit based on the change in the interest rates specified by the contract for such extension of credit. Among the examples required to be provided under this clause is an example that reflects the maximum payment amount of the regular required payments on the extension of credit, based on the maximum interest rate allowed under the contract, in accordance with the rules of the Bureau. Prior to issuing any rules pursuant to this clause, the Bureau shall conduct consumer testing to determine the appropriate format for providing the disclosures required under this subparagraph to consumers so that such disclosures can be easily understood, including the fact that the initial regular payments are for a specific time period that will end on a certain date, that payments will adjust afterwards potentially to a higher amount, and that there is no guarantee that the borrower will be able to refinance to a lower amount.

(D) In any case in which the disclosure statement under subparagraph (A) contains an annual percentage rate of interest that is no longer accurate, as determined under section 1606(c) of this title, the creditor shall furnish an additional, corrected statement to the borrower, not later than 3 business days before the date of consummation of the transaction.

(E) The consumer shall receive the disclosures required under this paragraph before paying any fee to the creditor or other person in connection with the consumer's application for an extension of credit that is secured by the dwelling of a consumer. If the disclosures are mailed to the consumer, the consumer is considered to have received them 3 business days after they are mailed. A creditor or other person may impose a fee for obtaining the consumer's credit report before the consumer has received the disclosures under this paragraph, provided the fee is bona fide and reasonable in amount.

(F) WAIVER OF TIMELINESS OF DISCLOSURES.—To expedite consummation of a transaction, if the consumer determines that the extension of credit is needed to meet a bona fide personal financial emergency, the consumer may waive or modify the timing requirements for disclosures under subparagraph (A), provided that—

(i) the term "bona fide personal emergency" may be further defined in regulations issued by the Bureau;

(ii) the consumer provides to the creditor a dated, written statement describing the emergency and specifically waiving or modifying those timing requirements, which statement shall bear the signature of all consumers entitled to receive the disclosures required by this paragraph; and

(iii) the creditor provides to the consumers at or before the time of such waiver or modification, the final disclosures required by paragraph (1).

(G)(i) In the case of an extension of credit relating to a plan described in section 101(53D) of title 11—

(I) the requirements of subparagraphs (A) through (E) shall not apply; and

(II) a good faith estimate of the disclosures required under subsection (a) shall be made in accordance with regulations of the Bureau under section 1631(c) of this title before such credit is extended, or shall be delivered or placed in the mail not later than 3 business days after the date on which the creditor receives the written application of the consumer for such credit, whichever is earlier.

(ii) If a disclosure statement furnished within 3 business days of the written application (as provided under clause (i) (II)) contains an annual percentage rate which is subsequently rendered inaccurate, within the meaning of section 1606(c) of this title, the creditor shall furnish another disclosure statement at the time of settlement or consummation of the transaction.

(3) In the case of a credit transaction described in paragraph (15) of subsection (a), disclosures required by that paragraph shall be made to the consumer at the time of application for such extension of credit.

(4) Repayment analysis required to include escrow payments.—

(A) In general.—In the case of any consumer credit transaction secured by a first mortgage or lien on the principal dwelling of the consumer, other than a consumer credit transaction under an open end credit plan or a reverse mortgage, for which an impound, trust, or other type of account has been or will be established in connection with the transaction for the payment of property taxes, hazard and flood (if any) insurance premiums, or other periodic payments or premiums with respect to the property, the information required to be provided under subsection (a) with respect to the number, amount, and due dates or period of payments scheduled to repay the total of payments shall take into account the amount of any monthly payment to such account for each such repayment in accordance with section 10(a)(2) of the Real Estate Settlement Procedures Act of 1974 [12 U.S.C. 2609(a)(2)].

(B) Assessment value.—The amount taken into account under subparagraph (A) for the payment of property taxes, hazard and flood (if any) insurance premiums, or other periodic payments or premiums with respect to the property shall reflect the taxable assessed value of the real property securing the transaction after the consummation of the transaction, including the value of any improvements on the property or to be constructed on the property (whether or not such construction will be financed from the proceeds of the transaction), if known, and the replacement costs of the property for hazard insurance, in the initial year after the transaction.

(c) Timing of disclosures on unsolicited mailed or telephone purchase orders or loan requests

(1) If a creditor receives a purchase order by mail or telephone without personal solicitation, and the cash price and the total sale price and the terms of financing, including the annual percentage rate, are set forth in the creditor's catalog or other printed material distributed to the public, then the disclosures required under subsection (a) may be made at any time not later than the date the first payment is due.

(2) If a creditor receives a request for a loan by mail or telephone without personal solicitation and the terms of financing, including the annual percentage rate for representative amounts of credit, are set forth in the creditor's printed material distributed to the public, or in the contract of loan or other printed material delivered to the obligor, then the disclosures required under subsection (a) may be made at any time not later than the date the first payment is due.

(d) Timing of disclosure in cases of an addition of a deferred payment price to an existing outstanding balance

If a consumer credit sale is one of a series of consumer credit sales transactions made pursuant to an agreement providing for the addition of the deferred payment price of that sale to an existing outstanding balance, and the person to whom the credit is extended has approved in writing both the annual percentage rate or rates and the method of computing the finance charge or charges, and the creditor retains no security interest in any property as to which he has received payments aggregating the amount of the sales price including any finance charges attributable thereto, then the disclosure required under subsection (a) for the particular sale may be made at any time not later than the date the first payment for that sale is due. For the purposes of this subsection, in the case of items purchased on different dates, the first purchased shall be deemed first paid for, and in the case of items purchased on the same date, the lowest price shall be deemed first paid for.

(e) Terms and disclosure with respect to private education loans

(1) Disclosures required in private education loan applications and solicitations

In any application for a private education loan, or a solicitation for a private education loan without requiring an application, the private educational lender shall disclose to the borrower, clearly and conspicuously—

(A) the potential range of rates of interest applicable to the private education loan;

(B) whether the rate of interest applicable to the private education loan is fixed or variable;

(C) limitations on interest rate adjustments, both in terms of frequency and amount, or the lack thereof, if applicable;

(D) requirements for a co-borrower, including any changes in the applicable interest rates without a co-borrower;

(E) potential finance charges, late fees, penalties, and adjustments to principal, based on defaults or late payments of the borrower;

(F) fees or range of fees applicable to the private education loan;

(G) the term of the private education loan;

(H) whether interest will accrue while the student to whom the private education loan relates is enrolled at a covered educational institution;

(I) payment deferral options;

(J) general eligibility criteria for the private education loan;

(K) an example of the total cost of the private education loan over the life of the loan—

(i) which shall be calculated using the principal amount and the maximum rate of interest actually offered by the private educational lender; and

(ii) calculated both with and without capitalization of interest, if an option exists for postponing interest payments;

(L) that a covered educational institution may have school-specific education loan benefits and terms not detailed on the disclosure form;

(M) that the borrower may qualify for Federal student financial assistance through a program under title IV of the Higher Education Act of 1965 (20 U.S.C. 1070 et seq.), in lieu of, or in addition to, a loan from a non-Federal source;

(N) the interest rates available with respect to such Federal student financial assistance through a program under title IV of the Higher Education Act of 1965 (20 U.S.C. 1070 et seq.);

(O) that, as provided in paragraph (6)—

(i) the borrower shall have the right to accept the terms of the loan and consummate the transaction at any time within 30 calendar days (or such longer period as the private educational lender may provide) following the date on which the application for the private education loan is approved and the borrower receives the disclosure documents required under this subsection for the loan; and

(ii) except for changes based on adjustments to the index used for a loan, the rates and terms of the loan may not be changed by the private educational lender during the period described in clause (i);

(P) that, before a private education loan may be consummated, the borrower must obtain from the relevant institution of higher education the form required under paragraph (3), and complete, sign, and return such form to the private educational lender;

(Q) that the consumer may obtain additional information concerning such Federal student financial assistance from their institution of higher education, or at the website of the Department of Education; and

(R) such other information as the Bureau shall prescribe, by rule, as necessary or appropriate for consumers to make informed borrowing decisions.

(2) Disclosures at the time of private education loan approval

Contemporaneously with the approval of a private education loan application, and before the loan transaction is consummated, the private educational lender shall disclose to the borrower, clearly and conspicuously—

(A) the applicable rate of interest in effect on the date of approval;

(B) whether the rate of interest applicable to the private education loan is fixed or variable;

(C) limitations on interest rate adjustments, both in terms of frequency and amount, or the lack thereof, if applicable;

(D) the initial approved principal amount;

(E) applicable finance charges, late fees, penalties, and adjustments to principal, based on borrower defaults or late payments, including limitations on the discharge of a private education loan in bankruptcy;

(F) fees or range of fees applicable to the private education loan;

(G) the maximum term under the private education loan program;

(H) an estimate of the total amount for repayment, at both the interest rate in effect on the date of approval and at the maximum possible rate of interest offered by the private educational lender and applicable to the borrower, to the extent that such maximum rate may be determined, or if not, a good faith estimate thereof;

(I) any principal and interest payments required while the student for whom the private education loan is intended is enrolled at a covered educational institution and unpaid interest that will accrue during such enrollment;

(J) payment deferral options applicable to the borrower;

(K) whether monthly payments are graduated;

(L) that, as provided in paragraph (6)—

(i) the borrower shall have the right to accept the terms of the loan and consummate the transaction at any time within 30 calendar days (or such longer period as the private educational lender may provide) following the date on which the application for the private education loan is approved and the borrower receives the disclosure documents required under this subsection for the loan; and

(ii) except for changes based on adjustments to the index used for a loan, the rates and terms of the loan may not be changed by the private educational lender during the period described in clause (i);

(M) that the borrower—

(i) may qualify for Federal financial assistance through a program under title IV of the Higher Education Act of 1965 (20 U.S.C. 1070 et seq.), in lieu of, or in addition to, a loan from a non-Federal source; and

(ii) may obtain additional information concerning such assistance from their institution of higher education or the website of the Department of Education;

(N) the interest rates available with respect to such Federal financial assistance through a program under title IV of the Higher Education Act of 1965 (20 U.S.C. 1070 et seq.);

(O) the maximum monthly payment, calculated using the maximum rate of interest actually offered by the private educational lender and applicable to the borrower, to the extent that such maximum rate may be determined, or if not, a good faith estimate thereof; and

(P) such other information as the Bureau shall prescribe, by rule, as necessary or appropriate for consumers to make informed borrowing decisions.

(3) Self-certification of information

(A) In general

Before a private educational lender may consummate a private education loan with respect to a student attending an institution of higher education, the lender shall obtain from the applicant for the private education loan the form developed by the Secretary of Education under section 155 of the Higher Education Act of 1965 [20 U.S.C. 1019d], signed by the applicant, in written or electronic form.

(B) Rule of construction

No other provision of this subsection shall be construed to require a private educational lender to perform any additional duty under this paragraph, other than collecting the form required under subparagraph (A).

(4) Disclosures at the time of private education loan consummation

Contemporaneously with the consummation of a private education loan, a private educational lender shall make to the borrower each of the disclosures described in—

(A) paragraph (2)(A) (adjusted, as necessary, for the rate of interest in effect on the date of consummation, based on the index used for the loan);

(B) subparagraphs (B) through (K) and (M) through (P) of paragraph (2); and

(C) paragraph (7).

(5) Format of disclosures

(A) Model form

Not later than 2 years after August 14, 2008, the Bureau shall, based on consumer testing, and in consultation with the Secretary of Education, develop and issue model forms that may be used, at the option of the private educational lender, for the provision of disclosures required under this subsection.

(B) Format

Model forms developed under this paragraph shall—

(i) be comprehensible to borrowers, with a clear format and design;

(ii) provide for clear and conspicuous disclosures;

(iii) enable borrowers easily to identify material terms of the loan and to compare such terms among private education loans; and

(iv) be succinct, and use an easily readable type font.

(C) Safe harbor

Any private educational lender that elects to provide a model form developed under this subsection that accurately reflects the practices of the private educational lender shall be deemed to be in compliance with the disclosures required under this subsection.

(6) Effective period of approved rate of interest and loan terms

(A) In general

With respect to a private education loan, the borrower shall have the right to accept the terms of the loan and consummate the transaction at any time within 30 calendar days (or such longer period as the private educational lender may provide) following the date on which the application for the private education loan is approved and the borrower receives the disclosure documents required under this subsection for the loan, and the rates and terms of the loan may not be changed by the private educational lender during that period.

(B) Prohibition on changes

Except for changes based on adjustments to the index used for a loan, the rates and terms of the loan may not be changed by the private educational lender prior to the earlier of—

(i) the date of acceptance of the terms of the loan and consummation of the transaction by the borrower, as described in subparagraph (A); or

(ii) the expiration of the period described in subparagraph (A).

(7) Right to cancel

With respect to a private education loan, the borrower may cancel the loan, without penalty to the borrower, at any time within 3 business days of the date on which the loan is consummated, and the private educational lender shall disclose such right to the borrower in accordance with paragraph (4).

(8) Prohibition on disbursement

No funds may be disbursed with respect to a private education loan until the expiration of the 3-day period described in paragraph (7).

(9) Bureau regulations

In issuing regulations under this subsection, the Bureau shall prevent, to the extent possible, duplicative disclosure requirements for private educational lenders that are otherwise required to make disclosures under this subchapter, except that in any case in which the disclosure requirements of this subsection differ or conflict with the disclosure requirements of any other provision of this subchapter, the requirements of this subsection shall be controlling.

(10) Definitions

For purposes of this subsection, the terms "covered educational institution", "private educational lender", and "private education loan" have the same meanings as in section 1650 of this title.

(11) Duties of lenders participating in preferred lender arrangements

Each private educational lender that has a preferred lender arrangement with a covered educational institution shall annually, by a date determined by the Bureau, in consultation with the Secretary of Education, provide to the covered educational institution such information as the Bureau determines to include in the model form developed under paragraph (5) for each type of private education loan that the lender plans to offer to students attending the covered educational institution, or to the families of such students, for the next award year (as that term is defined in section 481 of the Higher Education Act of 1965 [20 U.S.C. 1088]).

(f) Periodic statements for residential mortgage loans

(1) In general

The creditor, assignee, or servicer with respect to any residential mortgage loan shall transmit to the obligor, for each billing cycle, a statement setting forth each of the following items, to the extent applicable, in a conspicuous and prominent manner:

(A) The amount of the principal obligation under the mortgage.

(B) The current interest rate in effect for the loan.

(C) The date on which the interest rate may next reset or adjust.

(D) The amount of any prepayment fee to be charged, if any.

(E) A description of any late payment fees.

(F) A telephone number and electronic mail address that may be used by the obligor to obtain information regarding the mortgage.

(G) The names, addresses, telephone numbers, and Internet addresses of counseling agencies or programs reasonably available to the consumer that have been certified or approved and made publicly available by the Secretary of Housing and Urban Development or a State housing finance authority (as defined in section 1441a–1 of title 12).

(H) Such other information as the Board [2] may prescribe in regulations.

(2) Development and use of standard form

The Board [2] shall develop and prescribe a standard form for the disclosure required under this subsection, taking into account that the statements required may be transmitted in writing or electronically.

(3) Exception

Paragraph (1) shall not apply to any fixed rate residential mortgage loan where the creditor, assignee, or servicer provides the obligor with a coupon book that provides the obligor with substantially the same information as required in paragraph (1).

(Pub. L. 90–321, title I, §128, May 29, 1968, 82 Stat. 155; Pub. L. 96–221, title VI, §614(a)–(c), Mar. 31, 1980, 94 Stat. 178, 179; Pub. L. 104–208, div. A, title II, §2105, Sept. 30, 1996, 110 Stat. 3009–402; Pub. L. 109–8, title XIII, §1302(b)(1), Apr. 20, 2005, 119 Stat. 208; Pub. L. 110–289, div. B, title V, §2502(a), July 30, 2008, 122 Stat. 2855; Pub. L. 110–315, title X, §1021(a), Aug. 14, 2008, 122 Stat. 3483; Pub. L. 110–343, div. A, title I, §130(a), Oct. 3, 2008, 122 Stat. 3797; Pub. L. 111–203, title X, §1100A(2), title XIV, §§1419, 1420, 1465, July 21, 2010, 124 Stat. 2107, 2154, 2155, 2185.)

Pub. L. 110–289, §2502(a)(5), (6), struck out ", whichever is earlier" after "consummation of the transaction" and "If the disclosure statement furnished within three days of the written application contains an annual percentage rate which is subsequently rendered inaccurate within the meaning of section 1606(c) of this title, the creditor shall furnish another statement at the time of settlement or consummation." at the end.

Pub. L. 110–289, §2502(a)(4), which directed insertion of ", which shall be at least 7 business days before consummation of the transaction" after "written application", was executed by making the insertion after "written application" the first place appearing.

Pub. L. 110–289, §2502(a)(2), (3), substituted "any extension of credit that is secured by the dwelling of a consumer" for "a residential mortgage transaction, as defined in section 1602(w) of this title" and "and" for "before the credit is extended, or".

Subsec. (b)(2)(B) to (F). Pub. L. 110–289, §2502(a)(6), added subpars. (B) to (F).

Subsec. (b)(2)(G). Pub. L. 110–343, §130(a)(2), amended subpar. (G) generally. Prior to amendment, subpar. (G) read as follows: "The requirements of subparagraphs (B), (C), (D) and (E) shall not apply to extensions of credit relating to plans described in section 101(53D) of title 11."

Pub. L. 110–289, §2502(a)(6), added subpar. (G).

Subsec. (e). Pub. L. 110–315 added subsec. (e).

2005—Subsec. (a)(15). Pub. L. 109–8, §1302(b)(1)(A), added par. (15).

Subsec. (b)(3). Pub. L. 109–8, §1302(b)(1)(B), added par. (3).

1996—Subsec. (a)(14). Pub. L. 104–208 added par. (14).

1980—Subsec. (a). Pub. L. 96–221, §614(a), substituted provisions setting forth required disclosures by the creditor for transactions other than under an open end credit plan, for provisions setting forth required disclosures by the creditor for sales not under open end credit plans.

Subsec. (b). Pub. L. 96–221, §614(b), designated existing provisions as par. (1), inserted provisions relating to the conspicuous segregation of required disclosures, and struck out provisions authorizing the required information to be disclosed in the signed evidence of indebtedness, and added par. (2).

Subsec. (c). Pub. L. 96–221, §614(c), designated existing provisions as par. (1), substituted "total sale" for "deferred payment", and added par. (2).

STATUTORY NOTES AND RELATED SUBSIDIARIES

EFFECTIVE DATE OF 2010 AMENDMENT

Amendment by section 1100A(2) of Pub. L. 111–203 effective on the designated transfer date, see section 1100H of Pub. L. 111–203, set out as a note under section 552a of Title 5, Government Organization and Employees.

Amendment by sections 1419, 1420, and 1465 of Pub. L. 111–203 effective on the date on which final regulations implementing that amendment take effect, or on the date that is 18 months after the designated transfer date if such regulations have not been issued by that date, see section 1400(c) of Pub. L. 111–203, set out as a note under section 1601 of this title.

EFFECTIVE DATE OF 2008 AMENDMENT

Pub. L. 110–343, div. A, title I, §130(b), Oct. 3, 2008, 122 Stat. 3797, provided that: "The amendments made by subsection (a) [amending this section] shall take effect as if included in the amendments made by section 2502 of the Mortgage Disclosure Improvement Act of 2008 (Public Law 110–289) [amending this section and section 1640 of this title]."

Pub. L. 110–315, title X, §1003, Aug. 14, 2008, 122 Stat. 3478, provided that:

"(a) IN GENERAL.—Except as provided in subsection (b) and as otherwise provided in this title [see Short Title of 2008 Amendment note set out under section 1601 of this title], this title and the amendments made by this title shall become effective on the date of enactment of this Act [Aug. 14, 2008].

"(b) EFFECT NOTWITHSTANDING REGULATIONS.—Paragraphs (1), (2), (3), (4), (6), (7), and (8) of section 128(e) [15 U.S.C. 1638(e)] and section 140(c) of the Truth in Lending Act [15 U.S.C. 1650(c)], as added by this title, shall become effective on the earlier of the date on which regulations issued under section 1002 [set out as a note below] become effective [Such regulations were issued effective Sept. 14, 2009, with compliance optional until Feb. 14, 2010. See 74 F.R. 41194.] or 18 months after the date of enactment of this Act [Aug. 14, 2008]."

Pub. L. 110–289, div. B, title V, §2502(c), July 30, 2008, 122 Stat. 2857, provided that:

"(1) GENERAL DISCLOSURES.—Except as provided in paragraph (2), the amendments made by subsection (a) [amending this section] shall become effective 12 months after the date of enactment of this Act [July 30, 2008].

"(2) VARIABLE INTEREST RATES.—Subparagraph (C) of section 128(b)(2) of the Truth in Lending Act (15 U.S.C. 1638(b)(2)(C)), as added by subsection (a) of this section, shall become effective on the earlier of—
"(A) the compliance date established by the Board for such purpose, by regulation; or
"(B) 30 months after the date of enactment of this Act [July 30, 2008]."

EFFECTIVE DATE OF 2005 AMENDMENT

Amendment by Pub. L. 109–8 effective 180 days after Apr. 20, 2005, and not applicable with respect to cases commenced under Title 11, Bankruptcy, before such effective date, except as otherwise provided, see section 1501 of Pub. L. 109–8, set out as a note under section 101 of Title 11.

EFFECTIVE DATE OF 1980 AMENDMENT

Amendment by Pub. L. 96–221 effective on expiration of two years and six months after Mar. 31, 1980, with all regulations, forms, and clauses required to be prescribed to be promulgated at least one year prior to such effective date, and allowing any creditor to comply with any amendments, in accordance with the regulations, forms, and clauses prescribed by the Board prior to such effective date, see section 625 of Pub. L. 96–221, set out as a note under section 1602 of this title.

REGULATIONS

Pub. L. 110–315, title X, §1002, Aug. 14, 2008, 122 Stat. 3478, provided that: "Not later than 365 days after the date of enactment of this Act [Aug. 14, 2008], the Board of Governors of the Federal Reserve System shall issue regulations in final form to implement paragraphs (1), (2), (3), (4), (6), (7), and (8) of section 128(e) [15 U.S.C. 1638(e)] and section 140(c) of the Truth in Lending Act [15 U.S.C. 1650(c)], as added by this title, which regulations shall become effective not later than 6 months after their date of issuance."

[1] So in original. The comma probably should not appear.

[2] So in original. Probably should be "Bureau".

§1638a. Reset of hybrid adjustable rate mortgages

(a) Hybrid adjustable rate mortgages defined

For purposes of this section, the term "hybrid adjustable rate mortgage" means a consumer credit transaction secured by the consumer's principal residence with a fixed interest rate for an introductory period that adjusts or resets to a variable interest rate after such period.

(b) Notice of reset and alternatives

During the 1-month period that ends 6 months before the date on which the interest rate in effect during the introductory period of a hybrid adjustable rate mortgage adjusts or resets to a variable interest rate or, in the case of such an adjustment or resetting that occurs within the first 6 months after consummation of such loan, at consummation, the creditor or servicer of such loan shall provide a written notice, separate and distinct from all other correspondence to the consumer, that includes the following:

(1) Any index or formula used in making adjustments to or resetting the interest rate and a source of information about the index or formula.

(2) An explanation of how the new interest rate and payment would be determined, including an explanation of how the index was adjusted, such as by the addition of a margin.

(3) A good faith estimate, based on accepted industry standards, of the creditor or servicer of the amount of the monthly payment that will apply after the date of the adjustment or reset, and the assumptions on which this estimate is based.

(4) A list of alternatives consumers may pursue before the date of adjustment or reset, and descriptions of the actions consumers must take to pursue these alternatives, including—

(A) refinancing;

(B) renegotiation of loan terms;

(C) payment forbearances; and

(D) pre-foreclosure sales.

(5) The names, addresses, telephone numbers, and Internet addresses of counseling agencies or programs reasonably available to the consumer that have been certified or approved and made publicly available by the Secretary of Housing and Urban Development or a State housing finance authority (as defined in section 1441a–1 of title 12).

(6) The address, telephone number, and Internet address for the State housing finance authority (as so defined) for the State in which the consumer resides.

(c) Savings clause

The Board may require the notice in paragraph (b) or other notice consistent with this chapter for adjustable rate mortgage loans that are not hybrid adjustable rate mortgage loans.

(Pub. L. 90–321, title I, §128A, as added Pub. L. 111–203, title XIV, §1418(a), July 21, 2010, 124 Stat. 2153.)

EDITORIAL NOTES

REFERENCES IN TEXT

This chapter, referred to in subsec. (c), was in the original "this Act" meaning Pub. L. 90–321, May 29, 1968, 82 Stat. 146, which is classified principally to this chapter. For complete classification of this Act to the Code, see Short Title note set out under section 1601 of this title and Tables.

STATUTORY NOTES AND RELATED SUBSIDIARIES

EFFECTIVE DATE

Section effective on the date on which final regulations implementing such section take effect, or on the date that is 18 months after the designated transfer date, if such regulations have not been issued by that date, see section 1400(c) of Pub. L. 111–203, set out as an Effective Date of 2010 Amendment note under section 1601 of this title.

§1639. Requirements for certain mortgages

(a) Disclosures

(1) Specific disclosures

In addition to other disclosures required under this subchapter, for each mortgage referred to in section 1602(aa) [1] of this title, the creditor shall provide the following disclosures in conspicuous type size:

(A) "You are not required to complete this agreement merely because you have received these disclosures or have signed a loan application.".

(B) "If you obtain this loan, the lender will have a mortgage on your home. You could lose your home, and any money you have put into it, if you do not meet your obligations under the loan.".

(2) Annual percentage rate

In addition to the disclosures required under paragraph (1), the creditor shall disclose—

(A) in the case of a credit transaction with a fixed rate of interest, the annual percentage rate and the amount of the regular monthly payment; or

(B) in the case of any other credit transaction, the annual percentage rate of the loan, the amount of the regular monthly payment, a statement that the interest rate and monthly payment may increase, and the amount of the maximum monthly payment, based on the maximum interest rate allowed pursuant to section 3806 of title 12.

(b) Time of disclosures

(1) In general

The disclosures required by this section shall be given not less than 3 business days prior to consummation of the transaction.

(2) New disclosures required

(A) In general

After providing the disclosures required by this section, a creditor may not change the terms of the extension of credit if such changes make the disclosures inaccurate, unless new disclosures are provided that meet the requirements of this section.

(B) Telephone disclosure

A creditor may provide new disclosures pursuant to subparagraph (A) by telephone, if—

(i) the change is initiated by the consumer; and

(ii) at the consummation of the transaction under which the credit is extended—

(I) the creditor provides to the consumer the new disclosures, in writing; and

(II) the creditor and consumer certify in writing that the new disclosures were provided by telephone, by not later than 3 days prior to the date of consummation of the transaction.

(3) No wait for lower rate

If a creditor extends to a consumer a second offer of credit with a lower annual percentage rate, the transaction may be consummated without regard to the period specified in paragraph (1) with respect to the second offer.

(4) Modifications

The Bureau may, if it finds that such action is necessary to permit homeowners to meet bona fide personal financial emergencies, prescribe regulations authorizing the modification or waiver of rights created under this subsection, to the extent and under the circumstances set forth in those regulations.

(c) No prepayment penalty

(1) In general [2]

(A) Limitation on terms

A mortgage referred to in section 1602(aa) [1] of this title may not contain terms under which a consumer must pay a prepayment penalty for paying all or part of the principal before the date on which the principal is due.

(B) Construction

For purposes of this subsection, any method of computing a refund of unearned scheduled interest is a prepayment penalty if it is less favorable to the consumer than the actuarial method (as that term is defined in section 1615(d) of this title).

(d) Limitations after default

A mortgage referred to in section 1602(aa) [1] of this title may not provide for an interest rate applicable after default that is higher than the interest rate that applies before default. If the date of maturity of a mortgage referred to in subsection [3] 1602(aa) [1] of this title is accelerated due to default and the consumer is entitled to a rebate of interest, that rebate shall be computed by any method that is not less favorable than the actuarial method (as that term is defined in section 1615(d) of this title).

(e) No balloon payments

No high-cost mortgage may contain a scheduled payment that is more than twice as large as the average of earlier scheduled payments. This subsection shall not apply when the payment schedule is adjusted to the seasonal or irregular income of the consumer.

(f) No negative amortization

A mortgage referred to in section 1602(aa) [1] of this title may not include terms under which the outstanding principal balance will increase at any time over the course of the loan because the regular periodic payments do not cover the full amount of interest due.

(g) No prepaid payments

A mortgage referred to in section 1602(aa) [1] of this title may not include terms under which more than 2 periodic payments required under the loan are consolidated and paid in advance from the loan proceeds provided to the consumer.

(h) Prohibition on extending credit without regard to payment ability of consumer

A creditor shall not engage in a pattern or practice of extending credit to consumers under mortgages referred to in section 1602(aa) [1] of this title based on the consumers' collateral without regard to the consumers' repayment ability, including the consumers' current and expected income, current obligations, and employment.

(i) Requirements for payments under home improvement contracts

A creditor shall not make a payment to a contractor under a home improvement contract from amounts extended as credit under a mortgage referred to in section 1602(aa) [1] of this title, other than—
(1) in the form of an instrument that is payable to the consumer or jointly to the consumer and the contractor; or
(2) at the election of the consumer, by a third party escrow agent in accordance with terms established in a written agreement signed by the consumer, the creditor, and the contractor before the date of payment.

(j) Recommended default

No creditor shall recommend or encourage default on an existing loan or other debt prior to and in connection with the closing or planned closing of a high-cost mortgage that refinances all or any portion of such existing loan or debt.

(k) Late fees

(1) In general

No creditor may impose a late payment charge or fee in connection with a high-cost mortgage—
(A) in an amount in excess of 4 percent of the amount of the payment past due;
(B) unless the loan documents specifically authorize the charge or fee;
(C) before the end of the 15-day period beginning on the date the payment is due, or in the case of a loan on which interest on each installment is paid in advance, before the end of the 30-day period beginning on the date

the payment is due; or

(D) more than once with respect to a single late payment.

(2) Coordination with subsequent late fees

If a payment is otherwise a full payment for the applicable period and is paid on its due date or within an applicable grace period, and the only delinquency or insufficiency of payment is attributable to any late fee or delinquency charge assessed on any earlier payment, no late fee or delinquency charge may be imposed on such payment.

(3) Failure to make installment payment

If, in the case of a loan agreement the terms of which provide that any payment shall first be applied to any past due principal balance, the consumer fails to make an installment payment and the consumer subsequently resumes making installment payments but has not paid all past due installments, the creditor may impose a separate late payment charge or fee for any principal due (without deduction due to late fees or related fees) until the default is cured.

(l) Acceleration of debt

No high-cost mortgage may contain a provision which permits the creditor to accelerate the indebtedness, except when repayment of the loan has been accelerated by default in payment, or pursuant to a due-on-sale provision, or pursuant to a material violation of some other provision of the loan document unrelated to payment schedule.

(m) Restriction on financing points and fees

No creditor may directly or indirectly finance, in connection with any high-cost mortgage, any of the following:

(1) Any prepayment fee or penalty payable by the consumer in a refinancing transaction if the creditor or an affiliate of the creditor is the noteholder of the note being refinanced.

(2) Any points or fees.

(n) Consequence of failure to comply

Any mortgage that contains a provision prohibited by this section shall be deemed a failure to deliver the material disclosures required under this subchapter, for the purpose of section 1635 of this title.

(o) "Affiliate" defined

For purposes of this section, the term "affiliate" has the same meaning as in section 1841(k) of title 12.

(p) Discretionary regulatory authority of Bureau

(1) Exemptions

The Bureau may, by regulation or order, exempt specific mortgage products or categories of mortgages from any or all of the prohibitions specified in subsections (c) through (i), if the Bureau finds that the exemption—

(A) is in the interest of the borrowing public; and

(B) will apply only to products that maintain and strengthen home ownership and equity protection.

(2) Prohibitions

The Bureau, by regulation or order, shall prohibit acts or practices in connection with—

(A) mortgage loans that the Bureau finds to be unfair, deceptive, or designed to evade the provisions of this section; and

(B) refinancing of mortgage loans that the Bureau finds to be associated with abusive lending practices, or that are otherwise not in the interest of the borrower.

(q) Civil penalties in Federal Trade Commission enforcement actions

For purposes of enforcement by the Federal Trade Commission, any violation of a regulation issued by the Bureau pursuant to subsection (l)(2) shall be treated as a violation of a rule promulgated under section 57a of this title regarding unfair or deceptive acts or practices.

(r) Prohibitions on evasions, structuring of transactions, and reciprocal arrangements

A creditor may not take any action in connection with a high-cost mortgage—

(1) to structure a loan transaction as an open-end credit plan or another form of loan for the purpose and with the intent of evading the provisions of this subchapter; or

(2) to divide any loan transaction into separate parts for the purpose and with the intent of evading provisions of this subchapter.

(s) Modification and deferral fees prohibited

A creditor, successor in interest, assignee, or any agent of any of the above, may not charge a consumer any fee to modify, renew, extend, or amend a high-cost mortgage, or to defer any payment due under the terms of such mortgage.

(t) Payoff statement

(1) Fees

(A) In general

Except as provided in subparagraph (B), no creditor or servicer may charge a fee for informing or transmitting to any person the balance due to pay off the outstanding balance on a high-cost mortgage.

(B) Transaction fee

When payoff information referred to in subparagraph (A) is provided by facsimile transmission or by a courier service, a creditor or servicer may charge a processing fee to cover the cost of such transmission or service in an amount not to exceed an amount that is comparable to fees imposed for similar services provided in connection with consumer credit transactions that are secured by the consumer's principal dwelling and are not high-cost mortgages.

(C) Fee disclosure

Prior to charging a transaction fee as provided in subparagraph (B), a creditor or servicer shall disclose that payoff balances are available for free pursuant to subparagraph (A).

(D) Multiple requests

If a creditor or servicer has provided payoff information referred to in subparagraph (A) without charge, other than the transaction fee allowed by subparagraph (B), on 4 occasions during a calendar year, the creditor or servicer may thereafter charge a reasonable fee for providing such information during the remainder of the calendar year.

(2) Prompt delivery

Payoff balances shall be provided within 5 business days after receiving a request by a consumer or a person authorized by the consumer to obtain such information.

(u) Pre-loan counseling

(1) In general

A creditor may not extend credit to a consumer under a high-cost mortgage without first receiving certification from a counselor that is approved by the Secretary of Housing and Urban Development, or at the discretion of the Secretary, a State housing finance authority, that the consumer has received counseling on the advisability of the mortgage. Such counselor shall not be employed by the creditor or an affiliate of the creditor or be affiliated with the creditor.

(2) Disclosures required prior to counseling

No counselor may certify that a consumer has received counseling on the advisability of the high-cost mortgage unless the counselor can verify that the consumer has received each statement required (in connection with such loan) by this section or the Real Estate Settlement Procedures Act of 1974 [12 U.S.C. 2601 et seq.] with respect to the transaction.

(3) Regulations

The Board [4] may prescribe such regulations as the Board determines to be appropriate to carry out the requirements of paragraph (1).

(v) Corrections and unintentional violations

A creditor or assignee in a high-cost mortgage who, when acting in good faith, fails to comply with any requirement under this section will not be deemed to have violated such requirement if the creditor or assignee establishes that either—

(1) within 30 days of the loan closing and prior to the institution of any action, the consumer is notified of or discovers the violation, appropriate restitution is made, and whatever adjustments are necessary are made to the loan to either, at the choice of the consumer—

(A) make the loan satisfy the requirements of this part; or

(B) in the case of a high-cost mortgage, change the terms of the loan in a manner beneficial to the consumer so that the loan will no longer be a high-cost mortgage; or

(2) within 60 days of the creditor's discovery or receipt of notification of an unintentional violation or bona fide error and prior to the institution of any action, the consumer is notified of the compliance failure, appropriate restitution is made, and whatever adjustments are necessary are made to the loan to either, at the choice of the consumer—

(A) make the loan satisfy the requirements of this part; or

(B) in the case of a high-cost mortgage, change the terms of the loan in a manner beneficial so that the loan will no longer be a high-cost mortgage.

(Pub. L. 90–321, title I, §129, as added Pub. L. 103–325, title I, §152(d), Sept. 23, 1994, 108 Stat. 2191; amended Pub. L. 111–8, div. D, title VI, §626(c), Mar. 11, 2009, 123 Stat. 679; Pub. L. 111–203, title X, §1100A(2), (9), title XIV, §§1432, 1433, July 21, 2010, 124 Stat. 2107, 2109, 2160; Pub. L. 115–174, title I, §109(a), May 24, 2018, 132 Stat. 1305.)

EDITORIAL NOTES

References in Text

Section 1602(aa) of this title, referred to in text, was redesignated section 1602(bb) of this title by Pub. L. 111–203, title X, §1100A(1)(A), July 21, 2010, 124 Stat. 2107.

The Real Estate Settlement Procedures Act of 1974, referred to in subsec. (u)(2), is Pub. L. 93–533, Dec. 22, 1974, 88 Stat. 1724, which is classified principally to chapter 27 (§2601 et seq.) of Title 12, Banks and Banking. For complete classification of this Act to the Code, see Short Title note set out under section 2601 of Title 12 and Tables.

Prior Provisions

A prior section 1639, Pub. L. 90–321, title I, §129, May 29, 1968, 82 Stat. 156, related to consumer loans not under open end credit plans, prior to repeal by Pub. L. 96–221, title VI, §614(d)(1), Mar. 31, 1980, 94 Stat. 180. Repeal effective on expiration of two years and six months after Mar. 31, 1980, with all regulations, forms, and clauses required to be prescribed to be promulgated at least one year prior to such effective date, and allowing any creditor to comply with any amendments, in accordance with the regulations, forms, and clauses prescribed by the Board prior to such effective date, see section 625 of Pub. L. 96–221, set out as an Effective Date of 1980 Amendment note under section 1602 of this title.

Amendments

2018—Subsec. (b)(3), (4). Pub. L. 115–174 added par. (3) and redesignated former par. (3) as (4).

2010—Pub. L. 111–203, §1100A(2), substituted "Bureau" for "Board" wherever appearing.

Subsec. (c)(2). Pub. L. 111–203, §1432(a), struck out par. (2) which related to exception to prepayment penalty prohibition.

Subsec. (e). Pub. L. 111–203, §1432(b), amended subsec. (e) generally. Prior to amendment, text read as follows: "A mortgage referred to in section 1602(aa) of this title having a term of less than 5 years may not include terms under which the aggregate amount of the regular periodic payments would not fully amortize the outstanding principal balance."

Subsecs. (j) to (l). Pub. L. 111–203, §1433(a)(2), added subsecs. (j) to (l). Former subsecs. (j) to (l) redesignated (n) to (p), respectively.

Subsec. (m). Pub. L. 111–203, §1433(a)(2), added subsec. (m). Former subsec. (m) redesignated (q).

Pub. L. 111–203, §1100A(9), added subsec. (m) and struck out former subsec. (m). Prior to amendment, text read as follows: "For purposes of enforcement by the Federal Trade Commission, any violation of a regulation issued by the Federal Reserve Board pursuant to subsection (l)(2) of this section shall be treated as a violation of a rule promulgated under section 57a of this title regarding unfair or deceptive acts or practices."

Subsecs. (n) to (q). Pub. L. 111–203, §1433(a)(1), redesignated former subsecs. (j) to (m) as (n) to (q), respectively.

Subsecs. (r) to (v). Pub. L. 111–203, §1433(b)–(f), added subsecs. (r) to (v).

2009—Subsec. (m). Pub. L. 111–8 added subsec. (m).

STATUTORY NOTES AND RELATED SUBSIDIARIES

Effective Date of 2010 Amendment

Amendment by section 1100A(2), (9) of Pub. L. 111–203 effective on the designated transfer date, see section 1100H of Pub. L. 111–203, set out as a note under section 552a of Title 5, Government Organization and Employees.

Amendment by sections 1432 and 1433 of Pub. L. 111–203 effective on the date on which final regulations implementing that amendment take effect, or on the date that is 18 months after the designated transfer date if such regulations have not been issued by that date, see section 1400(c) of Pub. L. 111–203, set out as a note under section 1601 of this title.

[1] See References in Text note below.

[2] So in original. There is no par. (2).

[3] So in original. Probably should be "section".

[4] So in original. Probably should be "Bureau".

§1639a. Duty of servicers of residential mortgages

(a) In general

Notwithstanding any other provision of law, whenever a servicer of residential mortgages agrees to enter into a qualified loss mitigation plan with respect to 1 or more residential mortgages originated before May 20, 2009, including mortgages held in a securitization or other investment vehicle—

(1) to the extent that the servicer owes a duty to investors or other parties to maximize the net present value of such mortgages, the duty shall be construed to apply to all such investors and parties, and not to any individual party or group of parties; and

(2) the servicer shall be deemed to have satisfied the duty set forth in paragraph (1) if, before December 31, 2012, the servicer implements a qualified loss mitigation plan that meets the following criteria:

(A) Default on the payment of such mortgage has occurred, is imminent, or is reasonably foreseeable, as such terms are defined by guidelines issued by the Secretary of the Treasury or his designee under the Emergency Economic Stabilization Act of 2008 [12 U.S.C. 5201 et seq.].

(B) The mortgagor occupies the property securing the mortgage as his or her principal residence.

(C) The servicer reasonably determined, consistent with the guidelines issued by the Secretary of the Treasury or his designee, that the application of such qualified loss mitigation plan to a mortgage or class of mortgages will likely provide an anticipated recovery on the outstanding principal mortgage debt that will exceed the anticipated recovery through foreclosures.

(b) No liability

A servicer that is deemed to be acting in the best interests of all investors or other parties under this section shall not be liable to any party who is owed a duty under subsection (a)(1), and shall not be subject to any injunction, stay, or other equitable relief to such party, based solely upon the implementation by the servicer of a qualified loss mitigation plan.

(c) Standard industry practice

The qualified loss mitigation plan guidelines issued by the Secretary of the Treasury under the Emergency Economic Stabilization Act of 2008 [12 U.S.C. 5201 et seq.] shall constitute standard industry practice for purposes of all Federal and State laws.

(d) Scope of safe harbor

Any person, including a trustee, issuer, and loan originator, shall not be liable for monetary damages or be subject to an injunction, stay, or other equitable relief, based solely upon the cooperation of such person with a servicer when such cooperation is necessary for the servicer to implement a qualified loss mitigation plan that meets the requirements of subsection (a).

(e) Reporting

Each servicer that engages in qualified loss mitigation plans under this section shall regularly report to the Secretary of the Treasury the extent, scope, and results of the servicer's modification activities. The Secretary of the Treasury shall prescribe regulations or guidance specifying the form, content, and timing of such reports.

(f) Definitions

As used in this section—

(1) the term "qualified loss mitigation plan" means—

(A) a residential loan modification, workout, or other loss mitigation plan, including to the extent that the Secretary of the Treasury determines appropriate, a loan sale, real property disposition, trial modification, pre-foreclosure sale, and deed in lieu of foreclosure, that is described or authorized in guidelines issued by the Secretary of the Treasury or his designee under the Emergency Economic Stabilization Act of 2008 [12 U.S.C. 5201 et seq.]; and

(B) a refinancing of a mortgage under the Hope for Homeowners program;

(2) the term "servicer" means the person responsible for the servicing for others of residential mortgage loans (including of a pool of residential mortgage loans); and

(3) the term "securitization vehicle" means a trust, special purpose entity, or other legal structure that is used to facilitate the issuing of securities, participation certificates, or similar instruments backed by or referring to a pool of assets that includes residential mortgages (or instruments that are related to residential mortgages such as credit-linked notes).

(g) Rule of construction

No provision of subsection (b) or (d) shall be construed as affecting the liability of any servicer or person as described in subsection (d) for actual fraud in the origination or servicing of a loan or in the implementation of a qualified loss mitigation plan, or for the violation of a State or Federal law, including laws regulating the origination of mortgage loans, commonly referred to as predatory lending laws.

(Pub. L. 90–321, title I, §129A, as added Pub. L. 110–289, div. A, title IV, §1403, July 30, 2008, 122 Stat. 2809; renumbered §129 and amended Pub. L. 111–22, div. A, title II, §201(b), May 20, 2009, 123 Stat. 1638; renumbered §129A, Pub. L. 111–203, title XIV, §1402(a)(1), July 21, 2010, 124 Stat. 2138.)

EDITORIAL NOTES

REFERENCES IN TEXT

The Emergency Economic Stabilization Act of 2008, referred to in subsecs. (a)(2)(A), (c), (f)(1)(A), is div. A of Pub. L. 110–343, Oct. 3, 2008, 122 Stat. 3765, which is classified principally to chapter 52 (§5201 et seq.) of Title 12, Banks and Banking. For complete classification of this Act to the Code, see Short Title note set out under section 5201 of Title 12 and Tables.

AMENDMENTS

2009—Pub. L. 111–22 amended section generally. Prior to amendment, section related to fiduciary duty of servicers of pooled residential mortgages without providing for date limitation for implementing modifications or workout plans.

STATUTORY NOTES AND RELATED SUBSIDIARIES

FINDINGS

Pub. L. 111–22, div. A, title II, §201(a), May 20, 2009, 123 Stat. 1638, provided that: "Congress finds the following:

"(1) Increasing numbers of mortgage foreclosures are not only depriving many Americans of their homes, but are also destabilizing property values and negatively affecting State and local economies as well as the national economy.

"(2) In order to reduce the number of foreclosures and to stabilize property values, local economies, and the national economy, servicers must be given—

"(A) authorization to—

"(i) modify mortgage loans and engage in other loss mitigation activities consistent with applicable guidelines issued by the Secretary of the Treasury or his designee under the Emergency Economic Stabilization Act of 2008 [12 U.S.C. 5201 et seq.]; and

"(ii) refinance mortgage loans under the Hope for Homeowners program; and

"(B) a safe harbor to enable such servicers to exercise these authorities."

§1639b. Residential mortgage loan origination

(a) Finding and purpose

(1) Finding

The Congress finds that economic stabilization would be enhanced by the protection, limitation, and regulation of the terms of residential mortgage credit and the practices related to such credit, while ensuring that responsible, affordable mortgage credit remains available to consumers.

(2) Purpose

It is the purpose of this section and section 1639c of this title to assure that consumers are offered and receive residential mortgage loans on terms that reasonably reflect their ability to repay the loans and that are understandable and not unfair, deceptive or abusive.

(b) Duty of care

(1) Standard

Subject to regulations prescribed under this subsection, each mortgage originator shall, in addition to the duties imposed by otherwise applicable provisions of State or Federal law—

(A) be qualified and, when required, registered and licensed as a mortgage originator in accordance with applicable State or Federal law, including the Secure and Fair Enforcement for Mortgage Licensing Act of 2008 [12 U.S.C. 5101 et seq.]; and

(B) include on all loan documents any unique identifier of the mortgage originator provided by the Nationwide Mortgage Licensing System and Registry.

(2) Compliance procedures required

The Bureau shall prescribe regulations requiring depository institutions to establish and maintain procedures reasonably designed to assure and monitor the compliance of such depository institutions, the subsidiaries of such institutions, and the employees of such institutions or subsidiaries with the requirements of this section and the registration procedures established under section 1507 of the Secure and Fair Enforcement for Mortgage Licensing Act of 2008 [12 U.S.C. 5106].

(c) Prohibition on steering incentives

(1) In general

For any residential mortgage loan, no mortgage originator shall receive from any person and no person shall pay to a mortgage originator, directly or indirectly, compensation that varies based on the terms of the loan (other than the amount of the principal).

(2) Restructuring of financing origination fee

(A) In general

For any mortgage loan, a mortgage originator may not receive from any person other than the consumer and no person, other than the consumer, who knows or has reason to know that a consumer has directly compensated or will directly compensate a mortgage originator may pay a mortgage originator any origination fee or charge except bona fide third party charges not retained by the creditor, mortgage originator, or an affiliate of the creditor or mortgage originator.

(B) Exception

Notwithstanding subparagraph (A), a mortgage originator may receive from a person other than the consumer an origination fee or charge, and a person other than the consumer may pay a mortgage originator an origination fee or charge, if—

(i) the mortgage originator does not receive any compensation directly from the consumer; and

(ii) the consumer does not make an upfront payment of discount points, origination points, or fees, however denominated (other than bona fide third party charges not retained by the mortgage originator, creditor, or an affiliate of the creditor or originator), except that the Bureau may, by rule, waive or provide exemptions to this clause if the Bureau determines that such waiver or exemption is in the interest of consumers and in the public interest.

(3) Regulations

The Bureau shall prescribe regulations to prohibit—

(A) mortgage originators from steering any consumer to a residential mortgage loan that—

(i) the consumer lacks a reasonable ability to repay (in accordance with regulations prescribed under section 1639c(a) of this title); or

(ii) has predatory characteristics or effects (such as equity stripping, excessive fees, or abusive terms);

(B) mortgage originators from steering any consumer from a residential mortgage loan for which the consumer is qualified that is a qualified mortgage (as defined in section 1639c(b)(2) of this title) to a residential mortgage loan that is not a qualified mortgage;

(C) abusive or unfair lending practices that promote disparities among consumers of equal credit worthiness but of different race, ethnicity, gender, or age; and

(D) mortgage originators from—

(i) mischaracterizing the credit history of a consumer or the residential mortgage loans available to a consumer;

(ii) mischaracterizing or suborning the mischaracterization of the appraised value of the property securing the extension of credit; or

(iii) if unable to suggest, offer, or recommend to a consumer a loan that is not more expensive than a loan for which the consumer qualifies, discouraging a consumer from seeking a residential mortgage loan secured by a consumer's principal dwelling from another mortgage originator.

(4) Rules of construction

No provision of this subsection shall be construed as—

(A) permitting any yield spread premium or other similar compensation that would, for any residential mortgage loan, permit the total amount of direct and indirect compensation from all sources permitted to a mortgage originator to vary based on the terms of the loan (other than the amount of the principal);

(B) limiting or affecting the amount of compensation received by a creditor upon the sale of a consummated loan to a subsequent purchaser;

(C) restricting a consumer's ability to finance, at the option of the consumer, including through principal or rate, any origination fees or costs permitted under this subsection, or the mortgage originator's right to receive such fees or costs (including compensation) from any person, subject to paragraph (2)(B), so long as such fees or costs do not vary based on the terms of the loan (other than the amount of the principal) or the consumer's decision about whether to finance such fees or costs; or

(D) prohibiting incentive payments to a mortgage originator based on the number of residential mortgage loans originated within a specified period of time.

(d) Liability for violations

(1) In general

For purposes of providing a cause of action for any failure by a mortgage originator, other than a creditor, to comply with any requirement imposed under this section and any regulation prescribed under this section, section 1640 of this title shall be applied with respect to any such failure by substituting "mortgage originator" for "creditor" each place such term appears in each such subsection.[1]

(2) Maximum

The maximum amount of any liability of a mortgage originator under paragraph (1) to a consumer for any violation of this section shall not exceed the greater of actual damages or an amount equal to 3 times the total amount of direct and indirect compensation or gain accruing to the mortgage originator in connection with the residential mortgage loan involved in the violation, plus the costs to the consumer of the action, including a reasonable attorney's fee.

(e) Discretionary regulatory authority

(1) In general

The Bureau shall, by regulations, prohibit or condition terms, acts or practices relating to residential mortgage loans that the Bureau finds to be abusive, unfair, deceptive, predatory, necessary or proper to ensure that responsible, affordable mortgage credit remains available to consumers in a manner consistent with the purposes of this section and section 1639c of this title, necessary or proper to effectuate the purposes of this section and section 1639c of this title, to prevent circumvention or evasion thereof, or to facilitate compliance with such sections, or are not in the interest of the borrower.

(2) Application

The regulations prescribed under paragraph (1) shall be applicable to all residential mortgage loans and shall be applied in the same manner as regulations prescribed under section 1604 of this title.

(f) Timeshare plans

This section and any regulations promulgated thereunder do not apply to an extension of credit relating to a plan described in section 101(53D) of title 11.

(Pub. L. 90–321, title I, §129B, as added and amended Pub. L. 111–203, title X, §1100A(2), title XIV, §§1402(a)(2), 1403–1405(a), July 21, 2010, 124 Stat. 2107, 2139-2141.)

EDITORIAL NOTES

REFERENCES IN TEXT

The Secure and Fair Enforcement for Mortgage Licensing Act of 2008, referred to in subsec. (b)(1)(A), is title V of div. A of Pub. L. 110–289, July 30, 2008, 122 Stat. 2810, also known as the S.A.F.E. Mortgage Licensing Act of 2008, which is classified generally to chapter 51 (§5101 et seq.) of Title 12, Banks and Banking. For complete classification of this Act to the Code, see Short Title note set out under section 5101 of Title 12 and Tables.

AMENDMENTS

2010—Pub. L. 111–203, §1100A(2), substituted "Bureau" for "Board" wherever appearing.
Subsec. (c). Pub. L. 111–203, §1403, added subsec. (c).
Subsec. (d). Pub. L. 111–203, §1404, added subsec. (d).
Subsecs. (e), (f). Pub. L. 111–203, §1405(a), added subsecs. (e) and (f).

EFFECTIVE DATE OF 2010 AMENDMENT

Amendment by section 1100A(2) of Pub. L. 111–203 effective on the designated transfer date, see section 1100H of Pub. L. 111–203, set out as a note under section 552a of Title 5, Government Organization and Employees.

Amendment by sections 1403–1405(a) of Pub. L. 111–203 effective on the date on which final regulations implementing that amendment take effect, or on the date that is 18 months after the designated transfer date if such regulations have not been issued by that date, see section 1400(c) of Pub. L. 111–203, set out as a note under section 1601 of this title.

STATUTORY NOTES AND RELATED SUBSIDIARIES

EFFECTIVE DATE

Section effective on the date on which final regulations implementing such section take effect, or on the date that is 18 months after the designated transfer date if such regulations have not been issued by that date, see section 1400(c) of Pub. L. 111–203, set out as an Effective Date of 2010 Amendment note under section 1601 of this title.

[1] *So in original. Probably should be "in such section."*

§1639c. Minimum standards for residential mortgage loans

(a) Ability to repay

(1) In general

In accordance with regulations prescribed by the Bureau, no creditor may make a residential mortgage loan unless the creditor makes a reasonable and good faith determination based on verified and documented information that, at the time the loan is consummated, the consumer has a reasonable ability to repay the loan, according to its terms, and all applicable taxes, insurance (including mortgage guarantee insurance), and assessments.

(2) Multiple loans

If the creditor knows, or has reason to know, that 1 or more residential mortgage loans secured by the same dwelling will be made to the same consumer, the creditor shall make a reasonable and good faith determination, based on verified and documented information, that the consumer has a reasonable ability to repay the combined payments of all loans on the same dwelling according to the terms of those loans and all applicable taxes, insurance (including mortgage guarantee insurance), and assessments.

(3) Basis for determination

A determination under this subsection of a consumer's ability to repay a residential mortgage loan shall include consideration of the consumer's credit history, current income, expected income the consumer is reasonably assured of receiving, current obligations, debt-to-income ratio or the residual income the consumer will have after paying non-mortgage debt and mortgage-related obligations, employment status, and other financial resources other than the consumer's equity in the dwelling or real property that secures repayment of the loan. A creditor shall determine the ability of the consumer to repay using a payment schedule that fully amortizes the loan over the term of the loan.

(4) Income verification

A creditor making a residential mortgage loan shall verify amounts of income or assets that such creditor relies on to determine repayment ability, including expected income or assets, by reviewing the consumer's Internal Revenue Service Form W–2, tax returns, payroll receipts, financial institution records, or other third-party documents that provide reasonably reliable evidence of the consumer's income or assets. In order to safeguard against fraudulent reporting, any consideration of a consumer's income history in making a determination under this subsection shall include the verification of such income by the use of—

(A) Internal Revenue Service transcripts of tax returns; or

(B) a method that quickly and effectively verifies income documentation by a third party subject to rules prescribed by the Bureau.

(5) Exemption

With respect to loans made, guaranteed, or insured by Federal departments or agencies identified in subsection (b)(3)(B)(ii), such departments or agencies may exempt refinancings under a streamlined refinancing from this income verification requirement as long as the following conditions are met:

(A) The consumer is not 30 days or more past due on the prior existing residential mortgage loan.

(B) The refinancing does not increase the principal balance outstanding on the prior existing residential mortgage loan, except to the extent of fees and charges allowed by the department or agency making, guaranteeing, or insuring the refinancing.

(C) Total points and fees (as defined in section 1602(aa)(4) [1] of this title, other than bona fide third party charges not retained by the mortgage originator, creditor, or an affiliate of the creditor or mortgage originator) payable in connection with the refinancing do not exceed 3 percent of the total new loan amount.

(D) The interest rate on the refinanced loan is lower than the interest rate of the original loan, unless the borrower is refinancing from an adjustable rate to a fixed-rate loan, under guidelines that the department or agency shall establish for loans they make, guarantee, or issue.

(E) The refinancing is subject to a payment schedule that will fully amortize the refinancing in accordance with the regulations prescribed by the department or agency making, guaranteeing, or insuring the refinancing.

(F) The terms of the refinancing do not result in a balloon payment, as defined in subsection (b)(2)(A)(ii).

(G) Both the residential mortgage loan being refinanced and the refinancing satisfy all requirements of the department or agency making, guaranteeing, or insuring the refinancing.

(6) Nonstandard loans

(A) Variable rate loans that defer repayment of any principal or interest

For purposes of determining, under this subsection, a consumer's ability to repay a variable rate residential mortgage loan that allows or requires the consumer to defer the repayment of any principal or interest, the creditor shall use a fully amortizing repayment schedule.

(B) Interest-only loans

For purposes of determining, under this subsection, a consumer's ability to repay a residential mortgage loan that permits or requires the payment of interest only, the creditor shall use the payment amount required to amortize the loan by its final maturity.

(C) Calculation for negative amortization

In making any determination under this subsection, a creditor shall also take into consideration any balance increase that may accrue from any negative amortization provision.

(D) Calculation process

For purposes of making any determination under this subsection, a creditor shall calculate the monthly payment amount for principal and interest on any residential mortgage loan by assuming—

(i) the loan proceeds are fully disbursed on the date of the consummation of the loan;

(ii) the loan is to be repaid in substantially equal monthly amortizing payments for principal and interest over the entire term of the loan with no balloon payment, unless the loan contract requires more rapid repayment (including balloon payment), in which case the calculation shall be made (I) in accordance with regulations prescribed by the Bureau, with respect to any loan which has an annual percentage rate that does not exceed the average prime offer rate for a comparable transaction, as of the date the interest rate is set, by 1.5 or more percentage points for a first lien residential mortgage loan; and by 3.5 or more percentage points for a subordinate lien residential mortgage loan; or (II) using the contract's repayment schedule, with respect to a loan which has an annual percentage rate, as of the date the interest rate is set, that is at least 1.5 percentage points above the average prime offer rate for a first lien residential mortgage loan; and 3.5 percentage points above the average prime offer rate for a subordinate lien residential mortgage loan; and

(iii) the interest rate over the entire term of the loan is a fixed rate equal to the fully indexed rate at the time of the loan closing, without considering the introductory rate.

(E) Refinance of hybrid loans with current lender

In considering any application for refinancing an existing hybrid loan by the creditor into a standard loan to be made by the same creditor in any case in which there would be a reduction in monthly payment and the mortgagor has not been delinquent on any payment on the existing hybrid loan, the creditor may—

(i) consider the mortgagor's good standing on the existing mortgage;

(ii) consider if the extension of new credit would prevent a likely default should the original mortgage reset and give such concerns a higher priority as an acceptable underwriting practice; and

(iii) offer rate discounts and other favorable terms to such mortgagor that would be available to new customers with high credit ratings based on such underwriting practice.

(7) Fully-indexed rate defined

For purposes of this subsection, the term "fully indexed rate" means the index rate prevailing on a residential mortgage loan at the time the loan is made plus the margin that will apply after the expiration of any introductory interest rates.

(8) Reverse mortgages and bridge loans

This subsection shall not apply with respect to any reverse mortgage or temporary or bridge loan with a term of 12 months or less, including to any loan to purchase a new dwelling where the consumer plans to sell a different dwelling within 12 months.

(9) Seasonal income

If documented income, including income from a small business, is a repayment source for a residential mortgage loan, a creditor may consider the seasonality and irregularity of such income in the underwriting of and scheduling of payments for such credit.

(b) Presumption of ability to repay

(1) In general

Any creditor with respect to any residential mortgage loan, and any assignee of such loan subject to liability under this subchapter, may presume that the loan has met the requirements of subsection (a), if the loan is a qualified mortgage.

(2) Definitions

For purposes of this subsection, the following definitions shall apply:

(A) Qualified mortgage

The term "qualified mortgage" means any residential mortgage loan—
(i) for which the regular periodic payments for the loan may not—
(I) result in an increase of the principal balance; or
(II) except as provided in subparagraph (E), allow the consumer to defer repayment of principal;

(ii) except as provided in subparagraph (E), the terms of which do not result in a balloon payment, where a "balloon payment" is a scheduled payment that is more than twice as large as the average of earlier scheduled payments;
(iii) for which the income and financial resources relied upon to qualify the obligors on the loan are verified and documented;
(iv) in the case of a fixed rate loan, for which the underwriting process is based on a payment schedule that fully amortizes the loan over the loan term and takes into account all applicable taxes, insurance, and assessments;
(v) in the case of an adjustable rate loan, for which the underwriting is based on the maximum rate permitted under the loan during the first 5 years, and a payment schedule that fully amortizes the loan over the loan term and takes into account all applicable taxes, insurance, and assessments;
(vi) that complies with any guidelines or regulations established by the Bureau relating to ratios of total monthly debt to monthly income or alternative measures of ability to pay regular expenses after payment of total monthly debt, taking into account the income levels of the borrower and such other factors as the Bureau may determine relevant and consistent with the purposes described in paragraph (3)(B)(i);
(vii) for which the total points and fees (as defined in subparagraph (C)) payable in connection with the loan do not exceed 3 percent of the total loan amount;
(viii) for which the term of the loan does not exceed 30 years, except as such term may be extended under paragraph (3), such as in high-cost areas; and
(ix) in the case of a reverse mortgage (except for the purposes of subsection (a) of this section, to the extent that such mortgages are exempt altogether from those requirements), a reverse mortgage which meets the standards for a qualified mortgage, as set by the Bureau in rules that are consistent with the purposes of this subsection.

(B) Average prime offer rate

The term "average prime offer rate" means the average prime offer rate for a comparable transaction as of the date on which the interest rate for the transaction is set, as published by the Bureau..[2]

(C) Points and fees

(i) In general

For purposes of subparagraph (A), the term "points and fees" means points and fees as defined by section 1602(aa)(4) [1] of this title (other than bona fide third party charges not retained by the mortgage originator, creditor, or an affiliate of the creditor or mortgage originator).

(ii) Computation

For purposes of computing the total points and fees under this subparagraph, the total points and fees shall exclude either of the amounts described in the following subclauses, but not both:
(I) Up to and including 2 bona fide discount points payable by the consumer in connection with the mortgage, but only if the interest rate from which the mortgage's interest rate will be discounted does not exceed by more than 1 percentage point the average prime offer rate.
(II) Unless 2 bona fide discount points have been excluded under subclause (I), up to and including 1 bona fide discount point payable by the consumer in connection with the mortgage, but only if the interest rate from which the mortgage's interest rate will be discounted does not exceed by more than 2 percentage points the average prime offer rate.

(iii) Bona fide discount points defined

For purposes of clause (ii), the term "bona fide discount points" means loan discount points which are knowingly paid by the consumer for the purpose of reducing, and which in fact result in a bona fide reduction of, the interest rate or time-price differential applicable to the mortgage.

(iv) Interest rate reduction

Subclauses (I) and (II) of clause (ii) shall not apply to discount points used to purchase an interest rate reduction unless the amount of the interest rate reduction purchased is reasonably consistent with established industry norms and practices for secondary mortgage market transactions.

(D) Smaller loans

The Bureau shall prescribe rules adjusting the criteria under subparagraph (A)(vii) in order to permit lenders that extend smaller loans to meet the requirements of the presumption of compliance under paragraph (1). In prescribing such rules, the Bureau shall consider the potential impact of such rules on rural areas and other areas where home values are lower.

(E) Balloon loans

The Bureau may, by regulation, provide that the term "qualified mortgage" includes a balloon loan—

(i) that meets all of the criteria for a qualified mortgage under subparagraph (A) (except clauses (i)(II), (ii), (iv), and (v) of such subparagraph);

(ii) for which the creditor makes a determination that the consumer is able to make all scheduled payments, except the balloon payment, out of income or assets other than the collateral;

(iii) for which the underwriting is based on a payment schedule that fully amortizes the loan over a period of not more than 30 years and takes into account all applicable taxes, insurance, and assessments; and

(iv) that is extended by a creditor that—

(I) operates in rural or underserved areas;

(II) together with all affiliates, has total annual residential mortgage loan originations that do not exceed a limit set by the Bureau;

(III) retains the balloon loans in portfolio; and

(IV) meets any asset size threshold and any other criteria as the Bureau may establish, consistent with the purposes of this part.

(F) Safe harbor

(i) Definitions

In this subparagraph—

(I) the term "covered institution" means an insured depository institution or an insured credit union that, together with its affiliates, has less than $10,000,000,000 in total consolidated assets;

(II) the term "insured credit union" has the meaning given the term in section 1752 of title 12;

(III) the term "insured depository institution" has the meaning given the term in section 1813 of title 12;

(IV) the term "interest-only" means that, under the terms of the legal obligation, one or more of the periodic payments may be applied solely to accrued interest and not to loan principal; and

(V) the term "negative amortization" means payment of periodic payments that will result in an increase in the principal balance under the terms of the legal obligation.

(ii) Safe harbor

In this section—

(I) the term "qualified mortgage" includes any residential mortgage loan—

(aa) that is originated and retained in portfolio by a covered institution;

(bb) that is in compliance with the limitations with respect to prepayment penalties described in subsections (c)(1) and (c)(3);

(cc) that is in compliance with the requirements of clause (vii) of subparagraph (A);

(dd) that does not have negative amortization or interest-only features; and

(ee) for which the covered institution considers and documents the debt, income, and financial resources of the consumer in accordance with clause (iv); and

(II) a residential mortgage loan described in subclause (I) shall be deemed to meet the requirements of subsection (a).

(iii) Exception for certain transfers

A residential mortgage loan described in clause (ii)(I) shall not qualify for the safe harbor under clause (ii) if the legal title to the residential mortgage loan is sold, assigned, or otherwise transferred to another person unless the residential mortgage loan is sold, assigned, or otherwise transferred—

(I) to another person by reason of the bankruptcy or failure of a covered institution;

(II) to a covered institution so long as the loan is retained in portfolio by the covered institution to which the loan is sold, assigned, or otherwise transferred;

(III) pursuant to a merger of a covered institution with another person or the acquisition of a covered institution by another person or of another person by a covered institution, so long as the loan is retained in portfolio by the person to whom the loan is sold, assigned, or otherwise transferred; or

(IV) to a wholly owned subsidiary of a covered institution, provided that, after the sale, assignment, or transfer, the residential mortgage loan is considered to be an asset of the covered institution for regulatory accounting purposes.

(iv) Consideration and documentation requirements

The consideration and documentation requirements described in clause (ii)(I)(ee) shall—

(I) not be construed to require compliance with, or documentation in accordance with, appendix Q to part 1026 of title 12, Code of Federal Regulations, or any successor regulation; and

(II) be construed to permit multiple methods of documentation.

(3) Regulations

(A) In general

The Bureau shall prescribe regulations to carry out the purposes of this subsection.

(B) Revision of safe harbor criteria

(i) In general

The Bureau may prescribe regulations that revise, add to, or subtract from the criteria that define a qualified mortgage upon a finding that such regulations are necessary or proper to ensure that responsible, affordable mortgage credit remains available to consumers in a manner consistent with the purposes of this section, necessary and appropriate to effectuate the purposes of this section and section 1639b of this title, to prevent circumvention or evasion thereof, or to facilitate compliance with such sections.

(ii) Loan definition

The following agencies shall, in consultation with the Bureau, prescribe rules defining the types of loans they insure, guarantee, or administer, as the case may be, that are qualified mortgages for purposes of paragraph (2) (A), and such rules may revise, add to, or subtract from the criteria used to define a qualified mortgage under paragraph (2)(A), upon a finding that such rules are consistent with the purposes of this section and section 1639b of this title, to prevent circumvention or evasion thereof, or to facilitate compliance with such sections:

(I) The Department of Housing and Urban Development, with regard to mortgages insured under the National Housing Act [12 U.S.C. 1701 et seq.].

(II) The Department of Veterans Affairs, with regard to a loan made or guaranteed by the Secretary of Veterans Affairs.

(III) The Department of Agriculture, with regard [3] loans guaranteed by the Secretary of Agriculture pursuant to section 1472(h) of title 42.

(IV) The Rural Housing Service, with regard to loans insured by the Rural Housing Service.

(C) Consideration of underwriting requirements for Property Assessed Clean Energy financing

(i) Definition

In this subparagraph, the term "Property Assessed Clean Energy financing" means financing to cover the costs of home improvements that results in a tax assessment on the real property of the consumer.

(ii) Regulations

The Bureau shall prescribe regulations that carry out the purposes of subsection (a) and apply section 1640 of this title with respect to violations under subsection (a) of this section with respect to Property Assessed Clean Energy financing, which shall account for the unique nature of Property Assessed Clean Energy financing.

(iii) Collection of information and consultation

In prescribing the regulations under this subparagraph, the Bureau—
(I) may collect such information and data that the Bureau determines is necessary; and
(II) shall consult with State and local governments and bond-issuing authorities.

(c) Prohibition on certain prepayment penalties

(1) Prohibited on certain loans

(A) In general

A residential mortgage loan that is not a "qualified mortgage", as defined under subsection (b)(2), may not contain terms under which a consumer must pay a prepayment penalty for paying all or part of the principal after the loan is consummated.

(B) Exclusions

For purposes of this subsection, a "qualified mortgage" may not include a residential mortgage loan that—
(i) has an adjustable rate; or
(ii) has an annual percentage rate that exceeds the average prime offer rate for a comparable transaction, as of the date the interest rate is set—

(I) by 1.5 or more percentage points, in the case of a first lien residential mortgage loan having a original principal obligation amount that is equal to or less than the amount of the maximum limitation on the original principal obligation of mortgage in effect for a residence of the applicable size, as of the date of such interest rate set, pursuant to the 6th sentence of section 1454(a)(2) of title 12;

(II) by 2.5 or more percentage points, in the case of a first lien residential mortgage loan having a original principal obligation amount that is more than the amount of the maximum limitation on the original principal obligation of mortgage in effect for a residence of the applicable size, as of the date of such interest rate set, pursuant to the 6th sentence of section 1454(a)(2) of title 12; and

(III) by 3.5 or more percentage points, in the case of a subordinate lien residential mortgage loan.

(2) Publication of average prime offer rate and APR thresholds

The Bureau—

(A) shall publish, and update at least weekly, average prime offer rates;

(B) may publish multiple rates based on varying types of mortgage transactions; and

(C) shall adjust the thresholds established under subclause (I), (II), and (III) of paragraph (1)(B)(ii) as necessary to reflect significant changes in market conditions and to effectuate the purposes of the Mortgage Reform and Anti-Predatory Lending Act.

(3) Phased-out penalties on qualified mortgages

A qualified mortgage (as defined in subsection (b)(2)) may not contain terms under which a consumer must pay a prepayment penalty for paying all or part of the principal after the loan is consummated in excess of the following limitations:

(A) During the 1-year period beginning on the date the loan is consummated, the prepayment penalty shall not exceed an amount equal to 3 percent of the outstanding balance on the loan.

(B) During the 1-year period beginning after the period described in subparagraph (A), the prepayment penalty shall not exceed an amount equal to 2 percent of the outstanding balance on the loan.

(C) During the 1-year period beginning after the 1-year period described in subparagraph (B), the prepayment penalty shall not exceed an amount equal to 1 percent of the outstanding balance on the loan.

(D) After the end of the 3-year period beginning on the date the loan is consummated, no prepayment penalty may be imposed on a qualified mortgage.

(4) Option for no prepayment penalty required

A creditor may not offer a consumer a residential mortgage loan product that has a prepayment penalty for paying all or part of the principal after the loan is consummated as a term of the loan without offering the consumer a residential mortgage loan product that does not have a prepayment penalty as a term of the loan.

(d) Single premium credit insurance prohibited

No creditor may finance, directly or indirectly, in connection with any residential mortgage loan or with any extension of credit under an open end consumer credit plan secured by the principal dwelling of the consumer, any credit life, credit disability, credit unemployment, or credit property insurance, or any other accident, loss-of-income, life, or health insurance, or any payments directly or indirectly for any debt cancellation or suspension agreement or contract, except that—

(1) insurance premiums or debt cancellation or suspension fees calculated and paid in full on a monthly basis shall not be considered financed by the creditor; and

(2) this subsection shall not apply to credit unemployment insurance for which the unemployment insurance premiums are reasonable, the creditor receives no direct or indirect compensation in connection with the unemployment insurance premiums, and the unemployment insurance premiums are paid pursuant to another insurance contract and not paid to an affiliate of the creditor.

(e) Arbitration

(1) In general

No residential mortgage loan and no extension of credit under an open end consumer credit plan secured by the principal dwelling of the consumer may include terms which require arbitration or any other nonjudicial procedure as the method for resolving any controversy or settling any claims arising out of the transaction.

(2) Post-controversy agreements

Subject to paragraph (3), paragraph (1) shall not be construed as limiting the right of the consumer and the creditor or any assignee to agree to arbitration or any other nonjudicial procedure as the method for resolving any controversy at any time after a dispute or claim under the transaction arises.

(3) No waiver of statutory cause of action

No provision of any residential mortgage loan or of any extension of credit under an open end consumer credit plan secured by the principal dwelling of the consumer, and no other agreement between the consumer and the creditor relating to the residential mortgage loan or extension of credit referred to in paragraph (1), shall be applied or interpreted so as to bar a consumer from bringing an action in an appropriate district court of the United States, or any other court of competent jurisdiction, pursuant to section 1640 of this title or any other provision of law, for damages or other relief in connection with any alleged violation of this section, any other provision of this subchapter, or any other Federal law.

(f) Mortgages with negative amortization

No creditor may extend credit to a borrower in connection with a consumer credit transaction under an open or closed end consumer credit plan secured by a dwelling or residential real property that includes a dwelling, other than a reverse mortgage, that provides or permits a payment plan that may, at any time over the term of the extension of credit, result in negative amortization unless, before such transaction is consummated—

(1) the creditor provides the consumer with a statement that—

(A) the pending transaction will or may, as the case may be, result in negative amortization;

(B) describes negative amortization in such manner as the Bureau shall prescribe;

(C) negative amortization increases the outstanding principal balance of the account; and

(D) negative amortization reduces the consumer's equity in the dwelling or real property; and

(2) in the case of a first-time borrower with respect to a residential mortgage loan that is not a qualified mortgage, the first-time borrower provides the creditor with sufficient documentation to demonstrate that the consumer received homeownership counseling from organizations or counselors certified by the Secretary of Housing and Urban Development as competent to provide such counseling.

(g) Protection against loss of anti-deficiency protection

(1) Definition

For purposes of this subsection, the term "anti-deficiency law" means the law of any State which provides that, in the event of foreclosure on the residential property of a consumer securing a mortgage, the consumer is not liable, in accordance with the terms and limitations of such State law, for any deficiency between the sale price obtained on such property through foreclosure and the outstanding balance of the mortgage.

(2) Notice at time of consummation

In the case of any residential mortgage loan that is, or upon consummation will be, subject to protection under an anti-deficiency law, the creditor or mortgage originator shall provide a written notice to the consumer describing the protection provided by the anti-deficiency law and the significance for the consumer of the loss of such protection before such loan is consummated.

(3) Notice before refinancing that would cause loss of protection

In the case of any residential mortgage loan that is subject to protection under an anti-deficiency law, if a creditor or mortgage originator provides an application to a consumer, or receives an application from a consumer, for any type of refinancing for such loan that would cause the loan to lose the protection of such anti-deficiency law, the creditor or mortgage originator shall provide a written notice to the consumer describing the protection provided by the anti-deficiency law and the significance for the consumer of the loss of such protection before any agreement for any such refinancing is consummated.

(h) Policy regarding acceptance of partial payment

In the case of any residential mortgage loan, a creditor shall disclose prior to settlement or, in the case of a person becoming a creditor with respect to an existing residential mortgage loan, at the time such person becomes a creditor—

(1) the creditor's policy regarding the acceptance of partial payments; and

(2) if partial payments are accepted, how such payments will be applied to such mortgage and if such payments will be placed in escrow.

(i) Timeshare plans

This section and any regulations promulgated under this section do not apply to an extension of credit relating to a plan described in section 101(53D) of title 11.

(Pub. L. 90–321, title I, §129C, as added and amended Pub. L. 111–203, title X, §1100A(2), title XIV, §§1411(a)(2), 1412, 1414(a), (c), (d), July 21, 2010, 124 Stat. 2107, 2142, 2145, 2149, 2152; Pub. L. 114–94, div. G, title LXXXIX, §89003(1), Dec. 4, 2015, 129 Stat. 1800; Pub. L. 115–174, title I, §101, title III, §307, May 24, 2018, 132 Stat. 1297, 1347.)

Editorial Notes

References in Text

Section 1602(aa)(4) of this title, referred to in subsecs. (a)(5)(C) and (b)(2)(C)(i), was redesignated section 1602(bb)(4) of this title by Pub. L. 111–203, title X, §1100A(1)(A), July 21, 2010, 124 Stat. 2107.

This part, referred to in subsec. (b)(2)(E)(iv)(IV), was in the original "this subtitle", and was translated as reading "this chapter", meaning chapter 2 of title I of Pub. L. 90–321, to reflect the probable intent of Congress. Title I of Pub. L. 90–321 does not contain subtitles.

The National Housing Act, referred to in subsec. (b)(3)(B)(ii)(I), is act June 27, 1934, ch. 847, 48 Stat. 1246, which is classified principally to chapter 13 (§1701 et seq.) of Title 12, Banks and Banking. For complete classification of this Act to the Code, see section 1701 of Title 12 and Tables.

The Mortgage Reform and Anti-Predatory Lending Act, referred to in subsec. (c)(2)(C), is title XIV of Pub. L. 111–203, July 21, 2010, 124 Stat. 2136. For complete classification of this Act to the Code, see Short Title of 2010 Amendment note set out under section 1601 of this title and Tables.

Amendments

2018—Subsec. (b)(2)(F). Pub. L. 115–174, §101, added subpar. (F).

Subsec. (b)(3)(C). Pub. L. 115–174, §307, added subpar. (C).

2015—Subsec. (b)(2)(E)(iv)(I). Pub. L. 114–94 struck out "predominantly" after "operates".
2010—Pub. L. 111–203, §1100A(2), substituted "Bureau" for "Board" wherever appearing.
Subsec. (b). Pub. L. 111–203, §1412, added subsec. (b).
Subsecs. (c) to (f). Pub. L. 111–203, §1414(a), added subsecs. (c) to (f).
Subsec. (g). Pub. L. 111–203, §1414(c), added subsec. (g).
Subsecs. (h), (i). Pub. L. 111–203, §1414(d), added subsecs. (h) and (i).

EFFECTIVE DATE OF 2010 AMENDMENT

Amendment by section 1100A(2) of Pub. L. 111–203 effective on the designated transfer date, see section 1100H of Pub. L. 111–203, set out as a note under section 552a of Title 5, Government Organization and Employees.

Amendment by sections 1412 and 1414(a), (c), (d) of Pub. L. 111–203 effective on the date on which final regulations implementing that amendment take effect, or on the date that is 18 months after the designated transfer date, if such regulations have not been issued by that date, see section 1400(c) of Pub. L. 111–203, set out as a note under section 1601 of this title.

EFFECTIVE DATE

Section effective on the date on which final regulations implementing such section take effect, or on the date that is 18 months after the designated transfer date if such regulations have not been issued by that date, see section 1400(c) of Pub. L. 111–203, set out as an Effective Date of 2010 Amendment note under section 1601 of this title.

RULE OF CONSTRUCTION

Pub. L. 111–203, title XIV, §1411(a)(1), July 21, 2010, 124 Stat. 2142, provided that: "No regulation, order, or guidance issued by the Bureau under this title [see Tables for classification] shall be construed as requiring a depository institution to apply mortgage underwriting standards that do not meet the minimum underwriting standards required by the appropriate prudential regulator of the depository institution."

[For definitions of "Bureau" and "depository institution" as used in section 1411(a)(1) of Pub. L. 111–203, set out above, see section 5301 of Title 12, Banks and Banking.]

[1] See References in Text note below.

[2] So in original.

[3] So in original. Probably should be followed by "to".

§1639d. Escrow or impound accounts relating to certain consumer credit transactions

(a) In general

Except as provided in subsection (b), (c), (d), or (e), a creditor, in connection with the consummation of a consumer credit transaction secured by a first lien on the principal dwelling of the consumer, other than a consumer credit transaction under an open end credit plan or a reverse mortgage, shall establish, before the consummation of such transaction, an escrow or impound account for the payment of taxes and hazard insurance, and, if applicable, flood insurance, mortgage insurance, ground rents, and any other required periodic payments or premiums with respect to the property or the loan terms, as provided in, and in accordance with, this section.

(b) When required

No impound, trust, or other type of account for the payment of property taxes, insurance premiums, or other purposes relating to the property may be required as a condition of a real property sale contract or a loan secured by a first deed of trust or mortgage on the principal dwelling of the consumer, other than a consumer credit transaction under an open end credit plan or a reverse mortgage, except when—

(1) any such impound, trust, or other type of escrow or impound account for such purposes is required by Federal or State law;

(2) a loan is made, guaranteed, or insured by a State or Federal governmental lending or insuring agency;

(3) the transaction is secured by a first mortgage or lien on the consumer's principal dwelling having an original principal obligation amount that—

(A) does not exceed the amount of the maximum limitation on the original principal obligation of mortgage in effect for a residence of the applicable size, as of the date such interest rate set, pursuant to the sixth sentence of section 1454(a)(2) of title 12, and the annual percentage rate will exceed the average prime offer rate as defined in section 1639c of this title by 1.5 or more percentage points; or

(B) exceeds the amount of the maximum limitation on the original principal obligation of mortgage in effect for a residence of the applicable size, as of the date such interest rate set, pursuant to the sixth sentence of section 1454(a)(2) of title 12, and the annual percentage rate will exceed the average prime offer rate as defined in section 1639c of this title by 2.5 or more percentage points; or

(4) so required pursuant to regulation.

(c) Exemptions

(1) In general

The Bureau may, by regulation, exempt from the requirements of subsection (a) a creditor that—
(A) operates in rural or underserved areas;
(B) together with all affiliates, has total annual mortgage loan originations that do not exceed a limit set by the Bureau;
(C) retains its mortgage loan originations in portfolio; and
(D) meets any asset size threshold and any other criteria the Bureau may establish, consistent with the purposes of this part.

(2) Treatment of loans held by smaller institutions

The Bureau shall, by regulation, exempt from the requirements of subsection (a) any loan made by an insured depository institution or an insured credit union secured by a first lien on the principal dwelling of a consumer if—
(A) the insured depository institution or insured credit union has assets of $10,000,000,000 or less;
(B) during the preceding calendar year, the insured depository institution or insured credit union and its affiliates originated 1,000 or fewer loans secured by a first lien on a principal dwelling; and
(C) the transaction satisfies the criteria in sections 1026.35(b)(2)(iii)(A), 1026.35(b)(2)(iii)(D), and 1026.35(b)(2)(v) of title 12, Code of Federal Regulations, or any successor regulation.

(d) Duration of mandatory escrow or impound account

An escrow or impound account established pursuant to subsection (b) shall remain in existence for a minimum period of 5 years, beginning with the date of the consummation of the loan, unless and until—
(1) such borrower has sufficient equity in the dwelling securing the consumer credit transaction so as to no longer be required to maintain private mortgage insurance;
(2) such borrower is delinquent;
(3) such borrower otherwise has not complied with the legal obligation, as established by rule; or
(4) the underlying mortgage establishing the account is terminated.

(e) Limited exemptions for loans secured by shares in a cooperative or in which an association must maintain a master insurance policy

Escrow accounts need not be established for loans secured by shares in a cooperative. Insurance premiums need not be included in escrow accounts for loans secured by dwellings or units, where the borrower must join an association as a condition of ownership, and that association has an obligation to the dwelling or unit owners to maintain a master policy insuring the dwellings or units.

(f) Clarification on escrow accounts for loans not meeting statutory test

For mortgages not covered by the requirements of subsection (b), no provision of this section shall be construed as precluding the establishment of an impound, trust, or other type of account for the payment of property taxes, insurance premiums, or other purposes relating to the property—
(1) on terms mutually agreeable to the parties to the loan;
(2) at the discretion of the lender or servicer, as provided by the contract between the lender or servicer and the borrower; or
(3) pursuant to the requirements for the escrowing of flood insurance payments for regulated lending institutions in section 102(d) of the Flood Disaster Protection Act of 1973 [42 U.S.C. 4012a(d)].

(g) Administration of mandatory escrow or impound accounts

(1) In general

Except as may otherwise be provided for in this subchapter or in regulations prescribed by the Bureau, escrow or impound accounts established pursuant to subsection (b) shall be established in a federally insured depository institution or credit union.

(2) Administration

Except as provided in this section or regulations prescribed under this section, an escrow or impound account subject to this section shall be administered in accordance with—

(A) the Real Estate Settlement Procedures Act of 1974 [12 U.S.C. 2601 et seq.] and regulations prescribed under such Act;

(B) the Flood Disaster Protection Act of 1973 and regulations prescribed under such Act; and

(C) the law of the State, if applicable, where the real property securing the consumer credit transaction is located.

(3) Applicability of payment of interest

If prescribed by applicable State or Federal law, each creditor shall pay interest to the consumer on the amount held in any impound, trust, or escrow account that is subject to this section in the manner as prescribed by that applicable State or Federal law.

(4) Penalty coordination with RESPA

Any action or omission on the part of any person which constitutes a violation of the Real Estate Settlement Procedures Act of 1974 or any regulation prescribed under such Act for which the person has paid any fine, civil money penalty, or other damages shall not give rise to any additional fine, civil money penalty, or other damages under this section, unless the action or omission also constitutes a direct violation of this section.

(h) Disclosures relating to mandatory escrow or impound account

In the case of any impound, trust, or escrow account that is required under subsection (b), the creditor shall disclose by written notice to the consumer at least 3 business days before the consummation of the consumer credit transaction giving rise to such account or in accordance with timeframes established in prescribed regulations the following information:

(1) The fact that an escrow or impound account will be established at consummation of the transaction.

(2) The amount required at closing to initially fund the escrow or impound account.

(3) The amount, in the initial year after the consummation of the transaction, of the estimated taxes and hazard insurance, including flood insurance, if applicable, and any other required periodic payments or premiums that reflects, as appropriate, either the taxable assessed value of the real property securing the transaction, including the value of any improvements on the property or to be constructed on the property (whether or not such construction will be financed from the proceeds of the transaction) or the replacement costs of the property.

(4) The estimated monthly amount payable to be escrowed for taxes, hazard insurance (including flood insurance, if applicable) and any other required periodic payments or premiums.

(5) The fact that, if the consumer chooses to terminate the account in the future, the consumer will become responsible for the payment of all taxes, hazard insurance, and flood insurance, if applicable, as well as any other required periodic payments or premiums on the property unless a new escrow or impound account is established.

(6) Such other information as the Bureau determines necessary for the protection of the consumer.

(i) Definitions

For purposes of this section, the following definitions shall apply:

(1) Flood insurance

The term "flood insurance" means flood insurance coverage provided under the national flood insurance program pursuant to the National Flood Insurance Act of 1968 [42 U.S.C. 4001 et seq.].

(2) Hazard insurance

The term "hazard insurance" shall have the same meaning as provided for "hazard insurance", "casualty insurance", "homeowner's insurance", or other similar term under the law of the State where the real property securing the consumer credit transaction is located.

(3) Insured credit union

The term "insured credit union" has the meaning given the term in section 1752 of title 12.

(4) Insured depository institution

The term "insured depository institution" has the meaning given the term in section 1813 of title 12.

(j) Disclosure notice required for consumers who waive escrow services

(1) In general

If—

(A) an impound, trust, or other type of account for the payment of property taxes, insurance premiums, or other purposes relating to real property securing a consumer credit transaction is not established in connection with the transaction; or

(B) a consumer chooses, and provides written notice to the creditor or servicer of such choice, at any time after such an account is established in connection with any such transaction and in accordance with any statute, regulation, or contractual agreement, to close such account,

the creditor or servicer shall provide a timely and clearly written disclosure to the consumer that advises the consumer of the responsibilities of the consumer and implications for the consumer in the absence of any such account.

(2) Disclosure requirements

Any disclosure provided to a consumer under paragraph (1) shall include the following:

(A) Information concerning any applicable fees or costs associated with either the non-establishment of any such account at the time of the transaction, or any subsequent closure of any such account.

(B) A clear and prominent statement that the consumer is responsible for personally and directly paying the non-escrowed items, in addition to paying the mortgage loan payment, in the absence of any such account, and the fact that the costs for taxes, insurance, and related fees can be substantial.

(C) A clear explanation of the consequences of any failure to pay non-escrowed items, including the possible requirement for the forced placement of insurance by the creditor or servicer and the potentially higher cost (including any potential commission payments to the servicer) or reduced coverage for the consumer in the event of any such creditor-placed insurance.

(D) Such other information as the Bureau determines necessary for the protection of the consumer.

(Pub. L. 90–321, title I, §129D, as added and amended Pub. L. 111–203, title X, §1100A(2), title XIV, §§1461(a), 1462, July 21, 2010, 124 Stat. 2107, 2178, 2181; Pub. L. 114–94, div. G, title LXXXIX, §89003(2), Dec. 4, 2015, 129 Stat. 1801; Pub. L. 115–174, title I, §108, May 24, 2018, 132 Stat. 1304.)

EDITORIAL NOTES

REFERENCES IN TEXT

This part, referred to in subsec. (c)(1)(D), was in the original "this subtitle", and was translated as reading "this chapter", meaning chapter 2 of title I of Pub. L. 90–321, to reflect the probable intent of Congress. Title I of Pub. L. 90–321 does not contain subtitles.

The Real Estate Settlement Procedures Act of 1974, referred to in subsec. (g)(2)(A), (4), is Pub. L. 93–533, Dec. 22, 1974, 88 Stat. 1724, which is classified principally to chapter 27 (§2601 et seq.) of Title 12, Banks and Banking. For complete classification of this Act to the Code, see Short Title note set out under section 2601 of Title 12 and Tables.

The Flood Disaster Protection Act of 1973, referred to in subsec. (g)(2)(B), is Pub. L. 93–234, Dec. 31, 1973, 87 Stat. 975. For complete classification of this Act to the Code, see Short Title of 1973 Amendment note set out under section 4001 of Title 42, The Public Health and Welfare, and Tables.

The National Flood Insurance Act of 1968, referred to in subsec. (i)(1), is title XIII of Pub. L. 90–448, Aug. 1, 1968, 82 Stat. 572, which is classified principally to chapter 50 (§4001 et seq.) of Title 42, The Public Health and Welfare. For complete classification of this Act to the Code, see Short Title note set out under section 4001 of Title 42 and Tables.

AMENDMENTS

2018—Subsec. (c). Pub. L. 115–174, §108(1)(A), (B), (D), designated existing provisions as par. (1) and inserted heading, redesignated former pars. (1) to (4) as subpars. (A) to (D), respectively, of par. (1) and realigned margins, and added par. (2).

Subsec. (c)(1). Pub. L. 115–174, §108(1)(B), (C), which directed substitution of "The Bureau" for "The Board" in introductory provisions, and "the Bureau" for "the Board" wherever appearing, duplicated the amendment made by Pub. L. 111–203, §1100A(2), which had already been executed. See 2010 Amendment note below.

Subsec. (i)(3), (4). Pub. L. 115–174, §108(2), added pars. (3) and (4).

2015—Subsec. (c)(1). Pub. L. 114–94 struck out "predominantly" after "operates".

2010—Pub. L. 111–203, §1100A(2), which directed substitution of "Bureau" for "Board" wherever appearing in Pub. L. 90–321, was executed to this section, which was added to Pub. L. 90–321 by section 1461(a) of Pub. L. 111–203.

Subsec. (j). Pub. L. 111–203, §1462, added subsec. (j).

STATUTORY NOTES AND RELATED SUBSIDIARIES

EFFECTIVE DATE OF 2010 AMENDMENT

Amendment by section 1100A(2) of Pub. L. 111–203 effective on the designated transfer date, see section 1100H of Pub. L. 111–203, set out as a note under section 552a of Title 5, Government Organization and Employees.

Amendment by section 1462 of Pub. L. 111–203 effective on the date on which final regulations implementing that amendment take effect, or on the date that is 18 months after the designated transfer date if such regulations have not been issued by that date, see section 1400(c) of Pub. L. 111–203, set out as a note under section 1601 of this title.

Section effective on the date on which final regulations implementing such section take effect, or on the date that is 18 months after the designated transfer date if such regulations have not been issued by that date, see section 1400(c) of Pub. L. 111–203, set out as an Effective Date of 2010 Amendment note under section 1601 of this title.

EXEMPTIONS AND MODIFICATIONS

Pub. L. 111–203, title XIV, §1461(b), July 21, 2010, 124 Stat. 2181, provided that: "The Board may prescribe rules that revise, add to, or subtract from the criteria of section 129D(b) of the Truth in Lending Act [15 U.S.C. 1639d(b)] if the Board determines that such rules are in the interest of consumers and in the public interest."

§1639e. Appraisal independence requirements

(a) In general

It shall be unlawful, in extending credit or in providing any services for a consumer credit transaction secured by the principal dwelling of the consumer, to engage in any act or practice that violates appraisal independence as described in or pursuant to regulations prescribed under this section.

(b) Appraisal independence

For purposes of subsection (a), acts or practices that violate appraisal independence shall include—

(1) any appraisal of a property offered as security for repayment of the consumer credit transaction that is conducted in connection with such transaction in which a person with an interest in the underlying transaction compensates, coerces, extorts, colludes, instructs, induces, bribes, or intimidates a person, appraisal management company, firm, or other entity conducting or involved in an appraisal, or attempts, to compensate, coerce, extort, collude, instruct, induce, bribe, or intimidate such a person, for the purpose of causing the appraised value assigned, under the appraisal, to the property to be based on any factor other than the independent judgment of the appraiser;

(2) mischaracterizing, or suborning any mischaracterization of, the appraised value of the property securing the extension of the credit;

(3) seeking to influence an appraiser or otherwise to encourage a targeted value in order to facilitate the making or pricing of the transaction; and

(4) withholding or threatening to withhold timely payment for an appraisal report or for appraisal services rendered when the appraisal report or services are provided for in accordance with the contract between the parties.

(c) Exceptions

The requirements of subsection (b) shall not be construed as prohibiting a mortgage lender, mortgage broker, mortgage banker, real estate broker, appraisal management company, employee of an appraisal management company, consumer, or any other person with an interest in a real estate transaction from asking an appraiser to undertake 1 or more of the following:

(1) Consider additional, appropriate property information, including the consideration of additional comparable properties to make or support an appraisal.

(2) Provide further detail, substantiation, or explanation for the appraiser's value conclusion.

(3) Correct errors in the appraisal report.

(d) Prohibitions on conflicts of interest

No certified or licensed appraiser conducting, and no appraisal management company procuring or facilitating, an appraisal in connection with a consumer credit transaction secured by the principal dwelling of a consumer may have a direct or indirect interest, financial or otherwise, in the property or transaction involving the appraisal.

(e) Mandatory reporting

Any mortgage lender, mortgage broker, mortgage banker, real estate broker, appraisal management company, employee of an appraisal management company, or any other person involved in a real estate transaction involving an appraisal in connection with a consumer credit transaction secured by the principal dwelling of a consumer who has a reasonable basis to believe an appraiser is failing to comply with the Uniform Standards of Professional Appraisal Practice, is violating applicable laws, or is otherwise engaging in unethical or unprofessional conduct, shall refer the matter to the applicable State appraiser certifying and licensing agency.

(f) No extension of credit

In connection with a consumer credit transaction secured by a consumer's principal dwelling, a creditor who knows, at or before loan consummation, of a violation of the appraisal independence standards established in subsections [1] (b) or (d) shall not extend credit based on such appraisal unless the creditor documents that the creditor has acted with reasonable diligence to determine that the appraisal does not materially misstate or misrepresent the value of such dwelling.

(g) Rules and interpretive guidelines

(1) In general

Except as provided under paragraph (2), the Board, the Comptroller of the Currency, the Federal Deposit Insurance Corporation, the National Credit Union Administration Board, the Federal Housing Finance Agency, and the Bureau may jointly issue rules, interpretive guidelines, and general statements of policy with respect to acts or practices that violate appraisal independence in the provision of mortgage lending services for a consumer credit transaction secured by the principal dwelling of the consumer and mortgage brokerage services for such a transaction, within the meaning of subsections (a), (b), (c), (d), (e), (f), (h), and (i).

(2) Interim final regulations

The Board shall, for purposes of this section, prescribe interim final regulations no later than 90 days after July 21, 2010, defining with specificity acts or practices that violate appraisal independence in the provision of mortgage lending services for a consumer credit transaction secured by the principal dwelling of the consumer or mortgage brokerage services for such a transaction and defining any terms in this section or such regulations. Rules prescribed by the Board under this paragraph shall be deemed to be rules prescribed by the agencies jointly under paragraph (1).

(h) Appraisal report portability

Consistent with the requirements of this section, the Board, the Comptroller of the Currency, the Federal Deposit Insurance Corporation, the National Credit Union Administration Board, the Federal Housing Finance Agency, and the Bureau may jointly issue regulations that address the issue of appraisal report portability, including regulations that ensure the portability of the appraisal report between lenders for a consumer credit transaction secured by a 1-4 unit single family residence that is the principal dwelling of the consumer, or mortgage brokerage services for such a transaction.

(i) Customary and reasonable fee

(1) In general

Lenders and their agents shall compensate fee appraisers at a rate that is customary and reasonable for appraisal services performed in the market area of the property being appraised. Evidence for such fees may be established by objective third-party information, such as government agency fee schedules, academic studies, and independent private sector surveys. Fee studies shall exclude assignments ordered by known appraisal management companies.

(2) Fee appraiser definition

(A) In general

For purposes of this section, the term "fee appraiser" means a person who is not an employee of the mortgage loan originator or appraisal management company engaging the appraiser and is—

(i) a State licensed or certified appraiser who receives a fee for performing an appraisal and certifies that the appraisal has been prepared in accordance with the Uniform Standards of Professional Appraisal Practice; or

(ii) a company not subject to the requirements of section 3353 of title 12 that utilizes the services of State licensed or certified appraisers and receives a fee for performing appraisals in accordance with the Uniform Standards of Professional Appraisal Practice.

(B) Rule of construction related to appraisal donations

If a fee appraiser voluntarily donates appraisal services to an organization eligible to receive tax-deductible charitable contributions, such voluntary donation shall be considered customary and reasonable for the purposes of paragraph (1).

(3) Exception for complex assignments

In the case of an appraisal involving a complex assignment, the customary and reasonable fee may reflect the increased time, difficulty, and scope of the work required for such an appraisal and include an amount over and above the customary and reasonable fee for non-complex assignments.

(j) Sunset

Effective on the date the interim final regulations are promulgated pursuant to subsection (g), the Home Valuation Code of Conduct announced by the Federal Housing Finance Agency on December 23, 2008, shall have no force or effect.

(k) Penalties

(1) First violation

In addition to the enforcement provisions referred to in section 1640 of this title, each person who violates this section shall forfeit and pay a civil penalty of not more than $10,000 for each day any such violation continues.

(2) Subsequent violations

In the case of any person on whom a civil penalty has been imposed under paragraph (1), paragraph (1) shall be applied by substituting "$20,000" for "$10,000" with respect to all subsequent violations.

(3) Assessment

The agency referred to in subsection (a) or (c) of section 1607 of this title with respect to any person described in paragraph (1) shall assess any penalty under this subsection to which such person is subject.

(Pub. L. 90–321, title I, §129E, as added Pub. L. 111–203, title XIV, §1472(a), July 21, 2010, 124 Stat. 2187; amended Pub. L. 115–174, title I, §102, May 24, 2018, 132 Stat. 1299.)

EDITORIAL NOTES

AMENDMENTS

2018—Subsec. (i)(2). Pub. L. 115–174 designated existing provisions as subpar. (A) and inserted heading, redesignated former subpars. (A) and (B) as cls. (i) and (ii), respectively, of subpar. (A) and realigned margins, and added subpar. (B).

STATUTORY NOTES AND RELATED SUBSIDIARIES

EFFECTIVE DATE

Section effective on the date on which final regulations implementing such section take effect, or on the date that is 18 months after the designated transfer date if such regulations have not been issued by that date, see section 1400(c) of Pub. L. 111–203, set out as an Effective Date of 2010 Amendment note under section 1601 of this title.

¹ So in original. Probably should be "subsection".

§1639f. Requirements for prompt crediting of home loan payments

(a) In general

In connection with a consumer credit transaction secured by a consumer's principal dwelling, no servicer shall fail to credit a payment to the consumer's loan account as of the date of receipt, except when a delay in crediting does not result in any charge to the consumer or in the reporting of negative information to a consumer reporting agency, except as required in subsection (b).

(b) Exception

If a servicer specifies in writing requirements for the consumer to follow in making payments, but accepts a payment that does not conform to the requirements, the servicer shall credit the payment as of 5 days after receipt.

(Pub. L. 90–321, title I, §129F, as added Pub. L. 111–203, title XIV, §1464(a), July 21, 2010, 124 Stat. 2184.)

STATUTORY NOTES AND RELATED SUBSIDIARIES

EFFECTIVE DATE

Section effective on the date on which final regulations implementing such section take effect, or on the date that is 18 months after the designated transfer date if such regulations have not been issued by that date, see section 1400(c) of Pub. L. 111–203, set out as an Effective Date of 2010 Amendment note under section 1601 of this title.

§1639g. Requests for payoff amounts of home loan

A creditor or servicer of a home loan shall send an accurate payoff balance within a reasonable time, but in no case more than 7 business days, after the receipt of a written request for such balance from or on behalf of the borrower.

(Pub. L. 90–321, title I, §129G, as added Pub. L. 111–203, title XIV, §1464(b), July 21, 2010, 124 Stat. 2184.)

STATUTORY NOTES AND RELATED SUBSIDIARIES

EFFECTIVE DATE

Section effective on the date on which final regulations implementing such section take effect, or on the date that is 18 months after the designated transfer date if such regulations have not been issued by that date, see section 1400(c) of Pub. L. 111–203, set out as an Effective Date of 2010 Amendment note under section 1601 of this title.

§1639h. Property appraisal requirements

(a) In general

A creditor may not extend credit in the form of a higher-risk mortgage to any consumer without first obtaining a written appraisal of the property to be mortgaged prepared in accordance with the requirements of this section.

(b) Appraisal requirements

(1) Physical property visit

Subject to the rules prescribed under paragraph (4), an appraisal of property to be secured by a higher-risk mortgage does not meet the requirement of this section unless it is performed by a certified or licensed appraiser who conducts a physical property visit of the interior of the mortgaged property.

(2) Second appraisal under certain circumstances

(A) In general

If the purpose of a higher-risk mortgage is to finance the purchase or acquisition of the mortgaged property from a person within 180 days of the purchase or acquisition of such property by that person at a price that was lower than the current sale price of the property, the creditor shall obtain a second appraisal from a different certified or licensed appraiser. The second appraisal shall include an analysis of the difference in sale prices, changes in market conditions, and any improvements made to the property between the date of the previous sale and the current sale.

(B) No cost to applicant

The cost of any second appraisal required under subparagraph (A) may not be charged to the applicant.

(3) Certified or licensed appraiser defined

For purposes of this section, the term "certified or licensed appraiser" means a person who—
(A) is, at a minimum, certified or licensed by the State in which the property to be appraised is located; and
(B) performs each appraisal in conformity with the Uniform Standards of Professional Appraisal Practice and title XI of the Financial Institutions Reform, Recovery, and Enforcement Act of 1989 [12 U.S.C. 3331 et seq.], and the regulations prescribed under such title, as in effect on the date of the appraisal.

(4) Regulations

(A) In general

The Board, the Comptroller of the Currency, the Federal Deposit Insurance Corporation, the National Credit Union Administration Board, the Federal Housing Finance Agency, and the Bureau shall jointly prescribe regulations to implement this section.

(B) Exemption

The agencies listed in subparagraph (A) may jointly exempt, by rule, a class of loans from the requirements of this subsection or subsection (a) if the agencies determine that the exemption is in the public interest and promotes the safety and soundness of creditors.

(c) Free copy of appraisal

A creditor shall provide 1 copy of each appraisal conducted in accordance with this section in connection with a higher-risk mortgage to the applicant without charge, and at least 3 days prior to the transaction closing date.

(d) Consumer notification

At the time of the initial mortgage application, the applicant shall be provided with a statement by the creditor that any appraisal prepared for the mortgage is for the sole use of the creditor, and that the applicant may choose to have a separate appraisal conducted at the expense of the applicant.

(e) Violations

In addition to any other liability to any person under this subchapter, a creditor found to have willfully failed to obtain an appraisal as required in this section shall be liable to the applicant or borrower for the sum of $2,000.

(f) Higher-risk mortgage defined

For purposes of this section, the term "higher-risk mortgage" means a residential mortgage loan, other than a reverse mortgage loan that is a qualified mortgage, as defined in section 1639c of this title, secured by a principal dwelling—
(1) that is not a qualified mortgage, as defined in section 1639c of this title; and
(2) with an annual percentage rate that exceeds the average prime offer rate for a comparable transaction, as defined in section 1639c of this title, as of the date the interest rate is set—

(A) by 1.5 or more percentage points, in the case of a first lien residential mortgage loan having an original principal obligation amount that does not exceed the amount of the maximum limitation on the original principal obligation of mortgage in effect for a residence of the applicable size, as of the date of such interest rate set, pursuant to the sixth sentence of section 1454(a)(2) of title 12;

(B) by 2.5 or more percentage points, in the case of a first lien residential mortgage loan having an original principal obligation amount that exceeds the amount of the maximum limitation on the original principal obligation of mortgage in effect for a residence of the applicable size, as of the date of such interest rate set, pursuant to the sixth sentence of section 1454(a)(2) of title 12; and

(C) by 3.5 or more percentage points for a subordinate lien residential mortgage loan.

(Pub. L. 90–321, title I, §129H, as added Pub. L. 111–203, title XIV, §1471, July 21, 2010, 124 Stat. 2185.)

EDITORIAL NOTES

REFERENCES IN TEXT

The Financial Institutions Reform, Recovery, and Enforcement Act of 1989, referred to in subsec. (b)(3) (B), is Pub. L. 101–73, Aug. 9, 1989, 103 Stat. 183. Title XI of the Act is classified principally to chapter 34A (§3331 et seq.) of Title 12, Banks and Banking. For complete classification of this Act to the Code, see Short Title of 1989 Amendment note set out under section 1811 of Title 12 and Tables.

STATUTORY NOTES AND RELATED SUBSIDIARIES

EFFECTIVE DATE

Section effective on the date on which final regulations implementing such section take effect, or on the date that is 18 months after the designated transfer date if such regulations have not been issued by that date, see section 1400(c) of Pub. L. 111–203, set out as an Effective Date of 2010 Amendment note under section 1601 of this title.

§1640. Civil liability

(a) Individual or class action for damages; amount of award; factors determining amount of award

Except as otherwise provided in this section, any creditor who fails to comply with any requirement imposed under this part, including any requirement under section 1635 of this title, subsection (f) or (g) of section 1641 of this title, or part D or E of this subchapter with respect to any person is liable to such person in an amount equal to the sum of—

(1) any actual damage sustained by such person as a result of the failure;

(2)(A)(i) in the case of an individual action twice the amount of any finance charge in connection with the transaction, (ii) in the case of an individual action relating to a consumer lease under part E of this subchapter, 25 per centum of the total amount of monthly payments under the lease, except that the liability under this subparagraph shall not be less than $200 nor greater than $2,000, (iii) in the case of an individual action relating to an open end consumer credit plan that is not secured by real property or a dwelling, twice the amount of any finance charge in connection with the transaction, with a minimum of $500 and a maximum of $5,000, or such higher amount as may be appropriate in the case of an established pattern or practice of such failures; [1] or (iv) in the case of an individual action relating to a credit transaction not under an open end credit plan that is secured by real property or a dwelling, not less than $400 or greater than $4,000; or

(B) in the case of a class action, such amount as the court may allow, except that as to each member of the class no minimum recovery shall be applicable, and the total recovery under this subparagraph in any class action or series of class actions arising out of the same failure to comply by the same creditor shall not be more than the lesser of $1,000,000 or 1 per centum of the net worth of the creditor;

(3) in the case of any successful action to enforce the foregoing liability or in any action in which a person is determined to have a right of rescission under section 1635 or 1638(e)(7) of this title, the costs of the action, together with a reasonable attorney's fee as determined by the court; and

(4) in the case of a failure to comply with any requirement under section 1639 of this title, paragraph (1) or (2) of section 1639b(c) of this title, or section 1639c(a) of this title, an amount equal to the sum of all finance charges and fees paid by the consumer, unless the creditor demonstrates that the failure to comply is not material.

In determining the amount of award in any class action, the court shall consider, among other relevant factors, the amount of any actual damages awarded, the frequency and persistence of failures of compliance by the creditor, the resources of the creditor, the number of persons adversely affected, and the extent to which the creditor's failure of compliance was intentional. In connection with the disclosures referred to in subsections (a) and (b) of section 1637 of this title, a creditor shall have a liability determined under paragraph (2) only for failing to comply with the requirements of section 1635 of this title, 1637(a) ^{2} of this title, or any of paragraphs (4) through (13) of section 1637(b) of this title, or for failing to comply with disclosure requirements under State law for any term or item that the Bureau has determined to be substantially the same in meaning under section 1610(a)(2) of this title as any of the terms or items referred to in section 1637(a) of this title, or any of paragraphs (4) through (13) of section 1637(b) of this title. In connection with the disclosures referred to in subsection (c) or (d) of section 1637 of this title, a card issuer shall have a liability under this section only to a cardholder who pays a fee described in section 1637(c)(1)(A)(ii)(I) or section 1637(c)(4)(A)(i) of this title or who uses the credit card or charge card. In connection with the disclosures referred to in section 1638 of this title, a creditor shall have a liability determined under paragraph (2) only for failing to comply with the requirements of section 1635 of this title, of paragraph (2) (insofar as it requires a disclosure of the "amount financed"), (3), (4), (5), (6), or (9) of section 1638(a) of this title, or section 1638(b)(2)(C)(ii) of this title, of subparagraphs (A), (B), (D), (F), or (J) of section 1638(e)(2) of this title (for purposes of paragraph (2) or (4) of section 1638(e) of this title), or paragraph (4)(C), (6), (7), or (8) of section 1638(e) of this title, or for failing to comply with disclosure requirements under State law for any term which the Bureau has determined to be substantially the same in meaning under section 1610(a)(2) of this title as any of the terms referred to in any of those paragraphs of section 1638(a) of this title or section 1638(b)(2)(C)(ii) of this title. With respect to any failure to make disclosures required under this part or part D or E of this subchapter, liability shall be imposed only upon the creditor required to make disclosure, except as provided in section 1641 of this title.

(b) Correction of errors

A creditor or assignee has no liability under this section or section 1607 of this title or section 1611 of this title for any failure to comply with any requirement imposed under this part or part E, if within sixty days after discovering an error, whether pursuant to a final written examination report or notice issued under section 1607(e)(1) of this title or through the creditor's or assignee's own procedures, and prior to the institution of an action under this section or the receipt of written notice of the error from the obligor, the creditor or assignee notifies the person concerned of the error and makes whatever adjustments in the appropriate account are necessary to assure that the person will not be required to pay an amount in excess of the charge actually disclosed, or the dollar equivalent of the annual percentage rate actually disclosed, whichever is lower.

(c) Unintentional violations; bona fide errors

A creditor or assignee may not be held liable in any action brought under this section or section 1635 of this title for a violation of this subchapter if the creditor or assignee shows by a preponderance of evidence that the violation was not intentional and resulted from a bona fide error notwithstanding the maintenance of procedures reasonably adapted to avoid any such error. Examples of a bona fide error include, but are not limited to, clerical, calculation, computer malfunction and programing, and printing errors, except that an error of legal judgment with respect to a person's obligations under this subchapter is not a bona fide error.

(d) Liability in transaction or lease involving multiple obligors

When there are multiple obligors in a consumer credit transaction or consumer lease, there shall be no more than one recovery of damages under subsection (a)(2) for a violation of this subchapter.

(e) Jurisdiction of courts; limitations on actions; State attorney general enforcement

Except as provided in the subsequent sentence, any action under this section may be brought in any United States district court, or in any other court of competent jurisdiction, within one year from the date of the occurrence of the violation or, in the case of a violation involving a private education loan (as that term is defined in section 1650(a) of this title), 1 year from the date on which the first regular payment of principal is due under the loan. Any action under this section with respect to any violation of section 1639, 1639b, or 1639c of this title may be brought in any United States district court, or in any other court of competent jurisdiction, before the end of the 3-year period beginning on the date of the occurrence of the violation. This subsection does not bar a person from asserting a violation of this subchapter in an action to collect the debt which was brought more than one year from the date of the occurrence of the violation as a matter of defense by recoupment or set-off in such action, except as otherwise provided by State law. An action to enforce a violation of section 1639, 1639b, 1639c, 1639d, 1639e, 1639f, 1639g, or 1639h of this title may also be brought by the appropriate State attorney general in any appropriate United States district court, or any other court of competent jurisdiction, not later than 3 years after the date on which the violation occurs. The State attorney general shall provide prior written notice of any such civil action to the Federal agency responsible for enforcement under section 1607 of this title and shall provide the agency with a copy of the complaint. If prior notice is not feasible, the State attorney general shall provide notice to such agency immediately upon instituting the action. The Federal agency may—

(1) intervene in the action;

(2) upon intervening—

(A) remove the action to the appropriate United States district court, if it was not originally brought there; and

(B) be heard on all matters arising in the action; and

(3) file a petition for appeal.

(f) Good faith compliance with rule, regulation, or interpretation of Bureau or with interpretation or approval of duly authorized official or employee of Federal Reserve System

No provision of this section, section 1607(b) of this title, section 1607(c) of this title, section 1607(e) of this title, or section 1611 of this title imposing any liability shall apply to any act done or omitted in good faith in conformity with any rule, regulation, or interpretation thereof by the Bureau or in conformity with any interpretation or approval by an official or employee of the Federal Reserve System duly authorized by the Bureau to issue such interpretations or approvals under such procedures as the Bureau may prescribe therefor, notwithstanding that after such act or omission has occurred, such rule, regulation, interpretation, or approval is amended, rescinded, or determined by judicial or other authority to be invalid for any reason.

(g) Recovery for multiple failures to disclose

The multiple failure to disclose to any person any information required under this part or part D or E of this subchapter to be disclosed in connection with a single account under an open end consumer credit plan, other single consumer credit sale, consumer loan, consumer lease, or other extension of consumer credit, shall entitle the person to a single recovery under this section but continued failure to disclose after a recovery has been granted shall give rise to rights to additional recoveries. This subsection does not bar any remedy permitted by section 1635 of this title.

(h) Offset from amount owed to creditor or assignee; rights of defaulting consumer

A person may not take any action to offset any amount for which a creditor or assignee is potentially liable to such person under subsection (a)(2) against any amount owed by such person, unless the amount of the creditor's or assignee's liability under this subchapter has been determined by judgment of a court of competent jurisdiction in an action of which such person was a party. This subsection does not bar a consumer then in default on the obligation from asserting a violation of this subchapter as an original action, or as a defense or counterclaim to an action to collect amounts owed by the consumer brought by a person liable under this subchapter.

(i) Class action moratorium

(1) In general

During the period beginning on May 18, 1995, and ending on October 1, 1995, no court may enter any order certifying any class in any action under this subchapter—
(A) which is brought in connection with any credit transaction not under an open end credit plan which is secured by a first lien on real property or a dwelling and constitutes a refinancing or consolidation of an existing extension of credit; and
(B) which is based on the alleged failure of a creditor—
(i) to include a charge actually incurred (in connection with the transaction) in the finance charge disclosed pursuant to section 1638 of this title;
(ii) to properly make any other disclosure required under section 1638 of this title as a result of the failure described in clause (i); or
(iii) to provide proper notice of rescission rights under section 1635(a) of this title due to the selection by the creditor of the incorrect form from among the model forms prescribed by the Bureau or from among forms based on such model forms.

(2) Exceptions for certain alleged violations

Paragraph (1) shall not apply with respect to any action—
(A) described in clause (i) or (ii) of paragraph (1)(B), if the amount disclosed as the finance charge results in an annual percentage rate that exceeds the tolerance provided in section 1606(c) of this title; or
(B) described in paragraph (1)(B)(iii), if—
(i) no notice relating to rescission rights under section 1635(a) of this title was provided in any form; or
(ii) proper notice was not provided for any reason other than the reason described in such paragraph.

(j) Private educational lender

A private educational lender (as that term is defined in section 1650(a) of this title) has no liability under this section for failure to comply with section 1638(e)(3) of this title).[3]

(k) Defense to foreclosure

(1) In general

Notwithstanding any other provision of law, when a creditor, assignee, or other holder of a residential mortgage loan or anyone acting on behalf of such creditor, assignee, or holder, initiates a judicial or nonjudicial foreclosure of the residential mortgage loan, or any other action to collect the debt in connection with such loan, a consumer may assert a violation by a creditor of paragraph (1) or (2) of section 1639b(c) of this title, or of section 1639c(a) of this title, as a matter of defense by recoupment or set off without regard for the time limit on a private action for damages under subsection (e).

(2) Amount of recoupment or setoff

(A) In general

The amount of recoupment or set-off under paragraph (1) shall equal the amount to which the consumer would be entitled under subsection (a) for damages for a valid claim brought in an original action against the creditor, plus the costs to the consumer of the action, including a reasonable attorney's fee.

(B) Special rule

Where such judgment is rendered after the expiration of the applicable time limit on a private action for damages under subsection (e), the amount of recoupment or set-off under paragraph (1) derived from damages under subsection (a)(4) shall not exceed the amount to which the consumer would have been entitled under subsection (a)(4) for damages computed up to the day preceding the expiration of the applicable time limit.

(l) Exemption from liability and rescission in case of borrower fraud or deception

In addition to any other remedy available by law or contract, no creditor or assignee shall be liable to an obligor under this section, if such obligor, or co-obligor has been convicted of obtaining by actual fraud such residential mortgage loan.

(Pub. L. 90–321, title I, §130, May 29, 1968, 82 Stat. 157; Pub. L. 93–495, title IV, §§406, 407, 408(a)–(d), Oct. 28, 1974, 88 Stat. 1518; Pub. L. 94–222, §3(b), Feb. 27, 1976, 90 Stat. 197; Pub. L. 94–240, §4, Mar. 23, 1976, 90 Stat. 260; Pub. L. 96–221, title VI, §615, Mar. 31, 1980, 94 Stat. 180; Pub. L. 100–583, §3, Nov. 3, 1988, 102 Stat. 2966; Pub. L. 103–325, title I, §153(a), (b), Sept. 23, 1994, 108 Stat. 2195; Pub. L. 104–12, §2, May 18, 1995, 109 Stat. 161; Pub. L. 104–29, §6, Sept. 30, 1995, 109 Stat. 274; Pub. L. 110–289, div. B, title V, §2502(b), July 30, 2008, 122 Stat. 2857; Pub. L. 110–315, title X, §1012(a), Aug. 14, 2008, 122 Stat. 3482; Pub. L. 111–22, div. A, title IV, §404(b), May 20, 2009, 123 Stat. 1658; Pub. L. 111–24, title I, §107, title II, §201(b), May 22, 2009, 123 Stat. 1743, 1745; Pub. L. 111–203, title X, §1100A(2), title XIV, §§1413, 1416, 1417, 1422, July 21, 2010, 124 Stat. 2107, 2148, 2153, 2157.)

Editorial Notes

AMENDMENTS

2010—Pub. L. 111–203, §1100A(2), substituted "Bureau" for "Board" wherever appearing.

Subsec. (a)(2)(A)(ii). Pub. L. 111–203, §1416(a)(1), substituted "$200" for "$100" and "$2,000" for "$1,000".

Subsec. (a)(2)(B). Pub. L. 111–203, §1416(a)(2), substituted "$1,000,000" for "$500,000".

Subsec. (a)(4). Pub. L. 111–203, §1416(a)(3), inserted ", paragraph (1) or (2) of section 1639b(c) of this title, or section 1639c(a) of this title" after "section 1639 of this title".

Subsec. (e). Pub. L. 111–203, §1422, substituted "section 1639, 1639b, 1639c, 1639d, 1639e, 1639f, 1639g, or 1639h of this title may also" for "section 1639 of this title may also".

Pub. L. 111–203, §1416(b), in first sentence substituted "Except as provided in the subsequent sentence, any action" for "Any action" and inserted after first sentence "Any action under this section with respect to any violation of section 1639, 1639b, or 1639c of this title may be brought in any United States district court, or in any other court of competent jurisdiction, before the end of the 3-year period beginning on the date of the occurrence of the violation."

Subsec. (k). Pub. L. 111–203, §1413, added subsec. (k).

Subsec. (l). Pub. L. 111–203, §1417, added subsec. (l).

2009—Subsec. (a). Pub. L. 111–24, §201(b), in concluding provisions, substituted "In connection with the disclosures referred to in subsections (a) and (b) of section 1637 of this title, a creditor shall have a liability determined under paragraph (2) only for failing to comply with the requirements of section 1635 of this title, 1637(a) of this title, or any of paragraphs (4) through (13) of section 1637(b) of this title, or for failing to comply with disclosure requirements under State law for any term or item that the Board has determined to be substantially the same in meaning under section 1610(a)(2) of this title as any of the terms or items referred to in section 1637(a) of this title, or any of paragraphs (4) through (13) of section 1637(b) of this title." for "In connection with the disclosures referred to in subsections (a) and (b) of section 1637 of this title, a creditor shall have a liability determined under paragraph (2) only for failing to comply with the requirements of section 1635 of this title, section 1637(a) of this title, or of paragraph (4), (5), (6), (7), (8), (9), or (10) of section 1637(b) of this title or for failing to comply with disclosure requirements under State law for any term or item which the Board has determined to be substantially the same in meaning under section 1610(a)(2) of this title as any of the terms or items referred to in section 1637(a) of this title or any of those paragraphs of section 1637(b) of this title."

Pub. L. 111–22, §404(b), which directed insertion of "subsection (f) or (g) of section 1641 of this title," after "section 1635 of this title,", was executed by making the insertion only in the introductory provisions to reflect the probable intent of Congress.

Subsec. (a)(2)(A)(iii), (iv). Pub. L. 111–24, §107, added cl. (iii) and redesignated former cl. (iii) as (iv).

2008—Subsec. (a). Pub. L. 110–315, §1012(a)(1)(B), in fourth sentence of concluding provisions, substituted "1635 of this title," for "1635 of this title or" and inserted "of subparagraphs (A), (B), (D), (F), or (J) of section 1638(e)(2) of this title (for purposes of paragraph (2) or (4) of section 1638(e) of this title), or paragraph (4)(C), (6), (7), or (8) of section 1638(e) of this title," before "or for failing".

Pub. L. 110–289, §2502(b)(2), in concluding provisions, inserted "or section 1638(b)(2)(C)(ii) of this title," before "or for failing to comply" and "or section 1638(b)(2)(C)(ii) of this title" before ". With respect to".

Subsec. (a)(2)(A)(iii). Pub. L. 110–289, §2502(b)(1), substituted "not less than $400 or greater than $4,000" for "not less than $200 or greater than $2,000".

Subsec. (a)(3). Pub. L. 110–315, §1012(a)(1)(A), inserted "or 1638(e)(7)" after "section 1635".

Subsec. (e). Pub. L. 110–315, §1012(a)(2), inserted before period at end of first sentence "or, in the case of a violation involving a private education loan (as that term is defined in section 1650(a) of this title), 1 year from the date on which the first regular payment of principal is due under the loan".

Subsec. (j). Pub. L. 110–315, §1012(a)(3), added subsec. (j).

1995—Subsec. (a)(2)(A)(iii). Pub. L. 104–29 added cl. (iii).

Subsec. (i). Pub. L. 104–12 added subsec. (i).

1994—Subsec. (a)(4). Pub. L. 103–325, §153(a), added par. (4).

Subsec. (e). Pub. L. 103–325, §153(b), inserted at end "An action to enforce a violation of section 1639 of this title may also be brought by the appropriate State attorney general in any appropriate United States district court, or any other court of competent jurisdiction, not later than 3 years after the date on which the violation occurs. The State attorney general shall provide prior written notice of any such civil action to the Federal agency responsible for enforcement under section 1607 of this title and shall provide the agency with a copy of the complaint. If prior notice is not feasible, the State attorney general shall provide notice to such agency immediately upon instituting the action. The Federal agency may—

"(1) intervene in the action;

"(2) upon intervening—

"(A) remove the action to the appropriate United States district court, if it was not originally brought there; and

"(B) be heard on all matters arising in the action; and

"(3) file a petition for appeal."

1988—Subsec. (a). Pub. L. 100–583 substituted "in subsections (a) and (b) of section 1637" for "in section 1637" in third sentence and inserted provisions limiting liability of card issuer under this section to cardholders who pay fee or use credit card or charge card.

1980—Subsec. (a). Pub. L. 96–221, §615(b), in introductory text inserted provisions respecting applicability of section 1635 of this title, and in text following numbered pars. inserted provisions relating to disclosures required under sections 1637 and 1638 of this title.

Subsec. (a)(2)(B). Pub. L. 96–221, §615(a)(1), substituted provisions respecting recovery under this subparagraph in any class action or series of class actions, for provisions respecting recovery in a class action.

Subsec. (a)(3). Pub. L. 96–221, §615(a)(2), inserted provisions relating to right of rescission under section 1635 of this title.

Subsec. (b). Pub. L. 96–221, §615(a)(3), substituted provisions relating to correction of errors within sixty days by a creditor or assignee, for provisions relating to correction of errors within fifteen days by a creditor.

Subsec. (c). Pub. L. 96–221, §615(a)(3), substituted provisions relating to liability of a creditor or assignee in any action brought under this section or section 1635 of this title, for provisions relating to liability of a creditor in any action brought under this section.

Subsec. (d). Pub. L. 96–221, §615(a)(3), substituted provisions relating to liability in transaction or lease involving multiple obligors, for provisions relating to liability of subsequent assignees original creditor.

Subsec. (e). Pub. L. 96–221, §615(a)(4), inserted provisions relating to limitations on actions.

Subsec. (f). Pub. L. 96–221, §615(a)(5), inserted references to section 1607(b), (c), and (e) of this title.

Subsec. (g). Pub. L. 96–221, §615(a)(6), inserted provisions relating to remedy under section 1635 of this title.

Subsec. (h). Pub. L. 96–221, §615(a)(7), substituted provisions relating to offset from amounts owed to the creditor or assignee, and rights of defaulting consumer, for provisions relating to offset from amounts owed to the creditor.

1976—Subsec. (a). Pub. L. 94–240, §4(1), inserted "or E" after "part D".

Subsec. (a)(2)(A). Pub. L. 94–240, §4(2), designated existing provision as cl. (i) and added cl. (ii).

Subsec. (a)(2)(B). Pub. L. 94–240, §4(3), substituted "lesser of $500,000" for "lesser of $100,000".

Subsec. (b). Pub. L. 94–240, §4(4), inserted "or part E of this subchapter" after "this part" and struck out "finance" after "required to pay a".

Subsec. (f). Pub. L. 94–222 inserted "or in conformity with any interpretation or approval by an official or employee of the Federal Reserve System duly authorized by the Board to issue such interpretations or approvals under such procedures as the Board may prescribe therefor" after "by the Board", and substituted "interpretation, or approval" for "or interpretation" before "is amended".

Subsec. (g). Pub. L. 94–240, §4(5), inserted "or part D or E of this subchapter" after "this part", and "consumer lease" after "consumer loan".

1974—Subsec. (a). Pub. L. 93–495, §408(a), substituted provisions setting forth determination of amount of liability of any creditor failing to comply with any requirement imposed under part D of this subchapter or this part, for provisions setting forth determination of amount of liability of any creditor failing to disclose in connection with any consumer credit transaction any information required under this part to be disclosed to specified persons.

Subsec. (b). Pub. L. 93–495, §408(b), inserted "for any failure to comply with any requirement imposed under this part," before "if within".

Subsec. (c). Pub. L. 93–495, §408(c), substituted "subchapter" for "part".

Subsec. (f). Pub. L. 93–495, §406, added subsec. (f).

Subsec. (g). Pub. L. 93–495, §407, added subsec. (g).

Subsec. (h). Pub. L. 93–495, §408(d), added subsec. (h).

STATUTORY NOTES AND RELATED SUBSIDIARIES

EFFECTIVE DATE OF 2010 AMENDMENT

Amendment by section 1100A(2) of Pub. L. 111–203 effective on the designated transfer date, see section 1100H of Pub. L. 111–203, set out as a note under section 552a of Title 5, Government Organization and Employees.

Amendment by sections 1413, 1416, 1417, and 1422 of Pub. L. 111–203 effective on the date on which final regulations implementing that amendment take effect, or on the date that is 18 months after the designated transfer date, if such regulations have not been issued by that date, see section 1400(c) of Pub. L. 111–203, set out as a note under section 1601 of this title.

EFFECTIVE DATE OF 2009 AMENDMENT

Amendment by Pub. L. 111–24 effective 9 months after May 22, 2009, except as otherwise specifically provided, see section 3 of Pub. L. 111–24, set out as a note under section 1602 of this title.

EFFECTIVE DATE OF 2008 AMENDMENT

Pub. L. 110–315, title X, §1012(b), Aug. 14, 2008, 122 Stat. 3482, provided that: "The amendments made by this section [amending this section] shall have the same effective date as provisions referred to in section 1003(b) [set out as a note under section 1638 of this title]."

EFFECTIVE DATE OF 1980 AMENDMENT

Amendment by Pub. L. 96–221 effective on expiration of two years and six months after Mar. 31, 1980, with all regulations, forms, and clauses required to be prescribed to be promulgated at least one year prior to such effective date, and allowing any creditor to comply with any amendments, in accordance with the regulations, forms, and clauses prescribed by the Board prior to such effective date, see section 625 of Pub. L. 96–221, set out as a note under section 1602 of this title.

EFFECTIVE DATE OF 1976 AMENDMENT

Amendment by Pub. L. 94–240 effective on expiration of one year after Mar. 23, 1976, see section 6 of Pub. L. 94–240, set out as an Effective Date note under section 1667 of this title.

EFFECTIVE DATE OF 1974 AMENDMENT

Amendment by Pub. L. 93–495 effective Oct. 28, 1974, see section 416 of Pub. L. 93–495, set out as an Effective Date note under section 1665a of this title.

DETERMINATION OF LIABILITY PRIOR TO OCTOBER 28, 1974

Pub. L. 93–495, title IV, §408(e), Oct. 28, 1974, 88 Stat. 1519, provided that: "The amendments made by sections 406, 407, and 408 [amending this section] shall apply in determining the liability of any person under chapter 2 or 4 of the Truth in Lending Act [this part or part D of this subchapter], unless prior to the date of enactment of this Act [Oct. 28, 1974] such liability has been determined by final judgment of a court of competent jurisdiction and no further review of such judgment may be had by appeal or otherwise."

---

[1] *So in original. The semicolon probably should be a comma.*

[2] *So in original. Probably should be preceded by "section".*

§1641. Liability of assignees

(a) Prerequisites

Except as otherwise specifically provided in this subchapter, any civil action for a violation of this subchapter or proceeding under section 1607 of this title which may be brought against a creditor may be maintained against any assignee of such creditor only if the violation for which such action or proceeding is brought is apparent on the face of the disclosure statement, except where the assignment was involuntary. For the purpose of this section, a violation apparent on the face of the disclosure statement includes, but is not limited to (1) a disclosure which can be determined to be incomplete or inaccurate from the face of the disclosure statement or other documents assigned, or (2) a disclosure which does not use the terms required to be used by this subchapter.

(b) Proof of compliance with statutory provisions

Except as provided in section 1635(c) of this title, in any action or proceeding by or against any subsequent assignee of the original creditor without knowledge to the contrary by the assignee when he acquires the obligation, written acknowledgement of receipt by a person to whom a statement is required to be given pursuant to this subchapter shall be conclusive proof of the delivery thereof and, except as provided in subsection (a), of compliance with this part. This section does not affect the rights of the obligor in any action against the original creditor.

(c) Right of rescission by consumer unaffected

Any consumer who has the right to rescind a transaction under section 1635 of this title may rescind the transaction as against any assignee of the obligation.

(d) Rights upon assignment of certain mortgages

(1) In general

Any person who purchases or is otherwise assigned a mortgage referred to in section 1602(aa) [1] of this title shall be subject to all claims and defenses with respect to that mortgage that the consumer could assert against the creditor of the mortgage, unless the purchaser or assignee demonstrates, by a preponderance of the evidence, that a reasonable person exercising ordinary due diligence, could not determine, based on the documentation required by this subchapter, the itemization of the amount financed, and other disclosure of disbursements that the mortgage was a mortgage referred to in section 1602(aa) [1] of this title. The preceding sentence does not affect rights of a consumer under subsection (a), (b), or (c) of this section or any other provision of this subchapter.

(2) Limitation on damages

Notwithstanding any other provision of law, relief provided as a result of any action made permissible by paragraph (1) may not exceed—
  (A) with respect to actions based upon a violation of this subchapter, the amount specified in section 1640 of this title; and
  (B) with respect to all other causes of action, the sum of—
    (i) the amount of all remaining indebtedness; and
    (ii) the total amount paid by the consumer in connection with the transaction.

(3) Offset

The amount of damages that may be awarded under paragraph (2)(B) shall be reduced by the amount of any damages awarded under paragraph (2)(A).

(4) Notice

Any person who sells or otherwise assigns a mortgage referred to in section 1602(aa) [1] of this title shall include a prominent notice of the potential liability under this subsection as determined by the Bureau.

(e) Liability of assignee for consumer credit transactions secured by real property

(1) In general

Except as otherwise specifically provided in this subchapter, any civil action against a creditor for a violation of this subchapter, and any proceeding under section 1607 of this title against a creditor, with respect to a consumer credit transaction secured by real property may be maintained against any assignee of such creditor only if—
  (A) the violation for which such action or proceeding is brought is apparent on the face of the disclosure statement provided in connection with such transaction pursuant to this subchapter; and
  (B) the assignment to the assignee was voluntary.

(2) Violation apparent on the face of the disclosure described

For the purpose of this section, a violation is apparent on the face of the disclosure statement if—
  (A) the disclosure can be determined to be incomplete or inaccurate by a comparison among the disclosure statement, any itemization of the amount financed, the note, or any other disclosure of disbursement; or

(B) the disclosure statement does not use the terms or format required to be used by this subchapter.

(f) Treatment of servicer

(1) In general

A servicer of a consumer obligation arising from a consumer credit transaction shall not be treated as an assignee of such obligation for purposes of this section unless the servicer is or was the owner of the obligation.

(2) Servicer not treated as owner on basis of assignment for administrative convenience

A servicer of a consumer obligation arising from a consumer credit transaction shall not be treated as the owner of the obligation for purposes of this section on the basis of an assignment of the obligation from the creditor or another assignee to the servicer solely for the administrative convenience of the servicer in servicing the obligation. Upon written request by the obligor, the servicer shall provide the obligor, to the best knowledge of the servicer, with the name, address, and telephone number of the owner of the obligation or the master servicer of the obligation.

(3) "Servicer" defined

For purposes of this subsection, the term "servicer" has the same meaning as in section 2605(i)(2) of title 12.

(4) Applicability

This subsection shall apply to all consumer credit transactions in existence or consummated on or after September 30, 1995.

(g) Notice of new creditor

(1) In general

In addition to other disclosures required by this subchapter, not later than 30 days after the date on which a mortgage loan is sold or otherwise transferred or assigned to a third party, the creditor that is the new owner or assignee of the debt shall notify the borrower in writing of such transfer, including—

(A) the identity, address, telephone number of the new creditor;
(B) the date of transfer;
(C) how to reach an agent or party having authority to act on behalf of the new creditor;
(D) the location of the place where transfer of ownership of the debt is recorded; and
(E) any other relevant information regarding the new creditor.

(2) Definition

As used in this subsection, the term "mortgage loan" means any consumer credit transaction that is secured by the principal dwelling of a consumer.

(Pub. L. 90–321, title I, §131, May 29, 1968, 82 Stat. 157; Pub. L. 96–221, title VI, §616(a), Mar. 31, 1980, 94 Stat. 182; Pub. L. 103–325, title I, §153(c), Sept. 23, 1994, 108 Stat. 2195; Pub. L. 104–29, §7, Sept. 30, 1995, 109 Stat. 274; Pub. L. 111–22, div. A, title IV, §404(a), May 20, 2009, 123 Stat. 1658; Pub. L. 111–203, title X, §1100A(2), July 21, 2010, 124 Stat. 2107.)

EDITORIAL NOTES

REFERENCES IN TEXT

Section 1602(aa) of this title, referred to in subsec. (d)(1), (4), was redesignated section 1602(bb) of this title by Pub. L. 111–203, title X, §1100A(1)(A), July 21, 2010, 124 Stat. 2107.

AMENDMENTS

2010—Subsec. (d)(4). Pub. L. 111–203 substituted "Bureau" for "Board".
2009—Subsec. (g). Pub. L. 111–22 added subsec. (g).
1995—Subsec. (e). Pub. L. 104–29, §7(a), added subsec. (e).
Subsec. (f). Pub. L. 104–29, §7(b), added subsec. (f).
1994—Subsec. (d). Pub. L. 103–325 added subsec. (d).
1980—Pub. L. 96–221 added subsecs. (a) and (c), designated existing provisions as subsec. (b), substituted "excepted as provided in subsection (a)" for "unless the violation is apparent on the face of the statement", and struck out exception for actions under section 1640(d) of this title.

STATUTORY NOTES AND RELATED SUBSIDIARIES

EFFECTIVE DATE OF 2010 AMENDMENT

Amendment by Pub. L. 111–203 effective on the designated transfer date, see section 1100H of Pub. L. 111–203, set out as a note under section 552a of Title 5, Government Organization and Employees.

Amendment by Pub. L. 96–221 effective on expiration of two years and six months after Mar. 31, 1980, with all regulations, forms, and clauses required to be prescribed to be promulgated at least one year prior to such effective date, and allowing any creditor to comply with any amendments, in accordance with the regulations, forms, and clauses prescribed by the Board prior to such effective date, see section 625 of Pub. L. 96–221, set out as a note under section 1602 of this title.

[1] *See References in Text note below.*

§1642. Issuance of credit cards

No credit card shall be issued except in response to a request or application therefor. This prohibition does not apply to the issuance of a credit card in renewal of, or in substitution for, an accepted credit card.

(Pub. L. 90–321, title I, §132, as added Pub. L. 91–508, title V, §502(a), Oct. 26, 1970, 84 Stat. 1126.)

STATUTORY NOTES AND RELATED SUBSIDIARIES

EFFECTIVE DATE

Pub. L. 91–508, title V, §503(1), Oct. 26, 1970, 84 Stat. 1127, provided that: "Section 132 of such Act [this section] takes effect on date of enactment of this title [Oct. 26, 1970]."

§1643. Liability of holder of credit card

(a) Limits on liability

(1) A cardholder shall be liable for the unauthorized use of a credit card only if—

(A) the card is an accepted credit card;

(B) the liability is not in excess of $50;

(C) the card issuer gives adequate notice to the cardholder of the potential liability;

(D) the card issuer has provided the cardholder with a description of a means by which the card issuer may be notified of loss or theft of the card, which description may be provided on the face or reverse side of the statement required by section 1637(b) of this title or on a separate notice accompanying such statement;

(E) the unauthorized use occurs before the card issuer has been notified that an unauthorized use of the credit card has occurred or may occur as the result of loss, theft, or otherwise; and

(F) the card issuer has provided a method whereby the user of such card can be identified as the person authorized to use it.

(2) For purposes of this section, a card issuer has been notified when such steps as may be reasonably required in the ordinary course of business to provide the card issuer with the pertinent information have been taken, whether or not any particular officer, employee, or agent of the card issuer does in fact receive such information.

(b) Burden of proof

In any action by a card issuer to enforce liability for the use of a credit card, the burden of proof is upon the card issuer to show that the use was authorized or, if the use was unauthorized, then the burden of proof is upon the card issuer to show that the conditions of liability for the unauthorized use of a credit card, as set forth in subsection (a), have been met.

(c) Liability imposed by other laws or by agreement with issuer

Nothing in this section imposes liability upon a cardholder for the unauthorized use of a credit card in excess of his liability for such use under other applicable law or under any agreement with the card issuer.

(d) Exclusiveness of liability

Except as provided in this section, a cardholder incurs no liability from the unauthorized use of a credit card.

(Pub. L. 90–321, title I, §133, as added Pub. L. 91–508, title V, §502(a), Oct. 26, 1970, 84 Stat. 1126; amended Pub. L. 96–221, title VI, §617, Mar. 31, 1980, 94 Stat. 182.)

EDITORIAL NOTES

AMENDMENTS

1980—Subsec. (a). Pub. L. 96–221 revised existing provisions into pars. (1) and (2) and, as so revised, in par. (1) made changes in structure and phraseology and revised means of notice and verification, and in par. (2) made changes in phraseology.

STATUTORY NOTES AND RELATED SUBSIDIARIES

EFFECTIVE DATE OF 1980 AMENDMENT

Amendment by Pub. L. 96–221 effective on expiration of two years and six months after Mar. 31, 1980, with all regulations, forms, and clauses required to be prescribed to be promulgated at least one year prior to such effective date, and allowing any creditor to comply with any amendments, in accordance with the regulations, forms, and clauses prescribed by the Board prior to such effective date, see section 625 of Pub. L. 96–221, set out as a note under section 1602 of this title.

EFFECTIVE DATE

Pub. L. 91–508, title V, §503(2), Oct. 26, 1970, 84 Stat. 1127, provided that: "Section 133 of such Act [this section] takes effect upon the expiration of 90 days after such date of enactment [Oct. 26, 1970]."

§1644. Fraudulent use of credit cards; penalties

(a) Use, attempt or conspiracy to use card in transaction affecting interstate or foreign commerce

Whoever knowingly in a transaction affecting interstate or foreign commerce, uses or attempts or conspires to use any counterfeit, fictitious, altered, forged, lost, stolen, or fraudulently obtained credit card to obtain money, goods, services, or anything else of value which within any one-year period has a value aggregating $1,000 or more; or

(b) Transporting, attempting or conspiring to transport card in interstate commerce

Whoever, with unlawful or fraudulent intent, transports or attempts or conspires to transport in interstate or foreign commerce a counterfeit, fictitious, altered, forged, lost, stolen, or fraudulently obtained credit card knowing the same to be counterfeit, fictitious, altered, forged, lost, stolen, or fraudulently obtained; or

(c) Use of interstate commerce to sell or transport card

Whoever, with unlawful or fraudulent intent, uses any instrumentality of interstate or foreign commerce to sell or transport a counterfeit, fictitious, altered, forged, lost, stolen, or fraudulently obtained credit card knowing the same to be counterfeit, fictitious, altered, forged, lost, stolen, or fraudulently obtained; or

(d) Receipt, concealment, etc., of goods obtained by use of card

Whoever knowingly receives, conceals, uses, or transports money, goods, services, or anything else of value (except tickets for interstate or foreign transportation) which (1) within any one-year period has a value aggregating $1,000 or more, (2) has moved in or is part of, or which constitutes interstate or foreign commerce, and (3) has been obtained with a counterfeit, fictitious, altered, forged, lost, stolen, or fraudulently obtained credit card; or

(e) Receipt, concealment, etc., of tickets for interstate or foreign transportation obtained by use of card

Whoever knowingly receives, conceals, uses, sells, or transports in interstate or foreign commerce one or more tickets for interstate or foreign transportation, which (1) within any one-year period have a value aggregating $500 or more, and (2) have been purchased or obtained with one or more counterfeit, fictitious, altered, forged, lost, stolen, or fraudulently obtained credit cards; or

(f) Furnishing of money, etc., through use of card

Whoever in a transaction affecting interstate or foreign commerce furnishes money, property, services, or anything else of value, which within any one-year period has a value aggregating $1,000 or more, through the use of any counterfeit, fictitious, altered, forged, lost, stolen, or fraudulently obtained credit card knowing the same to be counterfeit, fictitious, altered, forged, lost, stolen, or fraudulently obtained—

shall be fined not more than $10,000 or imprisoned not more than ten years, or both.

(Pub. L. 90–321, title I, §134, as added Pub. L. 91–508, title V, §502(a), Oct. 26, 1970, 84 Stat. 1127; amended Pub. L. 93–495, title IV, §414, Oct. 28, 1974, 88 Stat. 1520.)

EDITORIAL NOTES

AMENDMENTS

1974—Pub. L. 93–495 generally reorganized provisions by designating former unlettered paragraph cls. (a) to (f), and as so designated, expanded prohibitions relating to fraudulent use of credit cards, decreased amount required for fraudulent use from a retail value aggregating $5,000, or more, to enumerated amounts for particular activities, and increased the punishment from a sentence of not more than five years to a sentence of not more than ten years.

STATUTORY NOTES AND RELATED SUBSIDIARIES

EFFECTIVE DATE OF 1974 AMENDMENT

Amendment by Pub. L. 93–495 effective Oct. 28, 1974, see section 416 of Pub. L. 93–495, set out as an Effective Date note under section 1665a of this title.

EFFECTIVE DATE

Pub. L. 91–508, title V, §503(3), Oct. 26, 1970, 84 Stat. 1127, provided that: "Section 134 of such Act [this section] applies to offenses committed on or after such date of enactment [Oct. 26, 1970]."

§1645. Business credit cards; limits on liability of employees

The exemption provided by section 1603(1) of this title does not apply to the provisions of sections 1642, 1643, and 1644 of this title, except that a card issuer and a business or other organization which provides credit cards issued by the same card issuer to ten or more of its employees may by contract agree as to liability of the business or other organization with respect to unauthorized use of such credit cards without regard to the provisions of section 1643 of this title, but in no case may such business or other organization or card issuer impose liability upon any employee with respect to unauthorized use of such a credit card except in accordance with and subject to the limitations of section 1643 of this title.

(Pub. L. 90–321, title I, §135, as added Pub. L. 93–495, title IV, §410(a), Oct. 28, 1974, 88 Stat. 1519.)

STATUTORY NOTES AND RELATED SUBSIDIARIES

EFFECTIVE DATE

Section effective Oct. 28, 1974, see section 416 of Pub. L. 93–495, set out as a note under section 1665a of this title.

§1646. Dissemination of annual percentage rates; implementation, etc.

(a) Annual percentage rates

The Bureau shall collect, publish, and disseminate to the public, on a demonstration basis in a number of standard metropolitan statistical areas to be determined by the Bureau, the annual percentage rates charged for representative types of nonsale credit by creditors in such areas. For the purpose of this section, the Bureau is authorized to require creditors in such areas to furnish information necessary for the Bureau to collect, publish, and disseminate such information.

(b) Credit card price and availability information

(1) Collection required

The Bureau shall collect, on a semiannual basis, credit card price and availability information, including the information required to be disclosed under section 1637(c) of this title, from a broad sample of financial institutions which offer credit card services.

(2) Sample requirements

The broad sample of financial institutions required under paragraph (1) shall include—
(A) the 25 largest issuers of credit cards; and
(B) not less than 125 additional financial institutions selected by the Bureau in a manner that ensures—
(i) an equitable geographical distribution within the sample; and
(ii) the representation of a wide spectrum of institutions within the sample.

(3) Report of information from sample

Each financial institution in the broad sample established pursuant to paragraph (2) shall report the information to the Bureau in accordance with such regulations or orders as the Bureau may prescribe.

(4) Public availability of collected information; report to Congress

The Bureau shall—
(A) make the information collected pursuant to this subsection available to the public upon request; and

(B) report such information semiannually to Congress.

(c) Implementation

The Bureau is authorized to enter into contracts or other arrangements with appropriate persons, organizations, or State agencies to carry out its functions under subsections (a) and (b) and to furnish financial assistance in support thereof.

(Pub. L. 90–321, title I, §136, as added Pub. L. 96–221, title VI, §618(a), Mar. 31, 1980, 94 Stat. 183; amended Pub. L. 100–583, §5, Nov. 3, 1988, 102 Stat. 2967; Pub. L. 111–203, title X, §1100A(2), July 21, 2010, 124 Stat. 2107.)

Editorial Notes

Amendments

2010—Pub. L. 111–203 substituted "Bureau" for "Board" wherever appearing.

1988—Subsecs. (b), (c). Pub. L. 100–583 added subsec. (b), redesignated former subsec. (b) as (c), and substituted "subsections (a) and (b)" for "subsection (a)".

Statutory Notes and Related Subsidiaries

Effective Date of 2010 Amendment

Amendment by Pub. L. 111–203 effective on the designated transfer date, see section 1100H of Pub. L. 111–203, set out as a note under section 552a of Title 5, Government Organization and Employees.

Effective Date

Section effective on expiration of two years and six months after Mar. 31, 1980, with all regulations, forms, and clauses required to be prescribed to be promulgated at least one year prior to such effective date, and allowing any creditor to comply with any amendments, in accordance with the regulations, forms, and clauses prescribed by the Board prior to such effective date, see section 625 of Pub. L. 96–221, set out as an Effective Date of 1980 Amendment note under section 1602 of this title.

§1647. Home equity plans

(a) Index requirement

In the case of extensions of credit under an open end consumer credit plan which are subject to a variable rate and are secured by a consumer's principal dwelling, the index or other rate of interest to which changes in the annual percentage rate are related shall be based on an index or rate of interest which is publicly available and is not under the control of the creditor.

(b) Grounds for acceleration of outstanding balance

A creditor may not unilaterally terminate any account under an open end consumer credit plan under which extensions of credit are secured by a consumer's principal dwelling and require the immediate repayment of any outstanding balance at such time, except in the case of—

(1) fraud or material misrepresentation on the part of the consumer in connection with the account;

(2) failure by the consumer to meet the repayment terms of the agreement for any outstanding balance; or

(3) any other action or failure to act by the consumer which adversely affects the creditor's security for the account or any right of the creditor in such security.

This subsection does not apply to reverse mortgage transactions.

(c) Change in terms

(1) In general

No open end consumer credit plan under which extensions of credit are secured by a consumer's principal dwelling may contain a provision which permits a creditor to change unilaterally any term required to be disclosed under section 1637a(a) of this title or any other term, except a change in insignificant terms such as the address of the creditor for billing purposes.

(2) Certain changes not precluded

Notwithstanding the provisions of subsection [1] (1), a creditor may make any of the following changes:

(A) Change the index and margin applicable to extensions of credit under such plan if the index used by the creditor is no longer available and the substitute index and margin would result in a substantially similar interest rate.

(B) Prohibit additional extensions of credit or reduce the credit limit applicable to an account under the plan during any period in which the value of the consumer's principal dwelling which secures any outstanding balance is significantly less than the original appraisal value of the dwelling.

(C) Prohibit additional extensions of credit or reduce the credit limit applicable to the account during any period in which the creditor has reason to believe that the consumer will be unable to comply with the repayment requirements of the account due to a material change in the consumer's financial circumstances.

(D) Prohibit additional extensions of credit or reduce the credit limit applicable to the account during any period in which the consumer is in default with respect to any material obligation of the consumer under the agreement.

(E) Prohibit additional extensions of credit or reduce the credit limit applicable to the account during any period in which—

(i) the creditor is precluded by government action from imposing the annual percentage rate provided for in the account agreement; or

(ii) any government action is in effect which adversely affects the priority of the creditor's security interest in the account to the extent that the value of the creditor's secured interest in the property is less than 120 percent of the amount of the credit limit applicable to the account.

(F) Any change that will benefit the consumer.

(3) Material obligations

Upon the request of the consumer and at the time an agreement is entered into by a consumer to open an account under an open end consumer credit plan under which extensions of credit are secured by the consumer's principal dwelling, the consumer shall be given a list of the categories of contract obligations which are deemed by the creditor to be material obligations of the consumer under the agreement for purposes of paragraph (2)(D).

(4) Consumer benefit

(A) In general

For purposes of paragraph (2)(F), a change shall be deemed to benefit the consumer if the change is unequivocally beneficial to the borrower and the change is beneficial through the entire term of the agreement.

(B) Bureau categorization

The Bureau may, by regulation, determine categories of changes that benefit the consumer.

(d) Terms changed after application

If any term or condition described in section 1637a(a) of this title which is disclosed to a consumer in connection with an application to open an account under an open end consumer credit plan described in such section (other than a variable feature of the plan) changes before the account is opened, and if, as a result of such change, the consumer elects not to enter into the plan agreement, the creditor shall refund all fees paid by the consumer in connection with such application.

(e) Additional requirements relating to refunds and imposition of nonrefundable fees

(1) In general

No nonrefundable fee may be imposed by a creditor or any other person in connection with any application by a consumer to establish an account under any open end consumer credit plan which provides for extensions of credit which are secured by a consumer's principal dwelling before the end of the 3-day period beginning on the date such consumer receives the disclosure required under section 1637a(a) of this title and the pamphlet required under section 1637a(e) of this title with respect to such application.

(2) Constructive receipt

For purposes of determining when a nonrefundable fee may be imposed in accordance with this subsection if the disclosures and pamphlet referred to in paragraph (1) are mailed to the consumer, the date of the receipt of the disclosures by such consumer shall be deemed to be 3 business days after the date of mailing by the creditor.

(Pub. L. 90–321, title I, §137, as added Pub. L. 100–709, §3, Nov. 23, 1988, 102 Stat. 4731; amended Pub. L. 103–325, title I, §154(c), Sept. 23, 1994, 108 Stat. 2197; Pub. L. 111–203, title X, §1100A(2), July 21, 2010, 124 Stat. 2107.)

EDITORIAL NOTES

AMENDMENTS

2010—Subsec. (c)(4)(B). Pub. L. 111–203 substituted "Bureau" for "Board" in heading and text.

1994—Subsec. (b). Pub. L. 103–325 inserted at end "This subsection does not apply to reverse mortgage transactions."

STATUTORY NOTES AND RELATED SUBSIDIARIES

EFFECTIVE DATE OF 2010 AMENDMENT

Amendment by Pub. L. 111–203 effective on the designated transfer date, see section 1100H of Pub. L. 111–203, set out as a note under section 552a of Title 5, Government Organization and Employees.

EFFECTIVE DATE

For effective date of section, see Regulations; Effective Date note below.

REGULATIONS; EFFECTIVE DATE

For provisions relating to promulgation of regulations to implement amendment by Pub. L. 100–709 [enacting this section], and effective date of such amendment in connection with those regulations, see section 7 of Pub. L. 100–709, set out as a note under section 1637a of this title.

---

¹ So in original. Probably should be "paragraph".

§1648. Reverse mortgages

(a) In general

In addition to the disclosures required under this subchapter, for each reverse mortgage, the creditor shall, not less than 3 days prior to consummation of the transaction, disclose to the consumer in conspicuous type a good faith estimate of the projected total cost of the mortgage to the consumer expressed as a table of annual interest rates. Each annual interest rate shall be based on a projected total future credit extension balance under a projected appreciation rate for the dwelling and a term for the mortgage. The disclosure shall include—

(1) statements of the annual interest rates for not less than 3 projected appreciation rates and not less than 3 credit transaction periods, as determined by the Bureau, including—

(A) a short-term reverse mortgage;

(B) a term equaling the actuarial life expectancy of the consumer; and

(C) such longer term as the Bureau deems appropriate; and

(2) a statement that the consumer is not obligated to complete the reverse mortgage transaction merely because the consumer has received the disclosure required under this section or has signed an application for the reverse mortgage.

(b) Projected total cost

In determining the projected total cost of the mortgage to be disclosed to the consumer under subsection (a), the creditor shall take into account—

(1) any shared appreciation or equity that the lender will, by contract, be entitled to receive;

(2) all costs and charges to the consumer, including the costs of any associated annuity that the consumer elects or is required to purchase as part of the reverse mortgage transaction;

(3) all payments to and for the benefit of the consumer, including, in the case in which an associated annuity is purchased (whether or not required by the lender as a condition of making the reverse mortgage), the annuity payments received by the consumer and financed from the proceeds of the loan, instead of the proceeds used to finance the annuity; and

(4) any limitation on the liability of the consumer under reverse mortgage transactions (such as nonrecourse limits and equity conservation agreements).

(Pub. L. 90–321, title I, §138, as added Pub. L. 103–325, title I, §154(b), Sept. 23, 1994, 108 Stat. 2196; amended Pub. L. 111–203, title X, §1100A(2), July 21, 2010, 124 Stat. 2107.)

EDITORIAL NOTES

AMENDMENTS

2010—Subsec. (a)(1). Pub. L. 111–203 substituted "Bureau" for "Board" in two places.

STATUTORY NOTES AND RELATED SUBSIDIARIES

EFFECTIVE DATE OF 2010 AMENDMENT

Amendment by Pub. L. 111–203 effective on the designated transfer date, see section 1100H of Pub. L. 111–203, set out as a note under section 552a of Title 5, Government Organization and Employees.

§1649. Certain limitations on liability

(a) Limitations on liability

For any closed end consumer credit transaction that is secured by real property or a dwelling, that is subject to this subchapter, and that is consummated before September 30, 1995, a creditor or any assignee of a creditor shall have no civil, administrative, or criminal liability under this subchapter for, and a consumer shall have no extended rescission rights under section 1635(f) of this title with respect to—

    (1) the creditor's treatment, for disclosure purposes, of—

        (A) taxes described in section 1605(d)(3) of this title;

        (B) fees described in section 1605(e)(2) and (5) of this title;

        (C) fees and amounts referred to in the 3rd sentence of section 1605(a) of this title; or

        (D) borrower-paid mortgage broker fees referred to in section 1605(a)(6) of this title;

    (2) the form of written notice used by the creditor to inform the obligor of the rights of the obligor under section 1635 of this title if the creditor provided the obligor with a properly dated form of written notice published and adopted by the Bureau or a comparable written notice, and otherwise complied with all the requirements of this section regarding notice; or

    (3) any disclosure relating to the finance charge imposed with respect to the transaction if the amount or percentage actually disclosed—

        (A) may be treated as accurate for purposes of this subchapter if the amount disclosed as the finance charge does not vary from the actual finance charge by more than $200;

        (B) may, under section 1605(f)(2) of this title, be treated as accurate for purposes of section 1635 of this title; or

        (C) is greater than the amount or percentage required to be disclosed under this subchapter.

(b) Exceptions

Subsection (a) shall not apply to—

    (1) any individual action or counterclaim brought under this subchapter which was filed before June 1, 1995;

    (2) any class action brought under this subchapter for which a final order certifying a class was entered before January 1, 1995;

    (3) the named individual plaintiffs in any class action brought under this subchapter which was filed before June 1, 1995; or

    (4) any consumer credit transaction with respect to which a timely notice of rescission was sent to the creditor before June 1, 1995.

(Pub. L. 90–321, title I, §139, as added Pub. L. 104–29, §4(a), Sept. 30, 1995, 109 Stat. 273; amended Pub. L. 104–208, div. A, title II, §2107(a), Sept. 30, 1996, 110 Stat. 3009–402; Pub. L. 111–203, title X, §1100A(2), July 21, 2010, 124 Stat. 2107.)

EDITORIAL NOTES

AMENDMENTS

2010—Subsec. (a)(2). Pub. L. 111–203 substituted "Bureau" for "Board".

1996—Subsec. (a). Pub. L. 104–208 substituted "For any closed end consumer credit transaction that is secured by real property or a dwelling, that is subject to this subchapter, and" for "For any consumer credit transaction subject to this subchapter".

STATUTORY NOTES AND RELATED SUBSIDIARIES

EFFECTIVE DATE OF 2010 AMENDMENT

Amendment by Pub. L. 111–203 effective on the designated transfer date, see section 1100H of Pub. L. 111–203, set out as a note under section 552a of Title 5, Government Organization and Employees.

EFFECTIVE DATE OF 1996 AMENDMENT

Pub. L. 104–208, div. A, title II, §2107(b), Sept. 30, 1996, 110 Stat. 3009–402, provided that: "The amendment made by subsection (a) [amending this section] shall be effective as of September 30, 1995."

§1650. Preventing unfair and deceptive private educational lending practices and eliminating conflicts of interest

(a) Definitions

As used in this section—

(1) the term "cosigner"—

(A) means any individual who is liable for the obligation of another without compensation, regardless of how designated in the contract or instrument with respect to that obligation, other than an obligation under a private education loan extended to consolidate a consumer's pre-existing private education loans;

(B) includes any person the signature of which is requested as condition to grant credit or to forbear on collection; and

(C) does not include a spouse of an individual described in subparagraph (A), the signature of whom is needed to perfect the security interest in a loan.

(2) the term "covered educational institution"—

(A) means any educational institution that offers a postsecondary educational degree, certificate, or program of study (including any institution of higher education); and

(B) includes an agent, officer, or employee of the educational institution;

(3) the term "gift"—

(A)(i) means any gratuity, favor, discount, entertainment, hospitality, loan, or other item having more than a de minimis monetary value, including services, transportation, lodging, or meals, whether provided in kind, by purchase of a ticket, payment in advance, or reimbursement after the expense has been incurred; and

(ii) includes an item described in clause (i) provided to a family member of an officer, employee, or agent of a covered educational institution, or to any other individual based on that individual's relationship with the officer, employee, or agent, if—

(I) the item is provided with the knowledge and acquiescence of the officer, employee, or agent; and

(II) the officer, employee, or agent has reason to believe the item was provided because of the official position of the officer, employee, or agent; and

(B) does not include—

(i) standard informational material related to a loan, default aversion, default prevention, or financial literacy;

(ii) food, refreshments, training, or informational material furnished to an officer, employee, or agent of a covered educational institution, as an integral part of a training session or through participation in an advisory council that is designed to improve the service of the private educational lender to the covered educational institution, if such training or participation contributes to the professional development of the officer, employee, or agent of the covered educational institution;

(iii) favorable terms, conditions, and borrower benefits on a private education loan provided to a student employed by the covered educational institution, if such terms, conditions, or benefits are not provided because of the student's employment with the covered educational institution;

(iv) the provision of financial literacy counseling or services, including counseling or services provided in coordination with a covered educational institution, to the extent that such counseling or services are not undertaken to secure—

(I) applications for private education loans or private education loan volume;

(II) applications or loan volume for any loan made, insured, or guaranteed under title IV of the Higher Education Act of 1965 (20 U.S.C. 1070 et seq.); or

(III) the purchase of a product or service of a specific private educational lender;

(v) philanthropic contributions to a covered educational institution from a private educational lender that are unrelated to private education loans and are not made in exchange for any advantage related to private education loans; or

(vi) State education grants, scholarships, or financial aid funds administered by or on behalf of a State;

(4) the term "institution of higher education" has the same meaning as in section 102 of the Higher Education Act of 1965 (20 U.S.C. 1002);

(5) the term "postsecondary educational expenses" means any of the expenses that are included as part of the cost of attendance of a student, as defined under section 472 of the Higher Education Act of 1965 (20 U.S.C. 1087ll);

(6) the term "preferred lender arrangement" has the same meaning as in section 151 of the Higher Education Act of 1965 [20 U.S.C. 1019];

(7) the term "private educational lender" means—

(A) a financial institution, as defined in section 1813 of title 12 that solicits, makes, or extends private education loans;

(B) a Federal credit union, as defined in section 1752 of title 12 that solicits, makes, or extends private education loans; and

(C) any other person engaged in the business of soliciting, making, or extending private education loans;

(8) the term "private education loan"—

(A) means a loan provided by a private educational lender that—

(i) is not made, insured, or guaranteed under of [1] title IV of the Higher Education Act of 1965 (20 U.S.C. 1070 et seq.); and

(ii) is issued expressly for postsecondary educational expenses to a borrower, regardless of whether the loan is provided through the educational institution that the subject student attends or directly to the borrower from the private educational lender; and

(B) does not include an extension of credit under an open end consumer credit plan, a reverse mortgage transaction, a residential mortgage transaction, or any other loan that is secured by real property or a dwelling; and

(9) the term "revenue sharing" means an arrangement between a covered educational institution and a private educational lender under which—

(A) a private educational lender provides or issues private education loans with respect to students attending the covered educational institution;

(B) the covered educational institution recommends to students or others the private educational lender or the private education loans of the private educational lender; and

(C) the private educational lender pays a fee or provides other material benefits, including profit sharing, to the covered educational institution in connection with the private education loans provided to students attending the covered educational institution or a borrower acting on behalf of a student.

(b) Prohibition on certain gifts and arrangements

A private educational lender may not, directly or indirectly—

(1) offer or provide any gift to a covered educational institution in exchange for any advantage or consideration provided to such private educational lender related to its private education loan activities; or

(2) engage in revenue sharing with a covered educational institution.

(c) Prohibition on co-branding

A private educational lender may not use the name, emblem, mascot, or logo of the covered educational institution, or other words, pictures, or symbols readily identified with the covered educational institution, in the marketing of private education loans in any way that implies that the covered educational institution endorses the private education loans offered by the private educational lender.

(d) Advisory Board compensation

Any person who is employed in the financial aid office of a covered educational institution, or who otherwise has responsibilities with respect to private education loans or other financial aid of the institution, and who serves on an advisory board, commission, or group established by a private educational lender or group of such lenders shall be prohibited from receiving anything of value from the private educational lender or group of lenders. Nothing in this subsection prohibits the reimbursement of reasonable expenses incurred by an employee of a covered educational institution as part of their service on an advisory board, commission, or group described in this subsection.

(e) Prohibition on prepayment or repayment fees or penalty

It shall be unlawful for any private educational lender to impose a fee or penalty on a borrower for early repayment or prepayment of any private education loan.

(f) Credit card protections for college students

(1) Disclosure required

An institution of higher education shall publicly disclose any contract or other agreement made with a card issuer or creditor for the purpose of marketing a credit card.

(2) Inducements prohibited

No card issuer or creditor may offer to a student at an institution of higher education any tangible item to induce such student to apply for or participate in an open end consumer credit plan offered by such card issuer or creditor, if such offer is made—

(A) on the campus of an institution of higher education;

(B) near the campus of an institution of higher education, as determined by rule of the Bureau; or

(C) at an event sponsored by or related to an institution of higher education.

(3) Sense of the Congress

It is the sense of the Congress that each institution of higher education should consider adopting the following policies relating to credit cards:

(A) That any card issuer that markets a credit card on the campus of such institution notify the institution of the location at which such marketing will take place.

(B) That the number of locations on the campus of such institution at which the marketing of credit cards takes place be limited.

(C) That credit card and debt education and counseling sessions be offered as a regular part of any orientation program for new students of such institution.

(g) Additional protections relating to borrower or cosigner of a private education loan

(1) Prohibition on automatic default in case of death or bankruptcy of non-student obligor

With respect to a private education loan involving a student obligor and 1 or more cosigners, the creditor shall not declare a default or accelerate the debt against the student obligor on the sole basis of a bankruptcy or death of a cosigner.

(2) Cosigner release in case of death of borrower

(A) Release of cosigner

The holder of a private education loan, when notified of the death of a student obligor, shall release within a reasonable timeframe any cosigner from the obligations of the cosigner under the private education loan.

(B) Notification of release

A holder or servicer of a private education loan, as applicable, shall within a reasonable time-frame notify any cosigners for the private education loan if a cosigner is released from the obligations of the cosigner for the private education loan under this paragraph.

(C) Designation of individual to act on behalf of the borrower

Any lender that extends a private education loan shall provide the student obligor an option to designate an individual to have the legal authority to act on behalf of the student obligor with respect to the private education loan in the event of the death of the student obligor.

(Pub. L. 90–321, title I, §140, as added Pub. L. 110–315, title X, §1011(a), Aug. 14, 2008, 122 Stat. 3479; amended Pub. L. 111–24, title III, §304, May 22, 2009, 123 Stat. 1749; Pub. L. 111–203, title X, §1100A(2), July 21, 2010, 124 Stat. 2107; Pub. L. 115–174, title VI, §601(a), May 24, 2018, 132 Stat. 1365.)

months after Aug. 14, 2008, see section 1003(b) of Pub. L. 110–315, set out as an Effective Date of 2008 Amendment note under section 1638 of this title. Such regulations were issued effective Sept. 14, 2009, with compliance optional until Feb. 14, 2010.

[1] *So in original. The word "of" probably should not appear.*

§1651. Procedure for timely settlement of estates of decedent obligors

The Bureau, in consultation with the Bureau [1] and each other agency referred to in section 1607(a) of this title, shall prescribe regulations to require any creditor, with respect to any credit card account under an open end consumer credit plan, to establish procedures to ensure that any administrator of an estate of any deceased obligor with respect to such account can resolve outstanding credit balances in a timely manner.

(Pub. L. 90–321, title I, §140A, as added Pub. L. 111–24, title V, §504(a), May 22, 2009, 123 Stat. 1756; amended Pub. L. 111–203, title X, §1100A(2), (3), July 21, 2010, 124 Stat. 2107.)

EDITORIAL NOTES

AMENDMENTS

2010—Pub. L. 111–203, §1100A(3), substituted "the Bureau" for "the Federal Trade Commission".
Pub. L. 111–203, §1100A(2), substituted "The Bureau" for "The Board".

STATUTORY NOTES AND RELATED SUBSIDIARIES

EFFECTIVE DATE OF 2010 AMENDMENT

Amendment by Pub. L. 111–203 effective on the designated transfer date, see section 1100H of Pub. L. 111–203, set out as a note under section 552a of Title 5, Government Organization and Employees.

EFFECTIVE DATE

Section effective 9 months after May 22, 2009, except as otherwise specifically provided, see section 3 of Pub. L. 111–24, set out as an Effective Date of 2009 Amendment note under section 1602 of this title.

[1] *So in original.*

PART C—CREDIT ADVERTISING AND LIMITS ON CREDIT CARD FEES

§1661. Catalogs and multiple-page advertisements

For the purposes of this part, a catalog or other multiple-page advertisement shall be considered a single advertisement if it clearly and conspicuously displays a credit terms table on which the information required to be stated under this part is clearly set forth.

(Pub. L. 90–321, title I, §141, May 29, 1968, 82 Stat. 158.)

STATUTORY NOTES AND RELATED SUBSIDIARIES

EFFECTIVE DATE

Pub. L. 90–321, title V, §504(b), May 29, 1968, 82 Stat. 167, provided that chapter 3 of title I, which enacted sections 1661 to 1665 of this title, is effective July 1, 1969.

§1662. Advertising of downpayments and installments

No advertisement to aid, promote, or assist directly or indirectly any extension of consumer credit may state
(1) that a specific periodic consumer credit amount or installment amount can be arranged, unless the creditor usually and customarily arranges credit payments or installments for that period and in that amount.

(2) that a specified downpayment is required in connection with any extension of consumer credit, unless the creditor usually and customarily arranges downpayments in that amount.

(Pub. L. 90–321, title I, §142, May 29, 1968, 82 Stat. 158.)

§1663. Advertising of open end credit plans

No advertisement to aid, promote, or assist directly or indirectly the extension of consumer credit under an open end credit plan may set forth any of the specific terms of that plan unless it also clearly and conspicuously sets forth all of the following items:

(1) Any minimum or fixed amount which could be imposed.

(2) In any case in which periodic rates may be used to compute the finance charge, the periodic rates expressed as annual percentage rates.

(3) Any other term that the Bureau may by regulation require to be disclosed.

(Pub. L. 90–321, title I, §143, May 29, 1968, 82 Stat. 158; Pub. L. 96–221, title VI, §§613(f), 619(a), Mar. 31, 1980, 94 Stat. 177, 183; Pub. L. 111–203, title X, §1100A(2), July 21, 2010, 124 Stat. 2107.)

EDITORIAL NOTES

AMENDMENTS

2010—Par. (3). Pub. L. 111–203 substituted "Bureau" for "Board".

1980—Pub. L. 96–221 in existing introductory text struck out applicability of rate determined under section 1637(a)(5) of this title, and amended section generally substituting items setting forth minimum or fixed amount, etc., set out in pars. (1) to (3), for items time period, etc., set out in pars. (1) to (5).

STATUTORY NOTES AND RELATED SUBSIDIARIES

EFFECTIVE DATE OF 2010 AMENDMENT

Amendment by Pub. L. 111–203 effective on the designated transfer date, see section 1100H of Pub. L. 111–203, set out as a note under section 552a of Title 5, Government Organization and Employees.

EFFECTIVE DATE OF 1980 AMENDMENT

Amendment by Pub. L. 96–221 effective on expiration of two years and six months after Mar. 31, 1980, with all regulations, forms, and clauses required to be prescribed to be promulgated at least one year prior to such effective date, and allowing any creditor to comply with any amendments, in accordance with the regulations, forms, and clauses prescribed by the Board prior to such effective date, see section 625 of Pub. L. 96–221, set out as a note under section 1602 of this title.

§1664. Advertising of credit other than open end plans

(a) Exclusion of open end credit plans

Except as provided in subsection (b), this section applies to any advertisement to aid, promote, or assist directly or indirectly any consumer credit sale, loan, or other extension of credit subject to the provisions of this subchapter, other than an open end credit plan.

(b) Advertisements of residential real estate

The provisions of this section do not apply to advertisements of residential real estate except to the extent that the Bureau may by regulation require.

(c) Rate of finance charge expressed as annual percentage rate

If any advertisement to which this section applies states the rate of a finance charge, the advertisement shall state the rate of that charge expressed as an annual percentage rate.

(d) Requisite disclosures in advertisement

If any advertisement to which this section applies states the amount of the downpayment, if any, the amount of any installment payment, the dollar amount of any finance charge, or the number of installments or the period of repayment, then the advertisement shall state all of the following items:

(1) The downpayment, if any.

(2) The terms of repayment.

(3) The rate of the finance charge expressed as an annual percentage rate.

(e) Credit transaction secured by principal dwelling of consumer

Each advertisement to which this section applies that relates to a consumer credit transaction that is secured by the principal dwelling of a consumer in which the extension of credit may exceed the fair market value of the dwelling, and which advertisement is disseminated in paper form to the public or through the Internet, as opposed to by radio or television, shall clearly and conspicuously state that—

(1) the interest on the portion of the credit extension that is greater than the fair market value of the dwelling is not tax deductible for Federal income tax purposes; and

(2) the consumer should consult a tax adviser for further information regarding the deductibility of interest and charges.

(Pub. L. 90–321, title I, §144, May 29, 1968, 82 Stat. 158; Pub. L. 96–221, title VI, §619(b), Mar. 31, 1980, 94 Stat. 183; Pub. L. 109–8, title XIII, §1302(b)(2), Apr. 20, 2005, 119 Stat. 209; Pub. L. 111–203, title X, §1100A(2), July 21, 2010, 124 Stat. 2107.)

Editorial Notes

Amendments

2010—Subsec. (b). Pub. L. 111–203 substituted "Bureau" for "Board".
2005—Subsec. (e). Pub. L. 109–8 added subsec. (e).
1980—Subsec. (d). Pub. L. 97–221 substituted items setting forth downpayment, etc., set out in pars. (1) to (3), for items setting forth cash price or amount of loan, etc., set out in pars. (1) to (4).

Statutory Notes and Related Subsidiaries

Effective Date of 2010 Amendment

Amendment by Pub. L. 111–203 effective on the designated transfer date, see section 1100H of Pub. L. 111–203, set out as a note under section 552a of Title 5, Government Organization and Employees.

Effective Date of 2005 Amendment

Amendment by Pub. L. 109–8 effective 180 days after Apr. 20, 2005, and not applicable with respect to cases commenced under Title 11, Bankruptcy, before such effective date, except as otherwise provided, see section 1501 of Pub. L. 109–8, set out as a note under section 101 of Title 11.

Effective Date of 1980 Amendment

Amendment by Pub. L. 96–221 effective on expiration of two years and six months after Mar. 31, 1980, with all regulations, forms, and clauses required to be prescribed to be promulgated at least one year prior to such effective date, and allowing any creditor to comply with any amendments, in accordance with the regulations, forms, and clauses prescribed by the Board prior to such effective date, see section 625 of Pub. L. 96–221, set out as a note under section 1602 of this title.

§1665. Nonliability of advertising media

There is no liability under this part on the part of any owner or personnel, as such, of any medium in which an advertisement appears or through which it is disseminated.

(Pub. L. 90–321, title I, §145, May 29, 1968, 82 Stat. 159.)

§1665a. Use of annual percentage rate in oral disclosures; exceptions

In responding orally to any inquiry about the cost of credit, a creditor, regardless of the method used to compute finance charges, shall state rates only in terms of the annual percentage rate, except that in the case of an open end credit plan, the periodic rate also may be stated and, in the case of an other than open end credit plan where a major component of the finance charge consists of interest computed at a simple annual rate, the simple annual rate also may be stated. The Bureau may, by regulation, modify the requirements of this section or provide an exception from this section for a transaction or class of transactions for which the creditor cannot determine in advance the applicable annual percentage rate.

(Pub. L. 90–321, title I, §146, as added Pub. L. 93–495, title IV, §401(a), Oct. 28, 1974, 88 Stat. 1517; amended Pub. L. 96–221, title VI, §623(a), Mar. 31, 1980, 94 Stat. 185; Pub. L. 111–203, title X, §1100A(2), July 21, 2010, 124 Stat. 2107.)

AMENDMENTS

2010—Pub. L. 111–203 substituted "Bureau" for "Board".

1980—Pub. L. 96–221 substituted provisions relating to use of annual percentage rate in oral disclosures by creditors, for provisions setting forth requirements for advertisements concerning consumer credit repayable in more than four installments.

EFFECTIVE DATE OF 2010 AMENDMENT

Amendment by Pub. L. 111–203 effective on the designated transfer date, see section 1100H of Pub. L. 111–203, set out as a note under section 552a of Title 5, Government Organization and Employees.

EFFECTIVE DATE OF 1980 AMENDMENT

Amendment by Pub. L. 96–221 effective on expiration of two years and six months after Mar. 31, 1980, with all regulations, forms, and clauses required to be prescribed to be promulgated at least one year prior to such effective date, and allowing any creditor to comply with any amendments, in accordance with the regulations, forms, and clauses prescribed by the Board prior to such effective date, see section 625 of Pub. L. 96–221, set out as a note under section 1602 of this title.

EFFECTIVE DATE

Pub. L. 93–495, title IV, §416, Oct. 28, 1974, 88 Stat. 1521, provided that: "This title [enacting this section and sections 1614 and 1645 of this title, amending sections 1603, 1607, 1635, 1637, 1640, and 1644 of this title, and enacting provision set out as a note under section 1640 of this title] takes effect upon the date of its enactment [Oct. 28, 1974], except that sections 409 [amending section 1631 of this title] and 411 [amending section 1637 of this title] take effect upon the expiration of one year after the date of its enactment [Oct. 28, 1974]."

§1665b. Advertising of open end consumer credit plans secured by consumer's principal dwelling

(a) In general

If any advertisement to aid, promote, or assist, directly or indirectly, the extension of consumer credit through an open end consumer credit plan under which extensions of credit are secured by the consumer's principal dwelling states, affirmatively or negatively, any of the specific terms of the plan, including any periodic payment amount required under such plan, such advertisement shall also clearly and conspicuously set forth the following information, in such form and manner as the Bureau may require:

(1) Loan fees and opening cost estimates

Any loan fee the amount of which is determined as a percentage of the credit limit applicable to an account under the plan and an estimate of the aggregate amount of other fees for opening the account, based on the creditor's experience with the plan and stated as a single amount or as a reasonable range.

(2) Periodic rates

In any case in which periodic rates may be used to compute the finance charge, the periodic rates expressed as an annual percentage rate.

(3) Highest annual percentage rate

The highest annual percentage rate which may be imposed under the plan.

(4) Other information

Any other information the Bureau may by regulation require.

(b) Tax deductibility

(1) In general

If any advertisement described in subsection (a) contains a statement that any interest expense incurred with respect to the plan is or may be tax deductible, the advertisement shall not be misleading with respect to such deductibility.

(2) Credit in excess of fair market value

Each advertisement described in subsection (a) that relates to an extension of credit that may exceed the fair market value of the dwelling, and which advertisement is disseminated in paper form to the public or through the Internet, as opposed to by radio or television, shall include a clear and conspicuous statement that—

(A) the interest on the portion of the credit extension that is greater than the fair market value of the dwelling is not tax deductible for Federal income tax purposes; and

(B) the consumer should consult a tax adviser for further information regarding the deductibility of interest and charges.

(c) Certain terms prohibited

No advertisement described in subsection (a) with respect to any home equity account may refer to such loan as "free money" or use other terms determined by the Bureau by regulation to be misleading.

(d) Discounted initial rate

(1) In general

If any advertisement described in subsection (a) includes an initial annual percentage rate that is not determined by the index or formula used to make later interest rate adjustments, the advertisement shall also state with equal prominence the current annual percentage rate that would have been applied using the index or formula if such initial rate had not been offered.

(2) Quoted rate must be reasonably current

The annual percentage rate required to be disclosed under the paragraph (1) rate must be current as of a reasonable time given the media involved.

(3) Period during which initial rate is in effect

Any advertisement to which paragraph (1) applies shall also state the period of time during which the initial annual percentage rate referred to in such paragraph will be in effect.

(e) Balloon payment

If any advertisement described in subsection (a) contains a statement regarding the minimum monthly payment under the plan, the advertisement shall also disclose, if applicable, the fact that the plan includes a balloon payment.

(f) "Balloon payment" defined

For purposes of this section and section 1637a of this title, the term "balloon payment" means, with respect to any open end consumer credit plan under which extensions of credit are secured by the consumer's principal dwelling, any repayment option under which—

(1) the account holder is required to repay the entire amount of any outstanding balance as of a specified date or at the end of a specified period of time, as determined in accordance with the terms of the agreement pursuant to which such credit is extended; and

(2) the aggregate amount of the minimum periodic payments required would not fully amortize such outstanding balance by such date or at the end of such period.

(Pub. L. 90–321, title I, §147, as added Pub. L. 100–709, §2(c), Nov. 23, 1988, 102 Stat. 4730; amended Pub. L. 109–8, title XIII, §1302(a)(2), Apr. 20, 2005, 119 Stat. 208; Pub. L. 111–203, title X, §1100A(2), July 21, 2010, 124 Stat. 2107.)

EDITORIAL NOTES

AMENDMENTS

2010—Subsecs. (a), (c). Pub. L. 111–203 substituted "Bureau" for "Board" wherever appearing.

2005—Subsec. (b). Pub. L. 109–8 designated existing provisions as par. (1), inserted par. heading, and added par. (2).

STATUTORY NOTES AND RELATED SUBSIDIARIES

EFFECTIVE DATE OF 2010 AMENDMENT

Amendment by Pub. L. 111–203 effective on the designated transfer date, see section 1100H of Pub. L. 111–203, set out as a note under section 552a of Title 5, Government Organization and Employees.

EFFECTIVE DATE OF 2005 AMENDMENT

Amendment by Pub. L. 109–8 effective 180 days after Apr. 20, 2005, and not applicable with respect to cases commenced under Title 11, Bankruptcy, before such effective date, except as otherwise provided, see section 1501 of Pub. L. 109–8, set out as a note under section 101 of Title 11.

EFFECTIVE DATE

For effective date of section, see Regulations; Effective Date note below.

REGULATIONS; EFFECTIVE DATE

For provisions relating to promulgation of regulations to implement amendment by Pub. L. 100–709 [enacting this section], and effective date of such amendment in connection with those regulations, see section 7 of Pub. L. 100–709, set out as a note under section 1637a of this title.

§1665c. Interest rate reduction on open end consumer credit plans

(a) In general

If a creditor increases the annual percentage rate applicable to a credit card account under an open end consumer credit plan, based on factors including the credit risk of the obligor, market conditions, or other factors, the creditor shall consider changes in such factors in subsequently determining whether to reduce the annual percentage rate for such obligor.

(b) Requirements

With respect to any credit card account under an open end consumer credit plan, the creditor shall—

(1) maintain reasonable methodologies for assessing the factors described in subsection (a);

(2) not less frequently than once every 6 months, review accounts as to which the annual percentage rate has been increased since January 1, 2009, to assess whether such factors have changed (including whether any risk has declined);

(3) reduce the annual percentage rate previously increased when a reduction is indicated by the review; and

(4) in the event of an increase in the annual percentage rate, provide in the written notice required under section 1637(i) of this title a statement of the reasons for the increase.

(c) Rule of construction

This section shall not be construed to require a reduction in any specific amount.

(d) Rulemaking

The Bureau [1] shall issue final rules not later than 9 months after May 22, 2009, to implement the requirements of and evaluate compliance with this section, and subsections (a), (b), and (c) shall become effective 15 months after May 22, 2009.

(Pub. L. 90–321, title I, §148, as added Pub. L. 111–24, title I, §101(c), May 22, 2009, 123 Stat. 1737; amended Pub. L. 111–203, title X, §1100A(2), July 21, 2010, 124 Stat. 2107.)

EDITORIAL NOTES

AMENDMENTS

2010—Subsec. (d). Pub. L. 111–203 substituted "Bureau" for "Board".

STATUTORY NOTES AND RELATED SUBSIDIARIES

EFFECTIVE DATE OF 2010 AMENDMENT

Amendment by Pub. L. 111–203 effective on the designated transfer date, see section 1100H of Pub. L. 111–203, set out as a note under section 552a of Title 5, Government Organization and Employees.

EFFECTIVE DATE

Section effective 9 months after May 22, 2009, except as otherwise specifically provided, see section 3 of Pub. L. 111–24, set out as an Effective Date of 2009 Amendment note under section 1602 of this title.

[1] So in original. Probably should be "Board".

§1665d. Reasonable penalty fees on open end consumer credit plans

(a) In general

The amount of any penalty fee or charge that a card issuer may impose with respect to a credit card account under an open end consumer credit plan in connection with any omission with respect to, or violation of, the cardholder agreement, including any late payment fee, over-the-limit fee, or any other penalty fee or charge, shall be reasonable and proportional to such omission or violation.

(b) Rulemaking required

The Bureau, in consultation with the Comptroller of the Currency, the Board of Directors of the Federal Deposit Insurance Corporation, the Director of the Office of Thrift Supervision, and the National Credit Union Administration Board, shall issue final rules not later than 9 months after May 22, 2009, to establish standards for assessing whether the amount of any penalty fee or charge described under subsection (a) is reasonable and proportional to the omission or violation to which the fee or charge relates. Subsection (a) shall become effective 15 months after May 22, 2009.

(c) Considerations

In issuing rules required by this section, the Bureau shall consider—

(1) the cost incurred by the creditor from such omission or violation;
(2) the deterrence of such omission or violation by the cardholder;
(3) the conduct of the cardholder; and
(4) such other factors as the Bureau may deem necessary or appropriate.

(d) Differentiation permitted

In issuing rules required by this subsection, the Bureau may establish different standards for different types of fees and charges, as appropriate.

(e) Safe harbor rule authorized

The Bureau, in consultation with the Comptroller of the Currency, the Board of Directors of the Federal Deposit Insurance Corporation, the Director of the Office of Thrift Supervision, and the National Credit Union Administration Board, may issue rules to provide an amount for any penalty fee or charge described under subsection (a) that is presumed to be reasonable and proportional to the omission or violation to which the fee or charge relates.

(Pub. L. 90–321, title I, §149, as added Pub. L. 111–24, title I, §102(b)(1), May 22, 2009, 123 Stat. 1740; amended Pub. L. 111–203, title X, §1100A(2), July 21, 2010, 124 Stat. 2107.)

EDITORIAL NOTES

AMENDMENTS

2010—Subsecs. (b) to (e). Pub. L. 111–203, §1100A(2), which directed amendment of this section by substituting "Bureau" for "Board" wherever appearing, was executed by making the substitution for "Board" the first time appearing in subsecs. (b) and (e), and wherever appearing in subsecs. (c) and (d), to reflect the probable intent of Congress.

STATUTORY NOTES AND RELATED SUBSIDIARIES

EFFECTIVE DATE OF 2010 AMENDMENT

Amendment by Pub. L. 111–203 effective on the designated transfer date, see section 1100H of Pub. L. 111–203, set out as a note under section 552a of Title 5, Government Organization and Employees.

EFFECTIVE DATE

Section effective 9 months after May 22, 2009, except as otherwise specifically provided, see section 3 of Pub. L. 111–24, set out as an Effective Date of 2009 Amendment note under section 1602 of this title.

§1665e. Consideration of ability to repay

A card issuer may not open any credit card account for any consumer under an open end consumer credit plan, or increase any credit limit applicable to such account, unless the card issuer considers the ability of the consumer to make the required payments under the terms of such account.

(Pub. L. 90–321, title I, §150, as added Pub. L. 111–24, title I, §109(a), May 22, 2009, 123 Stat. 1743.)

STATUTORY NOTES AND RELATED SUBSIDIARIES

EFFECTIVE DATE

Section effective 9 months after May 22, 2009, except as otherwise specifically provided, see section 3 of Pub. L. 111–24, set out as an Effective Date of 2009 Amendment note under section 1602 of this title.

§1666. Correction of billing errors

(a) Written notice by obligor to creditor; time for and contents of notice; procedure upon receipt of notice by creditor

If a creditor, within sixty days after having transmitted to an obligor a statement of the obligor's account in connection with an extension of consumer credit, receives at the address disclosed under section 1637(b)(10) of this title a written notice (other than notice on a payment stub or other payment medium supplied by the creditor if the creditor so stipulates with the disclosure required under section 1637(a)(7) of this title) from the obligor in which the obligor—

(1) sets forth or otherwise enables the creditor to identify the name and account number (if any) of the obligor,

(2) indicates the obligor's belief that the statement contains a billing error and the amount of such billing error, and

(3) sets forth the reasons for the obligor's belief (to the extent applicable) that the statement contains a billing error,

the creditor shall, unless the obligor has, after giving such written notice and before the expiration of the time limits herein specified, agreed that the statement was correct—

(A) not later than thirty days after the receipt of the notice, send a written acknowledgment thereof to the obligor, unless the action required in subparagraph (B) is taken within such thirty-day period, and

(B) not later than two complete billing cycles of the creditor (in no event later than ninety days) after the receipt of the notice and prior to taking any action to collect the amount, or any part thereof, indicated by the obligor under paragraph (2) either—

(i) make appropriate corrections in the account of the obligor, including the crediting of any finance charges on amounts erroneously billed, and transmit to the obligor a notification of such corrections and the creditor's explanation of any change in the amount indicated by the obligor under paragraph (2) and, if any such change is made and the obligor so requests, copies of documentary evidence of the obligor's indebtedness; or

(ii) send a written explanation or clarification to the obligor, after having conducted an investigation, setting forth to the extent applicable the reasons why the creditor believes the account of the obligor was correctly shown in the statement and, upon request of the obligor, provide copies of documentary evidence of the obligor's indebtedness. In the case of a billing error where the obligor alleges that the creditor's billing statement reflects goods not delivered to the obligor or his designee in accordance with the agreement made at the time of the transaction, a creditor may not construe such amount to be correctly shown unless he determines that such goods were actually delivered, mailed, or otherwise sent to the obligor and provides the obligor with a statement of such determination.

After complying with the provisions of this subsection with respect to an alleged billing error, a creditor has no further responsibility under this section if the obligor continues to make substantially the same allegation with respect to such error.

(b) Billing error

For the purpose of this section, a "billing error" consists of any of the following:

(1) A reflection on a statement of an extension of credit which was not made to the obligor or, if made, was not in the amount reflected on such statement.

(2) A reflection on a statement of an extension of credit for which the obligor requests additional clarification including documentary evidence thereof.

(3) A reflection on a statement of goods or services not accepted by the obligor or his designee or not delivered to the obligor or his designee in accordance with the agreement made at the time of a transaction.

(4) The creditor's failure to reflect properly on a statement a payment made by the obligor or a credit issued to the obligor.

(5) A computation error or similar error of an accounting nature of the creditor on a statement.

(6) Failure to transmit the statement required under section 1637(b) of this title to the last address of the obligor which has been disclosed to the creditor, unless that address was furnished less than twenty days before the end of the billing cycle for which the statement is required.

(7) Any other error described in regulations of the Bureau.

(c) Action by creditor to collect amount or any part thereof regarded by obligor to be a billing error

For the purposes of this section, "action to collect the amount, or any part thereof, indicated by an obligor under paragraph (2)" does not include the sending of statements of account, which may include finance charges on amounts in dispute, to the obligor following written notice from the obligor as specified under subsection (a), if—

(1) the obligor's account is not restricted or closed because of the failure of the obligor to pay the amount indicated under paragraph (2) of subsection (a), and

(2) the creditor indicates the payment of such amount is not required pending the creditor's compliance with this section.

Nothing in this section shall be construed to prohibit any action by a creditor to collect any amount which has not been indicated by the obligor to contain a billing error.

(d) Restricting or closing by creditor of account regarded by obligor to contain a billing error

Pursuant to regulations of the Bureau, a creditor operating an open end consumer credit plan may not, prior to the sending of the written explanation or clarification required under paragraph (B)(ii), restrict or close an account with respect to which the obligor has indicated pursuant to subsection (a) that he believes such account to contain a billing error solely because of the obligor's failure to pay the amount indicated to be in error. Nothing in this subsection shall be deemed to prohibit a creditor from applying against the credit limit on the obligor's account the amount indicated to be in error.

(e) Effect of noncompliance with requirements by creditor

Any creditor who fails to comply with the requirements of this section or section 1666a of this title forfeits any right to collect from the obligor the amount indicated by the obligor under paragraph (2) of subsection (a) of this section, and any finance charges thereon, except that the amount required to be forfeited under this subsection may not exceed $50.

(Pub. L. 90–321, title I, §161, as added Pub. L. 93–495, title III, §306, Oct. 28, 1974, 88 Stat. 1512; amended Pub. L. 96–221, title VI §§613(g), 620, Mar. 31, 1980, 94 Stat. 177, 184; Pub. L. 111–203, title X, §§1087, 1100A(2), July 21, 2010, 124 Stat. 2086, 2107.)

EDITORIAL NOTES

CODIFICATION

Pub L. 111–203, §1100A(2), which directed the substitution of "Bureau" for "Board" wherever appearing in title I of Pub. L. 90–321, was executed to this section, which is section 161 of title I of Pub. L. 90–321. Section 1087 of Pub. L. 111–203, which directed the making of an identical amendment in title III of Pub. L. 93–495, which added this section to title I of Pub. L. 90–321, has not been executed.

AMENDMENTS

2010—Subsecs. (b)(7), (d). Pub. L. 111–203, §1100A(2), substituted "Bureau" for "Board". See Codification note above.

1980—Subsec. (a). Pub. L. 96–221, §613(g), substituted "(b)(10)" for "(b)(11)" and "(a)(7)" for "(a)(8)". Subsec. (b)(6), (7). Pub. L. 96–221, §620(a), added par. (6) and redesignated former par. (6) as (7). Subsec. (c). Pub. L. 96–221, §620(b), inserted provisions respecting finance charges on amounts in dispute.

STATUTORY NOTES AND RELATED SUBSIDIARIES

EFFECTIVE DATE OF 2010 AMENDMENT

Amendment by Pub. L. 111–203 effective on the designated transfer date, see section 1100H of Pub. L. 111–203, set out as a note under section 552a of Title 5, Government Organization and Employees.

EFFECTIVE DATE OF 1980 AMENDMENT

Amendment by Pub. L. 96–221 effective on expiration of two years and six months after Mar. 31, 1980, with all regulations, forms, and clauses required to be prescribed to be promulgated at least one year prior to such effective date, and allowing any creditor to comply with any amendments, in accordance with the regulations, forms, and clauses prescribed by the Board prior to such effective date, see section 625 of Pub. L. 96–221, set out as a note under section 1602 of this title.

EFFECTIVE DATE

Pub. L. 93–495, title III, §308, Oct. 28, 1974, 88 Stat. 1517, provided that: "This title [enacting this section and sections 1666a to 1666j of this title, amending sections 1601, 1602, 1610, 1631, 1632, and 1637 of this title, and enacting provision set out as a note under section 1601 of this title] takes effect upon the expiration of one year after the date of its enactment [Oct. 28, 1974]."

SHORT TITLE

Title III of Pub. L. 93–495, which is classified principally to this part, is known as the "Fair Credit Billing Act". For complete classification of Title III to the Code, see Short Title of 1974 Amendment note set out under section 1601 of this title and Tables.

§1666a. Regulation of credit reports

(a) Reports by creditor on obligor's failure to pay amount regarded as billing error

After receiving a notice from an obligor as provided in section 1666(a) of this title, a creditor or his agent may not directly or indirectly threaten to report to any person adversely on the obligor's credit rating or credit standing because of the obligor's failure to pay the amount indicated by the obligor under section 1666(a)(2) of this title, and such amount may not be reported as delinquent to any third party until the creditor has met the requirements of section 1666 of this title and has allowed the obligor the same number of days (not less than ten) thereafter to make payment as is provided under the credit agreement with the obligor for the payment of undisputed amounts.

(b) Reports by creditor on delinquent amounts in dispute; notification of obligor of parties notified of delinquency

If a creditor receives a further written notice from an obligor that an amount is still in dispute within the time allowed for payment under subsection (a) of this section, a creditor may not report to any third party that the amount of the obligor is delinquent because the obligor has failed to pay an amount which he has indicated under section 1666(a)(2) of this title, unless the creditor also reports that the amount is in dispute and, at the same time, notifies the obligor of the name and address of each party to whom the creditor is reporting information concerning the delinquency.

(c) Reports by creditor of subsequent resolution of delinquent amounts

A creditor shall report any subsequent resolution of any delinquencies reported pursuant to subsection (b) to the parties to whom such delinquencies were initially reported.

(Pub. L. 90–321, title I, §162, as added Pub. L. 93–495, title III, §306, Oct. 28, 1974, 88 Stat. 1513.)

§1666b. Timing of payments

(a) Time to make payments

A creditor may not treat a payment on a credit card account under an open end consumer credit plan as late for any purpose, unless the creditor has adopted reasonable procedures designed to ensure that each periodic statement including the information required by section 1637(b) of this title is mailed or delivered to the consumer not later than 21 days before the payment due date.

(b) Grace period

If an open end consumer credit plan provides a time period within which an obligor may repay any portion of the credit extended without incurring an additional finance charge, such additional finance charge may not be imposed with respect to such portion of the credit extended for the billing cycle of which such period is a part, unless a statement which includes the amount upon which the finance charge for the period is based was mailed or delivered to the consumer not later than 21 days before the date specified in the statement by which payment must be made in order to avoid imposition of that finance charge.

(Pub. L. 90–321, title I, §163, as added Pub. L. 93–495, title III, §306, Oct. 28, 1974, 88 Stat. 1514; amended Pub. L. 111–24, title I, §106(b)(1), May 22, 2009, 123 Stat. 1742; Pub. L. 111–93, §2, Nov. 6, 2009, 123 Stat. 2998.)

EDITORIAL NOTES

AMENDMENTS

2009—Pub. L. 111–24 amended section generally, adding provisions relating to late payments and delivery of periodic statements, substituting provisions requiring a 21-day statement delivery period for provisions requiring a 14-day period before the imposition of additional finance charges, and striking provisions relating to excusable cause for creditor's failure to make timely mailing or delivery of periodic statements.

Subsec. (a). Pub. L. 111–93 inserted "a credit card account under" after "payment on".

STATUTORY NOTES AND RELATED SUBSIDIARIES

EFFECTIVE DATE

Pub. L. 111–24, title I, §106(b)(2), May 22, 2009, 123 Stat. 1742, provided that: "Notwithstanding section 3 [see Effective Date of 2009 Amendment note set out under section 1602 of this title], section 163 of the Truth in Lending Act [15 U.S.C. 1666b], as amended by this subsection, shall become effective 90 days after the date of enactment of this Act [May 22, 2009]."

§1666c. Prompt and fair crediting of payments

(a) In general

Payments received from an obligor under an open end consumer credit plan by the creditor shall be posted promptly to the obligor's account as specified in regulations of the Bureau. Such regulations shall prevent a finance charge from being imposed on any obligor if the creditor has received the obligor's payment in readily identifiable form, by 5:00 p.m. on the date on which such payment is due, in the amount, manner, and location indicated by the creditor to avoid the imposition thereof.

(b) Application of payments

(1) In general

Upon receipt of a payment from a cardholder, the card issuer shall apply amounts in excess of the minimum payment amount first to the card balance bearing the highest rate of interest, and then to each successive balance bearing the next highest rate of interest, until the payment is exhausted.

(2) Clarification relating to certain deferred interest arrangements

A creditor shall allocate the entire amount paid by the consumer in excess of the minimum payment amount to a balance on which interest is deferred during the last 2 billing cycles immediately preceding the expiration of the period during which interest is deferred.

(c) Changes by card issuer

If a card issuer makes a material change in the mailing address, office, or procedures for handling cardholder payments, and such change causes a material delay in the crediting of a cardholder payment made during the 60-day period following the date on which such change took effect, the card issuer may not impose any late fee or finance charge for a late payment on the credit card account to which such payment was credited.

(Pub. L. 90–321, title I, §164, as added Pub. L. 93–495, title III, §306, Oct. 28, 1974, 88 Stat. 1514; amended Pub. L. 111–24, title I, §104, May 22, 2009, 123 Stat. 1741; Pub. L. 111–203, title X, §§1087, 1100A(2), July 21, 2010, 124 Stat. 2086, 2107.)

EDITORIAL NOTES

CODIFICATION

Pub L. 111–203, §1100A(2), which directed the substitution of "Bureau" for "Board" wherever appearing in title I of Pub. L. 90–321, was executed to this section, which is section 164 of title I of Pub. L. 90–321. Section 1087 of Pub. L. 111–203, which directed the making of an identical amendment in title III of Pub. L. 93–495, which added this section to title I of Pub. L. 90–321, has not been executed.

AMENDMENTS

2010—Subsec. (a). Pub. L. 111–203, §1100A(2), substituted "Bureau" for "Board". See Codification note above.

2009—Pub. L. 111–24, §104(1), substituted "Prompt and fair crediting of payments" for "Prompt crediting of payments" in section catchline, designated existing provisions as subsec. (a), and inserted subsec. (a) heading.

Subsec. (a). Pub. L. 111–24, §104(2), (3), inserted ", by 5:00 p.m. on the date on which such payment is due," after "in readily identifiable form" and substituted "manner, and location" for "manner, location, and time".

Subsecs. (b), (c). Pub. L. 111–24, §104(4), added subsecs. (b) and (c).

STATUTORY NOTES AND RELATED SUBSIDIARIES

EFFECTIVE DATE OF 2010 AMENDMENT

Amendment by Pub. L. 111–203 effective on the designated transfer date, see section 1100H of Pub. L. 111–203, set out as a note under section 552a of Title 5, Government Organization and Employees.

EFFECTIVE DATE OF 2009 AMENDMENT

Amendment by Pub. L. 111–24 effective 9 months after May 22, 2009, except as otherwise specifically provided, see section 3 of Pub. L. 111–24, set out as a note under section 1602 of this title.

§1666d. Treatment of credit balances

Whenever a credit balance in excess of $1 is created in connection with a consumer credit transaction through (1) transmittal of funds to a creditor in excess of the total balance due on an account, (2) rebates of unearned finance charges or insurance premiums, or (3) amounts otherwise owed to or held for the benefit of an obligor, the creditor shall—

  (A) credit the amount of the credit balance to the consumer's account;

  (B) refund any part of the amount of the remaining credit balance, upon request of the consumer; and

  (C) make a good faith effort to refund to the consumer by cash, check, or money order any part of the amount of the credit balance remaining in the account for more than six months, except that no further action is required in any case in which the consumer's current location is not known by the creditor and cannot be traced through the consumer's last known address or telephone number.

(Pub. L. 90–321, title I, §165, as added Pub. L. 93–495, title III, §306, Oct. 28, 1974, 88 Stat. 1514; amended Pub. L. 96–221, title VI, §621(a), Mar. 31, 1980, 94 Stat. 184.)

EDITORIAL NOTES

AMENDMENTS

1980—Pub. L. 96–221 substituted provisions relating to duties of creditor whenever a credit balance in excess of $1 is created in connection with a consumer credit transaction, for provisions relating to duties of creditor whenever an obligor transmits funds to creditor in excess of the total balance due on an open end consumer credit account.

STATUTORY NOTES AND RELATED SUBSIDIARIES

EFFECTIVE DATE OF 1980 AMENDMENT

Amendment by Pub. L. 96–221 effective on expiration of two years and six months after Mar. 31, 1980, with all regulations, forms, and clauses required to be prescribed to be promulgated at least one year prior to such effective date, and allowing any creditor to comply with any amendments, in accordance with the regulations, forms, and clauses prescribed by the Board prior to such effective date, see section 625 of Pub. L. 96–221, set out as a note under section 1602 of this title.

§1666e. Notification of credit card issuer by seller of return of goods, etc., by obligor; credit for account of obligor

With respect to any sales transaction where a credit card has been used to obtain credit, where the seller is a person other than the card issuer, and where the seller accepts or allows a return of the goods or forgiveness of a debit for services which were the subject of such sale, the seller shall promptly transmit to the credit card issuer, a credit statement with respect thereto and the credit card issuer shall credit the account of the obligor for the amount of the transaction.

(Pub. L. 90–321, title I, §166, as added Pub. L. 93–495, title III, §306, Oct. 28, 1974, 88 Stat. 1514.)

§1666f. Inducements to cardholders by sellers of cash discounts for payments by cash, check or similar means; finance charge for sales transactions involving cash discounts

(a) Cash discounts

With respect to credit [1] card which may be used for extensions of credit in sales transactions in which the seller is a person other than the card issuer, the card issuer may not, by contract or otherwise, prohibit any such seller from offering a discount to a cardholder to induce the cardholder to pay by cash, check, or similar means rather than use a credit card.

(b) Finance charge

With respect to any sales transaction, any discount from the regular price offered by the seller for the purpose of inducing payment by cash, checks, or other means not involving the use of an open-end credit plan or a credit card shall not constitute a finance charge as determined under section 1605 of this title if such discount is offered to all prospective buyers and its availability is disclosed clearly and conspicuously.

(Pub. L. 90–321, title I, §167, as added Pub. L. 93–495, title III, §306, Oct. 28, 1974, 88 Stat. 1515; amended Pub. L. 94–222, §3(c)(1), Feb. 27, 1976, 90 Stat. 197; Pub. L. 97–25, title I, §101, July 27, 1981, 95 Stat. 144.)

AMENDMENTS

1981—Subsec. (b). Pub. L. 97–25 substituted "With respect to any sales transaction, any discount from the regular price offered by the seller for the purpose of inducing payment by cash, checks, or other means not involving the use of an open-end credit plan or a credit card shall not constitute a finance charge as determined under section 1605 of this title if such discount is offered to all prospective buyers and its availability is disclosed clearly and conspicuously" for "With respect to any sales transaction, any discount not in excess of 5 per centum offered by the seller for the purpose of inducing payment by cash, check, or other means not involving the use of a credit card shall not constitute a finance charge as determined under section 1605 of this title, if such discount is offered to all prospective buyers and its availability is disclosed to all prospective buyers clearly and conspicuously in accordance with regulations of the Board".

1976—Subsec. (a). Pub. L. 94–222 temporarily designated existing provisions as par. (1) and added par. (2). See Termination Date of 1976 Amendment note below.

TERMINATION DATE OF 1976 AMENDMENT

Section 3(c)(2) of Pub. L. 94–222, as amended by Pub. L. 95–630, title XV, §1501, Nov. 10, 1978, 92 Stat. 3713; Pub. L. 97–25, title II, §201, July 27, 1981, 95 Stat. 44, provided that: "The amendments made by paragraph (1) [amending this section] shall cease to be effective on February 27, 1984."

NULLIFICATION OF BOARD RULES AND REGULATIONS UNDER SUBSECTION (B) OF THIS SECTION IN EFFECT ON JULY 26, 1981

Pub. L. 97–25, title I, §103, July 27, 1981, 95 Stat. 144, provided that: "Any rule or regulation of the Board of Governors of the Federal Reserve System pursuant to section 167(b) of the Truth in Lending Act [subsec. (b) of this section], as such section was in effect on the day before the date of enactment of this Act [July 27, 1981], is null and void."

---

[1] So in original. Probably should be preceded by "a".

§1666g. Tie-in services prohibited for issuance of credit card

Notwithstanding any agreement to the contrary, a card issuer may not require a seller, as a condition to participating in a credit card plan, to open an account with or procure any other service from the card issuer or its subsidiary or agent.

(Pub. L. 90–321, title I, §168, as added Pub. L. 93–495, title III, §306, Oct. 28, 1974, 88 Stat. 1515.)

§1666h. Offset of cardholder's indebtedness by issuer of credit card with funds deposited with issuer by cardholder; remedies of creditors under State law not affected

(a) Offset against consumer's funds

A card issuer may not take any action to offset a cardholder's indebtedness arising in connection with a consumer credit transaction under the relevant credit card plan against funds of the cardholder held on deposit with the card issuer unless—

(1) such action was previously authorized in writing by the cardholder in accordance with a credit plan whereby the cardholder agrees periodically to pay debts incurred in his open end credit account by permitting the card issuer periodically to deduct all or a portion of such debt from the cardholder's deposit account, and

(2) such action with respect to any outstanding disputed amount not be taken by the card issuer upon request of the cardholder.

In the case of any credit card account in existence on the effective date of this section, the previous written authorization referred to in clause (1) shall not be required until the date (after such effective date) when such account is renewed, but in no case later than one year after such effective date. Such written authorization shall be deemed to exist if the card issuer has previously notified the cardholder that the use of his credit card account will subject any funds which the card issuer holds in deposit accounts of such cardholder to offset against any amounts due and payable on his credit card account which have not been paid in accordance with the terms of the agreement between the card issuer and the cardholder.

(b) Attachments and levies

This section does not alter or affect the right under State law of a card issuer to attach or otherwise levy upon funds of a cardholder held on deposit with the card issuer if that remedy is constitutionally available to creditors generally.

(Pub. L. 90–321, title I, §169, as added Pub. L. 93–495, title III, §306, Oct. 28, 1974, 88 Stat. 1515.)

EDITORIAL NOTES

REFERENCES IN TEXT

For effective date of this section, referred to in subsec. (a), see Effective Date note set out under section 1666 of this title.

§1666i. Assertion by cardholder against card issuer of claims and defenses arising out of credit card transaction; prerequisites; limitation on amount of claims or defenses

(a) Claims and defenses assertible

Subject to the limitation contained in subsection (b), a card issuer who has issued a credit card to a cardholder pursuant to an open end consumer credit plan shall be subject to all claims (other than tort claims) and defenses arising out of any transaction in which the credit card is used as a method of payment or extension of credit if (1) the obligor has made a good faith attempt to obtain satisfactory resolution of a disagreement or problem relative to the transaction from the person honoring the credit card; (2) the amount of the initial transaction exceeds $50; and (3) the place where the initial transaction occurred was in the same State as the mailing address previously provided by the cardholder or was within 100 miles from such address, except that the limitations set forth in clauses (2) and (3) with respect to an obligor's right to assert claims and defenses against a card issuer shall not be applicable to any transaction in which the person honoring the credit card (A) is the same person as the card issuer, (B) is controlled by the card issuer, (C) is under direct or indirect common control with the card issuer, (D) is a franchised dealer in the card issuer's products or services, or (E) has obtained the order for such transaction through a mail solicitation made by or participated in by the card issuer in which the cardholder is solicited to enter into such transaction by using the credit card issued by the card issuer.

(b) Amount of claims and defenses assertible

The amount of claims or defenses asserted by the cardholder may not exceed the amount of credit outstanding with respect to such transaction at the time the cardholder first notifies the card issuer or the person honoring the credit card of such claim or defense. For the purpose of determining the amount of credit outstanding in the preceding sentence, payments and credits to the cardholder's account are deemed to have been applied, in the order indicated, to the payment of: (1) late charges in the order of their entry to the account; (2) finance charges in order of their entry to the account; and (3) debits to the account other than those set forth above, in the order in which each debit entry to the account was made.

(Pub. L. 90–321, title I, §170, as added Pub. L. 93–495, title III, §306, Oct. 28, 1974, 88 Stat. 1515.)

§1666i–1. Limits on interest rate, fee, and finance charge increases applicable to outstanding balances

(a) In general

In the case of any credit card account under an open end consumer credit plan, no creditor may increase any annual percentage rate, fee, or finance charge applicable to any outstanding balance, except as permitted under subsection (b).

(b) Exceptions

The prohibition under subsection (a) shall not apply to—
 (1) an increase in an annual percentage rate upon the expiration of a specified period of time, provided that—
  (A) prior to commencement of that period, the creditor disclosed to the consumer, in a clear and conspicuous manner, the length of the period and the annual percentage rate that would apply after expiration of the period;
  (B) the increased annual percentage rate does not exceed the rate disclosed pursuant to subparagraph (A); and
  (C) the increased annual percentage rate is not applied to transactions that occurred prior to commencement of the period;

(2) an increase in a variable annual percentage rate in accordance with a credit card agreement that provides for changes in the rate according to operation of an index that is not under the control of the creditor and is available to the general public;

(3) an increase due to the completion of a workout or temporary hardship arrangement by the obligor or the failure of the obligor to comply with the terms of a workout or temporary hardship arrangement, provided that—

(A) the annual percentage rate, fee, or finance charge applicable to a category of transactions following any such increase does not exceed the rate, fee, or finance charge that applied to that category of transactions prior to commencement of the arrangement; and

(B) the creditor has provided the obligor, prior to the commencement of such arrangement, with clear and conspicuous disclosure of the terms of the arrangement (including any increases due to such completion or failure); or

(4) an increase due solely to the fact that a minimum payment by the obligor has not been received by the creditor within 60 days after the due date for such payment, provided that the creditor shall—

(A) include, together with the notice of such increase required under section 1637(i) of this title, a clear and conspicuous written statement of the reason for the increase and that the increase will terminate not later than 6 months after the date on which it is imposed, if the creditor receives the required minimum payments on time from the obligor during that period; and

(B) terminate such increase not later than 6 months after the date on which it is imposed, if the creditor receives the required minimum payments on time during that period.

(c) Repayment of outstanding balance

(1) In general

The creditor shall not change the terms governing the repayment of any outstanding balance, except that the creditor may provide the obligor with one of the methods described in paragraph (2) of repaying any outstanding balance, or a method that is no less beneficial to the obligor than one of those methods.

(2) Methods

The methods described in this paragraph are—

(A) an amortization period of not less than 5 years, beginning on the effective date of the increase set forth in the notice required under section 1637(i) of this title; or

(B) a required minimum periodic payment that includes a percentage of the outstanding balance that is equal to not more than twice the percentage required before the effective date of the increase set forth in the notice required under section 1637(i) of this title.

(d) Outstanding balance defined

For purposes of this section, the term "outstanding balance" means the amount owed on a credit card account under an open end consumer credit plan as of the end of the 14th day after the date on which the creditor provides notice of an increase in the annual percentage rate, fee, or finance charge in accordance with section 1637(i) of this title.

(Pub. L. 90–321, title I, §171, as added Pub. L. 111–24, title I, §101(b)(2), May 22, 2009, 123 Stat. 1736.)

EDITORIAL NOTES

PRIOR PROVISIONS

A prior section 171 of Pub. L. 90–321 was renumbered section 173 and is classified to section 1666j of this title.

STATUTORY NOTES AND RELATED SUBSIDIARIES

EFFECTIVE DATE

Section effective 9 months after May 22, 2009, except as otherwise specifically provided, see section 3 of Pub. L. 111–24, set out as an Effective Date of 2009 Amendment note under section 1602 of this title.

§1666i–2. Additional limits on interest rate increases

(a) Limitation on increases within first year

Except in the case of an increase described in paragraph (1), (2), (3), or (4) of section 1666i–1(b) of this title, no increase in any annual percentage rate, fee, or finance charge on any credit card account under an open end consumer credit plan shall be effective before the end of the 1-year period beginning on the date on which the account is opened.

(b) Promotional rate minimum term

No increase in any annual percentage rate applicable to a credit card account under an open end consumer credit plan that is a promotional rate (as that term is defined by the Bureau) shall be effective before the end of the 6-month period beginning on the date on which the promotional rate takes effect, subject to such reasonable exceptions as the Bureau may establish, by rule.

(Pub. L. 90–321, title I, §172, as added Pub. L. 111–24, title I, §101(d), May 22, 2009, 123 Stat. 1738; amended Pub. L. 111–203, title X, §1100A(2), July 21, 2010, 124 Stat. 2107.)

EDITORIAL NOTES

AMENDMENTS

2010—Subsec. (b). Pub. L. 111–203 substituted "Bureau" for "Board" in two places.

STATUTORY NOTES AND RELATED SUBSIDIARIES

EFFECTIVE DATE OF 2010 AMENDMENT

Amendment by Pub. L. 111–203 effective on the designated transfer date, see section 1100H of Pub. L. 111–203, set out as a note under section 552a of Title 5, Government Organization and Employees.

EFFECTIVE DATE

Section effective 9 months after May 22, 2009, except as otherwise specifically provided, see section 3 of Pub. L. 111–24, set out as an Effective Date of 2009 Amendment note under section 1602 of this title.

§1666j. Applicability of State laws

(a) Consistency of provisions

This part does not annul, alter, or affect, or exempt any person subject to the provisions of this part from complying with, the laws of any State with respect to credit billing practices, except to the extent that those laws are inconsistent with any provision of this part, and then only to the extent of the inconsistency. The Bureau is authorized to determine whether such inconsistencies exist. The Bureau may not determine that any State law is inconsistent with any provision of this part if the Bureau determines that such law gives greater protection to the consumer.

(b) Exemptions by Bureau from credit billing requirements

The Bureau shall by regulation exempt from the requirements of this part any class of credit transactions within any State if it determines that under the law of that State that class of transactions is subject to requirements substantially similar to those imposed under this part or that such law gives greater protection to the consumer, and that there is adequate provision for enforcement.

(c) Finance charge or other charge for credit for sales transactions involving cash discounts

Notwithstanding any other provisions of this subchapter, any discount offered under section 1666f(b) of this title shall not be considered a finance charge or other charge for credit under the usury laws of any State or under the laws of any State relating to disclosure of information in connection with credit transactions, or relating to the types, amounts or rates of charges, or to any element or elements of charges permissible under such laws in connection with the extension or use of credit.

(Pub. L. 90–321, title I, §173, formerly §171, as added Pub. L. 93–495, title III, §306, Oct. 28, 1974, 88 Stat. 1516; amended Pub. L. 94–222, §3(d), Feb. 27, 1976, 90 Stat. 198; renumbered §173, Pub. L. 111–24, title I, §101(b)(1), May 22, 2009, 123 Stat. 1736; Pub. L. 111–203, title X, §§1087, 1100A(2), July 21, 2010, 124 Stat. 2086, 2107.)

EDITORIAL NOTES

CODIFICATION

Pub L. 111–203, §1100A(2), which directed the substitution of "Bureau" for "Board" wherever appearing in title I of Pub. L. 90–321, was executed to this section, which is section 173 of title I of Pub. L. 90–321. Section 1087 of Pub. L. 111–203, which directed the making of an identical amendment in title III of Pub. L. 93–495, which added this section to title I of Pub. L. 90–321, has not been executed.

AMENDMENTS

2010—Subsecs. (a), (b). Pub. L. 111–203, §1100A(2), substituted "Bureau" for "Board" wherever appearing. See Codification note above.

1976—Subsec. (c). Pub. L. 94–222 added subsec. (c).

EFFECTIVE DATE OF 2010 AMENDMENT

Amendment by Pub. L. 111–203 effective on the designated transfer date, see section 1100H of Pub. L. 111–203, set out as a note under section 552a of Title 5, Government Organization and Employees.

PART E—CONSUMER LEASES

§1667. Definitions

For purposes of this part—

(1) The term "consumer lease" means a contract in the form of a lease or bailment for the use of personal property by a natural person for a period of time exceeding four months, and for a total contractual obligation not exceeding $50,000,[1] primarily for personal, family, or household purposes, whether or not the lessee has the option to purchase or otherwise become the owner of the property at the expiration of the lease, except that such term shall not include any credit sale as defined in section 1602(g) [2] of this title. Such term does not include a lease for agricultural, business, or commercial purposes, or to a government or governmental agency or instrumentality, or to an organization.

(2) The term "lessee" means a natural person who leases or is offered a consumer lease.

(3) The term "lessor" means a person who is regularly engaged in leasing, offering to lease, or arranging to lease under a consumer lease.

(4) The term "personal property" means any property which is not real property under the laws of the State where situated at the time offered or otherwise made available for lease.

(5) The terms "security" and "security interest" mean any interest in property which secures payment or performance of an obligation.

(Pub. L. 90–321, title I, §181, as added Pub. L. 94–240, §3, Mar. 23, 1976, 90 Stat. 257; amended Pub. L. 111–203, title X, §1100E(a)(2), July 21, 2010, 124 Stat. 2111.)

EDITORIAL NOTES

REFERENCES IN TEXT

Section 1602(g) of this title, referred to in par. (1), was redesignated section 1602(h) of this title by Pub. L. 111–203, title X, §1100A(1)(A), July 21, 2010, 124 Stat. 2107.

AMENDMENTS

2010—Par. (1). Pub. L. 111–203 substituted "$50,000" for "$25,000".

EFFECTIVE DATE OF 2010 AMENDMENT

Amendment by Pub. L. 111–203 effective on the designated transfer date, see section 1100H of Pub. L. 111–203, set out as a note under section 552a of Title 5, Government Organization and Employees.

EFFECTIVE DATE

Pub. L. 94–240, §6, Mar. 23, 1976, 90 Stat. 261, provided that: "This Act [enacting this section and sections 1667a to 1667e of this title, amending sections 1601 and 1640 of this title, and enacting provisions set out as a note under section 1601 of this title] takes effect one year after the date of its enactment [Mar. 23, 1976]."

ADJUSTMENTS FOR INFLATION

On and after Dec. 31, 2011, dollar amount described in par. (1) of this section to be adjusted annually by the annual percentage increase in the Consumer Price Index for Urban Wage Earners and Clerical Workers, see section 1100E(b) of Pub. L. 111–203, set out as a note under section 1603 of this title.

§1667a. Consumer lease disclosures

Each lessor shall give a lessee prior to the consummation of the lease a dated written statement on which the lessor and lessee are identified setting out accurately and in a clear and conspicuous manner the following information with respect to that lease, as applicable:

(1) A brief description or identification of the leased property;

(2) The amount of any payment by the lessee required at the inception of the lease;

(3) The amount paid or payable by the lessee for official fees, registration, certificate of title, or license fees or taxes;

(4) The amount of other charges payable by the lessee not included in the periodic payments, a description of the charges and that the lessee shall be liable for the differential, if any, between the anticipated fair market value of the leased property and its appraised actual value at the termination of the lease, if the lessee has such liability;

(5) A statement of the amount or method of determining the amount of any liabilities the lease imposes upon the lessee at the end of the term and whether or not the lessee has the option to purchase the leased property and at what price and time;

(6) A statement identifying all express warranties and guarantees made by the manufacturer or lessor with respect to the leased property, and identifying the party responsible for maintaining or servicing the leased property together with a description of the responsibility;

(7) A brief description of insurance provided or paid for by the lessor or required of the lessee, including the types and amounts of the coverages and costs;

(8) A description of any security interest held or to be retained by the lessor in connection with the lease and a clear identification of the property to which the security interest relates;

(9) The number, amount, and due dates or periods of payments under the lease and the total amount of such periodic payments;

(10) Where the lease provides that the lessee shall be liable for the anticipated fair market value of the property on expiration of the lease, the fair market value of the property at the inception of the lease, the aggregate cost of the lease on expiration, and the differential between them; and

(11) A statement of the conditions under which the lessee or lessor may terminate the lease prior to the end of the term and the amount or method of determining any penalty or other charge for delinquency, default, late payments, or early termination.

The disclosures required under this section may be made in the lease contract to be signed by the lessee. The Bureau may provide by regulation that any portion of the information required to be disclosed under this section may be given in the form of estimates where the lessor is not in a position to know exact information.

(Pub. L. 90–321, title I, §182, as added Pub. L. 94–240, §3, Mar. 23, 1976, 90 Stat. 258; amended Pub. L. 111–203, title X, §1100A(2), (10)(B), July 21, 2010, 124 Stat. 2107, 2109.)

EDITORIAL NOTES

AMENDMENTS

2010—Pub. L. 111–203, §1100A(2), (10)(B), made similar amendments, resulting in the substitution of "The Bureau" for "The Board" in concluding provisions.

STATUTORY NOTES AND RELATED SUBSIDIARIES

EFFECTIVE DATE OF 2010 AMENDMENT

Amendment by Pub. L. 111–203 effective on the designated transfer date, see section 1100H of Pub. L. 111–203, set out as a note under section 552a of Title 5, Government Organization and Employees.

§1667b. Lessee's liability on expiration or termination of lease

(a) Estimated residual value of property as basis; presumptions; action by lessor for excess liability; mutually agreeable final adjustment

Where the lessee's liability on expiration of a consumer lease is based on the estimated residual value of the property such estimated residual value shall be a reasonable approximation of the anticipated actual fair market value of the property on lease expiration. There shall be a rebuttable presumption that the estimated residual value is unreasonable to the extent that the estimated residual value exceeds the actual residual value by more than three times the average payment allocable to a monthly period under the lease. In addition, where the lessee has such liability on expiration of a consumer lease there shall be a rebuttable presumption that the lessor's estimated residual value is not in good faith to the extent that the estimated residual value exceeds the actual residual value by more than three times the average payment allocable to a monthly period under the lease and such lessor shall not collect from the lessee the amount of such excess liability on expiration of a consumer lease unless the lessor brings a successful action with respect to such excess liability. In all actions, the lessor shall pay the lessee's reasonable attorney's fees. The presumptions stated in this section shall not apply to the extent the excess of estimated over actual residual value is due to physical damage to the property beyond reasonable wear and use, or to excessive use, and the lease may set standards for such wear and use if such standards are not unreasonable. Nothing in this subsection shall preclude the right of a willing lessee to make any mutually agreeable final adjustment with respect to such excess residual liability, provided such an agreement is reached after termination of the lease.

(b) Penalties and charges for delinquency, default, or early termination

Penalties or other charges for delinquency, default, or early termination may be specified in the lease but only at an amount which is reasonable in the light of the anticipated or actual harm caused by the delinquency, default, or early termination, the difficulties of proof of loss, and the inconvenience or nonfeasibility of otherwise obtaining an adequate remedy.

(c) Independent professional appraisal of residual value of property at termination of lease; finality

If a lease has a residual value provision at the termination of the lease, the lessee may obtain at his expense, a professional appraisal of the leased property by an independent third party agreed to by both parties. Such appraisal shall be final and binding on the parties.

(Pub. L. 90–321, title I, §183, as added Pub. L. 94–240, §3, Mar. 23, 1976, 90 Stat. 259.)

§1667c. Consumer lease advertising; liability of advertising media

(a) In general

If an advertisement for a consumer lease includes a statement of the amount of any payment or a statement that any or no initial payment is required, the advertisement shall clearly and conspicuously state, as applicable—

(1) the transaction advertised is a lease;

(2) the total amount of any initial payments required on or before consummation of the lease or delivery of the property, whichever is later;

(3) that a security deposit is required;

(4) the number, amount, and timing of scheduled payments; and

(5) with respect to a lease in which the liability of the consumer at the end of the lease term is based on the anticipated residual value of the property, that an extra charge may be imposed at the end of the lease term.

(b) Advertising medium not liable

No owner or employee of any entity that serves as a medium in which an advertisement appears or through which an advertisement is disseminated, shall be liable under this section.

(c) Radio advertisements

(1) In general

An advertisement by radio broadcast to aid, promote, or assist, directly or indirectly, any consumer lease shall be deemed to be in compliance with the requirements of subsection (a) if such advertisement clearly and conspicuously—

(A) states the information required by paragraphs (1) and (2) of subsection (a);

(B) states the number, amounts, due dates or periods of scheduled payments, and the total of such payments under the lease;

(C) includes—

(i) a referral to—

(I) a toll-free telephone number established in accordance with paragraph (2) that may be used by consumers to obtain the information required under subsection (a); or

(II) a written advertisement that—

(aa) appears in a publication in general circulation in the community served by the radio station on which such advertisement is broadcast during the period beginning 3 days before any such broadcast and ending 10 days after such broadcast; and

(bb) includes the information required to be disclosed under subsection (a); and

(ii) the name and dates of any publication referred to in clause (i)(II); and

(D) includes any other information which the Bureau determines necessary to carry out this part.

(2) Establishment of toll-free number

(A) In general

In the case of a radio broadcast advertisement described in paragraph (1) that includes a referral to a toll-free telephone number, the lessor who offers the consumer lease shall—

(i) establish such a toll-free telephone number not later than the date on which the advertisement including the referral is broadcast;

(ii) maintain such telephone number for a period of not less than 10 days, beginning on the date of any such broadcast; and

(iii) provide the information required under subsection (a) with respect to the lease to any person who calls such number.

(B) Form of information

The information required to be provided under subparagraph (A)(iii) shall be provided verbally or, if requested by the consumer, in written form.

(3) No effect on other law

Nothing in this subsection shall affect the requirements of Federal law as such requirements apply to advertisement by any medium other than radio broadcast.

(Pub. L. 90–321, title I, §184, as added Pub. L. 94–240, §3, Mar. 23, 1976, 90 Stat. 259; amended Pub. L. 103–325, title III, §336(a), Sept. 23, 1994, 108 Stat. 2234; Pub. L. 104–208, div. A, title II, §2605(c), Sept. 30, 1996, 110 Stat. 3009–473; Pub. L. 111–203, title X, §1100A(2), (10)(A), July 21, 2010, 124 Stat. 2107, 2109.)

EDITORIAL NOTES

AMENDMENTS

2010—Subsec. (c)(1)(D). Pub. L. 111–203, §1100A(2), (10)(A), made similar amendments, resulting in the substitution of "the Bureau" for "the Board".

1996—Subsec. (a). Pub. L. 104–208, §2605(c)(1), (3), added subsec. (a) and struck out former subsec. (a) consisting of introductory provisions and 5 pars. relating to contents of lease agreements required if consumer lease advertisement stated amount of payment, number of required payments, or that any or no payments were required at lease inception.

Subsec. (b). Pub. L. 104–208, §2605(c)(3), added subsec. (b). Former subsec. (b) redesignated (c).

Subsec. (c). Pub. L. 104–208, §2605(c)(1), (2), redesignated subsec. (b) as (c) and struck out former subsec. (c) which read as follows: "There is no liability under this section on the part of any owner or personnel, as such, of any medium in which an advertisement appears or through which it is disseminated."

1994—Subsecs. (b), (c). Pub. L. 103–325 added subsec. (b) and redesignated former subsec. (b) as (c).

STATUTORY NOTES AND RELATED SUBSIDIARIES

EFFECTIVE DATE OF 2010 AMENDMENT

Amendment by Pub. L. 111–203 effective on the designated transfer date, see section 1100H of Pub. L. 111–203, set out as a note under section 552a of Title 5, Government Organization and Employees.

STUDY OF ADVERTISING RULES

Pub. L. 103–325, title III, §336(b), Sept. 23, 1994, 108 Stat. 2235, provided that not later than 365 days after Sept. 23, 1994, the Board of Governors of the Federal Reserve System shall submit a report to the Congress on credit advertising rules.

§1667d. Civil liability of lessors

(a) Grounds for maintenance of action

Any lessor who fails to comply with any requirement imposed under section 1667a or 1667b of this title with respect to any person is liable to such person as provided in section 1640 of this title.

(b) Additional grounds for maintenance of action; "creditor" defined

Any lessor who fails to comply with any requirement imposed under section 1667c of this title with respect to any person who suffers actual damage from the violation is liable to such person as provided in section 1640 of this title. For the purposes of this section, the term "creditor" as used in sections 1640 and 1641 of this title shall include a lessor as defined in this part.

(c) Jurisdiction of courts; time limitation

Notwithstanding section 1640(e) of this title, any action under this section may be brought in any United States district court or in any other court of competent jurisdiction. Such actions alleging a failure to disclose or otherwise comply with the requirements of this part shall be brought within one year of the termination of the lease agreement.

(Pub. L. 90–321, title I, §185, as added Pub. L. 94–240, §3, Mar. 23, 1976, 90 Stat. 260; amended Pub. L. 96–221, title VI, §624, Mar. 31, 1980, 94 Stat. 185.)

EDITORIAL NOTES

AMENDMENTS

1980—Subsec. (b). Pub. L. 96–221 struck out applicability of section 1614 of this title to term "creditor".

STATUTORY NOTES AND RELATED SUBSIDIARIES

EFFECTIVE DATE OF 1980 AMENDMENT

Amendment by Pub. L. 96–221 effective on expiration of two years and six months after Mar. 31, 1980, with all regulations, forms, and clauses required to be prescribed to be promulgated at least one year prior to such effective date, and allowing any creditor to comply with any amendments, in accordance with the regulations, forms, and clauses prescribed by the Board prior to such effective date, see section 625 of Pub. L. 96–221, set out as a note under section 1602 of this title.

§1667e. Applicability of State laws; exemptions by Bureau from leasing requirements

(a) This part does not annul, alter, or affect, or exempt any person subject to the provisions of this part from complying with, the laws of any State with respect to consumer leases, except to the extent that those laws are inconsistent with any provision of this part, and then only to the extent of the inconsistency. The Bureau is authorized to determine whether such inconsistencies exist. The Bureau may not determine that any State law is inconsistent with any provision of this part if the Bureau determines that such law gives greater protection and benefit to the consumer.

(b) The Bureau shall by regulation exempt from the requirements of this part any class of lease transactions within any State if it determines that under the law of that State that class of transactions is subject to requirements substantially similar to those imposed under this part or that such law gives greater protection and benefit to the consumer, and that there is adequate provision for enforcement.

(Pub. L. 90–321, title I, §186, as added Pub. L. 94–240, §3, Mar. 23, 1976, 90 Stat. 260; amended Pub. L. 111–203, title X, §1100A(2), (10), July 21, 2010, 124 Stat. 2107, 2109.)

EDITORIAL NOTES

AMENDMENTS

2010—Pub. L. 111–203, §1100A(2), (10), substituted "Bureau" for "Board", "the Bureau" for "the Board", and "The Bureau" for "The Board" wherever appearing.

STATUTORY NOTES AND RELATED SUBSIDIARIES

EFFECTIVE DATE OF 2010 AMENDMENT

Amendment by Pub. L. 111–203 effective on the designated transfer date, see section 1100H of Pub. L. 111–203, set out as a note under section 552a of Title 5, Government Organization and Employees.

§1667f. Regulations

(a) Regulations authorized

(1) In general

The Bureau shall prescribe regulations to update and clarify the requirements and definitions applicable to lease disclosures and contracts, and any other issues specifically related to consumer leasing, to the extent that the Bureau determines such action to be necessary—

    (A) to carry out this part;

(B) to prevent any circumvention of this part; or

(C) to facilitate compliance with the requirements of the ^{1} part.

(2) Classifications, adjustments

Any regulations prescribed under paragraph (1) may contain classifications and differentiations, and may provide for adjustments and exceptions for any class of transactions, as the Bureau considers appropriate.

(b) Model disclosure

(1) Publication

The Bureau shall establish and publish model disclosure forms to facilitate compliance with the disclosure requirements of this part and to aid the consumer in understanding the transaction to which the subject disclosure form relates.

(2) Use of automated equipment

In establishing model forms under this subsection, the Bureau shall consider the use by lessors of data processing or similar automated equipment.

(3) Use optional

A lessor may utilize a model disclosure form established by the Bureau under this subsection for purposes of compliance with this part, at the discretion of the lessor.

(4) Effect of use

Any lessor who properly uses the material aspects of any model disclosure form established by the Bureau under this subsection shall be deemed to be in compliance with the disclosure requirements to which the form relates.

(Pub. L. 90–321, title I, §187, as added Pub. L. 104–208, div. A, title II, §2605(b)(1), Sept. 30, 1996, 110 Stat. 3009–471; amended Pub. L. 111–203, title X, §1100A(2), (10), July 21, 2010, 124 Stat. 2107, 2109.)

EDITORIAL NOTES

AMENDMENTS

2010—Pub. L. 111–203, §1100A(2), (10), substituted "Bureau" for "Board", "the Bureau" for "the Board", and "The Bureau" for "The Board " wherever appearing.

STATUTORY NOTES AND RELATED SUBSIDIARIES

EFFECTIVE DATE OF 2010 AMENDMENT

Amendment by Pub. L. 111–203 effective on the designated transfer date, see section 1100H of Pub. L. 111–203, set out as a note under section 552a of Title 5, Government Organization and Employees.

EFFECTIVE DATE

Section 2605(b)(2) of div. A of Pub. L. 104–208 provided that:

"(A) IN GENERAL.—Any regulation of the Board, or any amendment or interpretation of any regulation of the Board issued pursuant to section 187 of the Truth in Lending Act [15 U.S.C. 1667f] (as added by paragraph (1) of this subsection), shall become effective on the first October 1 that follows the date of promulgation of that regulation, amendment, or interpretation by not less than 6 months.

"(B) LONGER PERIOD.—The Board may, at the discretion of the Board, extend the time period referred to in subparagraph (A) in accordance with subparagraph (C), to permit lessors to adjust their disclosure forms to accommodate the requirements of section 127 [187] of the Truth in Lending Act (as added by paragraph (1) of this subsection).

"(C) SHORTER PERIOD.—The Board may shorten the time period referred to in subparagraph (A), if the Board makes a specific finding that such action is necessary to comply with the findings of a court or to prevent an unfair or deceptive practice.

"(D) COMPLIANCE BEFORE EFFECTIVE DATE.—Any lessor may comply with any means of disclosure provided for in section 127 [187] of the Truth in Lending Act (as added by paragraph (1) of this subsection) before the effective date of such requirement.

"(E) DEFINITIONS.—For purposes of this subsection, the term 'lessor' has the same meaning as in section 181 of the Truth in Lending Act [15 U.S.C. 1667]."

CONGRESSIONAL FINDINGS AND DECLARATION OF PURPOSES

Section 2605(a) of div. A of Pub. L. 104–208 provided that:

"(1) FINDINGS.—The Congress finds that—

"(A) competition among the various financial institutions and other firms engaged in the business of consumer leasing is greatest when there is informed use of leasing;

"(B) the informed use of leasing results from an awareness of the cost of leasing by consumers; and

"(C) there has been a continued trend toward leasing automobiles and other durable goods for consumer use as an alternative to installment credit sales and that leasing product advances have occurred such that lessors have been unable to provide consistent industry-wide disclosures to fully account for the competitive progress that has occurred.

"(2) PURPOSES.—The purposes of this section are—

"(A) to assure a simple, meaningful disclosure of leasing terms so that the consumer will be able to compare more readily the various leasing terms available to the consumer and avoid the uninformed use of leasing, and to protect the consumer against inaccurate and unfair leasing practices;

"(B) to provide for adequate cost disclosures that reflect the marketplace without impairing competition and the development of new leasing products; and

"(C) to provide the Board with the regulatory authority to assure a simplified, meaningful definition and disclosure of the terms of certain leases of personal property for personal, family, or household purposes so as to—

"(i) enable the lessee to compare more readily the various lease terms available to the lessee;

"(ii) enable comparison of lease terms with credit terms, as appropriate; and

"(iii) assure meaningful and accurate disclosures of lease terms in advertisements."

---

¹ So in original. Probably should be "this".

This marks the end of the Truth In Lending Act
15 U.S.C. §§ 1601-1667f

RESTRICTIONS ON GARNISHMENT

15 U.S.C. §§ 1671-1677, as amended

The wage garnishment provisions of the Consumer Credit Protection Act protect employees from discharge by their employers because their wages have been garnished for any one debt, and it limits the amount of an employee's earnings that may be garnished in any one week. This also applies to all employers and individuals who receive earnings for personal services (including wages, salaries, commissions, bonuses and income from a pension or retirement program, but ordinarily not including tips).

Subchapter II, Restrictions on Garnishment

SUBCHAPTER II—RESTRICTIONS ON GARNISHMENT

§1671. Congressional findings and declaration of purpose

(a) Disadvantages of garnishment

The Congress finds:

(1) The unrestricted garnishment of compensation due for personal services encourages the making of predatory extensions of credit. Such extensions of credit divert money into excessive credit payments and thereby hinder the production and flow of goods in interstate commerce.

(2) The application of garnishment as a creditors' remedy frequently results in loss of employment by the debtor, and the resulting disruption of employment, production, and consumption constitutes a substantial burden on interstate commerce.

(3) The great disparities among the laws of the several States relating to garnishment have, in effect, destroyed the uniformity of the bankruptcy laws and frustrated the purposes thereof in many areas of the country.

(b) Necessity for regulation

On the basis of the findings stated in subsection (a) of this section, the Congress determines that the provisions of this subchapter are necessary and proper for the purpose of carrying into execution the powers of the Congress to regulate commerce and to establish uniform bankruptcy laws.

(Pub. L. 90–321, title III, §301, May 29, 1968, 82 Stat. 163.)

STATUTORY NOTES AND RELATED SUBSIDIARIES

EFFECTIVE DATE

Pub. L. 90–321, title V, §504(c), May 29, 1968, 82 Stat. 167, provided that: "Title III [enacting this section and sections 1672 to 1677 of this title] takes effect on July 1, 1970."

§1672. Definitions

For the purposes of this subchapter:

(a) The term "earnings" means compensation paid or payable for personal services, whether denominated as wages, salary, commission, bonus, or otherwise, and includes periodic payments pursuant to a pension or retirement program.

(b) The term "disposable earnings" means that part of the earnings of any individual remaining after the deduction from those earnings of any amounts required by law to be withheld.

(c) The term "garnishment" means any legal or equitable procedure through which the earnings of any individual are required to be withheld for payment of any debt.

(Pub. L. 90–321, title III, §302, May 29, 1968, 82 Stat. 163.)

§1673. Restriction on garnishment

(a) Maximum allowable garnishment

Except as provided in subsection (b) and in section 1675 of this title, the maximum part of the aggregate disposable earnings of an individual for any workweek which is subjected to garnishment may not exceed

(1) 25 per centum of his disposable earnings for that week, or

(2) the amount by which his disposable earnings for that week exceed thirty times the Federal minimum hourly wage prescribed by section 206(a)(1) of title 29 in effect at the time the earnings are payable,

whichever is less. In the case of earnings for any pay period other than a week, the Secretary of Labor shall by regulation prescribe a multiple of the Federal minimum hourly wage equivalent in effect to that set forth in paragraph

(2).

(b) Exceptions

(1) The restrictions of subsection (a) do not apply in the case of

(A) any order for the support of any person issued by a court of competent jurisdiction or in accordance with an administrative procedure, which is established by State law, which affords substantial due process, and which is subject to judicial review.

(B) any order of any court of the United States having jurisdiction over cases under chapter 13 of title 11.

(C) any debt due for any State or Federal tax.

(2) The maximum part of the aggregate disposable earnings of an individual for any workweek which is subject to garnishment to enforce any order for the support of any person shall not exceed—

(A) where such individual is supporting his spouse or dependent child (other than a spouse or child with respect to whose support such order is used), 50 per centum of such individual's disposable earnings for that week; and

(B) where such individual is not supporting such a spouse or dependent child described in clause (A), 60 per centum of such individual's disposable earnings for that week;

except that, with respect to the disposable earnings of any individual for any workweek, the 50 per centum specified in clause (A) shall be deemed to be 55 per centum and the 60 per centum specified in clause (B) shall be deemed to be 65 per centum, if and to the extent that such earnings are subject to garnishment to enforce a support order with respect to a period which is prior to the twelve-week period which ends with the beginning of such workweek.

(c) Execution or enforcement of garnishment order or process prohibited

No court of the United States or any State, and no State (or officer or agency thereof), may make, execute, or enforce any order or process in violation of this section.

(Pub. L. 90–321, title III, §303, May 29, 1968, 82 Stat. 163; Pub. L. 95–30, title V, §501(e)(1)–(3), May 23, 1977, 91 Stat. 161, 162; Pub. L. 95–598, title III, §312(a), Nov. 6, 1978, 92 Stat. 2676.)

EDITORIAL NOTES

AMENDMENTS

1978—Subsec. (b)(1)(B). Pub. L. 95–598 substituted "court of the United States having jurisdiction over cases under chapter 13 of title 11" for "court of bankruptcy under chapter XIII of the Bankruptcy Act".

1977—Subsec. (b). Pub. L. 95–30, §501(e)(1), (2), designated existing provisions as par. (1) and existing pars. (1), (2), and (3) as subpars. (A), (B), and (C) thereof, substituted "for the support of any person issued by a court of competent jurisdiction or in accordance with an administrative procedure, which is established by State law, which affords substantial due process, and which is subject to judicial review" for "of any court for the support of any person" in subpar. (A) as so redesignated, and added par. (2).

Subsec. (c). Pub. L. 95–30, §501(e)(3), inserted ", and no State (or officer or agency thereof)," after "or any State".

STATUTORY NOTES AND RELATED SUBSIDIARIES

EFFECTIVE DATE OF 1978 AMENDMENT

Amendment by Pub. L. 95–598 effective Oct. 1, 1979, see section 402(a) of Pub. L. 95–598, set out as an Effective Date note preceding section 101 of Title 11, Bankruptcy.

EFFECTIVE DATE OF 1977 AMENDMENT

Pub. L. 95–30, title V, §501(e)(5), May 23, 1977, 91 Stat. 162, provided that: "The amendments made by this subsection [amending this section and section 1675 of this title] shall take effect on the first day of the first calendar month which begins after the date of enactment of this Act [May 23, 1977]."

§1674. Restriction on discharge from employment by reason of garnishment

(a) Termination of employment

No employer may discharge any employee by reason of the fact that his earnings have been subjected to garnishment for any one indebtedness.

(b) Penalties

Whoever willfully violates subsection (a) of this section shall be fined not more than $1,000, or imprisoned not more than one year, or both.

(Pub. L. 90–321, title III, §304, May 29, 1968, 82 Stat. 163.)

§1675. Exemption for State-regulated garnishments

The Secretary of Labor may by regulation exempt from the provisions of section 1673(a) and (b)(2) of this title garnishments issued under the laws of any State if he determines that the laws of that State provide restrictions on garnishment which are substantially similar to those provided in section 1673(a) and (b)(2) of this title.

(Pub. L. 90–321, title III, §305, May 29, 1968, 82 Stat. 164; Pub. L. 95–30, title V, §501(e)(4), May 23, 1977, 91 Stat. 162.)

EDITORIAL NOTES

AMENDMENTS

1977—Pub. L. 95–30 substituted "section 1673(a) and (b)(2) of this title" for "section 1673(a) of this title" in two places.

§1676. Enforcement by Secretary of Labor

The Secretary of Labor, acting through the Wage and Hour Division of the Department of Labor, shall enforce the provisions of this subchapter.

(Pub. L. 90–321, title III, §306, May 29, 1968, 82 Stat. 164.)

§1677. Effect on State laws

This subchapter does not annul, alter, or affect, or exempt any person from complying with, the laws of any State
  (1) prohibiting garnishments or providing for more limited garnishment than are allowed under this subchapter, or
  (2) prohibiting the discharge of any employee by reason of the fact that his earnings have been subjected to garnishment for more than one indebtedness.

(Pub. L. 90–321, title III, §307, May 29, 1968, 82 Stat. 164.)

This marks the end of Restrictions On Garnishment
15 U.S.C. §§ 1671-1677

CREDIT REPAIR ORGANIZATIONS

15 U.S.C. § 1679, as amended

This Act, Title IV of the Consumer Credit Protection Act, prohibits untrue or misleading representations and requires certain affirmative disclosures in the offering or sale of "credit repair" services. The Act bars companies offering credit repair services from demanding advance payment, requires that credit repair contracts be in writing, and gives consumers certain contract cancellation rights.

Subchapter II-A, Credit Repair Organizations

SUBCHAPTER II–A—CREDIT REPAIR ORGANIZATIONS

§1679. Findings and purposes

(a) Findings

The Congress makes the following findings:

(1) Consumers have a vital interest in establishing and maintaining their credit worthiness and credit standing in order to obtain and use credit. As a result, consumers who have experienced credit problems may seek assistance from credit repair organizations which offer to improve the credit standing of such consumers.

(2) Certain advertising and business practices of some companies engaged in the business of credit repair services have worked a financial hardship upon consumers, particularly those of limited economic means and who are inexperienced in credit matters.

(b) Purposes

The purposes of this subchapter are—

(1) to ensure that prospective buyers of the services of credit repair organizations are provided with the information necessary to make an informed decision regarding the purchase of such services; and

(2) to protect the public from unfair or deceptive advertising and business practices by credit repair organizations.

(Pub. L. 90–321, title IV, §402, as added Pub. L. 104–208, div. A, title II, §2451, Sept. 30, 1996, 110 Stat. 3009–455.)

Editorial Notes

Prior Provisions

A prior title IV of Pub. L. 90–321, May 29, 1968, 82 Stat. 164, as amended by Pub. L. 91–344, July 20, 1970, 84 Stat. 440; Pub. L. 92–321, June 30, 1972, 86 Stat. 382, which was set out as a note under section 1601 of this title, established a bipartisan National Commission on Consumer Finance to study the functioning and structure of the consumer finance industry as well as consumer credit transactions generally. The Commission was to submit a final report by Dec. 31, 1972, and was to cease to exist thereafter.

Statutory Notes and Related Subsidiaries

Effective Date

Pub. L. 90–321, title IV, §413, as added by Pub. L. 104–208, div. A, title II, §2451, Sept. 30, 1996, 110 Stat. 3009–462, provided that: "This title [enacting this subchapter] shall apply after the end of the 6-month period beginning on the date of the enactment of the Credit Repair Organizations Act [Sept. 30, 1996], except with respect to contracts entered into by a credit repair organization before the end of such period."

Short Title

This subchapter known as the "Credit Repair Organizations Act", see Short Title note set out under section 1601 of this title.

§1679a. Definitions

For purposes of this subchapter, the following definitions apply:

(1) Consumer

The term "consumer" means an individual.

(2) Consumer credit transaction

The term "consumer credit transaction" means any transaction in which credit is offered or extended to an individual for personal, family, or household purposes.

(3) Credit repair organization

The term "credit repair organization"—

(A) means any person who uses any instrumentality of interstate commerce or the mails to sell, provide, or perform (or represent that such person can or will sell, provide, or perform) any service, in return for the payment of money or other valuable consideration, for the express or implied purpose of—

(i) improving any consumer's credit record, credit history, or credit rating; or

(ii) providing advice or assistance to any consumer with regard to any activity or service described in clause (i); and

(B) does not include—

(i) any nonprofit organization which is exempt from taxation under section 501(c)(3) of title 26;

(ii) any creditor (as defined in section 1602 of this title), with respect to any consumer, to the extent the creditor is assisting the consumer to restructure any debt owed by the consumer to the creditor; or

(iii) any depository institution (as that term is defined in section 1813 of title 12) or any Federal or State credit union (as those terms are defined in section 1752 of title 12), or any affiliate or subsidiary of such a depository institution or credit union.

(4) Credit

The term "credit" has the meaning given to such term in section 1602(e) [1] of this title.

(Pub. L. 90–321, title IV, §403, as added Pub. L. 104–208, div. A, title II, §2451, Sept. 30, 1996, 110 Stat. 3009–455.)

§1679b. Prohibited practices

(a) In general

No person may—

(1) make any statement, or counsel or advise any consumer to make any statement, which is untrue or misleading (or which, upon the exercise of reasonable care, should be known by the credit repair organization, officer, employee, agent, or other person to be untrue or misleading) with respect to any consumer's credit worthiness, credit standing, or credit capacity to—

(A) any consumer reporting agency (as defined in section 1681a(f) of this title); or

(B) any person—

(i) who has extended credit to the consumer; or

(ii) to whom the consumer has applied or is applying for an extension of credit;

(2) make any statement, or counsel or advise any consumer to make any statement, the intended effect of which is to alter the consumer's identification to prevent the display of the consumer's credit record, history, or rating for the purpose of concealing adverse information that is accurate and not obsolete to—

(A) any consumer reporting agency;

(B) any person—

(i) who has extended credit to the consumer; or

(ii) to whom the consumer has applied or is applying for an extension of credit;

(3) make or use any untrue or misleading representation of the services of the credit repair organization; or

(4) engage, directly or indirectly, in any act, practice, or course of business that constitutes or results in the commission of, or an attempt to commit, a fraud or deception on any person in connection with the offer or sale of the services of the credit repair organization.

(b) Payment in advance

No credit repair organization may charge or receive any money or other valuable consideration for the performance of any service which the credit repair organization has agreed to perform for any consumer before such service is fully performed.

(Pub. L. 90–321, title IV, §404, as added Pub. L. 104–208, div. A, title II, §2451, Sept. 30, 1996, 110 Stat. 3009–456.)

EDITORIAL NOTES

PRIOR PROVISIONS

For a prior section 404 of Pub. L. 90–321, see note set out under section 1679 of this title.

STATUTORY NOTES AND RELATED SUBSIDIARIES

EFFECTIVE DATE

Section applicable after the end of the 6-month period beginning on Sept. 30, 1996, except with respect to contracts entered into by a credit repair organization before the end of such period, see section 413 of Pub. L. 90–321, as added by Pub. L. 104–208, set out as a note under section 1679 of this title.

§1679c. Disclosures

(a) Disclosure required

Any credit repair organization shall provide any consumer with the following written statement before any contract or agreement between the consumer and the credit repair organization is executed:

"Consumer Credit File Rights Under State and Federal Law

"You have a right to dispute inaccurate information in your credit report by contacting the credit bureau directly. However, neither you nor any 'credit repair' company or credit repair organization has the right to have accurate, current, and verifiable information removed from your credit report. The credit bureau must remove accurate, negative information from your report only if it is over 7 years old. Bankruptcy information can be reported for 10 years.

"You have a right to obtain a copy of your credit report from a credit bureau. You may be charged a reasonable fee. There is no fee, however, if you have been turned down for credit, employment, insurance, or a rental dwelling because of information in your credit report within the preceding 60 days. The credit bureau must provide someone to help you interpret the information in your credit file. You are entitled to receive a free copy of your credit report if you are unemployed and intend to apply for employment in the next 60 days, if you are a recipient of public welfare assistance, or if you have reason to believe that there is inaccurate information in your credit report due to fraud.

"You have a right to sue a credit repair organization that violates the Credit Repair Organization Act. This law prohibits deceptive practices by credit repair organizations.

"You have the right to cancel your contract with any credit repair organization for any reason within 3 business days from the date you signed it.

"Credit bureaus are required to follow reasonable procedures to ensure that the information they report is accurate. However, mistakes may occur.

"You may, on your own, notify a credit bureau in writing that you dispute the accuracy of information in your credit file. The credit bureau must then reinvestigate and modify or remove inaccurate or incomplete information. The credit bureau may not charge any fee for this service. Any pertinent information and copies of all documents you have concerning an error should be given to the credit bureau.

"If the credit bureau's reinvestigation does not resolve the dispute to your satisfaction, you may send a brief statement to the credit bureau, to be kept in your file, explaining why you think the record is inaccurate. The credit bureau must include a summary of your statement about disputed information with any report it issues about you.

"The Federal Trade Commission regulates credit bureaus and credit repair organizations. For more information contact:

"The Public Reference Branch

"Federal Trade Commission

"Washington, D.C. 20580".

(b) Separate statement requirement

The written statement required under this section shall be provided as a document which is separate from any written contract or other agreement between the credit repair organization and the consumer or any other written material provided to the consumer.

(c) Retention of compliance records

(1) In general

The credit repair organization shall maintain a copy of the statement signed by the consumer acknowledging receipt of the statement.

(2) Maintenance for 2 years

The copy of any consumer's statement shall be maintained in the organization's files for 2 years after the date on which the statement is signed by the consumer.

(Pub. L. 90–321, title IV, §405, as added Pub. L. 104–208, div. A, title II, §2451, Sept. 30, 1996, 110 Stat. 3009–457.)

§1679d. Credit repair organizations contracts

(a) Written contracts required

No services may be provided by any credit repair organization for any consumer—

(1) unless a written and dated contract (for the purchase of such services) which meets the requirements of subsection (b) has been signed by the consumer; or

(2) before the end of the 3-business-day period beginning on the date the contract is signed.

(b) Terms and conditions of contract

No contract referred to in subsection (a) meets the requirements of this subsection unless such contract includes (in writing)—

(1) the terms and conditions of payment, including the total amount of all payments to be made by the consumer to the credit repair organization or to any other person;

(2) a full and detailed description of the services to be performed by the credit repair organization for the consumer, including—

(A) all guarantees of performance; and

(B) an estimate of—

(i) the date by which the performance of the services (to be performed by the credit repair organization or any other person) will be complete; or

(ii) the length of the period necessary to perform such services;

(3) the credit repair organization's name and principal business address; and

(4) a conspicuous statement in bold face type, in immediate proximity to the space reserved for the consumer's signature on the contract, which reads as follows: "You may cancel this contract without penalty or obligation at any time before midnight of the 3rd business day after the date on which you signed the contract. See the attached notice of cancellation form for an explanation of this right.".

(Pub. L. 90–321, title IV, §406, as added Pub. L. 104–208, div. A, title II, §2451, Sept. 30, 1996, 110 Stat. 3009–458.)

EDITORIAL NOTES

PRIOR PROVISIONS

For a prior section 406 of Pub. L. 90–321, see note set out under section 1679 of this title.

STATUTORY NOTES AND RELATED SUBSIDIARIES

EFFECTIVE DATE

Section applicable after the end of the 6-month period beginning on Sept. 30, 1996, except with respect to contracts entered into by a credit repair organization before the end of such period, see section 413 of Pub. L. 90–321, as added by Pub. L. 104–208, set out as a note under section 1679 of this title.

§1679e. Right to cancel contract

(a) In general

Any consumer may cancel any contract with any credit repair organization without penalty or obligation by notifying the credit repair organization of the consumer's intention to do so at any time before midnight of the 3rd business day which begins after the date on which the contract or agreement between the consumer and the credit repair organization is executed or would, but for this subsection, become enforceable against the parties.

(b) Cancellation form and other information

Each contract shall be accompanied by a form, in duplicate, which has the heading "Notice of Cancellation" and contains in bold face type the following statement:

"You may cancel this contract, without any penalty or obligation, at any time before midnight of the 3rd day which begins after the date the contract is signed by you.

"To cancel this contract, mail or deliver a signed, dated copy of this cancellation notice, or any other written notice to [name of credit repair organization] at [address of credit repair organization] before midnight on [date]

"I hereby cancel this transaction,

[date]

[purchaser's signature].".

(c) Consumer copy of contract required

Any consumer who enters into any contract with any credit repair organization shall be given, by the organization—

(1) a copy of the completed contract and the disclosure statement required under section 1679c of this title; and

(2) a copy of any other document the credit repair organization requires the consumer to sign,

at the time the contract or the other document is signed.

(Pub. L. 90–321, title IV, §407, as added Pub. L. 104–208, div. A, title II, §2451, Sept. 30, 1996, 110 Stat. 3009–459.)

EDITORIAL NOTES

PRIOR PROVISIONS

For a prior section 407 of Pub. L. 90–321, see note set out under section 1679 of this title.

STATUTORY NOTES AND RELATED SUBSIDIARIES

EFFECTIVE DATE

Section applicable after the end of the 6-month period beginning on Sept. 30, 1996, except with respect to contracts entered into by a credit repair organization before the end of such period, see section 413 of Pub. L. 90–321, as added by Pub. L. 104–208, set out as a note under section 1679 of this title.

§1679f. Noncompliance with this subchapter

(a) Consumer waivers invalid

Any waiver by any consumer of any protection provided by or any right of the consumer under this subchapter—
(1) shall be treated as void; and
(2) may not be enforced by any Federal or State court or any other person.

(b) Attempt to obtain waiver

Any attempt by any person to obtain a waiver from any consumer of any protection provided by or any right of the consumer under this subchapter shall be treated as a violation of this subchapter.

(c) Contracts not in compliance

Any contract for services which does not comply with the applicable provisions of this subchapter—
(1) shall be treated as void; and
(2) may not be enforced by any Federal or State court or any other person.

(Pub. L. 90–321, title IV, §408, as added Pub. L. 104–208, div. A, title II, §2451, Sept. 30, 1996, 110 Stat. 3009–459.)

STATUTORY NOTES AND RELATED SUBSIDIARIES

EFFECTIVE DATE

Section applicable after the end of the 6-month period beginning on Sept. 30, 1996, except with respect to contracts entered into by a credit repair organization before the end of such period, see section 413 of Pub. L. 90–321, as added by Pub. L. 104–208, set out as a note under section 1679 of this title.

§1679g. Civil liability

(a) Liability established

Any person who fails to comply with any provision of this subchapter with respect to any other person shall be liable to such person in an amount equal to the sum of the amounts determined under each of the following paragraphs:

(1) Actual damages

The greater of—
(A) the amount of any actual damage sustained by such person as a result of such failure; or
(B) any amount paid by the person to the credit repair organization.

(2) Punitive damages

(A) Individual actions

In the case of any action by an individual, such additional amount as the court may allow.

(B) Class actions

In the case of a class action, the sum of—
(i) the aggregate of the amount which the court may allow for each named plaintiff; and
(ii) the aggregate of the amount which the court may allow for each other class member, without regard to any minimum individual recovery.

(3) Attorneys' fees

In the case of any successful action to enforce any liability under paragraph (1) or (2), the costs of the action, together with reasonable attorneys' fees.

(b) Factors to be considered in awarding punitive damages

In determining the amount of any liability of any credit repair organization under subsection (a)(2), the court shall consider, among other relevant factors—
(1) the frequency and persistence of noncompliance by the credit repair organization;
(2) the nature of the noncompliance;
(3) the extent to which such noncompliance was intentional; and
(4) in the case of any class action, the number of consumers adversely affected.

(Pub. L. 90–321, title IV, §409, as added Pub. L. 104–208, div. A, title II, §2451, Sept. 30, 1996, 110 Stat. 3009–459.)

STATUTORY NOTES AND RELATED SUBSIDIARIES

EFFECTIVE DATE

Section applicable after the end of the 6-month period beginning on Sept. 30, 1996, except with respect to contracts entered into by a credit repair organization before the end of such period, see section 413 of Pub. L. 90–321, as added by Pub. L. 104–208, set out as a note under section 1679 of this title.

§1679h. Administrative enforcement

(a) In general

Compliance with the requirements imposed under this subchapter with respect to credit repair organizations shall be enforced under the Federal Trade Commission Act [15 U.S.C. 41 et seq.] by the Federal Trade Commission.

(b) Violations of this subchapter treated as violations of Federal Trade Commission Act

(1) In general

For the purpose of the exercise by the Federal Trade Commission of the Commission's functions and powers under the Federal Trade Commission Act [15 U.S.C. 41 et seq.], any violation of any requirement or prohibition imposed under this subchapter with respect to credit repair organizations shall constitute an unfair or deceptive act or practice in commerce in violation of section 5(a) of the Federal Trade Commission Act [15 U.S.C. 45(a)].

(2) Enforcement authority under other law

All functions and powers of the Federal Trade Commission under the Federal Trade Commission Act shall be available to the Commission to enforce compliance with this subchapter by any person subject to enforcement by the Federal Trade Commission pursuant to this subsection, including the power to enforce the provisions of this subchapter in the same manner as if the violation had been a violation of any Federal Trade Commission trade regulation rule, without regard to whether the credit repair organization—

    (A) is engaged in commerce; or

    (B) meets any other jurisdictional tests in the Federal Trade Commission Act.

(c) State action for violations

(1) Authority of States

In addition to such other remedies as are provided under State law, whenever the chief law enforcement officer of a State, or an official or agency designated by a State, has reason to believe that any person has violated or is violating this subchapter, the State—

    (A) may bring an action to enjoin such violation;

    (B) may bring an action on behalf of its residents to recover damages for which the person is liable to such residents under section 1679g of this title as a result of the violation; and

    (C) in the case of any successful action under subparagraph (A) or (B), shall be awarded the costs of the action and reasonable attorney fees as determined by the court.

(2) Rights of Commission

(A) Notice to Commission

The State shall serve prior written notice of any civil action under paragraph (1) upon the Federal Trade Commission and provide the Commission with a copy of its complaint, except in any case where such prior notice is not feasible, in which case the State shall serve such notice immediately upon instituting such action.

(B) Intervention

The Commission shall have the right—

    (i) to intervene in any action referred to in subparagraph (A);

    (ii) upon so intervening, to be heard on all matters arising in the action; and

    (iii) to file petitions for appeal.

(3) Investigatory powers

For purposes of bringing any action under this subsection, nothing in this subsection shall prevent the chief law enforcement officer, or an official or agency designated by a State, from exercising the powers conferred on the chief law enforcement officer or such official by the laws of such State to conduct investigations or to administer oaths or affirmations or to compel the attendance of witnesses or the production of documentary and other evidence.

(4) Limitation

Whenever the Federal Trade Commission has instituted a civil action for violation of this subchapter, no State may, during the pendency of such action, bring an action under this section against any defendant named in the complaint of the Commission for any violation of this subchapter that is alleged in that complaint.

(Pub. L. 90–321, title IV, §410, as added Pub. L. 104–208, div. A, title II, §2451, Sept. 30, 1996, 110 Stat. 3009–460.)

EDITORIAL NOTES

The Federal Trade Commission Act, referred to in subsecs. (a) and (b), is act Sept. 26, 1914, ch. 311, 38 Stat. 717, which is classified generally to subchapter I (§41 et seq.) of chapter 2 of this title. For complete classification of this Act to the Code, see section 58 of this title and Tables.

STATUTORY NOTES AND RELATED SUBSIDIARIES

EFFECTIVE DATE

Section applicable after the end of the 6-month period beginning on Sept. 30, 1996, except with respect to contracts entered into by a credit repair organization before the end of such period, see section 413 of Pub. L. 90–321, as added by Pub. L. 104–208, set out as a note under section 1679 of this title.

§1679i. Statute of limitations

Any action to enforce any liability under this subchapter may be brought before the later of—
(1) the end of the 5-year period beginning on the date of the occurrence of the violation involved; or
(2) in any case in which any credit repair organization has materially and willfully misrepresented any information which—

(A) the credit repair organization is required, by any provision of this subchapter, to disclose to any consumer; and

(B) is material to the establishment of the credit repair organization's liability to the consumer under this subchapter,

the end of the 5-year period beginning on the date of the discovery by the consumer of the misrepresentation.

(Pub. L. 90–321, title IV, §411, as added Pub. L. 104–208, div. A, title II, §2451, Sept. 30, 1996, 110 Stat. 3009–461.)

STATUTORY NOTES AND RELATED SUBSIDIARIES

EFFECTIVE DATE

Section applicable after the end of the 6-month period beginning on Sept. 30, 1996, except with respect to contracts entered into by a credit repair organization before the end of such period, see section 413 of Pub. L. 90–321, as added by Pub. L. 104–208, set out as a note under section 1679 of this title.

§1679j. Relation to State law

This subchapter shall not annul, alter, affect, or exempt any person subject to the provisions of this subchapter from complying with any law of any State except to the extent that such law is inconsistent with any provision of this subchapter, and then only to the extent of the inconsistency.

(Pub. L. 90–321, title IV, §412, as added Pub. L. 104–208, div. A, title II, §2451, Sept. 30, 1996, 110 Stat. 3009–462.)

STATUTORY NOTES AND RELATED SUBSIDIARIES

EFFECTIVE DATE

Section applicable after the end of the 6-month period beginning on Sept. 30, 1996, except with respect to contracts entered into by a credit repair organization before the end of such period, see section 413 of Pub. L. 90–321, as added by Pub. L. 104–208, set out as a note under section 1679 of this title.

This marks the end of Credit Repair Organizations
15 U.S.C. § 1679

FAIR CREDIT REPORTING ACT

15 U.S.C. § 1681

The Act (Title VI of the Consumer Credit Protection Act) protects information collected by consumer reporting agencies such as credit bureaus, medical information companies and tenant screening services. Information in a consumer report cannot be provided to anyone who does not have a purpose specified in the Act. Companies that provide information to consumer reporting agencies also have specific legal obligations, including the duty to investigate disputed information. In addition, users of the information for credit, insurance, or employment purposes must notify the consumer when an adverse action is taken on the basis of such reports. The Fair and Accurate Credit Transactions Act added many provisions to this Act primarily relating to record accuracy and identity theft. The Dodd-Frank Act transferred to the Consumer Financial Protection Bureau most of the rulemaking responsibilities added to this Act by the Fair and Accurate Credit Transactions Act and the Credit CARD Act, but the Commission retains all its enforcement authority.

Subchapter III, Credit Reporting Agencies

SUBCHAPTER III—CREDIT REPORTING AGENCIES

§1681. Congressional findings and statement of purpose

(a) Accuracy and fairness of credit reporting

The Congress makes the following findings:

(1) The banking system is dependent upon fair and accurate credit reporting. Inaccurate credit reports directly impair the efficiency of the banking system, and unfair credit reporting methods undermine the public confidence which is essential to the continued functioning of the banking system.

(2) An elaborate mechanism has been developed for investigating and evaluating the credit worthiness, credit standing, credit capacity, character, and general reputation of consumers.

(3) Consumer reporting agencies have assumed a vital role in assembling and evaluating consumer credit and other information on consumers.

(4) There is a need to insure that consumer reporting agencies exercise their grave responsibilities with fairness, impartiality, and a respect for the consumer's right to privacy.

(b) Reasonable procedures

It is the purpose of this subchapter to require that consumer reporting agencies adopt reasonable procedures for meeting the needs of commerce for consumer credit, personnel, insurance, and other information in a manner which is fair and equitable to the consumer, with regard to the confidentiality, accuracy, relevancy, and proper utilization of such information in accordance with the requirements of this subchapter.

(Pub. L. 90–321, title VI, §602, as added Pub. L. 91–508, title VI, §601, Oct. 26, 1970, 84 Stat. 1128.)

STATUTORY NOTES AND RELATED SUBSIDIARIES

EFFECTIVE DATE OF 2003 AMENDMENT

Pub. L. 108–159, §3, Dec. 4, 2003, 117 Stat. 1953, provided that: "Except as otherwise specifically provided in this Act [see Short Title of 2003 Amendment note set out under section 1601 of this title] and the amendments made by this Act—

"(1) before the end of the 2-month period beginning on the date of enactment of this Act [Dec. 4, 2003], the Board and the Commission shall jointly prescribe regulations in final form establishing effective dates for each provision of this Act; and

"(2) the regulations prescribed under paragraph (1) shall establish effective dates that are as early as possible, while allowing a reasonable time for the implementation of the provisions of this Act, but in no case shall any such effective date be later than 10 months after the date of issuance of such regulations in final form."

[For final rules adopted by Board of Governors of the Federal Reserve System and Federal Trade Commission establishing effective dates for provisions of Pub. L. 108–159, see 68 F.R. 74467 (joint interim final rules) and 69 F.R. 6526 (joint final rules).]

EFFECTIVE DATE

Pub. L. 90–321, title V, §504(d), as added by Pub. L. 91–508, title VI, §602, Oct. 26, 1970, 84 Stat. 1136, provided that: "Title VI [enacting this subchapter] takes effect upon the expiration of one hundred and eighty days following the date of its enactment [Oct. 26, 1970]."

SHORT TITLE

This subchapter known as the "Fair Credit Reporting Act", see Short Title note set out under section 1601 of this title.

STUDY OF EFFECTS OF CREDIT SCORES AND CREDIT-BASED INSURANCE SCORES ON AVAILABILITY AND AFFORDABILITY OF FINANCIAL PRODUCTS

Pub. L. 108–159, title II, §215, Dec. 4, 2003, 117 Stat. 1984, provided that:

"(a) STUDY REQUIRED.—The Commission and the Board, in consultation with the Office of Fair Housing and Equal Opportunity of the Department of Housing and Urban Development, shall conduct a study of—

"(1) the effects of the use of credit scores and credit-based insurance scores on the availability and affordability of financial products and services, including credit cards, mortgages, auto loans, and property and casualty insurance;

"(2) the statistical relationship, utilizing a multivariate analysis that controls for prohibited factors under the Equal Credit Opportunity Act [15 U.S.C. 1691 et seq.] and other known risk factors, between credit scores and credit-based insurance scores and the quantifiable risks and actual losses experienced by businesses;

"(3) the extent to which, if any, the use of credit scoring models, credit scores, and credit-based insurance scores impact on the availability and affordability of credit and insurance to the extent information is currently available or is available through proxies, by geography, income, ethnicity, race, color, religion, national origin, age, sex, marital status, and creed, including the extent to which the consideration or lack of consideration of certain factors by credit scoring systems could result in negative or differential treatment of protected classes under the Equal Credit Opportunity Act, and the extent to which, if any, the use of underwriting systems relying on these models could achieve comparable results through the use of factors with less negative impact; and

"(4) the extent to which credit scoring systems are used by businesses, the factors considered by such systems, and the effects of variables which are not considered by such systems.

"(b) PUBLIC PARTICIPATION.—The Commission shall seek public input about the prescribed methodology and research design of the study described in subsection (a), including from relevant Federal regulators, State insurance regulators, community, civil rights, consumer, and housing groups.

"(c) REPORT REQUIRED.—

"(1) IN GENERAL.—Before the end of the 24-month period beginning on the date of enactment of this Act [Dec. 4, 2003], the Commission shall submit a detailed report on the study conducted pursuant to subsection (a) to the Committee on Financial Services of the House of Representatives and the Committee on Banking, Housing, and Urban Affairs of the Senate.

"(2) CONTENTS OF REPORT.—The report submitted under paragraph (1) shall include the findings and conclusions of the Commission, recommendations to address specific areas of concerns addressed in the study, and recommendations for legislative or administrative action that the Commission may determine to be necessary to ensure that credit and credit-based insurance scores are used appropriately and fairly to avoid negative effects."

FTC STUDY OF ISSUES RELATING TO THE FAIR CREDIT REPORTING ACT

Pub. L. 108–159, title III, §318, Dec. 4, 2003, 117 Stat. 1998, provided that:

"(a) STUDY REQUIRED.—

"(1) IN GENERAL.—The Commission shall conduct a study on ways to improve the operation of the Fair Credit Reporting Act [15 U.S.C. 1681 et seq.].

"(2) AREAS FOR STUDY.—In conducting the study under paragraph (1), the Commission shall review—

"(A) the efficacy of increasing the number of points of identifying information that a credit reporting agency is required to match to ensure that a consumer is the correct individual to whom a consumer report relates before releasing a consumer report to a user, including—

"(i) the extent to which requiring additional points of such identifying information to match would—

"(I) enhance the accuracy of credit reports; and

"(II) combat the provision of incorrect consumer reports to users;

"(ii) the extent to which requiring an exact match of the first and last name, social security number, and address and ZIP Code of the consumer would enhance the likelihood of increasing credit report accuracy; and

"(iii) the effects of allowing consumer reporting agencies to use partial matches of social security numbers and name recognition software on the accuracy of credit reports;

"(B) requiring notification to consumers when negative information has been added to their credit reports, including—

"(i) the potential impact of such notification on the ability of consumers to identify errors on their credit reports; and

"(ii) the potential impact of such notification on the ability of consumers to remove fraudulent information from their credit reports;

"(C) the effects of requiring that a consumer who has experienced an adverse action based on a credit report receives a copy of the same credit report that the creditor relied on in taking the adverse action, including—

"(i) the extent to which providing such reports to consumers would increase the ability of consumers to identify errors in their credit reports; and

"(ii) the extent to which providing such reports to consumers would increase the ability of consumers to remove fraudulent information from their credit reports;

"(D) any common financial transactions that are not generally reported to the consumer reporting agencies, but would provide useful information in determining the credit worthiness of consumers; and

"(E) any actions that might be taken within a voluntary reporting system to encourage the reporting of the types of transactions described in subparagraph (D).

"(3) COSTS AND BENEFITS.—With respect to each area of study described in paragraph (2), the Commission shall consider the extent to which such requirements would benefit consumers, balanced against the cost of implementing such provisions.

"(b) REPORT REQUIRED.—Not later than 1 year after the date of enactment of this Act [Dec. 4, 2003], the chairman of the Commission shall submit a report to the Committee on Banking, Housing, and Urban Affairs of the Senate and the Committee on Financial Services of the House of Representatives containing a detailed summary of the findings and conclusions of the study under this section, together with such recommendations for legislative or administrative actions as may be appropriate."

FTC STUDY OF THE ACCURACY OF CONSUMER REPORTS

Pub. L. 108–159, title III, §319, Dec. 4, 2003, 117 Stat. 1999, provided that:

"(a) STUDY REQUIRED.—Until the final report is submitted under subsection (b)(2), the Commission shall conduct an ongoing study of the accuracy and completeness of information contained in consumer reports prepared or maintained by consumer reporting agencies and methods for improving the accuracy and completeness of such information.

"(b) BIENNIAL REPORTS REQUIRED.—

"(1) INTERIM REPORTS.—The Commission shall submit an interim report to the Congress on the study conducted under subsection (a) at the end of the 1-year period beginning on the date of enactment of this Act [Dec. 4, 2003] and biennially thereafter for 8 years.

"(2) FINAL REPORT.—The Commission shall submit a final report to the Congress on the study conducted under subsection (a) at the end of the 2-year period beginning on the date on which the final interim report is submitted to the Congress under paragraph (1).

"(3) CONTENTS.—Each report submitted under this subsection shall contain a detailed summary of the findings and conclusions of the Commission with respect to the study required under subsection (a) and such recommendations for legislative and administrative action as the Commission may determine to be appropriate."

DEFINITIONS

Pub. L. 108–159, §2, Dec. 4, 2003, 117 Stat. 1953, provided that: "As used in this Act [see Short Title of 2003 Amendment note set out under section 1601 of this title]—

"(1) the term 'Board' means the Board of Governors of the Federal Reserve System;

"(2) the term 'Commission', other than as used in title V [20 U.S.C. 9701 et seq.], means the Federal Trade Commission;

"(3) the terms 'consumer', 'consumer report', 'consumer reporting agency', 'creditor', 'Federal banking agencies', and 'financial institution' have the same meanings as in section 603 of the Fair Credit Reporting Act [15 U.S.C. 1681a], as amended by this Act; and

"(4) the term 'affiliates' means persons that are related by common ownership or affiliated by corporate control."

§1681a. Definitions; rules of construction

(a) Definitions and rules of construction set forth in this section are applicable for the purposes of this subchapter.

(b) The term "person" means any individual, partnership, corporation, trust, estate, cooperative, association, government or governmental subdivision or agency, or other entity.

(c) The term "consumer" means an individual.

(d) CONSUMER REPORT.—

(1) IN GENERAL.—The term "consumer report" means any written, oral, or other communication of any information by a consumer reporting agency bearing on a consumer's credit worthiness, credit standing, credit capacity, character, general reputation, personal characteristics, or mode of living which is used or expected to be used or collected in whole or in part for the purpose of serving as a factor in establishing the consumer's eligibility for—

(A) credit or insurance to be used primarily for personal, family, or household purposes;

(B) employment purposes; or

(C) any other purpose authorized under section 1681b of this title.

(2) EXCLUSIONS.—Except as provided in paragraph (3), the term "consumer report" does not include—

(A) subject to section 1681s–3 of this title, any—

(i) report containing information solely as to transactions or experiences between the consumer and the person making the report;

(ii) communication of that information among persons related by common ownership or affiliated by corporate control; or

(iii) communication of other information among persons related by common ownership or affiliated by corporate control, if it is clearly and conspicuously disclosed to the consumer that the information may be communicated among such persons and the consumer is given the opportunity, before the time that the information is initially communicated, to direct that such information not be communicated among such persons;

(B) any authorization or approval of a specific extension of credit directly or indirectly by the issuer of a credit card or similar device;

(C) any report in which a person who has been requested by a third party to make a specific extension of credit directly or indirectly to a consumer conveys his or her decision with respect to such request, if the third party advises the consumer of the name and address of the person to whom the request was made, and such person makes the disclosures to the consumer required under section 1681m of this title; or

(D) a communication described in subsection (o) or (x).[1]

(3) RESTRICTION ON SHARING OF MEDICAL INFORMATION.—Except for information or any communication of information disclosed as provided in section 1681b(g)(3) of this title, the exclusions in paragraph (2) shall not apply with respect to information disclosed to any person related by common ownership or affiliated by corporate control, if the information is—

(A) medical information;

(B) an individualized list or description based on the payment transactions of the consumer for medical products or services; or

(C) an aggregate list of identified consumers based on payment transactions for medical products or services.

(e) The term "investigative consumer report" means a consumer report or portion thereof in which information on a consumer's character, general reputation, personal characteristics, or mode of living is obtained through personal interviews with neighbors, friends, or associates of the consumer reported on or with others with whom he is acquainted or who may have knowledge concerning any such items of information. However, such information shall not include specific factual information on a consumer's credit record obtained directly from a creditor of the consumer or from a consumer reporting agency when such information was obtained directly from a creditor of the consumer or from the consumer.

(f) The term "consumer reporting agency" means any person which, for monetary fees, dues, or on a cooperative nonprofit basis, regularly engages in whole or in part in the practice of assembling or evaluating consumer credit information or other information on consumers for the purpose of furnishing consumer reports to third parties, and which uses any means or facility of interstate commerce for the purpose of preparing or furnishing consumer reports.

(g) The term "file", when used in connection with information on any consumer, means all of the information on that consumer recorded and retained by a consumer reporting agency regardless of how the information is stored.

(h) The term "employment purposes" when used in connection with a consumer report means a report used for the purpose of evaluating a consumer for employment, promotion, reassignment or retention as an employee.

(i) MEDICAL INFORMATION.—The term "medical information"—

(1) means information or data, whether oral or recorded, in any form or medium, created by or derived from a health care provider or the consumer, that relates to—

(A) the past, present, or future physical, mental, or behavioral health or condition of an individual;

(B) the provision of health care to an individual; or

(C) the payment for the provision of health care to an individual.[2]

(2) does not include the age or gender of a consumer, demographic information about the consumer, including a consumer's residence address or e-mail address, or any other information about a consumer that does not relate to the physical, mental, or behavioral health or condition of a consumer, including the existence or value of any insurance policy.

(j) DEFINITIONS RELATING TO CHILD SUPPORT OBLIGATIONS.—

(1) OVERDUE SUPPORT.—The term "overdue support" has the meaning given to such term in section 666(e) of title 42.

(2) STATE OR LOCAL CHILD SUPPORT ENFORCEMENT AGENCY.—The term "State or local child support enforcement agency" means a State or local agency which administers a State or local program for establishing and enforcing child support obligations.

(k) ADVERSE ACTION.—
    (1) ACTIONS INCLUDED.—The term "adverse action"—
        (A) has the same meaning as in section 1691(d)(6) of this title; and
        (B) means—
           (i) a denial or cancellation of, an increase in any charge for, or a reduction or other adverse or unfavorable change in the terms of coverage or amount of, any insurance, existing or applied for, in connection with the underwriting of insurance;
           (ii) a denial of employment or any other decision for employment purposes that adversely affects any current or prospective employee;
           (iii) a denial or cancellation of, an increase in any charge for, or any other adverse or unfavorable change in the terms of, any license or benefit described in section 1681b(a)(3)(D) of this title; and
           (iv) an action taken or determination that is—
              (I) made in connection with an application that was made by, or a transaction that was initiated by, any consumer, or in connection with a review of an account under section 1681b(a)(3)(F)(ii) of this title; and
              (II) adverse to the interests of the consumer.

    (2) APPLICABLE FINDINGS, DECISIONS, COMMENTARY, AND ORDERS.—For purposes of any determination of whether an action is an adverse action under paragraph (1)(A), all appropriate final findings, decisions, commentary, and orders issued under section 1691(d)(6) of this title by the Bureau or any court shall apply.

(l) FIRM OFFER OF CREDIT OR INSURANCE.—The term "firm offer of credit or insurance" means any offer of credit or insurance to a consumer that will be honored if the consumer is determined, based on information in a consumer report on the consumer, to meet the specific criteria used to select the consumer for the offer, except that the offer may be further conditioned on one or more of the following:
    (1) The consumer being determined, based on information in the consumer's application for the credit or insurance, to meet specific criteria bearing on credit worthiness or insurability, as applicable, that are established—
        (A) before selection of the consumer for the offer; and
        (B) for the purpose of determining whether to extend credit or insurance pursuant to the offer.

    (2) Verification—
        (A) that the consumer continues to meet the specific criteria used to select the consumer for the offer, by using information in a consumer report on the consumer, information in the consumer's application for the credit or insurance, or other information bearing on the credit worthiness or insurability of the consumer; or
        (B) of the information in the consumer's application for the credit or insurance, to determine that the consumer meets the specific criteria bearing on credit worthiness or insurability.

    (3) The consumer furnishing any collateral that is a requirement for the extension of the credit or insurance that was—
        (A) established before selection of the consumer for the offer of credit or insurance; and
        (B) disclosed to the consumer in the offer of credit or insurance.

(m) CREDIT OR INSURANCE TRANSACTION THAT IS NOT INITIATED BY THE CONSUMER.—The term "credit or insurance transaction that is not initiated by the consumer" does not include the use of a consumer report by a person with which the consumer has an account or insurance policy, for purposes of—
    (1) reviewing the account or insurance policy; or
    (2) collecting the account.

(n) STATE.—The term "State" means any State, the Commonwealth of Puerto Rico, the District of Columbia, and any territory or possession of the United States.
(o) EXCLUDED COMMUNICATIONS.—A communication is described in this subsection if it is a communication—
    (1) that, but for subsection (d)(2)(D), would be an investigative consumer report;
    (2) that is made to a prospective employer for the purpose of—
        (A) procuring an employee for the employer; or
        (B) procuring an opportunity for a natural person to work for the employer;

    (3) that is made by a person who regularly performs such procurement;
    (4) that is not used by any person for any purpose other than a purpose described in subparagraph (A) or (B) of paragraph (2); and
    (5) with respect to which—

(A) the consumer who is the subject of the communication—

(i) consents orally or in writing to the nature and scope of the communication, before the collection of any information for the purpose of making the communication;

(ii) consents orally or in writing to the making of the communication to a prospective employer, before the making of the communication; and

(iii) in the case of consent under clause (i) or (ii) given orally, is provided written confirmation of that consent by the person making the communication, not later than 3 business days after the receipt of the consent by that person;

(B) the person who makes the communication does not, for the purpose of making the communication, make any inquiry that if made by a prospective employer of the consumer who is the subject of the communication would violate any applicable Federal or State equal employment opportunity law or regulation; and

(C) the person who makes the communication—

(i) discloses in writing to the consumer who is the subject of the communication, not later than 5 business days after receiving any request from the consumer for such disclosure, the nature and substance of all information in the consumer's file at the time of the request, except that the sources of any information that is acquired solely for use in making the communication and is actually used for no other purpose, need not be disclosed other than under appropriate discovery procedures in any court of competent jurisdiction in which an action is brought; and

(ii) notifies the consumer who is the subject of the communication, in writing, of the consumer's right to request the information described in clause (i).

(p) CONSUMER REPORTING AGENCY THAT COMPILES AND MAINTAINS FILES ON CONSUMERS ON A NATIONWIDE BASIS. —The term "consumer reporting agency that compiles and maintains files on consumers on a nationwide basis" means a consumer reporting agency that regularly engages in the practice of assembling or evaluating, and maintaining, for the purpose of furnishing consumer reports to third parties bearing on a consumer's credit worthiness, credit standing, or credit capacity, each of the following regarding consumers residing nationwide:

(1) Public record information.

(2) Credit account information from persons who furnish that information regularly and in the ordinary course of business.

(q) DEFINITIONS RELATING TO FRAUD ALERTS.—

(1) ACTIVE DUTY MILITARY CONSUMER.—The term "active duty military consumer" means a consumer in military service who—

(A) is on active duty (as defined in section 101(d)(1) of title 10) or is a reservist performing duty under a call or order to active duty under a provision of law referred to in section 101(a)(13) of title 10; and

(B) is assigned to service away from the usual duty station of the consumer.

(2) FRAUD ALERT; ACTIVE DUTY ALERT.—The terms "fraud alert" and "active duty alert" mean a statement in the file of a consumer that—

(A) notifies all prospective users of a consumer report relating to the consumer that the consumer may be a victim of fraud, including identity theft, or is an active duty military consumer, as applicable; and

(B) is presented in a manner that facilitates a clear and conspicuous view of the statement described in subparagraph (A) by any person requesting such consumer report.

(3) IDENTITY THEFT.—The term "identity theft" means a fraud committed using the identifying information of another person, subject to such further definition as the Bureau may prescribe, by regulation.

(4) IDENTITY THEFT REPORT.—The term "identity theft report" has the meaning given that term by rule of the Bureau, and means, at a minimum, a report—

(A) that alleges an identity theft;

(B) that is a copy of an official, valid report filed by a consumer with an appropriate Federal, State, or local law enforcement agency, including the United States Postal Inspection Service, or such other government agency deemed appropriate by the Bureau; and

(C) the filing of which subjects the person filing the report to criminal penalties relating to the filing of false information if, in fact, the information in the report is false.

(5) NEW CREDIT PLAN.—The term "new credit plan" means a new account under an open end credit plan (as defined in section 1602(i) [1] of this title) or a new credit transaction not under an open end credit plan.

(r) CREDIT AND DEBIT RELATED TERMS—

(1) CARD ISSUER.—The term "card issuer" means—

(A) a credit card issuer, in the case of a credit card; and

(B) a debit card issuer, in the case of a debit card.

(2) CREDIT CARD.—The term "credit card" has the same meaning as in section 1602 of this title.

(3) DEBIT CARD.—The term "debit card" means any card issued by a financial institution to a consumer for use in initiating an electronic fund transfer from the account of the consumer at such financial institution, for the purpose of transferring money between accounts or obtaining money, property, labor, or services.

(4) ACCOUNT AND ELECTRONIC FUND TRANSFER.—The terms "account" and "electronic fund transfer" have the same meanings as in section 1693a of this title.

(5) CREDIT AND CREDITOR.—The terms "credit" and "creditor" have the same meanings as in section 1691a of this title.

(s) FEDERAL BANKING AGENCY.—The term "Federal banking agency" has the same meaning as in section 1813 of title 12.

(t) FINANCIAL INSTITUTION.—The term "financial institution" means a State or National bank, a State or Federal savings and loan association, a mutual savings bank, a State or Federal credit union, or any other person that, directly or indirectly, holds a transaction account (as defined in section 461(b) of title 12) belonging to a consumer.

(u) RESELLER.—The term "reseller" means a consumer reporting agency that—

(1) assembles and merges information contained in the database of another consumer reporting agency or multiple consumer reporting agencies concerning any consumer for purposes of furnishing such information to any third party, to the extent of such activities; and

(2) does not maintain a database of the assembled or merged information from which new consumer reports are produced.

(v) COMMISSION.—The term "Commission" means the Bureau.[3]

(w) The term "Bureau" means the Bureau of Consumer Financial Protection.

(x) NATIONWIDE SPECIALTY CONSUMER REPORTING AGENCY.—The term "nationwide specialty consumer reporting agency" means a consumer reporting agency that compiles and maintains files on consumers on a nationwide basis relating to—

(1) medical records or payments;

(2) residential or tenant history;

(3) check writing history;

(4) employment history; or

(5) insurance claims.

(y) EXCLUSION OF CERTAIN COMMUNICATIONS FOR EMPLOYEE INVESTIGATIONS.—

(1) COMMUNICATIONS DESCRIBED IN THIS SUBSECTION.—A communication is described in this subsection if—

(A) but for subsection (d)(2)(D), the communication would be a consumer report;

(B) the communication is made to an employer in connection with an investigation of—

(i) suspected misconduct relating to employment; or

(ii) compliance with Federal, State, or local laws and regulations, the rules of a self-regulatory organization, or any preexisting written policies of the employer;

(C) the communication is not made for the purpose of investigating a consumer's credit worthiness, credit standing, or credit capacity; and

(D) the communication is not provided to any person except—

(i) to the employer or an agent of the employer;

(ii) to any Federal or State officer, agency, or department, or any officer, agency, or department of a unit of general local government;

(iii) to any self-regulatory organization with regulatory authority over the activities of the employer or employee;

(iv) as otherwise required by law; or

(v) pursuant to section 1681f of this title.

(2) SUBSEQUENT DISCLOSURE.—After taking any adverse action based in whole or in part on a communication described in paragraph (1), the employer shall disclose to the consumer a summary containing the nature and substance of the communication upon which the adverse action is based, except that the sources of information acquired solely for use in preparing what would be but for subsection (d)(2)(D) an investigative consumer report need not be disclosed.

(3) SELF-REGULATORY ORGANIZATION DEFINED.—For purposes of this subsection, the term "self-regulatory organization" includes any self-regulatory organization (as defined in section 78c(a)(26) of this title), any entity established under title I of the Sarbanes-Oxley Act of 2002 [15 U.S.C. 7211 et seq.], any board of trade designated by the Commodity Futures Trading Commission, and any futures association registered with such Commission.

(z) VETERAN.—The term "veteran" has the meaning given the term in section 101 of title 38.

(aa) VETERAN'S MEDICAL DEBT.—The term "veteran's medical debt"—

    (1) means a medical collection debt of a veteran owed to a non-Department of Veterans Affairs health care provider that was submitted to the Department for payment for health care authorized by the Department of Veterans Affairs; and

    (2) includes medical collection debt that the Department of Veterans Affairs has wrongfully charged a veteran.

(Pub. L. 90–321, title VI, §603, as added Pub. L. 91–508, title VI, §601, Oct. 26, 1970, 84 Stat. 1128; amended Pub. L. 102–537, §2(b), Oct. 27, 1992, 106 Stat. 3531; Pub. L. 104–208, div. A, title II, §2402, Sept. 30, 1996, 110 Stat. 3009–426; Pub. L. 105–347, §6(1)–(3), Nov. 2, 1998, 112 Stat. 3211; Pub. L. 108–159, title I, §111, title II, §214(c)(1), title IV, §411(b), (c), title VI, §611, Dec. 4, 2003, 117 Stat. 1954, 1983, 2001, 2010; Pub. L. 111–203, title X, §1088(a)(1), (2)(A), (C), (3), July 21, 2010, 124 Stat. 2086, 2087; Pub. L. 115–174, title III, §302(b)(1), May 24, 2018, 132 Stat. 1333.)

EDITORIAL NOTES

REFERENCES IN TEXT

Subsection (x) of this section, referred to in subsec. (d)(2)(D), was redesignated subsection (y) of this section by Pub. L. 111–203, title X, §1088(a)(1), July 21, 2010, 124 Stat. 2086.

Section 1602(i) of this title, referred to in subsec. (q)(5), was redesignated section 1602(j) of this title by Pub. L. 111–203, title X, §1100A(1)(A), July 21, 2010, 124 Stat. 2107.

The Sarbanes-Oxley Act of 2002, referred to in subsec. (y)(3), is Pub. L. 107–204, July 30, 2002, 116 Stat. 745. Title I of the Act is classified principally to subchapter I (§7211 et seq.) of chapter 98 of this title. For complete classification of this Act to the Code, see Short Title note set out under section 7201 of this title and Tables.

AMENDMENTS

2018—Subsecs. (z), (aa). Pub. L. 115–174 added subsecs. (z) and (aa).

2010—Subsec. (k)(2). Pub. L. 111–203, §1088(a)(3), substituted "Bureau" for "Board of Governors of the Federal Reserve System".

Subsec. (q)(3), (4). Pub. L. 111–203, §1088(a)(2)(C), substituted "the Bureau" for "the Commission" wherever appearing.

Subsec. (v). Pub. L. 111–203, §1088(a)(2)(A), substituted "Bureau" for "Federal Trade Commission".

Subsecs. (w) to (y). Pub. L. 111–203, §1088(a)(1), added subsec. (w) and redesignated former subsecs. (w) and (x) as (x) and (y), respectively.

2003—Subsec. (d)(2). Pub. L. 108–159, §411(b)(1), substituted "Except as provided in paragraph (3), the term" for "The term" in introductory provisions.

Subsec. (d)(2)(A). Pub. L. 108–159, §214(c)(1), inserted "subject to section 1681s–3 of this title," after "(A)" in introductory provisions.

Subsec. (d)(2)(D). Pub. L. 108–159, §611(b), inserted "or (x)" after "subsection (o)".

Subsec. (d)(3). Pub. L. 108–159, §411(b)(2), added par. (3).

Subsec. (i). Pub. L. 108–159, §411(c), inserted heading and amended text of subsec. (i) generally. Prior to amendment, text read as follows: "The term 'medical information' means information or records obtained, with the consent of the individual to whom it relates, from licensed physicians or medical practitioners, hospitals, clinics, or other medical or medically related facilities."

Subsecs. (q) to (w). Pub. L. 108–159, §111, added subsecs. (q) to (w).

Subsec. (x). Pub. L. 108–159, §611(a), added subsec. (x).

1998—Subsec. (d)(2)(A)(iii). Pub. L. 105–347, §6(1), struck out "any" before "communication of other".

Subsec. (o)(1). Pub. L. 105–347, §6(2), substituted "(d)(2)(D)" for "(d)(2)(E)".

Subsec. (o)(4). Pub. L. 105–347, §6(3), substituted "and" for "or" at end.

1996—Subsec. (d). Pub. L. 104–208, §2402(e), inserted subsec. heading, designated existing provisions as par. (1) and inserted heading, redesignated cls. (1) to (3) as subpars. (A) to (C), respectively, added par. (2), and struck out at end "The term does not include (A) any report containing information solely as to transactions or experiences between the consumer and the person making the report; (B) any authorization or approval of a specific extension of credit directly or indirectly by the issuer of a credit card or similar device; or (C) any report in which a person who has been requested by a third party to make a specific extension of credit directly or indirectly to a consumer conveys his decision with respect to such request, if the third party advises the consumer of the name and address of the person to whom the request was made and such person makes the disclosures to the consumer required under section 1681m of this title."

Subsec. (k). Pub. L. 104–208, §2402(a), added subsec. (k).

Subsec. (l). Pub. L. 104–208, §2402(b), added subsec. (l).

Subsec. (m). Pub. L. 104–208, §2402(c), added subsec. (m).

Subsec. (n). Pub. L. 104–208, §2402(d), added subsec. (n).
Subsec. (o). Pub. L. 104–208, §2402(f), added subsec. (o).
Subsec. (p). Pub. L. 104–208, §2402(g), added subsec. (p).
1992—Subsec. (j). Pub. L. 102–537 added subsec. (j).

STATUTORY NOTES AND RELATED SUBSIDIARIES

EFFECTIVE DATE OF 2018 AMENDMENT

Pub. L. 115–174, title III, §302(e), May 24, 2018, 132 Stat. 1335, provided that: "The amendments made by this section [amending this section and sections 1681c, 1681c–1, 1681i, and 1681t of this title and enacting provisions set out as a note under section 1681c of this title] shall take effect on the date that is 1 year after the date of enactment of this Act [May 24, 2018]."

EFFECTIVE DATE OF 2010 AMENDMENT

Amendment by Pub. L. 111–203 effective on the designated transfer date, see section 1100H of Pub. L. 111–203, set out as a note under section 552a of Title 5, Government Organization and Employees.

EFFECTIVE DATE OF 2003 AMENDMENT

Amendment by Pub. L. 108–159 subject to joint regulations establishing effective dates as prescribed by Federal Reserve Board and Federal Trade Commission, except as otherwise provided, see section 3 of Pub. L. 108–159, set out as a note under section 1681 of this title.

Pub. L. 108–159, title IV, §411(d), Dec. 4, 2003, 117 Stat. 2002, provided that: "This section [amending this section and section 1681b of this title] shall take effect at the end of the 180-day period beginning on the date of enactment of this Act [Dec. 4, 2003], except that paragraph (2) of section 604(g) of the Fair Credit Reporting Act [15 U.S.C. 1681b(g)(2)] (as amended by subsection (a) of this section) shall take effect on the later of—

"(1) the end of the 90-day period beginning on the date on which the regulations required under paragraph (5)(B) of such section 604(g) are issued in final form; or

"(2) the date specified in the regulations referred to in paragraph (1)."

EFFECTIVE DATE OF 1998 AMENDMENT

Pub. L. 105–347, §7, Nov. 2, 1998, 112 Stat. 3211, provided that: "The amendments made by this Act [amending this section and sections 1681b, 1681c, 1681g, 1681i, 1681k, and 1681s of this title] shall be deemed to have the same effective date [see section 2420 of Pub. L. 104–208, set out as a note below] as the amendments made by section 2403 of the Consumer Credit Reporting Reform Act of 1996 (Public Law 104–208; 110 Stat. 3009–1257 [3009–430]) [amending section 1681b of this title]."

EFFECTIVE DATE OF 1996 AMENDMENT

Pub. L. 104–208, div. A, title II, §2420, Sept. 30, 1996, 110 Stat. 3009–454, provided that:

"(a) IN GENERAL.—Except as otherwise specifically provided in this chapter [chapter 1 (§§2401–2422) of subtitle D of title II of div. A of Pub. L. 104–208, see Short Title of 1996 Amendment note set out under section 1601 of this title], the amendments made by this chapter shall become effective 365 days after the date of enactment of this Act [Sept. 30, 1996].

"(b) EARLY COMPLIANCE.—Any person or other entity that is subject to the requirements of this chapter may, at its option, comply with any provision of this chapter before the date on which that provision becomes effective under this chapter, in which case, each of the corresponding provisions of this chapter shall be fully applicable to such person or entity."

EFFECTIVE DATE OF 1992 AMENDMENT

Pub. L. 102–537, §2(d), Oct. 27, 1992, 106 Stat. 3532, provided that: "The amendments made by this section [enacting section 1681s–1 of this title and amending this section] shall take effect on January 1, 1993."

EFFECTIVE DATE

Section effective upon the expiration of one hundred and eighty days following Oct. 26, 1970, see section 504(d) of Pub. L. 90–321, as added by Pub. L. 91–508, set out as a note under section 1681 of this title.

CONSTRUCTION OF 1996 AMENDMENT

Pub. L. 104–208, div. A, title II, §2421, Sept. 30, 1996, 110 Stat. 3009–454, provided that: "Nothing in this chapter [chapter 1 (§§2401–2422) of subtitle D of title II of div. A of Pub. L. 104–208, see Short Title of 1996 Amendment note set out under section 1601 of this title] or the amendments made by this chapter shall be considered to supersede or otherwise affect section 2721 of title 18, United States Code, with respect to motor vehicle records for surveys, marketing, or solicitations."

§1681b. Permissible purposes of consumer reports

(a) In general

Subject to subsection (c), any consumer reporting agency may furnish a consumer report under the following circumstances and no other:

(1) In response to the order of a court having jurisdiction to issue such an order, a subpoena issued in connection with proceedings before a Federal grand jury, or a subpoena issued in accordance with section 5318 of title 31 or section 3486 of title 18.

(2) In accordance with the written instructions of the consumer to whom it relates.

(3) To a person which it has reason to believe—

(A) intends to use the information in connection with a credit transaction involving the consumer on whom the information is to be furnished and involving the extension of credit to, or review or collection of an account of, the consumer; or

(B) intends to use the information for employment purposes; or

(C) intends to use the information in connection with the underwriting of insurance involving the consumer; or

(D) intends to use the information in connection with a determination of the consumer's eligibility for a license or other benefit granted by a governmental instrumentality required by law to consider an applicant's financial responsibility or status; or

(E) intends to use the information, as a potential investor or servicer, or current insurer, in connection with a valuation of, or an assessment of the credit or prepayment risks associated with, an existing credit obligation; or

(F) otherwise has a legitimate business need for the information—

(i) in connection with a business transaction that is initiated by the consumer; or

(ii) to review an account to determine whether the consumer continues to meet the terms of the account.

(G) executive departments and agencies in connection with the issuance of government-sponsored individually-billed travel charge cards.

(4) In response to a request by the head of a State or local child support enforcement agency (or a State or local government official authorized by the head of such an agency), if the person making the request certifies to the consumer reporting agency that—

(A) the consumer report is needed for the purpose of establishing an individual's capacity to make child support payments, determining the appropriate level of such payments, or enforcing a child support order, award, agreement, or judgment;

(B) the parentage of the consumer for the child to which the obligation relates has been established or acknowledged by the consumer in accordance with State laws under which the obligation arises (if required by those laws); and

(C) the consumer report will be kept confidential, will be used solely for a purpose described in subparagraph (A), and will not be used in connection with any other civil, administrative, or criminal proceeding, or for any other purpose.

(5) To an agency administering a State plan under section 654 of title 42 for use to set an initial or modified child support award.

(6) To the Federal Deposit Insurance Corporation or the National Credit Union Administration as part of its preparation for its appointment or as part of its exercise of powers, as conservator, receiver, or liquidating agent for an insured depository institution or insured credit union under the Federal Deposit Insurance Act [12 U.S.C. 1811 et seq.] or the Federal Credit Union Act [12 U.S.C. 1751 et seq.], or other applicable Federal or State law, or in connection with the resolution or liquidation of a failed or failing insured depository institution or insured credit union, as applicable.

(b) Conditions for furnishing and using consumer reports for employment purposes

(1) Certification from user

A consumer reporting agency may furnish a consumer report for employment purposes only if—

(A) the person who obtains such report from the agency certifies to the agency that—

(i) the person has complied with paragraph (2) with respect to the consumer report, and the person will comply with paragraph (3) with respect to the consumer report if paragraph (3) becomes applicable; and

(ii) information from the consumer report will not be used in violation of any applicable Federal or State equal employment opportunity law or regulation; and

(B) the consumer reporting agency provides with the report, or has previously provided, a summary of the consumer's rights under this subchapter, as prescribed by the Bureau under section 1681g(c)(3) [1] of this title.

(2) Disclosure to consumer

(A) In general

Except as provided in subparagraph (B), a person may not procure a consumer report, or cause a consumer report to be procured, for employment purposes with respect to any consumer, unless—

(i) a clear and conspicuous disclosure has been made in writing to the consumer at any time before the report is procured or caused to be procured, in a document that consists solely of the disclosure, that a consumer report may be obtained for employment purposes; and

(ii) the consumer has authorized in writing (which authorization may be made on the document referred to in clause (i)) the procurement of the report by that person.

(B) Application by mail, telephone, computer, or other similar means

If a consumer described in subparagraph (C) applies for employment by mail, telephone, computer, or other similar means, at any time before a consumer report is procured or caused to be procured in connection with that application—

(i) the person who procures the consumer report on the consumer for employment purposes shall provide to the consumer, by oral, written, or electronic means, notice that a consumer report may be obtained for employment purposes, and a summary of the consumer's rights under section 1681m(a)(3) [1] of this title; and

(ii) the consumer shall have consented, orally, in writing, or electronically to the procurement of the report by that person.

(C) Scope

Subparagraph (B) shall apply to a person procuring a consumer report on a consumer in connection with the consumer's application for employment only if—

(i) the consumer is applying for a position over which the Secretary of Transportation has the power to establish qualifications and maximum hours of service pursuant to the provisions of section 31502 of title 49, or a position subject to safety regulation by a State transportation agency; and

(ii) as of the time at which the person procures the report or causes the report to be procured the only interaction between the consumer and the person in connection with that employment application has been by mail, telephone, computer, or other similar means.

(3) Conditions on use for adverse actions

(A) In general

Except as provided in subparagraph (B), in using a consumer report for employment purposes, before taking any adverse action based in whole or in part on the report, the person intending to take such adverse action shall provide to the consumer to whom the report relates—

(i) a copy of the report; and

(ii) a description in writing of the rights of the consumer under this subchapter, as prescribed by the Bureau under section 1681g(c)(3) [1] of this title.

(B) Application by mail, telephone, computer, or other similar means

(i) If a consumer described in subparagraph (C) applies for employment by mail, telephone, computer, or other similar means, and if a person who has procured a consumer report on the consumer for employment purposes takes adverse action on the employment application based in whole or in part on the report, then the person must provide to the consumer to whom the report relates, in lieu of the notices required under subparagraph (A) of this section and under section 1681m(a) of this title, within 3 business days of taking such action, an oral, written or electronic notification—

(I) that adverse action has been taken based in whole or in part on a consumer report received from a consumer reporting agency;

(II) of the name, address and telephone number of the consumer reporting agency that furnished the consumer report (including a toll-free telephone number established by the agency if the agency compiles and maintains files on consumers on a nationwide basis);

(III) that the consumer reporting agency did not make the decision to take the adverse action and is unable to provide to the consumer the specific reasons why the adverse action was taken; and

(IV) that the consumer may, upon providing proper identification, request a free copy of a report and may dispute with the consumer reporting agency the accuracy or completeness of any information in a report.

(ii) If, under clause (B)(i)(IV), the consumer requests a copy of a consumer report from the person who procured the report, then, within 3 business days of receiving the consumer's request, together with proper identification, the person must send or provide to the consumer a copy of a report and a copy of the consumer's rights as prescribed by the Bureau under section 1681g(c)(3) [1] of this title.

(C) Scope

Subparagraph (B) shall apply to a person procuring a consumer report on a consumer in connection with the consumer's application for employment only if—

(i) the consumer is applying for a position over which the Secretary of Transportation has the power to establish qualifications and maximum hours of service pursuant to the provisions of section 31502 of title 49, or a position subject to safety regulation by a State transportation agency; and

(ii) as of the time at which the person procures the report or causes the report to be procured the only interaction between the consumer and the person in connection with that employment application has been by mail, telephone, computer, or other similar means.

(4) Exception for national security investigations

(A) In general

In the case of an agency or department of the United States Government which seeks to obtain and use a consumer report for employment purposes, paragraph (3) shall not apply to any adverse action by such agency or department which is based in part on such consumer report, if the head of such agency or department makes a written finding that—

(i) the consumer report is relevant to a national security investigation of such agency or department;

(ii) the investigation is within the jurisdiction of such agency or department;

(iii) there is reason to believe that compliance with paragraph (3) will—

(I) endanger the life or physical safety of any person;

(II) result in flight from prosecution;

(III) result in the destruction of, or tampering with, evidence relevant to the investigation;

(IV) result in the intimidation of a potential witness relevant to the investigation;

(V) result in the compromise of classified information; or

(VI) otherwise seriously jeopardize or unduly delay the investigation or another official proceeding.

(B) Notification of consumer upon conclusion of investigation

Upon the conclusion of a national security investigation described in subparagraph (A), or upon the determination that the exception under subparagraph (A) is no longer required for the reasons set forth in such subparagraph, the official exercising the authority in such subparagraph shall provide to the consumer who is the subject of the consumer report with regard to which such finding was made—

(i) a copy of such consumer report with any classified information redacted as necessary;

(ii) notice of any adverse action which is based, in part, on the consumer report; and

(iii) the identification with reasonable specificity of the nature of the investigation for which the consumer report was sought.

(C) Delegation by head of agency or department

For purposes of subparagraphs (A) and (B), the head of any agency or department of the United States Government may delegate his or her authorities under this paragraph to an official of such agency or department who has personnel security responsibilities and is a member of the Senior Executive Service or equivalent civilian or military rank.

(D) Definitions

For purposes of this paragraph, the following definitions shall apply:

(i) Classified information

The term "classified information" means information that is protected from unauthorized disclosure under Executive Order No. 12958 or successor orders.

(ii) National security investigation

The term "national security investigation" means any official inquiry by an agency or department of the United States Government to determine the eligibility of a consumer to receive access or continued access to classified information or to determine whether classified information has been lost or compromised.

(c) Furnishing reports in connection with credit or insurance transactions that are not initiated by consumer

(1) In general

A consumer reporting agency may furnish a consumer report relating to any consumer pursuant to subparagraph (A) or (C) of subsection (a)(3) in connection with any credit or insurance transaction that is not initiated by the consumer only if—

(A) the consumer authorizes the agency to provide such report to such person; or

(B)(i) the transaction consists of a firm offer of credit or insurance;

(ii) the consumer reporting agency has complied with subsection (e);

(iii) there is not in effect an election by the consumer, made in accordance with subsection (e), to have the consumer's name and address excluded from lists of names provided by the agency pursuant to this paragraph; and

(iv) the consumer report does not contain a date of birth that shows that the consumer has not attained the age of 21, or, if the date of birth on the consumer report shows that the consumer has not attained the age of 21, such consumer consents to the consumer reporting agency to such furnishing.

(2) Limits on information received under paragraph (1)(B)

A person may receive pursuant to paragraph (1)(B) only—

(A) the name and address of a consumer;

(B) an identifier that is not unique to the consumer and that is used by the person solely for the purpose of verifying the identity of the consumer; and

(C) other information pertaining to a consumer that does not identify the relationship or experience of the consumer with respect to a particular creditor or other entity.

(3) Information regarding inquiries

Except as provided in section 1681g(a)(5) of this title, a consumer reporting agency shall not furnish to any person a record of inquiries in connection with a credit or insurance transaction that is not initiated by a consumer.

(d) Reserved

(e) Election of consumer to be excluded from lists

(1) In general

A consumer may elect to have the consumer's name and address excluded from any list provided by a consumer reporting agency under subsection (c)(1)(B) in connection with a credit or insurance transaction that is not initiated by the consumer, by notifying the agency in accordance with paragraph (2) that the consumer does not consent to any use of a consumer report relating to the consumer in connection with any credit or insurance transaction that is not initiated by the consumer.

(2) Manner of notification

A consumer shall notify a consumer reporting agency under paragraph (1)—

(A) through the notification system maintained by the agency under paragraph (5); or

(B) by submitting to the agency a signed notice of election form issued by the agency for purposes of this subparagraph.

(3) Response of agency after notification through system

Upon receipt of notification of the election of a consumer under paragraph (1) through the notification system maintained by the agency under paragraph (5), a consumer reporting agency shall—

(A) inform the consumer that the election is effective only for the 5-year period following the election if the consumer does not submit to the agency a signed notice of election form issued by the agency for purposes of paragraph (2)(B); and

(B) provide to the consumer a notice of election form, if requested by the consumer, not later than 5 business days after receipt of the notification of the election through the system established under paragraph (5), in the case of a request made at the time the consumer provides notification through the system.

(4) Effectiveness of election

An election of a consumer under paragraph (1)—

(A) shall be effective with respect to a consumer reporting agency beginning 5 business days after the date on which the consumer notifies the agency in accordance with paragraph (2);

(B) shall be effective with respect to a consumer reporting agency—

(i) subject to subparagraph (C), during the 5-year period beginning 5 business days after the date on which the consumer notifies the agency of the election, in the case of an election for which a consumer notifies the agency only in accordance with paragraph (2)(A); or

(ii) until the consumer notifies the agency under subparagraph (C), in the case of an election for which a consumer notifies the agency in accordance with paragraph (2)(B);

(C) shall not be effective after the date on which the consumer notifies the agency, through the notification system established by the agency under paragraph (5), that the election is no longer effective; and

(D) shall be effective with respect to each affiliate of the agency.

(5) Notification system

(A) In general

Each consumer reporting agency that, under subsection (c)(1)(B), furnishes a consumer report in connection with a credit or insurance transaction that is not initiated by a consumer, shall—

(i) establish and maintain a notification system, including a toll-free telephone number, which permits any consumer whose consumer report is maintained by the agency to notify the agency, with appropriate identification, of the consumer's election to have the consumer's name and address excluded from any such list of names and addresses provided by the agency for such a transaction; and

(ii) publish by not later than 365 days after September 30, 1996, and not less than annually thereafter, in a publication of general circulation in the area served by the agency—

(I) a notification that information in consumer files maintained by the agency may be used in connection with such transactions; and

(II) the address and toll-free telephone number for consumers to use to notify the agency of the consumer's election under clause (i).

(B) Establishment and maintenance as compliance

Establishment and maintenance of a notification system (including a toll-free telephone number) and publication by a consumer reporting agency on the agency's own behalf and on behalf of any of its affiliates in accordance with this paragraph is deemed to be compliance with this paragraph by each of those affiliates.

(6) Notification system by agencies that operate nationwide

Each consumer reporting agency that compiles and maintains files on consumers on a nationwide basis shall establish and maintain a notification system for purposes of paragraph (5) jointly with other such consumer reporting agencies.

(f) Certain use or obtaining of information prohibited

A person shall not use or obtain a consumer report for any purpose unless—

(1) the consumer report is obtained for a purpose for which the consumer report is authorized to be furnished under this section; and

(2) the purpose is certified in accordance with section 1681e of this title by a prospective user of the report through a general or specific certification.

(g) Protection of medical information

(1) Limitation on consumer reporting agencies

A consumer reporting agency shall not furnish for employment purposes, or in connection with a credit or insurance transaction, a consumer report that contains medical information (other than medical contact information treated in the manner required under section 1681c(a)(6) of this title) about a consumer, unless—

(A) if furnished in connection with an insurance transaction, the consumer affirmatively consents to the furnishing of the report;

(B) if furnished for employment purposes or in connection with a credit transaction—

(i) the information to be furnished is relevant to process or effect the employment or credit transaction; and

(ii) the consumer provides specific written consent for the furnishing of the report that describes in clear and conspicuous language the use for which the information will be furnished; or

(C) the information to be furnished pertains solely to transactions, accounts, or balances relating to debts arising from the receipt of medical services, products, or devises, where such information, other than account status or amounts, is restricted or reported using codes that do not identify, or do not provide information sufficient to infer, the specific provider or the nature of such services, products, or devices, as provided in section 1681c(a)(6) of this title.

(2) Limitation on creditors

Except as permitted pursuant to paragraph (3)(C) or regulations prescribed under paragraph (5)(A), a creditor shall not obtain or use medical information (other than medical information treated in the manner required under section 1681c(a)(6) of this title) pertaining to a consumer in connection with any determination of the consumer's eligibility, or continued eligibility, for credit.

(3) Actions authorized by Federal law, insurance activities and regulatory determinations

Section 1681a(d)(3) of this title shall not be construed so as to treat information or any communication of information as a consumer report if the information or communication is disclosed—

(A) in connection with the business of insurance or annuities, including the activities described in section 18B of the model Privacy of Consumer Financial and Health Information Regulation issued by the National Association of Insurance Commissioners (as in effect on January 1, 2003);

(B) for any purpose permitted without authorization under the Standards for Individually Identifiable Health Information promulgated by the Department of Health and Human Services pursuant to the Health Insurance Portability and Accountability Act of 1996, or referred to under section 1179 of such Act,[1] or described in section 6802(e) of this title; or

(C) as otherwise determined to be necessary and appropriate, by regulation or order, by the Bureau or the applicable State insurance authority (with respect to any person engaged in providing insurance or annuities).

(4) Limitation on redisclosure of medical information

Any person that receives medical information pursuant to paragraph (1) or (3) shall not disclose such information to any other person, except as necessary to carry out the purpose for which the information was initially disclosed, or as otherwise permitted by statute, regulation, or order.

(5) Regulations and effective date for paragraph (2)

(A) ^{2} Regulations required

The Bureau may, after notice and opportunity for comment, prescribe regulations that permit transactions under paragraph (2) that are determined to be necessary and appropriate to protect legitimate operational, transactional, risk, consumer, and other needs (and which shall include permitting actions necessary for administrative verification purposes), consistent with the intent of paragraph (2) to restrict the use of medical information for inappropriate purposes.

(6) Coordination with other laws

No provision of this subsection shall be construed as altering, affecting, or superseding the applicability of any other provision of Federal law relating to medical confidentiality.

(Pub. L. 90–321, title VI, §604, as added Pub. L. 91–508, title VI, §601, Oct. 26, 1970, 84 Stat. 1129; amended Pub. L. 101–73, title IX, §964(c), Aug. 9, 1989, 103 Stat. 506; Pub. L. 104–193, title III, §352, Aug. 22, 1996, 110 Stat. 2240; Pub. L. 104–208, div. A, title II, §§2403, 2404(a), (b), 2405, Sept. 30, 1996, 110 Stat. 3009–430, 3009-431, 3009-433, 3009-434; Pub. L. 105–107, title III, §311(a), Nov. 20, 1997, 111 Stat. 2255; Pub. L. 105–347, §§2, 3, 6(4), Nov. 2, 1998, 112 Stat. 3208, 3210, 3211; Pub. L. 107–306, title VIII, §811(b)(8)(A), Nov. 27, 2002, 116 Stat. 2426; Pub. L. 108–159, title II, §213(c), title IV, §§411(a), 412(f), title VIII, §811(b), Dec. 4, 2003, 117 Stat. 1979, 1999, 2003, 2011; Pub. L. 108–177, title III, §361(j), Dec. 13, 2003, 117 Stat. 2625; Pub. L. 109–351, title VII, §719, Oct. 13, 2006, 120 Stat. 1998; Pub. L. 110–161, div. D, title VII, §743, Dec. 26, 2007, 121 Stat. 2033; Pub. L. 111–24, title III, §302, May 22, 2009, 123 Stat. 1748; Pub. L. 111–203, title X, §1088(a)(2)(A), (4), July 21, 2010, 124 Stat. 2087; Pub. L. 114–94, div. G, title LXXX, §80001, Dec. 4, 2015, 129 Stat. 1792; Pub. L. 116–283, div. F, title LXIII, §6308(b), Jan. 1, 2021, 134 Stat. 4594.)

EDITORIAL NOTES

REFERENCES IN TEXT

The Federal Deposit Insurance Act, referred to in subsec. (a)(6), is act Sept. 21, 1950, ch. 967, §2, 64 Stat. 873, which is classified generally to chapter 16 (§1811 et seq.) of Title 12, Banks and Banking. For complete classification of this Act to the Code, see Short Title note set out under section 1811 of Title 12 and Tables.

The Federal Credit Union Act, referred to in subsec. (a)(6), is act June 26, 1934, ch. 750, 48 Stat. 1216, which is classified principally to chapter 14 (§1751 et seq.) of Title 12, Banks and Banking. For complete classification of this Act to the Code, see section 1751 of Title 12 and Tables.

Section 1681g(c) of this title, referred to in subsec. (b)(1)(B), (3)(A)(ii), (B)(ii), was amended generally by Pub. L. 108–159, title II, §211(c), Dec. 4, 2003, 117 Stat. 1970, and, as so amended, no longer contains a par. (3).

Section 1681m(a)(3) of this title, referred to in subsec. (b)(2)(B)(i), was redesignated section 1681m(a)(4) of this title by Pub. L. 111–203, title X, §1100F(1)(A), July 21, 2010, 124 Stat. 2112.

Executive Order No. 12958, referred to in subsec. (b)(4)(D)(i), which was formerly set out under section 435 (now section 3161) of Title 50, War and National Defense, was revoked by Ex. Ord. No. 13526, §6.2(g), Dec. 29, 2009, 75 F.R. 731.

The Health Insurance Portability and Accountability Act of 1996, referred to in subsec. (g)(3)(B), is Pub. L. 104–191, Aug. 21, 1996, 110 Stat. 1936. For complete classification of this Act to the Code, see Short Title of 1996 Amendments note set out under section 201 of Title 42, The Public Health and Welfare, and Tables.

Section 1179 of such Act, referred to in subsec. (g)(3)(B), probably means section 1179 of the Social Security Act, as added by section 262(a) of Pub. L. 104–191, title II, Aug. 21, 1996, 110 Stat. 2030, which is classified to section 1320d–8 of Title 42, The Public Health and Welfare.

AMENDMENTS

2021—Subsec. (a)(1). Pub. L. 116–283 substituted "such an order, a" for "such an order, or a" and inserted ", or a subpoena issued in accordance with section 5318 of title 31 or section 3486 of title 18" after "grand jury".

2015—Subsec. (a)(4)(A). Pub. L. 114–94, §80001(1), substituted ", determining the appropriate level of such payments, or enforcing a child support order, award, agreement, or judgment" for "or determining the appropriate level of such payments".

Subsec. (a)(4)(B). Pub. L. 114–94, §80001(2)(A), substituted "parentage" for "paternity" and inserted "and" at end.

Subsec. (a)(4)(C), (D). Pub. L. 114–94, §80001(3), (4), redesignated subpar. (D) as (C) and struck out former subpar. (C) which read as follows: "the person has provided at least 10 days' prior notice to the consumer whose report is requested, by certified or registered mail to the last known address of the consumer, that the report will be requested; and".

2010—Subsec. (b)(1)(B), (3)(A)(ii), (B)(ii). Pub. L. 111–203, §1088(a)(2)(A), substituted "Bureau" for "Federal Trade Commission".

Subsec. (g)(3)(C). Pub. L. 111–203, §1088(a)(4)(A), added subpar. (C) and struck out former subpar. (C) which read as follows: "as otherwise determined to be necessary and appropriate, by regulation or order and subject to paragraph (6), by the Commission, any Federal banking agency or the National Credit Union Administration (with respect to any financial institution subject to the jurisdiction of such agency or Administration under paragraph (1), (2), or (3) of section 1681s(b) of this title, or the applicable State insurance authority (with respect to any person engaged in providing insurance or annuities)."

Subsec. (g)(5). Pub. L. 111–203, §1088(a)(4)(B), added par. (5) and struck out former par. (5) which related to prescription of par. (2) regulations by each Federal banking agency and the National Credit Union Administration and required issuance of final regulations before the end of the 6-month period beginning on Dec. 4, 2003.

2009—Subsec. (c)(1)(B)(iv). Pub. L. 111–24 added cl. (iv).

2007—Subsec. (a)(3)(G). Pub. L. 110–161 added subpar. (G).

2006—Subsec. (a)(6). Pub. L. 109–351 added par. (6).

2003—Subsec. (a). Pub. L. 108–159, §811(b), realigned margins.

Subsec. (b)(4)(D) to (F). Pub. L. 108–177 struck out subpars. (D) and (E) and redesignated subpar. (F) as (D). Prior to amendment, subpars. (D) and (E) read as follows:

"(D) REPORT TO THE CONGRESS.—Except as provided in subparagraph (E), not later than January 31 of each year, the head of each agency and department of the United States Government that exercised authority under this paragraph during the preceding year shall submit a report to the Congress on the number of times the department or agency exercised such authority during the year.

"(E) REPORTS TO CONGRESSIONAL INTELLIGENCE COMMITTEES.—In the case of a report to be submitted under subparagraph (D) to the congressional intelligence committees (as defined in section 401a of title 50), the submittal date for such report shall be as provided in section 415b of title 50."

Subsec. (e)(3)(A), (4)(B)(i). Pub. L. 108–159, §213(c), substituted "5-year period" for "2-year period".

Subsec. (g). Pub. L. 108–159, §411(a), amended heading and text of subsec. (g) generally. Prior to amendment, text read as follows: "A consumer reporting agency shall not furnish for employment purposes, or in connection with a credit or insurance transaction, a consumer report that contains medical information about a consumer, unless the consumer consents to the furnishing of the report."

Subsec. (g)(1). Pub. L. 108–159, §412(f)(1), inserted "(other than medical contact information treated in the manner required under section 1681c(a)(6) of this title)" after "a consumer report that contains medical information" in introductory provisions.

Subsec. (g)(2). Pub. L. 108–159, §412(f)(2), inserted "(other than medical information treated in the manner required under section 1681c(a)(6) of this title)" after "a creditor shall not obtain or use medical information".

2002—Subsec. (b)(4)(D). Pub. L. 107–306, §811(b)(8)(A)(i), substituted "Except as provided in subparagraph (E), not later than" for "Not later than".

Subsec. (b)(4)(E), (F). Pub. L. 107–306, §811(b)(8)(A)(ii), (iii), added subpar. (E) and redesignated former subpar. (E) as (F).

1998—Subsec. (b)(1)(B). Pub. L. 105–347, §3, inserted ", or has previously provided," before "a summary".

Subsec. (b)(2). Pub. L. 105–347, §2(a), amended heading and text of par. (2) generally. Prior to amendment, text read as follows: "A person may not procure a consumer report, or cause a consumer report to be procured, for employment purposes with respect to any consumer, unless—

"(A) a clear and conspicuous disclosure has been made in writing to the consumer at any time before the report is procured or caused to be procured, in a document that consists solely of the disclosure, that a consumer report may be obtained for employment purposes; and

"(B) the consumer has authorized in writing the procurement of the report by that person."

Subsec. (b)(3). Pub. L. 105–347, §2(b), amended heading and text of par. (3) generally. Prior to amendment, text read as follows: "In using a consumer report for employment purposes, before taking any adverse action based in whole or in part on the report, the person intending to take such adverse action shall provide to the consumer to whom the report relates—

"(A) a copy of the report; and

"(B) a description in writing of the rights of the consumer under this subchapter, as prescribed by the Federal Trade Commission under section 1681g(c)(3) of this title."

Subsec. (g). Pub. L. 105–347, §6(4), struck out "or a direct marketing transaction" after "or insurance transaction".

1997—Subsec. (b)(4). Pub. L. 105–107 added par. (4).

1996—Pub. L. 104–208, §§2403(a), 2404(a)(1), designated existing provisions as subsec. (a) and inserted heading, substituted "Subject to subsection (c), any consumer reporting agency" for "A consumer reporting agency" in introductory provisions, added subpars. (E) and (F) of par. (3), and struck out former subpar. (E) of par. (3) which read as follows: "otherwise has a legitimate business need for the information in connection with a business transaction involving the consumer."

Subsec. (b). Pub. L. 104–208, §2403(b), added subsec. (b).

Subsecs. (c) to (e). Pub. L. 104–208, §2404(a)(2), added subsecs. (c) to (e).

Subsec. (f). Pub. L. 104–208, §2404(b), added subsec. (f).

Subsec. (g). Pub. L. 104–208, §2405, added subsec. (g).

Pars. (4), (5). Pub. L. 104–193 added pars. (4) and (5).

1989—Par. (1). Pub. L. 101–73 inserted ", or a subpoena issued in connection with proceedings before a Federal grand jury" before period at end.

STATUTORY NOTES AND RELATED SUBSIDIARIES

EFFECTIVE DATE OF 2010 AMENDMENT

Amendment by Pub. L. 111–203 effective on the designated transfer date, see section 1100H of Pub. L. 111–203, set out as a note under section 552a of Title 5, Government Organization and Employees.

EFFECTIVE DATE OF 2009 AMENDMENT

Amendment by Pub. L. 111–24 effective 9 months after May 22, 2009, except as otherwise specifically provided, see section 3 of Pub. L. 111–24, set out as a note under section 1602 of this title.

EFFECTIVE DATE OF 2003 AMENDMENTS

Amendment by Pub. L. 108–177 effective Dec. 31, 2003, see section 361(n) of Pub. L. 108–177, set out as a note under section 1611 of Title 10, Armed Forces.

Amendment by Pub. L. 108–159 subject to joint regulations establishing effective dates as prescribed by Federal Reserve Board and Federal Trade Commission, except as otherwise provided, see section 3 of Pub. L. 108–159, set out as a note under section 1681 of this title.

Amendment by section 411 of Pub. L. 108–159 effective at end of 180-day period beginning on Dec. 4, 2003, with certain exceptions, see section 411(d) of Pub. L. 108–159, set out as an Effective Date of 2003 Amendment note under section 1681a of this title.

Pub. L. 108–159, title IV, §412(g), Dec. 4, 2003, 117 Stat. 2003, provided that: "The amendments made by this section [amending this section and sections 1681c, 1681s, and 1681s–2 of this title] shall take effect at the end of the 15-month period beginning on the date of enactment of this Act [Dec. 4, 2003]."

EFFECTIVE DATE OF 1998 AMENDMENT

Amendment by Pub. L. 105–347 deemed to have same effective date as amendments made by section 2403 of Pub. L. 104–208, see section 7 of Pub. L. 105–347, set out as a note under section 1681a of this title.

EFFECTIVE DATE OF 1997 AMENDMENT

Pub. L. 105–107, title III, §311(c), Nov. 20, 1997, 111 Stat. 2256, provided that: "The amendments made by subsections (a) and (b) [amending this section and section 1681e of this title] shall take effect as if such amendments had been included in chapter 1 of subtitle D of the Economic Growth and Regulatory Paperwork Reduction Act of 1996 [chapter 1 (§§2401–2422) of subtitle D of title II of div. A of Pub. L. 104–208], as of the date of the enactment of such Act [Sept. 30, 1996]."

EFFECTIVE DATE OF 1996 AMENDMENTS

Amendment by Pub. L. 104–208 effective 365 days after Sept. 30, 1996, with special rule for early compliance, see section 2420 of Pub. L. 104–208, set out as a note under section 1681a of this title.

For effective date of amendment by Pub. L. 104–193, see section 395(a)–(c) of Pub. L. 104–193, set out as a note under section 654 of Title 42, The Public Health and Welfare.

EFFECTIVE DATE

Section effective upon the expiration of one hundred and eighty days following Oct. 26, 1970, see section 504(d) of Pub. L. 90–321, as added by Pub. L. 91–508, set out as a note under section 1681 of this title.

PUBLIC AWARENESS CAMPAIGN

Pub. L. 108–159, title II, §213(d), Dec. 4, 2003, 117 Stat. 1979, provided that: "The Commission shall actively publicize and conspicuously post on its website any address and the toll-free telephone number established as part of a notification system for opting out of prescreening under section 604(e) of the Fair Credit Reporting Act (15 U.S.C. 1681b(e)), and otherwise take measures to increase public awareness regarding the availability of the right to opt out of prescreening."

[For definitions of terms used in section 213(d) of Pub. L. 108–159, set out above, see section 2 of Pub. L. 108–159, set out as a Definitions note under section 1681 of this title.]

COORDINATION WITH FEDERAL LAWS RELATING TO MEDICAL CONFIDENTIALITY

Pub. L. 108–159, title IV, §412(d), Dec. 4, 2003, 117 Stat. 2002, provided that: "No provision of any amendment made by this section [amending this section and sections 1681c, 1681s, and 1681s–2 of this title] shall be construed as altering, affecting, or superseding the applicability of any other provision of Federal law relating to medical confidentiality."

FTC GUIDELINES REGARDING PRESCREENING FOR INSURANCE TRANSACTIONS

Pub. L. 104–208, div. A, title II, §2404(c), Sept. 30, 1996, 110 Stat. 3009–434, provided that: "The Federal Trade Commission may issue such guidelines as it deems necessary with respect to the use of consumer reports in connection with insurance transactions that are not initiated by the consumer pursuant to section 604(c) of the Fair Credit Reporting Act [15 U.S.C. 1681b(c)], as added by subsection (a) of this section."

[1] *See References in Text note below.*

[2] *So in original. No subpar. (B) has been enacted.*

§1681c. Requirements relating to information contained in consumer reports

(a) Information excluded from consumer reports

Except as authorized under subsection (b), no consumer reporting agency may make any consumer report containing any of the following items of information:

(1) Cases under title 11 or under the Bankruptcy Act that, from the date of entry of the order for relief or the date of adjudication, as the case may be, antedate the report by more than 10 years.

(2) Civil suits, civil judgments, and records of arrest that, from date of entry, antedate the report by more than seven years or until the governing statute of limitations has expired, whichever is the longer period.

(3) Paid tax liens which, from date of payment, antedate the report by more than seven years.

(4) Accounts placed for collection or charged to profit and loss which antedate the report by more than seven years.

(5) Any other adverse item of information, other than records of convictions of crimes which antedates the report by more than seven years.

(6) The name, address, and telephone number of any medical information furnisher that has notified the agency of its status, unless—

   (A) such name, address, and telephone number are restricted or reported using codes that do not identify, or provide information sufficient to infer, the specific provider or the nature of such services, products, or devices to a person other than the consumer; or

   (B) the report is being provided to an insurance company for a purpose relating to engaging in the business of insurance other than property and casualty insurance.

(7) With respect to a consumer reporting agency described in section 1681a(p) of this title, any information related to a veteran's medical debt if the date on which the hospital care, medical services, or extended care services was rendered relating to the debt antedates the report by less than 1 year if the consumer reporting agency has actual knowledge that the information is related to a veteran's medical debt and the consumer reporting agency is in compliance with its obligation under section 302(c)(5) of the Economic Growth, Regulatory Relief, and Consumer Protection Act.

(8) With respect to a consumer reporting agency described in section 1681a(p) of this title, any information related to a fully paid or settled veteran's medical debt that had been characterized as delinquent, charged off, or in collection if the consumer reporting agency has actual knowledge that the information is related to a veteran's medical debt and the consumer reporting agency is in compliance with its obligation under section 302(c)(5) of the Economic Growth, Regulatory Relief, and Consumer Protection Act.

(b) Exempted cases

The provisions of paragraphs (1) through (5) of subsection (a) are not applicable in the case of any consumer credit report to be used in connection with—

(1) a credit transaction involving, or which may reasonably be expected to involve, a principal amount of $150,000 or more;

(2) the underwriting of life insurance involving, or which may reasonably be expected to involve, a face amount of $150,000 or more; or

(3) the employment of any individual at an annual salary which equals, or which may reasonably be expected to equal $75,000, or more.

(c) Running of reporting period

(1) In general

The 7-year period referred to in paragraphs (4) and (6) of subsection (a) shall begin, with respect to any delinquent account that is placed for collection (internally or by referral to a third party, whichever is earlier), charged to profit and loss, or subjected to any similar action, upon the expiration of the 180-day period beginning on the date of the commencement of the delinquency which immediately preceded the collection activity, charge to profit and loss, or similar action.

(2) Effective date

Paragraph (1) shall apply only to items of information added to the file of a consumer on or after the date that is 455 days after September 30, 1996.

(d) Information required to be disclosed

(1) Title 11 information

Any consumer reporting agency that furnishes a consumer report that contains information regarding any case involving the consumer that arises under title 11 shall include in the report an identification of the chapter of such title 11 under which such case arises if provided by the source of the information. If any case arising or filed under title 11 is withdrawn by the consumer before a final judgment, the consumer reporting agency shall include in the report that such case or filing was withdrawn upon receipt of documentation certifying such withdrawal.

(2) Key factor in credit score information

Any consumer reporting agency that furnishes a consumer report that contains any credit score or any other risk score or predictor on any consumer shall include in the report a clear and conspicuous statement that a key factor (as defined in section 1681g(f)(2)(B) of this title) that adversely affected such score or predictor was the number of enquiries, if such a predictor was in fact a key factor that adversely affected such score. This paragraph shall not apply to a check services company, acting as such, which issues authorizations for the purpose of approving or processing negotiable instruments, electronic fund transfers, or similar methods of payments, but only to the extent that such company is engaged in such activities.

(e) Indication of closure of account by consumer

If a consumer reporting agency is notified pursuant to section 1681s–2(a)(4) of this title that a credit account of a consumer was voluntarily closed by the consumer, the agency shall indicate that fact in any consumer report that includes information related to the account.

(f) Indication of dispute by consumer

If a consumer reporting agency is notified pursuant to section 1681s–2(a)(3) of this title that information regarding a consumer who [1] was furnished to the agency is disputed by the consumer, the agency shall indicate that fact in each consumer report that includes the disputed information.

(g) Truncation of credit card and debit card numbers

(1) In general

Except as otherwise provided in this subsection, no person that accepts credit cards or debit cards for the transaction of business shall print more than the last 5 digits of the card number or the expiration date upon any receipt provided to the cardholder at the point of the sale or transaction.

(2) Limitation

This subsection shall apply only to receipts that are electronically printed, and shall not apply to transactions in which the sole means of recording a credit card or debit card account number is by handwriting or by an imprint or copy of the card.

(3) Effective date

This subsection shall become effective—

(A) 3 years after December 4, 2003, with respect to any cash register or other machine or device that electronically prints receipts for credit card or debit card transactions that is in use before January 1, 2005; and

(B) 1 year after December 4, 2003, with respect to any cash register or other machine or device that electronically prints receipts for credit card or debit card transactions that is first put into use on or after January 1,

2005.

(h) Notice of discrepancy in address

(1) In general

If a person has requested a consumer report relating to a consumer from a consumer reporting agency described in section 1681a(p) of this title, the request includes an address for the consumer that substantially differs from the addresses in the file of the consumer, and the agency provides a consumer report in response to the request, the consumer reporting agency shall notify the requester of the existence of the discrepancy.

(2) Regulations

(A) Regulations required

The Bureau shall,,[2] in consultation with the Federal banking agencies, the National Credit Union Administration, and the Federal Trade Commission,,[2] prescribe regulations providing guidance regarding reasonable policies and procedures that a user of a consumer report should employ when such user has received a notice of discrepancy under paragraph (1).

(B) Policies and procedures to be included

The regulations prescribed under subparagraph (A) shall describe reasonable policies and procedures for use by a user of a consumer report—

(i) to form a reasonable belief that the user knows the identity of the person to whom the consumer report pertains; and

(ii) if the user establishes a continuing relationship with the consumer, and the user regularly and in the ordinary course of business furnishes information to the consumer reporting agency from which the notice of discrepancy pertaining to the consumer was obtained, to reconcile the address of the consumer with the consumer reporting agency by furnishing such address to such consumer reporting agency as part of information regularly furnished by the user for the period in which the relationship is established.

(Pub. L. 90–321, title VI, §605, as added Pub. L. 91–508, title VI, §601, Oct. 26, 1970, 84 Stat. 1129; amended Pub. L. 95–598, title III, §312(b), Nov. 6, 1978, 92 Stat. 2676; Pub. L. 104–208, div. A, title II, §2406(a)–(e)(1), Sept. 30, 1996, 110 Stat. 3009–434, 3009-435; Pub. L. 105–347, §5, Nov. 2, 1998, 112 Stat. 3211; Pub. L. 108–159, title I, §113, title II, §212(d), title III, §315, title IV, §412(b), (c), title VIII, §811(c)(1), (2)(A), Dec. 4, 2003, 117 Stat. 1959, 1977, 1996, 2002, 2011; Pub. L. 111–203, title X, §1088(a)(2)(D), (5), July 21, 2010, 124 Stat. 2087; Pub. L. 115–174, title III, §302(b)(2), May 24, 2018, 132 Stat. 1333.)

EDITORIAL NOTES

REFERENCES IN TEXT

The Bankruptcy Act, referred to in subsec. (a)(1), was act July 1, 1898, ch. 541, 30 Stat. 544, which was classified to section 1 et seq. of former Title 11, Bankruptcy, prior to its repeal by Pub. L. 95–598, Nov. 6, 1978, 92 Stat. 2549, section 101 of which enacted revised Title 11.

Section 302(c)(5) of the Economic Growth, Regulatory Relief, and Consumer Protection Act, referred to in subsec. (a)(7), (8), is section 302(c)(5) of Pub. L. 115–174, which is set out as a note below.

AMENDMENTS

2018—Subsec. (a)(7), (8). Pub. L. 115–174 added pars. (7) and (8).

2010—Subsec. (h)(2)(A). Pub. L. 111–203, §1088(a)(5), substituted ", in consultation with the Federal banking agencies, the National Credit Union Administration, and the Federal Trade Commission," for "with respect to the entities that are subject to their respective enforcement authority under section 1681s of this title".

Pub. L. 111–203, §1088(a)(2)(D), substituted "The Bureau shall" for "The Federal banking agencies, the National Credit Union Administration, and the Commission shall jointly".

2003—Subsec. (a)(1). Pub. L. 108–159, §811(c)(1), substituted "(1) Cases" for "(1) cases".

Subsec. (a)(2). Pub. L. 108–159, §811(c)(2)(A), made technical correction to directory language of Pub. L. 105–347, §5(1). See 1998 Amendment note below.

Subsec. (a)(6). Pub. L. 108–159, §412(b), added par. (6).

Subsec. (b). Pub. L. 108–159, §412(c), substituted "The provisions of paragraphs (1) through (5) of subsection (a)" for "The provisions of subsection (a)" in introductory provisions.

Subsec. (d). Pub. L. 108–159, §212(d), designated existing provisions as par. (1), inserted heading, and added par. (2).

Subsec. (g). Pub. L. 108–159, §113, added subsec. (g).

Subsec. (h). Pub. L. 108–159, §315, added subsec. (h).

1998—Subsec. (a)(2). Pub. L. 105–347, §5(1), as amended by Pub. L. 108–159, §811(c)(2)(A), substituted "Civil suits, civil judgments, and records of arrest that" for "Suits and judgments which".

Subsec. (a)(5), (6). Pub. L. 105–347, §5(2)–(4), redesignated par. (6) as (5), inserted ", other than records of convictions of crimes" after "of information", and struck out former par. (5) which read as follows: "Records of arrest, indictment, or conviction of crime which, from date of disposition, release, or parole, antedate the report by more than seven years."

1996—Pub. L. 104–208, §2406(e)(1), amended section catchline.

Subsec. (a). Pub. L. 104–208, §2406(a)(1), inserted heading.

Subsec. (b). Pub. L. 104–208, §2406(a)(2), substituted "$150,000" for "$50,000" in pars. (1) and (2) and "$75,000" for "$20,000" in par. (3).

Subsec. (c). Pub. L. 104–208, §2406(b), added subsec. (c).

Subsec. (d). Pub. L. 104–208, §2406(c), added subsec. (d).

Subsecs. (e), (f). Pub. L. 104–208, §2406(d), added subsecs. (e) and (f).

1978—Subsec. (a)(1). Pub. L. 95–598 substituted "cases under title 11 or under the Bankruptcy Act that, from the date of entry of the order for relief or the date of adjudication, as the case may be, antedate the report by more than 10 years" for "Bankruptcies which, from date of adjudication of the most recent bankruptcy, antedate the report by more than fourteen years".

STATUTORY NOTES AND RELATED SUBSIDIARIES

EFFECTIVE DATE OF 2018 AMENDMENT

Amendment by Pub. L. 115–174 effective 1 year after May 24, 2018, see section 302(e) of Pub. L. 115–174, set out as a note under section 1681a of this title.

EFFECTIVE DATE OF 2010 AMENDMENT

Amendment by Pub. L. 111–203 effective on the designated transfer date, see section 1100H of Pub. L. 111–203, set out as a note under section 552a of Title 5, Government Organization and Employees.

EFFECTIVE DATE OF 2003 AMENDMENT

Amendment by Pub. L. 108–159 subject to joint regulations establishing effective dates as prescribed by Federal Reserve Board and Federal Trade Commission, except as otherwise provided, see section 3 of Pub. L. 108–159, set out as a note under section 1681 of this title.

Amendment by section 412 of Pub. L. 108–159 effective at end of 15-month period beginning on Dec. 4, 2003, see section 412(g) of Pub. L. 108–159, set out as a note under section 1681b of this title.

Pub. L. 108–159, title VIII, §811(c)(2)(B), Dec. 4, 2003, 117 Stat. 2011, provided that: "The amendment made by subparagraph (A) [amending this section] shall be deemed to have the same effective date as section 5(1) of Public Law 105–347 (112 Stat. 3211) [see Effective Date of 1998 Amendment note below]."

EFFECTIVE DATE OF 1998 AMENDMENT

Amendment by Pub. L. 105–347 deemed to have same effective date as amendments made by section 2403 of Pub. L. 104–208, see section 7 of Pub. L. 105–347, set out as a note under section 1681a of this title.

EFFECTIVE DATE OF 1996 AMENDMENT

Amendment by Pub. L. 104–208 effective 365 days after Sept. 30, 1996, with special rule for early compliance, see section 2420 of Pub. L. 104–208, set out as a note under section 1681a of this title.

EFFECTIVE DATE OF 1978 AMENDMENT

Amendment by Pub. L. 95–598 effective Oct. 1, 1979, see section 402(a) of Pub. L. 95–598, set out as an Effective Date note preceding section 101 of Title 11, Bankruptcy.

EFFECTIVE DATE

Section effective upon the expiration of one hundred and eighty days following Oct. 26, 1970, see section 504(d) of Pub. L. 90–321, as added by Pub. L. 91–508, set out as a note under section 1681 of this title.

VERIFICATION OF VETERAN'S MEDICAL DEBT

Pub. L. 115–174, title III, §302(c), May 24, 2018, 132 Stat. 1334, provided that:

"(1) DEFINITIONS.—For purposes of this subsection—

"(A) the term 'consumer reporting agency' means a consumer reporting agency described in section 603(p) of the Fair Credit Reporting Act (15 U.S.C. 1681a(p)); and

"(B) the terms 'veteran' and 'veteran's medical debt' have the meanings given those terms in section 603 of the Fair Credit Reporting Act (15 U.S.C. 1681a), as added by subsection (b)(1).

"(2) ESTABLISHMENT.—Not later than 1 year after the date of enactment of this Act [May 24, 2018], the Secretary of Veterans Affairs shall establish a database to allow consumer reporting agencies to verify whether a debt furnished to a consumer reporting agency is a veteran's medical debt.

"(3) DATABASE FEATURES.—The Secretary of Veterans Affairs shall ensure that the database established under paragraph (2), to the extent permitted by law, provides consumer reporting agencies with—

"(A) sufficiently detailed and specific information to verify whether a debt being furnished to the consumer reporting agency is a veteran's medical debt;

"(B) access to verification information in a secure electronic format;

"(C) timely access to verification information; and

"(D) any other features that would promote the efficient, timely, and secure delivery of information that consumer reporting agencies could use to verify whether a debt is a veteran's medical debt.

"(4) STAKEHOLDER INPUT.—Prior to establishing the database for verification under paragraph (2), the Secretary of Veterans Affairs shall publish in the Federal Register a notice and request for comment that solicits input from consumer reporting agencies and other stakeholders.

"(5) VERIFICATION.—Provided the database established under paragraph (2) is fully functional and the data available to consumer reporting agencies, a consumer reporting agency shall use the database as a means to identify a veteran's medical debt pursuant to paragraphs (7) and (8) of section 605(a) of the Fair Credit Reporting Act (15 U.S.C. 1681c(a)), as added by subsection (b)(2)."

---

1 _So In original. Probably should be "which"._

2 _So in original._

---

§1681c–1. Identity theft prevention; fraud alerts and active duty alerts

(a) One-call fraud alerts

(1) Initial alerts

Upon the direct request of a consumer, or an individual acting on behalf of or as a personal representative of a consumer, who asserts in good faith a suspicion that the consumer has been or is about to become a victim of fraud or related crime, including identity theft, a consumer reporting agency described in section 1681a(p) of this title that maintains a file on the consumer and has received appropriate proof of the identity of the requester shall—

(A) include a fraud alert in the file of that consumer, and also provide that alert along with any credit score generated in using that file, for a period of not less than 1 year, beginning on the date of such request, unless the consumer or such representative requests that such fraud alert be removed before the end of such period, and the agency has received appropriate proof of the identity of the requester for such purpose; and

(B) refer the information regarding the fraud alert under this paragraph to each of the other consumer reporting agencies described in section 1681a(p) of this title, in accordance with procedures developed under section 1681s(f) of this title.

(2) Access to free reports

In any case in which a consumer reporting agency includes a fraud alert in the file of a consumer pursuant to this subsection, the consumer reporting agency shall—

(A) disclose to the consumer that the consumer may request a free copy of the file of the consumer pursuant to section 1681j(d) of this title; and

(B) provide to the consumer all disclosures required to be made under section 1681g of this title, without charge to the consumer, not later than 3 business days after any request described in subparagraph (A).

(b) Extended alerts

(1) In general

Upon the direct request of a consumer, or an individual acting on behalf of or as a personal representative of a consumer, who submits an identity theft report to a consumer reporting agency described in section 1681a(p) of this title that maintains a file on the consumer, if the agency has received appropriate proof of the identity of the requester, the agency shall—

(A) include a fraud alert in the file of that consumer, and also provide that alert along with any credit score generated in using that file, during the 7-year period beginning on the date of such request, unless the consumer or such representative requests that such fraud alert be removed before the end of such period and the agency has received appropriate proof of the identity of the requester for such purpose;

(B) during the 5-year period beginning on the date of such request, exclude the consumer from any list of consumers prepared by the consumer reporting agency and provided to any third party to offer credit or insurance to the consumer as part of a transaction that was not initiated by the consumer, unless the consumer or such representative requests that such exclusion be rescinded before the end of such period; and

(C) refer the information regarding the extended fraud alert under this paragraph to each of the other consumer reporting agencies described in section 1681a(p) of this title, in accordance with procedures developed under section 1681s(f) of this title.

(2) Access to free reports

In any case in which a consumer reporting agency includes a fraud alert in the file of a consumer pursuant to this subsection, the consumer reporting agency shall—

(A) disclose to the consumer that the consumer may request 2 free copies of the file of the consumer pursuant to section 1681j(d) of this title during the 12-month period beginning on the date on which the fraud alert was included in the file; and

(B) provide to the consumer all disclosures required to be made under section 1681g of this title, without charge to the consumer, not later than 3 business days after any request described in subparagraph (A).

(c) Active duty alerts

Upon the direct request of an active duty military consumer, or an individual acting on behalf of or as a personal representative of an active duty military consumer, a consumer reporting agency described in section 1681a(p) of this title that maintains a file on the active duty military consumer and has received appropriate proof of the identity of the requester shall—

(1) include an active duty alert in the file of that active duty military consumer, and also provide that alert along with any credit score generated in using that file, during a period of not less than 12 months, or such longer period as the Bureau shall determine, by regulation, beginning on the date of the request, unless the active duty military consumer or such representative requests that such fraud alert be removed before the end of such period, and the agency has received appropriate proof of the identity of the requester for such purpose;

(2) during the 2-year period beginning on the date of such request, exclude the active duty military consumer from any list of consumers prepared by the consumer reporting agency and provided to any third party to offer credit or insurance to the consumer as part of a transaction that was not initiated by the consumer, unless the consumer requests that such exclusion be rescinded before the end of such period; and

(3) refer the information regarding the active duty alert to each of the other consumer reporting agencies described in section 1681a(p) of this title, in accordance with procedures developed under section 1681s(f) of this title.

(d) Procedures

Each consumer reporting agency described in section 1681a(p) of this title shall establish policies and procedures to comply with this section, including procedures that inform consumers of the availability of initial, extended, and active duty alerts and procedures that allow consumers and active duty military consumers to request initial, extended, or active duty alerts (as applicable) in a simple and easy manner, including by telephone.

(e) Referrals of alerts

Each consumer reporting agency described in section 1681a(p) of this title that receives a referral of a fraud alert or active duty alert from another consumer reporting agency pursuant to this section shall, as though the agency received the request from the consumer directly, follow the procedures required under—

(1) paragraphs (1)(A) and (2) of subsection (a), in the case of a referral under subsection (a)(1)(B);

(2) paragraphs (1)(A), (1)(B), and (2) of subsection (b), in the case of a referral under subsection (b)(1)(C); and

(3) paragraphs (1) and (2) of subsection (c), in the case of a referral under subsection (c)(3).

(f) Duty of reseller to reconvey alert

A reseller shall include in its report any fraud alert or active duty alert placed in the file of a consumer pursuant to this section by another consumer reporting agency.

(g) Duty of other consumer reporting agencies to provide contact information

If a consumer contacts any consumer reporting agency that is not described in section 1681a(p) of this title to communicate a suspicion that the consumer has been or is about to become a victim of fraud or related crime, including identity theft, the agency shall provide information to the consumer on how to contact the Bureau and the consumer reporting agencies described in section 1681a(p) of this title to obtain more detailed information and request alerts under this section.

(h) Limitations on use of information for credit extensions

(1) Requirements for initial and active duty alerts

(A) Notification

Each initial fraud alert and active duty alert under this section shall include information that notifies all prospective users of a consumer report on the consumer to which the alert relates that the consumer does not authorize the establishment of any new credit plan or extension of credit, other than under an open-end credit plan (as defined in section 1602(i) [1] of this title), in the name of the consumer, or issuance of an additional card on an existing credit account requested by a consumer, or any increase in credit limit on an existing credit account requested by a consumer, except in accordance with subparagraph (B).

(B) Limitation on users

(i) In general

No prospective user of a consumer report that includes an initial fraud alert or an active duty alert in accordance with this section may establish a new credit plan or extension of credit, other than under an open-end credit plan (as defined in section 1602(i) ^{1} of this title), in the name of the consumer, or issue an additional card on an existing credit account requested by a consumer, or grant any increase in credit limit on an existing credit account requested by a consumer, unless the user utilizes reasonable policies and procedures to form a reasonable belief that the user knows the identity of the person making the request.

(ii) Verification

If a consumer requesting the alert has specified a telephone number to be used for identity verification purposes, before authorizing any new credit plan or extension described in clause (i) in the name of such consumer, a user of such consumer report shall contact the consumer using that telephone number or take reasonable steps to verify the consumer's identity and confirm that the application for a new credit plan is not the result of identity theft.

(2) Requirements for extended alerts

(A) Notification

Each extended alert under this section shall include information that provides all prospective users of a consumer report relating to a consumer with—
(i) notification that the consumer does not authorize the establishment of any new credit plan or extension of credit described in clause (i), other than under an open-end credit plan (as defined in section 1602(i) ^{1} of this title), in the name of the consumer, or issuance of an additional card on an existing credit account requested by a consumer, or any increase in credit limit on an existing credit account requested by a consumer, except in accordance with subparagraph (B); and
(ii) a telephone number or other reasonable contact method designated by the consumer.

(B) Limitation on users

No prospective user of a consumer report or of a credit score generated using the information in the file of a consumer that includes an extended fraud alert in accordance with this section may establish a new credit plan or extension of credit, other than under an open-end credit plan (as defined in section 1602(i) ^{1} of this title), in the name of the consumer, or issue an additional card on an existing credit account requested by a consumer, or any increase in credit limit on an existing credit account requested by a consumer, unless the user contacts the consumer in person or using the contact method described in subparagraph (A)(ii) to confirm that the application for a new credit plan or increase in credit limit, or request for an additional card is not the result of identity theft.

(i) National security freeze

(1) Definitions

For purposes of this subsection:
(A) The term "consumer reporting agency" means a consumer reporting agency described in section 1681a(p) of this title.
(B) The term "proper identification" has the meaning of such term as used under section 1681h of this title.
(C) The term "security freeze" means a restriction that prohibits a consumer reporting agency from disclosing the contents of a consumer report that is subject to such security freeze to any person requesting the consumer report.

(2) Placement of security freeze

(A) In general

Upon receiving a direct request from a consumer that a consumer reporting agency place a security freeze, and upon receiving proper identification from the consumer, the consumer reporting agency shall, free of charge, place the security freeze not later than—
(i) in the case of a request that is by toll-free telephone or secure electronic means, 1 business day after receiving the request directly from the consumer; or
(ii) in the case of a request that is by mail, 3 business days after receiving the request directly from the consumer.

(B) Confirmation and additional information

Not later than 5 business days after placing a security freeze under subparagraph (A), a consumer reporting agency shall—
(i) send confirmation of the placement to the consumer; and
(ii) inform the consumer of—
(I) the process by which the consumer may remove the security freeze, including a mechanism to authenticate the consumer; and
(II) the consumer's right described in section 1681m(d)(1)(D) of this title.

(C) Notice to third parties

A consumer reporting agency may advise a third party that a security freeze has been placed with respect to a consumer under subparagraph (A).

(3) Removal of security freeze

(A) In general

A consumer reporting agency shall remove a security freeze placed on the consumer report of a consumer only in the following cases:

(i) Upon the direct request of the consumer.

(ii) The security freeze was placed due to a material misrepresentation of fact by the consumer.

(B) Notice if removal not by request

If a consumer reporting agency removes a security freeze under subparagraph (A)(ii), the consumer reporting agency shall notify the consumer in writing prior to removing the security freeze.

(C) Removal of security freeze by consumer request

Except as provided in subparagraph (A)(ii), a security freeze shall remain in place until the consumer directly requests that the security freeze be removed. Upon receiving a direct request from a consumer that a consumer reporting agency remove a security freeze, and upon receiving proper identification from the consumer, the consumer reporting agency shall, free of charge, remove the security freeze not later than—

(i) in the case of a request that is by toll-free telephone or secure electronic means, 1 hour after receiving the request for removal; or

(ii) in the case of a request that is by mail, 3 business days after receiving the request for removal.

(D) Third-party requests

If a third party requests access to a consumer report of a consumer with respect to which a security freeze is in effect, where such request is in connection with an application for credit, and the consumer does not allow such consumer report to be accessed, the third party may treat the application as incomplete.

(E) Temporary removal of security freeze

Upon receiving a direct request from a consumer under subparagraph (A)(i), if the consumer requests a temporary removal of a security freeze, the consumer reporting agency shall, in accordance with subparagraph (C), remove the security freeze for the period of time specified by the consumer.

(4) Exceptions

A security freeze shall not apply to the making of a consumer report for use of the following:

(A) A person or entity, or a subsidiary, affiliate, or agent of that person or entity, or an assignee of a financial obligation owed by the consumer to that person or entity, or a prospective assignee of a financial obligation owed by the consumer to that person or entity in conjunction with the proposed purchase of the financial obligation, with which the consumer has or had prior to assignment an account or contract including a demand deposit account, or to whom the consumer issued a negotiable instrument, for the purposes of reviewing the account or collecting the financial obligation owed for the account, contract, or negotiable instrument. For purposes of this subparagraph, "reviewing the account" includes activities related to account maintenance, monitoring, credit line increases, and account upgrades and enhancements.

(B) Any Federal, State, or local agency, law enforcement agency, trial court, or private collection agency acting pursuant to a court order, warrant, or subpoena.

(C) A child support agency acting pursuant to part D of title IV of the Social Security Act (42 U.S.C. 651 et seq.).

(D) A Federal agency or a State or its agents or assigns acting to investigate fraud or acting to investigate or collect delinquent taxes or unpaid court orders or to fulfill any of its other statutory responsibilities, provided such responsibilities are consistent with a permissible purpose under section 1681b of this title.

(E) By a person using credit information for the purposes described under section 1681b(c) of this title.

(F) Any person or entity administering a credit file monitoring subscription or similar service to which the consumer has subscribed.

(G) Any person or entity for the purpose of providing a consumer with a copy of the consumer's consumer report or credit score, upon the request of the consumer.

(H) Any person using the information in connection with the underwriting of insurance.

(I) Any person using the information for employment, tenant, or background screening purposes.

(J) Any person using the information for assessing, verifying, or authenticating a consumer's identity for purposes other than the granting of credit, or for investigating or preventing actual or potential fraud.

(5) Notice of rights

At any time a consumer is required to receive a summary of rights required under section 1681g of this title, the following notice shall be included:

"CONSUMERS HAVE THE RIGHT TO OBTAIN A SECURITY FREEZE

"You have a right to place a 'security freeze' on your credit report, which will prohibit a consumer reporting agency from releasing information in your credit report without your express authorization. The security freeze is designed to prevent credit, loans, and services from being approved in your name without your consent. However, you should be aware that using a security freeze to take control over who gets access to the personal and financial information in your credit report may delay, interfere with, or prohibit the timely approval of any subsequent request or application you make regarding a new loan, credit, mortgage, or any other account involving the extension of credit.

"As an alternative to a security freeze, you have the right to place an initial or extended fraud alert on your credit file at no cost. An initial fraud alert is a 1-year alert that is placed on a consumer's credit file. Upon seeing a fraud alert display on a consumer's credit file, a business is required to take steps to verify the consumer's identity before extending new credit. If you are a victim of identity theft, you are entitled to an extended fraud alert, which is a fraud alert lasting 7 years.

"A security freeze does not apply to a person or entity, or its affiliates, or collection agencies acting on behalf of the person or entity, with which you have an existing account that requests information in your credit report for the purposes of reviewing or collecting the account. Reviewing the account includes activities related to account maintenance, monitoring, credit line increases, and account upgrades and enhancements.".

(6) Webpage

(A) Consumer reporting agencies

A consumer reporting agency shall establish a webpage that—
(i) allows a consumer to request a security freeze;
(ii) allows a consumer to request an initial fraud alert;
(iii) allows a consumer to request an extended fraud alert;
(iv) allows a consumer to request an active duty fraud alert;
(v) allows a consumer to opt-out of the use of information in a consumer report to send the consumer a solicitation of credit or insurance, in accordance with section 1681m(d) of this title; and
(vi) shall not be the only mechanism by which a consumer may request a security freeze.

(B) FTC

The Federal Trade Commission shall establish a single webpage that includes a link to each webpage established under subparagraph (A) within the Federal Trade Commission's website www.Identitytheft.gov, or a successor website.

(j) National protection for files and credit records of protected consumers

(1) Definitions

As used in this subsection:
(A) The term "consumer reporting agency" means a consumer reporting agency described in section 1681a(p) of this title.
(B) The term "protected consumer" means an individual who is—
(i) under the age of 16 years at the time a request for the placement of a security freeze is made; or
(ii) an incapacitated person or a protected person for whom a guardian or conservator has been appointed.

(C) The term "protected consumer's representative" means a person who provides to a consumer reporting agency sufficient proof of authority to act on behalf of a protected consumer.
(D) The term "record" means a compilation of information that—
(i) identifies a protected consumer;
(ii) is created by a consumer reporting agency solely for the purpose of complying with this subsection; and
(iii) may not be created or used to consider the protected consumer's credit worthiness, credit standing, credit capacity, character, general reputation, personal characteristics, or mode of living.

(E) The term "security freeze" means a restriction that prohibits a consumer reporting agency from disclosing the contents of a consumer report that is the subject of such security freeze or, in the case of a protected consumer for whom the consumer reporting agency does not have a file, a record that is subject to such security freeze to any person requesting the consumer report for the purpose of opening a new account involving the extension of credit.
(F) The term "sufficient proof of authority" means documentation that shows a protected consumer's representative has authority to act on behalf of a protected consumer and includes—
(i) an order issued by a court of law;
(ii) a lawfully executed and valid power of attorney;
(iii) a document issued by a Federal, State, or local government agency in the United States showing proof of parentage, including a birth certificate; or
(iv) with respect to a protected consumer who has been placed in a foster care setting, a written communication from a county welfare department or its agent or designee, or a county probation department or its agent or designee, certifying that the protected consumer is in a foster care setting under its jurisdiction.

(G) The term "sufficient proof of identification" means information or documentation that identifies a protected consumer and a protected consumer's representative and includes—

    (i) a social security number or a copy of a social security card issued by the Social Security Administration;

    (ii) a certified or official copy of a birth certificate issued by the entity authorized to issue the birth certificate; or

    (iii) a copy of a driver's license, an identification card issued by the motor vehicle administration, or any other government issued identification.

(2) Placement of security freeze for a protected consumer

(A) In general

Upon receiving a direct request from a protected consumer's representative that a consumer reporting agency place a security freeze, and upon receiving sufficient proof of identification and sufficient proof of authority, the consumer reporting agency shall, free of charge, place the security freeze not later than—

    (i) in the case of a request that is by toll-free telephone or secure electronic means, 1 business day after receiving the request directly from the protected consumer's representative; or

    (ii) in the case of a request that is by mail, 3 business days after receiving the request directly from the protected consumer's representative.

(B) Confirmation and additional information

Not later than 5 business days after placing a security freeze under subparagraph (A), a consumer reporting agency shall—

    (i) send confirmation of the placement to the protected consumer's representative; and

    (ii) inform the protected consumer's representative of the process by which the protected consumer may remove the security freeze, including a mechanism to authenticate the protected consumer's representative.

(C) Creation of file

If a consumer reporting agency does not have a file pertaining to a protected consumer when the consumer reporting agency receives a direct request under subparagraph (A), the consumer reporting agency shall create a record for the protected consumer.

(3) Prohibition on release of record or file of protected consumer

After a security freeze has been placed under paragraph (2)(A), and unless the security freeze is removed in accordance with this subsection, a consumer reporting agency may not release the protected consumer's consumer report, any information derived from the protected consumer's consumer report, or any record created for the protected consumer.

(4) Removal of a protected consumer security freeze

(A) In general

A consumer reporting agency shall remove a security freeze placed on the consumer report of a protected consumer only in the following cases:

    (i) Upon the direct request of the protected consumer's representative.

    (ii) Upon the direct request of the protected consumer, if the protected consumer is not under the age of 16 years at the time of the request.

    (iii) The security freeze was placed due to a material misrepresentation of fact by the protected consumer's representative.

(B) Notice if removal not by request

If a consumer reporting agency removes a security freeze under subparagraph (A)(iii), the consumer reporting agency shall notify the protected consumer's representative in writing prior to removing the security freeze.

(C) Removal of freeze by request

Except as provided in subparagraph (A)(iii), a security freeze shall remain in place until a protected consumer's representative or protected consumer described in subparagraph (A)(ii) directly requests that the security freeze be removed. Upon receiving a direct request from the protected consumer's representative or protected consumer described in subparagraph (A)(ii) that a consumer reporting agency remove a security freeze, and upon receiving sufficient proof of identification and sufficient proof of authority, the consumer reporting agency shall, free of charge, remove the security freeze not later than—

    (i) in the case of a request that is by toll-free telephone or secure electronic means, 1 hour after receiving the request for removal; or

    (ii) in the case of a request that is by mail, 3 business days after receiving the request for removal.

(D) Temporary removal of security freeze

Upon receiving a direct request from a protected consumer or a protected consumer's representative under subparagraph (A)(i), if the protected consumer or protected consumer's representative requests a temporary removal of a security freeze, the consumer reporting agency shall, in accordance with subparagraph (C), remove the security freeze for the period of time specified by the protected consumer or protected consumer's representative.

(k) Credit monitoring

(1) Definitions

In this subsection:

(A) The term "active duty military consumer" includes a member of the National Guard.

(B) The term "National Guard" has the meaning given the term in section 101(c) of title 10.

(2) Credit monitoring

A consumer reporting agency described in section 1681a(p) of this title shall provide a free electronic credit monitoring service that, at a minimum, notifies a consumer of material additions or modifications to the file of the consumer at the consumer reporting agency to any consumer who provides to the consumer reporting agency—

(A) appropriate proof that the consumer is an active duty military consumer; and

(B) contact information of the consumer.

(3) Rulemaking

Not later than 1 year after May 24, 2018, the Federal Trade Commission shall promulgate regulations regarding the requirements of this subsection, which shall at a minimum include—

(A) a definition of an electronic credit monitoring service and material additions or modifications to the file of a consumer; and

(B) what constitutes appropriate proof.

(4) Applicability

(A) Sections 1681n and 1681o of this title shall not apply to any violation of this subsection.

(B) This subsection shall be enforced exclusively under section 1681s of this title by the Federal agencies and Federal and State officials identified in that section.

(Pub. L. 90–321, title VI, §605A, as added Pub. L. 108–159, title I, §112(a), Dec. 4, 2003, 117 Stat. 1955; amended Pub. L. 111–203, title X, §1088(a)(2)(C), July 21, 2010, 124 Stat. 2087; Pub. L. 115–174, title III, §§301(a), 302(d)(1), May 24, 2018, 132 Stat. 1326, 1334.)

EDITORIAL NOTES

REFERENCES IN TEXT

Section 1602(i) of this title, referred to in subsec. (h), was redesignated section 1602(j) of this title by Pub. L. 111–203, title X, §1100A(1)(A), July 21, 2010, 124 Stat. 2107.

The Social Security Act, referred to in subsec. (i)(4)(C), is act Aug. 14, 1935, ch. 531, 49 Stat. 620. Part D of title IV of the Act is classified generally to part D (§651 et seq.) of subchapter IV of chapter 7 of Title 42, The Public Health and Welfare. For complete classification of this Act to the Code, see section 1305 of Title 42 and Tables.

AMENDMENTS

2018—Subsec. (a)(1)(A). Pub. L. 115–174, §301(a)(1), substituted "1 year" for "90 days".

Subsecs. (i), (j). Pub. L. 115–174, §301(a)(2), added subsecs. (i) and (j).

Subsec. (k). Pub. L. 115–174, §302(d)(1), added subsec. (k).

2010—Subsecs. (c)(1), (g). Pub. L. 111–203 substituted "the Bureau" for "the Commission".

STATUTORY NOTES AND RELATED SUBSIDIARIES

EFFECTIVE DATE OF 2018 AMENDMENT

Pub. L. 115–174, title III, §301(c), May 24, 2018, 132 Stat. 1332, provided that: "The amendments made by this section [amending this section and section 1681t of this title] shall take effect on the date that is 120 days after the date of enactment of this Act [May 24, 2018]."

Amendment by section 302(d)(1) of Pub. L. 115–174 effective 1 year after May 24, 2018, see section 302(e) of Pub. L. 115–174, set out as a note under section 1681a of this title.

EFFECTIVE DATE OF 2010 AMENDMENT

Amendment by Pub. L. 111–203 effective on the designated transfer date, see section 1100H of Pub. L. 111–203, set out as a note under section 552a of Title 5, Government Organization and Employees.

EFFECTIVE DATE

Section subject to joint regulations establishing effective dates as prescribed by Federal Reserve Board and Federal Trade Commission, except as otherwise provided, see section 3 of Pub. L. 108–159, set out as an Effective Date of 2003 Amendment note under section 1681 of this title.

Pub. L. 108–159, title I, §112(b), Dec. 4, 2003, 117 Stat. 1959, as amended by Pub. L. 111–203, title X, §1088(b)(1), July 21, 2010, 124 Stat. 2092, provided that: "The Bureau shall prescribe regulations to define what constitutes appropriate proof of identity for purposes of sections 605A , 605B, and 609(a)(1) of the Fair Credit Reporting Act [15 U.S.C. 1681c–1, 1681c–2, 1681g(a)(1)], as amended by this Act."

PUBLIC CAMPAIGN TO PREVENT IDENTITY THEFT

Pub. L. 108–159, title I, §151(b), Dec. 4, 2003, 117 Stat. 1964, provided that: "Not later than 2 years after the date of enactment of this Act [Dec. 4, 2003], the Commission shall establish and implement a media and distribution campaign to teach the public how to prevent identity theft. Such campaign shall include existing Commission education materials, as well as radio, television, and print public service announcements, video cassettes, interactive digital video discs (DVD's) or compact audio discs (CD's), and Internet resources."

[For definitions of terms used in section 151(b) of Pub. L. 108–159, set out above, see section 2 of Pub. L. 108–159, set out as a Definitions note under section 1681 of this title.]

[1] *See References in Text note below.*

§1681c–2. Block of information resulting from identity theft

(a) Block

Except as otherwise provided in this section, a consumer reporting agency shall block the reporting of any information in the file of a consumer that the consumer identifies as information that resulted from an alleged identity theft, not later than 4 business days after the date of receipt by such agency of—

(1) appropriate proof of the identity of the consumer;

(2) a copy of an identity theft report;

(3) the identification of such information by the consumer; and

(4) a statement by the consumer that the information is not information relating to any transaction by the consumer.

(b) Notification

A consumer reporting agency shall promptly notify the furnisher of information identified by the consumer under subsection (a)—

(1) that the information may be a result of identity theft;

(2) that an identity theft report has been filed;

(3) that a block has been requested under this section; and

(4) of the effective dates of the block.

(c) Authority to decline or rescind

(1) In general

A consumer reporting agency may decline to block, or may rescind any block, of information relating to a consumer under this section, if the consumer reporting agency reasonably determines that—

(A) the information was blocked in error or a block was requested by the consumer in error;

(B) the information was blocked, or a block was requested by the consumer, on the basis of a material misrepresentation of fact by the consumer relevant to the request to block; or

(C) the consumer obtained possession of goods, services, or money as a result of the blocked transaction or transactions.

(2) Notification to consumer

If a block of information is declined or rescinded under this subsection, the affected consumer shall be notified promptly, in the same manner as consumers are notified of the reinsertion of information under section 1681i(a)(5)(B) of this title.

(3) Significance of block

For purposes of this subsection, if a consumer reporting agency rescinds a block, the presence of information in the file of a consumer prior to the blocking of such information is not evidence of whether the consumer knew or should have known that the consumer obtained possession of any goods, services, or money as a result of the block.

(d) Exception for resellers

(1) No reseller file

This section shall not apply to a consumer reporting agency, if the consumer reporting agency—

(A) is a reseller;

(B) is not, at the time of the request of the consumer under subsection (a), otherwise furnishing or reselling a consumer report concerning the information identified by the consumer; and

(C) informs the consumer, by any means, that the consumer may report the identity theft to the Bureau to obtain consumer information regarding identity theft.

(2) Reseller with file

The sole obligation of the consumer reporting agency under this section, with regard to any request of a consumer under this section, shall be to block the consumer report maintained by the consumer reporting agency from any subsequent use, if—

(A) the consumer, in accordance with the provisions of subsection (a), identifies, to a consumer reporting agency, information in the file of the consumer that resulted from identity theft; and

(B) the consumer reporting agency is a reseller of the identified information.

(3) Notice

In carrying out its obligation under paragraph (2), the reseller shall promptly provide a notice to the consumer of the decision to block the file. Such notice shall contain the name, address, and telephone number of each consumer reporting agency from which the consumer information was obtained for resale.

(e) Exception for verification companies

The provisions of this section do not apply to a check services company, acting as such, which issues authorizations for the purpose of approving or processing negotiable instruments, electronic fund transfers, or similar methods of payments, except that, beginning 4 business days after receipt of information described in paragraphs (1) through (3) of subsection (a), a check services company shall not report to a national consumer reporting agency described in section 1681a(p) of this title, any information identified in the subject identity theft report as resulting from identity theft.

(f) Access to blocked information by law enforcement agencies

No provision of this section shall be construed as requiring a consumer reporting agency to prevent a Federal, State, or local law enforcement agency from accessing blocked information in a consumer file to which the agency could otherwise obtain access under this subchapter.

(Pub. L. 90–321, title VI, §605B, as added Pub. L. 108–159, title I, §152(a), Dec. 4, 2003, 117 Stat. 1964; amended Pub. L. 111–203, title X, §1088(a)(2)(C), July 21, 2010, 124 Stat. 2087.)

EDITORIAL NOTES

AMENDMENTS

2010—Subsec. (d)(1)(C). Pub. L. 111–203 substituted "the Bureau" for "the Commission".

STATUTORY NOTES AND RELATED SUBSIDIARIES

EFFECTIVE DATE OF 2010 AMENDMENT

Amendment by Pub. L. 111–203 effective on the designated transfer date, see section 1100H of Pub. L. 111–203, set out as a note under section 552a of Title 5, Government Organization and Employees.

EFFECTIVE DATE

Section subject to joint regulations establishing effective dates as prescribed by Federal Reserve Board and Federal Trade Commission, except as otherwise provided, see section 3 of Pub. L. 108–159, set out as an Effective Date of 2003 Amendment note under section 1681 of this title.

§1681c–3. Adverse information in cases of trafficking

(a) Definitions

In this section:

(1) Trafficking documentation

The term "trafficking documentation" means—

(A) documentation of—

(i) a determination that a consumer is a victim of trafficking made by a Federal, State, or Tribal governmental entity; or

(ii) by a court of competent jurisdiction; and

(B) documentation that identifies items of adverse information that should not be furnished by a consumer reporting agency because the items resulted from a severe form of trafficking in persons or sex trafficking of which the consumer is a victim.

(2) Trafficking Victims Protection Act of 2000 definitions

The terms "severe forms of trafficking in persons" and "sex trafficking" have the meanings given, respectively, in section 103 of the Trafficking Victims Protection Act of 2000 (22 U.S.C. 7102).

(3) Victim of trafficking

The term "victim of trafficking" means a person who is a victim of a severe form of trafficking in persons or sex trafficking.

(b) Adverse information

A consumer reporting agency may not furnish a consumer report containing any adverse item of information about a consumer that resulted from a severe form of trafficking in persons or sex trafficking if the consumer has provided trafficking documentation to the consumer reporting agency.

(c) Rulemaking

(1) In general

Not later than 180 days after December 27, 2021, the Director shall issue rules to implement subsection (a).

(2) Contents

The rules issued pursuant to paragraph (1) shall establish a method by which consumers shall submit trafficking documentation to consumer reporting agencies.

(Pub. L. 90–321, title VI, §605C, as added Pub. L. 117–81, div. F, title LXI, §6102(a), Dec. 27, 2021, 135 Stat. 2383.)

STATUTORY NOTES AND RELATED SUBSIDIARIES

EFFECTIVE DATE

Pub. L. 117–81, div. F, title LXI, §6102(c), Dec. 27, 2021, 135 Stat. 2384, provided that: "The amendments made by this section [enacting this section] shall apply on the date that is 30 days after the date on which the Director of the Bureau of Consumer Financial Protection issues a rule pursuant to section 605C(c) of the Fair Credit Reporting Act [15 U.S.C. 1681c–3(c)], as added by subsection (a) of this section. Any rule issued by the Director to implement such section 605C [15 U.S.C. 1681c–3] shall be limited to preventing a consumer reporting agency from furnishing a consumer report containing any adverse item of information about a consumer (as such terms are defined, respectively, in section 603 the Fair Credit Reporting Act (15 U.S.C. 1681a)) that resulted from trafficking."

§1681d. Disclosure of investigative consumer reports

(a) Disclosure of fact of preparation

A person may not procure or cause to be prepared an investigative consumer report on any consumer unless—
(1) it is clearly and accurately disclosed to the consumer that an investigative consumer report including information as to his character, general reputation, personal characteristics, and mode of living, whichever are applicable, may be made, and such disclosure (A) is made in a writing mailed, or otherwise delivered, to the consumer, not later than three days after the date on which the report was first requested, and (B) includes a statement informing the consumer of his right to request the additional disclosures provided for under subsection (b) of this section and the written summary of the rights of the consumer prepared pursuant to section 1681g(c) of this title; and
(2) the person certifies or has certified to the consumer reporting agency that—
(A) the person has made the disclosures to the consumer required by paragraph (1); and
(B) the person will comply with subsection (b).

(b) Disclosure on request of nature and scope of investigation

Any person who procures or causes to be prepared an investigative consumer report on any consumer shall, upon written request made by the consumer within a reasonable period of time after the receipt by him of the disclosure required by subsection (a)(1), make a complete and accurate disclosure of the nature and scope of the investigation requested. This disclosure shall be made in a writing mailed, or otherwise delivered, to the consumer not later than five days after the date on which the request for such disclosure was received from the consumer or such report was first requested, whichever is the later.

(c) Limitation on liability upon showing of reasonable procedures for compliance with provisions

No person may be held liable for any violation of subsection (a) or (b) of this section if he shows by a preponderance of the evidence that at the time of the violation he maintained reasonable procedures to assure compliance with subsection (a) or (b).

(d) Prohibitions

(1) Certification

A consumer reporting agency shall not prepare or furnish an investigative consumer report unless the agency has received a certification under subsection (a)(2) from the person who requested the report.

(2) Inquiries

A consumer reporting agency shall not make an inquiry for the purpose of preparing an investigative consumer report on a consumer for employment purposes if the making of the inquiry by an employer or prospective employer of the consumer would violate any applicable Federal or State equal employment opportunity law or regulation.

(3) Certain public record information

Except as otherwise provided in section 1681k of this title, a consumer reporting agency shall not furnish an investigative consumer report that includes information that is a matter of public record and that relates to an arrest, indictment, conviction, civil judicial action, tax lien, or outstanding judgment, unless the agency has verified the accuracy of the information during the 30-day period ending on the date on which the report is furnished.

(4) Certain adverse information

A consumer reporting agency shall not prepare or furnish an investigative consumer report on a consumer that contains information that is adverse to the interest of the consumer and that is obtained through a personal interview with a neighbor, friend, or associate of the consumer or with another person with whom the consumer is acquainted or who has knowledge of such item of information, unless—

(A) the agency has followed reasonable procedures to obtain confirmation of the information, from an additional source that has independent and direct knowledge of the information; or

(B) the person interviewed is the best possible source of the information.

(Pub. L. 90–321, title VI, §606, as added Pub. L. 91–508, title VI, §601, Oct. 26, 1970, 84 Stat. 1130; amended Pub. L. 104–208, div. A, title II, §§2408(d)(2), 2414, Sept. 30, 1996, 110 Stat. 3009–438, 3009-449.)

EDITORIAL NOTES

AMENDMENTS

1996—Subsec. (a)(1)(B). Pub. L. 104–208, §§2408(d)(2), 2414(1), inserted "and the written summary of the rights of the consumer prepared pursuant to section 1681g(c) of this title" before the semicolon and substituted "and" for "or" at end.

Subsec. (a)(2). Pub. L. 104–208, §2414(2), added par. (2) and struck out former par. (2) which read as follows: "the report is to be used for employment purposes for which the consumer has not specifically applied."

Subsec. (b). Pub. L. 104–208, §2414(3), substituted ", make a complete" for ", shall make a complete".

Subsec. (d). Pub. L. 104–208, §2414(4), added subsec. (d).

STATUTORY NOTES AND RELATED SUBSIDIARIES

EFFECTIVE DATE OF 1996 AMENDMENT

Amendment by Pub. L. 104–208 effective 365 days after Sept. 30, 1996, with special rule for early compliance, see section 2420 of Pub. L. 104–208, set out as a note under section 1681a of this title.

EFFECTIVE DATE

Section effective upon the expiration of one hundred and eighty days following Oct. 26, 1970, see section 504(d) of Pub. L. 90–321, as added by Pub. L. 91–508, set out as a note under section 1681 of this title.

§1681e. Compliance procedures

(a) Identity and purposes of credit users

Every consumer reporting agency shall maintain reasonable procedures designed to avoid violations of section 1681c of this title and to limit the furnishing of consumer reports to the purposes listed under section 1681b of this title. These procedures shall require that prospective users of the information identify themselves, certify the purposes for which the information is sought, and certify that the information will be used for no other purpose. Every consumer reporting agency shall make a reasonable effort to verify the identity of a new prospective user and the uses certified by such prospective user prior to furnishing such user a consumer report. No consumer reporting agency may furnish a consumer report to any person if it has reasonable grounds for believing that the consumer report will not be used for a purpose listed in section 1681b of this title.

(b) Accuracy of report

Whenever a consumer reporting agency prepares a consumer report it shall follow reasonable procedures to assure maximum possible accuracy of the information concerning the individual about whom the report relates.

(c) Disclosure of consumer reports by users allowed

A consumer reporting agency may not prohibit a user of a consumer report furnished by the agency on a consumer from disclosing the contents of the report to the consumer, if adverse action against the consumer has been taken by the user based in whole or in part on the report.

(d) Notice to users and furnishers of information

(1) Notice requirement

A consumer reporting agency shall provide to any person—
(A) who regularly and in the ordinary course of business furnishes information to the agency with respect to any consumer; or
(B) to whom a consumer report is provided by the agency;

a notice of such person's responsibilities under this subchapter.

(2) Content of notice

The Bureau shall prescribe the content of notices under paragraph (1), and a consumer reporting agency shall be in compliance with this subsection if it provides a notice under paragraph (1) that is substantially similar to the Bureau prescription under this paragraph.

(e) Procurement of consumer report for resale

(1) Disclosure

A person may not procure a consumer report for purposes of reselling the report (or any information in the report) unless the person discloses to the consumer reporting agency that originally furnishes the report—
(A) the identity of the end-user of the report (or information); and
(B) each permissible purpose under section 1681b of this title for which the report is furnished to the end-user of the report (or information).

(2) Responsibilities of procurers for resale

A person who procures a consumer report for purposes of reselling the report (or any information in the report) shall—
(A) establish and comply with reasonable procedures designed to ensure that the report (or information) is resold by the person only for a purpose for which the report may be furnished under section 1681b of this title, including by requiring that each person to which the report (or information) is resold and that resells or provides the report (or information) to any other person—
(i) identifies each end user of the resold report (or information);
(ii) certifies each purpose for which the report (or information) will be used; and
(iii) certifies that the report (or information) will be used for no other purpose; and

(B) before reselling the report, make reasonable efforts to verify the identifications and certifications made under subparagraph (A).

(3) Resale of consumer report to a Federal agency or department

Notwithstanding paragraph (1) or (2), a person who procures a consumer report for purposes of reselling the report (or any information in the report) shall not disclose the identity of the end-user of the report under paragraph (1) or (2) if—
(A) the end user is an agency or department of the United States Government which procures the report from the person for purposes of determining the eligibility of the consumer concerned to receive access or continued access to classified information (as defined in section 1681b(b)(4)(E)(i) [1] of this title); and
(B) the agency or department certifies in writing to the person reselling the report that nondisclosure is necessary to protect classified information or the safety of persons employed by or contracting with, or undergoing investigation for work or contracting with the agency or department.

(Pub. L. 90–321, title VI, §607, as added Pub. L. 91–508, title VI, §601, Oct. 26, 1970, 84 Stat. 1130; amended Pub. L. 104–208, div. A, title II, §2407, Sept. 30, 1996, 110 Stat. 3009–435; Pub. L. 105–107, title III, §311(b), Nov. 20, 1997, 111 Stat. 2256; Pub. L. 111–203, title X, §1088(a)(2)(A), July 21, 2010, 124 Stat. 2087.)

EDITORIAL NOTES

Section 1681b(b)(4) of this title, referred to in subsec. (e)(3)(A), was subsequently amended, and section 1681b(b)(4)(E) no longer defines the term "classified information". However, such term is defined elsewhere in that section.

AMENDMENTS

2010—Subsec. (d)(2). Pub. L. 111–203 substituted "Bureau" for "Federal Trade Commission" in two places.

1997—Subsec. (e)(3). Pub. L. 105–107 added par. (3).

1996—Subsecs. (c) to (e). Pub. L. 104–208 added subsecs. (c) to (e).

STATUTORY NOTES AND RELATED SUBSIDIARIES

EFFECTIVE DATE OF 2010 AMENDMENT

Amendment by Pub. L. 111–203 effective on the designated transfer date, see section 1100H of Pub. L. 111–203, set out as a note under section 552a of Title 5, Government Organization and Employees.

EFFECTIVE DATE OF 1997 AMENDMENT

Amendment by Pub. L. 105–107 effective as if included in chapter 1 of subtitle D of the Economic Growth and Regulatory Paperwork Reduction Act of 1996, Pub. L. 104–208, as of Sept. 30, 1996, see section 311(c) of Pub. L. 105–107, set out as a note under section 1681b of this title.

EFFECTIVE DATE OF 1996 AMENDMENT

Amendment by Pub. L. 104–208 effective 365 days after Sept. 30, 1996, with special rule for early compliance, see section 2420 of Pub. L. 104–208, set out as a note under section 1681a of this title.

EFFECTIVE DATE

Section effective upon the expiration of one hundred and eighty days following Oct. 26, 1970, see section 504(d) of Pub. L. 90–321, as added by Pub. L. 91–508, set out as a note under section 1681 of this title.

[1] *See References in Text note below.*

§1681f. Disclosures to governmental agencies

Notwithstanding the provisions of section 1681b of this title, a consumer reporting agency may furnish identifying information respecting any consumer, limited to his name, address, former addresses, places of employment, or former places of employment, to a governmental agency.

(Pub. L. 90–321, title VI, §608, as added Pub. L. 91–508, title VI, §601, Oct. 26, 1970, 84 Stat. 1131.)

STATUTORY NOTES AND RELATED SUBSIDIARIES

EFFECTIVE DATE

Section effective upon the expiration of one hundred and eighty days following Oct. 26, 1970, see section 504(d) of Pub. L. 90–321, as added by Pub. L. 91–508, set out as a note under section 1681 of this title.

§1681g. Disclosures to consumers

(a) Information on file; sources; report recipients

Every consumer reporting agency shall, upon request, and subject to section 1681h(a)(1) of this title, clearly and accurately disclose to the consumer:

(1) All information in the consumer's file at the time of the request, except that—

(A) if the consumer to whom the file relates requests that the first 5 digits of the social security number (or similar identification number) of the consumer not be included in the disclosure and the consumer reporting agency has received appropriate proof of the identity of the requester, the consumer reporting agency shall so truncate such number in such disclosure; and

(B) nothing in this paragraph shall be construed to require a consumer reporting agency to disclose to a consumer any information concerning credit scores or any other risk scores or predictors relating to the consumer.

(2) The sources of the information; except that the sources of information acquired solely for use in preparing an investigative consumer report and actually used for no other purpose need not be disclosed: *Provided,* That in the event an action is brought under this subchapter, such sources shall be available to the plaintiff under appropriate discovery procedures in the court in which the action is brought.

(3)(A) Identification of each person (including each end-user identified under section 1681e(e)(1) of this title) that procured a consumer report—

(i) for employment purposes, during the 2-year period preceding the date on which the request is made; or

(ii) for any other purpose, during the 1-year period preceding the date on which the request is made.

(B) An identification of a person under subparagraph (A) shall include—

(i) the name of the person or, if applicable, the trade name (written in full) under which such person conducts business; and

(ii) upon request of the consumer, the address and telephone number of the person.

(C) Subparagraph (A) does not apply if—

(i) the end user is an agency or department of the United States Government that procures the report from the person for purposes of determining the eligibility of the consumer to whom the report relates to receive access or continued access to classified information (as defined in section 1681b(b)(4)(E)(i) [1] of this title); and

(ii) the head of the agency or department makes a written finding as prescribed under section 1681b(b)(4)(A) of this title.

(4) The dates, original payees, and amounts of any checks upon which is based any adverse characterization of the consumer, included in the file at the time of the disclosure.

(5) A record of all inquiries received by the agency during the 1-year period preceding the request that identified the consumer in connection with a credit or insurance transaction that was not initiated by the consumer.

(6) If the consumer requests the credit file and not the credit score, a statement that the consumer may request and obtain a credit score.

(b) Exempt information

The requirements of subsection (a) respecting the disclosure of sources of information and the recipients of consumer reports do not apply to information received or consumer reports furnished prior to the effective date of this subchapter except to the extent that the matter involved is contained in the files of the consumer reporting agency on that date.

(c) Summary of rights to obtain and dispute information in consumer reports and to obtain credit scores

(1) Commission [2] summary of rights required

(A) In general

The Commission [2] shall prepare a model summary of the rights of consumers under this subchapter.

(B) Content of summary

The summary of rights prepared under subparagraph (A) shall include a description of—

(i) the right of a consumer to obtain a copy of a consumer report under subsection (a) from each consumer reporting agency;

(ii) the frequency and circumstances under which a consumer is entitled to receive a consumer report without charge under section 1681j of this title;

(iii) the right of a consumer to dispute information in the file of the consumer under section 1681i of this title;

(iv) the right of a consumer to obtain a credit score from a consumer reporting agency, and a description of how to obtain a credit score;

(v) the method by which a consumer can contact, and obtain a consumer report from, a consumer reporting agency without charge, as provided in the regulations of the Bureau prescribed under section 211(c) [1] of the Fair and Accurate Credit Transactions Act of 2003; and

(vi) the method by which a consumer can contact, and obtain a consumer report from, a consumer reporting agency described in section 1681a(w) [1] of this title, as provided in the regulations of the Bureau prescribed under section 1681j(a)(1)(C) of this title.

(C) Availability of summary of rights

The Commission [2] shall—

(i) actively publicize the availability of the summary of rights prepared under this paragraph;

(ii) conspicuously post on its Internet website the availability of such summary of rights; and

(iii) promptly make such summary of rights available to consumers, on request.

(2) Summary of rights required to be included with agency disclosures

A consumer reporting agency shall provide to a consumer, with each written disclosure by the agency to the consumer under this section—

(A) the summary of rights prepared by the Bureau under paragraph (1);

(B) in the case of a consumer reporting agency described in section 1681a(p) of this title, a toll-free telephone number established by the agency, at which personnel are accessible to consumers during normal business hours;

(C) a list of all Federal agencies responsible for enforcing any provision of this subchapter, and the address and any appropriate phone number of each such agency, in a form that will assist the consumer in selecting the appropriate agency;

(D) a statement that the consumer may have additional rights under State law, and that the consumer may wish to contact a State or local consumer protection agency or a State attorney general (or the equivalent thereof) to learn of those rights; and

(E) a statement that a consumer reporting agency is not required to remove accurate derogatory information from the file of a consumer, unless the information is outdated under section 1681c of this title or cannot be verified.

(d) Summary of rights of identity theft victims

(1) In general

The Commission,[2] in consultation with the Federal banking agencies and the National Credit Union Administration, shall prepare a model summary of the rights of consumers under this subchapter with respect to the procedures for remedying the effects of fraud or identity theft involving credit, an electronic fund transfer, or an account or transaction at or with a financial institution or other creditor.

(2) Summary of rights and contact information

Beginning 60 days after the date on which the model summary of rights is prescribed in final form by the Bureau pursuant to paragraph (1), if any consumer contacts a consumer reporting agency and expresses a belief that the consumer is a victim of fraud or identity theft involving credit, an electronic fund transfer, or an account or transaction at or with a financial institution or other creditor, the consumer reporting agency shall, in addition to any other action that the agency may take, provide the consumer with a summary of rights that contains all of the information required by the Bureau under paragraph (1), and information on how to contact the Bureau to obtain more detailed information.

(e) Information available to victims

(1) In general

For the purpose of documenting fraudulent transactions resulting from identity theft, not later than 30 days after the date of receipt of a request from a victim in accordance with paragraph (3), and subject to verification of the identity of the victim and the claim of identity theft in accordance with paragraph (2), a business entity that has provided credit to, provided for consideration products, goods, or services to, accepted payment from, or otherwise entered into a commercial transaction for consideration with, a person who has allegedly made unauthorized use of the means of identification of the victim, shall provide a copy of application and business transaction records in the control of the business entity, whether maintained by the business entity or by another person on behalf of the business entity, evidencing any transaction alleged to be a result of identity theft to—

(A) the victim;

(B) any Federal, State, or local government law enforcement agency or officer specified by the victim in such a request; or

(C) any law enforcement agency investigating the identity theft and authorized by the victim to take receipt of records provided under this subsection.

(2) Verification of identity and claim

Before a business entity provides any information under paragraph (1), unless the business entity, at its discretion, otherwise has a high degree of confidence that it knows the identity of the victim making a request under paragraph (1), the victim shall provide to the business entity—

(A) as proof of positive identification of the victim, at the election of the business entity—

(i) the presentation of a government-issued identification card;

(ii) personally identifying information of the same type as was provided to the business entity by the unauthorized person; or

(iii) personally identifying information that the business entity typically requests from new applicants or for new transactions, at the time of the victim's request for information, including any documentation described in clauses (i) and (ii); and

(B) as proof of a claim of identity theft, at the election of the business entity—

(i) a copy of a police report evidencing the claim of the victim of identity theft; and

(ii) a properly completed—

(I) copy of a standardized affidavit of identity theft developed and made available by the Bureau; or

(II) an [3] affidavit of fact that is acceptable to the business entity for that purpose.

(3) Procedures

The request of a victim under paragraph (1) shall—

(A) be in writing;

(B) be mailed to an address specified by the business entity, if any; and

(C) if asked by the business entity, include relevant information about any transaction alleged to be a result of identity theft to facilitate compliance with this section including—

(i) if known by the victim (or if readily obtainable by the victim), the date of the application or transaction; and

(ii) if known by the victim (or if readily obtainable by the victim), any other identifying information such as an account or transaction number.

(4) No charge to victim

Information required to be provided under paragraph (1) shall be so provided without charge.

(5) Authority to decline to provide information

A business entity may decline to provide information under paragraph (1) if, in the exercise of good faith, the business entity determines that—

(A) this subsection does not require disclosure of the information;

(B) after reviewing the information provided pursuant to paragraph (2), the business entity does not have a high degree of confidence in knowing the true identity of the individual requesting the information;

(C) the request for the information is based on a misrepresentation of fact by the individual requesting the information relevant to the request for information; or

(D) the information requested is Internet navigational data or similar information about a person's visit to a website or online service.

(6) Limitation on liability

Except as provided in section 1681s of this title, sections 1681n and 1681o of this title do not apply to any violation of this subsection.

(7) Limitation on civil liability

No business entity may be held civilly liable under any provision of Federal, State, or other law for disclosure, made in good faith pursuant to this subsection.

(8) No new recordkeeping obligation

Nothing in this subsection creates an obligation on the part of a business entity to obtain, retain, or maintain information or records that are not otherwise required to be obtained, retained, or maintained in the ordinary course of its business or under other applicable law.

(9) Rule of construction

(A) In general

No provision of subtitle A of title V of Public Law 106–102 [15 U.S.C. 6801 et seq.], prohibiting the disclosure of financial information by a business entity to third parties shall be used to deny disclosure of information to the victim under this subsection.

(B) Limitation

Except as provided in subparagraph (A), nothing in this subsection permits a business entity to disclose information, including information to law enforcement under subparagraphs (B) and (C) of paragraph (1), that the business entity is otherwise prohibited from disclosing under any other applicable provision of Federal or State law.

(10) Affirmative defense

In any civil action brought to enforce this subsection, it is an affirmative defense (which the defendant must establish by a preponderance of the evidence) for a business entity to file an affidavit or answer stating that—

(A) the business entity has made a reasonably diligent search of its available business records; and

(B) the records requested under this subsection do not exist or are not reasonably available.

(11) Definition of victim

For purposes of this subsection, the term "victim" means a consumer whose means of identification or financial information has been used or transferred (or has been alleged to have been used or transferred) without the authority of that consumer, with the intent to commit, or to aid or abet, an identity theft or a similar crime.

(12) Effective date

This subsection shall become effective 180 days after December 4, 2003.

(13) Effectiveness study

Not later than 18 months after December 4, 2003, the Comptroller General of the United States shall submit a report to Congress assessing the effectiveness of this provision.

(f) Disclosure of credit scores

(1) In general

Upon the request of a consumer for a credit score, a consumer reporting agency shall supply to the consumer a statement indicating that the information and credit scoring model may be different than the credit score that may be used by the lender, and a notice which shall include—

(A) the current credit score of the consumer or the most recent credit score of the consumer that was previously calculated by the credit reporting agency for a purpose related to the extension of credit;

(B) the range of possible credit scores under the model used;

(C) all of the key factors that adversely affected the credit score of the consumer in the model used, the total number of which shall not exceed 4, subject to paragraph (9);

(D) the date on which the credit score was created; and

(E) the name of the person or entity that provided the credit score or credit file upon which the credit score was created.

(2) Definitions

For purposes of this subsection, the following definitions shall apply:

(A) Credit score

The term "credit score"—

(i) means a numerical value or a categorization derived from a statistical tool or modeling system used by a person who makes or arranges a loan to predict the likelihood of certain credit behaviors, including default (and the numerical value or the categorization derived from such analysis may also be referred to as a "risk predictor" or "risk score"); and

(ii) does not include—

(I) any mortgage score or rating of an automated underwriting system that considers one or more factors in addition to credit information, including the loan to value ratio, the amount of down payment, or the financial assets of a consumer; or

(II) any other elements of the underwriting process or underwriting decision.

(B) Key factors

The term "key factors" means all relevant elements or reasons adversely affecting the credit score for the particular individual, listed in the order of their importance based on their effect on the credit score.

(3) Timeframe and manner of disclosure

The information required by this subsection shall be provided in the same timeframe and manner as the information described in subsection (a).

(4) Applicability to certain uses

This subsection shall not be construed so as to compel a consumer reporting agency to develop or disclose a score if the agency does not—

(A) distribute scores that are used in connection with residential real property loans; or

(B) develop scores that assist credit providers in understanding the general credit behavior of a consumer and predicting the future credit behavior of the consumer.

(5) Applicability to credit scores developed by another person

(A) In general

This subsection shall not be construed to require a consumer reporting agency that distributes credit scores developed by another person or entity to provide a further explanation of them, or to process a dispute arising pursuant to section 1681i of this title, except that the consumer reporting agency shall provide the consumer with the name and address and website for contacting the person or entity who developed the score or developed the methodology of the score.

(B) Exception

This paragraph shall not apply to a consumer reporting agency that develops or modifies scores that are developed by another person or entity.

(6) Maintenance of credit scores not required

This subsection shall not be construed to require a consumer reporting agency to maintain credit scores in its files.

(7) Compliance in certain cases

In complying with this subsection, a consumer reporting agency shall—

(A) supply the consumer with a credit score that is derived from a credit scoring model that is widely distributed to users by that consumer reporting agency in connection with residential real property loans or with a credit score that assists the consumer in understanding the credit scoring assessment of the credit behavior of the consumer and predictions about the future credit behavior of the consumer; and

(B) a statement indicating that the information and credit scoring model may be different than that used by the lender.

(8) Fair and reasonable fee

A consumer reporting agency may charge a fair and reasonable fee, as determined by the Bureau, for providing the information required under this subsection.

(9) Use of enquiries as a key factor

If a key factor that adversely affects the credit score of a consumer consists of the number of enquiries made with respect to a consumer report, that factor shall be included in the disclosure pursuant to paragraph (1)(C) without regard to the numerical limitation in such paragraph.

(g) Disclosure of credit scores by certain mortgage lenders

(1) In general

Any person who makes or arranges loans and who uses a consumer credit score, as defined in subsection (f), in connection with an application initiated or sought by a consumer for a closed end loan or the establishment of an open end loan for a consumer purpose that is secured by 1 to 4 units of residential real property (hereafter in this subsection referred to as the "lender") shall provide the following to the consumer as soon as reasonably practicable:

(A) Information required under subsection (f)

(i) In general

A copy of the information identified in subsection (f) that was obtained from a consumer reporting agency or was developed and used by the user of the information.

(ii) Notice under subparagraph (D)

In addition to the information provided to it by a third party that provided the credit score or scores, a lender is only required to provide the notice contained in subparagraph (D).

(B) Disclosures in case of automated underwriting system

(i) In general

If a person that is subject to this subsection uses an automated underwriting system to underwrite a loan, that person may satisfy the obligation to provide a credit score by disclosing a credit score and associated key factors supplied by a consumer reporting agency.

(ii) Numerical credit score

However, if a numerical credit score is generated by an automated underwriting system used by an enterprise, and that score is disclosed to the person, the score shall be disclosed to the consumer consistent with subparagraph (C).

(iii) Enterprise defined

For purposes of this subparagraph, the term "enterprise" has the same meaning as in paragraph (6) of section 4502 of title 12.

(C) Disclosures of credit scores not obtained from a consumer reporting agency

A person that is subject to the provisions of this subsection and that uses a credit score, other than a credit score provided by a consumer reporting agency, may satisfy the obligation to provide a credit score by disclosing a credit score and associated key factors supplied by a consumer reporting agency.

(D) Notice to home loan applicants

A copy of the following notice, which shall include the name, address, and telephone number of each consumer reporting agency providing a credit score that was used:

"NOTICE TO THE HOME LOAN APPLICANT

"In connection with your application for a home loan, the lender must disclose to you the score that a consumer reporting agency distributed to users and the lender used in connection with your home loan, and the key factors affecting your credit scores.

"The credit score is a computer generated summary calculated at the time of the request and based on information that a consumer reporting agency or lender has on file. The scores are based on data about your credit history and payment patterns. Credit scores are important because they are used to assist the lender in determining whether you will obtain a loan. They may also be used to determine what interest rate you may be offered on the mortgage. Credit scores can change over time, depending on your conduct, how your credit history and payment patterns change, and how credit scoring technologies change.

"Because the score is based on information in your credit history, it is very important that you review the credit-related information that is being furnished to make sure it is accurate. Credit records may vary from one company to another.

"If you have questions about your credit score or the credit information that is furnished to you, contact the consumer reporting agency at the address and telephone number provided with this notice, or contact the lender, if the lender developed or generated the credit score. The consumer reporting agency plays no part in the decision to take any action on the loan application and is unable to provide you with specific reasons for the decision on a loan application. "If you have questions concerning the terms of the loan, contact the lender.".

(E) Actions not required under this subsection

This subsection shall not require any person to—

(i) explain the information provided pursuant to subsection (f);

(ii) disclose any information other than a credit score or key factors, as defined in subsection (f);

(iii) disclose any credit score or related information obtained by the user after a loan has closed;

(iv) provide more than 1 disclosure per loan transaction; or

(v) provide the disclosure required by this subsection when another person has made the disclosure to the consumer for that loan transaction.

(F) No obligation for content

(i) In general

The obligation of any person pursuant to this subsection shall be limited solely to providing a copy of the information that was received from the consumer reporting agency.

(ii) Limit on liability

No person has liability under this subsection for the content of that information or for the omission of any information within the report provided by the consumer reporting agency.

(G) Person defined as excluding enterprise

As used in this subsection, the term "person" does not include an enterprise (as defined in paragraph (6) of section 4502 of title 12).

(2) Prohibition on disclosure clauses null and void

(A) In general

Any provision in a contract that prohibits the disclosure of a credit score by a person who makes or arranges loans or a consumer reporting agency is void.

(B) No liability for disclosure under this subsection

A lender shall not have liability under any contractual provision for disclosure of a credit score pursuant to this subsection.

(Pub. L. 90–321, title VI, §609, as added Pub. L. 91–508, title VI, §601, Oct. 26, 1970, 84 Stat. 1131; amended Pub. L. 103–325, title III, §339, Sept. 23, 1994, 108 Stat. 2237; Pub. L. 104–208, div. A, title II, §2408(a)–(d)(1), (e)(5)(A), Sept. 30, 1996, 110 Stat. 3009–436, 3009-437, 3009-439; Pub. L. 105–347, §4(a), Nov. 2, 1998, 112 Stat. 3210; Pub. L. 108–159, title I, §§115, 151(a)(1), title II, §§211(c), 212(a)–(c), title VIII, §811(d), Dec. 4, 2003, 117 Stat. 1961, 1970, 1973-1975, 2011; Pub. L. 111–203, title X, §1088(a)(2)(C), July 21, 2010, 124 Stat. 2087.)

EDITORIAL NOTES

REFERENCES IN TEXT

Section 1681b(b)(4) of this title, referred to in subsec. (a)(3)(C)(i), was subsequently amended, and section 1681b(b)(4)(E) no longer defines the term "classified information". However, such term is defined elsewhere in that section.

For the effective date of this subchapter, referred to in subsec. (b), see section 504(d) of Pub. L. 90–321, set out as an Effective Date note under section 1681 of this title.

Section 211(c) of the Fair and Accurate Credit Transactions Act of 2003, referred to in subsec. (c)(1)(B)(v), probably means section 211(d) of Pub. L. 108–159, which is set out as a note under section 1681j of this title and relates to the promulgation of regulations. Section 211(c) of Pub. L. 108–159 amended this section.

Section 1681a(w) of this title, referred to in subsec. (c)(1)(B)(vi), was redesignated section 1681a(x) of this title by Pub. L. 111–203, title X, §1088(a)(1), July 21, 2010, 124 Stat. 2086.

Public Law 106–102, referred to in subsec. (e)(9)(A), is Pub. L. 106–102, Nov. 12, 1999, 113 Stat. 1338, known as the Gramm-Leach-Bliley Act. Subtitle A of title V of the Act is classified principally to subchapter I (§ 6801 et seq.) of chapter 94 of this title. For complete classification of this Act to the Code, see Short Title of 1999 Amendment note set out under section 1811 of Title 12, Banks and Banking, and Tables.

AMENDMENTS

2010—Pub. L. 111–203 substituted "the Bureau" for "the Commission" wherever appearing.

2003—Subsec. (a)(1). Pub. L. 108–159, §115, substituted "except that—

"(A) if the consumer to whom the file relates requests that the first 5 digits of the social security number (or similar identification number) of the consumer not be included in the disclosure and the consumer reporting agency has received appropriate proof of the identity of the requester, the consumer reporting agency shall so truncate such number in such disclosure; and

"(B) nothing"

for "except that nothing".

Subsec. (a)(2), (3)(C). Pub. L. 108–159, §811(d), realigned margins.

Subsec. (a)(6). Pub. L. 108–159, §212(a), added par. (6).

Subsec. (c). Pub. L. 108–159, §211(c), amended subsec. (c) generally. Prior to amendment, subsec. (c) related to the summary of rights required to be included with disclosure to consumers by consumer reporting agencies.

Subsecs. (d), (e). Pub. L. 108–159, §151(a)(1), added subsecs. (d) and (e).

Subsec. (f). Pub. L. 108–159, §212(b), added subsec. (f).

Subsec. (g). Pub. L. 108–159, §212(c), added subsec. (g).

1998—Subsec. (a)(3)(C). Pub. L. 105–347 added subpar. (C).

1996—Subsec. (a). Pub. L. 104–208, §2408(e)(5)(A), in introductory provisions substituted ", and subject to section 1681h(a)(1) of this title" for "and proper identification of any consumer".

Subsec. (a)(1). Pub. L. 104–208, §2408(a), amended par. (1) generally. Prior to amendment, par. (1) read as follows: "The nature and substance of all information (except medical information) in its files on the consumer at the time of the request."

Subsec. (a)(3). Pub. L. 104–208, §2408(b), amended par. (3) generally. Prior to amendment, par. (3) read as follows: "The recipients of any consumer report on the consumer which it has furnished—

"(A) for employment purposes within the two-year period preceding the request, and

"(B) for any other purpose within the six-month period preceding the request."

Subsec. (a)(5). Pub. L. 104–208, §2408(c), added par. (5).

Subsec. (c). Pub. L. 104–208, §2408(d)(1), added subsec. (c).

1994—Subsec. (a)(4). Pub. L. 103–325 added par. (4).

EFFECTIVE DATE OF 2010 AMENDMENT

Amendment by Pub. L. 111–203 effective on the designated transfer date, see section 1100H of Pub. L. 111–203, set out as a note under section 552a of Title 5, Government Organization and Employees.

EFFECTIVE DATE OF 2003 AMENDMENT

Amendment by Pub. L. 108–159 subject to joint regulations establishing effective dates as prescribed by Federal Reserve Board and Federal Trade Commission, except as otherwise provided, see section 3 of Pub. L. 108–159, set out as a note under section 1681 of this title.

EFFECTIVE DATE OF 1998 AMENDMENT

Amendment by Pub. L. 105–347 deemed to have same effective date as amendments made by section 2403 of Pub. L. 104–208, see section 7 of Pub. L. 105–347, set out as a note under section 1681a of this title.

EFFECTIVE DATE OF 1996 AMENDMENT

Amendment by Pub. L. 104–208 effective 365 days after Sept. 30, 1996, with special rule for early compliance, see section 2420 of Pub. L. 104–208, set out as a note under section 1681a of this title.

EFFECTIVE DATE

Section effective upon the expiration of one hundred and eighty days following Oct. 26, 1970, see section 504(d) of Pub. L. 90–321, as added by Pub. L. 91–508, set out as a note under section 1681 of this title.

SIMPLIFIED DISCLOSURE TO MAXIMIZE COMPREHENSIBILITY AND STANDARDIZATION

Pub. L. 104–208, div. A, title II, §2408(e)(2), (3), Sept. 30, 1996, 110 Stat. 3009–438, 3009-439, provided that:

"(2) SIMPLIFIED DISCLOSURE.—Not later than 90 days after the date of enactment of this Act [Sept. 30, 1996], each consumer reporting agency shall develop a form on which such consumer reporting agency shall make the disclosures required under section 609(a) of the Fair Credit Reporting Act [15 U.S.C. 1681g(a)], for the purpose of maximizing the comprehensibility and standardization of such disclosures.

"(3) GOALS.—The Federal Trade Commission shall take appropriate action to assure that the goals of comprehensibility and standardization are achieved in accordance with paragraph (2)."

§1681h. Conditions and form of disclosure to consumers

(a) In general

(1) Proper identification

A consumer reporting agency shall require, as a condition of making the disclosures required under section 1681g of this title, that the consumer furnish proper identification.

(2) Disclosure in writing

Except as provided in subsection (b), the disclosures required to be made under section 1681g of this title shall be provided under that section in writing.

(b) Other forms of disclosure

(1) In general

If authorized by a consumer, a consumer reporting agency may make the disclosures required under [1] 1681g of this title—
   (A) other than in writing; and
   (B) in such form as may be—
      (i) specified by the consumer in accordance with paragraph (2); and
      (ii) available from the agency.

(2) Form

A consumer may specify pursuant to paragraph (1) that disclosures under section 1681g of this title shall be made—

   (A) in person, upon the appearance of the consumer at the place of business of the consumer reporting agency where disclosures are regularly provided, during normal business hours, and on reasonable notice;
   (B) by telephone, if the consumer has made a written request for disclosure by telephone;
   (C) by electronic means, if available from the agency; or
   (D) by any other reasonable means that is available from the agency.

(c) Trained personnel

Any consumer reporting agency shall provide trained personnel to explain to the consumer any information furnished to him pursuant to section 1681g of this title.

(d) Persons accompanying consumer

The consumer shall be permitted to be accompanied by one other person of his choosing, who shall furnish reasonable identification. A consumer reporting agency may require the consumer to furnish a written statement granting permission to the consumer reporting agency to discuss the consumer's file in such person's presence.

(e) Limitation of liability

Except as provided in sections 1681n and 1681o of this title, no consumer may bring any action or proceeding in the nature of defamation, invasion of privacy, or negligence with respect to the reporting of information against any consumer reporting agency, any user of information, or any person who furnishes information to a consumer reporting agency, based on information disclosed pursuant to section 1681g, 1681h, or 1681m of this title, or based on information disclosed by a user of a consumer report to or for a consumer against whom the user has taken adverse action, based in whole or in part on the report [2] except as to false information furnished with malice or willful intent to injure such consumer.

(Pub. L. 90–321, title VI, §610, as added Pub. L. 91–508, title VI, §601, Oct. 26, 1970, 84 Stat. 1131; amended Pub. L. 104–208, div. A, title II, §2408(e)(1), (4), (5)(B), Sept. 30, 1996, 110 Stat. 3009–438, 3009-439.)

EDITORIAL NOTES

AMENDMENTS

1996—Pub. L. 104–208, §2408(e)(5)(B), inserted "and form" after "Conditions" in section catchline.
   Subsec. (a). Pub. L. 104–208, §2408(e)(1), inserted heading and amended text of subsec. (a) generally. Prior to amendment, text read as follows: "A consumer reporting agency shall make the disclosures

required under section 1681g of this title during normal business hours and on reasonable notice."

Subsec. (b). Pub. L. 104–208, §2408(e)(1), inserted heading and amended text of subsec. (b) generally. Prior to amendment, text read as follows: "The disclosures required under section 1681g of this title shall be made to the consumer—

"(1) in person if he appears in person and furnishes proper identification; or

"(2) by telephone if he has made a written request, with proper identification, for telephone disclosure and the toll charge, if any, for the telephone call is prepaid by or charged directly to the consumer."

Subsec. (e). Pub. L. 104–208, §2408(e)(4), inserted "or based on information disclosed by a user of a consumer report to or for a consumer against whom the user has taken adverse action, based in whole or in part on the report" before "except".

STATUTORY NOTES AND RELATED SUBSIDIARIES

EFFECTIVE DATE OF 1996 AMENDMENT

Amendment by Pub. L. 104–208 effective 365 days after Sept. 30, 1996, with special rule for early compliance, see section 2420 of Pub. L. 104–208, set out as a note under section 1681a of this title.

EFFECTIVE DATE

Section effective upon the expiration of one hundred and eighty days following Oct. 26, 1970, see section 504(d) of Pub. L. 90–321, as added by Pub. L. 91–508, set out as a note under section 1681 of this title.

¹ So in original. Probably should be followed by "section".

² So in original. Probably should be followed by a comma.

§1681i. Procedure in case of disputed accuracy

(a) Reinvestigations of disputed information

(1) Reinvestigation required

(A) In general

Subject to subsection (f) and except as provided in subsection (g), if the completeness or accuracy of any item of information contained in a consumer's file at a consumer reporting agency is disputed by the consumer and the consumer notifies the agency directly, or indirectly through a reseller, of such dispute, the agency shall, free of charge, conduct a reasonable reinvestigation to determine whether the disputed information is inaccurate and record the current status of the disputed information, or delete the item from the file in accordance with paragraph (5), before the end of the 30-day period beginning on the date on which the agency receives the notice of the dispute from the consumer or reseller.

(B) Extension of period to reinvestigate

Except as provided in subparagraph (C), the 30-day period described in subparagraph (A) may be extended for not more than 15 additional days if the consumer reporting agency receives information from the consumer during that 30-day period that is relevant to the reinvestigation.

(C) Limitations on extension of period to reinvestigate

Subparagraph (B) shall not apply to any reinvestigation in which, during the 30-day period described in subparagraph (A), the information that is the subject of the reinvestigation is found to be inaccurate or incomplete or the consumer reporting agency determines that the information cannot be verified.

(2) Prompt notice of dispute to furnisher of information

(A) In general

Before the expiration of the 5-business-day period beginning on the date on which a consumer reporting agency receives notice of a dispute from any consumer or a reseller in accordance with paragraph (1), the agency shall provide notification of the dispute to any person who provided any item of information in dispute, at the address and in the manner established with the person. The notice shall include all relevant information regarding the dispute that the agency has received from the consumer or reseller.

(B) Provision of other information

The consumer reporting agency shall promptly provide to the person who provided the information in dispute all relevant information regarding the dispute that is received by the agency from the consumer or the reseller after the period referred to in subparagraph (A) and before the end of the period referred to in paragraph (1)(A).

(3) Determination that dispute is frivolous or irrelevant

(A) In general

Notwithstanding paragraph (1), a consumer reporting agency may terminate a reinvestigation of information disputed by a consumer under that paragraph if the agency reasonably determines that the dispute by the consumer is frivolous or irrelevant, including by reason of a failure by a consumer to provide sufficient information to investigate the disputed information.

(B) Notice of determination

Upon making any determination in accordance with subparagraph (A) that a dispute is frivolous or irrelevant, a consumer reporting agency shall notify the consumer of such determination not later than 5 business days after making such determination, by mail or, if authorized by the consumer for that purpose, by any other means available to the agency.

(C) Contents of notice

A notice under subparagraph (B) shall include—
(i) the reasons for the determination under subparagraph (A); and
(ii) identification of any information required to investigate the disputed information, which may consist of a standardized form describing the general nature of such information.

(4) Consideration of consumer information

In conducting any reinvestigation under paragraph (1) with respect to disputed information in the file of any consumer, the consumer reporting agency shall review and consider all relevant information submitted by the consumer in the period described in paragraph (1)(A) with respect to such disputed information.

(5) Treatment of inaccurate or unverifiable information

(A) In general

If, after any reinvestigation under paragraph (1) of any information disputed by a consumer, an item of the information is found to be inaccurate or incomplete or cannot be verified, the consumer reporting agency shall—
(i) promptly delete that item of information from the file of the consumer, or modify that item of information, as appropriate, based on the results of the reinvestigation; and
(ii) promptly notify the furnisher of that information that the information has been modified or deleted from the file of the consumer.

(B) Requirements relating to reinsertion of previously deleted material

(i) Certification of accuracy of information

If any information is deleted from a consumer's file pursuant to subparagraph (A), the information may not be reinserted in the file by the consumer reporting agency unless the person who furnishes the information certifies that the information is complete and accurate.

(ii) Notice to consumer

If any information that has been deleted from a consumer's file pursuant to subparagraph (A) is reinserted in the file, the consumer reporting agency shall notify the consumer of the reinsertion in writing not later than 5 business days after the reinsertion or, if authorized by the consumer for that purpose, by any other means available to the agency.

(iii) Additional information

As part of, or in addition to, the notice under clause (ii), a consumer reporting agency shall provide to a consumer in writing not later than 5 business days after the date of the reinsertion—
(I) a statement that the disputed information has been reinserted;
(II) the business name and address of any furnisher of information contacted and the telephone number of such furnisher, if reasonably available, or of any furnisher of information that contacted the consumer reporting agency, in connection with the reinsertion of such information; and
(III) a notice that the consumer has the right to add a statement to the consumer's file disputing the accuracy or completeness of the disputed information.

(C) Procedures to prevent reappearance

A consumer reporting agency shall maintain reasonable procedures designed to prevent the reappearance in a consumer's file, and in consumer reports on the consumer, of information that is deleted pursuant to this paragraph (other than information that is reinserted in accordance with subparagraph (B)(i)).

(D) Automated reinvestigation system

Any consumer reporting agency that compiles and maintains files on consumers on a nationwide basis shall implement an automated system through which furnishers of information to that consumer reporting agency may report the results of a reinvestigation that finds incomplete or inaccurate information in a consumer's file to other such consumer reporting agencies.

(6) Notice of results of reinvestigation

(A) In general

A consumer reporting agency shall provide written notice to a consumer of the results of a reinvestigation under this subsection not later than 5 business days after the completion of the reinvestigation, by mail or, if authorized by the consumer for that purpose, by other means available to the agency.

(B) Contents

As part of, or in addition to, the notice under subparagraph (A), a consumer reporting agency shall provide to a consumer in writing before the expiration of the 5-day period referred to in subparagraph (A)—

(i) a statement that the reinvestigation is completed;

(ii) a consumer report that is based upon the consumer's file as that file is revised as a result of the reinvestigation;

(iii) a notice that, if requested by the consumer, a description of the procedure used to determine the accuracy and completeness of the information shall be provided to the consumer by the agency, including the business name and address of any furnisher of information contacted in connection with such information and the telephone number of such furnisher, if reasonably available;

(iv) a notice that the consumer has the right to add a statement to the consumer's file disputing the accuracy or completeness of the information; and

(v) a notice that the consumer has the right to request under subsection (d) that the consumer reporting agency furnish notifications under that subsection.

(7) Description of reinvestigation procedure

A consumer reporting agency shall provide to a consumer a description referred to in paragraph (6)(B)(iii) by not later than 15 days after receiving a request from the consumer for that description.

(8) Expedited dispute resolution

If a dispute regarding an item of information in a consumer's file at a consumer reporting agency is resolved in accordance with paragraph (5)(A) by the deletion of the disputed information by not later than 3 business days after the date on which the agency receives notice of the dispute from the consumer in accordance with paragraph (1)(A), then the agency shall not be required to comply with paragraphs (2), (6), and (7) with respect to that dispute if the agency—

(A) provides prompt notice of the deletion to the consumer by telephone;

(B) includes in that notice, or in a written notice that accompanies a confirmation and consumer report provided in accordance with subparagraph (C), a statement of the consumer's right to request under subsection (d) that the agency furnish notifications under that subsection; and

(C) provides written confirmation of the deletion and a copy of a consumer report on the consumer that is based on the consumer's file after the deletion, not later than 5 business days after making the deletion.

(b) Statement of dispute

If the reinvestigation does not resolve the dispute, the consumer may file a brief statement setting forth the nature of the dispute. The consumer reporting agency may limit such statements to not more than one hundred words if it provides the consumer with assistance in writing a clear summary of the dispute.

(c) Notification of consumer dispute in subsequent consumer reports

Whenever a statement of a dispute is filed, unless there is reasonable grounds to believe that it is frivolous or irrelevant, the consumer reporting agency shall, in any subsequent consumer report containing the information in question, clearly note that it is disputed by the consumer and provide either the consumer's statement or a clear and accurate codification or summary thereof.

(d) Notification of deletion of disputed information

Following any deletion of information which is found to be inaccurate or whose accuracy can no longer be verified or any notation as to disputed information, the consumer reporting agency shall, at the request of the consumer, furnish notification that the item has been deleted or the statement, codification or summary pursuant to subsection (b) or (c) to any person specifically designated by the consumer who has within two years prior thereto received a consumer report for employment purposes, or within six months prior thereto received a consumer report for any other purpose, which contained the deleted or disputed information.

(e) Treatment of complaints and report to Congress

(1) In general

The Commission [1] shall—

(A) compile all complaints that it receives that a file of a consumer that is maintained by a consumer reporting agency described in section 1681a(p) of this title contains incomplete or inaccurate information, with respect to which, the consumer appears to have disputed the completeness or accuracy with the consumer reporting agency or otherwise utilized the procedures provided by subsection (a); and

(B) transmit each such complaint to each consumer reporting agency involved.

(2) Exclusion

Complaints received or obtained by the Bureau pursuant to its investigative authority under the Consumer Financial Protection Act of 2010 shall not be subject to paragraph (1).

(3) Agency responsibilities

Each consumer reporting agency described in section 1681a(p) of this title that receives a complaint transmitted by the Bureau pursuant to paragraph (1) shall—

(A) review each such complaint to determine whether all legal obligations imposed on the consumer reporting agency under this subchapter (including any obligation imposed by an applicable court or administrative order) have been met with respect to the subject matter of the complaint;

(B) provide reports on a regular basis to the Bureau regarding the determinations of and actions taken by the consumer reporting agency, if any, in connection with its review of such complaints; and

(C) maintain, for a reasonable time period, records regarding the disposition of each such complaint that is sufficient to demonstrate compliance with this subsection.

(4) Rulemaking authority

The Commission [1] may prescribe regulations, as appropriate to implement this subsection.

(5) Annual report

The Commission [1] shall submit to the Committee on Banking, Housing, and Urban Affairs of the Senate and the Committee on Financial Services of the House of Representatives an annual report regarding information gathered by the Bureau under this subsection.

(f) Reinvestigation requirement applicable to resellers

(1) Exemption from general reinvestigation requirement

Except as provided in paragraph (2), a reseller shall be exempt from the requirements of this section.

(2) Action required upon receiving notice of a dispute

If a reseller receives a notice from a consumer of a dispute concerning the completeness or accuracy of any item of information contained in a consumer report on such consumer produced by the reseller, the reseller shall, within 5 business days of receiving the notice, and free of charge—

(A) determine whether the item of information is incomplete or inaccurate as a result of an act or omission of the reseller; and

(B) if—

(i) the reseller determines that the item of information is incomplete or inaccurate as a result of an act or omission of the reseller, not later than 20 days after receiving the notice, correct the information in the consumer report or delete it; or

(ii) if the reseller determines that the item of information is not incomplete or inaccurate as a result of an act or omission of the reseller, convey the notice of the dispute, together with all relevant information provided by the consumer, to each consumer reporting agency that provided the reseller with the information that is the subject of the dispute, using an address or a notification mechanism specified by the consumer reporting agency for such notices.

(3) Responsibility of consumer reporting agency to notify consumer through reseller

Upon the completion of a reinvestigation under this section of a dispute concerning the completeness or accuracy of any information in the file of a consumer by a consumer reporting agency that received notice of the dispute from a reseller under paragraph (2)—

(A) the notice by the consumer reporting agency under paragraph (6), (7), or (8) of subsection (a) shall be provided to the reseller in lieu of the consumer; and

(B) the reseller shall immediately reconvey such notice to the consumer, including any notice of a deletion by telephone in the manner required under paragraph (8)(A).

(4) Reseller reinvestigations

No provision of this subsection shall be construed as prohibiting a reseller from conducting a reinvestigation of a consumer dispute directly.

(g) Dispute process for veteran's medical debt

(1) In general

With respect to a veteran's medical debt, the veteran may submit a notice described in paragraph (2), proof of liability of the Department of Veterans Affairs for payment of that debt, or documentation that the Department of Veterans Affairs is in the process of making payment for authorized hospital care, medical services, or extended care services rendered to a consumer reporting agency or a reseller to dispute the inclusion of that debt on a consumer report of the veteran.

(2) Notification to veteran

The Department of Veterans Affairs shall submit to a veteran a notice that the Department of Veterans Affairs has assumed liability for part or all of a veteran's medical debt.

(3) Deletion of information from file

If a consumer reporting agency receives notice, proof of liability, or documentation under paragraph (1), the consumer reporting agency shall delete all information relating to the veteran's medical debt from the file of the veteran and notify the furnisher and the veteran of that deletion.

(Pub. L. 90–321, title VI, §611, as added Pub. L. 91–508, title VI, §601, Oct. 26, 1970, 84 Stat. 1132; amended Pub. L. 104–208, div. A, title II, §2409, Sept. 30, 1996, 110 Stat. 3009–439; Pub. L. 105–347, §6(5), Nov. 2, 1998, 112 Stat. 3211; Pub. L. 108–159, title III, §§313(a), 314(a), 316, 317, Dec. 4, 2003, 117 Stat. 1994–1996, 1998; Pub. L. 111–203, title X, §1088(a)(2)(C), (6), July 21, 2010, 124 Stat. 2087; Pub. L. 115–174, title III, §302(b)(3), May 24, 2018, 132 Stat. 1333.)

Editorial Notes

References in Text

The Consumer Financial Protection Act of 2010, referred to in subsec. (e)(2), is title X of Pub. L. 111–203, July 21, 2010, 124 Stat. 1955, which enacted subchapter V (§5481 et seq.) of chapter 53 of Title 12, Banks and Banking, and enacted and amended numerous other sections and notes in the Code. For complete classification of this Act to the Code, see Short Title note set out under section 5301 of Title 12 and Tables.

Amendments

2018—Subsec. (a)(1)(A). Pub. L. 115–174, §302(b)(3)(A), inserted "and except as provided in subsection (g)" after "subsection (f)".

Subsec. (g). Pub. L. 115–174, §302(b)(3)(B), added subsec. (g).

2010—Subsec. (e)(2). Pub. L. 111–203, §1088(a)(6), added par. (2) and struck out former par. (2) which read as follows: "Complaints received or obtained by the Commission pursuant to its investigative authority under the Federal Trade Commission Act shall not be subject to paragraph (1)."

Subsec. (e)(3), (5). Pub. L. 111–203, §1088(a)(2)(C), substituted "the Bureau" for "the Commission" wherever appearing.

2003—Subsec. (a)(1)(A). Pub. L. 108–159, §317, substituted "shall, free of charge, conduct a reasonable reinvestigation to determine whether the disputed information is inaccurate" for "shall reinvestigate free of charge".

Pub. L. 108–159, §316(a)(1), substituted "Subject to subsection (f), if the completeness" for "If the completeness" and inserted ", or indirectly through a reseller," after "notifies the agency directly" and "or reseller" before period at end.

Subsec. (a)(2)(A). Pub. L. 108–159, §316(a)(2), inserted "or a reseller" after "dispute from any consumer" and "or reseller" before period at end.

Subsec. (a)(2)(B). Pub. L. 108–159, §316(c), struck out "from consumer" after "information" in heading.

Pub. L. 108–159, §316(a)(3), inserted "or the reseller" after "from the consumer".

Subsec. (a)(5)(A). Pub. L. 108–159, §314(a), substituted "shall—" and cls. (i) and (ii) for "shall promptly delete that item of information from the consumer's file or modify that item of information, as appropriate, based on the results of the reinvestigation."

Subsec. (e). Pub. L. 108–159, §313(a), added subsec. (e).

Subsec. (f). Pub. L. 108–159, §316(b), added subsec. (f).

1998—Subsec. (a)(7). Pub. L. 105–347 substituted "(6)(B)(iii)" for "(6)(B)(iv)".

1996—Subsec. (a). Pub. L. 104–208, §2409(a), inserted heading and amended text of subsec. (a) generally. Prior to amendment, text read as follows: "If the completeness or accuracy of any item of information contained in his file is disputed by a consumer, and such dispute is directly conveyed to the consumer reporting agency by the consumer, the consumer reporting agency shall within a reasonable period of time reinvestigate and record the current status of that information unless it has reasonable grounds to believe that the dispute by the consumer is frivolous or irrelevant. If after such reinvestigation such information is found to be inaccurate or can no longer be verified, the consumer reporting agency shall promptly delete such information. The presence of contradictory information in the consumer's file does not in and of itself constitute reasonable grounds for believing the dispute is frivolous or irrelevant."

Subsec. (d). Pub. L. 104–208, §2409(b), struck out at end "The consumer reporting agency shall clearly and conspicuously disclose to the consumer his rights to make such a request. Such disclosure shall be made at or prior to the time the information is deleted or the consumer's statement regarding the disputed information is received."

EFFECTIVE DATE OF 2018 AMENDMENT

Amendment by Pub. L. 115–174 effective 1 year after May 24, 2018, see section 302(e) of Pub. L. 115–174, set out as a note under section 1681a of this title.

EFFECTIVE DATE OF 2010 AMENDMENT

Amendment by Pub. L. 111–203 effective on the designated transfer date, see section 1100H of Pub. L. 111–203, set out as a note under section 552a of Title 5, Government Organization and Employees.

EFFECTIVE DATE OF 2003 AMENDMENT

Amendment by Pub. L. 108–159 subject to joint regulations establishing effective dates as prescribed by Federal Reserve Board and Federal Trade Commission, except as otherwise provided, see section 3 of Pub. L. 108–159, set out as a note under section 1681 of this title.

EFFECTIVE DATE OF 1998 AMENDMENT

Amendment by Pub. L. 105–347 deemed to have same effective date as amendments made by section 2403 of Pub. L. 104–208, see section 7 of Pub. L. 105–347, set out as a note under section 1681a of this title.

EFFECTIVE DATE OF 1996 AMENDMENT

Amendment by Pub. L. 104–208 effective 365 days after Sept. 30, 1996, with special rule for early compliance, see section 2420 of Pub. L. 104–208, set out as a note under section 1681a of this title.

EFFECTIVE DATE

Section effective upon the expiration of one hundred and eighty days following Oct. 26, 1970, see section 504(d) of Pub. L. 90–321, as added by Pub. L. 91–508, set out as a note under section 1681 of this title.

PROMPT INVESTIGATION OF DISPUTED CONSUMER INFORMATION

Pub. L. 108–159, title III, §313(b), Dec. 4, 2003, 117 Stat. 1994, provided that:

"(1) STUDY REQUIRED.—The Board and the Commission shall jointly study the extent to which, and the manner in which, consumer reporting agencies and furnishers of consumer information to consumer reporting agencies are complying with the procedures, time lines, and requirements under the Fair Credit Reporting Act [this subchapter] for the prompt investigation of the disputed accuracy of any consumer information, the completeness of the information provided to consumer reporting agencies, and the prompt correction or deletion, in accordance with such Act, of any inaccurate or incomplete information or information that cannot be verified.

"(2) REPORT REQUIRED.—Before the end of the 12-month period beginning on the date of enactment of this Act [Dec. 4, 2003], the Board and the Commission shall jointly submit a progress report to the Congress on the results of the study required under paragraph (1).

"(3) CONSIDERATIONS.—In preparing the report required under paragraph (2), the Board and the Commission shall consider information relating to complaints compiled by the Commission under section 611(e) of the Fair Credit Reporting Act [15 U.S.C. 1681i(e)], as added by this section.

"(4) RECOMMENDATIONS.—The report required under paragraph (2) shall include such recommendations as the Board and the Commission jointly determine to be appropriate for legislative or administrative action, to ensure that—

"(A) consumer disputes with consumer reporting agencies over the accuracy or completeness of information in a consumer's file are promptly and fully investigated and any incorrect, incomplete, or unverifiable information is corrected or deleted immediately thereafter;

"(B) furnishers of information to consumer reporting agencies maintain full and prompt compliance with the duties and responsibilities established under section 623 of the Fair Credit Reporting Act [15 U.S.C. 1681s–2]; and

"(C) consumer reporting agencies establish and maintain appropriate internal controls and management review procedures for maintaining full and continuous compliance with the procedures, time lines, and requirements under the Fair Credit Reporting Act [this subchapter] for the prompt investigation of the disputed accuracy of any consumer information and the prompt correction or deletion, in accordance with such Act, of any inaccurate or incomplete information or information that cannot be verified."

[For definitions of terms used in section 313(b) of Pub. L. 108–159, set out above, see section 2 of Pub. L. 108–159, set out as a Definitions note under section 1681 of this title.]

§1681j. Charges for certain disclosures

(a) Free annual disclosure

(1) Nationwide consumer reporting agencies

(A) In general

All consumer reporting agencies described in subsections (p) and (w) [1] of section 1681a of this title shall make all disclosures pursuant to section 1681g of this title once during any 12-month period upon request of the consumer and without charge to the consumer.

(B) Centralized source

Subparagraph (A) shall apply with respect to a consumer reporting agency described in section 1681a(p) of this title only if the request from the consumer is made using the centralized source established for such purpose in accordance with section 211(c) [1] of the Fair and Accurate Credit Transactions Act of 2003.

(C) Nationwide specialty consumer reporting agency

(i) In general

The Commission [2] shall prescribe regulations applicable to each consumer reporting agency described in section 1681a(w) [1] of this title to require the establishment of a streamlined process for consumers to request consumer reports under subparagraph (A), which shall include, at a minimum, the establishment by each such agency of a toll-free telephone number for such requests.

(ii) Considerations

In prescribing regulations under clause (i), the Bureau shall consider—
(I) the significant demands that may be placed on consumer reporting agencies in providing such consumer reports;
(II) appropriate means to ensure that consumer reporting agencies can satisfactorily meet those demands, including the efficacy of a system of staggering the availability to consumers of such consumer reports; and
(III) the ease by which consumers should be able to contact consumer reporting agencies with respect to access to such consumer reports.

(iii) Date of issuance

The Commission [2] shall issue the regulations required by this subparagraph in final form not later than 6 months after December 4, 2003.

(iv) Consideration of ability to comply

The regulations of the Bureau under this subparagraph shall establish an effective date by which each nationwide specialty consumer reporting agency (as defined in section 1681a(w) [1] of this title) shall be required to comply with subsection (a), which effective date—
(I) shall be established after consideration of the ability of each nationwide specialty consumer reporting agency to comply with subsection (a); and
(II) shall be not later than 6 months after the date on which such regulations are issued in final form (or such additional period not to exceed 3 months, as the Bureau determines appropriate).

(2) Timing

A consumer reporting agency shall provide a consumer report under paragraph (1) not later than 15 days after the date on which the request is received under paragraph (1).

(3) Reinvestigations

Notwithstanding the time periods specified in section 1681i(a)(1) of this title, a reinvestigation under that section by a consumer reporting agency upon a request of a consumer that is made after receiving a consumer report under this subsection shall be completed not later than 45 days after the date on which the request is received.

(4) Exception for first 12 months of operation

This subsection shall not apply to a consumer reporting agency that has not been furnishing consumer reports to third parties on a continuing basis during the 12-month period preceding a request under paragraph (1), with respect to consumers residing nationwide.

(b) Free disclosure after adverse notice to consumer

Each consumer reporting agency that maintains a file on a consumer shall make all disclosures pursuant to section 1681g of this title without charge to the consumer if, not later than 60 days after receipt by such consumer of a notification pursuant to section 1681m of this title, or of a notification from a debt collection agency affiliated with that consumer reporting agency stating that the consumer's credit rating may be or has been adversely affected, the consumer makes a request under section 1681g of this title.

(c) Free disclosure under certain other circumstances

Upon the request of the consumer, a consumer reporting agency shall make all disclosures pursuant to section 1681g of this title once during any 12-month period without charge to that consumer if the consumer certifies in writing that the consumer—

(1) is unemployed and intends to apply for employment in the 60-day period beginning on the date on which the certification is made;

(2) is a recipient of public welfare assistance; or

(3) has reason to believe that the file on the consumer at the agency contains inaccurate information due to fraud.

(d) Free disclosures in connection with fraud alerts

Upon the request of a consumer, a consumer reporting agency described in section 1681a(p) of this title shall make all disclosures pursuant to section 1681g of this title without charge to the consumer, as provided in subsections (a)(2) and (b)(2) of section 1681c–1 of this title, as applicable.

(e) Other charges prohibited

A consumer reporting agency shall not impose any charge on a consumer for providing any notification required by this subchapter or making any disclosure required by this subchapter, except as authorized by subsection (f).

(f) Reasonable charges allowed for certain disclosures

(1) In general

In the case of a request from a consumer other than a request that is covered by any of subsections (a) through (d), a consumer reporting agency may impose a reasonable charge on a consumer—

(A) for making a disclosure to the consumer pursuant to section 1681g of this title, which charge—

(i) shall not exceed $8; and

(ii) shall be indicated to the consumer before making the disclosure; and

(B) for furnishing, pursuant to section 1681i(d) of this title, following a reinvestigation under section 1681i(a) of this title, a statement, codification, or summary to a person designated by the consumer under that section after the 30-day period beginning on the date of notification of the consumer under paragraph (6) or (8) of section 1681i(a) of this title with respect to the reinvestigation, which charge—

(i) shall not exceed the charge that the agency would impose on each designated recipient for a consumer report; and

(ii) shall be indicated to the consumer before furnishing such information.

(2) Modification of amount

The Bureau shall increase the amount referred to in paragraph (1)(A)(i) on January 1 of each year, based proportionally on changes in the Consumer Price Index, with fractional changes rounded to the nearest fifty cents.

(g) Prevention of deceptive marketing of credit reports

(1) In general

Subject to rulemaking pursuant to section 205(b) of the Credit CARD Act of 2009, any advertisement for a free credit report in any medium shall prominently disclose in such advertisement that free credit reports are available under Federal law at: "AnnualCreditReport.com" (or such other source as may be authorized under Federal law).

(2) Television and radio advertisement

In the case of an advertisement broadcast by television, the disclosures required under paragraph (1) shall be included in the audio and visual part of such advertisement. In the case of an advertisement broadcast by televison [3] or radio, the disclosure required under paragraph (1) shall consist only of the following: "This is not the free credit report provided for by Federal law".

(Pub. L. 90–321, title VI, §612, as added Pub. L. 91–508, title VI, §601, Oct. 26, 1970, 84 Stat. 1132; amended Pub. L. 104–208, div. A, title II, §2410, Sept. 30, 1996, 110 Stat. 3009–442; Pub. L. 108–159, title II, §211(a), Dec. 4, 2003, 117 Stat. 1968; Pub. L. 111–24, title II, §205(a), May 22, 2009, 123 Stat. 1747; Pub. L. 111–203, title X, §1088(a)(2)(A), (C), July 21, 2010, 124 Stat. 2087.)

Editorial Notes

References in Text

Section 1681a(w) of this title, referred to in subsec. (a)(1)(A), (C)(i), (iv), was redesignated section 1681a(x) of this title by Pub. L. 111–203, title X, §1088(a)(1), July 21, 2010, 124 Stat. 2086.

Section 211(c) of the Fair and Accurate Credit Transactions Act of 2003, referred to in subsec. (a)(1)(B), probably means section 211(d) of Pub. L. 108–159, which is set out as a note below and relates to the establishment of a centralized source. Section 211(c) of Pub. L. 108–159 amended section 1681g of this title.

Section 205(b) of the Credit CARD Act of 2009, referred to in subsec. (g), is section 205(b) of Pub. L. 111–24, which is set out as a note below.

AMENDMENTS

2010—Subsec. (a)(1)(C). Pub. L. 111–203, §1088(a)(2)(C), substituted "the Bureau" for "the Commission" wherever appearing.

Subsec. (f)(2). Pub. L. 111–203, §1088(a)(2)(A), substituted "Bureau" for "Federal Trade Commission".

2009—Subsec. (g). Pub. L. 111–24 added subsec. (g).

2003—Subsec. (a). Pub. L. 108–159, §211(a)(2), added subsec. (a). Former subsec. (a) redesignated (f).

Subsec. (d). Pub. L. 108–159, §211(a)(4), added subsec. (d). Former subsec. (d) redesignated (e).

Subsec. (e). Pub. L. 108–159, §211(a)(3), (5), redesignated subsec. (d) as (e) and substituted "subsection (f)" for "subsection (a)".

Subsec. (f). Pub. L. 108–159, §211(a)(1), (6), redesignated subsec. (a) as (f) and substituted "In the case of a request from a consumer other than a request that is covered by any of subsections (a) through (d), a" for "Except as provided in subsections (b), (c), and (d), a" in par. (1).

1996—Pub. L. 104–208 amended section generally. Prior to amendment, section read as follows: "A consumer reporting agency shall make all disclosures pursuant to section 1681g of this title and furnish all consumer reports pursuant to section 1681i(d) of this title without charge to the consumer if, within thirty days after receipt by such consumer of a notification pursuant to section 1681m of this title or notification from a debt collection agency affiliated with such consumer reporting agency stating that the consumer's credit rating may be or has been adversely affected, the consumer makes a request under section 1681g or 1681i(d) of this title. Otherwise, the consumer reporting agency may impose a reasonable charge on the consumer for making disclosure to such consumer pursuant to section 1681g of this title, the charge for which shall be indicated to the consumer prior to making disclosure; and for furnishing notifications, statements, summaries, or codifications to person designated by the consumer pursuant to section 1681i(d) of this title, the charge for which shall be indicated to the consumer prior to furnishing such information and shall not exceed the charge that the consumer reporting agency would impose on each designated recipient for a consumer report except that no charge may be made for notifying such persons of the deletion of information which is found to be inaccurate or which can no longer be verified."

STATUTORY NOTES AND RELATED SUBSIDIARIES

EFFECTIVE DATE OF 2010 AMENDMENT

Amendment by Pub. L. 111–203 effective on the designated transfer date, see section 1100H of Pub. L. 111–203, set out as a note under section 552a of Title 5, Government Organization and Employees.

EFFECTIVE DATE OF 2009 AMENDMENT

Amendment by Pub. L. 111–24 effective 9 months after May 22, 2009, except as otherwise specifically provided, see section 3 of Pub. L. 111–24, set out as a note under section 1602 of this title.

EFFECTIVE DATE OF 2003 AMENDMENT

Amendment by Pub. L. 108–159 subject to joint regulations establishing effective dates as prescribed by Federal Reserve Board and Federal Trade Commission, except as otherwise provided, see section 3 of Pub. L. 108–159, set out as a note under section 1681 of this title.

EFFECTIVE DATE OF 1996 AMENDMENT

Amendment by Pub. L. 104–208 effective 365 days after Sept. 30, 1996, with special rule for early compliance, see section 2420 of Pub. L. 104–208, set out as a note under section 1681a of this title.

EFFECTIVE DATE

Section effective upon the expiration of one hundred and eighty days following Oct. 26, 1970, see section 504(d) of Pub. L. 90–321, as added by Pub. L. 91–508, set out as a note under section 1681 of this title.

REGULATIONS

Pub. L. 111–24, title II, §205(b), May 22, 2009, 123 Stat. 1747, provided that:

"(1) IN GENERAL.—Not later than 9 months after the date of enactment of this Act [May 22, 2009], the Federal Trade Commission shall issue a final rule to carry out this section.

"(2) CONTENT.—The rule required by this subsection—

"(A) shall include specific wording to be used in advertisements in accordance with this section; and

"(B) for advertisements on the Internet, shall include whether the disclosure required under section 612(g)(1) of the Fair Credit Reporting Act [15 U.S.C. 1681j(g)(1)] (as added by this section) shall appear on the advertisement or the website on which the free credit report is made available.

"(3) INTERIM DISCLOSURES.—If an advertisement subject to section 612(g) of the Fair Credit Reporting Act [15 U.S.C. 1681j(g)], as added by this section, is made public after the 9-month deadline specified in paragraph (1), but before the rule required by paragraph (1) is finalized, such advertisement shall include the disclosure: 'Free credit reports are available under Federal law at: "AnnualCreditReport.com".' "

Pub. L. 108–159, title II, §211(d), Dec. 4, 2003, 117 Stat. 1972, as amended by Pub. L. 111–203, §1088(b) (2), July 21, 2010, 124 Stat. 2092, provided that:

"(1) IN GENERAL.—The Bureau [probably means the Bureau of Consumer Financial Protection] shall prescribe regulations applicable to consumer reporting agencies described in section 603(p) of the Fair Credit Reporting Act [15 U.S.C. 1681a(p)], to require the establishment of—

"(A) a centralized source through which consumers may obtain a consumer report from each such consumer reporting agency, using a single request, and without charge to the consumer, as provided in section 612(a) of the Fair Credit Reporting Act [15 U.S.C. 1681j(a)] (as amended by this section); and

"(B) a standardized form for a consumer to make such a request for a consumer report by mail or through an Internet website.

"(2) CONSIDERATIONS.—In prescribing regulations under paragraph (1), the Bureau shall consider—

"(A) the significant demands that may be placed on consumer reporting agencies in providing such consumer reports;

"(B) appropriate means to ensure that consumer reporting agencies can satisfactorily meet those demands, including the efficacy of a system of staggering the availability to consumers of such consumer reports; and

"(C) the ease by which consumers should be able to contact consumer reporting agencies with respect to access to such consumer reports.

"(3) CENTRALIZED SOURCE.—The centralized source for a request for a consumer report from a consumer required by this subsection shall provide for—

"(A) a toll-free telephone number for such purpose;

"(B) use of an Internet website for such purpose; and

"(C) a process for requests by mail for such purpose.

"(4) TRANSITION.—The regulations of the Bureau under paragraph (1) shall provide for an orderly transition by consumer reporting agencies described in section 603(p) of the Fair Credit Reporting Act [15 U.S.C. 1681a(p)] to the centralized source for consumer report distribution required by section 612(a)(1)(B) [15 U.S.C. 1681j(a)(1)(B)], as amended by this section, in a manner that—

"(A) does not temporarily overwhelm such consumer reporting agencies with requests for disclosures of consumer reports beyond their capacity to deliver; and

"(B) does not deny creditors, other users, and consumers access to consumer reports on a time-sensitive basis for specific purposes, such as home purchases or suspicions of identity theft, during the transition period.

"(5) TIMING.—Regulations required by this subsection shall—

"(A) be issued in final form not later than 6 months after the date of enactment of this Act [Dec. 4, 2003]; and

"(B) become effective not later than 6 months after the date on which they are issued in final form.

"(6) SCOPE OF REGULATIONS.—

"(A) IN GENERAL.—The Bureau shall, by rule, determine whether to require a consumer reporting agency that compiles and maintains files on consumers on substantially a nationwide basis, other than one described in section 603(p) of the Fair Credit Reporting Act [15 U.S.C. 1681a(p)], to make free consumer reports available upon consumer request, and if so, whether such consumer reporting agencies should make such free reports available through the centralized source described in paragraph (1)(A).

"(B) CONSIDERATIONS.—Before making any determination under subparagraph (A), the Bureau shall consider—

"(i) the number of requests for consumer reports to, and the number of consumer reports generated by, the consumer reporting agency, in comparison with consumer reporting agencies described in subsections (p) and (w) [now (x)] of section 603 of the Fair Credit Reporting Act [15 U.S.C. 1681a(p), (w) [x]];

"(ii) the overall scope of the operations of the consumer reporting agency;

"(iii) the needs of consumers for access to consumer reports provided by consumer reporting agencies free of charge;

"(iv) the costs of providing access to consumer reports by consumer reporting agencies free of charge; and

"(v) the effects on the ongoing competitive viability of such consumer reporting agencies if such free access is required."

[For definitions of terms used in section 211(d) of Pub. L. 108–159, set out above, see section 2 of Pub. L. 108–159, set out as a Definitions note under section 1681 of this title.]

[1] *See References in Text note below.*

[2] *So in original. Probably should be "Bureau".*

[3] *So in original. Probably should be "television".*

§1681k. Public record information for employment purposes

(a) In general

A consumer reporting agency which furnishes a consumer report for employment purposes and which for that purpose compiles and reports items of information on consumers which are matters of public record and are likely to have an adverse effect upon a consumer's ability to obtain employment shall—

(1) at the time such public record information is reported to the user of such consumer report, notify the consumer of the fact that public record information is being reported by the consumer reporting agency, together with the name and address of the person to whom such information is being reported; or

(2) maintain strict procedures designed to insure that whenever public record information which is likely to have an adverse effect on a consumer's ability to obtain employment is reported it is complete and up to date. For purposes of this paragraph, items of public record relating to arrests, indictments, convictions, suits, tax liens, and outstanding judgments shall be considered up to date if the current public record status of the item at the time of the report is reported.

(b) Exemption for national security investigations

Subsection (a) does not apply in the case of an agency or department of the United States Government that seeks to obtain and use a consumer report for employment purposes, if the head of the agency or department makes a written finding as prescribed under section 1681b(b)(4)(A) of this title.

(Pub. L. 90–321, title VI, §613, as added Pub. L. 91–508, title VI, §601, Oct. 26, 1970, 84 Stat. 1133; amended Pub. L. 105–347, §4(b), Nov. 2, 1998, 112 Stat. 3210.)

EDITORIAL NOTES

AMENDMENTS

1998—Pub. L. 105–347 designated existing provisions as subsec. (a), inserted heading, and added subsec. (b).

STATUTORY NOTES AND RELATED SUBSIDIARIES

EFFECTIVE DATE OF 1998 AMENDMENT

Amendment by Pub. L. 105–347 deemed to have same effective date as amendments made by section 2403 of Pub. L. 104–208, see section 7 of Pub. L. 105–347, set out as a note under section 1681a of this title.

EFFECTIVE DATE

Section effective upon the expiration of one hundred and eighty days following Oct. 26, 1970, see section 504(d) of Pub. L. 90–321, as added by Pub. L. 91–508, set out as a note under section 1681 of this title.

§1681*l*. Restrictions on investigative consumer reports

Whenever a consumer reporting agency prepares an investigative consumer report, no adverse information in the consumer report (other than information which is a matter of public record) may be included in a subsequent consumer report unless such adverse information has been verified in the process of making such subsequent consumer report, or the adverse information was received within the three-month period preceding the date the subsequent report is furnished.

(Pub. L. 90–321, title VI, §614, as added Pub. L. 91–508, title VI, §601, Oct. 26, 1970, 84 Stat. 1133.)

STATUTORY NOTES AND RELATED SUBSIDIARIES

EFFECTIVE DATE

Section effective upon the expiration of one hundred and eighty days following Oct. 26, 1970, see section 504(d) of Pub. L. 90–321, as added by Pub. L. 91–508, set out as a note under section 1681 of this title.

§1681m. Requirements on users of consumer reports

(a) Duties of users taking adverse actions on basis of information contained in consumer reports

If any person takes any adverse action with respect to any consumer that is based in whole or in part on any information contained in a consumer report, the person shall—

(1) provide oral, written, or electronic notice of the adverse action to the consumer;

(2) provide to the consumer written or electronic disclosure—

(A) of a numerical credit score as defined in section 1681g(f)(2)(A) of this title used by such person in taking any adverse action based in whole or in part on any information in a consumer report; and

(B) of the information set forth in subparagraphs (B) through (E) of section 1681g(f)(1) of this title;

(3) provide to the consumer orally, in writing, or electronically—

(A) the name, address, and telephone number of the consumer reporting agency (including a toll-free telephone number established by the agency if the agency compiles and maintains files on consumers on a nationwide basis) that furnished the report to the person; and

(B) a statement that the consumer reporting agency did not make the decision to take the adverse action and is unable to provide the consumer the specific reasons why the adverse action was taken; and

(4) provide to the consumer an oral, written, or electronic notice of the consumer's right—

(A) to obtain, under section 1681j of this title, a free copy of a consumer report on the consumer from the consumer reporting agency referred to in paragraph (3), which notice shall include an indication of the 60-day period under that section for obtaining such a copy; and

(B) to dispute, under section 1681i of this title, with a consumer reporting agency the accuracy or completeness of any information in a consumer report furnished by the agency.

(b) Adverse action based on information obtained from third parties other than consumer reporting agencies

(1) In general

Whenever credit for personal, family, or household purposes involving a consumer is denied or the charge for such credit is increased either wholly or partly because of information obtained from a person other than a consumer reporting agency bearing upon the consumer's credit worthiness, credit standing, credit capacity, character, general reputation, personal characteristics, or mode of living, the user of such information shall, within a reasonable period of time, upon the consumer's written request for the reasons for such adverse action received within sixty days after learning of such adverse action, disclose the nature of the information to the consumer. The user of such information shall clearly and accurately disclose to the consumer his right to make such written request at the time such adverse action is communicated to the consumer.

(2) Duties of person taking certain actions based on information provided by affiliate

(A) Duties, generally

If a person takes an action described in subparagraph (B) with respect to a consumer, based in whole or in part on information described in subparagraph (C), the person shall—

(i) notify the consumer of the action, including a statement that the consumer may obtain the information in accordance with clause (ii); and

(ii) upon a written request from the consumer received within 60 days after transmittal of the notice required by clause (i), disclose to the consumer the nature of the information upon which the action is based by not later than 30 days after receipt of the request.

(B) Action described

An action referred to in subparagraph (A) is an adverse action described in section 1681a(k)(1)(A) of this title, taken in connection with a transaction initiated by the consumer, or any adverse action described in clause (i) or (ii) of section 1681a(k)(1)(B) of this title.

(C) Information described

Information referred to in subparagraph (A)—

(i) except as provided in clause (ii), is information that—

(I) is furnished to the person taking the action by a person related by common ownership or affiliated by common corporate control to the person taking the action; and

(II) bears on the credit worthiness, credit standing, credit capacity, character, general reputation, personal characteristics, or mode of living of the consumer; and

(ii) does not include—

(I) information solely as to transactions or experiences between the consumer and the person furnishing the information; or

(II) information in a consumer report.

(c) Reasonable procedures to assure compliance

No person shall be held liable for any violation of this section if he shows by a preponderance of the evidence that at the time of the alleged violation he maintained reasonable procedures to assure compliance with the provisions of this section.

(d) Duties of users making written credit or insurance solicitations on basis of information contained in consumer files

(1) In general

Any person who uses a consumer report on any consumer in connection with any credit or insurance transaction that is not initiated by the consumer, that is provided to that person under section 1681b(c)(1)(B) of this title, shall provide with each written solicitation made to the consumer regarding the transaction a clear and conspicuous statement that—

(A) information contained in the consumer's consumer report was used in connection with the transaction;

(B) the consumer received the offer of credit or insurance because the consumer satisfied the criteria for credit worthiness or insurability under which the consumer was selected for the offer;

(C) if applicable, the credit or insurance may not be extended if, after the consumer responds to the offer, the consumer does not meet the criteria used to select the consumer for the offer or any applicable criteria bearing on credit worthiness or insurability or does not furnish any required collateral;

(D) the consumer has a right to prohibit information contained in the consumer's file with any consumer reporting agency from being used in connection with any credit or insurance transaction that is not initiated by the consumer; and

(E) the consumer may exercise the right referred to in subparagraph (D) by notifying a notification system established under section 1681b(e) of this title.

(2) Disclosure of address and telephone number; format

A statement under paragraph (1) shall—

(A) include the address and toll-free telephone number of the appropriate notification system established under section 1681b(e) of this title; and

(B) be presented in such format and in such type size and manner as to be simple and easy to understand, as established by the Bureau, by rule, in consultation with the Federal Trade Commission, the Federal banking agencies, and the National Credit Union Administration.

(3) Maintaining criteria on file

A person who makes an offer of credit or insurance to a consumer under a credit or insurance transaction described in paragraph (1) shall maintain on file the criteria used to select the consumer to receive the offer, all criteria bearing on credit worthiness or insurability, as applicable, that are the basis for determining whether or not to extend credit or insurance pursuant to the offer, and any requirement for the furnishing of collateral as a condition of the extension of credit or insurance, until the expiration of the 3-year period beginning on the date on which the offer is made to the consumer.

(4) Authority of Federal agencies regarding unfair or deceptive acts or practices not affected

This section is not intended to affect the authority of any Federal or State agency to enforce a prohibition against unfair or deceptive acts or practices, including the making of false or misleading statements in connection with a credit or insurance transaction that is not initiated by the consumer.

(e) Red flag guidelines and regulations required

(1) Guidelines

The Federal banking agencies, the National Credit Union Administration, the Federal Trade Commission, the Commodity Futures Trading Commission, and the Securities and Exchange Commission shall jointly, with respect to the entities that are subject to their respective enforcement authority under section 1681s of this title—

(A) establish and maintain guidelines for use by each financial institution and each creditor regarding identity theft with respect to account holders at, or customers of, such entities, and update such guidelines as often as necessary;

(B) prescribe regulations requiring each financial institution and each creditor to establish reasonable policies and procedures for implementing the guidelines established pursuant to subparagraph (A), to identify possible risks to account holders or customers or to the safety and soundness of the institution or customers; and

(C) prescribe regulations applicable to card issuers to ensure that, if a card issuer receives notification of a change of address for an existing account, and within a short period of time (during at least the first 30 days after such notification is received) receives a request for an additional or replacement card for the same account, the card issuer may not issue the additional or replacement card, unless the card issuer, in accordance with reasonable policies and procedures—

(i) notifies the cardholder of the request at the former address of the cardholder and provides to the cardholder a means of promptly reporting incorrect address changes;

(ii) notifies the cardholder of the request by such other means of communication as the cardholder and the card issuer previously agreed to; or

(iii) uses other means of assessing the validity of the change of address, in accordance with reasonable policies and procedures established by the card issuer in accordance with the regulations prescribed under subparagraph (B).

(2) Criteria

(A) In general

In developing the guidelines required by paragraph (1)(A), the agencies described in paragraph (1) shall identify patterns, practices, and specific forms of activity that indicate the possible existence of identity theft.

(B) Inactive accounts

In developing the guidelines required by paragraph (1)(A), the agencies described in paragraph (1) shall consider including reasonable guidelines providing that when a transaction occurs with respect to a credit or deposit account that has been inactive for more than 2 years, the creditor or financial institution shall follow reasonable policies and procedures that provide for notice to be given to a consumer in a manner reasonably designed to reduce the likelihood of identity theft with respect to such account.

(3) Consistency with verification requirements

Guidelines established pursuant to paragraph (1) shall not be inconsistent with the policies and procedures required under section 5318(l) of title 31.

(4) Definitions

As used in this subsection, the term "creditor"—

(A) means a creditor, as defined in section 1691a of this title, that regularly and in the ordinary course of business—

(i) obtains or uses consumer reports, directly or indirectly, in connection with a credit transaction;

(ii) furnishes information to consumer reporting agencies, as described in section 1681s–2 of this title, in connection with a credit transaction; or

(iii) advances funds to or on behalf of a person, based on an obligation of the person to repay the funds or repayable from specific property pledged by or on behalf of the person;

(B) does not include a creditor described in subparagraph (A)(iii) that advances funds on behalf of a person for expenses incidental to a service provided by the creditor to that person; and

(C) includes any other type of creditor, as defined in that section 1691a of this title, as the agency described in paragraph (1) having authority over that creditor may determine appropriate by rule promulgated by that agency, based on a determination that such creditor offers or maintains accounts that are subject to a reasonably foreseeable risk of identity theft.

(f) Prohibition on sale or transfer of debt caused by identity theft

(1) In general

No person shall sell, transfer for consideration, or place for collection a debt that such person has been notified under section 1681c–2 of this title has resulted from identity theft.

(2) Applicability

The prohibitions of this subsection shall apply to all persons collecting a debt described in paragraph (1) after the date of a notification under paragraph (1).

(3) Rule of construction

Nothing in this subsection shall be construed to prohibit—

(A) the repurchase of a debt in any case in which the assignee of the debt requires such repurchase because the debt has resulted from identity theft;

(B) the securitization of a debt or the pledging of a portfolio of debt as collateral in connection with a borrowing; or

(C) the transfer of debt as a result of a merger, acquisition, purchase and assumption transaction, or transfer of substantially all of the assets of an entity.

(g) Debt collector communications concerning identity theft

If a person acting as a debt collector (as that term is defined in subchapter V) on behalf of a third party that is a creditor or other user of a consumer report is notified that any information relating to a debt that the person is attempting to collect may be fraudulent or may be the result of identity theft, that person shall—

(1) notify the third party that the information may be fraudulent or may be the result of identity theft; and

(2) upon request of the consumer to whom the debt purportedly relates, provide to the consumer all information to which the consumer would otherwise be entitled if the consumer were not a victim of identity theft, but wished to dispute the debt under provisions of law applicable to that person.

(h) Duties of users in certain credit transactions

(1) In general

Subject to rules prescribed as provided in paragraph (6), if any person uses a consumer report in connection with an application for, or a grant, extension, or other provision of, credit on material terms that are materially less favorable than the most favorable terms available to a substantial proportion of consumers from or through that person, based in whole or in part on a consumer report, the person shall provide an oral, written, or electronic notice to the consumer in the form and manner required by regulations prescribed in accordance with this subsection.

(2) Timing

The notice required under paragraph (1) may be provided at the time of an application for, or a grant, extension, or other provision of, credit or the time of communication of an approval of an application for, or grant, extension, or other provision of, credit, except as provided in the regulations prescribed under paragraph (6).

(3) Exceptions

No notice shall be required from a person under this subsection if—

(A) the consumer applied for specific material terms and was granted those terms, unless those terms were initially specified by the person after the transaction was initiated by the consumer and after the person obtained a consumer report; or

(B) the person has provided or will provide a notice to the consumer under subsection (a) in connection with the transaction.

(4) Other notice not sufficient

A person that is required to provide a notice under subsection (a) cannot meet that requirement by providing a notice under this subsection.

(5) Content and delivery of notice

A notice under this subsection shall, at a minimum—

(A) include a statement informing the consumer that the terms offered to the consumer are set based on information from a consumer report;

(B) identify the consumer reporting agency furnishing the report;

(C) include a statement informing the consumer that the consumer may obtain a copy of a consumer report from that consumer reporting agency without charge;

(D) include the contact information specified by that consumer reporting agency for obtaining such consumer reports (including a toll-free telephone number established by the agency in the case of a consumer reporting agency described in section 1681a(p) of this title); and

(E) include a statement informing the consumer of—

(i) a numerical credit score as defined in section 1681g(f)(2)(A) of this title, used by such person in making the credit decision described in paragraph (1) based in whole or in part on any information in a consumer report; and

(ii) the information set forth in subparagraphs (B) through (E) of section 1681g(f)(1) of this title.

(6) Rulemaking

(A) Rules required

The Bureau shall prescribe rules to carry out this subsection.

(B) Content

Rules required by subparagraph (A) shall address, but are not limited to—

(i) the form, content, time, and manner of delivery of any notice under this subsection;

(ii) clarification of the meaning of terms used in this subsection, including what credit terms are material, and when credit terms are materially less favorable;

(iii) exceptions to the notice requirement under this subsection for classes of persons or transactions regarding which the agencies determine that notice would not significantly benefit consumers;

(iv) a model notice that may be used to comply with this subsection; and

(v) the timing of the notice required under paragraph (1), including the circumstances under which the notice must be provided after the terms offered to the consumer were set based on information from a consumer report.

(7) Compliance

A person shall not be liable for failure to perform the duties required by this section if, at the time of the failure, the person maintained reasonable policies and procedures to comply with this section.

(8) Enforcement

(A) No civil actions

Sections 1681n and 1681o of this title shall not apply to any failure by any person to comply with this section.

(B) Administrative enforcement

This section shall be enforced exclusively under section 1681s of this title by the Federal agencies and officials identified in that section.

(Pub. L. 90–321, title VI, §615, as added Pub. L. 91–508, title VI, §601, Oct. 26, 1970, 84 Stat. 1133; amended Pub. L. 104–208, div. A, title II, §2411, Sept. 30, 1996, 110 Stat. 3009–443; Pub. L. 108–159, title I, §§114, 154(b), 155, title II, §213(a), title III, §311(a), title VIII, §811(h), Dec. 4, 2003, 117 Stat. 1960, 1967, 1978, 1988, 2012; Pub. L. 111–203, title X, §§1088(a)(2)(C), (7)–(9), 1100F, July 21, 2010, 124 Stat. 2087, 2088, 2112; Pub. L. 111–319, §2(a), Dec. 18, 2010, 124 Stat. 3457.)

EDITORIAL NOTES

AMENDMENTS

2010—Subsec. (a)(2) to (4). Pub. L. 111–203, §1100F(1), added par. (2), redesignated former pars. (2) and (3) as (3) and (4), respectively, and substituted "paragraph (3)" for "paragraph (2)" in par. (4).

Subsec. (d)(2)(B). Pub. L. 111–203, §1088(a)(7), substituted "the Federal Trade Commission, the Federal banking agencies," for "the Federal banking agencies".

Pub. L. 111–203, §1088(a)(2)(C), substituted "the Bureau" for "the Commission".

Subsec. (e)(1). Pub. L. 111–203, §1088(a)(8), substituted "the Federal Trade Commission, the Commodity Futures Trading Commission, and the Securities and Exchange Commission" for "and the Commission" in introductory provisions.

Subsec. (e)(4). Pub. L. 111–319 added par. (4).

Subsec. (h)(5)(E). Pub. L. 111–203, §1100F(2), added subpar. (E).

Subsec. (h)(6)(A). Pub. L. 111–203, §1088(a)(9), added subpar. (A) and struck out former subpar. (A). Prior to amendment, text read as follows: "The Commission and the Board shall jointly prescribe rules."

2003—Subsec. (d)(2). Pub. L. 108–159, §213(a), amended heading and text of par. (2) generally. Prior to amendment, text read as follows: "A statement under paragraph (1) shall include the address and toll-free telephone number of the appropriate notification system established under section 1681b(e) of this title."

Subsec. (e). Pub. L. 108–159, §811(h), repealed Pub. L. 104–208, §2411(c). See 1996 Amendment note below.

Pub. L. 108–159, §114, added subsec. (e) and struck out former subsec. (e) designation that had been added with no heading or text by Pub. L. 104–208, §2411(c). See note above and 1996 Amendment note below.

Subsec. (f). Pub. L. 108–159, §154(b), added subsec. (f).

Subsec. (g). Pub. L. 108–159, §155, added subsec. (g).

Subsec. (h). Pub. L. 108–159, §311(a), added subsec. (h).

1996—Subsec. (a). Pub. L. 104–208, §2411(a), inserted heading and amended text of subsec. (a) generally. Prior to amendment, text read as follows: "Whenever credit or insurance for personal, family, or household purposes, or employment involving a consumer is denied or the charge for such credit or insurance is increased either wholly or partly because of information contained in a consumer report from a consumer reporting agency, the user of the consumer report shall so advise the consumer against whom such adverse action has been taken and supply the name and address of the consumer reporting agency making the report."

Subsec. (b). Pub. L. 104–208, §2411(e), inserted subsec. heading, designated existing provisions as par. (1) and inserted heading, and added par. (2).

Subsec. (c). Pub. L. 104–208, §2411(d), substituted "this section" for "subsections (a) and (b) of this section".

Subsec. (d). Pub. L. 104–208, §2411(b), added subsec. (d).

Subsec. (e). Pub. L. 104–208, §2411(c), which added subsec. (e) containing subsec. designation, but no heading or text, was repealed by Pub. L. 108–159, §811(h).

STATUTORY NOTES AND RELATED SUBSIDIARIES

EFFECTIVE DATE OF 2010 AMENDMENT

Pub. L. 111–319, §2(b), Dec. 18, 2010, 124 Stat. 3458, provided that: "The amendment made by this section [amending this section] shall become effective on the date of enactment of this Act [Dec. 18, 2010]."

Amendment by Pub. L. 111–203 effective on the designated transfer date, see section 1100H of Pub. L. 111–203, set out as a note under section 552a of Title 5, Government Organization and Employees.

EFFECTIVE DATE OF 2003 AMENDMENT

Amendment by Pub. L. 108–159 subject to joint regulations establishing effective dates as prescribed by Federal Reserve Board and Federal Trade Commission, except as otherwise provided, see section 3 of Pub. L. 108–159, set out as a note under section 1681 of this title.

EFFECTIVE DATE OF 1996 AMENDMENT

Amendment by Pub. L. 104–208 effective 365 days after Sept. 30, 1996, with special rule for early compliance, see section 2420 of Pub. L. 104–208, set out as a note under section 1681a of this title.

EFFECTIVE DATE

Section effective upon the expiration of one hundred and eighty days following Oct. 26, 1970, see section 504(d) of Pub. L. 90–321, as added by Pub. L. 91–508, set out as a note under section 1681 of this title.

REGULATIONS

Pub. L. 108–159, title II, §213(b), Dec. 4, 2003, 117 Stat. 1979, provided that: "Regulations required by section 615(d)(2) of the Fair Credit Reporting Act [15 U.S.C. 1681m(d)(2)], as amended by this section, shall be issued in final form not later than 1 year after the date of enactment of this Act [Dec. 4, 2003]."

§1681n. Civil liability for willful noncompliance

(a) In general

Any person who willfully fails to comply with any requirement imposed under this subchapter with respect to any consumer is liable to that consumer in an amount equal to the sum of—

(1)(A) any actual damages sustained by the consumer as a result of the failure or damages of not less than $100 and not more than $1,000; or

(B) in the case of liability of a natural person for obtaining a consumer report under false pretenses or knowingly without a permissible purpose, actual damages sustained by the consumer as a result of the failure or $1,000, whichever is greater;

(2) such amount of punitive damages as the court may allow; and

(3) in the case of any successful action to enforce any liability under this section, the costs of the action together with reasonable attorney's fees as determined by the court.

(b) Civil liability for knowing noncompliance

Any person who obtains a consumer report from a consumer reporting agency under false pretenses or knowingly without a permissible purpose shall be liable to the consumer reporting agency for actual damages sustained by the consumer reporting agency or $1,000, whichever is greater.

(c) Attorney's fees

Upon a finding by the court that an unsuccessful pleading, motion, or other paper filed in connection with an action under this section was filed in bad faith or for purposes of harassment, the court shall award to the prevailing party attorney's fees reasonable in relation to the work expended in responding to the pleading, motion, or other paper.

(d) Clarification of willful noncompliance

For the purposes of this section, any person who printed an expiration date on any receipt provided to a consumer cardholder at a point of sale or transaction between December 4, 2004, and June 3, 2008, but otherwise complied with the requirements of section 1681c(g) of this title for such receipt shall not be in willful noncompliance with section 1681c(g) of this title by reason of printing such expiration date on the receipt.

(Pub. L. 90–321, title VI, §616, as added Pub. L. 91–508, title VI, §601, Oct. 26, 1970, 84 Stat. 1134; amended Pub. L. 104–208, div. A, title II, §2412(a)–(c), (e)(1), Sept. 30, 1996, 110 Stat. 3009–446; Pub. L. 110–241, §3(a), June 3, 2008, 122 Stat. 1566.)

EDITORIAL NOTES

AMENDMENTS

2008—Subsec. (d). Pub. L. 110–241 added subsec. (d).

1996—Subsec. (a). Pub. L. 104–208, §2412(a), designated existing provisions as subsec. (a), inserted heading, and in introductory provisions substituted "Any person who" for "Any consumer reporting agency or user of information which".

Subsec. (a)(1). Pub. L. 104–208, §2412(b), amended par. (1) generally. Prior to amendment, par. (1) read as follows: "any actual damages sustained by the consumer as a result of the failure;".

Subsec. (b). Pub. L. 104–208, §2412(c), added subsec. (b).

Subsec. (c). Pub. L. 104–208, §2412(e)(1), added subsec. (c).

STATUTORY NOTES AND RELATED SUBSIDIARIES

EFFECTIVE DATE OF 1996 AMENDMENT

Amendment by Pub. L. 104–208 effective 365 days after Sept. 30, 1996, with special rule for early compliance, see section 2420 of Pub. L. 104–208, set out as a note under section 1681a of this title.

EFFECTIVE DATE

Section effective upon the expiration of one hundred and eighty days following Oct. 26, 1970, see section 504(d) of Pub. L. 90–321, as added by Pub. L. 91–508, set out as a note under section 1681 of this title.

CONSTRUCTION

Pub. L. 108–159, title III, §312(f), Dec. 4, 2003, 117 Stat. 1993, provided that: "Nothing in this section, the amendments made by this section, or any other provision of this Act [see Short Title of 2003 Amendment note set out under section 1601 of this title] shall be construed to affect any liability under section 616 or 617 of the Fair Credit Reporting Act (15 U.S.C. 1681n, 1681o) that existed on the day before the date of enactment of this Act [Dec. 4, 2003]."

STATEMENT OF FINDINGS AND PURPOSE FOR 2008 AMENDMENT

Pub. L. 110–241, §2, June 3, 2008, 122 Stat. 1565, provided that:

"(a) FINDINGS.—The Congress finds as follows:

"(1) The Fair and Accurate Credit Transactions Act [of 2003] (commonly referred to as 'FACTA') [Pub. L. 108–159, see Short Title of 2003 Amendment note set out under section 1601 of this title] was enacted into law in 2003 and 1 of the purposes of such Act is to prevent criminals from obtaining access to consumers' private financial and credit information in order to reduce identity theft and credit card fraud.

"(2) As part of that law, the Congress enacted a requirement, through an amendment to the Fair Credit Reporting Act [15 U.S.C. 1681 et seq.], that no person that accepts credit cards or debit cards for the transaction of business shall print more than the last 5 digits of the card number or the expiration date upon any receipt provided to the card holder at the point of the sale or transaction.

"(3) Many merchants understood that this requirement would be satisfied by truncating the account number down to the last 5 digits based in part on the language of the provision as well as the publicity in the aftermath of the passage of the law.

"(4) Almost immediately after the deadline for compliance passed, hundreds of lawsuits were filed alleging that the failure to remove the expiration date was a willful violation of the Fair Credit Reporting Act even where the account number was properly truncated.

"(5) None of these lawsuits contained an allegation of harm to any consumer's identity.

"(6) Experts in the field agree that proper truncation of the card number, by itself as required by the amendment made by the Fair and Accurate Credit Transactions Act [of 2003], regardless of the inclusion of the expiration date, prevents a potential fraudster from perpetrating identity theft or credit card fraud.

"(7) Despite repeatedly being denied class certification, the continued appealing and filing of these lawsuits represents a significant burden on the hundreds of companies that have been sued and could well raise prices to consumers without corresponding consumer protection benefit.

"(b) PURPOSE.—The purpose of this Act [amending this section and enacting provisions set out as notes under this section and section 1601 of this title] is to ensure that consumers suffering from any actual harm to their credit or identity are protected while simultaneously limiting abusive lawsuits that do not protect consumers but only result in increased cost to business and potentially increased prices to consumers."

RETROACTIVE EFFECT OF 2008 AMENDMENT

Pub. L. 110–241, §3(b), June 3, 2008, 122 Stat. 1566, provided that: "The amendment made by subsection (a) [amending this section] shall apply to any action, other than an action which has become final, that is brought for a violation of [section] 605(g) of the Fair Credit Reporting Act [15 U.S.C. 1681c(g)] to which such amendment applies without regard to whether such action is brought before or after the date of the enactment of this Act [June 3, 2008]."

§1681o. Civil liability for negligent noncompliance

(a) In general

Any person who is negligent in failing to comply with any requirement imposed under this subchapter with respect to any consumer is liable to that consumer in an amount equal to the sum of—

(1) any actual damages sustained by the consumer as a result of the failure; and

(2) in the case of any successful action to enforce any liability under this section, the costs of the action together with reasonable attorney's fees as determined by the court.

(b) Attorney's fees

On a finding by the court that an unsuccessful pleading, motion, or other paper filed in connection with an action under this section was filed in bad faith or for purposes of harassment, the court shall award to the prevailing party attorney's fees reasonable in relation to the work expended in responding to the pleading, motion, or other paper.

(Pub. L. 90–321, title VI, §617, as added Pub. L. 91–508, title VI, §601, Oct. 26, 1970, 84 Stat. 1134; amended Pub. L. 104–208, div. A, title II, §2412(d), (e)(2), Sept. 30, 1996, 110 Stat. 3009–446, 3009-447; Pub. L. 108–159, title VIII, §811(e), Dec. 4, 2003, 117 Stat. 2012.)

EDITORIAL NOTES

AMENDMENTS

2003—Subsec. (a)(1). Pub. L. 108–159 inserted "and" after semicolon at end.

1996—Subsec. (a). Pub. L. 104–208, §2412(d), designated existing provisions as subsec. (a), inserted heading, and substituted "Any person who" for "Any consumer reporting agency or user of information which".

Subsec. (b). Pub. L. 104–208, §2412(e)(2), added subsec. (b).

STATUTORY NOTES AND RELATED SUBSIDIARIES

EFFECTIVE DATE OF 2003 AMENDMENT

Amendment by Pub. L. 108–159 subject to joint regulations establishing effective dates as prescribed by Federal Reserve Board and Federal Trade Commission, except as otherwise provided, see section 3 of Pub. L. 108–159, set out as a note under section 1681 of this title.

EFFECTIVE DATE OF 1996 AMENDMENT

Amendment by Pub. L. 104–208 effective 365 days after Sept. 30, 1996, with special rule for early compliance, see section 2420 of Pub. L. 104–208, set out as a note under section 1681a of this title.

EFFECTIVE DATE

Section effective upon the expiration of one hundred and eighty days following Oct. 26, 1970, see section 504(d) of Pub. L. 90–321, as added by Pub. L. 91–508, set out as a note under section 1681 of this title.

§1681p. Jurisdiction of courts; limitation of actions

An action to enforce any liability created under this subchapter may be brought in any appropriate United States district court, without regard to the amount in controversy, or in any other court of competent jurisdiction, not later than the earlier of—

(1) 2 years after the date of discovery by the plaintiff of the violation that is the basis for such liability; or

(2) 5 years after the date on which the violation that is the basis for such liability occurs.

(Pub. L. 90–321, title VI, §618, as added Pub. L. 91–508, title VI, §601, Oct. 26, 1970, 84 Stat. 1134; amended Pub. L. 108–159, title I, §156, Dec. 4, 2003, 117 Stat. 1968.)

EDITORIAL NOTES

AMENDMENTS

2003—Pub. L. 108–159 reenacted section catchline without change and amended text generally. Prior to amendment, text read as follows: "An action to enforce any liability created under this subchapter may be brought in any appropriate United States district court without regard to the amount in controversy, or in any other court of competent jurisdiction, within two years from the date on which the liability arises, except that where a defendant has materially and willfully misrepresented any information required under this subchapter to be disclosed to an individual and the information so misrepresented is material to the establishment of the defendant's liability to that individual under this subchapter, the action may be brought at any time within two years after discovery by the individual of the misrepresentation."

Statutory Notes and Related Subsidiaries

Effective Date of 2003 Amendment

Amendment by Pub. L. 108–159 subject to joint regulations establishing effective dates as prescribed by Federal Reserve Board and Federal Trade Commission, except as otherwise provided, see section 3 of Pub. L. 108–159, set out as a note under section 1681 of this title.

Effective Date

Section effective upon the expiration of one hundred and eighty days following Oct. 26, 1970, see section 504(d) of Pub. L. 90–321, as added by Pub. L. 91–508, set out as a note under section 1681 of this title.

§1681q. Obtaining information under false pretenses

Any person who knowingly and willfully obtains information on a consumer from a consumer reporting agency under false pretenses shall be fined under title 18, imprisoned for not more than 2 years, or both.

(Pub. L. 90–321, title VI, §619, as added Pub. L. 91–508, title VI, §601, Oct. 26, 1970, 84 Stat. 1134; amended Pub. L. 104–208, div. A, title II, §2415(a), Sept. 30, 1996, 110 Stat. 3009–450.)

Editorial Notes

Amendments

1996—Pub. L. 104–208 substituted "fined under title 18, imprisoned for not more than 2 years, or both" for "fined not more than $5,000 or imprisoned not more than one year, or both".

Statutory Notes and Related Subsidiaries

Effective Date of 1996 Amendment

Amendment by Pub. L. 104–208 effective 365 days after Sept. 30, 1996, with special rule for early compliance, see section 2420 of Pub. L. 104–208, set out as a note under section 1681a of this title.

Effective Date

Section effective upon the expiration of one hundred and eighty days following Oct. 26, 1970, see section 504(d) of Pub. L. 90–321, as added by Pub. L. 91–508, set out as a note under section 1681 of this title.

§1681r. Unauthorized disclosures by officers or employees

Any officer or employee of a consumer reporting agency who knowingly and willfully provides information concerning an individual from the agency's files to a person not authorized to receive that information shall be fined under title 18, imprisoned for not more than 2 years, or both.

(Pub. L. 90–321, title VI, §620, as added Pub. L. 91–508, title VI, §601, Oct. 26, 1970, 84 Stat. 1134; amended Pub. L. 104–208, div. A, title II, §2415(b), Sept. 30, 1996, 110 Stat. 3009–450.)

Editorial Notes

Amendments

1996—Pub. L. 104–208 substituted "fined under title 18, imprisoned for not more than 2 years, or both" for "fined not more than $5,000 or imprisoned not more than one year, or both".

EFFECTIVE DATE OF 1996 AMENDMENT

Amendment by Pub. L. 104–208 effective 365 days after Sept. 30, 1996, with special rule for early compliance, see section 2420 of Pub. L. 104–208, set out as a note under section 1681a of this title.

EFFECTIVE DATE

Section effective upon the expiration of one hundred and eighty days following Oct. 26, 1970, see section 504(d) of Pub. L. 90–321, as added by Pub. L. 91–508, set out as a note under section 1681 of this title.

§1681s. Administrative enforcement

(a) Enforcement by Federal Trade Commission

(1) In general

The Federal Trade Commission shall be authorized to enforce compliance with the requirements imposed by this subchapter under the Federal Trade Commission Act (15 U.S.C. 41 et seq.), with respect to consumer reporting agencies and all other persons subject thereto, except to the extent that enforcement of the requirements imposed under this subchapter is specifically committed to some other Government agency under any of subparagraphs (A) through (G) of subsection (b)(1), and subject to subtitle B of the Consumer Financial Protection Act of 2010 [12 U.S.C. 5511 et seq.], subsection (b).[1] For the purpose of the exercise by the Federal Trade Commission of its functions and powers under the Federal Trade Commission Act, a violation of any requirement or prohibition imposed under this subchapter shall constitute an unfair or deceptive act or practice in commerce, in violation of section 5(a) of the Federal Trade Commission Act (15 U.S.C. 45(a)), and shall be subject to enforcement by the Federal Trade Commission under section 5(b) of that Act [15 U.S.C. 45(b)] with respect to any consumer reporting agency or person that is subject to enforcement by the Federal Trade Commission pursuant to this subsection, irrespective of whether that person is engaged in commerce or meets any other jurisdictional tests under the Federal Trade Commission Act. The Federal Trade Commission shall have such procedural, investigative, and enforcement powers, including the power to issue procedural rules in enforcing compliance with the requirements imposed under this subchapter and to require the filing of reports, the production of documents, and the appearance of witnesses, as though the applicable terms and conditions of the Federal Trade Commission Act were part of this subchapter. Any person violating any of the provisions of this subchapter shall be subject to the penalties and entitled to the privileges and immunities provided in the Federal Trade Commission Act as though the applicable terms and provisions of such Act are part of this subchapter.

(2) Penalties

(A) Knowing violations

Except as otherwise provided by subtitle B of the Consumer Financial Protection Act of 2010, in the event of a knowing violation, which constitutes a pattern or practice of violations of this subchapter, the Federal Trade Commission may commence a civil action to recover a civil penalty in a district court of the United States against any person that violates this subchapter. In such action, such person shall be liable for a civil penalty of not more than $2,500 per violation.

(B) Determining penalty amount

In determining the amount of a civil penalty under subparagraph (A), the court shall take into account the degree of culpability, any history of such prior conduct, ability to pay, effect on ability to continue to do business, and such other matters as justice may require.

(C) Limitation

Notwithstanding paragraph (2), a court may not impose any civil penalty on a person for a violation of section 1681s–2(a)(1) of this title, unless the person has been enjoined from committing the violation, or ordered not to commit the violation, in an action or proceeding brought by or on behalf of the Federal Trade Commission, and has violated the injunction or order, and the court may not impose any civil penalty for any violation occurring before the date of the violation of the injunction or order.

(b) Enforcement by other agencies

(1) In general

Subject to subtitle B of the Consumer Financial Protection Act of 2010, compliance with the requirements imposed under this subchapter with respect to consumer reporting agencies, persons who use consumer reports from such agencies, persons who furnish information to such agencies, and users of information that are subject to section 1681m(d) of this title shall be enforced under—

(A) section 8 of the Federal Deposit Insurance Act (12 U.S.C. 1818), by the appropriate Federal banking agency, as defined in section 3(q) of the Federal Deposit Insurance Act (12 U.S.C. 1813(q)), with respect to—

(i) any national bank or State savings association, and any Federal branch or Federal agency of a foreign bank;

(ii) any member bank of the Federal Reserve System (other than a national bank), a branch or agency of a foreign bank (other than a Federal branch, Federal agency, or insured State branch of a foreign bank), a commercial lending company owned or controlled by a foreign bank, and any organization operating under section 25 or 25A of the Federal Reserve Act [12 U.S.C. 601 et seq., 611 et seq.]; and

(iii) any bank or Federal savings association insured by the Federal Deposit Insurance Corporation (other than a member of the Federal Reserve System) and any insured State branch of a foreign bank;

(B) the Federal Credit Union Act (12 U.S.C. 1751 et seq.), by the Administrator of the National Credit Union Administration with respect to any Federal credit union;

(C) subtitle IV of title 49, by the Secretary of Transportation, with respect to all carriers subject to the jurisdiction of the Surface Transportation Board;

(D) part A of subtitle VII of title 49, by the Secretary of Transportation, with respect to any air carrier or foreign air carrier subject to that part;

(E) the Packers and Stockyards Act, 1921 (7 U.S.C. 181 et seq.) (except as provided in section 406 of that Act [7 U.S.C. 226, 227]), by the Secretary of Agriculture, with respect to any activities subject to that Act;

(F) the Commodity Exchange Act [7 U.S.C. 1 et seq.], with respect to a person subject to the jurisdiction of the Commodity Futures Trading Commission;

(G) the Federal securities laws, and any other laws that are subject to the jurisdiction of the Securities and Exchange Commission, with respect to a person that is subject to the jurisdiction of the Securities and Exchange Commission; and

(H) subtitle E of the Consumer Financial Protection Act of 2010 [12 U.S.C. 5561 et seq.], by the Bureau, with respect to any person subject to this subchapter.

(2) Incorporated definitions

The terms used in paragraph (1) that are not defined in this subchapter or otherwise defined in section 3(s) of the Federal Deposit Insurance Act (12 U.S.C. 1813(s)) have the same meanings as in section 1(b) of the International Banking Act of 1978 (12 U.S.C. 3101).

(c) State action for violations

(1) Authority of States

In addition to such other remedies as are provided under State law, if the chief law enforcement officer of a State, or an official or agency designated by a State, has reason to believe that any person has violated or is violating this subchapter, the State—

(A) may bring an action to enjoin such violation in any appropriate United States district court or in any other court of competent jurisdiction;

(B) subject to paragraph (5), may bring an action on behalf of the residents of the State to recover—

(i) damages for which the person is liable to such residents under sections 1681n and 1681o of this title as a result of the violation;

(ii) in the case of a violation described in any of paragraphs (1) through (3) of section 1681s–2(c) of this title, damages for which the person would, but for section 1681s–2(c) of this title, be liable to such residents as a result of the violation; or

(iii) damages of not more than $1,000 for each willful or negligent violation; and

(C) in the case of any successful action under subparagraph (A) or (B), shall be awarded the costs of the action and reasonable attorney fees as determined by the court.

(2) Rights of Federal regulators

The State shall serve prior written notice of any action under paragraph (1) upon the Bureau and the Federal Trade Commission or the appropriate Federal regulator determined under subsection (b) and provide the Bureau and the Federal Trade Commission or appropriate Federal regulator with a copy of its complaint, except in any case in which such prior notice is not feasible, in which case the State shall serve such notice immediately upon instituting such action. The Bureau and the Federal Trade Commission or appropriate Federal regulator shall have the right—

(A) to intervene in the action;

(B) upon so intervening, to be heard on all matters arising therein;

(C) to remove the action to the appropriate United States district court; and

(D) to file petitions for appeal.

(3) Investigatory powers

For purposes of bringing any action under this subsection, nothing in this subsection shall prevent the chief law enforcement officer, or an official or agency designated by a State, from exercising the powers conferred on the chief law enforcement officer or such official by the laws of such State to conduct investigations or to administer oaths or affirmations or to compel the attendance of witnesses or the production of documentary and other evidence.

(4) Limitation on State action while Federal action pending

If the Bureau, the Federal Trade Commission, or the appropriate Federal regulator has instituted a civil action or an administrative action under section 8 of the Federal Deposit Insurance Act [12 U.S.C. 1818] for a violation of this subchapter, no State may, during the pendency of such action, bring an action under this section against any defendant named in the complaint of the Bureau, the Federal Trade Commission, or the appropriate Federal regulator for any violation of this subchapter that is alleged in that complaint.

(5) Limitations on State actions for certain violations

(A) Violation of injunction required

A State may not bring an action against a person under paragraph (1)(B) for a violation described in any of paragraphs (1) through (3) of section 1681s–2(c) of this title, unless—

(i) the person has been enjoined from committing the violation, in an action brought by the State under paragraph (1)(A); and

(ii) the person has violated the injunction.

(B) Limitation on damages recoverable

In an action against a person under paragraph (1)(B) for a violation described in any of paragraphs (1) through (3) of section 1681s–2(c) of this title, a State may not recover any damages incurred before the date of the violation of an injunction on which the action is based.

(d) Enforcement under other authority

For the purpose of the exercise by any agency referred to in subsection (b) of its powers under any Act referred to in that subsection, a violation of any requirement imposed under this subchapter shall be deemed to be a violation of a requirement imposed under that Act. In addition to its powers under any provision of law specifically referred to in subsection (b), each of the agencies referred to in that subsection may exercise, for the purpose of enforcing compliance with any requirement imposed under this subchapter any other authority conferred on it by law.

(e) Regulatory authority

(1) In general

The Bureau shall prescribe such regulations as are necessary to carry out the purposes of this subchapter, except with respect to sections 1681m(e) and 1681w of this title. The Bureau may prescribe regulations as may be necessary or appropriate to administer and carry out the purposes and objectives of this subchapter, and to prevent evasions thereof or to facilitate compliance therewith. Except as provided in section 1029(a) of the Consumer Financial Protection Act of 2010 [12 U.S.C. 5519(a)], the regulations prescribed by the Bureau under this subchapter shall apply to any person that is subject to this subchapter, notwithstanding the enforcement authorities granted to other agencies under this section.

(2) Deference

Notwithstanding any power granted to any Federal agency under this subchapter, the deference that a court affords to a Federal agency with respect to a determination made by such agency relating to the meaning or interpretation of any provision of this subchapter that is subject to the jurisdiction of such agency shall be applied as if that agency were the only agency authorized to apply, enforce, interpret, or administer the provisions of this subchapter [2] The regulations prescribed by the Bureau under this subchapter shall apply to any person that is subject to this subchapter, notwithstanding the enforcement authorities granted to other agencies under this section.

(f) Coordination of consumer complaint investigations

(1) In general

Each consumer reporting agency described in section 1681a(p) of this title shall develop and maintain procedures for the referral to each other such agency of any consumer complaint received by the agency alleging identity theft, or requesting a fraud alert under section 1681c–1 of this title or a block under section 1681c–2 of this title.

(2) Model form and procedure for reporting identity theft

The Commission,[3] in consultation with the Federal Trade Commission, the Federal banking agencies, and the National Credit Union Administration, shall develop a model form and model procedures to be used by consumers who are victims of identity theft for contacting and informing creditors and consumer reporting agencies of the fraud.

(3) Annual summary reports

Each consumer reporting agency described in section 1681a(p) of this title shall submit an annual summary report to the Bureau on consumer complaints received by the agency on identity theft or fraud alerts.

(g) Bureau regulation of coding of trade names

If the Bureau determines that a person described in paragraph (9) of section 1681s–2(a) of this title has not met the requirements of such paragraph, the Bureau shall take action to ensure the person's compliance with such paragraph, which may include issuing model guidance or prescribing reasonable policies and procedures, as necessary to ensure that such person complies with such paragraph.

(Pub. L. 90–321, title VI, §621, as added Pub. L. 91–508, title VI, §601, Oct. 26, 1970, 84 Stat. 1134; amended Pub. L. 98–443, §9(n), Oct. 4, 1984, 98 Stat. 1708; Pub. L. 101–73, title VII, §744(l), Aug. 9, 1989, 103 Stat. 439; Pub. L. 102–242, title II, §212(c), Dec. 19, 1991, 105 Stat. 2300; Pub. L. 102–550, title XVI, §1604(a)(6), Oct. 28, 1992, 106 Stat. 4082; Pub. L. 104–88, title III, §314, Dec. 29, 1995, 109 Stat. 948; Pub. L. 104–208, div. A, title II, §§2416–2418, Sept. 30, 1996, 110 Stat. 3009–450 to 3009-452; Pub. L. 105–347, §6(6), Nov. 2, 1998, 112 Stat. 3211; Pub. L. 106–102, title V, §506(a), (b), Nov. 12, 1999, 113 Stat. 1441, 1442; Pub. L. 108–159, title I, §153, title III, §312(e)(2), title IV, §412(e), title VIII, §811(f), Dec. 4, 2003, 117 Stat. 1966, 1993, 2003, 2012; Pub. L. 111–203, title X, §1088(a)(2)(A)–(C), (10), July 21, 2010, 124 Stat. 2087, 2088.)

EDITORIAL NOTES

REFERENCES IN TEXT

The Federal Trade Commission Act, referred to in subsec. (a)(1), is act Sept. 26, 1914, ch. 311, 38 Stat. 717, which is classified generally to subchapter I (§41 et seq.) of chapter 2 of this title. For complete classification of this Act to the Code, see section 58 of this title and Tables.

The Consumer Financial Protection Act of 2010, referred to in subsecs. (a) and (b)(1), is title X of Pub. L. 111–203, July 21, 2010, 124 Stat. 1955. Subtitles B (§§1021–1029A) and E (§§1051–1058) of the Act are classified generally to parts B (§5511 et seq.) and E (§5561 et seq.), respectively, of subchapter V of chapter 53 of Title 12, Banks and Banking. For complete classification of subtitles B and E to the Code, see Tables.

Sections 25 and 25A of the Federal Reserve Act, referred to in subsec. (b)(1)(A)(ii), are classified to subchapters I (§601 et seq.) and II (§611 et seq.), respectively, of chapter 6 of Title 12, Banks and Banking.

The Federal Credit Union Act, referred to in subsec. (b)(1)(B), is act June 26, 1934, ch. 750, 48 Stat. 1216, which is classified generally to chapter 14 (§1751 et seq.) of Title 12. For complete classification of this Act to the Code, see section 1751 of Title 12 and Tables.

The Packers and Stockyards Act, 1921, referred to in subsec. (b)(1)(E), is act Aug. 15, 1921, ch. 64, 42 Stat. 159, which is classified to chapter 9 (§181 et seq.) of Title 7, Agriculture. For complete classification of this Act to the Code, see section 181 of Title 7 and Tables.

The Commodity Exchange Act, referred to in subsec. (b)(1)(F), is act Sept. 21, 1922, ch. 369, 42 Stat. 998, which is classified generally to chapter 1 (§1 et seq.) of Title 7, Agriculture. For complete classification of this Act to the Code, see section 1 of Title 7 and Tables.

CODIFICATION

In subsec. (b)(1)(D), "part A of subtitle VII of title 49" substituted for "the Federal Aviation Act of 1958 (49 App. U.S.C. 1301 et seq.)" and "that part" substituted for "that Act" on authority of Pub. L. 103–272, §6(b), July 5, 1994, 108 Stat. 1378, the first section of which enacted subtitles II, III, and V to X of Title 49.

AMENDMENTS

2010—Subsec. (a). Pub. L. 111–203, §1088(a)(10)(A), added subsec. (a) and struck out former subsec. (a) which related to enforcement by Federal Trade Commission.

Subsec. (b). Pub. L. 111–203, §1088(a)(10)(B), added subsec. (b) and struck out former subsec. (b) which related to enforcement under section 8 of the Federal Deposit Insurance Act, the Federal Credit Union Act, subtitle IV of title 49, part A of subtitle VII of title 49, and the Packers and Stockyards Act, 1921.

Subsec. (c)(2). Pub. L. 111–203, §1088(a)(10)(C), in introductory provisions, inserted "and the Federal Trade Commission" before "or the appropriate" and before "or appropriate" in two places.

Pub. L. 111–203, §1088(a)(2)(C), in introductory provisions, substituted "provide the Bureau" for "provide the Commission".

Pub. L. 111–203, §1088(a)(2)(A), in introductory provisions, substituted "upon the Bureau" for "upon the Federal Trade Commission" and "The Bureau" for "The Federal Trade Commission".

Subsec. (c)(4). Pub. L. 111–203, §1088(a)(10)(D), inserted ", the Federal Trade Commission," before "or the appropriate" in two places.

Pub. L. 111–203, §1088(a)(2)(C), substituted "complaint of the Bureau" for "complaint of the Commission".

Pub. L. 111–203, §1088(a)(2)(A), substituted "If the Bureau" for "If the Federal Trade Commission".

Subsec. (e). Pub. L. 111–203, §1088(a)(10)(E), added subsec. (e) and struck out former subsec. (e) which related to prescription of regulations by certain Federal banking agencies, the Board of Governors of the Federal Reserve System, and the Board of the National Credit Union Administration.

Subsec. (f)(2). Pub. L. 111–203, §1088(a)(10)(F), substituted "the Federal Trade Commission, the Federal banking agencies," for "the Federal banking agencies".

Subsec. (f)(3). Pub. L. 111–203, §1088(a)(2)(C), substituted "the Bureau" for "the Commission".

Subsec. (g). Pub. L. 111–203, §1088(a)(2)(C), substituted "the Bureau" for "the Commission" in two places.

Pub. L. 111–203, §1088(a)(2)(B), substituted "Bureau" for "FTC" in heading.

2003—Subsec. (b)(1)(B). Pub. L. 108–159, §811(f), substituted "25A" for "25(a)".

Subsec. (c)(1)(B)(ii). Pub. L. 108–159, §312(e)(2)(A), substituted "described in any of paragraphs (1) through (3) of section 1681s–2(c)" for "of section 1681s–2(a)".

Subsec. (c)(5). Pub. L. 108–159, §312(e)(2)(B)(ii), substituted "certain violations" for "violation of section 1681s–2(a)(1)" in heading.

Subsec. (c)(5)(A), (B). Pub. L. 108–159, §312(e)(2)(B)(i), substituted "described in any of paragraphs (1) through (3) of section 1681s–2(c)" for "of section 1681s–2(a)(1)".

Subsec. (f). Pub. L. 108–159, §153, added subsec. (f).

Subsec. (g). Pub. L. 108–159, §412(e), added subsec. (g).

1999—Subsec. (a)(4). Pub. L. 106–102, §506(b), struck out par. (4) which read as follows: "Neither the Commission nor any other agency referred to in subsection (b) of this section may prescribe trade regulation rules or other regulations with respect to this subchapter."

Subsec. (d). Pub. L. 106–102, §506(a)(1), struck out at the end "Notwithstanding the preceding, no agency referred to in subsection (b) of this section may conduct an examination of a bank, savings association, or credit union regarding compliance with the provisions of this subchapter, except in response to a complaint (or if the agency otherwise has knowledge) that the bank, savings association, or credit union has violated a provision of this subchapter, in which case, the agency may conduct an examination as necessary to investigate the complaint. If an agency determines during an investigation in response to a complaint that a violation of this subchapter has occurred, the agency may, during its next 2 regularly scheduled examinations of the bank, savings association, or credit union, examine for compliance with this subchapter."

Subsec. (e). Pub. L. 106–102, §506(a)(2), added subsec. (e) and struck out heading and text of former subsec. (e). Text read as follows: "The Board of Governors of the Federal Reserve System may issue interpretations of any provision of this subchapter as such provision may apply to any persons identified under paragraph (1), (2), and (3) of subsection (b) of this section, or to the holding companies and affiliates of such persons, in consultation with Federal agencies identified in paragraphs (1), (2), and (3) of subsection (b) of this section."

1998—Subsec. (b). Pub. L. 105–347 struck out "or (e)" after "subject to subsection (d)" in introductory provisions.

1996—Subsec. (a). Pub. L. 104–208, §2416(b)(1), which directed the amendment of subsec. (a) by inserting heading "Enforcement by Federal Trade Commission" before "Compliance with the requirements", was executed by making the insertion after "(a)", to reflect the probable intent of Congress and the amendment by Pub. L. 104–208, §2416(a). See below.

Pub. L. 104–208, §2416(a), inserted "(1)" after "(a)" and added pars. (2) to (4).

Subsec. (b). Pub. L. 104–208, §2416(b)(2), inserted heading and in introductory provisions substituted "Compliance with the requirements imposed under this subchapter with respect to consumer reporting agencies, persons who use consumer reports from such agencies, persons who furnish information to such agencies, and users of information that are subject to subsection (d) or (e) of section 1681m of this title shall be enforced under—" for "Compliance with the requirements imposed under this subchapter with respect to consumer reporting agencies and persons who use consumer reports from such agencies shall be enforced under—".

Subsec. (c). Pub. L. 104–208, §2417(2), added subsec. (c). Former subsec. (c) redesignated (d).

Pub. L. 104–208, §2416(c), inserted at end "Notwithstanding the preceding, no agency referred to in subsection (b) of this section may conduct an examination of a bank, savings association, or credit union regarding compliance with the provisions of this subchapter, except in response to a complaint (or if the agency otherwise has knowledge) that the bank, savings association, or credit union has violated a provision of this subchapter, in which case, the agency may conduct an examination as necessary to investigate the complaint. If an agency determines during an investigation in response to a complaint that a violation of this subchapter has occurred, the agency may, during its next 2 regularly scheduled examinations of the bank, savings association, or credit union, examine for compliance with this subchapter."

Subsec. (d). Pub. L. 104–208, §2417(1), redesignated subsec. (c) as (d).

Subsec. (e). Pub. L. 104–208, §2418, added subsec. (e).

1995—Subsec. (b)(4). Pub. L. 104–88 substituted "Secretary of Transportation, with respect to all carriers subject to the jurisdiction of the Surface Transportation Board" for "Interstate Commerce Commission with respect to any common carrier subject to those Acts".

1992—Subsec. (b)(1)(C). Pub. L. 102–550 substituted semicolon for period at end.

1991—Subsec. (b). Pub. L. 102–242, §212(c)(2), inserted at end "The terms used in paragraph (1) that are not defined in this subchapter or otherwise defined in section 3(s) of the Federal Deposit Insurance Act (12 U.S.C. 1813(s)) shall have the meaning given to them in section 1(b) of the International Banking Act of 1978 (12 U.S.C. 3101)."

Pub. L. 102–242, §212(c)(1), added par. (1) and struck out former par. (1) which read as follows: "section 8 of the Federal Deposit Insurance Act, in the case of:

"(A) national banks, by the Comptroller of the Currency;

"(B) member banks of the Federal Reserve System (other than national banks), by the Federal Reserve Board; and

"(C) banks insured by the Federal Deposit Insurance Corporation (other than members of the Federal Reserve System), by the Board of Directors of the Federal Deposit Insurance Corporation."

1989—Subsec. (b)(2). Pub. L. 101–73 amended par. (2) generally. Prior to amendment, par. (2) read as follows: "section 5(d) of the Home Owners Loan Act of 1933, section 407 of the National Housing Act, and sections 6(i) and 17 of the Federal Home Loan Bank Act, by the Federal Home Loan Bank Board (acting directly or through the Federal Savings and Loan Insurance Corporation), in the case of any institution subject to any of those provisions;".

1984—Subsec. (b)(5). Pub. L. 98–443 substituted "Secretary of Transportation" for "Civil Aeronautics Board".

EFFECTIVE DATE OF 2010 AMENDMENT

Amendment by Pub. L. 111–203 effective on the designated transfer date, see section 1100H of Pub. L. 111–203, set out as a note under section 552a of Title 5, Government Organization and Employees.

EFFECTIVE DATE OF 2003 AMENDMENT

Amendment by Pub. L. 108–159 subject to joint regulations establishing effective dates as prescribed by Federal Reserve Board and Federal Trade Commission, except as otherwise provided, see section 3 of Pub. L. 108–159, set out as a note under section 1681 of this title.

Amendment by section 412(e) of Pub. L. 108–159 effective at end of 15-month period beginning on Dec. 4, 2003, see section 412(g) of Pub. L. 108–159, set out as a note under section 1681b of this title.

EFFECTIVE DATE OF 1998 AMENDMENT

Amendment by Pub. L. 105–347 deemed to have same effective date as amendments made by section 2403 of Pub. L. 104–208, see section 7 of Pub. L. 105–347, set out as a note under section 1681a of this title.

EFFECTIVE DATE OF 1996 AMENDMENT

Amendment by Pub. L. 104–208 effective 365 days after Sept. 30, 1996, with special rule for early compliance, see section 2420 of Pub. L. 104–208, set out as a note under section 1681a of this title.

EFFECTIVE DATE OF 1995 AMENDMENT

Amendment by Pub. L. 104–88 effective Jan. 1, 1996, see section 2 of Pub. L. 104–88, set out as an Effective Date note under section 1301 of Title 49, Transportation.

EFFECTIVE DATE OF 1992 AMENDMENT

Amendment by Pub. L. 102–550 effective as if included in the Federal Deposit Insurance Corporation Improvement Act of 1991, Pub. L. 102–242, as of Dec. 19, 1991, see section 1609(a) of Pub. L. 102–550, set out as a note under section 191 of Title 12, Banks and Banking.

EFFECTIVE DATE OF 1984 AMENDMENT

Amendment by Pub. L. 98–443 effective Jan. 1, 1985, see section 9(v) of Pub. L. 98–443, set out as a note under section 5314 of Title 5, Government Organization and Employees.

EFFECTIVE DATE

Section effective upon the expiration of one hundred and eighty days following Oct. 26, 1970, see section 504(d) of Pub. L. 90–321, as added by Pub. L. 91–508, set out as a note under section 1681 of this title.

Functions vested in Administrator of National Credit Union Administration transferred and vested in National Credit Union Administration Board pursuant to section 1752a of Title 12, Banks and Banking.

---

[1] *So in original.*

[2] *So in original. Probably should be followed by a period.*

[3] *So in original. Probably should be "Bureau,".*

§1681s–1. Information on overdue child support obligations

Notwithstanding any other provision of this subchapter, a consumer reporting agency shall include in any consumer report furnished by the agency in accordance with section 1681b of this title, any information on the failure of the consumer to pay overdue support which—

(1) is provided—
    (A) to the consumer reporting agency by a State or local child support enforcement agency; or
    (B) to the consumer reporting agency and verified by any local, State, or Federal Government agency; and

(2) antedates the report by 7 years or less.

(Pub. L. 90–321, title VI, §622, as added Pub. L. 102–537, §2(a), Oct. 27, 1992, 106 Stat. 3531.)

EDITORIAL NOTES

PRIOR PROVISIONS

A prior section 622 of Pub. L. 90–321 was renumbered section 625 and is classified to section 1681t of this title.

STATUTORY NOTES AND RELATED SUBSIDIARIES

EFFECTIVE DATE

Section effective Jan. 1, 1993, see section 2(d) of Pub. L. 102–537, set out as an Effective Date of 1992 Amendment note under section 1681a of this title.

§1681s–2. Responsibilities of furnishers of information to consumer reporting agencies

(a) Duty of furnishers of information to provide accurate information

(1) Prohibition

(A) Reporting information with actual knowledge of errors

A person shall not furnish any information relating to a consumer to any consumer reporting agency if the person knows or has reasonable cause to believe that the information is inaccurate.

(B) Reporting information after notice and confirmation of errors

A person shall not furnish information relating to a consumer to any consumer reporting agency if—
    (i) the person has been notified by the consumer, at the address specified by the person for such notices, that specific information is inaccurate; and
    (ii) the information is, in fact, inaccurate.

(C) No address requirement

A person who clearly and conspicuously specifies to the consumer an address for notices referred to in subparagraph (B) shall not be subject to subparagraph (A); however, nothing in subparagraph (B) shall require a person to specify such an address.

(D) Definition

For purposes of subparagraph (A), the term "reasonable cause to believe that the information is inaccurate" means having specific knowledge, other than solely allegations by the consumer, that would cause a reasonable person to have substantial doubts about the accuracy of the information.

(E) Rehabilitation of private education loans

(i) In general

Notwithstanding any other provision of this section, a consumer may request a financial institution to remove from a consumer report a reported default regarding a private education loan, and such information shall not be considered inaccurate, if—

(I) the financial institution chooses to offer a loan rehabilitation program which includes, without limitation, a requirement of the consumer to make consecutive on-time monthly payments in a number that demonstrates, in the assessment of the financial institution offering the loan rehabilitation program, a renewed ability and willingness to repay the loan; and

(II) the requirements of the loan rehabilitation program described in subclause (I) are successfully met.

(ii) Banking agencies

(I) In general

If a financial institution is supervised by a Federal banking agency, the financial institution shall seek written approval concerning the terms and conditions of the loan rehabilitation program described in clause (i) from the appropriate Federal banking agency.

(II) Feedback

An appropriate Federal banking agency shall provide feedback to a financial institution within 120 days of a request for approval under subclause (I).

(iii) Limitation

(I) In general

A consumer may obtain the benefits available under this subsection with respect to rehabilitating a loan only 1 time per loan.

(II) Rule of construction

Nothing in this subparagraph may be construed to require a financial institution to offer a loan rehabilitation program or to remove any reported default from a consumer report as a consideration of a loan rehabilitation program, except as described in clause (i).

(iv) Definitions

For purposes of this subparagraph—

(I) the term "appropriate Federal banking agency" has the meaning given the term in section 1813 of title 12; and

(II) the term "private education loan" has the meaning given the term in section 1650(a) of this title.

(F) Reporting information during COVID–19 pandemic

(i) Definitions

In this subsection:

(I) Accommodation

The term "accommodation" includes an agreement to defer 1 or more payments, make a partial payment, forbear any delinquent amounts, modify a loan or contract, or any other assistance or relief granted to a consumer who is affected by the coronavirus disease 2019 (COVID–19) pandemic during the covered period.

(II) Covered period

The term "covered period" means the period beginning on January 31, 2020 and ending on the later of—

(aa) 120 days after March 27, 2020; or

(bb) 120 days after the date on which the national emergency concerning the novel coronavirus disease (COVID–19) outbreak declared by the President on March 13, 2020 under the National Emergencies Act (50 U.S.C. 1601 et seq.) terminates.

(ii) Reporting

Except as provided in clause (iii), if a furnisher makes an accommodation with respect to 1 or more payments on a credit obligation or account of a consumer, and the consumer makes the payments or is not required to make 1 or more payments pursuant to the accommodation, the furnisher shall—

(I) report the credit obligation or account as current; or

(II) if the credit obligation or account was delinquent before the accommodation—

(aa) maintain the delinquent status during the period in which the accommodation is in effect; and

(bb) if the consumer brings the credit obligation or account current during the period described in item (aa), report the credit obligation or account as current.

(iii) Exception

Clause (ii) shall not apply with respect to a credit obligation or account of a consumer that has been charged-off.

(2) Duty to correct and update information

A person who—

(A) regularly and in the ordinary course of business furnishes information to one or more consumer reporting agencies about the person's transactions or experiences with any consumer; and

(B) has furnished to a consumer reporting agency information that the person determines is not complete or accurate,

shall promptly notify the consumer reporting agency of that determination and provide to the agency any corrections to that information, or any additional information, that is necessary to make the information provided by the person to the agency complete and accurate, and shall not thereafter furnish to the agency any of the information that remains not complete or accurate.

(3) Duty to provide notice of dispute

If the completeness or accuracy of any information furnished by any person to any consumer reporting agency is disputed to such person by a consumer, the person may not furnish the information to any consumer reporting agency without notice that such information is disputed by the consumer.

(4) Duty to provide notice of closed accounts

A person who regularly and in the ordinary course of business furnishes information to a consumer reporting agency regarding a consumer who has a credit account with that person shall notify the agency of the voluntary closure of the account by the consumer, in information regularly furnished for the period in which the account is closed.

(5) Duty to provide notice of delinquency of accounts

(A) In general

A person who furnishes information to a consumer reporting agency regarding a delinquent account being placed for collection, charged to profit or loss, or subjected to any similar action shall, not later than 90 days after furnishing the information, notify the agency of the date of delinquency on the account, which shall be the month and year of the commencement of the delinquency on the account that immediately preceded the action.

(B) Rule of construction

For purposes of this paragraph only, and provided that the consumer does not dispute the information, a person that furnishes information on a delinquent account that is placed for collection, charged for profit or loss, or subjected to any similar action, complies with this paragraph, if—

(i) the person reports the same date of delinquency as that provided by the creditor to which the account was owed at the time at which the commencement of the delinquency occurred, if the creditor previously reported that date of delinquency to a consumer reporting agency;

(ii) the creditor did not previously report the date of delinquency to a consumer reporting agency, and the person establishes and follows reasonable procedures to obtain the date of delinquency from the creditor or another reliable source and reports that date to a consumer reporting agency as the date of delinquency; or

(iii) the creditor did not previously report the date of delinquency to a consumer reporting agency and the date of delinquency cannot be reasonably obtained as provided in clause (ii), the person establishes and follows reasonable procedures to ensure the date reported as the date of delinquency precedes the date on which the account is placed for collection, charged to profit or loss, or subjected to any similar action, and reports such date to the credit reporting agency.

(6) Duties of furnishers upon notice of identity theft-related information

(A) Reasonable procedures

A person that furnishes information to any consumer reporting agency shall have in place reasonable procedures to respond to any notification that it receives from a consumer reporting agency under section 1681c–2 of this title relating to information resulting from identity theft, to prevent that person from refurnishing such blocked information.

(B) Information alleged to result from identity theft

If a consumer submits an identity theft report to a person who furnishes information to a consumer reporting agency at the address specified by that person for receiving such reports stating that information maintained by such person that purports to relate to the consumer resulted from identity theft, the person may not furnish such information that purports to relate to the consumer to any consumer reporting agency, unless the person subsequently knows or is informed by the consumer that the information is correct.

(7) Negative information

(A) Notice to consumer required

(i) In general

If any financial institution that extends credit and regularly and in the ordinary course of business furnishes information to a consumer reporting agency described in section 1681a(p) of this title furnishes negative information to such an agency regarding credit extended to a customer, the financial institution shall provide a notice of such furnishing of negative information, in writing, to the customer.

(ii) Notice effective for subsequent submissions

After providing such notice, the financial institution may submit additional negative information to a consumer reporting agency described in section 1681a(p) of this title with respect to the same transaction, extension of credit, account, or customer without providing additional notice to the customer.

(B) Time of notice

(i) In general

The notice required under subparagraph (A) shall be provided to the customer prior to, or no later than 30 days after, furnishing the negative information to a consumer reporting agency described in section 1681a(p) of this title.

(ii) Coordination with new account disclosures

If the notice is provided to the customer prior to furnishing the negative information to a consumer reporting agency, the notice may not be included in the initial disclosures provided under section 1637(a) of this title.

(C) Coordination with other disclosures

The notice required under subparagraph (A)—
(i) may be included on or with any notice of default, any billing statement, or any other materials provided to the customer; and
(ii) must be clear and conspicuous.

(D) Model disclosure

(i) Duty of Bureau

The Bureau shall prescribe a brief model disclosure that a financial institution may use to comply with subparagraph (A), which shall not exceed 30 words.

(ii) Use of model not required

No provision of this paragraph may be construed to require a financial institution to use any such model form prescribed by the Bureau.

(iii) Compliance using model

A financial institution shall be deemed to be in compliance with subparagraph (A) if the financial institution uses any model form prescribed by the Bureau under this subparagraph, or the financial institution uses any such model form and rearranges its format.

(E) Use of notice without submitting negative information

No provision of this paragraph shall be construed as requiring a financial institution that has provided a customer with a notice described in subparagraph (A) to furnish negative information about the customer to a consumer reporting agency.

(F) Safe harbor

A financial institution shall not be liable for failure to perform the duties required by this paragraph if, at the time of the failure, the financial institution maintained reasonable policies and procedures to comply with this paragraph or the financial institution reasonably believed that the institution is prohibited, by law, from contacting the consumer.

(G) Definitions

For purposes of this paragraph, the following definitions shall apply:

(i) Negative information

The term "negative information" means information concerning a customer's delinquencies, late payments, insolvency, or any form of default.

(ii) Customer; financial institution

The terms "customer" and "financial institution" have the same meanings as in section 6809 of this title.

(8) Ability of consumer to dispute information directly with furnisher

(A) In general

The Bureau, in consultation with the Federal Trade Commission, the Federal banking agencies, and the National Credit Union Administration, shall prescribe regulations that shall identify the circumstances under which a furnisher shall be required to reinvestigate a dispute concerning the accuracy of information contained in a consumer report on the consumer, based on a direct request of a consumer.

(B) Considerations

In prescribing regulations under subparagraph (A), the agencies shall weigh—

(i) the benefits to consumers with the costs on furnishers and the credit reporting system;

(ii) the impact on the overall accuracy and integrity of consumer reports of any such requirements;

(iii) whether direct contact by the consumer with the furnisher would likely result in the most expeditious resolution of any such dispute; and

(iv) the potential impact on the credit reporting process if credit repair organizations, as defined in section 1679a(3) of this title, including entities that would be a credit repair organization, but for section 1679a(3)(B)(i) of this title, are able to circumvent the prohibition in subparagraph (G).

(C) Applicability

Subparagraphs (D) through (G) shall apply in any circumstance identified under the regulations promulgated under subparagraph (A).

(D) Submitting a notice of dispute

A consumer who seeks to dispute the accuracy of information shall provide a dispute notice directly to such person at the address specified by the person for such notices that—

(i) identifies the specific information that is being disputed;

(ii) explains the basis for the dispute; and

(iii) includes all supporting documentation required by the furnisher to substantiate the basis of the dispute.

(E) Duty of person after receiving notice of dispute

After receiving a notice of dispute from a consumer pursuant to subparagraph (D), the person that provided the information in dispute to a consumer reporting agency shall—

(i) conduct an investigation with respect to the disputed information;

(ii) review all relevant information provided by the consumer with the notice;

(iii) complete such person's investigation of the dispute and report the results of the investigation to the consumer before the expiration of the period under section 1681i(a)(1) of this title within which a consumer reporting agency would be required to complete its action if the consumer had elected to dispute the information under that section; and

(iv) if the investigation finds that the information reported was inaccurate, promptly notify each consumer reporting agency to which the person furnished the inaccurate information of that determination and provide to the agency any correction to that information that is necessary to make the information provided by the person accurate.

(F) Frivolous or irrelevant dispute

(i) In general

This paragraph shall not apply if the person receiving a notice of a dispute from a consumer reasonably determines that the dispute is frivolous or irrelevant, including—

(I) by reason of the failure of a consumer to provide sufficient information to investigate the disputed information; or

(II) the submission by a consumer of a dispute that is substantially the same as a dispute previously submitted by or for the consumer, either directly to the person or through a consumer reporting agency under subsection (b), with respect to which the person has already performed the person's duties under this paragraph or subsection (b), as applicable.

(ii) Notice of determination

Upon making any determination under clause (i) that a dispute is frivolous or irrelevant, the person shall notify the consumer of such determination not later than 5 business days after making such determination, by mail or, if authorized by the consumer for that purpose, by any other means available to the person.

(iii) Contents of notice

A notice under clause (ii) shall include—

(I) the reasons for the determination under clause (i); and

(II) identification of any information required to investigate the disputed information, which may consist of a standardized form describing the general nature of such information.

(G) Exclusion of credit repair organizations

This paragraph shall not apply if the notice of the dispute is submitted by, is prepared on behalf of the consumer by, or is submitted on a form supplied to the consumer by, a credit repair organization, as defined in section 1679a(3) of this title, or an entity that would be a credit repair organization, but for section 1679a(3)(B)(i) of this title.

(9) Duty to provide notice of status as medical information furnisher

A person whose primary business is providing medical services, products, or devices, or the person's agent or assignee, who furnishes information to a consumer reporting agency on a consumer shall be considered a medical information furnisher for purposes of this subchapter, and shall notify the agency of such status.

(b) Duties of furnishers of information upon notice of dispute

(1) In general

After receiving notice pursuant to section 1681i(a)(2) of this title of a dispute with regard to the completeness or accuracy of any information provided by a person to a consumer reporting agency, the person shall—

(A) conduct an investigation with respect to the disputed information;

(B) review all relevant information provided by the consumer reporting agency pursuant to section 1681i(a)(2) of this title;

(C) report the results of the investigation to the consumer reporting agency;

(D) if the investigation finds that the information is incomplete or inaccurate, report those results to all other consumer reporting agencies to which the person furnished the information and that compile and maintain files on consumers on a nationwide basis; and

(E) if an item of information disputed by a consumer is found to be inaccurate or incomplete or cannot be verified after any reinvestigation under paragraph (1), for purposes of reporting to a consumer reporting agency only, as appropriate, based on the results of the reinvestigation promptly—

(i) modify that item of information;

(ii) delete that item of information; or

(iii) permanently block the reporting of that item of information.

(2) Deadline

A person shall complete all investigations, reviews, and reports required under paragraph (1) regarding information provided by the person to a consumer reporting agency, before the expiration of the period under section 1681i(a)(1) of this title within which the consumer reporting agency is required to complete actions required by that section regarding that information.

(c) Limitation on liability

Except as provided in section 1681s(c)(1)(B) of this title, sections 1681n and 1681o of this title do not apply to any violation of—

(1) subsection (a) of this section, including any regulations issued thereunder;

(2) subsection (e) of this section, except that nothing in this paragraph shall limit, expand, or otherwise affect liability under section 1681n or 1681o of this title, as applicable, for violations of subsection (b) of this section; or

(3) subsection (e) of section 1681m of this title.

(d) Limitation on enforcement

The provisions of law described in paragraphs (1) through (3) of subsection (c) (other than with respect to the exception described in paragraph (2) of subsection (c)) shall be enforced exclusively as provided under section 1681s of this title by the Federal agencies and officials and the State officials identified in section 1681s of this title.

(e) Accuracy guidelines and regulations required

(1) Guidelines

The Bureau shall, with respect to persons or entities that are subject to the enforcement authority of the Bureau under section 1681s of this title—

(A) establish and maintain guidelines for use by each person that furnishes information to a consumer reporting agency regarding the accuracy and integrity of the information relating to consumers that such entities furnish to consumer reporting agencies, and update such guidelines as often as necessary; and

(B) prescribe regulations requiring each person that furnishes information to a consumer reporting agency to establish reasonable policies and procedures for implementing the guidelines established pursuant to subparagraph (A).

(2) Criteria

In developing the guidelines required by paragraph (1)(A), the Bureau shall—

(A) identify patterns, practices, and specific forms of activity that can compromise the accuracy and integrity of information furnished to consumer reporting agencies;

(B) review the methods (including technological means) used to furnish information relating to consumers to consumer reporting agencies;

(C) determine whether persons that furnish information to consumer reporting agencies maintain and enforce policies to ensure the accuracy and integrity of information furnished to consumer reporting agencies; and

(D) examine the policies and processes that persons that furnish information to consumer reporting agencies employ to conduct reinvestigations and correct inaccurate information relating to consumers that has been furnished to consumer reporting agencies.

(Pub. L. 90–321, title VI, §623, as added Pub. L. 104–208, div. A, title II, §2413(a)(2), Sept. 30, 1996, 110 Stat. 3009–447; amended Pub. L. 108–159, title I, §154(a), title II, §217(a), title III, §§312(a)–(e)(1), 314(b), title IV, §412(a), Dec. 4, 2003, 117 Stat. 1966, 1986, 1989-1993, 1995, 2002; Pub. L. 111–203, title X, §1088(a)(2)(D), (11), July 21, 2010, 124 Stat. 2087, 2090; Pub. L. 115–174, title VI, §602(a), May 24, 2018, 132 Stat. 1366; Pub. L. 116–136, div. A, title IV, §4021, Mar. 27, 2020, 134 Stat. 489.)

REFERENCES IN TEXT

The National Emergencies Act, referred to in subsec. (a)(1)(F)(i)(II)(bb), is Pub. L. 94–412, Sept. 14, 1976, 90 Stat. 1255, which is classified principally to chapter 34 (§1601 et seq.) of Title 50, War and National Defense. For complete classification of this Act to the Code, see Short Title note set out under section 1601 of Title 50 and Tables.

PRIOR PROVISIONS

A prior section 623 of Pub. L. 90–321 was renumbered section 625 and is classified to section 1681t of this title.

AMENDMENTS

2020—Subsec. (a)(1)(F). Pub. L. 116–136 added subpar. (F).

2018—Subsec. (a)(1)(E). Pub. L. 115–174 added subpar. (E).

2010—Subsec. (a)(7)(D). Pub. L. 111–203, §1088(a)(11)(A), added subpar. (D) and struck out former subpar. (D) which related to duty of Board to prescribe a model disclosure.

Subsec. (a)(8)(A). Pub. L. 111–203, §1088(a)(11)(B), which directed amendment of subpar. (A) by inserting ", in consultation with the Federal Trade Commission, the Federal banking agencies, and the National Credit Union Administration," before "shall jointly", was executed by making the insertion before "shall prescribe", to reflect the probable intent of Congress and the amendment by Pub. L. 111–203, §1088(a)(2)(D). See below.

Pub. L. 111–203, §1088(a)(2)(D), substituted "The Bureau shall" for "The Federal banking agencies, the National Credit Union Administration, and the Commission shall jointly".

Subsec. (e). Pub. L. 111–203, §1088(a)(11)(C), added subsec. (e) and struck out former subsec. (e) which related to establishment and maintenance of accuracy guidelines and prescription of implementing regulations by the Federal banking agencies, the National Credit Union Administration, and the Commission.

2003—Subsec. (a)(1)(A). Pub. L. 108–159, §312(b)(1), substituted "knows or has reasonable cause to believe that the information is inaccurate" for "knows or consciously avoids knowing that the information is inaccurate".

Subsec. (a)(1)(D). Pub. L. 108–159, §312(b)(2), added subpar. (D).

Subsec. (a)(5). Pub. L. 108–159, §312(d), designated existing provisions as subpar. (A), inserted heading, inserted "date of delinquency on the account, which shall be the" before "month" and "on the account" before "that immediately preceded", and added subpar. (B).

Subsec. (a)(6). Pub. L. 108–159, §154(a), added par. (6).

Subsec. (a)(7). Pub. L. 108–159, §217(a), added par. (7).

Subsec. (a)(8). Pub. L. 108–159, §312(c), added par. (8).

Subsec. (a)(9). Pub. L. 108–159, §412(a), added par. (9).

Subsec. (b)(1)(E). Pub. L. 108–159, §314(b), added subpar. (E).

Subsec. (c). Pub. L. 108–159, §312(e)(1), added subsec. (c) and struck out heading and text of former subsec. (c). Text read as follows: "Sections 1681n and 1681o of this title do not apply to any failure to comply with subsection (a) of this section, except as provided in section 1681s(c)(1)(B) of this title."

Subsec. (d). Pub. L. 108–159, §312(e)(1), added subsec. (d) and struck out heading and text of former subsec. (d). Text read as follows: "Subsection (a) of this section shall be enforced exclusively under section 1681s of this title by the Federal agencies and officials and the State officials identified in that section."

Subsec. (e). Pub. L. 108–159, §312(a), added subsec. (e).

EFFECTIVE DATE OF 2010 AMENDMENT

Amendment by Pub. L. 111–203 effective on the designated transfer date, see section 1100H of Pub. L. 111–203, set out as a note under section 552a of Title 5, Government Organization and Employees.

EFFECTIVE DATE OF 2003 AMENDMENT

Amendment by Pub. L. 108–159 subject to joint regulations establishing effective dates as prescribed by Federal Reserve Board and Federal Trade Commission, except as otherwise provided, see section 3 of Pub. L. 108–159, set out as a note under section 1681 of this title.

Amendment by section 412(a) of Pub. L. 108–159 effective at end of 15-month period beginning on Dec. 4, 2003, see section 412(g) of Pub. L. 108–159, set out as a note under section 1681b of this title.

§1681s–3. Affiliate sharing

(a) Special rule for solicitation for purposes of marketing

(1) Notice

Any person that receives from another person related to it by common ownership or affiliated by corporate control a communication of information that would be a consumer report, but for clauses (i), (ii), and (iii) of section 1681a(d)(2)(A) of this title, may not use the information to make a solicitation for marketing purposes to a consumer about its products or services, unless—

(A) it is clearly and conspicuously disclosed to the consumer that the information may be communicated among such persons for purposes of making such solicitations to the consumer; and

(B) the consumer is provided an opportunity and a simple method to prohibit the making of such solicitations to the consumer by such person.

(2) Consumer choice

(A) In general

The notice required under paragraph (1) shall allow the consumer the opportunity to prohibit all solicitations referred to in such paragraph, and may allow the consumer to choose from different options when electing to prohibit the sending of such solicitations, including options regarding the types of entities and information covered, and which methods of delivering solicitations the consumer elects to prohibit.

(B) Format

Notwithstanding subparagraph (A), the notice required under paragraph (1) shall be clear, conspicuous, and concise, and any method provided under paragraph (1)(B) shall be simple. The regulations prescribed to implement this section shall provide specific guidance regarding how to comply with such standards.

(3) Duration

(A) In general

The election of a consumer pursuant to paragraph (1)(B) to prohibit the making of solicitations shall be effective for at least 5 years, beginning on the date on which the person receives the election of the consumer, unless the consumer requests that such election be revoked.

(B) Notice upon expiration of effective period

At such time as the election of a consumer pursuant to paragraph (1)(B) is no longer effective, a person may not use information that the person receives in the manner described in paragraph (1) to make any solicitation for marketing purposes to the consumer, unless the consumer receives a notice and an opportunity, using a simple method, to extend the opt-out for another period of at least 5 years, pursuant to the procedures described in paragraph (1).

(4) Scope

This section shall not apply to a person—

(A) using information to make a solicitation for marketing purposes to a consumer with whom the person has a pre-existing business relationship;

(B) using information to facilitate communications to an individual for whose benefit the person provides employee benefit or other services pursuant to a contract with an employer related to and arising out of the current employment relationship or status of the individual as a participant or beneficiary of an employee benefit plan;

(C) using information to perform services on behalf of another person related by common ownership or affiliated by corporate control, except that this subparagraph shall not be construed as permitting a person to send solicitations on behalf of another person, if such other person would not be permitted to send the solicitation on its own behalf as a result of the election of the consumer to prohibit solicitations under paragraph (1)(B);

(D) using information in response to a communication initiated by the consumer;

(E) using information in response to solicitations authorized or requested by the consumer; or

(F) if compliance with this section by that person would prevent compliance by that person with any provision of State insurance laws pertaining to unfair discrimination in any State in which the person is lawfully doing business.

(5) No retroactivity

This subsection shall not prohibit the use of information to send a solicitation to a consumer if such information was received prior to the date on which persons are required to comply with regulations implementing this subsection.

(b) Notice for other purposes permissible

A notice or other disclosure under this section may be coordinated and consolidated with any other notice required to be issued under any other provision of law by a person that is subject to this section, and a notice or other disclosure that is equivalent to the notice required by subsection (a), and that is provided by a person described in subsection (a) to a consumer together with disclosures required by any other provision of law, shall satisfy the requirements of subsection (a).

(c) User requirements

Requirements with respect to the use by a person of information received from another person related to it by common ownership or affiliated by corporate control, such as the requirements of this section, constitute requirements with respect to the exchange of information among persons affiliated by common ownership or common corporate control, within the meaning of section 1681t(b)(2) of this title.

(d) Definitions

For purposes of this section, the following definitions shall apply:

(1) Pre-existing business relationship

The term "pre-existing business relationship" means a relationship between a person, or a person's licensed agent, and a consumer, based on—

(A) a financial contract between a person and a consumer which is in force;

(B) the purchase, rental, or lease by the consumer of that person's goods or services, or a financial transaction (including holding an active account or a policy in force or having another continuing relationship) between the consumer and that person during the 18-month period immediately preceding the date on which the consumer is sent a solicitation covered by this section;

(C) an inquiry or application by the consumer regarding a product or service offered by that person, during the 3-month period immediately preceding the date on which the consumer is sent a solicitation covered by this section; or

(D) any other pre-existing customer relationship defined in the regulations implementing this section.

(2) Solicitation

The term "solicitation" means the marketing of a product or service initiated by a person to a particular consumer that is based on an exchange of information described in subsection (a), and is intended to encourage the consumer to purchase such product or service, but does not include communications that are directed at the general public or determined not to be a solicitation by the regulations prescribed under this section.

(Pub. L. 90–321, title VI, §624, as added Pub. L. 108–159, title II, §214(a)(2), Dec. 4, 2003, 117 Stat. 1980.)

EDITORIAL NOTES

PRIOR PROVISIONS

A prior section 624 of Pub. L. 90–321 was renumbered section 625 and is classified to section 1681t of this title.

Another prior section 624 of Pub. L. 90–321 was renumbered section 626 and is classified to section 1681u of this title.

STATUTORY NOTES AND RELATED SUBSIDIARIES

EFFECTIVE DATE

Section subject to joint regulations establishing effective dates as prescribed by Federal Reserve Board and Federal Trade Commission, except as otherwise provided, see section 3 of Pub. L. 108–159, set out as an Effective Date of 2003 Amendment note under section 1681 of this title.

REGULATIONS

Pub. L. 108–159, title II, §214(b), Dec. 4, 2003, 117 Stat. 1982, as amended by Pub. L. 111–203, title X, §1088(b)(3), July 21, 2010, 124 Stat. 2092, provided that:

"(1) IN GENERAL.—Regulations to carry out section 624 of the Fair Credit Reporting Act (15 U.S.C. 1681s–3), shall be prescribed, as described in paragraph (2), by—

"(A) the Commodity Futures Trading Commission, with respect to entities subject to its enforcement authorities;

"(B) the Securities and Exchange Commission, with respect to entities subject to its enforcement authorities; and

"(C) the Bureau, with respect to other entities subject to this Act [see Short Title of 2003 Amendment note set out under section 1601 of this title].

"(2) COORDINATION.—Each agency required to prescribe regulations under paragraph (1) shall consult and coordinate with each other such agency so that, to the extent possible, the regulations prescribed by each such entity are consistent and comparable with the regulations prescribed by each other such agency.

"(3) CONSIDERATIONS.—In promulgating regulations under this subsection, each agency referred to in paragraph (1) shall—

"(A) ensure that affiliate sharing notification methods provide a simple means for consumers to make determinations and choices under section 624 of the Fair Credit Reporting Act [15 U.S.C. 1681s–3], as added by this section;

"(B) consider the affiliate sharing notification practices employed on the date of enactment of this Act [Dec. 4, 2003] by persons that will be subject to that section 624; and

"(C) ensure that notices and disclosures may be coordinated and consolidated, as provided in subsection (b) of that section 624.

"(4) TIMING.—Regulations required by this subsection shall—

"(A) be issued in final form not later than 9 months after the date of enactment of this Act [Dec. 4, 2003]; and

"(B) become effective not later than 6 months after the date on which they are issued in final form."

[For definitions of terms used in section 214(b) of Pub. L. 108–159, set out above, see section 2 of Pub. L. 108–159, set out as a Definitions note under section 1681 of this title.]

STUDIES OF INFORMATION SHARING PRACTICES

Pub. L. 108–159, title II, §214(e), Dec. 4, 2003, 117 Stat. 1983, as amended by Pub. L. 111–203, title X, §1088(b)(4), July 21, 2010, 124 Stat. 2092, provided that:

"(1) IN GENERAL.—The Federal banking agencies, the National Credit Union Administration, and the Bureau shall jointly conduct regular studies of the consumer information sharing practices by financial institutions and other persons that are creditors or users of consumer reports with their affiliates.

"(2) MATTERS FOR STUDY.—In conducting the studies required by paragraph (1), the agencies described in paragraph (1) shall—

"(A) identify—

"(i) the purposes for which financial institutions and other creditors and users of consumer reports share consumer information;

"(ii) the types of information shared by such entities with their affiliates;

"(iii) the number of choices provided to consumers with respect to the control of such sharing, and the degree to and manner in which consumers exercise such choices, if at all; and

"(iv) whether such entities share or may share personally identifiable transaction or experience information with affiliates for purposes—

"(I) that are related to employment or hiring, including whether the person that is the subject of such information is given notice of such sharing, and the specific uses of such shared information; or

"(II) of general publication of such information; and

"(B) specifically examine the information sharing practices that financial institutions and other creditors and users of consumer reports and their affiliates employ for the purpose of making underwriting decisions or credit evaluations of consumers.

"(3) REPORTS.—

"(A) INITIAL REPORT.—Not later than 3 years after the date of enactment of this Act [Dec. 4, 2003], the Federal banking agencies, the National Credit Union Administration, and the Commission shall jointly submit a report to the Congress on the results of the initial study conducted in accordance with this subsection, together with any recommendations for legislative or regulatory action.

"(B) Followup reports.—The Federal banking agencies, the National Credit Union Administration, and the Commission shall, not less frequently than once every 3 years following the date of submission of the initial report under subparagraph (A), jointly submit a report to the Congress that, together with any recommendations for legislative or regulatory action—

"(i) documents any changes in the areas of study referred to in paragraph (2)(A) occurring since the date of submission of the previous report;

"(ii) identifies any changes in the practices of financial institutions and other creditors and users of consumer reports in sharing consumer information with their affiliates for the purpose of making underwriting decisions or credit evaluations of consumers occurring since the date of submission of the previous report; and

"(iii) examines the effects that changes described in clause (ii) have had, if any, on the degree to which such affiliate sharing practices reduce the need for financial institutions, creditors, and other users of consumer reports to rely on consumer reports for such decisions."

[For definitions of terms used in section 214(e) of Pub. L. 108–159, set out above, see section 2 of Pub. L. 108–159, set out as a Definitions note under section 1681 of this title.]

§1681t. Relation to State laws

(a) In general

Except as provided in subsections (b) and (c), this subchapter does not annul, alter, affect, or exempt any person subject to the provisions of this subchapter from complying with the laws of any State with respect to the collection, distribution, or use of any information on consumers, or for the prevention or mitigation of identity theft, except to the extent that those laws are inconsistent with any provision of this subchapter, and then only to the extent of the inconsistency.

(b) General exceptions

No requirement or prohibition may be imposed under the laws of any State—

(1) with respect to any subject matter regulated under—

(A) subsection (c) or (e) of section 1681b of this title, relating to the prescreening of consumer reports;

(B) section 1681i of this title, relating to the time by which a consumer reporting agency must take any action, including the provision of notification to a consumer or other person, in any procedure related to the disputed accuracy of information in a consumer's file, except that this subparagraph shall not apply to any State law in effect on September 30, 1996;

(C) subsections (a) and (b) of section 1681m of this title, relating to the duties of a person who takes any adverse action with respect to a consumer;

(D) section 1681m(d) of this title, relating to the duties of persons who use a consumer report of a consumer in connection with any credit or insurance transaction that is not initiated by the consumer and that consists of a firm offer of credit or insurance;

(E) section 1681c of this title, relating to information contained in consumer reports, except that this subparagraph shall not apply to any State law in effect on September 30, 1996;

(F) section 1681s–2 of this title, relating to the responsibilities of persons who furnish information to consumer reporting agencies, except that this paragraph shall not apply—

(i) with respect to section 54A(a) of chapter 93 of the Massachusetts Annotated Laws (as in effect on September 30, 1996); or

(ii) with respect to section 1785.25(a) of the California Civil Code (as in effect on September 30, 1996);

(G) section 1681g(e) of this title, relating to information available to victims under section 1681g(e) of this title;

(H) section 1681s–3 of this title, relating to the exchange and use of information to make a solicitation for marketing purposes;

(I) section 1681m(h) of this title, relating to the duties of users of consumer reports to provide notice with respect to terms in certain credit transactions;

(J) subsections (i) and (j) of section 1681c–1 of this title relating to security freezes; or

(K) subsection (k) of section 1681c–1 of this title, relating to credit monitoring for active duty military consumers, as defined in that subsection;

(2) with respect to the exchange of information among persons affiliated by common ownership or common corporate control, except that this paragraph shall not apply with respect to subsection (a) or (c)(1) of section 2480e of title 9, Vermont Statutes Annotated (as in effect on September 30, 1996);

(3) with respect to the disclosures required to be made under subsection (c), (d), (e), or (g) of section 1681g of this title, or subsection (f) of section 1681g of this title relating to the disclosure of credit scores for credit granting purposes, except that this paragraph—

(A) shall not apply with respect to sections 1785.10, 1785.16, and 1785.20.2 of the California Civil Code (as in effect on December 4, 2003) and section 1785.15 through section 1785.15.2 of such Code (as in effect on such date);

(B) shall not apply with respect to sections 5–3–106(2) and 212–14.3–104.3 of the Colorado Revised Statutes (as in effect on December 4, 2003); and

(C) shall not be construed as limiting, annulling, affecting, or superseding any provision of the laws of any State regulating the use in an insurance activity, or regulating disclosures concerning such use, of a credit-based insurance score of a consumer by any person engaged in the business of insurance;

(4) with respect to the frequency of any disclosure under section 1681j(a) of this title, except that this paragraph shall not apply—

(A) with respect to section 12–14.3–105(1)(d) of the Colorado Revised Statutes (as in effect on December 4, 2003);

(B) with respect to section 10–1–393(29)(C) of the Georgia Code (as in effect on December 4, 2003);

(C) with respect to section 1316.2 of title 10 of the Maine Revised Statutes (as in effect on December 4, 2003);

(D) with respect to sections 14–1209(a)(1) and 14–1209(b)(1)(i) of the Commercial Law Article of the Code of Maryland (as in effect on December 4, 2003);

(E) with respect to section 59(d) and section 59(e) of chapter 93 of the General Laws of Massachusetts (as in effect on December 4, 2003);

(F) with respect to section 56:11–37.10(a)(1) of the New Jersey Revised Statutes (as in effect on December 4, 2003); or

(G) with respect to section 2480c(a)(1) of title 9 of the Vermont Statutes Annotated (as in effect on December 4, 2003); or

(5) with respect to the conduct required by the specific provisions of—

(A) section 1681c(g) of this title;

(B) section 1681c–1 of this title;

(C) section 1681c–2 of this title;

(D) section 1681g(a)(1)(A) of this title;

(E) section 1681j(a) of this title;

(F) subsections (e), (f), and (g) of section 1681m of this title;

(G) section 1681s(f) of this title;

(H) section 1681s–2(a)(6) of this title; or

(I) section 1681w of this title.

(c) "Firm offer of credit or insurance" defined

Notwithstanding any definition of the term "firm offer of credit or insurance" (or any equivalent term) under the laws of any State, the definition of that term contained in section 1681a(l) of this title shall be construed to apply in the enforcement and interpretation of the laws of any State governing consumer reports.

(d) Limitations

Subsections (b) and (c) do not affect any settlement, agreement, or consent judgment between any State Attorney General and any consumer reporting agency in effect on September 30, 1996.

(Pub. L. 90–321, title VI, §625, formerly §622, as added Pub. L. 91–508, title VI, §601, Oct. 26, 1970, 84 Stat. 1136; renumbered §623, Pub. L. 102–537, §2(a), Oct. 27, 1992, 106 Stat. 3531; renumbered §624 and amended Pub. L. 104–208, div. A, title II, §§2413(a)(1), 2419, Sept. 30, 1996, 110 Stat. 3009–447, 3009–452; renumbered §625 and amended Pub. L. 108–159, title I, §151(a)(2), title II, §§212(e), 214(a)(1), (c)(2), title III, §311(b), title VII, §711, Dec. 4, 2003, 117 Stat. 1964, 1977, 1980, 1983, 1989, 2011; Pub. L. 115–174, title III, §§301(b), 302(d)(2), May 24, 2018, 132 Stat. 1332, 1335.)

EDITORIAL NOTES

PRIOR PROVISIONS

A prior section 625 of Pub. L. 90–321 was renumbered section 626 and is classified to section 1681u of this title.

AMENDMENTS

2018—Subsec. (b)(1)(J). Pub. L. 115–174, §301(b), added subpar. (J).

Subsec. (b)(1)(K). Pub. L. 115–174, §302(d)(2), added subpar. (K).

2003—Subsec. (a). Pub. L. 108–159, §711(1), inserted "or for the prevention or mitigation of identity theft," after "information on consumers,".

Subsec. (b)(1)(E). Pub. L. 108–159, §214(c)(2)(A), struck out "or" after semicolon at end.

Subsec. (b)(1)(G). Pub. L. 108–159, §151(a)(2), added subpar. (G).

Subsec. (b)(1)(H). Pub. L. 108–159, §214(c)(2)(B), added subpar. (H).

Subsec. (b)(1)(I). Pub. L. 108–159, §311(b), added subpar. (I).

Subsec. (b)(3), (4). Pub. L. 108–159, §212(e), added pars. (3) and (4) and struck out former par. (3) which read as follows: "with respect to the form and content of any disclosure required to be made under section 1681g(c) of this title."

Subsec. (b)(5). Pub. L. 108–159, §711(2), added par. (5).

Subsec. (d). Pub. L. 108–159, §711(3), substituted "(b) and (c)" for "(b) and (c)—", struck out par. (1) designation before "do not affect", substituted "1996." for "1996; and", and struck out par. (2) which read as follows:

"(2) do not apply to any provision of State law (including any provision of a State constitution) that—

"(A) is enacted after January 1, 2004;

"(B) states explicitly that the provision is intended to supplement this subchapter; and

"(C) gives greater protection to consumers than is provided under this subchapter."

1996—Subsec. (a). Pub. L. 104–208, §2419(1), designated existing provisions as subsec. (a), inserted heading, and substituted "Except as provided in subsections (b) and (c), this subchapter" for "This subchapter".

Subsecs. (b) to (d). Pub. L. 104–208, §2419(2), added subsecs. (b) to (d).

STATUTORY NOTES AND RELATED SUBSIDIARIES

EFFECTIVE DATE OF 2018 AMENDMENT

Amendment by section 301(b) of Pub. L. 115–174 effective 120 days after May 24, 2018, see section 301(c) of Pub. L. 115–174, set out as a note under section 1681c–1 of this title.

Amendment by section 302(d)(2) of Pub. L. 115–174 effective 1 year after May 24, 2018, see section 302(e) of Pub. L. 115–174, set out as a note under section 1681a of this title.

EFFECTIVE DATE OF 2003 AMENDMENT

Amendment by Pub. L. 108–159 subject to joint regulations establishing effective dates as prescribed by Federal Reserve Board and Federal Trade Commission, except as otherwise provided, see section 3 of Pub. L. 108–159, set out as a note under section 1681 of this title.

EFFECTIVE DATE OF 1996 AMENDMENT

Amendment by Pub. L. 104–208 effective 365 days after Sept. 30, 1996, with special rule for early compliance, see section 2420 of Pub. L. 104–208, set out as a note under section 1681a of this title.

EFFECTIVE DATE

Section effective upon the expiration of one hundred and eighty days following Oct. 26, 1970, see section 504(d) of Pub. L. 90–321, as added by Pub. L. 91–508, set out as a note under section 1681 of this title.

§1681u. Disclosures to FBI for counterintelligence purposes

(a) Identity of financial institutions

Notwithstanding section 1681b of this title or any other provision of this subchapter, a consumer reporting agency shall furnish to the Federal Bureau of Investigation the names and addresses of all financial institutions (as that term is defined in section 3401 of title 12) at which a consumer maintains or has maintained an account, to the extent that information is in the files of the agency, when presented with a written request for that information that includes a term that specifically identifies a consumer or account to be used as the basis for the production of that information, signed by the Director of the Federal Bureau of Investigation, or the Director's designee in a position not lower than Deputy Assistant Director at Bureau headquarters or a Special Agent in Charge of a Bureau field office designated by the Director, which certifies compliance with this section. The Director or the Director's designee may make such a certification only if the Director or the Director's designee has determined in writing, that such information is sought for the conduct of an authorized investigation to protect against international terrorism or clandestine intelligence activities, provided that such an investigation of a United States person is not conducted solely upon the basis of activities protected by the first amendment to the Constitution of the United States.

(b) Identifying information

Notwithstanding the provisions of section 1681b of this title or any other provision of this subchapter, a consumer reporting agency shall furnish identifying information respecting a consumer, limited to name, address, former addresses, places of employment, or former places of employment, to the Federal Bureau of Investigation when presented with a written request that includes a term that specifically identifies a consumer or account to be used as the basis for the production of that information, signed by the Director or the Director's designee in a position not lower than Deputy Assistant Director at Bureau headquarters or a Special Agent in Charge of a Bureau field office designated by the Director, which certifies compliance with this subsection. The Director or the Director's designee may make such a certification only if the Director or the Director's designee has determined in writing that such information is sought for the conduct of an authorized investigation to protect against international terrorism or clandestine intelligence activities, provided that such an investigation of a United States person is not conducted solely upon the basis of activities protected by the first amendment to the Constitution of the United States.

(c) Court order for disclosure of consumer reports

Notwithstanding section 1681b of this title or any other provision of this subchapter, if requested in writing by the Director of the Federal Bureau of Investigation, or a designee of the Director in a position not lower than Deputy Assistant Director at Bureau headquarters or a Special Agent in Charge in a Bureau field office designated by the Director, a court may issue an order ex parte, which shall include a term that specifically identifies a consumer or account to be used as the basis for the production of the information, directing a consumer reporting agency to furnish a consumer report to the Federal Bureau of Investigation, upon a showing in camera that the consumer report is sought for the conduct of an authorized investigation to protect against international terrorism or clandestine intelligence activities, provided that such an investigation of a United States person is not conducted solely upon the basis of activities protected by the first amendment to the Constitution of the United States. The terms of an order issued under this subsection shall not disclose that the order is issued for purposes of a counterintelligence investigation.

(d) Prohibition of certain disclosure

(1) Prohibition

(A) In general

If a certification is issued under subparagraph (B) and notice of the right to judicial review under subsection (e) is provided, no consumer reporting agency that receives a request under subsection (a) or (b) or an order under subsection (c), or officer, employee, or agent thereof, shall disclose or specify in any consumer report, that the Federal Bureau of Investigation has sought or obtained access to information or records under subsection (a), (b), or (c).

(B) Certification

The requirements of subparagraph (A) shall apply if the Director of the Federal Bureau of Investigation, or a designee of the Director whose rank shall be no lower than Deputy Assistant Director at Bureau headquarters or a Special Agent in Charge of a Bureau field office, certifies that the absence of a prohibition of disclosure under this subsection may result in—
(i) a danger to the national security of the United States;
(ii) interference with a criminal, counterterrorism, or counterintelligence investigation;
(iii) interference with diplomatic relations; or
(iv) danger to the life or physical safety of any person.

(2) Exception

(A) In general

A consumer reporting agency that receives a request under subsection (a) or (b) or an order under subsection (c), or officer, employee, or agent thereof, may disclose information otherwise subject to any applicable nondisclosure requirement to—
(i) those persons to whom disclosure is necessary in order to comply with the request;
(ii) an attorney in order to obtain legal advice or assistance regarding the request; or
(iii) other persons as permitted by the Director of the Federal Bureau of Investigation or the designee of the Director.

(B) Application

A person to whom disclosure is made under subparagraph (A) shall be subject to the nondisclosure requirements applicable to a person to whom a request under subsection (a) or (b) or an order under subsection (c) is issued in the same manner as the person to whom the request is issued.

(C) Notice

Any recipient that discloses to a person described in subparagraph (A) information otherwise subject to a nondisclosure requirement shall inform the person of the applicable nondisclosure requirement.

(D) Identification of disclosure recipients

At the request of the Director of the Federal Bureau of Investigation or the designee of the Director, any person making or intending to make a disclosure under clause (i) or (iii) of subparagraph (A) shall identify to the Director or such designee the person to whom such disclosure will be made or to whom such disclosure was made prior to the request.

(e) Judicial review

(1) In general

A request under subsection (a) or (b) or an order under subsection (c) or a non-disclosure requirement imposed in connection with such request under subsection (d) shall be subject to judicial review under section 3511 of title 18.

(2) Notice

A request under subsection (a) or (b) or an order under subsection (c) shall include notice of the availability of judicial review described in paragraph (1).

(f) Payment of fees

The Federal Bureau of Investigation shall, subject to the availability of appropriations, pay to the consumer reporting agency assembling or providing report or information in accordance with procedures established under this section a fee for reimbursement for such costs as are reasonably necessary and which have been directly incurred in searching, reproducing, or transporting books, papers, records, or other data required or requested to be produced under this section.

(g) Limit on dissemination

The Federal Bureau of Investigation may not disseminate information obtained pursuant to this section outside of the Federal Bureau of Investigation, except to other Federal agencies as may be necessary for the approval or conduct of a foreign counterintelligence investigation, or, where the information concerns a person subject to the Uniform Code of Military Justice, to appropriate investigative authorities within the military department concerned as may be necessary for the conduct of a joint foreign counterintelligence investigation.

(h) Rules of construction

Nothing in this section shall be construed to prohibit information from being furnished by the Federal Bureau of Investigation pursuant to a subpoena or court order, in connection with a judicial or administrative proceeding to enforce the provisions of this subchapter. Nothing in this section shall be construed to authorize or permit the withholding of information from the Congress.

(i) Reports to Congress

(1) On a semiannual basis, the Attorney General shall fully inform the Permanent Select Committee on Intelligence and the Committee on Banking, Finance and Urban Affairs of the House of Representatives, and the Select Committee on Intelligence and the Committee on Banking, Housing, and Urban Affairs of the Senate concerning all requests made pursuant to subsections (a), (b), and (c).

(2) In the case of the semiannual reports required to be submitted under paragraph (1) to the Permanent Select Committee on Intelligence of the House of Representatives and the Select Committee on Intelligence of the Senate, the submittal dates for such reports shall be as provided in section 3106 of title 50.

(j) Damages

Any agency or department of the United States obtaining or disclosing any consumer reports, records, or information contained therein in violation of this section is liable to the consumer to whom such consumer reports, records, or information relate in an amount equal to the sum of—

(1) $100, without regard to the volume of consumer reports, records, or information involved;

(2) any actual damages sustained by the consumer as a result of the disclosure;

(3) if the violation is found to have been willful or intentional, such punitive damages as a court may allow; and

(4) in the case of any successful action to enforce liability under this subsection, the costs of the action, together with reasonable attorney fees, as determined by the court.

(k) Disciplinary actions for violations

If a court determines that any agency or department of the United States has violated any provision of this section and the court finds that the circumstances surrounding the violation raise questions of whether or not an officer or employee of the agency or department acted willfully or intentionally with respect to the violation, the agency or department shall promptly initiate a proceeding to determine whether or not disciplinary action is warranted against the officer or employee who was responsible for the violation.

(l) Good-faith exception

Notwithstanding any other provision of this subchapter, any consumer reporting agency or agent or employee thereof making disclosure of consumer reports or identifying information pursuant to this subsection in good-faith reliance upon a certification of the Federal Bureau of Investigation pursuant to provisions of this section shall not be liable to any person for such disclosure under this subchapter, the constitution of any State, or any law or regulation of any State or any political subdivision of any State.

(m) Limitation of remedies

Notwithstanding any other provision of this subchapter, the remedies and sanctions set forth in this section shall be the only judicial remedies and sanctions for violation of this section.

(n) Injunctive relief

In addition to any other remedy contained in this section, injunctive relief shall be available to require compliance with the procedures of this section. In the event of any successful action under this subsection, costs together with reasonable attorney fees, as determined by the court, may be recovered.

(Pub. L. 90–321, title VI, §626, formerly §624, as added Pub. L. 104–93, title VI, §601(a), Jan. 6, 1996, 109 Stat. 974; renumbered §625 and amended Pub. L. 107–56, title III, §358(g)(1)(A), title V, §505(c), Oct. 26, 2001, 115 Stat. 327, 366; Pub. L. 107–306, title VIII, §811(b)(8)(B), Nov. 27, 2002, 116 Stat. 2426; renumbered §626, Pub. L. 108–159, title II, §214(a)(1), Dec. 4, 2003, 117 Stat. 1980; Pub. L. 109–177, title I, §116(b), Mar. 9, 2006, 120 Stat. 214; Pub. L. 109–178, §4(c)(1), Mar. 9, 2006, 120 Stat. 280; Pub. L. 114–23, title V, §§501(c), 502(c), 503(c), June 2, 2015, 129 Stat. 282, 285, 290.)

EDITORIAL NOTES

REFERENCES IN TEXT

This subchapter, referred to in subsec. (h), was in the original, "this Act" and was translated as reading "this title", meaning title VI of Pub. L. 90–321, known as the Fair Credit Reporting Act, to reflect the probable intent of Congress.

PRIOR PROVISIONS

A prior section 626 of Pub. L. 90–321 was renumbered section 627 and is classified to section 1681v of this title.

AMENDMENTS

2015—Subsec. (a). Pub. L. 114–23, §501(c)(1), substituted "that information that includes a term that specifically identifies a consumer or account to be used as the basis for the production of that information," for "that information,".

Subsec. (b). Pub. L. 114–23, §501(c)(2), substituted "written request that includes a term that specifically identifies a consumer or account to be used as the basis for the production of that information," for "written request,".

Subsec. (c). Pub. L. 114–23, §501(c)(3), inserted ", which shall include a term that specifically identifies a consumer or account to be used as the basis for the production of the information," after "issue an order ex parte".

Subsec. (d). Pub. L. 114–23, §502(c), added subsec. (d) and struck out former subsec. (d) which related to confidentiality.

Subsecs. (e) to (n). Pub. L. 114–23, §503(c), added subsec. (e) and redesignated former subsecs. (e) to (m) as (f) to (n), respectively.

2006—Subsec. (d). Pub. L. 109–177 reenacted heading without change and amended text generally. Prior to amendment, text read as follows: "No consumer reporting agency or officer, employee, or agent of a consumer reporting agency shall disclose to any person, other than those officers, employees, or agents of a consumer reporting agency necessary to fulfill the requirement to disclose information to the Federal Bureau of Investigation under this section, that the Federal Bureau of Investigation has sought or obtained the identity of financial institutions or a consumer report respecting any consumer under subsection (a), (b), or (c) of this section, and no consumer reporting agency or officer, employee, or agent of a consumer reporting agency shall include in any consumer report any information that would indicate that the Federal Bureau of Investigation has sought or obtained such information or a consumer report."

Subsec. (d)(4). Pub. L. 109–178 amended par. (4) generally. Prior to amendment, par. (4) read as follows: "At the request of the Director of the Federal Bureau of Investigation or the designee of the Director, any person making or intending to make a disclosure under this section shall identify to the Director or such designee the person to whom such disclosure will be made or to whom such disclosure was made prior to the request, but in no circumstance shall a person be required to inform the Director or such designee that the person intends to consult an attorney to obtain legal advice or legal assistance."

2002—Subsec. (h). Pub. L. 107–306 designated existing provisions as par. (1) and added par. (2).

2001—Pub. L. 107–56, §505(c), which directed amendment of section 624 of the Fair Credit Reporting Act, was executed by making the amendment to this section to reflect the probable intent of Congress and the renumbering of section 624 as 625 by section 358(g)(1)(A) of Pub. L. 107–56. See below.

Subsec. (a). Pub. L. 107–56, §505(c)(1), inserted "in a position not lower than Deputy Assistant Director at Bureau headquarters or a Special Agent in Charge of a Bureau field office designated by the Director" after "Investigation, or the Director's designee" and substituted "in writing, that such information is sought for the conduct of an authorized investigation to protect against international terrorism or clandestine intelligence activities, provided that such an investigation of a United States person is not conducted solely upon the basis of activities protected by the first amendment to the Constitution of the United States." for pars. (1) and (2) requiring determination in writing that the information requested is necessary for the conduct of an authorized foreign counterintelligence investigation and that there are specific and articulable facts giving reason to believe that the consumer is a foreign power or a person who is not a United States person and is an official of a foreign power, or that the consumer is an agent of a foreign power and is engaging or has engaged in an act of international terrorism or clandestine intelligence activities that involve or may involve a violation of criminal statutes of the United States.

Subsec. (b). Pub. L. 107–56, §505(c)(2), inserted "in a position not lower than Deputy Assistant Director at Bureau headquarters or a Special Agent in Charge of a Bureau field office designated by the Director" after "signed by the Director or the Director's designee" and substituted "in writing that such information is sought for the conduct of an authorized investigation to protect against international terrorism or clandestine intelligence activities, provided that such an investigation of a United States person is not conducted solely upon the basis of activities protected by the first amendment to the Constitution of the United States." for pars. (1) and (2) requiring determination in writing that the information requested is necessary to the conduct of an authorized counterintelligence investigation and that there is information giving reason to believe that the consumer has been, or is about to be, in contact with a foreign power or an agent of a foreign power.

Subsec. (c). Pub. L. 107–56, §505(c)(3), inserted "in a position not lower than Deputy Assistant Director at Bureau headquarters or a Special Agent in Charge in a Bureau field office designated by the Director" after "designee of the Director" and substituted "in camera that the consumer report is sought for the conduct of an authorized investigation to protect against international terrorism or clandestine intelligence activities, provided that such an investigation of a United States person is not conducted solely upon the basis of activities protected by the first amendment to the Constitution of the United States." for pars. (1) and (2) requiring a showing in camera that the consumer report is necessary for the conduct of an authorized foreign counterintelligence investigation and there are specific and articulable facts giving reason to believe that the consumer whose consumer report is sought is an agent of a foreign power and is engaging or has engaged in an act of international terrorism or in clandestine intelligence activities that involve or may involve a violation of criminal statutes of the United States.

STATUTORY NOTES AND RELATED SUBSIDIARIES

CHANGE OF NAME

Committee on Banking, Finance and Urban Affairs of House of Representatives treated as referring to Committee on Banking and Financial Services of House of Representatives by section 1(a) of Pub. L. 104–14, set out as a note preceding section 21 of Title 2, The Congress. Committee on Banking and Financial Services of House of Representatives abolished and replaced by Committee on Financial Services of House of Representatives, and jurisdiction over matters relating to securities and exchanges and insurance generally transferred from Committee on Energy and Commerce of House of Representatives by House Resolution No. 5, One Hundred Seventh Congress, Jan. 3, 2001.

EFFECTIVE DATE OF 2001 AMENDMENT

Amendment by section 358(g)(1)(A) of Pub. L. 107–56 applicable with respect to reports filed or records maintained on, before, or after Oct. 26, 2001, see section 358(h) of Pub. L. 107–56, set out as a note under section 1829b of this Title 12, Banks and Banking.

§1681v. Disclosures to governmental agencies for counterterrorism purposes

(a) Disclosure

Notwithstanding section 1681b of this title or any other provision of this subchapter, a consumer reporting agency shall furnish a consumer report of a consumer and all other information in a consumer's file to a government agency authorized to conduct investigations of, or intelligence or counterintelligence activities or analysis related to, international terrorism when presented with a written certification by such government agency that such information is necessary for the agency's conduct or such investigation, activity or analysis and that includes a term that specifically identifies a consumer or account to be used as the basis for the production of such information.

(b) Form of certification

The certification described in subsection (a) shall be signed by a supervisory official designated by the head of a Federal agency or an officer of a Federal agency whose appointment to office is required to be made by the President, by and with the advice and consent of the Senate.

(c) Prohibition of certain disclosure

(1) Prohibition

(A) In general

If a certification is issued under subparagraph (B) and notice of the right to judicial review under subsection (d) is provided, no consumer reporting agency that receives a request under subsection (a), or officer, employee, or agent thereof, shall disclose or specify in any consumer report, that a government agency described in subsection (a) has sought or obtained access to information or records under subsection (a).

(B) Certification

The requirements of subparagraph (A) shall apply if the head of the government agency described in subsection (a), or a designee, certifies that the absence of a prohibition of disclosure under this subsection may result in—

(i) a danger to the national security of the United States;

(ii) interference with a criminal, counterterrorism, or counterintelligence investigation;

(iii) interference with diplomatic relations; or

(iv) danger to the life or physical safety of any person.

(2) Exception

(A) In general

A consumer reporting agency that receives a request under subsection (a), or officer, employee, or agent thereof, may disclose information otherwise subject to any applicable nondisclosure requirement to—

(i) those persons to whom disclosure is necessary in order to comply with the request;

(ii) an attorney in order to obtain legal advice or assistance regarding the request; or

(iii) other persons as permitted by the head of the government agency described in subsection (a) or a designee.

(B) Application

A person to whom disclosure is made under subparagraph (A) shall be subject to the nondisclosure requirements applicable to a person to whom a request under subsection (a) is issued in the same manner as the person to whom the request is issued.

(C) Notice

Any recipient that discloses to a person described in subparagraph (A) information otherwise subject to a nondisclosure requirement shall inform the person of the applicable nondisclosure requirement.

(D) Identification of disclosure recipients

At the request of the head of the government agency described in subsection (a) or a designee, any person making or intending to make a disclosure under clause (i) or (iii) of subparagraph (A) shall identify to the head or such designee the person to whom such disclosure will be made or to whom such disclosure was made prior to the request.

(d) Judicial review

(1) In general

A request under subsection (a) or a non-disclosure requirement imposed in connection with such request under subsection (c) shall be subject to judicial review under section 3511 of title 18.

(2) Notice

A request under subsection (a) shall include notice of the availability of judicial review described in paragraph (1).

(e) Rule of construction

Nothing in section 1681u of this title shall be construed to limit the authority of the Director of the Federal Bureau of Investigation under this section.

(f) Safe harbor

Notwithstanding any other provision of this subchapter, any consumer reporting agency or agent or employee thereof making disclosure of consumer reports or other information pursuant to this section in good-faith reliance upon a certification of a government agency pursuant to the provisions of this section shall not be liable to any person for such disclosure under this subchapter, the constitution of any State, or any law or regulation of any State or any political subdivision of any State.

(g) Reports to Congress

(1) On a semi-annual basis, the Attorney General shall fully inform the Committee on the Judiciary, the Committee on Financial Services, and the Permanent Select Committee on Intelligence of the House of Representatives and the Committee on the Judiciary, the Committee on Banking, Housing, and Urban Affairs, and the Select Committee on Intelligence of the Senate concerning all requests made pursuant to subsection (a).

(2) In the case of the semiannual reports required to be submitted under paragraph (1) to the Permanent Select Committee on Intelligence of the House of Representatives and the Select Committee on Intelligence of the Senate, the submittal dates for such reports shall be as provided in section 3106 of title 50.

(Pub. L. 90–321, title VI, §627, formerly §626, as added Pub. L. 107–56, title III, §358(g)(1)(B), Oct. 26, 2001, 115 Stat. 327; renumbered §627 and amended Pub. L. 108–159, title II, §214(a)(1), (c)(3), Dec. 4, 2003, 117 Stat. 1980, 1983; Pub. L. 108–458, title VI, §6203(l), Dec. 17, 2004, 118 Stat. 3747; Pub. L. 109–177, title I, §§116(c), 118(b), Mar. 9,

2006, 120 Stat. 214, 217; Pub. L. 109–178, §4(c)(2), Mar. 9, 2006, 120 Stat. 280; Pub. L. 114–23, title V, §§501(d), 502(d), 503(d), June 2, 2015, 129 Stat. 282, 286, 290.)

EDITORIAL NOTES

AMENDMENTS

2015—Subsec. (a). Pub. L. 114–23, §501(d), substituted "analysis and that includes a term that specifically identifies a consumer or account to be used as the basis for the production of such information." for "analysis."

Subsec. (c). Pub. L. 114–23, §502(d), added subsec. (c) and struck out former subsec. (c) which related to confidentiality.

Subsecs. (d) to (g). Pub. L. 114–23, §503(d), added subsec. (d) and redesignated former subsecs. (d) to (f) as (e) to (g), respectively.

2006—Subsec. (c). Pub. L. 109–177, §116(c), amended subsec. (c) generally. Prior to amendment, text read as follows: "No consumer reporting agency, or officer, employee, or agent of such consumer reporting agency, shall disclose to any person, or specify in any consumer report, that a government agency has sought or obtained access to information under subsection (a) of this section."

Subsec. (c)(4). Pub. L. 109–178 amended par. (4) generally. Prior to amendment, par. (4) read as follows: "At the request of the authorized Government agency, any person making or intending to make a disclosure under this section shall identify to the requesting official of the authorized Government agency the person to whom such disclosure will be made or to whom such disclosure was made prior to the request, but in no circumstance shall a person be required to inform such requesting official that the person intends to consult an attorney to obtain legal advice or legal assistance."

Subsec. (f). Pub. L. 109–177, §118(b), added subsec. (f).

2004—Subsec. (e). Pub. L. 108–458 substituted "government agency" for "governmental agency".

2003—Subsec. (d). Pub. L. 108–159, §214(c)(3), made technical amendment to reference in original act which appears in text as reference to section 1681u of this title.

STATUTORY NOTES AND RELATED SUBSIDIARIES

EFFECTIVE DATE OF 2004 AMENDMENT

Amendment by Pub. L. 108–458 effective as if included in Pub. L. 107–56, as of the date of enactment of such Act, see section 6205 of Pub. L. 108–458, set out as a note under section 1828 of Title 12, Banks and Banking.

EFFECTIVE DATE OF 2003 AMENDMENT

Amendment by Pub. L. 108–159 subject to joint regulations establishing effective dates as prescribed by Federal Reserve Board and Federal Trade Commission, except as otherwise provided, see section 3 of Pub. L. 108–159, set out as a note under section 1681 of this title.

EFFECTIVE DATE

Section applicable with respect to reports filed or records maintained on, before, or after Oct. 26, 2001, see section 358(h) of Pub. L. 107–56, set out as an Effective Date of 2001 Amendment note under section 1829b of this Title 12, Banks and Banking.

§1681w. Disposal of records

(a) Regulations

(1) In general

The Federal Trade Commission, the Securities and Exchange Commission, the Commodity Futures Trading Commission, the Federal banking agencies, and the National Credit Union Administration, with respect to the entities that are subject to their respective enforcement authority under section 1681s of this title, and in coordination as described in paragraph (2), shall issue final regulations requiring any person that maintains or otherwise possesses consumer information, or any compilation of consumer information, derived from consumer reports for a business purpose to properly dispose of any such information or compilation.

(2) Coordination

Each agency required to prescribe regulations under paragraph (1) shall—

(A) consult and coordinate with each other such agency so that, to the extent possible, the regulations prescribed by each such agency are consistent and comparable with the regulations by each such other agency; and

(B) ensure that such regulations are consistent with the requirements and regulations issued pursuant to Public Law 106–102 and other provisions of Federal law.

(3) Exemption authority

In issuing regulations under this section, the agencies identified in paragraph (1) may exempt any person or class of persons from application of those regulations, as such agency deems appropriate to carry out the purpose of this section.

(b) Rule of construction

Nothing in this section shall be construed—

(1) to require a person to maintain or destroy any record pertaining to a consumer that is not imposed under other law; or

(2) to alter or affect any requirement imposed under any other provision of law to maintain or destroy such a record.

(Pub. L. 90–321, title VI, §628, as added Pub. L. 108–159, title II, §216(a), Dec. 4, 2003, 117 Stat. 1985; amended Pub. L. 111–203, title X, §1088(a)(12), (13), July 21, 2010, 124 Stat. 2091, 2092.)

EDITORIAL NOTES

REFERENCES IN TEXT

Public Law 106–102, referred to in subsec. (a)(2)(B), is Pub. L. 106–102, Nov. 12, 1999, 113 Stat. 1338, known as the Gramm-Leach-Bliley Act. For complete classification of this Act to the Code, see Short Title of 1999 Amendment note set out under section 1811 of Title 12, Banks and Banking, and Tables.

AMENDMENTS

2010—Subsec. (a)(1). Pub. L. 111–203, §1088(a)(12), substituted "The Federal Trade Commission, the Securities and Exchange Commission, the Commodity Futures Trading Commission, the Federal banking agencies, and the National Credit Union Administration, with respect to the entities that are subject to their respective enforcement authority under section 1681s of this title," for "Not later than 1 year after December 4, 2003, the Federal banking agencies, the National Credit Union Administration, and the Commission with respect to the entities that are subject to their respective enforcement authority under section 1681s of this title, and the Securities and Exchange Commission,".

Subsec. (a)(3). Pub. L. 111–203, §1088(a)(13), substituted "the agencies identified in paragraph (1)" for "the Federal banking agencies, the National Credit Union Administration, the Commission, and the Securities and Exchange Commission".

STATUTORY NOTES AND RELATED SUBSIDIARIES

EFFECTIVE DATE OF 2010 AMENDMENT

Amendment by Pub. L. 111–203 effective on the designated transfer date, see section 1100H of Pub. L. 111–203, set out as a note under section 552a of Title 5, Government Organization and Employees.

EFFECTIVE DATE

Section subject to joint regulations establishing effective dates as prescribed by Federal Reserve Board and Federal Trade Commission, except as otherwise provided, see section 3 of Pub. L. 108–159, set out as an Effective Date of 2003 Amendment note under section 1681 of this title.

§1681x. Corporate and technological circumvention prohibited

The Commission shall prescribe regulations, to become effective not later than 90 days after December 4, 2003, to prevent a consumer reporting agency from circumventing or evading treatment as a consumer reporting agency described in section 1681a(p) of this title for purposes of this subchapter, including—

(1) by means of a corporate reorganization or restructuring, including a merger, acquisition, dissolution, divestiture, or asset sale of a consumer reporting agency; or

(2) by maintaining or merging public record and credit account information in a manner that is substantially equivalent to that described in paragraphs (1) and (2) of section 1681a(p) of this title, in the manner described in section 1681a(p) of this title.

(Pub. L. 90–321, title VI, §629, as added Pub. L. 108–159, title II, §211(b), Dec. 4, 2003, 117 Stat. 1970.)

STATUTORY NOTES AND RELATED SUBSIDIARIES

EFFECTIVE DATE

Section subject to joint regulations establishing effective dates as prescribed by Federal Reserve Board and Federal Trade Commission, except as otherwise provided, see section 3 of Pub. L. 108–159, set out as an Effective Date of 2003 Amendment note under section 1681 of this title.

This marks the end of the Fair Credit Reporting Act

15 U.S.C. § 1681

EQUAL CREDIT OPPORTUNITY ACT

15 U.S.C. §§ 1691-1691f, as amended

This Act (Title VII of the Consumer Credit Protection Act) prohibits discrimination on the basis of race, color, religion, national origin, sex, marital status, age, receipt of public assistance, or good faith exercise of any rights under the Consumer Credit Protection Act. The Act also requires creditors to provide applicants, upon request, with the reasons underlying decisions to deny credit. The Dodd-Frank Act added, among other things, a requirement that creditors provide to applicants a copy of all appraisals and other written valuations used in connection with the applicant's application for first lien loans secured by a dwelling.

Subchapter IV, Equal Credit Opportunity

SUBCHAPTER IV—EQUAL CREDIT OPPORTUNITY

§1691. Scope of prohibition

(a) Activities constituting discrimination

It shall be unlawful for any creditor to discriminate against any applicant, with respect to any aspect of a credit transaction—

(1) on the basis of race, color, religion, national origin, sex or marital status, or age (provided the applicant has the capacity to contract);

(2) because all or part of the applicant's income derives from any public assistance program; or

(3) because the applicant has in good faith exercised any right under this chapter.

(b) Activities not constituting discrimination

It shall not constitute discrimination for purposes of this subchapter for a creditor—

(1) to make an inquiry of marital status if such inquiry is for the purpose of ascertaining the creditor's rights and remedies applicable to the particular extension of credit and not to discriminate in a determination of credit-worthiness;

(2) to make an inquiry of the applicant's age or of whether the applicant's income derives from any public assistance program if such inquiry is for the purpose of determining the amount and probable continuance of income levels, credit history, or other pertinent element of credit-worthiness as provided in regulations of the Bureau;

(3) to use any empirically derived credit system which considers age if such system is demonstrably and statistically sound in accordance with regulations of the Bureau, except that in the operation of such system the age of an elderly applicant may not be assigned a negative factor or value;

(4) to make an inquiry or to consider the age of an elderly applicant when the age of such applicant is to be used by the creditor in the extension of credit in favor of such applicant; or

(5) to make an inquiry under section 1691c–2 of this title, in accordance with the requirements of that section.

(c) Additional activities not constituting discrimination

It is not a violation of this section for a creditor to refuse to extend credit offered pursuant to—

(1) any credit assistance program expressly authorized by law for an economically disadvantaged class of persons;

(2) any credit assistance program administered by a nonprofit organization for its members or an economically disadvantaged class of persons; or

(3) any special purpose credit program offered by a profit-making organization to meet special social needs which meets standards prescribed in regulations by the Bureau;

if such refusal is required by or made pursuant to such program.

(d) Reason for adverse action; procedure applicable; "adverse action" defined

(1) Within thirty days (or such longer reasonable time as specified in regulations of the Bureau for any class of credit transaction) after receipt of a completed application for credit, a creditor shall notify the applicant of its action on the application.

(2) Each applicant against whom adverse action is taken shall be entitled to a statement of reasons for such action from the creditor. A creditor satisfies this obligation by—

(A) providing statements of reasons in writing as a matter of course to applicants against whom adverse action is taken; or

(B) giving written notification of adverse action which discloses (i) the applicant's right to a statement of reasons within thirty days after receipt by the creditor of a request made within sixty days after such notification, and (ii) the identity of the person or office from which such statement may be obtained. Such statement may be given orally if the written notification advises the applicant of his right to have the statement of reasons confirmed in writing on written request.

(3) A statement of reasons meets the requirements of this section only if it contains the specific reasons for the adverse action taken.

(4) Where a creditor has been requested by a third party to make a specific extension of credit directly or indirectly to an applicant, the notification and statement of reasons required by this subsection may be made directly by such creditor, or indirectly through the third party, provided in either case that the identity of the creditor is disclosed.

(5) The requirements of paragraph (2), (3), or (4) may be satisfied by verbal statements or notifications in the case of any creditor who did not act on more than one hundred and fifty applications during the calendar year preceding the calendar year in which the adverse action is taken, as determined under regulations of the Bureau.

(6) For purposes of this subsection, the term "adverse action" means a denial or revocation of credit, a change in the terms of an existing credit arrangement, or a refusal to grant credit in substantially the amount or on substantially the terms requested. Such term does not include a refusal to extend additional credit under an existing credit arrangement where the applicant is delinquent or otherwise in default, or where such additional credit would exceed a previously established credit limit.

(e) Copies furnished to applicants

(1) In general

Each creditor shall furnish to an applicant a copy of any and all written appraisals and valuations developed in connection with the applicant's application for a loan that is secured or would have been secured by a first lien on a dwelling promptly upon completion, but in no case later than 3 days prior to the closing of the loan, whether the creditor grants or denies the applicant's request for credit or the application is incomplete or withdrawn.

(2) Waiver

The applicant may waive the 3 day requirement provided for in paragraph (1), except where otherwise required in law.

(3) Reimbursement

The applicant may be required to pay a reasonable fee to reimburse the creditor for the cost of the appraisal, except where otherwise required in law.

(4) Free copy

Notwithstanding paragraph (3), the creditor shall provide a copy of each written appraisal or valuation at no additional cost to the applicant.

(5) Notification to applicants

At the time of application, the creditor shall notify an applicant in writing of the right to receive a copy of each written appraisal and valuation under this subsection.

(6) Valuation defined

For purposes of this subsection, the term "valuation" shall include any estimate of the value of a dwelling developed in connection with a creditor's decision to provide credit, including those values developed pursuant to a policy of a government sponsored enterprise or by an automated valuation model, a broker price opinion, or other methodology or mechanism.

(Pub. L. 90–321, title VII, §701, as added Pub. L. 93–495, title V, §503, Oct. 28, 1974, 88 Stat. 1521; amended Pub. L. 94–239, §2, Mar. 23, 1976, 90 Stat. 251; Pub. L. 102–242, title II, §223(d), Dec. 19, 1991, 105 Stat. 2306; Pub. L. 111–203, title X, §§1071(b), 1085(1), title XIV, §1474, July 21, 2010, 124 Stat. 2059, 2083, 2199.)

EDITORIAL NOTES

AMENDMENTS

2010—Pub. L. 111–203, §1085(1), substituted "Bureau" for "Board" wherever appearing.

Subsec. (b)(5). Pub. L. 111–203, §1071(b), added par. (5).

Subsec. (e). Pub. L. 111–203, §1474, amended subsec. (e) generally. Prior to amendment, subsec. (e) read as follows: "Each creditor shall promptly furnish an applicant, upon written request by the applicant made within a reasonable period of time of the application, a copy of the appraisal report used in connection with the applicant's application for a loan that is or would have been secured by a lien on residential real property. The creditor may require the applicant to reimburse the creditor for the cost of the appraisal."

1991—Subsec. (e). Pub. L. 102–242 added subsec. (e).

1976—Subsec. (a). Pub. L. 94–239 designated existing provisions as cl. (1), expanded prohibition against discrimination to include race, color, religion, national origin and age, and added cls. (2) and (3).

Subsec. (b). Pub. L. 94–239 designated existing provisions as cl. (1) and added cls. (2) to (4).

Subsecs. (c), (d). Pub. L. 94–239 added subsecs. (c) and (d).

STATUTORY NOTES AND RELATED SUBSIDIARIES

EFFECTIVE DATE OF 2010 AMENDMENT

Pub. L. 111–203, title X, §1071(d), July 21, 2010, 124 Stat. 2059, provided that: "This section [enacting section 1691c–2 of this title and amending this section] shall become effective on the designated transfer date."

[The term "designated transfer date" is defined in section 5481(9) of Title 12, Banks and Banking, as the date established under section 5582 of Title 12.]

Amendment by section 1085(1) of Pub. L. 111–203 effective on the designated transfer date, see section 1100H of Pub. L. 111–203, set out as a note under section 552a of Title 5, Government Organization and Employees.

Amendment by section 1474 of Pub. L. 111–203 effective on the date on which final regulations implementing that amendment take effect, or on the date that is 18 months after the designated transfer date if such regulations have not been issued by that date, see section 1400(c) of Pub. L. 111–203, set out as a note under section 1601 of this title.

EFFECTIVE DATE

Section 708, formerly §707, of title VII of Pub. L. 90–321, as added by Pub. L. 93–495, title V, §503, Oct. 28, 1974, 88 Stat. 1525, renumbered and amended by Pub. L. 94–239, §§7, 8, Mar. 23, 1976, 90 Stat. 255, provided that: "This title [enacting this subchapter and provisions set out as notes under section 1691 of this title] takes effect upon the expiration of one year after the date of its enactment [Oct. 28, 1974]. The amendments made by the Equal Credit Opportunity Act Amendments of 1976 [enacting section 1691f of this title, amending this section and sections 1691b, 1691c, 1691d, and 1691e of this title, repealing section 1609 of this title, enacting provisions set out as notes under this section, and repealing provisions set out as a note under this section] shall take effect on the date of enactment thereof [Mar. 23, 1976] and shall apply to any violation occurring on or after such date, except that the amendments made to section 701 of the Equal Credit Opportunity Act [this section] shall take effect 12 months after the date of enactment [Mar. 23, 1976]."

SHORT TITLE

This subchapter known as the "Equal Credit Opportunity Act", see Short Title note set out under section 1601 of this title.

CONGRESSIONAL FINDINGS AND STATEMENT OF PURPOSE

Pub. L. 93–495, title V, §502, Oct. 28, 1974, 88 Stat. 1521, provided that: "The Congress finds that there is a need to insure that the various financial institutions and other firms engaged in the extensions of credit exercise their responsibility to make credit available with fairness, impartiality, and without discrimination on the basis of sex or marital status. Economic stabilization would be enhanced and competition among the various financial institutions and other firms engaged in the extension of credit would be strengthened by an absence of discrimination on the basis of sex or marital status, as well as by the informed use of credit which Congress has heretofore sought to promote. It is the purpose of this Act [see Short Title note set out under section 1601 of this title] to require that financial institutions and other firms engaged in the extension of credit make that credit equally available to all credit-worthy customers without regard to sex or marital status."

§1691a. Definitions; rules of construction

(a) The definitions and rules of construction set forth in this section are applicable for the purposes of this subchapter.

(b) The term "applicant" means any person who applies to a creditor directly for an extension, renewal, or continuation of credit, or applies to a creditor indirectly by use of an existing credit plan for an amount exceeding a previously established credit limit.

(c) The term "Bureau" means the Bureau of Consumer Financial Protection.

(d) The term "credit" means the right granted by a creditor to a debtor to defer payment of debt or to incur debts and defer its payment or to purchase property or services and defer payment therefor.

(e) The term "creditor" means any person who regularly extends, renews, or continues credit; any person who regularly arranges for the extension, renewal, or continuation of credit; or any assignee of an original creditor who participates in the decision to extend, renew, or continue credit.

(f) The term "person" means a natural person, a corporation, government or governmental subdivision or agency, trust, estate, partnership, cooperative, or association.

(g) Any reference to any requirement imposed under this subchapter or any provision thereof includes reference to the regulations of the Bureau under this subchapter or the provision thereof in question.

(Pub. L. 90–321, title VII, §702, as added Pub. L. 93–495, title V, §503, Oct. 28, 1974, 88 Stat. 1522; amended Pub. L. 111–203, title X, §1085(1), (2), July 21, 2010, 124 Stat. 2083.)

EDITORIAL NOTES

AMENDMENTS

2010—Subsec. (c). Pub. L. 111–203, §1085(2), added subsec. (c) and struck out former subsec. (c) which read as follows: "The term 'Board' refers to the Board of Governors of the Federal Reserve System."

Subsec. (g). Pub. L. 111–203, §1085(1), substituted "Bureau" for "Board".

STATUTORY NOTES AND RELATED SUBSIDIARIES

EFFECTIVE DATE OF 2010 AMENDMENT

Amendment by Pub. L. 111–203 effective on the designated transfer date, see section 1100H of Pub. L. 111–203, set out as a note under section 552a of Title 5, Government Organization and Employees.

§1691b. Promulgation of regulations by the Bureau

(a) In general

The Bureau shall prescribe regulations to carry out the purposes of this subchapter. These regulations may contain but are not limited to such classifications, differentiation, or other provision, and may provide for such adjustments and exceptions for any class of transactions, as in the judgment of the Bureau are necessary or proper to effectuate the purposes of this subchapter, to prevent circumvention or evasion thereof, or to facilitate or substantiate compliance therewith.

(b) Exempt transactions

Such regulations may exempt from the provisions of this subchapter any class of transactions that are not primarily for personal, family, or household purposes, or business or commercial loans made available by a financial institution, except that a particular type within a class of such transactions may be exempted if the Bureau determines, after making an express finding that the application of this subchapter or of any provision of this subchapter of such transaction would not contribute substantially to effecting the purposes of this subchapter.

(c) Limitation on exemptions

An exemption granted pursuant to subsection (b) shall be for no longer than five years and shall be extended only if the Bureau makes a subsequent determination, in the manner described by such paragraph,[1] that such exemption remains appropriate.

(d) Maintenance of records

Pursuant to Bureau regulations, entities making business or commercial loans shall maintain such records or other data relating to such loans as may be necessary to evidence compliance with this subsection [2] or enforce any action pursuant to the authority of this chapter. In no event shall such records or data be maintained for a period of less than one year. The Bureau shall promulgate regulations to implement this paragraph [3] in the manner prescribed by chapter 5 of title 5.

(e) Notice of denial of loan

The Bureau shall provide in regulations that an applicant for a business or commercial loan shall be provided a written notice of such applicant's right to receive a written statement of the reasons for the denial of such loan.

(f) Board authority

Notwithstanding subsection (a), the Board shall prescribe regulations to carry out the purposes of this subchapter with respect to a person described in section 5519(a) of title 12. These regulations may contain but are not limited to such classifications, differentiation, or other provision, and may provide for such adjustments and exceptions for any class of transactions, as in the judgment of the Board are necessary or proper to effectuate the purposes of this subchapter, to prevent circumvention or evasion thereof, or to facilitate or substantiate compliance therewith.

(g) Deference

Notwithstanding any power granted to any Federal agency under this subchapter, the deference that a court affords to a Federal agency with respect to a determination made by such agency relating to the meaning or interpretation of any provision of this subchapter that is subject to the jurisdiction of such agency shall be applied as if that agency were the only agency authorized to apply, enforce, interpret, or administer the provisions of this subchapter [4]

(Pub. L. 90–321, title VII, §703, as added Pub. L. 93–495, title V, §503, Oct. 28, 1974, 88 Stat. 1522; amended Pub. L. 94–239, §3(a), Mar. 23, 1976, 90 Stat. 252; Pub. L. 100–533, title III, §301, Oct. 25, 1988, 102 Stat. 2692; Pub. L. 111–203, title X, §1085(1), (3), July 21, 2010, 124 Stat. 2083.)

AMENDMENTS

2010—Pub. L. 111–203, §1085(3)(A), substituted "Promulgation of regulations by the Bureau" for "Regulations" in section catchline.

Pub. L. 111–203, §1085(1), substituted "Bureau" for "Board" wherever appearing.

Subsecs. (a) to (e). Pub. L. 111–203, §1085(3)(B)–(E), in subsec. (a), struck out "(a)" designation before "(1)", redesignated subsec. (a) pars. (1) to (5) as subsecs. (a) to (e), respectively, in subsec. (c) substituted "subsection (b)" for "paragraph (2)", and struck out former subsec. (b), which related to establishment of a Consumer Advisory Council to advise and consult with the Board.

Subsecs. (f), (g). Pub. L. 111–203, §1085(3)(F), added subsecs. (f) and (g).

1988—Subsec. (a). Pub. L. 100–533 amended subsec. (a) generally. Prior to amendment, subsec. (a) read as follows: "The Board shall prescribe regulations to carry out the purposes of this subchapter. These regulations may contain but are not limited to such classifications, differentiation, or other provision, and may provide for such adjustments and exceptions for any class of transactions, as in the judgment of the Board are necessary or proper to effectuate the purposes of this subchapter, to prevent circumvention or evasion thereof, or to facilitate or substantiate compliance therewith. In particular, such regulations may exempt from one or more of the provisions of this subchapter any class of transactions not primarily for personal, family, or household purposes, if the Board makes an express finding that the application of such provision or provisions would not contribute substantially to carrying out the purposes of this subchapter. Such regulations shall be prescribed as soon as possible after the date of enactment of this Act, but in no event later than the effective date of this Act."

1976—Pub. L. 94–239 designated existing provisions as subsec. (a), inserted provisions exempting from regulations of this subchapter any class of transactions not primarily for personal, family, or household purposes to be determined by the Board, and added subsec. (b).

EFFECTIVE DATE OF 2010 AMENDMENT

Amendment by Pub. L. 111–203 effective on the designated transfer date, see section 1100H of Pub. L. 111–203, set out as a note under section 552a of Title 5, Government Organization and Employees.

EFFECTIVE DATE OF 1976 AMENDMENT

Amendment by Pub. L. 94–239 effective Mar. 23, 1976, see section 708 of Pub. L. 90–321, set out as an Effective Date note under section 1691 of this title.

[1] *So in original. Probably should be "subsection,".*

[2] *So in original.*

[3] *So in original. Probably should be "subsection".*

[4] *So in original. Probably should be followed by a period.*

§1691c. Administrative enforcement

(a) Enforcing agencies

Subject to subtitle B of the Consumer Protection Financial Protection Act of 2010 [1] with [2] the requirements imposed under this subchapter shall be enforced under:

(1) section 8 of the Federal Deposit Insurance Act [12 U.S.C. 1818], by the appropriate Federal banking agency, as defined in section 3(q) of the Federal Deposit Insurance Act (12 U.S.C. 1813(q)), with respect to—

(A) national banks, Federal savings associations, and Federal branches and Federal agencies of foreign banks;

(B) member banks of the Federal Reserve System (other than national banks), branches and agencies of foreign banks (other than Federal branches, Federal agencies, and insured State branches of foreign banks), commercial lending companies owned or controlled by foreign banks, and organizations operating under section 25 or 25A of the Federal Reserve Act [12 U.S.C. 601 et seq., 611 et seq.]; and

(C) banks and State savings associations insured by the Federal Deposit Insurance Corporation (other than members of the Federal Reserve System), and insured State branches of foreign banks;

(2) The Federal Credit Union Act [12 U.S.C. 1751 et seq.], by the Administrator of the National Credit Union Administration with respect to any Federal Credit Union.

(3) Subtitle IV of title 49, by the Secretary of Transportation, with respect to all carriers subject to the jurisdiction of the Surface Transportation Board.

(4) Part A of subtitle VII of title 49, by the Secretary of Transportation with respect to any air carrier or foreign air carrier subject to that part.

(5) The Packers and Stockyards Act, 1921 [7 U.S.C. 181 et seq.] (except as provided in section 406 of that Act [7 U.S.C. 226, 227]), by the Secretary of Agriculture with respect to any activities subject to that Act.

(6) The Farm Credit Act of 1971 [12 U.S.C. 2001 et seq.], by the Farm Credit Administration with respect to any Federal land bank, Federal land bank association, Federal intermediate credit bank, and production credit association;

(7) The Securities Exchange Act of 1934 [15 U.S.C. 78a et seq.], by the Securities and Exchange Commission with respect to brokers and dealers;

(8) The Small Business Investment Act of 1958 [15 U.S.C. 661 et seq.], by the Small Business Administration, with respect to small business investment companies; and

(9) Subtitle E of the Consumer Financial Protection Act of 2010 [12 U.S.C. 5561 et seq.], by the Bureau, with respect to any person subject to this subchapter.

The terms used in paragraph (1) that are not defined in this subchapter or otherwise defined in section 3(s) of the Federal Deposit Insurance Act (12 U.S.C. 1813(s)) shall have the meaning given to them in section 1(b) of the International Banking Act of 1978 (12 U.S.C. 3101).

(b) Violations of subchapter deemed violations of preexisting statutory requirements; additional agency powers

For the purpose of the exercise by any agency referred to in subsection (a) of its powers under any Act referred to in that subsection, a violation of any requirement imposed under this subchapter shall be deemed to be a violation of a requirement imposed under that Act. In addition to its powers under any provision of law specifically referred to in subsection (a), each of the agencies referred to in that subsection may exercise for the purpose of enforcing compliance with any requirement imposed under this subchapter, any other authority conferred on it by law. The exercise of the authorities of any of the agencies referred to in subsection (a) for the purpose of enforcing compliance with any requirement imposed under this subchapter shall in no way preclude the exercise of such authorities for the purpose of enforcing compliance with any other provision of law not relating to the prohibition of discrimination on the basis of sex or marital status with respect to any aspect of a credit transaction.

(c) Overall enforcement authority of Federal Trade Commission

Except to the extent that enforcement of the requirements imposed under this subchapter is specifically committed to some other Government agency under any of paragraphs (1) through (8) of subsection (a), and subject to subtitle B of the Consumer Financial Protection Act of 2010, the Federal Trade Commission shall be authorized to enforce such requirements. For the purpose of the exercise by the Federal Trade Commission of its functions and powers under the Federal Trade Commission Act (15 U.S.C. 41 et seq.), a violation of any requirement imposed under this subchapter [3] shall be deemed a violation of a requirement imposed under that Act. All of the functions and powers of the Federal Trade Commission under the Federal Trade Commission Act are available to the Federal Trade Commission to enforce compliance by any person with the requirements imposed under this subchapter, irrespective of whether that person is engaged in commerce or meets any other jurisdictional tests under the Federal Trade Commission Act, including the power to enforce any rule prescribed by the Bureau under this subchapter in the same manner as if the violation had been a violation of a Federal Trade Commission trade regulation rule.

(d) Rules and regulations by enforcing agencies

The authority of the Bureau to issue regulations under this subchapter does not impair the authority of any other agency designated in this section to make rules respecting its own procedures in enforcing compliance with requirements imposed under this subchapter.

(Pub. L. 90–321, title VII, §704, as added Pub. L. 93–495, title V, §503, Oct. 28, 1974, 88 Stat. 1522; amended Pub. L. 94–239, §4, Mar. 23, 1976, 90 Stat. 253; Pub. L. 98–443, §9(n), Oct. 4, 1984, 98 Stat. 1708; Pub. L. 101–73, title VII, §744(m), Aug. 9, 1989, 103 Stat. 439; Pub. L. 102–242, title II, §212(d), Dec. 19, 1991, 105 Stat. 2300; Pub. L. 102–550, title XVI, §1604(a)(7), Oct. 28, 1992, 106 Stat. 4082; Pub. L. 104–88, title III, §315, Dec. 29, 1995, 109 Stat. 948; Pub. L. 111–203, title X, §1085(4), July 21, 2010, 124 Stat. 2084.)

EDITORIAL NOTES

References in Text

The Consumer Financial Protection Act of 2010, referred to in subsecs. (a) and (c), is title X of Pub. L. 111–203, July 21, 2010, 124 Stat. 1955. Subtitles B (§§1021–1029A) and E (§§1051–1058) of the Act are classified generally to parts B (§5511 et seq.) and E (§5561 et seq.), respectively, of subchapter V of chapter 53 of Title 12, Banks and Banking. For complete classification of subtitles B and E to the Code, see Tables.

Sections 25 and 25A of the Federal Reserve Act, referred to in subsec. (a)(1)(B), are classified to subchapters I (§601 et seq.) and II (§611 et seq.), respectively, of chapter 6 of Title 12, Banks and Banking.

The Federal Credit Union Act, referred to in subsec. (a)(2), is act June 26, 1934, ch. 750, 48 Stat. 1216, which is classified generally to chapter 14 (§1751 et seq.) of Title 12. For complete classification of this Act to the Code, see section 1751 of Title 12 and Tables.

The Packers and Stockyards Act, 1921, referred to in subsec. (a)(5), is act Aug. 15, 1921, ch. 64, 42 Stat. 159, which is classified to chapter 9 (§181 et seq.) of Title 7, Agriculture. For complete classification of this Act to the Code, see section 181 of Title 7 and Tables.

The Farm Credit Act of 1971, referred to in subsec. (a)(6), is Pub. L. 92–181, Dec. 10, 1971, 85 Stat. 583, which is classified generally to chapter 23 (§2001 et seq.) of Title 12, Banks and Banking. For complete classification of this Act to the Code, see Short Title note set out under section 2001 of Title 12 and Tables.

The Securities Exchange Act of 1934, referred to in subsec. (a)(7), is act June 6, 1934, ch. 404, 48 Stat. 881, which is classified principally to chapter 2B (§78a et seq.) of this title. For complete classification of this Act to the Code, see Codification note set out under section 78a of this title and Tables.

The Small Business Investment Act of 1958, referred to in subsec. (a)(8), is Pub. L. 85–699, Aug. 21, 1958, 72 Stat. 689, which is classified principally to chapter 14B (§661 et seq.) of this title. For complete classification of this Act to the Code, see Short Title note set out under section 661 of this title and Tables.

The Federal Trade Commission Act, referred to in subsec. (c), is act Sept. 26, 1914, ch. 311, 38 Stat. 717, which is classified generally to subchapter I (§41 et seq.) of chapter 2 of this title. For complete classification of this Act to the Code, see section 58 of this title and Tables.

This subchapter, referred to in subsec. (c) before "shall be deemed", probably should have been a reference to this title in the original, meaning title VII of Pub. L. 90–321 which is classified generally to this subchapter.

Codification

In subsec. (a)(3), "Subtitle IV of title 49" substituted for "The Acts to regulate commerce" on authority of Pub. L. 95–473, §3(b), Oct. 17, 1978, 92 Stat. 1466, the first section of which enacted subtitle IV of Title 49, Transportation.

In subsec. (a)(4), "Part A of subtitle VII of title 49" substituted for "The Federal Aviation Act of 1958 [49 App. U.S.C. 1301 et seq.]" and "that part" substituted for "that Act" on authority of Pub. L. 103–272, §6(b), July 5, 1994, 108 Stat. 1378, the first section of which enacted subtitles II, III, and V to X of Title 49.

Amendments

2010—Subsec. (a). Pub. L. 111–203, §1085(4)(A)(i), substituted "Subject to subtitle B of the Consumer Protection Financial Protection Act of 2010" for "Compliance" in introductory provisions.

Subsec. (a)(1). Pub. L. 111–203, §1085(4)(A)(ii), added par. (1) and struck out former par. (1) which read as follows: "section 8 of the Federal Deposit Insurance Act, in the case of—

"(A) national banks, and Federal branches and Federal agencies of foreign banks, by the Office of the Comptroller of the Currency;

"(B) member banks of the Federal Reserve System (other than national banks), branches and agencies of foreign banks (other than Federal branches, Federal agencies, and insured State branches of foreign banks), commercial lending companies owned or controlled by foreign banks, and organizations operating under section 25 or 25(a) of the Federal Reserve Act, by the Board; and

"(C) banks insured by the Federal Deposit Insurance Corporation (other than members of the Federal Reserve System) and insured State branches of foreign banks, by the Board of Directors of the Federal Deposit Insurance Corporation;".

Subsec. (a)(2) to (9). Pub. L. 111–203, §1085(4)(A)(ii)–(vi), added par. (9), redesignated former pars. (3) to (9) as (2) to (8), respectively, and struck out former par. (2) which read as follows: "Section 8 of the Federal Deposit Insurance Act, by the Director of the Office of Thrift Supervision, in the case of a savings association the deposits of which are insured by the Federal Deposit Insurance Corporation."

Subsec. (c). Pub. L. 111–203, §1085(4)(B), added subsec. (c) and struck out former subsec. (c) which read as follows: "Except to the extent that enforcement of the requirements imposed under this subchapter is specifically committed to some other Government agency under subsection (a) of this section, the Federal Trade Commission shall enforce such requirements. For the purpose of the exercise by the Federal Trade Commission of its functions and powers under the Federal Trade Commission Act, a violation of any requirement imposed under this subchapter shall be deemed a violation of a requirement imposed under that Act. All of the functions and powers of the Federal Trade Commission under the Federal Trade Commission Act are available to the Commission to enforce compliance by any person with the requirements imposed under this subchapter, irrespective of whether that person is engaged in commerce or meets any other jurisdictional tests in the Federal Trade Commission Act, including the power to enforce any Federal Reserve Board regulation promulgated under this subchapter in the same manner as if the violation had been a violation of a Federal Trade Commission trade regulation rule."

Subsec. (d). Pub. L. 111–203, §1085(4)(C), substituted "Bureau" for "Board".

1995—Subsec. (a)(4). Pub. L. 104–88 substituted "Secretary of Transportation, with respect to all carriers subject to the jurisdiction of the Surface Transportation Board" for "Interstate Commerce Commission with respect to any common carrier subject to those Acts".

1992—Subsec. (a)(1)(C). Pub. L. 102–550 substituted semicolon for period at end.

1991—Subsec. (a). Pub. L. 102–242, §212(d)(2), inserted at end "The terms used in paragraph (1) that are not defined in this subchapter or otherwise defined in section 3(s) of the Federal Deposit Insurance Act (12 U.S.C. 1813(s)) shall have the meaning given to them in section 1(b) of the International Banking Act of 1978 (12 U.S.C. 3101)."

Pub. L. 102–242, §212(d)(1), added par. (1) and struck out former par. (1) which read as follows: "Section 8 of Federal Deposit Insurance Act, in the case of—

"(A) national banks, by the Comptroller of the Currency,

"(B) member banks of the Federal Reserve System (other than national banks), by the Federal Reserve Board,

"(C) banks the deposits or accounts of which are insured by the Federal Deposit Insurance Corporation (other than members of the Federal Reserve System), by the Board of Directors of the Federal Deposit Insurance Corporation."

1989—Subsec. (a)(2). Pub. L. 101–73 amended par. (2) generally. Prior to amendment, par. (2) read as follows: "Section 5(d) of the Home Owners' Loan Act of 1933, section 407 of the National Housing Act, and sections 6(i) and 17 of the Federal Home Loan Bank Act, by the Federal Home Loan Bank Board (acting directly or through the Federal Savings and Loan Insurance Corporation), in the case of any institution subject to any of those provisions."

1984—Subsec. (a)(5). Pub. L. 98–443 substituted "Secretary of Transportation" for "Civil Aeronautics Board".

1976—Subsec. (c). Pub. L. 94–239 inserted provisions giving the Federal Trade Commission power to enforce any regulation of the Federal Reserve Board promulgated under this subchapter.

EFFECTIVE DATE OF 2010 AMENDMENT

Amendment by Pub. L. 111–203 effective on the designated transfer date, see section 1100H of Pub. L. 111–203, set out as a note under section 552a of Title 5, Government Organization and Employees.

EFFECTIVE DATE OF 1995 AMENDMENT

Amendment by Pub. L. 104–88 effective Jan. 1, 1996, see section 2 of Pub. L. 104–88, set out as an Effective Date note under section 1301 of Title 49, Transportation.

EFFECTIVE DATE OF 1992 AMENDMENT

Amendment by Pub. L. 102–550 effective as if included in the Federal Deposit Insurance Corporation Improvement Act of 1991, Pub. L. 102–242, as of Dec. 19, 1991, see section 1609(a) of Pub. L. 102–550, set out as a note under section 191 of Title 12, Banks and Banking.

EFFECTIVE DATE OF 1984 AMENDMENT

Amendment by Pub. L. 98–443 effective Jan. 1, 1985, see section 9(v) of Pub. L. 98–443, set out as a note under section 5314 of Title 5, Government Organization and Employees.

EFFECTIVE DATE OF 1976 AMENDMENT

Amendment by Pub. L. 94–239 effective Mar. 23, 1976, see section 708 of Pub. L. 90–321, set out as an Effective Date note under section 1691 of this title.

TRANSFER OF FUNCTIONS

Functions vested in Administrator of National Credit Union Administration transferred and vested in National Credit Union Administration Board pursuant to section 1752a of Title 12, Banks and Banking.

¹ *So in original. Probably should be "Consumer Financial Protection Act of 2010".*

² *So in original. Probably should be ", compliance with".*

³ *See References in Text note below.*

§1691c–1. Incentives for self-testing and self-correction

(a) Privileged information

(1) Conditions for privilege

A report or result of a self-test (as that term is defined by regulations of the Bureau) shall be considered to be privileged under paragraph (2) if a creditor—

(A) conducts, or authorizes an independent third party to conduct, a self-test of any aspect of a credit transaction by a creditor, in order to determine the level or effectiveness of compliance with this subchapter by the creditor; and

(B) has identified any possible violation of this subchapter by the creditor and has taken, or is taking, appropriate corrective action to address any such possible violation.

(2) Privileged self-test

If a creditor meets the conditions specified in subparagraphs (A) and (B) of paragraph (1) with respect to a self-test described in that paragraph, any report or results of that self-test—

(A) shall be privileged; and

(B) may not be obtained or used by any applicant, department, or agency in any—

(i) proceeding or civil action in which one or more violations of this subchapter are alleged; or

(ii) examination or investigation relating to compliance with this subchapter.

(b) Results of self-testing

(1) In general

No provision of this section may be construed to prevent an applicant, department, or agency from obtaining or using a report or results of any self-test in any proceeding or civil action in which a violation of this subchapter is alleged, or in any examination or investigation of compliance with this subchapter if—

(A) the creditor or any person with lawful access to the report or results—

(i) voluntarily releases or discloses all, or any part of, the report or results to the applicant, department, or agency, or to the general public; or

(ii) refers to or describes the report or results as a defense to charges of violations of this subchapter against the creditor to whom the self-test relates; or

(B) the report or results are sought in conjunction with an adjudication or admission of a violation of this subchapter for the sole purpose of determining an appropriate penalty or remedy.

(2) Disclosure for determination of penalty or remedy

Any report or results of a self-test that are disclosed for the purpose specified in paragraph (1)(B)—

(A) shall be used only for the particular proceeding in which the adjudication or admission referred to in paragraph (1)(B) is made; and

(B) may not be used in any other action or proceeding.

(c) Adjudication

An applicant, department, or agency that challenges a privilege asserted under this section may seek a determination of the existence and application of that privilege in—

(1) a court of competent jurisdiction; or

(2) an administrative law proceeding with appropriate jurisdiction.

(Pub. L. 90–321, title VII, §704A, as added Pub. L. 104–208, div. A, title II, §2302(a)(1), Sept. 30, 1996, 110 Stat. 3009–420; amended Pub. L. 111–203, title X, §1085(1), July 21, 2010, 124 Stat. 2083.)

EDITORIAL NOTES

AMENDMENTS

2010—Subsec. (a)(1). Pub. L. 111–203 substituted "Bureau" for "Board" in introductory provisions.

EFFECTIVE DATE OF 2010 AMENDMENT

Amendment by Pub. L. 111–203 effective on the designated transfer date, see section 1100H of Pub. L. 111–203, set out as a note under section 552a of Title 5, Government Organization and Employees.

EFFECTIVE DATE

Pub. L. 104–208, div. A, title II, §2302(c), Sept. 30, 1996, 110 Stat. 3009–423, provided that:

"(1) IN GENERAL.—Except as provided in paragraph (2), the privilege provided for in section 704A of the Equal Credit Opportunity Act [15 U.S.C. 1691c–1] or section 814A of the Fair Housing Act [42 U.S.C. 3614–1] (as those sections are added by this section) shall apply to a self-test (as that term is defined pursuant to the regulations prescribed under subsection (a)(2) [set out below] or (b)(2) of this section [42 U.S.C. 3614–1 note], as appropriate) conducted before, on, or after the effective date of the regulations prescribed under subsection (a)(2) or (b)(2), as appropriate.

"(2) EXCEPTION.—The privilege referred to in paragraph (1) does not apply to such a self-test conducted before the effective date of the regulations prescribed under subsection (a) or (b), as appropriate, if—

"(A) before that effective date, a complaint against the creditor or person engaged in residential real estate related lending activities (as the case may be) was—

"(i) formally filed in any court of competent jurisdiction; or

"(ii) the subject of an ongoing administrative law proceeding;

"(B) in the case of section 704A of the Equal Credit Opportunity Act, the creditor has waived the privilege pursuant to subsection (b)(1)(A)(i) of that section; or

"(C) in the case of section 814A of the Fair Housing Act, the person engaged in residential real estate related lending activities has waived the privilege pursuant to subsection (b)(1)(A)(i) of that section."

REGULATIONS

Pub. L. 104–208, div. A, title II, §2302(a)(2), Sept. 30, 1996, 110 Stat. 3009–421, provided that:

"(A) IN GENERAL.—Not later than 6 months after the date of enactment of this Act [Sept. 30, 1996], in consultation with the Secretary of Housing and Urban Development and the agencies referred to in section 704 of the Equal Credit Opportunity Act [15 U.S.C. 1691c], and after providing notice and an opportunity for public comment, the Board shall prescribe final regulations to implement section 704A of the Equal Credit Opportunity Act [15 U.S.C. 1691c–1], as added by this section.

"(B) SELF-TEST.—

"(i) DEFINITION.—The regulations prescribed under subparagraph (A) shall include a definition of the term 'self-test' for purposes of section 704A of the Equal Credit Opportunity Act, as added by this section.

"(ii) REQUIREMENT FOR SELF-TEST.—The regulations prescribed under subparagraph (A) shall specify that a self-test shall be sufficiently extensive to constitute a determination of the level and effectiveness of compliance by a creditor with the Equal Credit Opportunity Act [15 U.S.C. 1691 et seq.].

"(iii) SUBSTANTIAL SIMILARITY TO CERTAIN FAIR HOUSING ACT REGULATIONS.—The regulations prescribed under subparagraph (A) shall be substantially similar to the regulations prescribed by the Secretary of Housing and Urban Development to carry out section 814A(d) of the Fair Housing Act [42 U.S.C. 3614–1(d)], as added by this section."

§1691c–2. Small business loan data collection

(a) Purpose

The purpose of this section is to facilitate enforcement of fair lending laws and enable communities, governmental entities, and creditors to identify business and community development needs and opportunities of women-owned, minority-owned, and small businesses.

(b) Information gathering

Subject to the requirements of this section, in the case of any application to a financial institution for credit for women-owned, minority-owned, or small business, the financial institution shall—

(1) inquire whether the business is a women-owned, minority-owned, or small business, without regard to whether such application is received in person, by mail, by telephone, by electronic mail or other form of electronic transmission, or by any other means, and whether or not such application is in response to a solicitation by the financial institution; and

(2) maintain a record of the responses to such inquiry, separate from the application and accompanying information.

(c) Right to refuse

Any applicant for credit may refuse to provide any information requested pursuant to subsection (b) in connection with any application for credit.

(d) No access by underwriters

(1) Limitation

Where feasible, no loan underwriter or other officer or employee of a financial institution, or any affiliate of a financial institution, involved in making any determination concerning an application for credit shall have access to any information provided by the applicant pursuant to a request under subsection (b) in connection with such application.

(2) Limited access

If a financial institution determines that a loan underwriter or other officer or employee of a financial institution, or any affiliate of a financial institution, involved in making any determination concerning an application for credit should have access to any information provided by the applicant pursuant to a request under subsection (b), the financial institution shall provide notice to the applicant of the access of the underwriter to such information, along with notice that the financial institution may not discriminate on the basis of such information.

(e) Form and manner of information

(1) In general

Each financial institution shall compile and maintain, in accordance with regulations of the Bureau, a record of the information provided by any loan applicant pursuant to a request under subsection (b).

(2) Itemization

Information compiled and maintained under paragraph (1) shall be itemized in order to clearly and conspicuously disclose—

(A) the number of the application and the date on which the application was received;

(B) the type and purpose of the loan or other credit being applied for;

(C) the amount of the credit or credit limit applied for, and the amount of the credit transaction or the credit limit approved for such applicant;

(D) the type of action taken with respect to such application, and the date of such action;

(E) the census tract in which is located the principal place of business of the women-owned, minority-owned, or small business loan applicant;

(F) the gross annual revenue of the business in the last fiscal year of the women-owned, minority-owned, or small business loan applicant preceding the date of the application;

(G) the race, sex, and ethnicity of the principal owners of the business; and

(H) any additional data that the Bureau determines would aid in fulfilling the purposes of this section.

(3) No personally identifiable information

In compiling and maintaining any record of information under this section, a financial institution may not include in such record the name, specific address (other than the census tract required under paragraph (1)(E)),[1] telephone number, electronic mail address, or any other personally identifiable information concerning any individual who is, or is connected with, the women-owned, minority-owned, or small business loan applicant.

(4) Discretion to delete or modify publicly available data

The Bureau may, at its discretion, delete or modify data collected under this section which is or will be available to the public, if the Bureau determines that the deletion or modification of the data would advance a privacy interest.

(f) Availability of information

(1) Submission to Bureau

The data required to be compiled and maintained under this section by any financial institution shall be submitted annually to the Bureau.

(2) Availability of information

Information compiled and maintained under this section shall be—

(A) retained for not less than 3 years after the date of preparation;

(B) made available to any member of the public, upon request, in the form required under regulations prescribed by the Bureau;

(C) annually made available to the public generally by the Bureau, in such form and in such manner as is determined by the Bureau, by regulation.

(3) Compilation of aggregate data

The Bureau may, at its discretion—

(A) compile and aggregate data collected under this section for its own use; and

(B) make public such compilations of aggregate data.

(g) Bureau action

(1) In general

The Bureau shall prescribe such rules and issue such guidance as may be necessary to carry out, enforce, and compile data pursuant to this section.

(2) Exceptions

The Bureau, by rule or order, may adopt exceptions to any requirement of this section and may, conditionally or unconditionally, exempt any financial institution or class of financial institutions from the requirements of this section, as the Bureau deems necessary or appropriate to carry out the purposes of this section.

(3) Guidance

The Bureau shall issue guidance designed to facilitate compliance with the requirements of this section, including assisting financial institutions in working with applicants to determine whether the applicants are women-owned, minority-owned, or small businesses for purposes of this section.

(h) Definitions

For purposes of this section, the following definitions shall apply:

(1) Financial institution

The term "financial institution" means any partnership, company, corporation, association (incorporated or unincorporated), trust, estate, cooperative organization, or other entity that engages in any financial activity.

(2) Small business

The term "small business" has the same meaning as the term "small business concern" in section 632 of this title.

(3) Small business loan

The term "small business loan" means a loan made to a small business.

(4) Minority

The term "minority" has the same meaning as in section 1204(c)(3) of the Financial Institutions Reform, Recovery, and Enforcement Act of 1989.

(5) Minority-owned business

The term "minority-owned business" means a business—

(A) more than 50 percent of the ownership or control of which is held by 1 or more minority individuals; and

(B) more than 50 percent of the net profit or loss of which accrues to 1 or more minority individuals.

(6) Women-owned business

The term "women-owned business" means a business—

(A) more than 50 percent of the ownership or control of which is held by 1 or more women; and

(B) more than 50 percent of the net profit or loss of which accrues to 1 or more women.

(Pub. L. 90–321, title VII, §704B, as added Pub. L. 111–203, title X, §1071(a), July 21, 2010, 124 Stat. 2056.)

EDITORIAL NOTES

REFERENCES IN TEXT

Section 1204(c)(3) of the Financial Institutions Reform, Recovery, and Enforcement Act of 1989, referred to in subsec. (h)(4), is section 1204(c)(3) of Pub. L. 101–73, which is set out as a note under section 1811 of Title 12, Banks and Banking.

STATUTORY NOTES AND RELATED SUBSIDIARIES

EFFECTIVE DATE

Section effective on the designated transfer date, see section 1071(d) of Pub. L. 111–203, set out as an Effective Date of 2010 Amendment note under section 1691 of this title.

---

[1] So in original. Probably should be "(2)(E)),".

§1691d. Applicability of other laws

(a) Requests for signature of husband and wife for creation of valid lien, etc.

A request for the signature of both parties to a marriage for the purpose of creating a valid lien, passing clear title, waiving inchoate rights to property, or assigning earnings, shall not constitute discrimination under this subchapter: *Provided, however,* That this provision shall not be construed to permit a creditor to take sex or marital status into account in connection with the evaluation of creditworthiness of any applicant.

(b) State property laws affecting creditworthiness

Consideration or application of State property laws directly or indirectly affecting creditworthiness shall not constitute discrimination for purposes of this subchapter.

(c) State laws prohibiting separate extension of consumer credit to husband and wife

Any provision of State law which prohibits the separate extension of consumer credit to each party to a marriage shall not apply in any case where each party to a marriage voluntarily applies for separate credit from the same creditor: *Provided,* That in any case where such a State law is so preempted, each party to the marriage shall be solely responsible for the debt so contracted.

(d) Combining credit accounts of husband and wife with same creditor to determine permissible finance charges or loan ceilings under Federal or State laws

When each party to a marriage separately and voluntarily applies for and obtains separate credit accounts with the same creditor, those accounts shall not be aggregated or otherwise combined for purposes of determining permissible finance charges or permissible loan ceilings under the laws of any State or of the United States.

(e) Election of remedies under subchapter or State law; nature of relief determining applicability

Where the same act or omission constitutes a violation of this subchapter and of applicable State law, a person aggrieved by such conduct may bring a legal action to recover monetary damages either under this subchapter or under such State law, but not both. This election of remedies shall not apply to court actions in which the relief sought does not include monetary damages or to administrative actions.

(f) Compliance with inconsistent State laws; determination of inconsistency

This subchapter does not annul, alter, or affect, or exempt any person subject to the provisions of this subchapter from complying with, the laws of any State with respect to credit discrimination, except to the extent that those laws are inconsistent with any provision of this subchapter, and then only to the extent of the inconsistency. The Bureau is authorized to determine whether such inconsistencies exist. The Bureau may not determine that any State law is inconsistent with any provision of this subchapter if the Bureau determines that such law gives greater protection to the applicant.

(g) Exemption by regulation of credit transactions covered by State law; failure to comply with State law

The Bureau shall by regulation exempt from the requirements of sections 1691 and 1691a of this title any class of credit transactions within any State if it determines that under the law of that State that class of transactions is subject to requirements substantially similar to those imposed under this subchapter or that such law gives greater protection to the applicant, and that there is adequate provision for enforcement. Failure to comply with any requirement of such State law in any transaction so exempted shall constitute a violation of this subchapter for the purposes of section 1691e of this title.

(Pub. L. 90–321, title VII, §705, as added Pub. L. 93–495, title V, §503, Oct. 28, 1974, 88 Stat. 1523; amended Pub. L. 94–239, §5, Mar. 23, 1976, 90 Stat. 253; Pub. L. 111–203, title X, §1085(1), July 21, 2010, 124 Stat. 2083.)

EDITORIAL NOTES

AMENDMENTS

2010—Subsecs. (f), (g). Pub. L. 111–203 substituted "Bureau" for "Board" wherever appearing.

1976—Subsec. (e). Pub. L. 94–239, §5(1), substituted provisions requiring an election of remedies in legal actions involving the recovery of monetary damages, for provisions specifying a general election of remedies.

Subsecs. (f), (g). Pub. L. 94–239, §5(2), added subsecs. (f) and (g).

STATUTORY NOTES AND RELATED SUBSIDIARIES

EFFECTIVE DATE OF 2010 AMENDMENT

Amendment by Pub. L. 111–203 effective on the designated transfer date, see section 1100H of Pub. L. 111–203, set out as a note under section 552a of Title 5, Government Organization and Employees.

EFFECTIVE DATE OF 1976 AMENDMENT

Amendment by Pub. L. 94–239 effective Mar. 23, 1976, see section 708 of Pub. L. 90–321, set out as an Effective Date note under section 1691 of this title.

§1691e. Civil liability

(a) Individual or class action for actual damages

Any creditor who fails to comply with any requirement imposed under this subchapter shall be liable to the aggrieved applicant for any actual damages sustained by such applicant acting either in an individual capacity or as a member of a class.

(b) Recovery of punitive damages in individual and class action for actual damages; exemptions; maximum amount of punitive damages in individual actions; limitation on total recovery in class actions; factors determining amount of award

Any creditor, other than a government or governmental subdivision or agency, who fails to comply with any requirement imposed under this subchapter shall be liable to the aggrieved applicant for punitive damages in an amount not greater than $10,000, in addition to any actual damages provided in subsection (a), except that in the case of a class action the total recovery under this subsection shall not exceed the lesser of $500,000 or 1 per centum of the net worth of the creditor. In determining the amount of such damages in any action, the court shall consider, among other relevant factors, the amount of any actual damages awarded, the frequency and persistence of failures of compliance by the creditor, the resources of the creditor, the number of persons adversely affected, and the extent to which the creditor's failure of compliance was intentional.

(c) Action for equitable and declaratory relief

Upon application by an aggrieved applicant, the appropriate United States district court or any other court of competent jurisdiction may grant such equitable and declaratory relief as is necessary to enforce the requirements imposed under this subchapter.

(d) Recovery of costs and attorney fees

In the case of any successful action under subsection (a), (b), or (c), the costs of the action, together with a reasonable attorney's fee as determined by the court, shall be added to any damages awarded by the court under such subsection.

(e) Good faith compliance with rule, regulation, or interpretation of Bureau or interpretation or approval by an official or employee of Bureau of Consumer Financial Protection duly authorized by Bureau

No provision of this subchapter imposing liability shall apply to any act done or omitted in good faith in conformity with any official rule, regulation, or interpretation thereof by the Bureau or in conformity with any interpretation or approval by an official or employee of the Bureau of Consumer Financial Protection duly authorized by the Bureau to issue such interpretations or approvals under such procedures as the Bureau may prescribe therefor, notwithstanding that after such act or omission has occurred, such rule, regulation, interpretation, or approval is amended, rescinded, or determined by judicial or other authority to be invalid for any reason.

(f) Jurisdiction of courts; time for maintenance of action; exceptions

Any action under this section may be brought in the appropriate United States district court without regard to the amount in controversy, or in any other court of competent jurisdiction. No such action shall be brought later than 5 years after the date of the occurrence of the violation, except that—

(1) whenever any agency having responsibility for administrative enforcement under section 1691c of this title commences an enforcement proceeding within 5 years after the date of the occurrence of the violation,

(2) whenever the Attorney General commences a civil action under this section within 5 years after the date of the occurrence of the violation,

then any applicant who has been a victim of the discrimination which is the subject of such proceeding or civil action may bring an action under this section not later than one year after the commencement of that proceeding or action.

(g) Request by responsible enforcement agency to Attorney General for civil action

The agencies having responsibility for administrative enforcement under section 1691c of this title, if unable to obtain compliance with section 1691 of this title, are authorized to refer the matter to the Attorney General with a recommendation that an appropriate civil action be instituted. Each agency referred to in paragraphs (1), (2), and (9) of section 1691c(a) of this title shall refer the matter to the Attorney General whenever the agency has reason to believe that 1 or more creditors has engaged in a pattern or practice of discouraging or denying applications for credit in violation of section 1691(a) of this title. Each such agency may refer the matter to the Attorney General whenever the agency has reason to believe that 1 or more creditors has violated section 1691(a) of this title.

(h) Authority for Attorney General to bring civil action; jurisdiction

When a matter is referred to the Attorney General pursuant to subsection (g), or whenever he has reason to believe that one or more creditors are engaged in a pattern or practice in violation of this subchapter, the Attorney General may bring a civil action in any appropriate United States district court for such relief as may be appropriate, including actual and punitive damages and injunctive relief.

(i) Recovery under both subchapter and fair housing enforcement provisions prohibited for violation based on same transaction

No person aggrieved by a violation of this subchapter and by a violation of section 3605 of title 42 shall recover under this subchapter and section 3612 [1] of title 42, if such violation is based on the same transaction.

(j) Discovery of creditor's granting standards

Nothing in this subchapter shall be construed to prohibit the discovery of a creditor's credit granting standards under appropriate discovery procedures in the court or agency in which an action or proceeding is brought.

(k) Notice to HUD of violations

Whenever an agency referred to in paragraph (1), (2), or (3) [1] of section 1691c(a) of this title—

(1) has reason to believe, as a result of receiving a consumer complaint, conducting a consumer compliance examination, or otherwise, that a violation of this subchapter has occurred;

(2) has reason to believe that the alleged violation would be a violation of the Fair Housing Act [42 U.S.C. 3601 et seq.]; and

(3) does not refer the matter to the Attorney General pursuant to subsection (g),

the agency shall notify the Secretary of Housing and Urban Development of the violation, and shall notify the applicant that the Secretary of Housing and Urban Development has been notified of the alleged violation and that remedies for the violation may be available under the Fair Housing Act.

(Pub. L. 90–321, title VII, §706, as added Pub. L. 93–495, title V, §503, Oct. 28, 1974, 88 Stat. 1524; amended Pub. L. 94–239, §6, Mar. 23, 1976, 90 Stat. 253; Pub. L. 102–242, title II, §223(a)–(c), Dec. 19, 1991, 105 Stat. 2306; Pub. L. 111–203, title X, §1085(1), (5)–(7), July 21, 2010, 124 Stat. 2083, 2085.)

EDITORIAL NOTES

REFERENCES IN TEXT

Section 3612 of title 42, referred to in subsec. (i), which related to enforcement of the Fair Housing Act (42 U.S.C. 3601 et seq.) by private persons, was repealed by Pub. L. 100–430, §8(2), Sept. 13, 1988, 102 Stat. 1625. See section 3613 of Title 42, The Public Health and Welfare.

Paragraph (1), (2), or (3) of section 1691c(a) of this title, referred to in subsec. (k), probably means par. (1), (2), or (3) of section 1691c(a) of this title prior to repeal of pars. (1) and (2), enactment of new pars. (1) and (9), and redesignation of par. (3) as (2) by Pub. L. 111–203, title X, §1085(4)(A)(ii)–(vi), July 21, 2010, 124 Stat. 2084.

The Fair Housing Act, referred to in subsec. (k), is title VIII of Pub. L. 90–284, Apr. 11, 1968, 82 Stat. 81, which is classified principally to subchapter I (§3601 et seq.) of chapter 45 of Title 42. For complete classification of this Act to the Code, see Short Title note set out under section 3601 of Title 42 and Tables.

AMENDMENTS

2010—Subsec. (e). Pub. L. 111–203, §1085(5)(B), substituted "Bureau of Consumer Financial Protection" for "Federal Reserve System" in text.

Pub. L. 111–203, §1085(5)(A), which directed amendment of "subsection heading" by substituting "Bureau" for "Board" wherever appearing and "Bureau of Consumer Financial Protection" for "Federal Reserve System", was executed by making the substitutions in heading that had been supplied editorially, to reflect the probable intent of Congress.

Pub. L. 111–203, §1085(1), substituted "Bureau" for "Board" wherever appearing.

Subsec. (f). Pub. L. 111–203, §1085(7), substituted "5 years after" for "two years from" wherever appearing.

Subsec. (g). Pub. L. 111–203, §1085(6), substituted "(9)" for "(3)".

1991—Subsec. (g). Pub. L. 102–242, §223(a), inserted at end "Each agency referred to in paragraphs (1), (2), and (3) of section 1691c(a) of this title shall refer the matter to the Attorney General whenever the agency has reason to believe that 1 or more creditors has engaged in a pattern or practice of discouraging or denying applications for credit in violation of section 1691(a) of this title. Each such agency may refer the matter to the Attorney General whenever the agency has reason to believe that 1 or more creditors has violated section 1691(a) of this title."

Subsec. (h). Pub. L. 102–242, §223(b), inserted "actual and punitive damages and" after "be appropriate, including".

Subsec. (k). Pub. L. 102–242, §223(c), added subsec. (k).

1976—Subsec. (a). Pub. L. 94–239 substituted reference to member for reference to representative.

Subsec. (b). Pub. L. 94–239 inserted provisions exempting government or governmental subdivision or agency from requirements of this subchapter, incorporated provisions contained in former subsec. (c) relating to recovery in class actions and, as incorporated, raised the total amount of recovery under a class action from $100,000 to $500,000.

Subsec. (c). Pub. L. 94–239 redesignated subsec. (d) as (c) and specified United States district court or other court of competent jurisdiction as court in which to bring action, and substituted provisions authorizing such court to grant equitable and declaratory relief, for provisions authorizing civil actions for preventive relief. Provisions of former subsec. (c) were incorporated into present subsec. (b) and amended.

Subsec. (d). Pub. L. 94–239 redesignated subsec. (e) as (d) and made minor changes in phraseology. Former subsec. (d) redesignated (c) and amended.

Subsec. (e). Pub. L. 94–239 redesignated subsec. (f) as (e) and inserted reference to officially promulgated rule, regulation, or interpretation and provisions relating to approval and interpretations by an official or employee of the Federal Reserve System duly authorized by the Board. Former subsec. (e) redesignated (d) and amended.

Subsec. (f). Pub. L. 94–239 redesignated subsec. (g) as (f) and inserted provisions which substituted a two year limitation for one year limitation and provisions extending time in which to bring action under enumerated conditions. Former subsec. (f) redesignated (e) and amended.

Subsecs. (g) to (j). Pub. L. 94–239 added subsecs. (g) to (j). Former subsec. (g) redesignated (f) and amended.

STATUTORY NOTES AND RELATED SUBSIDIARIES

EFFECTIVE DATE OF 2010 AMENDMENT

Amendment by Pub. L. 111–203 effective on the designated transfer date, see section 1100H of Pub. L. 111–203, set out as a note under section 552a of Title 5, Government Organization and Employees.

EFFECTIVE DATE OF 1976 AMENDMENT

Amendment by Pub. L. 94–239 effective Mar. 23, 1976, see section 708 of Pub. L. 90–321, set out as an Effective Date note under section 1691 of this title.

[1] *See References in Text note below.*

§1691f. Annual reports to Congress; contents

Each year, the Bureau and the Attorney General shall, respectively, make reports to the Congress concerning the administration of their functions under this subchapter, including such recommendations as the Bureau and the Attorney General, respectively, deem necessary or appropriate. In addition, each report of the Bureau shall include its assessment of the extent to which compliance with the requirements of this subchapter is being achieved, and a summary of the enforcement actions taken by each of the agencies assigned administrative enforcement responsibilities under section 1691c of this title.

(Pub. L. 90–321, title VII, §707, as added Pub. L. 94–239, §7, Mar. 23, 1976, 90 Stat. 255; amended Pub. L. 96–221, title VI, §610(c), Mar. 31, 1980, 94 Stat. 174; Pub. L. 111–203, title X, §1085(1), July 21, 2010, 124 Stat. 2083.)

EDITORIAL NOTES

AMENDMENTS

2010—Pub. L. 111–203 substituted "Bureau" for "Board" wherever appearing.
1980—Pub. L. 96–221 substituted "Each year" for "Not later than February 1 of each year after 1976".

STATUTORY NOTES AND RELATED SUBSIDIARIES

EFFECTIVE DATE OF 2010 AMENDMENT

Amendment by Pub. L. 111–203 effective on the designated transfer date, see section 1100H of Pub. L. 111–203, set out as a note under section 552a of Title 5, Government Organization and Employees.

EFFECTIVE DATE OF 1980 AMENDMENT

Amendment by Pub. L. 96–221 effective on expiration of two years and six months after Mar. 31, 1980, with all regulations, forms, and clauses required to be prescribed to be promulgated at least one year prior to such effective date, and allowing any creditor to comply with any amendments, in accordance with the regulations, forms, and clauses prescribed by the Board prior to such effective date, see section 625 of Pub. L. 96–221, set out as a note under section 1602 of this title.

EFFECTIVE DATE

Section effective Mar. 23, 1976, see section 708 of Pub. L. 90–321, set out as a note under section 1691 of this title.

This marks the end of the Equal Credit opportunity Act
15 U.S.C. §§ 1691–1691f

FAIR DEBT COLLECTION PRACTICES ACT

15 U.S.C. §§ 1692-1692p, as amended

The FTC enforces the Fair Debt Collection Practices Act ("FDCPA"), which prohibits deceptive, unfair, and abusive debt collection practices. Among other things, the FDCPA bars collectors from using obscene or profane language, threatening violence, calling consumers repeatedly or at unreasonable hours, misrepresenting a consumer's legal rights, disclosing a consumer's personal affairs to third parties, and obtaining information about a consumer through false pretenses. Because certain practices that violate the FDCPA also violate the FTC Act, the FTC also uses the FTC Act to halt unfair or deceptive debt collection practices.

Subchapter V, Debt Collection Practices

SUBCHAPTER V—DEBT COLLECTION PRACTICES

§1692. Congressional findings and declaration of purpose

(a) Abusive practices

There is abundant evidence of the use of abusive, deceptive, and unfair debt collection practices by many debt collectors. Abusive debt collection practices contribute to the number of personal bankruptcies, to marital instability, to the loss of jobs, and to invasions of individual privacy.

(b) Inadequacy of laws

Existing laws and procedures for redressing these injuries are inadequate to protect consumers.

(c) Available non-abusive collection methods

Means other than misrepresentation or other abusive debt collection practices are available for the effective collection of debts.

(d) Interstate commerce

Abusive debt collection practices are carried on to a substantial extent in interstate commerce and through means and instrumentalities of such commerce. Even where abusive debt collection practices are purely intrastate in character, they nevertheless directly affect interstate commerce.

(e) Purposes

It is the purpose of this subchapter to eliminate abusive debt collection practices by debt collectors, to insure that those debt collectors who refrain from using abusive debt collection practices are not competitively disadvantaged, and to promote consistent State action to protect consumers against debt collection abuses.

(Pub. L. 90–321, title VIII, §802, as added Pub. L. 95–109, Sept. 20, 1977, 91 Stat. 874.)

STATUTORY NOTES AND RELATED SUBSIDIARIES

EFFECTIVE DATE

Pub. L. 90–321, title VIII, §819, formerly §818, as added by Pub. L. 95–109, Sept. 20, 1977, 91 Stat. 883, §818; renumbered §819, Pub. L. 109–351, title VIII, §801(a)(1), Oct. 13, 2006, 120 Stat. 2004, provided that: "This title [enacting this subchapter] takes effect upon the expiration of six months after the date of its enactment [Sept. 20, 1977], but section 809 [section 1692g of this title] shall apply only with respect to debts for which the initial attempt to collect occurs after such effective date."

SHORT TITLE

This subchapter known as the "Fair Debt Collection Practices Act", see Short Title note set out under section 1601 of this title.

§1692a. Definitions

As used in this subchapter—
    (1) The term "Bureau" means the Bureau of Consumer Financial Protection.
    (2) The term "communication" means the conveying of information regarding a debt directly or indirectly to any person through any medium.
    (3) The term "consumer" means any natural person obligated or allegedly obligated to pay any debt.
    (4) The term "creditor" means any person who offers or extends credit creating a debt or to whom a debt is owed, but such term does not include any person to the extent that he receives an assignment or transfer of a debt in default solely for the purpose of facilitating collection of such debt for another.
    (5) The term "debt" means any obligation or alleged obligation of a consumer to pay money arising out of a transaction in which the money, property, insurance, or services which are the subject of the transaction are primarily

for personal, family, or household purposes, whether or not such obligation has been reduced to judgment.

(6) The term "debt collector" means any person who uses any instrumentality of interstate commerce or the mails in any business the principal purpose of which is the collection of any debts, or who regularly collects or attempts to collect, directly or indirectly, debts owed or due or asserted to be owed or due another. Notwithstanding the exclusion provided by clause (F) of the last sentence of this paragraph, the term includes any creditor who, in the process of collecting his own debts, uses any name other than his own which would indicate that a third person is collecting or attempting to collect such debts. For the purpose of section 1692f(6) of this title, such term also includes any person who uses any instrumentality of interstate commerce or the mails in any business the principal purpose of which is the enforcement of security interests. The term does not include—

(A) any officer or employee of a creditor while, in the name of the creditor, collecting debts for such creditor;

(B) any person while acting as a debt collector for another person, both of whom are related by common ownership or affiliated by corporate control, if the person acting as a debt collector does so only for persons to whom it is so related or affiliated and if the principal business of such person is not the collection of debts;

(C) any officer or employee of the United States or any State to the extent that collecting or attempting to collect any debt is in the performance of his official duties;

(D) any person while serving or attempting to serve legal process on any other person in connection with the judicial enforcement of any debt;

(E) any nonprofit organization which, at the request of consumers, performs bona fide consumer credit counseling and assists consumers in the liquidation of their debts by receiving payments from such consumers and distributing such amounts to creditors; and

(F) any person collecting or attempting to collect any debt owed or due or asserted to be owed or due another to the extent such activity (i) is incidental to a bona fide fiduciary obligation or a bona fide escrow arrangement; (ii) concerns a debt which was originated by such person; (iii) concerns a debt which was not in default at the time it was obtained by such person; or (iv) concerns a debt obtained by such person as a secured party in a commercial credit transaction involving the creditor.

(7) The term "location information" means a consumer's place of abode and his telephone number at such place, or his place of employment.

(8) The term "State" means any State, territory, or possession of the United States, the District of Columbia, the Commonwealth of Puerto Rico, or any political subdivision of any of the foregoing.

(Pub. L. 90–321, title VIII, §803, as added Pub. L. 95–109, Sept. 20, 1977, 91 Stat. 875; amended Pub. L. 99–361, July 9, 1986, 100 Stat. 768; Pub. L. 111–203, title X, §1089(2), July 21, 2010, 124 Stat. 2092.)

EDITORIAL NOTES

AMENDMENTS

2010—Par. (1). Pub. L. 111–203 added par. (1) and struck out former par. (1) which read as follows: "The term 'Commission' means the Federal Trade Commission."

1986—Par. (6). Pub. L. 99–361 in provision preceding cl. (A) substituted "clause (F)" for "clause (G)", struck out cl. (F) which excluded any attorney-at-law collecting a debt as an attorney on behalf of and in the name of a client from term "debt collector", and redesignated cl. (G) as (F).

STATUTORY NOTES AND RELATED SUBSIDIARIES

EFFECTIVE DATE OF 2010 AMENDMENT

Amendment by Pub. L. 111–203 effective on the designated transfer date, see section 1100H of Pub. L. 111–203, set out as a note under section 552a of Title 5, Government Organization and Employees.

EFFECTIVE DATE

Section effective upon the expiration of six months after Sept. 20, 1977, see section 819 of Pub. L. 90–321, as added by Pub. L. 95–109, set out as a note under section 1692 of this title.

§1692b. Acquisition of location information

Any debt collector communicating with any person other than the consumer for the purpose of acquiring location information about the consumer shall—

(1) identify himself, state that he is confirming or correcting location information concerning the consumer, and, only if expressly requested, identify his employer;

(2) not state that such consumer owes any debt;

(3) not communicate with any such person more than once unless requested to do so by such person or unless the debt collector reasonably believes that the earlier response of such person is erroneous or incomplete and that such person now has correct or complete location information;

(4) not communicate by post card;

(5) not use any language or symbol on any envelope or in the contents of any communication effected by the mails or telegram that indicates that the debt collector is in the debt collection business or that the communication relates to the collection of a debt; and

(6) after the debt collector knows the consumer is represented by an attorney with regard to the subject debt and has knowledge of, or can readily ascertain, such attorney's name and address, not communicate with any person other than that attorney, unless the attorney fails to respond within a reasonable period of time to communication from the debt collector.

(Pub. L. 90–321, title VIII, §804, as added Pub. L. 95–109, Sept. 20, 1977, 91 Stat. 876.)

STATUTORY NOTES AND RELATED SUBSIDIARIES

EFFECTIVE DATE

Section effective upon the expiration of six months after Sept. 20, 1977, see section 819 of Pub. L. 90–321, as added by Pub. L. 95–109, set out as a note under section 1692 of this title.

§1692c. Communication in connection with debt collection

(a) Communication with the consumer generally

Without the prior consent of the consumer given directly to the debt collector or the express permission of a court of competent jurisdiction, a debt collector may not communicate with a consumer in connection with the collection of any debt—

(1) at any unusual time or place or a time or place known or which should be known to be inconvenient to the consumer. In the absence of knowledge of circumstances to the contrary, a debt collector shall assume that the convenient time for communicating with a consumer is after 8 o'clock antemeridian and before 9 o'clock postmeridian, local time at the consumer's location;

(2) if the debt collector knows the consumer is represented by an attorney with respect to such debt and has knowledge of, or can readily ascertain, such attorney's name and address, unless the attorney fails to respond within a reasonable period of time to a communication from the debt collector or unless the attorney consents to direct communication with the consumer; or

(3) at the consumer's place of employment if the debt collector knows or has reason to know that the consumer's employer prohibits the consumer from receiving such communication.

(b) Communication with third parties

Except as provided in section 1692b of this title, without the prior consent of the consumer given directly to the debt collector, or the express permission of a court of competent jurisdiction, or as reasonably necessary to effectuate a postjudgment judicial remedy, a debt collector may not communicate, in connection with the collection of any debt, with any person other than the consumer, his attorney, a consumer reporting agency if otherwise permitted by law, the creditor, the attorney of the creditor, or the attorney of the debt collector.

(c) Ceasing communication

If a consumer notifies a debt collector in writing that the consumer refuses to pay a debt or that the consumer wishes the debt collector to cease further communication with the consumer, the debt collector shall not communicate further with the consumer with respect to such debt, except—

(1) to advise the consumer that the debt collector's further efforts are being terminated;

(2) to notify the consumer that the debt collector or creditor may invoke specified remedies which are ordinarily invoked by such debt collector or creditor; or

(3) where applicable, to notify the consumer that the debt collector or creditor intends to invoke a specified remedy.

If such notice from the consumer is made by mail, notification shall be complete upon receipt.

(d) "Consumer" defined

For the purpose of this section, the term "consumer" includes the consumer's spouse, parent (if the consumer is a minor), guardian, executor, or administrator.

(Pub. L. 90–321, title VIII, §805, as added Pub. L. 95–109, Sept. 20, 1977, 91 Stat. 876.)

STATUTORY NOTES AND RELATED SUBSIDIARIES

Section effective upon the expiration of six months after Sept. 20, 1977, see section 819 of Pub. L. 90–321, as added by Pub. L. 95–109, set out as a note under section 1692 of this title.

§1692d. Harassment or abuse

A debt collector may not engage in any conduct the natural consequence of which is to harass, oppress, or abuse any person in connection with the collection of a debt. Without limiting the general application of the foregoing, the following conduct is a violation of this section:

(1) The use or threat of use of violence or other criminal means to harm the physical person, reputation, or property of any person.

(2) The use of obscene or profane language or language the natural consequence of which is to abuse the hearer or reader.

(3) The publication of a list of consumers who allegedly refuse to pay debts, except to a consumer reporting agency or to persons meeting the requirements of section 1681a(f) or 1681b(3) [1] of this title.

(4) The advertisement for sale of any debt to coerce payment of the debt.

(5) Causing a telephone to ring or engaging any person in telephone conversation repeatedly or continuously with intent to annoy, abuse, or harass any person at the called number.

(6) Except as provided in section 1692b of this title, the placement of telephone calls without meaningful disclosure of the caller's identity.

(Pub. L. 90–321, title VIII, §806, as added Pub. L. 95–109, Sept. 20, 1977, 91 Stat. 877.)

EDITORIAL NOTES

REFERENCES IN TEXT

Section 1681b(3) of this title, referred to in par. (3), was redesignated section 1681b(a)(3) of this title by Pub. L. 104–208, div. A, title II, §2403(a)(1), Sept. 30, 1996, 110 Stat. 3009–430.

STATUTORY NOTES AND RELATED SUBSIDIARIES

EFFECTIVE DATE

Section effective upon the expiration of six months after Sept. 20, 1977, see section 819 of Pub. L. 90–321, as added by Pub. L. 95–109, set out as a note under section 1692 of this title.

[1] See References in Text note below.

§1692e. False or misleading representations

A debt collector may not use any false, deceptive, or misleading representation or means in connection with the collection of any debt. Without limiting the general application of the foregoing, the following conduct is a violation of this section:

(1) The false representation or implication that the debt collector is vouched for, bonded by, or affiliated with the United States or any State, including the use of any badge, uniform, or facsimile thereof.

(2) The false representation of—

(A) the character, amount, or legal status of any debt; or

(B) any services rendered or compensation which may be lawfully received by any debt collector for the collection of a debt.

(3) The false representation or implication that any individual is an attorney or that any communication is from an attorney.

(4) The representation or implication that nonpayment of any debt will result in the arrest or imprisonment of any person or the seizure, garnishment, attachment, or sale of any property or wages of any person unless such action is lawful and the debt collector or creditor intends to take such action.

(5) The threat to take any action that cannot legally be taken or that is not intended to be taken.

(6) The false representation or implication that a sale, referral, or other transfer of any interest in a debt shall cause the consumer to—

(A) lose any claim or defense to payment of the debt; or

(B) become subject to any practice prohibited by this subchapter.

(7) The false representation or implication that the consumer committed any crime or other conduct in order to disgrace the consumer.

(8) Communicating or threatening to communicate to any person credit information which is known or which should be known to be false, including the failure to communicate that a disputed debt is disputed.

(9) The use or distribution of any written communication which simulates or is falsely represented to be a document authorized, issued, or approved by any court, official, or agency of the United States or any State, or which creates a false impression as to its source, authorization, or approval.

(10) The use of any false representation or deceptive means to collect or attempt to collect any debt or to obtain information concerning a consumer.

(11) The failure to disclose in the initial written communication with the consumer and, in addition, if the initial communication with the consumer is oral, in that initial oral communication, that the debt collector is attempting to collect a debt and that any information obtained will be used for that purpose, and the failure to disclose in subsequent communications that the communication is from a debt collector, except that this paragraph shall not apply to a formal pleading made in connection with a legal action.

(12) The false representation or implication that accounts have been turned over to innocent purchasers for value.

(13) The false representation or implication that documents are legal process.

(14) The use of any business, company, or organization name other than the true name of the debt collector's business, company, or organization.

(15) The false representation or implication that documents are not legal process forms or do not require action by the consumer.

(16) The false representation or implication that a debt collector operates or is employed by a consumer reporting agency as defined by section 1681a(f) of this title.

(Pub. L. 90–321, title VIII, §807, as added Pub. L. 95–109, Sept. 20, 1977, 91 Stat. 877; amended Pub. L. 104–208, div. A, title II, §2305(a), Sept. 30, 1996, 110 Stat. 3009–425.)

EDITORIAL NOTES

AMENDMENTS

1996—Par. (11). Pub. L. 104–208 amended par. (11) generally. Prior to amendment, par. (11) read as follows: "Except as otherwise provided for communications to acquire location information under section 1692b of this title, the failure to disclose clearly in all communications made to collect a debt or to obtain information about a consumer, that the debt collector is attempting to collect a debt and that any information obtained will be used for that purpose."

STATUTORY NOTES AND RELATED SUBSIDIARIES

EFFECTIVE DATE OF 1996 AMENDMENT

Pub. L. 104–208, div. A, title II, §2305(b), Sept. 30, 1996, 110 Stat. 3009–425, provided that: "The amendment made by subsection (a) [amending this section] shall take effect 90 days after the date of enactment of this Act [Sept. 30, 1996] and shall apply to all communications made after that date of enactment."

EFFECTIVE DATE

Section effective upon the expiration of six months after Sept. 20, 1977, see section 819 of Pub. L. 90–321, as added by Pub. L. 95–109, set out as a note under section 1692 of this title.

§1692f. Unfair practices

A debt collector may not use unfair or unconscionable means to collect or attempt to collect any debt. Without limiting the general application of the foregoing, the following conduct is a violation of this section:

(1) The collection of any amount (including any interest, fee, charge, or expense incidental to the principal obligation) unless such amount is expressly authorized by the agreement creating the debt or permitted by law.

(2) The acceptance by a debt collector from any person of a check or other payment instrument postdated by more than five days unless such person is notified in writing of the debt collector's intent to deposit such check or instrument not more than ten nor less than three business days prior to such deposit.

(3) The solicitation by a debt collector of any postdated check or other postdated payment instrument for the purpose of threatening or instituting criminal prosecution.

(4) Depositing or threatening to deposit any postdated check or other postdated payment instrument prior to the date on such check or instrument.

(5) Causing charges to be made to any person for communications by concealment of the true purpose of the communication. Such charges include, but are not limited to, collect telephone calls and telegram fees.

(6) Taking or threatening to take any nonjudicial action to effect dispossession or disablement of property if—

(A) there is no present right to possession of the property claimed as collateral through an enforceable security interest;

(B) there is no present intention to take possession of the property; or

(C) the property is exempt by law from such dispossession or disablement.

(7) Communicating with a consumer regarding a debt by post card.

(8) Using any language or symbol, other than the debt collector's address, on any envelope when communicating with a consumer by use of the mails or by telegram, except that a debt collector may use his business name if such name does not indicate that he is in the debt collection business.

(Pub. L. 90–321, title VIII, §808, as added Pub. L. 95–109, Sept. 20, 1977, 91 Stat. 879.)

STATUTORY NOTES AND RELATED SUBSIDIARIES

EFFECTIVE DATE

Section effective upon the expiration of six months after Sept. 20, 1977, see section 819 of Pub. L. 90–321, as added by Pub. L. 95–109, set out as a note under section 1692 of this title.

§1692g. Validation of debts

(a) Notice of debt; contents

Within five days after the initial communication with a consumer in connection with the collection of any debt, a debt collector shall, unless the following information is contained in the initial communication or the consumer has paid the debt, send the consumer a written notice containing—

(1) the amount of the debt;

(2) the name of the creditor to whom the debt is owed;

(3) a statement that unless the consumer, within thirty days after receipt of the notice, disputes the validity of the debt, or any portion thereof, the debt will be assumed to be valid by the debt collector;

(4) a statement that if the consumer notifies the debt collector in writing within the thirty-day period that the debt, or any portion thereof, is disputed, the debt collector will obtain verification of the debt or a copy of a judgment against the consumer and a copy of such verification or judgment will be mailed to the consumer by the debt collector; and

(5) a statement that, upon the consumer's written request within the thirty-day period, the debt collector will provide the consumer with the name and address of the original creditor, if different from the current creditor.

(b) Disputed debts

If the consumer notifies the debt collector in writing within the thirty-day period described in subsection (a) that the debt, or any portion thereof, is disputed, or that the consumer requests the name and address of the original creditor, the debt collector shall cease collection of the debt, or any disputed portion thereof, until the debt collector obtains verification of the debt or a copy of a judgment, or the name and address of the original creditor, and a copy of such verification or judgment, or name and address of the original creditor, is mailed to the consumer by the debt collector. Collection activities and communications that do not otherwise violate this subchapter may continue during the 30-day period referred to in subsection (a) unless the consumer has notified the debt collector in writing that the debt, or any portion of the debt, is disputed or that the consumer requests the name and address of the original creditor. Any collection activities and communication during the 30-day period may not overshadow or be inconsistent with the disclosure of the consumer's right to dispute the debt or request the name and address of the original creditor.

(c) Admission of liability

The failure of a consumer to dispute the validity of a debt under this section may not be construed by any court as an admission of liability by the consumer.

(d) Legal pleadings

A communication in the form of a formal pleading in a civil action shall not be treated as an initial communication for purposes of subsection (a).

(e) Notice provisions

The sending or delivery of any form or notice which does not relate to the collection of a debt and is expressly required by title 26, title V of Gramm-Leach-Bliley Act [15 U.S.C. 6801 et seq.], or any provision of Federal or State law relating to notice of data security breach or privacy, or any regulation prescribed under any such provision of law, shall not be treated as an initial communication in connection with debt collection for purposes of this section.

(Pub. L. 90–321, title VIII, §809, as added Pub. L. 95–109, Sept. 20, 1977, 91 Stat. 879; amended Pub. L. 109–351, title VIII, §802, Oct. 13, 2006, 120 Stat. 2006.)

REFERENCES IN TEXT

The Gramm-Leach-Bliley Act, referred to in subsec. (e), is Pub. L. 106–102, Nov. 12, 1999, 113 Stat. 1338. Title V of the Act is classified principally to chapter 94 (§ 6801 et seq.) of this title. For complete classification of this Act to the Code, see Short Title of 1999 Amendment note set out under section 1811 of Title 12, Banks and Banking, and Tables.

AMENDMENTS

2006—Subsec. (b). Pub. L. 109–351, §802(c), inserted at end "Collection activities and communications that do not otherwise violate this subchapter may continue during the 30-day period referred to in subsection (a) unless the consumer has notified the debt collector in writing that the debt, or any portion of the debt, is disputed or that the consumer requests the name and address of the original creditor. Any collection activities and communication during the 30-day period may not overshadow or be inconsistent with the disclosure of the consumer's right to dispute the debt or request the name and address of the original creditor."

Subsec. (d). Pub. L. 109–351, §802(a), added subsec. (d).

Subsec. (e). Pub. L. 109–351, §802(b), added subsec. (e).

STATUTORY NOTES AND RELATED SUBSIDIARIES

EFFECTIVE DATE

Section applicable only with respect to debts for which the initial attempt to collect occurs after the effective date of this subchapter, which takes effect upon the expiration of six months after Sept. 20, 1977, see section 819 of Pub. L. 90–321, as added by Pub. L. 95–109, set out as a note under section 1692 of this title.

§1692h. Multiple debts

If any consumer owes multiple debts and makes any single payment to any debt collector with respect to such debts, such debt collector may not apply such payment to any debt which is disputed by the consumer and, where applicable, shall apply such payment in accordance with the consumer's directions.

(Pub. L. 90–321, title VIII, §810, as added Pub. L. 95–109, Sept. 20, 1977, 91 Stat. 880.)

STATUTORY NOTES AND RELATED SUBSIDIARIES

EFFECTIVE DATE

Section effective upon the expiration of six months after Sept. 20, 1977, see section 819 of Pub. L. 90–321, as added by Pub. L. 95–109, set out as a note under section 1692 of this title.

§1692i. Legal actions by debt collectors

(a) Venue

Any debt collector who brings any legal action on a debt against any consumer shall—

(1) in the case of an action to enforce an interest in real property securing the consumer's obligation, bring such action only in a judicial district or similar legal entity in which such real property is located; or

(2) in the case of an action not described in paragraph (1), bring such action only in the judicial district or similar legal entity—

(A) in which such consumer signed the contract sued upon; or

(B) in which such consumer resides at the commencement of the action.

(b) Authorization of actions

Nothing in this subchapter shall be construed to authorize the bringing of legal actions by debt collectors.

(Pub. L. 90–321, title VIII, §811, as added Pub. L. 95–109, Sept. 20, 1977, 91 Stat. 880.)

EFFECTIVE DATE

Section effective upon the expiration of six months after Sept. 20, 1977, see section 819 of Pub. L. 90–321, as added by Pub. L. 95–109, set out as a note under section 1692 of this title.

§1692j. Furnishing certain deceptive forms

(a) It is unlawful to design, compile, and furnish any form knowing that such form would be used to create the false belief in a consumer that a person other than the creditor of such consumer is participating in the collection of or in an attempt to collect a debt such consumer allegedly owes such creditor, when in fact such person is not so participating.

(b) Any person who violates this section shall be liable to the same extent and in the same manner as a debt collector is liable under section 1692k of this title for failure to comply with a provision of this subchapter.

(Pub. L. 90–321, title VIII, §812, as added Pub. L. 95–109, Sept. 20, 1977, 91 Stat. 880.)

EFFECTIVE DATE

Section effective upon the expiration of six months after Sept. 20, 1977, see section 819 of Pub. L. 90–321, as added by Pub. L. 95–109, set out as a note under section 1692 of this title.

§1692k. Civil liability

(a) Amount of damages

Except as otherwise provided by this section, any debt collector who fails to comply with any provision of this subchapter with respect to any person is liable to such person in an amount equal to the sum of—

(1) any actual damage sustained by such person as a result of such failure;

(2)(A) in the case of any action by an individual, such additional damages as the court may allow, but not exceeding $1,000; or

(B) in the case of a class action, (i) such amount for each named plaintiff as could be recovered under subparagraph (A), and (ii) such amount as the court may allow for all other class members, without regard to a minimum individual recovery, not to exceed the lesser of $500,000 or 1 per centum of the net worth of the debt collector; and

(3) in the case of any successful action to enforce the foregoing liability, the costs of the action, together with a reasonable attorney's fee as determined by the court. On a finding by the court that an action under this section was brought in bad faith and for the purpose of harassment, the court may award to the defendant attorney's fees reasonable in relation to the work expended and costs.

(b) Factors considered by court

In determining the amount of liability in any action under subsection (a), the court shall consider, among other relevant factors—

(1) in any individual action under subsection (a)(2)(A), the frequency and persistence of noncompliance by the debt collector, the nature of such noncompliance, and the extent to which such noncompliance was intentional; or

(2) in any class action under subsection (a)(2)(B), the frequency and persistence of noncompliance by the debt collector, the nature of such noncompliance, the resources of the debt collector, the number of persons adversely affected, and the extent to which the debt collector's noncompliance was intentional.

(c) Intent

A debt collector may not be held liable in any action brought under this subchapter if the debt collector shows by a preponderance of evidence that the violation was not intentional and resulted from a bona fide error notwithstanding the maintenance of procedures reasonably adapted to avoid any such error.

(d) Jurisdiction

An action to enforce any liability created by this subchapter may be brought in any appropriate United States district court without regard to the amount in controversy, or in any other court of competent jurisdiction, within one year from the date on which the violation occurs.

(e) Advisory opinions of Bureau

No provision of this section imposing any liability shall apply to any act done or omitted in good faith in conformity with any advisory opinion of the Bureau, notwithstanding that after such act or omission has occurred, such opinion is amended, rescinded, or determined by judicial or other authority to be invalid for any reason.

(Pub. L. 90–321, title VIII, §813, as added Pub. L. 95–109, Sept. 20, 1977, 91 Stat. 881; amended Pub. L. 111–203, title X, §1089(1), July 21, 2010, 124 Stat. 2092.)

EDITORIAL NOTES

AMENDMENTS

2010—Subsec. (e). Pub. L. 111–203 substituted "Bureau" for "Commission".

STATUTORY NOTES AND RELATED SUBSIDIARIES

EFFECTIVE DATE OF 2010 AMENDMENT

Amendment by Pub. L. 111–203 effective on the designated transfer date, see section 1100H of Pub. L. 111–203, set out as a note under section 552a of Title 5, Government Organization and Employees.

EFFECTIVE DATE

Section effective upon the expiration of six months after Sept. 20, 1977, see section 819 of Pub. L. 90–321, as added by Pub. L. 95–109, set out as a note under section 1692 of this title.

§1692*l*. Administrative enforcement

(a) Federal Trade Commission

The Federal Trade Commission shall be authorized to enforce compliance with this subchapter, except to the extent that enforcement of the requirements imposed under this subchapter is specifically committed to another Government agency under any of paragraphs (1) through (5) of subsection (b), subject to subtitle B of the Consumer Financial Protection Act of 2010 [12 U.S.C. 5511 et seq.]. For purpose of the exercise by the Federal Trade Commission of its functions and powers under the Federal Trade Commission Act (15 U.S.C. 41 et seq.), a violation of this subchapter shall be deemed an unfair or deceptive act or practice in violation of that Act. All of the functions and powers of the Federal Trade Commission under the Federal Trade Commission Act are available to the Federal Trade Commission to enforce compliance by any person with this subchapter, irrespective of whether that person is engaged in commerce or meets any other jurisdictional tests under the Federal Trade Commission Act, including the power to enforce the provisions of this subchapter, in the same manner as if the violation had been a violation of a Federal Trade Commission trade regulation rule.

(b) Applicable provisions of law

Subject to subtitle B of the Consumer Financial Protection Act of 2010, compliance with any requirements imposed under this subchapter shall be enforced under—

(1) section 8 of the Federal Deposit Insurance Act [12 U.S.C. 1818], by the appropriate Federal banking agency, as defined in section 3(q) of the Federal Deposit Insurance Act (12 U.S.C. 1813(q)), with respect to—

(A) national banks, Federal savings associations, and Federal branches and Federal agencies of foreign banks;

(B) member banks of the Federal Reserve System (other than national banks), branches and agencies of foreign banks (other than Federal branches, Federal agencies, and insured State branches of foreign banks), commercial lending companies owned or controlled by foreign banks, and organizations operating under section 25 or 25A of the Federal Reserve Act [12 U.S.C. 601 et seq., 611 et seq.]; and

(C) banks and State savings associations insured by the Federal Deposit Insurance Corporation (other than members of the Federal Reserve System), and insured State branches of foreign banks;

(2) the Federal Credit Union Act [12 U.S.C. 1751 et seq.], by the Administrator of the National Credit Union Administration with respect to any Federal credit union;

(3) subtitle IV of title 49, by the Secretary of Transportation, with respect to all carriers subject to the jurisdiction of the Surface Transportation Board;

(4) part A of subtitle VII of title 49, by the Secretary of Transportation with respect to any air carrier or any foreign air carrier subject to that part;

(5) the Packers and Stockyards Act, 1921 [7 U.S.C. 181 et seq.] (except as provided in section 406 of that Act [7 U.S.C. 226, 227]), by the Secretary of Agriculture with respect to any activities subject to that Act; and

(6) subtitle E of the Consumer Financial Protection Act of 2010 [12 U.S.C. 5561 et seq.], by the Bureau, with respect to any person subject to this subchapter.

The terms used in paragraph (1) that are not defined in this subchapter or otherwise defined in section 3(s) of the Federal Deposit Insurance Act (12 U.S.C. 1813(s)) shall have the meaning given to them in section 1(b) of the International Banking Act of 1978 (12 U.S.C. 3101).

(c) Agency powers

For the purpose of the exercise by any agency referred to in subsection (b) of its powers under any Act referred to in that subsection, a violation of any requirement imposed under this subchapter shall be deemed to be a violation of a requirement imposed under that Act. In addition to its powers under any provision of law specifically referred to in subsection (b), each of the agencies referred to in that subsection may exercise, for the purpose of enforcing compliance with any requirement imposed under this subchapter any other authority conferred on it by law, except as provided in subsection (d).

(d) Rules and regulations

Except as provided in section 1029(a) of the Consumer Financial Protection Act of 2010 [12 U.S.C. 5519(a)], the Bureau may prescribe rules with respect to the collection of debts by debt collectors, as defined in this subchapter.

(Pub. L. 90–321, title VIII, §814, as added Pub. L. 95–109, Sept. 20, 1977, 91 Stat. 881; amended Pub. L. 98–443, §9(n), Oct. 4, 1984, 98 Stat. 1708; Pub. L. 101–73, title VII, §744(n), Aug. 9, 1989, 103 Stat. 440; Pub. L. 102–242, title II, §212(e), Dec. 19, 1991, 105 Stat. 2301; Pub. L. 102–550, title XVI, §1604(a)(8), Oct. 28, 1992, 106 Stat. 4082; Pub. L. 104–88, title III, §316, Dec. 29, 1995, 109 Stat. 949; Pub. L. 111–203, title X, §1089(3), (4), July 21, 2010, 124 Stat. 2092, 2093.)

EDITORIAL NOTES

REFERENCES IN TEXT

The Consumer Financial Protection Act of 2010, referred to in subsecs. (a) and (b), is title X of Pub. L. 111–203, July 21, 2010, 124 Stat. 1955. Subtitles B (§§1021–1029A) and E (§§1051–1058) of the Act are classified generally to parts B (§5511 et seq.) and E (§5561 et seq.), respectively, of subchapter V of chapter 53 of Title 12, Banks and Banking. For complete classification of subtitles B and E to the Code, see Tables.

The Federal Trade Commission Act, referred to in subsec. (a), is act Sept. 26, 1914, ch. 311, 38 Stat. 717, which is classified generally to subchapter I (§41 et seq.) of chapter 2 of this title. For complete classification of this Act to the Code, see section 58 of this title and Tables.

Sections 25 and 25A of the Federal Reserve Act, referred to in subsec. (b)(1)(B), are classified to subchapters I (§601 et seq.) and II (§611 et seq.), respectively, of chapter 6 of Title 12, Banks and Banking.

The Federal Credit Union Act, referred to in subsec. (b)(2), is act June 26, 1934, ch. 750, 48 Stat. 1216, which is classified generally to chapter 14 (§1751 et seq.) of Title 12. For complete classification of this Act to the Code, see section 1751 of Title 12 and Tables.

The Packers and Stockyards Act, 1921, referred to in subsec. (b)(5), is act Aug. 15, 1921, ch. 64, 42 Stat. 159, which is classified generally to chapter 9 (§181 et seq.) of Title 7, Agriculture. For complete classification of this Act to the Code, see section 181 of Title 7 and Tables.

CODIFICATION

In subsec. (b)(3), "subtitle IV of title 49" substituted for "the Acts to regulate commerce" on authority of Pub. L. 95–473, §3(b), Oct. 17, 1978, 92 Stat. 1466, the first section of which enacted subtitle IV of Title 49, Transportation.

In subsec. (b)(4), "part A of subtitle VII of title 49" substituted for "the Federal Aviation Act of 1958 [49 App. U.S.C. 1301 et seq.]" and "that part" substituted for "that Act" on authority of Pub. L. 103–272, §6(b), July 5, 1994, 108 Stat. 1378, the first section of which enacted subtitles II, III, and V to X of Title 49.

Section 1089(4) of Pub. L. 111–203, which directed amendment "in subsection (d)" of the Fair Debt Collection Practices Act, was executed in subsec. (d) of this section, which is section 814 of the Act, to reflect the probable intent of Congress. See 2010 Amendment note below.

AMENDMENTS

2010—Subsec. (a). Pub. L. 111–203, §1089(3)(A), added subsec. (a) and struck out former subsec. (a). Prior to amendment, text read as follows: "Compliance with this subchapter shall be enforced by the Commission, except to the extent that enforcement of the requirements imposed under this subchapter is specifically committed to another agency under subsection (b) of this section. For purpose of the exercise by the Commission of its functions and powers under the Federal Trade Commission Act, a violation of this subchapter shall be deemed an unfair or deceptive act or practice in violation of that Act. All of the functions and powers of the Commission under the Federal Trade Commission Act are available to the Commission to enforce compliance by any person with this subchapter, irrespective of whether that person is engaged in commerce or meets any other jurisdictional tests in the Federal Trade Commission Act, including the power to enforce the provisions of this subchapter in the same manner as if the violation had been a violation of a Federal Trade Commission trade regulation rule."

Subsec. (b). Pub. L. 111–203, §1089(3)(B)(i), substituted "Subject to subtitle B of the Consumer Financial Protection Act of 2010, compliance" for "Compliance" in introductory provisions.

Subsec. (b)(1). Pub. L. 111–203, §1089(3)(B)(ii), added par. (1) and struck out former par. (1) which read as follows: "section 8 of the Federal Deposit Insurance Act, in the case of—

"(A) national banks, and Federal branches and Federal agencies of foreign banks, by the Office of the Comptroller of the Currency;

"(B) member banks of the Federal Reserve System (other than national banks), branches and agencies of foreign banks (other than Federal branches, Federal agencies, and insured State branches of foreign banks), commercial lending companies owned or controlled by foreign banks, and organizations operating under section 25 or 25(a) of the Federal Reserve Act, by the Board of Governors of the Federal Reserve System; and

"(C) banks insured by the Federal Deposit Insurance Corporation (other than members of the Federal Reserve System) and insured State branches of foreign banks, by the Board of Directors of the Federal Deposit Insurance Corporation;".

Subsec. (b)(2) to (6). Pub. L. 111–203, §1089(3)(B)(ii)–(vi), added par. (6), redesignated former pars. (3) to (6) as (2) to (5), respectively, and struck out former par. (2) which read as follows: "section 8 of the Federal Deposit Insurance Act, by the Director of the Office of Thrift Supervision, in the case of a savings association the deposits of which are insured by the Federal Deposit Insurance Corporation;".

Subsec. (d). Pub. L. 111–203, §1089(4), substituted "Except as provided in section 1029(a) of the Consumer Financial Protection Act of 2010, the Bureau may prescribe rules with respect to the collection of debts by debt collectors, as defined in this subchapter" for "Neither the Commission nor any other agency referred to in subsection (b) of this section may promulgate trade regulation rules or other regulations with respect to the collection of debts by debt collectors as defined in this subchapter". See Codification note above.

1995—Subsec. (b)(4). Pub. L. 104–88 substituted "Secretary of Transportation, with respect to all carriers subject to the jurisdiction of the Surface Transportation Board" for "Interstate Commerce Commission with respect to any common carrier subject to those Acts".

1992—Subsec. (b)(1)(C). Pub. L. 102–550 substituted semicolon for period at end.

1991—Subsec. (b). Pub. L. 102–242, §212(e)(2), inserted at end "The terms used in paragraph (1) that are not defined in this subchapter or otherwise defined in section 3(s) of the Federal Deposit Insurance Act (12 U.S.C. 1813(s)) shall have the meaning given to them in section 1(b) of the International Banking Act of 1978 (12 U.S.C. 3101)."

Pub. L. 102–242, §212(e)(1), added par. (1) and struck out former par. (1) which read as follows: "section 8 of Federal Deposit Insurance Act, in the case of—

"(A) national banks, by the Comptroller of the Currency;

"(B) member banks of the Federal Reserve System (other than national banks), by the Federal Reserve Board; and

"(C) banks the deposits or accounts of which are insured by the Federal Deposit Insurance Corporation (other than members of the Federal Reserve System), by the Board of Directors of the Federal Deposit Insurance Corporation;".

1989—Subsec. (b)(2). Pub. L. 101–73 amended par. (2) generally. Prior to amendment, par. (2) read as follows: "section 5(d) of the Home Owners Loan Act of 1933, section 407 of the National Housing Act, and sections 6(i) and 17 of the Federal Home Loan Bank Act, by the Federal Home Loan Bank Board (acting directly or through the Federal Savings and Loan Insurance Corporation), in the case of any institution subject to any of those provisions;".

1984—Subsec. (b)(5). Pub. L. 98–443 substituted "Secretary of Transportation" for "Civil Aeronautics Board".

STATUTORY NOTES AND RELATED SUBSIDIARIES

EFFECTIVE DATE OF 2010 AMENDMENT

Amendment by Pub. L. 111–203 effective on the designated transfer date, see section 1100H of Pub. L. 111–203, set out as a note under section 552a of Title 5, Government Organization and Employees.

EFFECTIVE DATE OF 1995 AMENDMENT

Amendment by Pub. L. 104–88 effective Jan. 1, 1996, see section 2 of Pub. L. 104–88, set out as an Effective Date note under section 1301 of Title 49, Transportation.

EFFECTIVE DATE OF 1992 AMENDMENT

Amendment by Pub. L. 102–550 effective as if included in the Federal Deposit Insurance Corporation Improvement Act of 1991, Pub. L. 102–242, as of Dec. 19, 1991, see section 1609(a) of Pub. L. 102–550, set out as a note under section 191 of Title 12, Banks and Banking.

EFFECTIVE DATE OF 1984 AMENDMENT

Amendment by Pub. L. 98–443 effective Jan. 1, 1985, see section 9(v) of Pub. L. 98–443, set out as a note under section 5314 of Title 5, Government Organization and Employees.

EFFECTIVE DATE

Section effective upon the expiration of six months after Sept. 20, 1977, see section 819 of Pub. L. 90–321, as added by Pub. L. 95–109, set out as a note under section 1692 of this title.

TRANSFER OF FUNCTIONS

Functions vested in Administrator of National Credit Union Administration transferred and vested in National Credit Union Administration Board pursuant to section 1752a of Title 12, Banks and Banking.

§1692m. Reports to Congress by the Bureau; views of other Federal agencies

(a) Not later than one year after the effective date of this subchapter and at one-year intervals thereafter, the Bureau shall make reports to the Congress concerning the administration of its functions under this subchapter, including such recommendations as the Bureau deems necessary or appropriate. In addition, each report of the Bureau shall include its assessment of the extent to which compliance with this subchapter is being achieved and a summary of the enforcement actions taken by the Bureau under section 1692l of this title.

(b) In the exercise of its functions under this subchapter, the Bureau may obtain upon request the views of any other Federal agency which exercises enforcement functions under section 1692l of this title.

(Pub. L. 90–321, title VIII, §815, as added Pub. L. 95–109, Sept. 20, 1977, 91 Stat. 882; amended Pub. L. 111–203, title X, §1089(1), July 21, 2010, 124 Stat. 2092.)

EDITORIAL NOTES

REFERENCES IN TEXT

The effective date of this subchapter, referred to in subsec. (a), is the date occurring on expiration of six months after Sept. 20, 1977. See section 819 of Pub. L. 90–321, set out as an Effective Date note under section 1692 of this title.

AMENDMENTS

2010—Pub. L. 111–203 substituted "Bureau" for "Commission" wherever appearing.

STATUTORY NOTES AND RELATED SUBSIDIARIES

EFFECTIVE DATE OF 2010 AMENDMENT

Amendment by Pub. L. 111–203 effective on the designated transfer date, see section 1100H of Pub. L. 111–203, set out as a note under section 552a of Title 5, Government Organization and Employees.

EFFECTIVE DATE

Section effective upon the expiration of six months after Sept. 20, 1977, see section 819 of Pub. L. 90–321, as added by Pub. L. 95–109, set out as a note under section 1692 of this title.

§1692n. Relation to State laws

This subchapter does not annul, alter, or affect, or exempt any person subject to the provisions of this subchapter from complying with the laws of any State with respect to debt collection practices, except to the extent that those laws are inconsistent with any provision of this subchapter, and then only to the extent of the inconsistency. For purposes of this section, a State law is not inconsistent with this subchapter if the protection such law affords any consumer is greater than the protection provided by this subchapter.

(Pub. L. 90–321, title VIII, §816, as added Pub. L. 95–109, Sept. 20, 1977, 91 Stat. 883.)

EFFECTIVE DATE

Section effective upon the expiration of six months after Sept. 20, 1977, see section 819 of Pub. L. 90–321, as added by Pub. L. 95–109, set out as a note under section 1692 of this title.

§1692o. Exemption for State regulation

The Bureau shall by regulation exempt from the requirements of this subchapter any class of debt collection practices within any State if the Bureau determines that under the law of that State that class of debt collection practices is subject to requirements substantially similar to those imposed by this subchapter, and that there is adequate provision for enforcement.

(Pub. L. 90–321, title VIII, §817, as added Pub. L. 95–109, Sept. 20, 1977, 91 Stat. 883; amended Pub. L. 111–203, title X, §1089(1), July 21, 2010, 124 Stat. 2092.)

AMENDMENTS

2010—Pub. L. 111–203 substituted "Bureau" for "Commission" in two places.

EFFECTIVE DATE OF 2010 AMENDMENT

Amendment by Pub. L. 111–203 effective on the designated transfer date, see section 1100H of Pub. L. 111–203, set out as a note under section 552a of Title 5, Government Organization and Employees.

EFFECTIVE DATE

Section effective upon the expiration of six months after Sept. 20, 1977, see section 819 of Pub. L. 90–321, as added by Pub. L. 95–109, set out as a note under section 1692 of this title.

§1692p. Exception for certain bad check enforcement programs operated by private entities

(a) In general

(1) Treatment of certain private entities

Subject to paragraph (2), a private entity shall be excluded from the definition of a debt collector, pursuant to the exception provided in section 1692a(6) of this title, with respect to the operation by the entity of a program described in paragraph (2)(A) under a contract described in paragraph (2)(B).

(2) Conditions of applicability

Paragraph (1) shall apply if—

(A) a State or district attorney establishes, within the jurisdiction of such State or district attorney and with respect to alleged bad check violations that do not involve a check described in subsection (b), a pretrial diversion program for alleged bad check offenders who agree to participate voluntarily in such program to avoid criminal prosecution;

(B) a private entity, that is subject to an administrative support services contract with a State or district attorney and operates under the direction, supervision, and control of such State or district attorney, operates the pretrial diversion program described in subparagraph (A); and

(C) in the course of performing duties delegated to it by a State or district attorney under the contract, the private entity referred to in subparagraph (B)—

(i) complies with the penal laws of the State;

(ii) conforms with the terms of the contract and directives of the State or district attorney;

(iii) does not exercise independent prosecutorial discretion;

(iv) contacts any alleged offender referred to in subparagraph (A) for purposes of participating in a program referred to in such paragraph—

(I) only as a result of any determination by the State or district attorney that probable cause of a bad check violation under State penal law exists, and that contact with the alleged offender for purposes of participation in the program is appropriate; and

(II) the alleged offender has failed to pay the bad check after demand for payment, pursuant to State law, is made for payment of the check amount;

(v) includes as part of an initial written communication with an alleged offender a clear and conspicuous statement that—
(I) the alleged offender may dispute the validity of any alleged bad check violation;
(II) where the alleged offender knows, or has reasonable cause to believe, that the alleged bad check violation is the result of theft or forgery of the check, identity theft, or other fraud that is not the result of the conduct of the alleged offender, the alleged offender may file a crime report with the appropriate law enforcement agency; and
(III) if the alleged offender notifies the private entity or the district attorney in writing, not later than 30 days after being contacted for the first time pursuant to clause (iv), that there is a dispute pursuant to this subsection, before further restitution efforts are pursued, the district attorney or an employee of the district attorney authorized to make such a determination makes a determination that there is probable cause to believe that a crime has been committed; and

(vi) charges only fees in connection with services under the contract that have been authorized by the contract with the State or district attorney.

(b) Certain checks excluded

A check is described in this subsection if the check involves, or is subsequently found to involve—
(1) a postdated check presented in connection with a payday loan, or other similar transaction, where the payee of the check knew that the issuer had insufficient funds at the time the check was made, drawn, or delivered;
(2) a stop payment order where the issuer acted in good faith and with reasonable cause in stopping payment on the check;
(3) a check dishonored because of an adjustment to the issuer's account by the financial institution holding such account without providing notice to the person at the time the check was made, drawn, or delivered;
(4) a check for partial payment of a debt where the payee had previously accepted partial payment for such debt;
(5) a check issued by a person who was not competent, or was not of legal age, to enter into a legal contractual obligation at the time the check was made, drawn, or delivered; or
(6) a check issued to pay an obligation arising from a transaction that was illegal in the jurisdiction of the State or district attorney at the time the check was made, drawn, or delivered.

(c) Definitions

For purposes of this section, the following definitions shall apply:

(1) State or district attorney

The term "State or district attorney" means the chief elected or appointed prosecuting attorney in a district, county (as defined in section 2 of title 1), municipality, or comparable jurisdiction, including State attorneys general who act as chief elected or appointed prosecuting attorneys in a district, county (as so defined), municipality or comparable jurisdiction, who may be referred to by a variety of titles such as district attorneys, prosecuting attorneys, commonwealth's attorneys, solicitors, county attorneys, and state's attorneys, and who are responsible for the prosecution of State crimes and violations of jurisdiction-specific local ordinances.

(2) Check

The term "check" has the same meaning as in section 5002(6) of title 12.

(3) Bad check violation

The term "bad check violation" means a violation of the applicable State criminal law relating to the writing of dishonored checks.

(Pub. L. 90–321, title VIII, §818, as added Pub. L. 109–351, title VIII, §801(a)(2), Oct. 13, 2006, 120 Stat. 2004.)

This marks the end of the Fair Debt Collection Practices Act
U.S.C. 15 §§ 1692-1692p

ELECTRONIC FUND TRANSFER ACT

15 U.S.C. §§ 1693-1693r, as amended

This Act (Title IX of the Consumer Credit Protection Act) establishes the rights, liabilities and responsibilities of participants in electronic fund transfer systems. The Act requires financial institutions to adopt certain practices respecting such matters as transaction accounting, and error resolution, requires financial institutions and others to have certain procedures for preauthorized transfers, and sets liability limits for losses caused by unauthorized transfers. The Credit CARD Act and the Dodd-Frank Act made substantial amendments to this Act.

Subchapter VI, Electronic Fund Transfers

SUBCHAPTER VI—ELECTRONIC FUND TRANSFERS

§1693. Congressional findings and declaration of purpose

(a) Rights and liabilities undefined

The Congress finds that the use of electronic systems to transfer funds provides the potential for substantial benefits to consumers. However, due to the unique characteristics of such systems, the application of existing consumer protection legislation is unclear, leaving the rights and liabilities of consumers, financial institutions, and intermediaries in electronic fund transfers undefined.

(b) Purposes

It is the purpose of this subchapter to provide a basic framework establishing the rights, liabilities, and responsibilities of participants in electronic fund and remittance transfer systems. The primary objective of this subchapter, however, is the provision of individual consumer rights.

(Pub. L. 90–321, title IX, §902, as added Pub. L. 95–630, title XX, §2001, Nov. 10, 1978, 92 Stat. 3728; amended Pub. L. 111–203, title X, §1073(a)(1), July 21, 2010, 124 Stat. 2060.)

EDITORIAL NOTES

AMENDMENTS

2010—Subsec. (b). Pub. L. 111–203 inserted "and remittance" after "electronic fund".

STATUTORY NOTES AND RELATED SUBSIDIARIES

EFFECTIVE DATE OF 2010 AMENDMENT

Amendment by Pub. L. 111–203 effective 1 day after July 21, 2010, except as otherwise provided, see section 4 of Pub. L. 111–203, set out as an Effective Date note under section 5301 of Title 12, Banks and Banking.

EFFECTIVE DATE

Pub. L. 90–321, title IX, §923, formerly §921, as added by Pub. L. 95–630, title XX, §2001, Nov. 10, 1978, 92 Stat. 3741, renumbered §922, Pub. L. 111–24, title IV, §401(1), May 22, 2009, 123 Stat. 1751; renumbered §923, Pub. L. 111–203, title X, §1073(a)(3), July 21, 2010, 124 Stat. 2060, provided that: "This title [enacting this subchapter] takes effect upon the expiration of eighteen months from the date of its enactment [Nov. 10, 1978], except that sections 909 and 911 [sections 1693g, 1693i of this title] take effect upon the expiration of ninety days after the date of enactment."

[Pub. L. 111–203, §1073(a)(3), which directed renumbering of section 922 of Pub. L. 90–321 as section 923 effective 1 day after July 21, 2010, was executed after the renumbering of section 921 of Pub. L. 90–321 as section 922 by Pub. L. 111–24, §401(1), effective 15 months after May 22, 2009, to reflect the probable intent of Congress.]

SHORT TITLE

This subchapter known as the "Electronic Fund Transfer Act", see Short Title note set out under section 1601 of this title.

§1693a. Definitions

As used in this subchapter—

(1) the term "accepted card or other means of access" means a card, code, or other means of access to a consumer's account for the purpose of initiating electronic fund transfers when the person to whom such card or other means of access was issued has requested and received or has signed or has used, or authorized another to use, such card or other means of access for the purpose of transferring money between accounts or obtaining money, property, labor, or services;

(2) the term "account" means a demand deposit, savings deposit, or other asset account (other than an occasional or incidental credit balance in an open end credit plan as defined in section 1602(i) [1] of this title), as described in regulations of the Bureau, established primarily for personal, family, or household purposes, but such term does not include an account held by a financial institution pursuant to a bona fide trust agreement;

(4) [2] the term "Board" means the Board of Governors of the Federal Reserve System;

(4) [2] the term "Bureau" means the Bureau of Consumer Financial Protection;

(5) the term "business day" means any day on which the offices of the consumer's financial institution involved in an electronic fund transfer are open to the public for carrying on substantially all of its business functions;

(6) the term "consumer" means a natural person;

(7) the term "electronic fund transfer" means any transfer of funds, other than a transaction originated by check, draft, or similar paper instrument, which is initiated through an electronic terminal, telephonic instrument, or computer or magnetic tape so as to order, instruct, or authorize a financial institution to debit or credit an account. Such term includes, but is not limited to, point-of-sale transfers, automated teller machine transactions, direct deposits or withdrawals of funds, and transfers initiated by telephone. Such term does not include—

(A) any check guarantee or authorization service which does not directly result in a debit or credit to a consumer's account: [3]

(B) any transfer of funds, other than those processed by automated clearinghouse, made by a financial institution on behalf of a consumer by means of a service that transfers funds held at either Federal Reserve banks or other depository institutions and which is not designed primarily to transfer funds on behalf of a consumer;

(C) any transaction the primary purpose of which is the purchase or sale of securities or commodities through a broker-dealer registered with or regulated by the Securities and Exchange Commission;

(D) any automatic transfer from a savings account to a demand deposit account pursuant to an agreement between a consumer and a financial institution for the purpose of covering an overdraft or maintaining an agreed upon minimum balance in the consumer's demand deposit account; or

(E) any transfer of funds which is initiated by a telephone conversation between a consumer and an officer or employee of a financial institution which is not pursuant to a prearranged plan and under which periodic or recurring transfers are not contemplated;

as determined under regulations of the Bureau;

(8) the term "electronic terminal" means an electronic device, other than a telephone operated by a consumer, through which a consumer may initiate an electronic fund transfer. Such term includes, but is not limited to, point-of-sale terminals, automated teller machines, and cash dispensing machines;

(9) the term "financial institution" means a State or National bank, a State or Federal savings and loan association, a mutual savings bank, a State or Federal credit union, or any other person who, directly or indirectly, holds an account belonging to a consumer;

(10) the term "preauthorized electronic fund transfer" means an electronic fund transfer authorized in advance to recur at substantially regular intervals;

(11) the term "State" means any State, territory, or possession of the United States, the District of Columbia, the Commonwealth of Puerto Rico, or any political subdivision of any of the foregoing; and

(12) the term "unauthorized electronic fund transfer" means an electronic fund transfer from a consumer's account initiated by a person other than the consumer without actual authority to initiate such transfer and from which the consumer receives no benefit, but the term does not include any electronic fund transfer (A) initiated by a person other than the consumer who was furnished with the card, code, or other means of access to such consumer's account by such consumer, unless the consumer has notified the financial institution involved that transfers by such other person are no longer authorized, (B) initiated with fraudulent intent by the consumer or any person acting in concert with the consumer, or (C) which constitutes an error committed by a financial institution.

(Pub. L. 90–321, title IX, §903, as added Pub. L. 95–630, title XX, §2001, Nov. 10, 1978, 92 Stat. 3728; amended Pub. L. 111–203, title X, §1084(1), (2), July 21, 2010, 124 Stat. 2081.)

EDITORIAL NOTES

REFERENCES IN TEXT

Section 1602(i) of this title, referred to in par. (2), was redesignated section 1602(j) of this title by Pub. L. 111–203, title X, §1100A(1)(A), July 21, 2010, 124 Stat. 2107.

AMENDMENTS

2010—Pub. L. 111–203, §1084(1), which directed the substitution of "Bureau" for "Board" wherever appearing, was executed by making the substitution in pars. (2) and (6) but not in par. (3), to reflect the probable intent of Congress.

Par. (3). Pub. L. 111–203, §1084(2)(A), redesignated par. (3) as (4) defining the term "Board".

Par. (4). Pub. L. 111–203, §1084(2)(B), which directed addition of par. (4) defining the term "Bureau" after par. (3), was executed by making the addition after par. (4) defining the term "Board", to reflect the probable intent of Congress.

Pub. L. 111–203, §1084(2)(A), redesignated par. (3) as (4) defining the term "Board". Former par. (4) redesignated (5).

Pars. (5) to (12). Pub. L. 111–203, §1084(2)(A), redesignated pars. (4) to (11) as (5) to (12), respectively.

[1] See References in Text note below.

[2] So in original. There are two pars. designated "(4)" and no par. (3).

[3] So in original. The colon probably should be a semicolon.

§1693b. Regulations

(a) Prescription by the Bureau and the Board

(1) In general

Except as provided in paragraph (2), the Bureau shall prescribe rules to carry out the purposes of this subchapter.

(2) Authority of the Board

The Board shall have sole authority to prescribe rules—

(A) to carry out the purposes of this subchapter with respect to a person described in section 5519(a) of title 12; and

(B) to carry out the purposes of section 1693o–2 of this title.

In prescribing such regulations, the Board shall:

(1) [1] consult with the other agencies referred to in section 1693o [2] of this title and take into account, and allow for, the continuing evolution of electronic banking services and the technology utilized in such services,

(2) [1] prepare an analysis of economic impact which considers the costs and benefits to financial institutions, consumers, and other users of electronic fund transfers, including the extent to which additional documentation, reports, records, or other paper work would be required, and the effects upon competition in the provision of electronic banking services among large and small financial institutions and the availability of such services to different classes of consumers, particularly low income consumers,

(3) [1] to the extent practicable, the Board shall demonstrate that the consumer protections of the proposed regulations outweigh the compliance costs imposed upon consumers and financial institutions, and

(4) [1] any proposed regulations and accompanying analyses shall be sent promptly to Congress by the Board.

(b) Issuance of model clauses

The Bureau shall issue model clauses for optional use by financial institutions to facilitate compliance with the disclosure requirements of section 1693c of this title and to aid consumers in understanding the rights and responsibilities of participants in electronic fund transfers by utilizing readily understandable language. Such model clauses shall be adopted after notice duly given in the Federal Register and opportunity for public comment in accordance with section 553 of title 5. With respect to the disclosures required by section 1693c(a)(3) and (4) of this title, the Bureau shall take account of variations in the services and charges under different electronic fund transfer systems and, as appropriate, shall issue alternative model clauses for disclosure of these differing account terms.

(c) Criteria; modification of requirements

Regulations prescribed hereunder may contain such classifications, differentiations, or other provisions, and may provide for such adjustments and exceptions for any class of electronic fund transfers or remittance transfers, as in the judgment of the Bureau are necessary or proper to effectuate the purposes of this subchapter, to prevent circumvention or evasion thereof, or to facilitate compliance therewith. The Bureau shall by regulation modify the requirements imposed by this subchapter on small financial institutions if the Bureau determines that such modifications are necessary to alleviate any undue compliance burden on small financial institutions and such modifications are consistent with the purpose and objective of this subchapter.

(d) Applicability to service providers other than certain financial institutions

(1) In general

If electronic fund transfer services are made available to consumers by a person other than a financial institution holding a consumer's account, the Bureau shall by regulation assure that the disclosures, protections, responsibilities, and remedies created by this subchapter are made applicable to such persons and services.

(2) State and local government electronic benefit transfer systems

(A) "Electronic benefit transfer system" defined

In this paragraph, the term "electronic benefit transfer system"—

(i) means a system under which a government agency distributes needs-tested benefits by establishing accounts that may be accessed by recipients electronically, such as through automated teller machines or point-of-sale terminals; and

(ii) does not include employment-related payments, including salaries and pension, retirement, or unemployment benefits established by a Federal, State, or local government agency.

(B) Exemption generally

The disclosures, protections, responsibilities, and remedies established under this subchapter, and any regulation prescribed or order issued by the Bureau in accordance with this subchapter, shall not apply to any electronic benefit transfer system established under State or local law or administered by a State or local government.

(C) Exception for direct deposit into recipient's account

Subparagraph (B) shall not apply with respect to any electronic funds transfer under an electronic benefit transfer system for a deposit directly into a consumer account held by the recipient of the benefit.

(D) Rule of construction

No provision of this paragraph—

(i) affects or alters the protections otherwise applicable with respect to benefits established by any other provision [3] Federal, State, or local law; or

(ii) otherwise supersedes the application of any State or local law.

(3) Fee disclosures at automated teller machines

(A) In general

The regulations prescribed under paragraph (1) shall require any automated teller machine operator who imposes a fee on any consumer for providing host transfer services to such consumer to provide notice in accordance with subparagraph (B) to the consumer (at the time the service is provided) of—

(i) the fact that a fee is imposed by such operator for providing the service; and

(ii) the amount of any such fee.

(B) Notice requirement

The notice required under clauses (i) and (ii) of subparagraph (A) with respect to any fee described in such subparagraph shall appear on the screen of the automated teller machine, or on a paper notice issued from such machine, after the transaction is initiated and before the consumer is irrevocably committed to completing the transaction.

(C) Prohibition on fees not properly disclosed and explicitly assumed by consumer

No fee may be imposed by any automated teller machine operator in connection with any electronic fund transfer initiated by a consumer for which a notice is required under subparagraph (A), unless—

(i) the consumer receives such notice in accordance with subparagraph (B); and

(ii) the consumer elects to continue in the manner necessary to effect the transaction after receiving such notice.

(D) Definitions

For purposes of this paragraph, the following definitions shall apply:

(i) Automated teller machine operator

The term "automated teller machine operator" means any person who—

(I) operates an automated teller machine at which consumers initiate electronic fund transfers; and

(II) is not the financial institution that holds the account of such consumer from which the transfer is made.

(ii) Electronic fund transfer

The term "electronic fund transfer" includes a transaction that involves a balance inquiry initiated by a consumer in the same manner as an electronic fund transfer, whether or not the consumer initiates a transfer of funds in the course of the transaction.

(iii) Host transfer services

The term "host transfer services" means any electronic fund transfer made by an automated teller machine operator in connection with a transaction initiated by a consumer at an automated teller machine operated by such operator.

(e) Deference

No provision of this subchapter may be construed as altering, limiting, or otherwise affecting the deference that a court affords to—

(1) the Bureau in making determinations regarding the meaning or interpretation of any provision of this subchapter for which the Bureau has authority to prescribe regulations; or

(2) the Board in making determinations regarding the meaning or interpretation of section 1693o–2 of this title.

(Pub. L. 90–321, title IX, §904, as added Pub. L. 95–630, title XX, §2001, Nov. 10, 1978, 92 Stat. 3730; amended Pub. L. 104–193, title VIII, §891, title IX, §907, Aug. 22, 1996, 110 Stat. 2346, 2350; Pub. L. 106–102, title VII, §702, Nov. 12, 1999, 113 Stat. 1463; Pub. L. 111–203, title X, §§1073(a)(2), 1084(1), (3), July 21, 2010, 124 Stat. 2060, 2081; Pub. L. 112–216, §1, Dec. 20, 2012, 126 Stat. 1590.)

Editorial Notes

References in Text

Section 1693o of this title, referred to in subsec. (a)(1), was in the original "section 917", and was translated as meaning section 918 of Pub. L. 90–321 to reflect the probable intent of Congress and the renumbering of section 917 of Pub. L. 90–321 as section 918 by Pub. L. 111–24, title IV, §401, May 22, 2009, 123 Stat. 1751.

Amendments

2012—Subsec. (d)(3)(B). Pub. L. 112–216, in subpar. heading, substituted "requirement" for "requirements" and, in text, substituted "The notice required under clauses (i) and (ii)" for

"(i) On the machine.—The notice required under clause (i) of subparagraph (A) with respect to any fee described in such subparagraph shall be posted in a prominent and conspicuous location on or at the automated teller machine at which the electronic fund transfer is initiated by the consumer.

"(ii) On the screen.—The notice required under clauses (i) and (ii)"

and struck out ", except that during the period beginning on November 12, 1999, and ending on December 31, 2004, this clause shall not apply to any automated teller machine that lacks the technical capability to disclose the notice on the screen or to issue a paper notice after the transaction is initiated and before the consumer is irrevocably committed to completing the transaction" after "completing the transaction".

2010—Pub. L. 111–203, §1084(1), substituted "Bureau" for "Board" wherever appearing in subsecs. (b) to (d).

Subsec. (a). Pub. L. 111–203, §1084(3)(A), substituted "Prescription by the Bureau and the Board" for "Prescription by Board" in heading that had been supplied editorially and substituted initial pars. (1) and (2), relating to the Bureau's prescription of rules and authority of the Board, for first sentence of former introductory provisions which read as follows: "The Board shall prescribe regulations to carry out the purposes of this subchapter." Second sentence of former introductory provisions was redesignated as concluding provisions of par. (2) to reflect the probable intent of Congress.

Subsec. (c). Pub. L. 111–203, §1073(a)(2), inserted "or remittance transfers" after "electronic fund transfers".

Subsec. (e). Pub. L. 111–203, §1084(3)(B), added subsec. (e).

1999—Subsec. (d)(3). Pub. L. 106–102 added par. (3).

1996—Subsec. (d). Pub. L. 104–193, §907, which directed the amendment of subsec. (d), was not executed because of similar amendment by Pub. L. 104–193, §891. See below. Section 907 of Pub. L. 104–193 provided that subsec. (d) was to be amended by inserting subsec. (d) heading, by designating existing provisions as par. (1) and inserting heading, and by adding a new par. (2) reading as follows:

"(2) State and local government electronic benefit transfer programs.—

"(A) Exemption generally.—The disclosures, protections, responsibilities, and remedies established under this subchapter, and any regulation prescribed or order issued by the Board in accordance with this subchapter, shall not apply to any electronic benefit transfer program established under State or local law or administered by a State or local government.

"(B) Exception for direct deposit into recipient's account.—Subparagraph (A) shall not apply with respect to any electronic funds transfer under an electronic benefit transfer program for deposits directly into a consumer account held by the recipient of the benefit.

"(C) Rule of construction.—No provision of this paragraph may be construed as—

"(i) affecting or altering the protections otherwise applicable with respect to benefits established by Federal, State, or local law; or

"(ii) otherwise superseding the application of any State or local law.

"(D) Electronic benefit transfer program defined.—For purposes of this paragraph, the term 'electronic benefit transfer program'—

"(i) means a program under which a government agency distributes needs-tested benefits by establishing accounts to be accessed by recipients electronically, such as through automated teller machines, or point-of-sale terminals; and

"(ii) does not include employment-related payments, including salaries and pension, retirement, or unemployment benefits established by Federal, State, or local governments."

Pub. L. 104–193, §891, designated existing provisions as par. (1), inserted subsec. heading and par. (2), and substituted "If" for "In the event that".

STATUTORY NOTES AND RELATED SUBSIDIARIES

EFFECTIVE DATE OF 2010 AMENDMENT

Amendment by section 1073(a)(2) of Pub. L. 111–203 effective 1 day after July 21, 2010, except as otherwise provided, see section 4 of Pub. L. 111–203, set out as an Effective Date note under section 5301 of Title 12, Banks and Banking.

Amendment by section 1084(1), (3) of Pub. L. 111–203 effective on the designated transfer date, see section 1100H of Pub. L. 111–203, set out as a note under section 552a of Title 5, Government Organization and Employees.

[1] So in original. See 2010 Amendment note below.

[2] See References in Text note below.

[3] So in original. Probably should be followed by "of".

§1693c. Terms and conditions of transfers

(a) Disclosures; time; form; contents

The terms and conditions of electronic fund transfers involving a consumer's account shall be disclosed at the time the consumer contracts for an electronic fund transfer service, in accordance with regulations of the Bureau. Such disclosures shall be in readily understandable language and shall include, to the extent applicable—

(1) the consumer's liability for unauthorized electronic fund transfers and, at the financial institution's option, notice of the advisability of prompt reporting of any loss, theft, or unauthorized use of a card, code, or other means of access;

(2) the telephone number and address of the person or office to be notified in the event the consumer believes than [1] an unauthorized electronic fund transfer has been or may be effected;

(3) the type and nature of electronic fund transfers which the consumer may initiate, including any limitations on the frequency or dollar amount of such transfers, except that the details of such limitations need not be disclosed if their confidentiality is necessary to maintain the security of an electronic fund transfer system, as determined by the Bureau;

(4) any charges for electronic fund transfers or for the right to make such transfers;

(5) the consumer's right to stop payment of a preauthorized electronic fund transfer and the procedure to initiate such a stop payment order;

(6) the consumer's right to receive documentation of electronic fund transfers under section 1693d of this title;

(7) a summary, in a form prescribed by regulations of the Bureau, of the error resolution provisions of section 1693f of this title and the consumer's rights thereunder. The financial institution shall thereafter transmit such summary at least once per calendar year;

(8) the financial institution's liability to the consumer under section 1693h of this title;

(9) under what circumstances the financial institution will in the ordinary course of business disclose information concerning the consumer's account to third persons; and

(10) a notice to the consumer that a fee may be imposed by—

(A) an automated teller machine operator (as defined in section 1693b(d)(3)(D)(i) of this title) if the consumer initiates a transfer from an automated teller machine that is not operated by the person issuing the card or other means of access; and

(B) any national, regional, or local network utilized to effect the transaction.

(b) Notification of changes to consumer

A financial institution shall notify a consumer in writing at least twenty-one days prior to the effective date of any change in any term or condition of the consumer's account required to be disclosed under subsection (a) if such change would result in greater cost or liability for such consumer or decreased access to the consumer's account. A financial institution may, however, implement a change in the terms or conditions of an account without prior notice when such change is immediately necessary to maintain or restore the security of an electronic fund transfer system or a consumer's account. Subject to subsection (a)(3), the Bureau shall require subsequent notification if such a change is made permanent.

(c) Time for disclosures respecting accounts accessible prior to effective date of this subchapter

For any account of a consumer made accessible to electronic fund transfers prior to the effective date of this subchapter, the information required to be disclosed to the consumer under subsection (a) shall be disclosed not later than the earlier of—

(1) the first periodic statement required by section 1693d(c) of this title after the effective date of this subchapter; or

(2) thirty days after the effective date of this subchapter.

(Pub. L. 90–321, title IX, §905, as added Pub. L. 95–630, title XX, §2001, Nov. 10, 1978, 92 Stat. 3730; amended Pub. L. 106–102, title VII, §703, Nov. 12, 1999, 113 Stat. 1464; Pub. L. 111–203, title X, §1084(1), July 21, 2010, 124 Stat. 2081.)

EDITORIAL NOTES

REFERENCES IN TEXT

For effective date of this subchapter, referred to in subsec. (c), see section 921 of Pub. L. 90–321, set out as an Effective Date note under section 1693 of this title.

AMENDMENTS

2010—Subsecs. (a), (b). Pub. L. 111–203 substituted "Bureau" for "Board" wherever appearing.
1999—Subsec. (a)(10). Pub. L. 106–102 added par. (10).

STATUTORY NOTES AND RELATED SUBSIDIARIES

EFFECTIVE DATE OF 2010 AMENDMENT

Amendment by Pub. L. 111–203 effective on the designated transfer date, see section 1100H of Pub. L. 111–203, set out as a note under section 552a of Title 5, Government Organization and Employees.

1 So in original. Probably should be "that".

§1693d. Documentation of transfers

(a) Availability of written documentation to consumer; contents

For each electronic fund transfer initiated by a consumer from an electronic terminal, the financial institution holding such consumer's account shall, directly or indirectly, at the time the transfer is initiated, make available to the consumer written documentation of such transfer. The documentation shall clearly set forth to the extent applicable—

(1) the amount involved and date the transfer is initiated;

(2) the type of transfer;

(3) the identity of the consumer's account with the financial institution from which or to which funds are transferred;

(4) the identity of any third party to whom or from whom funds are transferred; and

(5) the location or identification of the electronic terminal involved.

(b) Notice of credit to consumer

For a consumer's account which is scheduled to be credited by a preauthorized electronic fund transfer from the same payor at least once in each successive sixty-day period, except where the payor provides positive notice of the transfer to the consumer, the financial institution shall elect to provide promptly either positive notice to the consumer when the credit is made as scheduled, or negative notice to the consumer when the credit is not made as scheduled, in accordance with regulations of the Bureau. The means of notice elected shall be disclosed to the consumer in accordance with section 1693c of this title.

(c) Periodic statement; contents

A financial institution shall provide each consumer with a periodic statement for each account of such consumer that may be accessed by means of an electronic fund transfer. Except as provided in subsections (d) and (e), such statement shall be provided at least monthly for each monthly or shorter cycle in which an electronic fund transfer affecting the account has occurred, or every three months, whichever is more frequent. The statement, which may include information regarding transactions other than electronic fund transfers, shall clearly set forth—

(1) with regard to each electronic fund transfer during the period, the information described in subsection (a), which may be provided on an accompanying document;

(2) the amount of any fee or charge assessed by the financial institution during the period for electronic fund transfers or for account maintenance;

(3) the balances in the consumer's account at the beginning of the period and at the close of the period; and

(4) the address and telephone number to be used by the financial institution for the purpose of receiving any statement inquiry or notice of account error from the consumer. Such address and telephone number shall be preceded by the caption "Direct Inquiries To:" or other similar language indicating that the address and number are to be used for such inquiries or notices.

(d) Consumer passbook accounts

In the case of a consumer's passbook account which may not be accessed by electronic fund transfers other than preauthorized electronic fund transfers crediting the account, a financial institution may, in lieu of complying with the requirements of subsection (c), upon presentation of the passbook provide the consumer in writing with the amount and date of each such transfer involving the account since the passbook was last presented.

(e) Accounts other than passbook accounts

In the case of a consumer's account, other than a passbook account, which may not be accessed by electronic fund transfers other than preauthorized electronic fund transfers crediting the account, the financial institution may provide a periodic statement on a quarterly basis which otherwise complies with the requirements of subsection (c).

(f) Documentation as evidence

In any action involving a consumer, any documentation required by this section to be given to the consumer which indicates that an electronic fund transfer was made to another person shall be admissible as evidence of such transfer and shall constitute prima facie proof that such transfer was made.

(Pub. L. 90–321, title IX, §906, as added Pub. L. 95–630, title XX, §2001, Nov. 10, 1978, 92 Stat. 3731; amended Pub. L. 111–203, title X, §1084(1), July 21, 2010, 124 Stat. 2081.)

EDITORIAL NOTES

AMENDMENTS

2010—Subsec. (b). Pub. L. 111–203 substituted "Bureau" for "Board".

STATUTORY NOTES AND RELATED SUBSIDIARIES

EFFECTIVE DATE OF 2010 AMENDMENT

Amendment by Pub. L. 111–203 effective on the designated transfer date, see section 1100H of Pub. L. 111–203, set out as a note under section 552a of Title 5, Government Organization and Employees.

§1693e. Preauthorized transfers

(a) A preauthorized electronic fund transfer from a consumer's account may be authorized by the consumer only in writing, and a copy of such authorization shall be provided to the consumer when made. A consumer may stop payment of a preauthorized electronic fund transfer by notifying the financial institution orally or in writing at any time up to three business days preceding the scheduled date of such transfer. The financial institution may require written confirmation to be provided to it within fourteen days of an oral notification if, when the oral notification is made, the consumer is advised of such requirement and the address to which such confirmation should be sent.

(b) In the case of preauthorized transfers from a consumer's account to the same person which may vary in amount, the financial institution or designated payee shall, prior to each transfer, provide reasonable advance notice to the consumer, in accordance with regulations of the Bureau, of the amount to be transferred and the scheduled date of the transfer.

(Pub. L. 90–321, title IX, §907, as added Pub. L. 95–630, title XX, §2001, Nov. 10, 1978, 92 Stat. 3733; amended Pub. L. 111–203, title X, §1084(1), July 21, 2010, 124 Stat. 2081.)

§1693f. Error resolution

(a) Notification to financial institution of error

If a financial institution, within sixty days after having transmitted to a consumer documentation pursuant to section 1693d(a), (c), or (d) of this title or notification pursuant to section 1693d(b) of this title, receives oral or written notice in which the consumer—

(1) sets forth or otherwise enables the financial institution to identify the name and account number of the consumer;

(2) indicates the consumer's belief that the documentation, or, in the case of notification pursuant to section 1693d(b) of this title, the consumer's account, contains an error and the amount of such error; and

(3) sets forth the reasons for the consumer's belief (where applicable) that an error has occurred,

the financial institution shall investigate the alleged error, determine whether an error has occurred, and report or mail the results of such investigation and determination to the consumer within ten business days. The financial institution may require written confirmation to be provided to it within ten business days of an oral notification of error if, when the oral notification is made, the consumer is advised of such requirement and the address to which such confirmation should be sent. A financial institution which requires written confirmation in accordance with the previous sentence need not provisionally recredit a consumer's account in accordance with subsection (c), nor shall the financial institution be liable under subsection (e) if the written confirmation is not received within the ten-day period referred to in the previous sentence.

(b) Correction of error; interest

If the financial institution determines that an error did occur, it shall promptly, but in no event more than one business day after such determination, correct the error, subject to section 1693g of this title, including the crediting of interest where applicable.

(c) Provisional recredit of consumer's account

If a financial institution receives notice of an error in the manner and within the time period specified in subsection (a), it may, in lieu of the requirements of subsections (a) and (b), within ten business days after receiving such notice provisionally recredit the consumer's account for the amount alleged to be in error, subject to section 1693g of this title, including interest where applicable, pending the conclusion of its investigation and its determination of whether an error has occurred. Such investigation shall be concluded not later than forty-five days after receipt of notice of the error. During the pendency of the investigation, the consumer shall have full use of the funds provisionally recredited.

(d) Absence of error; finding; explanation

If the financial institution determines after its investigation pursuant to subsection (a) or (c) that an error did not occur, it shall deliver or mail to the consumer an explanation of its findings within 3 business days after the conclusion of its investigation, and upon request of the consumer promptly deliver or mail to the consumer reproductions of all documents which the financial institution relied on to conclude that such error did not occur. The financial institution shall include notice of the right to request reproductions with the explanation of its findings.

(e) Treble damages

If in any action under section 1693m [1] of this title, the court finds that—

(1) the financial institution did not provisionally recredit a consumer's account within the ten-day period specified in subsection (c), and the financial institution (A) did not make a good faith investigation of the alleged error, or (B) did not have a reasonable basis for believing that the consumer's account was not in error; or

(2) the financial institution knowingly and willfully concluded that the consumer's account was not in error when such conclusion could not reasonably have been drawn from the evidence available to the financial institution at the time of its investigation,

then the consumer shall be entitled to treble damages determined under section 1693m(a)(1) [1] of this title.

(f) Acts constituting error

For the purpose of this section, an error consists of—

(1) an unauthorized electronic fund transfer;

(2) an incorrect electronic fund transfer from or to the consumer's account;

(3) the omission from a periodic statement of an electronic fund transfer affecting the consumer's account which should have been included;

(4) a computational error by the financial institution;

(5) the consumer's receipt of an incorrect amount of money from an electronic terminal;

(6) a consumer's request for additional information or clarification concerning an electronic fund transfer or any documentation required by this subchapter; or

(7) any other error described in regulations of the Bureau.

(Pub. L. 90–321, title IX, §908, as added Pub. L. 95–630, title XX, §2001, Nov. 10, 1978, 92 Stat. 3733; amended Pub. L. 111–203, title X, §1084(1), July 21, 2010, 124 Stat. 2081.)

EDITORIAL NOTES

REFERENCES IN TEXT

Section 1693m of this title, referred to in subsec. (e), was in the original a reference to section 915 of Pub. L. 90–321, and was translated as meaning section 916 of Pub. L. 90–321 to reflect the probable intent of Congress and the renumbering of section 915 of Pub. L. 90–321 as section 916 by Pub. L. 111–24, title IV, §401(1), May 22, 2009, 123 Stat. 1751.

AMENDMENTS

2010—Subsec. (f)(7). Pub. L. 111–203 substituted "Bureau" for "Board".

STATUTORY NOTES AND RELATED SUBSIDIARIES

EFFECTIVE DATE OF 2010 AMENDMENT

Amendment by Pub. L. 111–203 effective on the designated transfer date, see section 1100H of Pub. L. 111–203, set out as a note under section 552a of Title 5, Government Organization and Employees.

[1] See References in Text note below.

§1693g. Consumer liability

(a) Unauthorized electronic fund transfers; limit

A consumer shall be liable for any unauthorized electronic fund transfer involving the account of such consumer only if the card or other means of access utilized for such transfer was an accepted card or other meanas [1] of access and if the issuer of such card, code, or other means of access has provided a means whereby the user of such card, code, or other means of access can be identified as the person authorized to use it, such as by signature, photograph, or fingerprint or by electronic or mechanical confirmation. In no event, however, shall a consumer's liability for an unauthorized transfer exceed the lesser of—

(1) $50; or

(2) the amount of money or value of property or services obtained in such unauthorized electronic fund transfer prior to the time the financial institution is notified of, or otherwise becomes aware of, circumstances which lead to the reasonable belief that an unauthorized electronic fund transfer involving the consumer's account has been or may be effected. Notice under this paragraph is sufficient when such steps have been taken as may be reasonably required in the ordinary course of business to provide the financial institution with the pertinent information, whether or not any particular officer, employee, or agent of the financial institution does in fact receive such information.

Notwithstanding the foregoing, reimbursement need not be made to the consumer for losses the financial institution establishes would not have occurred but for the failure of the consumer to report within sixty days of transmittal of the statement (or in extenuating circumstances such as extended travel or hospitalization, within a reasonable time under the circumstances) any unauthorized electronic fund transfer or account error which appears on the periodic statement provided to the consumer under section 1693d of this title. In addition, reimbursement need not be made to the consumer for losses which the financial institution establishes would not have occurred but for the failure of the consumer to report any loss or theft of a card or other means of access within two business days after the consumer learns of the loss or theft (or in extenuating circumstances such as extended travel or hospitalization, within a longer period which is reasonable under the circumstances), but the consumer's liability under this subsection in any such case may not exceed a total of $500, or the amount of unauthorized electronic fund transfers which occur following the close of two business days (or such longer period) after the consumer learns of the loss or theft but prior to notice to the financial institution under this subsection, whichever is less.

(b) Burden of proof

In any action which involves a consumer's liability for an unauthorized electronic fund transfer, the burden of proof is upon the financial institution to show that the electronic fund transfer was authorized or, if the electronic fund transfer was unauthorized, then the burden of proof is upon the financial institution to establish that the conditions of liability set forth in subsection (a) have been met, and, if the transfer was initiated after the effective date of section 1693c of this title, that the disclosures required to be made to the consumer under section 1693c(a)(1) and (2) of this title were in fact made in accordance with such section.

(c) Determination of limitation on liability

In the event of a transaction which involves both an unauthorized electronic fund transfer and an extension of credit as defined in section 1602(e) [2] of this title pursuant to an agreement between the consumer and the financial institution to extend such credit to the consumer in the event the consumer's account is overdrawn, the limitation on the consumer's liability for such transaction shall be determined solely in accordance with this section.

(d) Restriction on liability

Nothing in this section imposes liability upon a consumer for an unauthorized electronic fund transfer in excess of his liability for such a transfer under other applicable law or under any agreement with the consumer's financial institution.

(e) Scope of liability

Except as provided in this section, a consumer incurs no liability from an unauthorized electronic fund transfer.

(Pub. L. 90–321, title IX, §909, as added Pub. L. 95–630, title XX, §2001, Nov. 10, 1978, 92 Stat. 3734.)

EDITORIAL NOTES

REFERENCES IN TEXT

Section 1602(e) of this title, referred to in subsec. (c), was redesignated section 1602(f) of this title by Pub. L. 111–203, title X, §1100A(1)(A), July 21, 2010, 124 Stat. 2107.

[1] So in original. Probably should be "means".

[2] See References in Text note below.

§1693h. Liability of financial institutions

(a) Action or failure to act proximately causing damages

Subject to subsections (b) and (c), a financial institution shall be liable to a consumer for all damages proximately caused by—

(1) the financial institution's failure to make an electronic fund transfer, in accordance with the terms and conditions of an account, in the correct amount or in a timely manner when properly instructed to do so by the consumer, except where—

(A) the consumer's account has insufficient funds;

(B) the funds are subject to legal process or other encumbrance restricting such transfer;

(C) such transfer would exceed an established credit limit;

(D) an electronic terminal has insufficient cash to complete the transaction; or

(E) as otherwise provided in regulations of the Bureau;

(2) the financial institution's failure to make an electronic fund transfer due to insufficient funds when the financial [1] institution failed to credit, in accordance with the terms and conditions of an account, a deposit of funds to the consumer's account which would have provided sufficient funds to make the transfer, and

(3) the financial institution's failure to stop payment of a preauthorized transfer from a consumer's account when instructed to do so in accordance with the terms and conditions of the account.

(b) Acts of God and technical malfunctions

A financial institution shall not be liable under subsection (a)(1) or (2) if the financial institution shows by a preponderance of the evidence that its action or failure to act resulted from—

(1) an act of God or other circumstance beyond its control, that it exercised reasonable care to prevent such an occurrence, and that it exercised such diligence as the circumstances required; or

(2) a technical malfunction which was known to the consumer at the time he attempted to initiate an electronic fund transfer or, in the case of a preauthorized transfer, at the time such transfer should have occurred.

(c) Intent

In the case of a failure described in subsection (a) which was not intentional and which resulted from a bona fide error, notwithstanding the maintenance of procedures reasonably adapted to avoid any such error, the financial institution shall be liable for actual damages proved.

(d) Exception for damaged notices

If the notice required to be posted pursuant to section 1693b(d)(3)(B)(i) of this title by an automated teller machine operator has been posted by such operator in compliance with such section and the notice is subsequently removed, damaged, or altered by any person other than the operator of the automated teller machine, the operator shall have no liability under this section for failure to comply with section 1693b(d)(3)(B)(i) of this title.

(Pub. L. 90–321, title IX, §910, as added Pub. L. 95–630, title XX, §2001, Nov. 10, 1978, 92 Stat. 3735; amended Pub. L. 106–102, title VII, §705, Nov. 12, 1999, 113 Stat. 1465; Pub. L. 111–203, title X, §1084(1), July 21, 2010, 124 Stat. 2081.)

EDITORIAL NOTES

AMENDMENTS

2010—Subsec. (a)(1)(E). Pub. L. 111–203 substituted "Bureau" for "Board".
1999—Subsec. (d). Pub. L. 106–102 added subsec. (d).

STATUTORY NOTES AND RELATED SUBSIDIARIES

EFFECTIVE DATE OF 2010 AMENDMENT

Amendment by Pub. L. 111–203 effective on the designated transfer date, see section 1100H of Pub. L. 111–203, set out as a note under section 552a of Title 5, Government Organization and Employees.

[1] *So in original. Probably should be "financial".*

§1693i. Issuance of cards or other means of access

(a) Prohibition; proper issuance

No person may issue to a consumer any card, code, or other means of access to such consumer's account for the purpose of initiating an electronic fund transfer other than—

(1) in response to a request or application therefor; or

(2) as a renewal of, or in substitution for, an accepted card, code, or other means of access, whether issued by the initial issuer or a successor.

(b) Exceptions

Notwithstanding the provisions of subsection (a), a person may distribute to a consumer on an unsolicited basis a card, code, or other means of access for use in initiating an electronic fund transfer from such consumer's account, if—

(1) such card, code, or other means of access is not validated;

(2) such distribution is accompanied by a complete disclosure, in accordance with section 1693c of this title, of the consumer's rights and liabilities which will apply if such card, code, or other means of access is validated;

(3) such distribution is accompanied by a clear explanation, in accordance with regulations of the Bureau, that such card, code, or other means of access is not validated and how the consumer may dispose of such code, card, or other means of access if validation is not desired; and

(4) such card, code, or other means of access is validated only in response to a request or application from the consumer, upon verification of the consumer's identity.

(c) Validation

For the purpose of subsection (b), a card, code, or other means of access is validated when it may be used to initiate an electronic fund transfer.

(Pub. L. 90–321, title IX, §911, as added Pub. L. 95–630, title XX, §2001, Nov. 10, 1978, 92 Stat. 3736; amended Pub. L. 111–203, title X, §1084(1), July 21, 2010, 124 Stat. 2081.)

2010—Subsec. (b)(3). Pub. L. 111–203 substituted "Bureau" for "Board".

STATUTORY NOTES AND RELATED SUBSIDIARIES

EFFECTIVE DATE OF 2010 AMENDMENT

Amendment by Pub. L. 111–203 effective on the designated transfer date, see section 1100H of Pub. L. 111–203, set out as a note under section 552a of Title 5, Government Organization and Employees.

§1693j. Suspension of obligations

If a system malfunction prevents the effectuation of an electronic fund transfer initiated by a consumer to another person, and such other person has agreed to accept payment by such means, the consumer's obligation to the other person shall be suspended until the malfunction is corrected and the electronic fund transfer may be completed, unless such other person has subsequently, by written request, demanded payment by means other than an electronic fund transfer.

(Pub. L. 90–321, title IX, §912, as added Pub. L. 95–630, title XX, §2001, Nov. 10, 1978, 92 Stat. 3737.)

§1693k. Compulsory use of electronic fund transfers

No person may—

(1) condition the extension of credit to a consumer on such consumer's repayment by means of preauthorized electronic fund transfers; or

(2) require a consumer to establish an account for receipt of electronic fund transfers with a particular financial institution as a condition of employment or receipt of a government benefit.

(Pub. L. 90–321, title IX, §913, as added Pub. L. 95–630, title XX, §2001, Nov. 10, 1978, 92 Stat. 3737.)

§1693l. Waiver of rights

No writing or other agreement between a consumer and any other person may contain any provision which constitutes a waiver of any right conferred or cause of action created by this subchapter. Nothing in this section prohibits, however, any writing or other agreement which grants to a consumer a more extensive right or remedy or greater protection than contained in this subchapter or a waiver given in settlement of a dispute or action.

(Pub. L. 90–321, title IX, §914, as added Pub. L. 95–630, title XX, §2001, Nov. 10, 1978, 92 Stat. 3737.)

§1693l–1. General-use prepaid cards, gift certificates, and store gift cards

(a) Definitions

In this section, the following definitions shall apply:

(1) Dormancy fee; inactivity charge or fee

The terms "dormancy fee" and "inactivity charge or fee" mean a fee, charge, or penalty for non-use or inactivity of a gift certificate, store gift card, or general-use prepaid card.

(2) General use [1] prepaid card, gift certificate, and store gift card

(A) General-use prepaid card

The term "general-use prepaid card" means a card or other payment code or device issued by any person that is—

(i) redeemable at multiple, unaffiliated merchants or service providers, or automated teller machines;

(ii) issued in a requested amount, whether or not that amount may, at the option of the issuer, be increased in value or reloaded if requested by the holder;

(iii) purchased or loaded on a prepaid basis; and

(iv) honored, upon presentation, by merchants for goods or services, or at automated teller machines.

(B) Gift certificate

The term "gift certificate" means an electronic promise that is—

(i) redeemable at a single merchant or an affiliated group of merchants that share the same name, mark, or logo;

(ii) issued in a specified amount that may not be increased or reloaded;

(iii) purchased on a prepaid basis in exchange for payment; and

(iv) honored upon presentation by such single merchant or affiliated group of merchants for goods or services.

(C) Store gift card

The term "store gift card" means an electronic promise, plastic card, or other payment code or device that is—

(i) redeemable at a single merchant or an affiliated group of merchants that share the same name, mark, or logo;

(ii) issued in a specified amount, whether or not that amount may be increased in value or reloaded at the request of the holder;

(iii) purchased on a prepaid basis in exchange for payment; and

(iv) honored upon presentation by such single merchant or affiliated group of merchants for goods or services.

(D) Exclusions

The terms "general-use prepaid card", "gift certificate", and "store gift card" do not include an electronic promise, plastic card, or payment code or device that is—

(i) used solely for telephone services;

(ii) reloadable and not marketed or labeled as a gift card or gift certificate;

(iii) a loyalty, award, or promotional gift card, as defined by the Bureau;

(iv) not marketed to the general public;

(v) issued in paper form only (including for tickets and events); or

(vi) redeemable solely for admission to events or venues at a particular location or group of affiliated locations, which may also include services or goods obtainable—

(I) at the event or venue after admission; or

(II) in conjunction with admission to such events or venues, at specific locations affiliated with and in geographic proximity to the event or venue.

(3) Service fee

(A) In general

The term "service fee" means a periodic fee, charge, or penalty for holding or use of a gift certificate, store gift card, or general-use prepaid card.

(B) Exclusion

With respect to a general-use prepaid card, the term "service fee" does not include a one-time initial issuance fee.

(b) Prohibition on imposition of fees or charges

(1) In general

Except as provided under paragraphs (2) through (4), it shall be unlawful for any person to impose a dormancy fee, an inactivity charge or fee, or a service fee with respect to a gift certificate, store gift card, or general-use prepaid card.

(2) Exceptions

A dormancy fee, inactivity charge or fee, or service fee may be charged with respect to a gift certificate, store gift card, or general-use prepaid card, if—

(A) there has been no activity with respect to the certificate or card in the 12-month period ending on the date on which the charge or fee is imposed;

(B) the disclosure requirements of paragraph (3) have been met;

(C) not more than one fee may be charged in any given month; and

(D) any additional requirements that the Bureau may establish through rulemaking under subsection (d) have been met.

(3) Disclosure requirements

The disclosure requirements of this paragraph are met if—

(A) the gift certificate, store gift card, or general-use prepaid card clearly and conspicuously states—

(i) that a dormancy fee, inactivity charge or fee, or service fee may be charged;

(ii) the amount of such fee or charge;

(iii) how often such fee or charge may be assessed; and

(iv) that such fee or charge may be assessed for inactivity; and

(B) the issuer or vendor of such certificate or card informs the purchaser of such charge or fee before such certificate or card is purchased, regardless of whether the certificate or card is purchased in person, over the Internet, or by telephone.

(4) Exclusion

The prohibition under paragraph (1) shall not apply to any gift certificate—

    (A) that is distributed pursuant to an award, loyalty, or promotional program, as defined by the Bureau; and

    (B) with respect to which, there is no money or other value exchanged.

(c) Prohibition on sale of gift cards with expiration dates

(1) In general

Except as provided under paragraph (2), it shall be unlawful for any person to sell or issue a gift certificate, store gift card, or general-use prepaid card that is subject to an expiration date.

(2) Exceptions

A gift certificate, store gift card, or general-use prepaid card may contain an expiration date if—

    (A) the expiration date is not earlier than 5 years after the date on which the gift certificate was issued, or the date on which card funds were last loaded to a store gift card or general-use prepaid card; and

    (B) the terms of expiration are clearly and conspicuously stated.

(d) Additional rulemaking

(1) In general

The Bureau shall—

    (A) prescribe regulations to carry out this section, in addition to any other rules or regulations required by this subchapter, including such additional requirements as appropriate relating to the amount of dormancy fees, inactivity charges or fees, or service fees that may be assessed and the amount of remaining value of a gift certificate, store gift card, or general-use prepaid card below which such charges or fees may be assessed; and

    (B) shall [2] determine the extent to which the individual definitions and provisions of this subchapter or Regulation E should apply to general-use prepaid cards, gift certificates, and store gift cards.

(2) Consultation

In prescribing regulations under this subsection, the Bureau shall consult with the Federal Trade Commission.

(3) Timing; effective date

The regulations required by this subsection shall be issued in final form not later than 9 months after May 22, 2009.

(Pub. L. 90–321, title IX, §915, as added Pub. L. 111–24, title IV, §401(2), May 22, 2009, 123 Stat. 1751; amended Pub. L. 111–203, title X, §1084(1), July 21, 2010, 124 Stat. 2081.)

"(A) comply with paragraphs (1) and (2) of section 915(b) of such Act [15 U.S.C. 1693l–1(b)(1), (2)];

"(B) consider any such certificate or card for which funds expire to have no expiration date with respect to the underlying funds;

"(C) at a consumer's request, replace such certificate or card that has funds remaining at no cost to the consumer; and

"(D) comply with the disclosure requirements of paragraph (2) of this subsection.

"(2) DISCLOSURE REQUIREMENTS.—The disclosure requirements of this subsection are met by providing notice to consumers, via in-store signage, messages during customer service calls, Web sites, and general advertising, that—

"(A) any such certificate or card for which funds expire shall be deemed to have no expiration date with respect to the underlying funds;

"(B) consumers holding such certificate or card shall have a right to a free replacement certificate or card that includes the packaging and materials, typically associated with such a certificate or card; and

"(C) any dormancy fee, inactivity fee, or service fee for such certificates or cards that might otherwise be charged shall not be charged if such fees do not comply with section 915 of the Electronic Funds [probably should be "Fund"] Transfer Act [15 U.S.C. 1693l–1].

"(3) PERIOD FOR DISCLOSURE REQUIREMENTS.—The notice requirements in paragraph (2) of this subsection shall continue until January 31, 2013."

Pub. L. 111–24, title IV, §403, May 22, 2009, 123 Stat. 1754, which provided that title IV of Pub. L. 111–24 was to become effective 15 months after May 22, 2009, was repealed by Pub. L. 111–209, §1, July 27, 2010, 124 Stat. 2254.

[1] So in original. Probably should be "General-use".

[2] So in original. The word "shall" probably should not appear.

§1693m. Civil liability

(a) Individual or class action for damages; amount of award

Except as otherwise provided by this section and section 1693h of this title, any person who fails to comply with any provision of this subchapter with respect to any consumer, except for an error resolved in accordance with section 1693f of this title, is liable to such consumer in an amount equal to the sum of—

(1) any actual damage sustained by such consumer as a result of such failure;

(2)(A) in the case of an individual action, an amount not less than $100 nor greater than $1,000; or

(B) in the case of a class action, such amount as the court may allow, except that (i) as to each member of the class no minimum recovery shall be applicable, and (ii) the total recovery under this subparagraph in any class action or series of class actions arising out of the same failure to comply by the same person shall not be more than the lesser of $500,000 or 1 per centum of the net worth of the defendant; and

(3) in the case of any successful action to enforce the foregoing liability, the costs of the action, together with a reasonable attorney's fee as determined by the court.

(b) Factors determining amount of award

In determining the amount of liability in any action under subsection (a), the court shall consider, among other relevant factors—

(1) in any individual action under subsection (a)(2)(A), the frequency and persistence of noncompliance, the nature of such noncompliance, and the extent to which the noncompliance was intentional; or

(2) in any class action under subsection (a)(2)(B), the frequency and persistence of noncompliance, the nature of such noncompliance, the resources of the defendant, the number of persons adversely affected, and the extent to which the noncompliance was intentional.

(c) Unintentional violations; bona fide error

Except as provided in section 1693h of this title, a person may not be held liable in any action brought under this section for a violation of this subchapter if the person shows by a preponderance of evidence that the violation was not intentional and resulted from a bona fide error notwithstanding the maintenance of procedures reasonably adapted to avoid any such error.

(d) Good faith compliance with rule, regulation, or interpretation

No provision of this section or section 1693n [1] of this title imposing any liability shall apply to—

(1) any act done or omitted in good faith in conformity with any rule, regulation, or interpretation thereof by the Bureau or the Board or in conformity with any interpretation or approval by an official or employee of the Bureau of

Consumer Financial Protection or the Federal Reserve System duly authorized by the Bureau or the Board to issue such interpretations or approvals under such procedures as the Bureau or the Board may prescribe therefor; or

(2) any failure to make disclosure in proper form if a financial institution utilized an appropriate model clause issued by the Bureau or the Board,

notwithstanding that after such act, omission, or failure has occurred, such rule, regulation, approval, or model clause is amended, rescinded, or determined by judicial or other authority to be invalid for any reason.

(e) Notification to consumer prior to action; adjustment of consumer's account

A person has no liability under this section for any failure to comply with any requirement under this subchapter if, prior to the institution of an action under this section, the person notifies the consumer concerned of the failure, complies with the requirements of this subchapter, and makes an appropriate adjustment to the consumer's account and pays actual damages or, where applicable, damages in accordance with section 1693h of this title.

(f) Action in bad faith or for harassment; attorney's fees

On a finding by the court that an unsuccessful action under this section was brought in bad faith or for purposes of harassment, the court shall award to the defendant attorney's fees reasonable in relation to the work expended and costs.

(g) Jurisdiction of courts; time for maintenance of action

Without regard to the amount in controversy, any action under this section may be brought in any United States district court, or in any other court of competent jurisdiction, within one year from the date of the occurrence of the violation.

(Pub. L. 90–321, title IX, §916, formerly §915, as added Pub. L. 95–630, title XX, §2001, Nov. 10, 1978, 92 Stat. 3737; renumbered §916, Pub. L. 111–24, title IV, §401(1), May 22, 2009, 123 Stat. 1751; amended Pub. L. 111–203, title X, §1084(1), (4), July 21, 2010, 124 Stat. 2081, 2082.)

Editorial Notes

References in Text

Section 1693n of this title, referred to in subsec. (d), was in the original a reference to section 916 of Pub. L. 90–321, and was translated as meaning section 917 of Pub. L. 90–321 to reflect the probable intent of Congress and the renumbering of section 916 of Pub. L. 90–321 as section 917 by Pub. L. 111–24, title IV, §401(1), May 22, 2009, 123 Stat. 1751.

Prior Provisions

A prior section 916 of Pub. L. 90–321 was renumbered section 917 and is classified to section 1693n of this title.

Amendments

2010—Pub. L. 111–203, §1084(1), which directed the substitution of "Bureau" for "Board" wherever appearing in section, was not executed in subsec. (d), which was the only place such term appeared, to reflect the probable intent of Congress and the amendment by Pub. L. 111–203, §1084(4). See below.

Subsec. (d). Pub. L. 111–203, §1084(4), struck out "of Board or approval of duly authorized official or employee of Federal Reserve System" after "interpretation" in heading that had been supplied editorially and inserted "Bureau of Consumer Financial Protection or the" before "Federal Reserve System" in par. (1) and "Bureau or the" before "Board" wherever appearing.

Statutory Notes and Related Subsidiaries

Effective Date of 2010 Amendment

Amendment by Pub. L. 111–203 effective on the designated transfer date, see section 1100H of Pub. L. 111–203, set out as a note under section 552a of Title 5, Government Organization and Employees.

[1] See References in Text note below.

§1693n. Criminal liability

(a) Violations respecting giving of false or inaccurate information, failure to provide information, and failure to comply with provisions of this subchapter

Whoever knowingly and willfully—

(1) gives false or inaccurate information or fails to provide information which he is required to disclose by this subchapter or any regulation issued thereunder; or

(2) otherwise fails to comply with any provision of this subchapter;

shall be fined not more than $5,000 or imprisoned not more than one year, or both.

(b) Violations affecting interstate or foreign commerce

Whoever—

(1) knowingly, in a transaction affecting interstate or foreign commerce, uses or attempts or conspires to use any counterfeit, fictitious, altered, forged, lost, stolen, or fraudulently obtained debit instrument to obtain money, goods, services, or anything else of value which within any one-year period has a value aggregating $1,000 or more; or

(2) with unlawful or fraudulent intent, transports or attempts or conspires to transport in interstate or foreign commerce a counterfeit, fictitious, altered, forged, lost, stolen, or fraudulently obtained debit instrument knowing the same to be counterfeit, fictitious, altered, forged, lost, stolen, or fraudulently obtained; or

(3) with unlawful or fraudulent intent, uses any instrumentality of interstate or foreign commerce to sell or transport a counterfeit, fictitious, altered, forged, lost, stolen, or fraudulently obtained debit instrument knowing the same to be counterfeit, fictitious, altered, forged, lost, stolen, or fraudulently obtained; or

(4) knowingly receives, conceals, uses, or transports money, goods, services, or anything else of value (except tickets for interstate or foreign transportation) which (A) within any one-year period has a value aggregating $1,000 or more, (B) has moved in or is part of, or which constitutes interstate or foreign commerce, and (C) has been obtained with a counterfeit, fictitious, altered, forged, lost, stolen, or fraudulently obtained debit instrument; or

(5) knowingly receives, conceals, uses, sells, or transports in interstate or foreign commerce one or more tickets for interstate or foreign transportation, which (A) within any one-year period have a value aggregating $500 or more, and (B) have been purchased or obtained with one or more counterfeit, fictitious, altered, forged, lost, stolen, or fraudulently obtained debit instrument; or

(6) in a transaction affecting interstate or foreign commerce, furnishes money, property, services, or anything else of value, which within any one-year period has a value aggregating $1,000 or more, through the use of any counterfeit, fictitious, altered, forged, lost, stolen, or fraudulently obtained debit instrument knowing the same to be counterfeit, fictitious, altered, forged, lost, stolen, or fraudulently obtained—

shall be fined not more than $10,000 or imprisoned not more than ten years, or both.

(c) "Debit instrument" defined

As used in this section, the term "debit instrument" means a card, code, or other device, other than a check, draft, or similar paper instrument, by the use of which a person may initiate an electronic fund transfer.

(Pub. L. 90–321, title IX, §917, formerly §916, as added Pub. L. 95–630, title XX, §2001, Nov. 10, 1978, 92 Stat. 3738; renumbered §917, Pub. L. 111–24, title IV, §401(1), May 22, 2009, 123 Stat. 1751.)

EDITORIAL NOTES

PRIOR PROVISIONS

A prior section 917 of Pub. L. 90–321 was renumbered section 918 and is classified to section 1693o of this title.

§1693o. Administrative enforcement

(a) Enforcing agencies

Subject to subtitle B of the Consumer Financial Protection Act of 2010 [12 U.S.C. 5511 et seq.], compliance with the requirements imposed under this subchapter shall be enforced under—

(1) section 8 of the Federal Deposit Insurance Act [12 U.S.C. 1818], by the appropriate Federal banking agency, as defined in section 3(q) of the Federal Deposit Insurance Act (12 U.S.C. 1813(q)), with respect to—

(A) national banks, Federal savings associations, and Federal branches and Federal agencies of foreign banks;

(B) member banks of the Federal Reserve System (other than national banks), branches and agencies of foreign banks (other than Federal branches, Federal agencies, and insured State branches of foreign banks), commercial lending companies owned or controlled by foreign banks, and organizations operating under section 25 or 25A of the Federal Reserve Act [12 U.S.C. 601 et seq., 611 et seq.]; and

(C) banks and State savings associations insured by the Federal Deposit Insurance Corporation (other than members of the Federal Reserve System), and insured State branches of foreign banks;

(2) the Federal Credit Union Act [12 U.S.C. 1751 et seq.], by the Administrator of the National Credit Union Administration with respect to any Federal credit union;

(3) part A of subtitle VII of title 49, by the Secretary of Transportation, with respect to any air carrier or foreign air carrier subject to that part;

(4) the Securities Exchange Act of 1934 [15 U.S.C. 78a et seq.], by the Securities and Exchange Commission, with respect to any broker or dealer subject to that Act and [1]

(5) subtitle E of the Consumer Financial Protection Act of 2010 [12 U.S.C. 5561 et seq.], by the Bureau, with respect to any person subject to this subchapter, except that the Bureau shall not have authority to enforce the requirements of section 1693o–2 of this title or any regulations prescribed by the Board under section 1693o–2 of this title.

The terms used in paragraph (1) that are not defined in this subchapter or otherwise defined in section 3(s) of the Federal Deposit Insurance Act (12 U.S.C. 1813(s)) shall have the meaning given to them in section 1(b) of the International Banking Act of 1978 (12 U.S.C. 3101).

(b) Violations of subchapter deemed violations of pre-existing statutory requirements; additional powers

For the purpose of the exercise by any agency referred to in any of paragraphs (1) through (4) of subsection (a) of its powers under any Act referred to in that subsection, a violation of any requirement imposed under this subchapter shall be deemed to be a violation of a requirement imposed under that Act. In addition to its powers under any provision of law specifically referred to in any of paragraphs (1) through (4) of subsection (a), each of the agencies referred to in that subsection may exercise, for the purpose of enforcing compliance with any requirement imposed under this subchapter, any other authority conferred on it by law.

(c) Overall enforcement authority of the Federal Trade Commission

Except to the extent that enforcement of the requirements imposed under this subchapter is specifically committed to some other Government agency under any of paragraphs (1) through (4) of subsection (a), and subject to subtitle B of the Consumer Financial Protection Act of 2010, the Federal Trade Commission shall be authorized to enforce such requirements. For the purpose of the exercise by the Federal Trade Commission of its functions and powers under the Federal Trade Commission Act [15 U.S.C. 41 et seq.], a violation of any requirement imposed under this subchapter shall be deemed a violation of a requirement imposed under that Act. All of the functions and powers of the Federal Trade Commission under the Federal Trade Commission Act are available to the Federal Trade Commission to enforce compliance by any person subject to the jurisdiction of the Federal Trade Commission with the requirements imposed under this subchapter, irrespective of whether that person is engaged in commerce or meets any other jurisdictional tests under the Federal Trade Commission Act.

(Pub. L. 90–321, title IX, §918, formerly §917, as added Pub. L. 95–630, title XX, §2001, Nov. 10, 1978, 92 Stat. 3739; amended Pub. L. 101–73, title VII, §744(o), Aug. 9, 1989, 103 Stat. 440; Pub. L. 102–242, title II, §212(f), Dec. 19, 1991, 105 Stat. 2301; Pub. L. 104–287, §6(h), Oct. 11, 1996, 110 Stat. 3399; renumbered §918, Pub. L. 111–24, title IV, §401(1), May 22, 2009, 123 Stat. 1751; Pub. L. 111–203, title X, §1084(5), July 21, 2010, 124 Stat. 2082.)

EDITORIAL NOTES

REFERENCES IN TEXT

The Consumer Financial Protection Act of 2010, referred to in subsecs. (a) and (c), is title X of Pub. L. 111–203, July 21, 2010, 124 Stat. 1955. Subtitles B (§§1021–1029A) and E (§§1051–1058) of the Act are classified generally to parts B (§5511 et seq.) and E (§5561 et seq.), respectively, of subchapter V of chapter 53 of Title 12, Banks and Banking. For complete classification of subtitles B and E to the Code, see Tables.

Sections 25 and 25A of the Federal Reserve Act, referred to in subsec. (a)(1)(B), are classified to subchapters I (§601 et seq.) and II (§611 et seq.), respectively, of chapter 6 of Title 12, Banks and Banking.

The Federal Credit Union Act, referred to in subsec. (a)(2), is act June 26, 1934, ch. 750, 48 Stat. 1216, which is classified generally to chapter 14 (§1751 et seq.) of Title 12. For complete classification of this Act to the Code, see section 1751 of Title 12 and Tables.

The Securities Exchange Act of 1934, referred to in subsec. (a)(4), is act June 6, 1934, ch. 404, 48 Stat. 881, which is classified principally to chapter 2B (§78a et seq.) of this title. For complete classification of this Act to the Code, see section 78a of this title and Tables.

The Federal Trade Commission Act, referred to in subsec. (c), is act Sept. 26, 1914, ch. 311, 38 Stat. 717, which is classified generally to subchapter I (§41 et seq.) of chapter 2 of this title. For complete classification of this Act to the Code, see section 58 of this title and Tables.

CODIFICATION

In subsec. (a)(3), "part A of subtitle VII of title 49" substituted for "the Federal Aviation Act of 1958 [49 App. U.S.C. 1301 et seq.]" and "that part" substituted for "that Act" on authority of Pub. L. 103–272, §6(b), July 5, 1994, 108 Stat. 1378, the first section of which enacted subtitles II, III, and V to X of Title 49, Transportation.

A prior section 918 of Pub. L. 90–321 was renumbered section 921 and is classified to section 1693p of this title.

AMENDMENTS

2010—Subsec. (a). Pub. L. 111–203, §1084(5)(A)(i), substituted "Subject to subtitle B of the Consumer Financial Protection Act of 2010, compliance" for "Compliance" in introductory provisions.

Subsec. (a)(1). Pub. L. 111–203, §1084(5)(A)(ii), added par. (1) and struck out former par. (1) which read as follows: "section 8 of the Federal Deposit Insurance Act, in the case of—

"(A) national banks, and Federal branches and Federal agencies of foreign banks, by the Office of the Comptroller of the Currency;

"(B) member banks of the Federal Reserve System (other than national banks), branches and agencies of foreign banks (other than Federal branches, Federal agencies, and insured State branches of foreign banks), commercial lending companies owned or controlled by foreign banks, and organizations operating under section 25 or 25(a) of the Federal Reserve Act, by the Board; and

"(C) banks insured by the Federal Deposit Insurance Corporation (other than members of the Federal Reserve System) and insured State branches of foreign banks, by the Board of Directors of the Federal Deposit Insurance Corporation;".

Subsec. (a)(2) to (5). Pub. L. 111–203, §1084(5)(A)(ii)–(vii), added par. (5), redesignated former pars. (3) to (5) as (2) to (4), respectively, and struck out former par. (2) which read as follows: "section 8 of the Federal Deposit Insurance Act, by the Director of the Office of Thrift Supervision, in the case of a savings association the deposits of which are insured by the Federal Deposit Insurance Corporation;".

Subsec. (b). Pub. L. 111–203, §1084(5)(B), inserted "any of paragraphs (1) through (4) of" before "subsection (a)" in two places.

Subsec. (c). Pub. L. 111–203, §1084(5)(C), added subsec. (c) and struck out former subsec. (c). Prior to amendment, text read as follows: "Except to the extent that enforcement of the requirements imposed under this subchapter is specifically committed to some other Government agency under subsection (a) of this section, the Federal Trade Commission shall enforce such requirements. For the purpose of the exercise by the Federal Trade Commission of its functions and powers under the Federal Trade Commission Act, a violation of any requirement imposed under this subchapter shall be deemed a violation of a requirement imposed under that Act. All of the functions and powers of the Federal Trade Commission under the Federal Trade Commission Act are available to the Commission to enforce compliance by any person subject to the jurisdiction of the Commission with the requirements imposed under this subchapter, irrespective of whether that person is engaged in commerce or meets any other jurisdictional tests in the Federal Trade Commission Act."

1996—Subsec. (a)(4). Pub. L. 104–287 substituted "Secretary of Transportation" for "Civil Aeronautics Board".

1991—Subsec. (a). Pub. L. 102–242, §212(f)(2), inserted at end "The terms used in paragraph (1) that are not defined in this subchapter or otherwise defined in section 3(s) of the Federal Deposit Insurance Act (12 U.S.C. 1813(s)) shall have the meaning given to them in section 1(b) of the International Banking Act of 1978 (12 U.S.C. 3101)."

Pub. L. 102–242, §212(f)(1), added par. (1) and struck out former par. (1) which read as follows: "section 8 of the Federal Deposit Insurance Act, in the case of—

"(A) national banks, by the Comptroller of the Currency;

"(B) member banks of the Federal Reserve System (other than national banks), by the Board;

"(C) banks insured by the Federal Deposit Insurance Corporation (other than members of the Federal Reserve System), by the Board of Directors of the Federal Deposit Insurance Corporation;".

1989—Subsec. (a)(2). Pub. L. 101–73 amended par. (2) generally. Prior to amendment, par. (2) read as follows: "section 5(d) of the Home Owners' Loan Act of 1933, section 407 of the National Housing Act, and sections 6(i) and 17 of the Federal Home Loan Bank Act, by the Federal Home Loan Bank Board (acting directly or through the Federal Savings and Loan Insurance Corporation), in the case of any institution subject to any of those provisions;".

STATUTORY NOTES AND RELATED SUBSIDIARIES

EFFECTIVE DATE OF 2010 AMENDMENT

Amendment by Pub. L. 111–203 effective on the designated transfer date, see section 1100H of Pub. L. 111–203, set out as a note under section 552a of Title 5, Government Organization and Employees.

Functions vested in Administrator of National Credit Union Administration transferred and vested in National Credit Union Administration Board pursuant to section 1752a of Title 12, Banks and Banking.

§1693o–1. Remittance transfers

(a) Disclosures required for remittance transfers

(1) In general

Each remittance transfer provider shall make disclosures as required under this section and in accordance with rules prescribed by the Bureau. Disclosures required under this section shall be in addition to any other disclosures applicable under this subchapter.

(2) Disclosures

Subject to rules prescribed by the Bureau, a remittance transfer provider shall provide, in writing and in a form that the sender may keep, to each sender requesting a remittance transfer, as applicable to the transaction—
    (A) at the time at which the sender requests a remittance transfer to be initiated, and prior to the sender making any payment in connection with the remittance transfer, a disclosure describing—
        (i) the amount of currency that will be received by the designated recipient, using the values of the currency into which the funds will be exchanged;
        (ii) the amount of transfer and any other fees charged by the remittance transfer provider for the remittance transfer; and
        (iii) any exchange rate to be used by the remittance transfer provider for the remittance transfer, to the nearest 1/100th of a point; and

    (B) at the time at which the sender makes payment in connection with the remittance transfer—
        (i) a receipt showing—
            (I) the information described in subparagraph (A);
            (II) the promised date of delivery to the designated recipient; and
            (III) the name and either the telephone number or the address of the designated recipient, if either the telephone number or the address of the designated recipient is provided by the sender; and

        (ii) a statement containing—
            (I) information about the rights of the sender under this section regarding the resolution of errors; and
            (II) appropriate contact information for—
                (aa) the remittance transfer provider; and
                (bb) the State agency that regulates the remittance transfer provider and the Bureau, including the toll-free telephone number established under section 5493 of title 12.

(3) Requirements relating to disclosures

With respect to each disclosure required to be provided under paragraph (2) a remittance transfer provider shall—
    (A) provide an initial notice and receipt, as required by subparagraphs (A) and (B) of paragraph (2), and an error resolution statement, as required by subsection (d), that clearly and conspicuously describe the information required to be disclosed therein; and
    (B) with respect to any transaction that a sender conducts electronically, comply with the Electronic Signatures in Global and National Commerce Act (15 U.S.C. 7001 et seq.).

(4) Exception for disclosures of amount received

(A) In general

Subject to the rules prescribed by the Bureau, and except as provided under subparagraph (B), the disclosures required regarding the amount of currency that will be received by the designated recipient shall be deemed to be accurate, so long as the disclosures provide a reasonably accurate estimate of the foreign currency to be received. This paragraph shall apply only to a remittance transfer provider who is an insured depository institution, as defined in section 1813 of title 12, or an insured credit union, as defined in section 1752 of title 12, and if—
    (i) a remittance transfer is conducted through a demand deposit, savings deposit, or other asset account that the sender holds with such remittance transfer provider; and
    (ii) at the time at which the sender requests the transaction, the remittance transfer provider is unable to know, for reasons beyond its control, the amount of currency that will be made available to the designated recipient.

(B) Deadline

The application of subparagraph (A) shall terminate 5 years after July 21, 2010, unless the Bureau determines that termination of such provision would negatively affect the ability of remittance transfer providers described in subparagraph (A) to send remittances to locations in foreign countries, in which case, the Bureau may, by rule, extend the application of subparagraph (A) to not longer than 10 years after July 21, 2010.

(5) Exemption authority

The Bureau may, by rule, permit a remittance transfer provider to satisfy the requirements of—

(A) paragraph (2)(A) orally, if the transaction is conducted entirely by telephone;

(B) paragraph (2)(B), in the case of a transaction conducted entirely by telephone, by mailing the disclosures required under such subparagraph to the sender, not later than 1 business day after the date on which the transaction is conducted, or by including such documents in the next periodic statement, if the telephone transaction is conducted through a demand deposit, savings deposit, or other asset account that the sender holds with the remittance transfer provider;

(C) subparagraphs (A) and (B) of paragraph (2) together in one written disclosure, but only to the extent that the information provided in accordance with paragraph (3)(A) is accurate at the time at which payment is made in connection with the subject remittance transfer; and

(D) paragraph (2)(A), without compliance with section 101(c) of the Electronic Signatures in Global Commerce Act [15 U.S.C. 7001(c)], if a sender initiates the transaction electronically and the information is displayed electronically in a manner that the sender can keep.

(6) Storefront and Internet notices

(A) In general

(i) Prominent posting

Subject to subparagraph (B), the Bureau may prescribe rules to require a remittance transfer provider to prominently post, and timely update, a notice describing a model remittance transfer for one or more amounts, as the Bureau may determine, which notice shall show the amount of currency that will be received by the designated recipient, using the values of the currency into which the funds will be exchanged.

(ii) Onsite displays

The Bureau may require the notice prescribed under this subparagraph to be displayed in every physical storefront location owned or controlled by the remittance transfer provider.

(iii) Internet notices

Subject to paragraph (3), the Bureau shall prescribe rules to require a remittance transfer provider that provides remittance transfers via the Internet to provide a notice, comparable to a storefront notice described in this subparagraph, located on the home page or landing page (with respect to such remittance transfer services) owned or controlled by the remittance transfer provider.

(iv) Rulemaking authority

In prescribing rules under this subparagraph, the Bureau may impose standards or requirements regarding the provision of the storefront and Internet notices required under this subparagraph and the provision of the disclosures required under paragraphs (2) and (3).

(B) Study and analysis

Prior to proposing rules under subparagraph (A), the Bureau shall undertake appropriate studies and analyses, which shall be consistent with section 1693b(a)(2) of this title, and may include an advanced notice of proposed rulemaking, to determine whether a storefront notice or Internet notice facilitates the ability of a consumer—

(i) to compare prices for remittance transfers; and

(ii) to understand the types and amounts of any fees or costs imposed on remittance transfers.

(b) Foreign language disclosures

The disclosures required under this section shall be made in English and in each of the foreign languages principally used by the remittance transfer provider, or any of its agents, to advertise, solicit, or market, either orally or in writing, at that office.

(c) Regulations regarding transfers to certain nations

If the Bureau determines that a recipient nation does not legally allow, or the method by which transactions are made in the recipient country do not allow, a remittance transfer provider to know the amount of currency that will be received by the designated recipient, the Bureau may prescribe rules (not later than 18 months after July 21, 2010) addressing the issue, which rules shall include standards for a remittance transfer provider to provide—

(1) a receipt that is consistent with subsections (a) and (b); and

(2) a reasonably accurate estimate of the foreign currency to be received, based on the rate provided to the sender by the remittance transfer provider at the time at which the transaction was initiated by the sender.

(d) Remittance transfer errors

(1) Error resolution

(A) In general

If a remittance transfer provider receives oral or written notice from the sender within 180 days of the promised date of delivery that an error occurred with respect to a remittance transfer, including the amount of currency designated in subsection (a)(3)(A) that was to be sent to the designated recipient of the remittance transfer, using the values of the currency into which the funds should have been exchanged, but was not made available to the designated recipient in the foreign country, the remittance transfer provider shall resolve the error pursuant to this subsection and investigate the reason for the error.

(B) Remedies

Not later than 90 days after the date of receipt of a notice from the sender pursuant to subparagraph (A), the remittance transfer provider shall, as applicable to the error and as designated by the sender—

(i) refund to the sender the total amount of funds tendered by the sender in connection with the remittance transfer which was not properly transmitted;

(ii) make available to the designated recipient, without additional cost to the designated recipient or to the sender, the amount appropriate to resolve the error;

(iii) provide such other remedy, as determined appropriate by rule of the Bureau for the protection of senders; or

(iv) provide written notice to the sender that there was no error with an explanation responding to the specific complaint of the sender.

(2) Rules

The Bureau shall establish, by rule issued not later than 18 months after July 21, 2010, clear and appropriate standards for remittance transfer providers with respect to error resolution relating to remittance transfers, to protect senders from such errors. Standards prescribed under this paragraph shall include appropriate standards regarding record keeping, as required, including documentation—

(A) of the complaint of the sender;

(B) that the sender provides the remittance transfer provider with respect to the alleged error; and

(C) of the findings of the remittance transfer provider regarding the investigation of the alleged error that the sender brought to their attention.

(3) Cancellation and refund policy rules

Not later than 18 months after July 21, 2010, the Bureau shall issue final rules regarding appropriate remittance transfer cancellation and refund policies for consumers.

(e) Applicability of this subchapter

(1) In general

A remittance transfer that is not an electronic fund transfer, as defined in section 1693a of this title, shall not be subject to any of the provisions of sections 1693c through 1693k of this title. A remittance transfer that is an electronic fund transfer, as defined in section 1693a of this title, shall be subject to all provisions of this subchapter, except for section 1693f of this title, that are otherwise applicable to electronic fund transfers under this subchapter.

(2) Rule of construction

Nothing in this section shall be construed—

(A) to affect the application to any transaction, to any remittance provider, or to any other person of any of the provisions of subchapter II of chapter 53 of title 31, section 1829b of title 12, or chapter 2 of title I of Public Law 91–508 (12 U.S.C. 1951–1959), or any regulations promulgated thereunder; or

(B) to cause any fund transfer that would not otherwise be treated as such under paragraph (1) to be treated as an electronic fund transfer, or as otherwise subject to this subchapter, for the purposes of any of the provisions referred to in subparagraph (A) or any regulations promulgated thereunder.

(f) Acts of agents

(1) In general

A remittance transfer provider shall be liable for any violation of this section by any agent, authorized delegate, or person affiliated with such provider, when such agent, authorized delegate, or affiliate acts for that remittance transfer provider.

(2) Obligations of remittance transfer providers

The Bureau shall prescribe rules to implement appropriate standards or conditions of, liability of a remittance transfer provider, including a provider who acts through an agent or authorized delegate. An agency charged with enforcing the requirements of this section, or rules prescribed by the Bureau under this section, may consider, in any action or other proceeding against a remittance transfer provider, the extent to which the provider had established and maintained policies or procedures for compliance, including policies, procedures, or other appropriate oversight measures designed to assure compliance by an agent or authorized delegate acting for such provider.

(g) Definitions

As used in this section—

(1) the term "designated recipient" means any person located in a foreign country and identified by the sender as the authorized recipient of a remittance transfer to be made by a remittance transfer provider, except that a designated recipient shall not be deemed to be a consumer for purposes of this chapter;

(2) the term "remittance transfer"—

(A) means the electronic (as defined in section 106(2) of the Electronic Signatures in Global and National Commerce Act (15 U.S.C. 7006(2))) transfer of funds requested by a sender located in any State to a designated recipient that is initiated by a remittance transfer provider, whether or not the sender holds an account with the remittance transfer provider or whether or not the remittance transfer is also an electronic fund transfer, as defined in section 1693a of this title; and

(B) does not include a transfer described in subparagraph (A) in an amount that is equal to or lesser than the amount of a small-value transaction determined, by rule, to be excluded from the requirements under section 1693d(a) of this title;

(3) the term "remittance transfer provider" means any person or financial institution that provides remittance transfers for a consumer in the normal course of its business, whether or not the consumer holds an account with such person or financial institution; and

(4) the term "sender" means a consumer who requests a remittance provider to send a remittance transfer for the consumer to a designated recipient.

(Pub. L. 90–321, title IX, §919, as added and amended Pub. L. 111–203, title X, §§1073(a)(4), 1084(1), July 21, 2010, 124 Stat. 2060, 2081.)

EDITORIAL NOTES

REFERENCES IN TEXT

The Electronic Signatures in Global and National Commerce Act, referred to in subsec. (a)(3)(B), is Pub. L. 106–229, June 30, 2000, 114 Stat. 464, which is classified principally to chapter 96 (§7001 et seq.) of this title. For complete classification of this Act to the Code, see Short Title note set out under section 7001 of this title and Tables.

Chapter 2 of title I of Public Law 91–508, referred to in subsec. (e)(2)(A), is chapter 2 (§§121–129) of title I of Pub. L. 91–508, Oct. 26, 1970, 84 Stat. 1116, which is classified generally to chapter 21 (§1951 et seq.) of Title 12, Banks and Banking. For complete classification of chapter 2 of title I of the Act to the Code, see Tables.

PRIOR PROVISIONS

A prior section 919 of Pub. L. 90–321 was renumbered section 921 and is classified to section 1693p of this title.

Another prior section 919 of Pub. L. 90–321 was renumbered section 922 and is classified to section 1693q of this title.

AMENDMENTS

2010—Pub. L. 111–203, §1084(1), substituted "Bureau" for "Board" wherever appearing.

STATUTORY NOTES AND RELATED SUBSIDIARIES

EFFECTIVE DATE OF 2010 AMENDMENT

Amendment by section 1084(1) of Pub. L. 111–203 effective on the designated transfer date, see section 1100H of Pub. L. 111–203, set out as a note under section 552a of Title 5, Government Organization and Employees.

EFFECTIVE DATE

Section effective 1 day after July 21, 2010, except as otherwise provided, see section 4 of Pub. L. 111–203, set out as a note under section 5301 of Title 12, Banks and Banking.

§1693o–2. Reasonable fees and rules for payment card transactions

(a) Reasonable interchange transaction fees for electronic debit transactions

(1) Regulatory authority over interchange transaction fees

The Board may prescribe regulations, pursuant to section 553 of title 5, regarding any interchange transaction fee that an issuer may receive or charge with respect to an electronic debit transaction, to implement this subsection (including related definitions), and to prevent circumvention or evasion of this subsection.

(2) Reasonable interchange transaction fees

The amount of any interchange transaction fee that an issuer may receive or charge with respect to an electronic debit transaction shall be reasonable and proportional to the cost incurred by the issuer with respect to the transaction.

(3) Rulemaking required

(A) In general

The Board shall prescribe regulations in final form not later than 9 months after July 21, 2010, to establish standards for assessing whether the amount of any interchange transaction fee described in paragraph (2) is reasonable and proportional to the cost incurred by the issuer with respect to the transaction.

(B) Information collection

The Board may require any issuer (or agent of an issuer) or payment card network to provide the Board with such information as may be necessary to carry out the provisions of this subsection and the Board, in issuing rules under subparagraph (A) and on at least a bi-annual basis thereafter, shall disclose such aggregate or summary information concerning the costs incurred, and interchange transaction fees charged or received, by issuers or payment card networks in connection with the authorization, clearance or settlement of electronic debit transactions as the Board considers appropriate and in the public interest.

(4) Considerations; consultation

In prescribing regulations under paragraph (3)(A), the Board shall—
   (A) consider the functional similarity between—
      (i) electronic debit transactions; and
      (ii) checking transactions that are required within the Federal Reserve bank system to clear at par;

   (B) distinguish between—
      (i) the incremental cost incurred by an issuer for the role of the issuer in the authorization, clearance, or settlement of a particular electronic debit transaction, which cost shall be considered under paragraph (2); and
      (ii) other costs incurred by an issuer which are not specific to a particular electronic debit transaction, which costs shall not be considered under paragraph (2); and

   (C) consult, as appropriate, with the Comptroller of the Currency, the Board of Directors of the Federal Deposit Insurance Corporation, the Director of the Office of Thrift Supervision, the National Credit Union Administration Board, the Administrator of the Small Business Administration, and the Director of the Bureau of Consumer Financial Protection.

(5) Adjustments to interchange transaction fees for fraud prevention costs

(A) Adjustments

The Board may allow for an adjustment to the fee amount received or charged by an issuer under paragraph (2), if—
      (i) such adjustment is reasonably necessary to make allowance for costs incurred by the issuer in preventing fraud in relation to electronic debit transactions involving that issuer; and
      (ii) the issuer complies with the fraud-related standards established by the Board under subparagraph (B), which standards shall—
         (I) be designed to ensure that any fraud-related adjustment of the issuer is limited to the amount described in clause (i) and takes into account any fraud-related reimbursements (including amounts from charge-backs) received from consumers, merchants, or payment card networks in relation to electronic debit transactions involving the issuer; and
         (II) require issuers to take effective steps to reduce the occurrence of, and costs from, fraud in relation to electronic debit transactions, including through the development and implementation of cost-effective fraud prevention technology.

(B) Rulemaking required

(i) In general

The Board shall prescribe regulations in final form not later than 9 months after July 21, 2010, to establish standards for making adjustments under this paragraph.

(ii) Factors for consideration

In issuing the standards and prescribing regulations under this paragraph, the Board shall consider—
      (I) the nature, type, and occurrence of fraud in electronic debit transactions;

(II) the extent to which the occurrence of fraud depends on whether authorization in an electronic debit transaction is based on signature, PIN, or other means;

(III) the available and economical means by which fraud on electronic debit transactions may be reduced;

(IV) the fraud prevention and data security costs expended by each party involved in electronic debit transactions (including consumers, persons who accept debit cards as a form of payment, financial institutions, retailers and payment card networks);

(V) the costs of fraudulent transactions absorbed by each party involved in such transactions (including consumers, persons who accept debit cards as a form of payment, financial institutions, retailers and payment card networks);

(VI) the extent to which interchange transaction fees have in the past reduced or increased incentives for parties involved in electronic debit transactions to reduce fraud on such transactions; and

(VII) such other factors as the Board considers appropriate.

(6) Exemption for small issuers

(A) In general

This subsection shall not apply to any issuer that, together with its affiliates, has assets of less than $10,000,000,000, and the Board shall exempt such issuers from regulations prescribed under paragraph (3)(A).

(B) Definition

For purposes of this paragraph, the term "issuer" shall be limited to the person holding the asset account that is debited through an electronic debit transaction.

(7) Exemption for government-administered payment programs and reloadable prepaid cards

(A) In general

This subsection shall not apply to an interchange transaction fee charged or received with respect to an electronic debit transaction in which a person uses—

(i) a debit card or general-use prepaid card that has been provided to a person pursuant to a Federal, State or local government-administered payment program, in which the person may only use the debit card or general-use prepaid card to transfer or debit funds, monetary value, or other assets that have been provided pursuant to such program; or

(ii) a plastic card, payment code, or device that is—

(I) linked to funds, monetary value, or assets which are purchased or loaded on a prepaid basis;

(II) not issued or approved for use to access or debit any account held by or for the benefit of the card holder (other than a subaccount or other method of recording or tracking funds purchased or loaded on the card on a prepaid basis);

(III) redeemable at multiple, unaffiliated merchants or service providers, or automated teller machines;

(IV) used to transfer or debit funds, monetary value, or other assets; and

(V) reloadable and not marketed or labeled as a gift card or gift certificate.

(B) Exception

Notwithstanding subparagraph (A), after the end of the 1-year period beginning on the effective date provided in paragraph (9), this subsection shall apply to an interchange transaction fee charged or received with respect to an electronic debit transaction described in subparagraph (A)(i) in which a person uses a general-use prepaid card, or an electronic debit transaction described in subparagraph (A)(ii), if any of the following fees may be charged to a person with respect to the card:

(i) A fee for an overdraft, including a shortage of funds or a transaction processed for an amount exceeding the account balance.

(ii) A fee imposed by the issuer for the first withdrawal per month from an automated teller machine that is part of the issuer's designated automated teller machine network.

(C) Definition

For purposes of subparagraph (B), the term "designated automated teller machine network" means either—

(i) all automated teller machines identified in the name of the issuer; or

(ii) any network of automated teller machines identified by the issuer that provides reasonable and convenient access to the issuer's customers.

(D) Reporting

Beginning 12 months after July 21, 2010, the Board shall annually provide a report to the Congress regarding —

(i) the prevalence of the use of general-use prepaid cards in Federal, State or local government-administered payment programs; and

(ii) the interchange transaction fees and cardholder fees charged with respect to the use of such general-use prepaid cards.

(8) Regulatory authority over network fees

(A) In general

The Board may prescribe regulations, pursuant to section 553 of title 5, regarding any network fee.

(B) Limitation

The authority under subparagraph (A) to prescribe regulations shall be limited to regulations to ensure that—

(i) a network fee is not used to directly or indirectly compensate an issuer with respect to an electronic debit transaction; and

(ii) a network fee is not used to circumvent or evade the restrictions of this subsection and regulations prescribed under such subsection.

(C) Rulemaking required

The Board shall prescribe regulations in final form before the end of the 9-month period beginning on July 21, 2010, to carry out the authorities provided under subparagraph (A).

(9) Effective date

This subsection shall take effect at the end of the 12-month period beginning on July 21, 2010.

(b) Limitation on payment card network restrictions

(1) Prohibitions against exclusivity arrangements

(A) No exclusive network

The Board shall, before the end of the 1-year period beginning on July 21, 2010, prescribe regulations providing that an issuer or payment card network shall not directly or through any agent, processor, or licensed member of a payment card network, by contract, requirement, condition, penalty, or otherwise, restrict the number of payment card networks on which an electronic debit transaction may be processed to—

(i) 1 such network; or

(ii) 2 or more such networks which are owned, controlled, or otherwise operated by —

(I) affiliated persons; or

(II) networks affiliated with such issuer.

(B) No routing restrictions

The Board shall, before the end of the 1-year period beginning on July 21, 2010, prescribe regulations providing that an issuer or payment card network shall not, directly or through any agent, processor, or licensed member of the network, by contract, requirement, condition, penalty, or otherwise, inhibit the ability of any person who accepts debit cards for payments to direct the routing of electronic debit transactions for processing over any payment card network that may process such transactions.

(2) Limitation on restrictions on offering discounts for use of a form of payment

(A) In general

A payment card network shall not, directly or through any agent, processor, or licensed member of the network, by contract, requirement, condition, penalty, or otherwise, inhibit the ability of any person to provide a discount or in-kind incentive for payment by the use of cash, checks, debit cards, or credit cards to the extent that—

(i) in the case of a discount or in-kind incentive for payment by the use of debit cards, the discount or in-kind incentive does not differentiate on the basis of the issuer or the payment card network;

(ii) in the case of a discount or in-kind incentive for payment by the use of credit cards, the discount or in-kind incentive does not differentiate on the basis of the issuer or the payment card network; and

(iii) to the extent required by Federal law and applicable State law, such discount or in-kind incentive is offered to all prospective buyers and disclosed clearly and conspicuously.

(B) Lawful discounts

For purposes of this paragraph, the network may not penalize any person for the providing of a discount that is in compliance with Federal law and applicable State law.

(3) Limitation on restrictions on setting transaction minimums or maximums

(A) In general

A payment card network shall not, directly or through any agent, processor, or licensed member of the network, by contract, requirement, condition, penalty, or otherwise, inhibit the ability—

(i) of any person to set a minimum dollar value for the acceptance by that person of credit cards, to the extent that—

(I) such minimum dollar value does not differentiate between issuers or between payment card networks; and

(II) such minimum dollar value does not exceed $10.00; or

(ii) of any Federal agency or institution of higher education to set a maximum dollar value for the acceptance by that Federal agency or institution of higher education of credit cards, to the extent that such maximum dollar value does not differentiate between issuers or between payment card networks.

(B) Increase in minimum dollar amount

The Board may, by regulation prescribed pursuant to section 553 of title 5, increase the amount of the dollar value listed in subparagraph (A)(i)(II).

(4) Rule of construction

No provision of this subsection shall be construed to authorize any person—

(A) to discriminate between debit cards within a payment card network on the basis of the issuer that issued the debit card; or

(B) to discriminate between credit cards within a payment card network on the basis of the issuer that issued the credit card.

(c) Definitions

For purposes of this section, the following definitions shall apply:

(1) Affiliate

The term "affiliate" means any company that controls, is controlled by, or is under common control with another company.

(2) Debit card

The term "debit card"—

(A) means any card, or other payment code or device, issued or approved for use through a payment card network to debit an asset account (regardless of the purpose for which the account is established), whether authorization is based on signature, PIN, or other means;

(B) includes a general-use prepaid card, as that term is defined in section 1693l–1(a)(2)(A) of this title; and

(C) does not include paper checks.

(3) Credit card

The term "credit card" has the same meaning as in section 1602 of this title.

(4) Discount

The term "discount"—

(A) means a reduction made from the price that customers are informed is the regular price; and

(B) does not include any means of increasing the price that customers are informed is the regular price.

(5) Electronic debit transaction

The term "electronic debit transaction" means a transaction in which a person uses a debit card.

(6) Federal agency

The term "Federal agency" means—

(A) an agency (as defined in section 101 of title 31); and

(B) a Government corporation (as defined in section 103 of title 5).

(7) Institution of higher education

The term "institution of higher education" has the same meaning as in 1001 [1] and 1002 of title 20.

(8) Interchange transaction fee

The term "interchange transaction fee" means any fee established, charged or received by a payment card network for the purpose of compensating an issuer for its involvement in an electronic debit transaction.

(9) Issuer

The term "issuer" means any person who issues a debit card, or credit card, or the agent of such person with respect to such card.

(10) Network fee

The term "network fee" means any fee charged and received by a payment card network with respect to an electronic debit transaction, other than an interchange transaction fee.

(11) Payment card network

The term "payment card network" means an entity that directly, or through licensed members, processors, or agents, provides the proprietary services, infrastructure, and software that route information and data to conduct debit card or credit card transaction authorization, clearance, and settlement, and that a person uses in order to accept as a form of payment a brand of debit card, credit card or other device that may be used to carry out debit or credit transactions.

(d) Enforcement

(1) In general

Compliance with the requirements imposed under this section shall be enforced under section 1693o of this title.

(2) Exception

Sections 1693m and 1693n of this title shall not apply with respect to this section or the requirements imposed pursuant to this section.

(Pub. L. 90–321, title IX, §920, as added Pub. L. 111–203, title X, §1075(a)(2), July 21, 2010, 124 Stat. 2068.)

EDITORIAL NOTES

PRIOR PROVISIONS

A prior section 920 of Pub. L. 90–321 was renumbered section 921 and is classified to section 1693p of this title.

Two other prior sections 920 of Pub. L. 90–321 were renumbered section 922 and are classified to sections 1693q and 1693r of this title.

STATUTORY NOTES AND RELATED SUBSIDIARIES

EFFECTIVE DATE

Section effective 1 day after July 21, 2010, except as otherwise provided, see section 4 of Pub. L. 111–203, set out as a note under section 5301 of Title 12, Banks and Banking.

[1] So in original. Probably should be preceded by "sections".

§1693p. Reports to Congress

(a) Not later than twelve months after the effective date of this subchapter and at one-year intervals thereafter, the Bureau shall make reports to the Congress concerning the administration of its functions under this subchapter, including such recommendations as the Bureau deems necessary and appropriate. In addition, each report of the Bureau shall include its assessment of the extent to which compliance with this subchapter is being achieved, and a summary of the enforcement actions taken under section 1693o [1] of this title. In such report, the Bureau shall particularly address the effects of this subchapter on the costs and benefits to financial institutions and consumers, on competition, on the introduction of new technology, on the operations of financial institutions, and on the adequacy of consumer protection.

(b) In the exercise of its functions under this subchapter, the Bureau may obtain upon request the views of any other Federal agency which, in the judgment of the Bureau, exercises regulatory or supervisory functions with respect to any class of persons subject to this subchapter.

(Pub. L. 90–321, title IX, §921, formerly §918, as added Pub. L. 95–630, title XX, §2001, Nov. 10, 1978, 92 Stat. 3740; amended Pub. L. 97–375, title II, §209(a), Dec. 21, 1982, 96 Stat. 1825; renumbered §919, Pub. L. 111–24, title IV, §401(1), May 22, 2009, 123 Stat. 1751; renumbered §920, renumbered §921, and amended Pub. L. 111–203, title X, §§1073(a)(3), 1075(a)(1), 1084(1), July 21, 2010, 124 Stat. 2060, 2068, 2081.)

EDITORIAL NOTES

REFERENCES IN TEXT

For effective date of this subchapter, referred to in subsec. (a), see section 921 of Pub. L. 90–321, set out as an Effective Date note under section 1693 of this title.

Section 1693o of this title, referred to in subsec. (a), was in the original "section 917 of this title", and was translated as meaning section 918 of title I of Pub. L. 90–321 to reflect the probable intent of Congress and the renumbering of section 917 of title I of Pub. L. 90–321 as section 918 by Pub. L. 111–24, title IV, §401(1), May 22, 2009, 123 Stat. 1751.

CODIFICATION

Renumbering of section 918 of Pub. L. 90–321 as section 919 by section 401(1) of Pub. L. 111–24 was executed prior to the renumberings of section 919 of Pub. L. 90–321 as section 920 and then as section 921 by sections 1073(a)(3) and 1075(a)(1) of Pub. L. 111–203 as the probable intent of Congress, notwithstanding section 403 of Pub. L. 111–24, set out as an Effective Date note under section 1693l–1 of this title and section 4 of Pub. L. 111–203, set out as an Effective Date note under section 5301 of Title 12, Banks and Banking, which provided that the renumbering by Pub. L. 111–24 was effective 15 months after May 22, 2009, and the renumberings by Pub. L. 111–203 were effective 1 day after July 21, 2010.

Two prior sections 921 of Pub. L. 90–321 were renumbered section 922 and are classified to sections 1693q and 1693r of this title.

Another prior section 921 of Pub. L. 90–321 was renumbered section 923 and is classified as an Effective Date note under section 1693 of this title.

AMENDMENTS

2010—Pub. L. 111–203, §1084(1), substituted "Bureau" for "Board" wherever appearing.

1982—Subsec. (a). Pub. L. 97–375 struck out requirement that the Attorney General make a report on the same terms as the Board, and that such report also contain an analysis of the impact of this subchapter on the operation, workload, and efficiency of the Federal courts, and substituted "necessary and appropriate" for "necessary or appropriate".

STATUTORY NOTES AND RELATED SUBSIDIARIES

EFFECTIVE DATE OF 2010 AMENDMENT

Amendment by section 1084(1) of Pub. L. 111–203 effective on the designated transfer date, see section 1100H of Pub. L. 111–203, set out as a note under section 552a of Title 5, Government Organization and Employees.

---

¹ *See References in Text note below.*

---

§1693q. Relation to State laws

This subchapter does not annul, alter, or affect the laws of any State relating to electronic fund transfers, dormancy fees, inactivity charges or fees, service fees, or expiration dates of gift certificates, store gift cards, or general-use prepaid cards, except to the extent that those laws are inconsistent with the provisions of this subchapter, and then only to the extent of the inconsistency. A State law is not inconsistent with this subchapter if the protection such law affords any consumer is greater than the protection afforded by this subchapter. The Bureau shall, upon its own motion or upon the request of any financial institution, State, or other interested party, submitted in accordance with procedures prescribed in regulations of the Bureau, determine whether a State requirement is inconsistent or affords greater protection. If the Bureau determines that a State requirement is inconsistent, financial institutions shall incur no liability under the law of that State for a good faith failure to comply with that law, notwithstanding that such determination is subsequently amended, rescinded, or determined by judicial or other authority to be invalid for any reason. This subchapter does not extend the applicability of any such law to any class of persons or transactions to which it would not otherwise apply.

(Pub. L. 90–321, title IX, §922, formerly §919, as added Pub. L. 95–630, title XX, §2001, Nov. 10, 1978, 92 Stat. 3741; renumbered §920 and amended Pub. L. 111–24, title IV, §§401(1), 402, May 22, 2009, 123 Stat. 1751, 1754; renumbered §921, renumbered §922, and amended Pub. L. 111–203, title X, §§1073(a)(3), 1075(a)(1), 1084(1), July 21, 2010, 124 Stat. 2060, 2068, 2081.)

EDITORIAL NOTES

CODIFICATION

Another section 922 of Pub. L. 90–321 is classified to section 1693r of this title.

Renumbering of section 919 of Pub. L. 90–321 as section 920 by section 401(1) of Pub. L. 111–24 was executed prior to the renumberings of section 920 of Pub. L. 90–321 as section 921 and then as section 922 by sections 1073(a)(3) and 1075(a)(1) of Pub. L. 111–203 as the probable intent of Congress, notwithstanding section 403 of Pub. L. 111–24, set out as an Effective Date note under section 1693l–1 of this title and section 4 of Pub. L. 111–203, set out as an Effective Date note under section 5301 of Title 12, Banks and Banking, which provided that the renumbering by Pub. L. 111–24 was effective 15 months after May 22, 2009, and the renumberings by Pub. L. 111–203 were effective 1 day after July 21, 2010.

PRIOR PROVISIONS

A prior section 922 of Pub. L. 90–321 was renumbered section 923 and is classified as an Effective Date note under section 1693 of this title.

AMENDMENTS

2010—Pub. L. 111–203, §1084(1), substituted "Bureau" for "Board" wherever appearing.

2009—Pub. L. 111–24, §402, inserted "dormancy fees, inactivity charges or fees, service fees, or expiration dates of gift certificates, store gift cards, or general-use prepaid cards," after "electronic fund transfers,".

STATUTORY NOTES AND RELATED SUBSIDIARIES

EFFECTIVE DATE OF 2010 AMENDMENT

Amendment by section 1084(1) of Pub. L. 111–203 effective on the designated transfer date, see section 1100H of Pub. L. 111–203, set out as a note under section 552a of Title 5, Government Organization and Employees.

EFFECTIVE DATE OF 2009 AMENDMENT

Amendment by Pub. L. 111–24 effective 15 months after May 22, 2009, see section 403 of Pub. L. 111–24, set out as an Effective Date note under section 1693l–1 of this title.

§1693r. Exemption for State regulation

The Bureau shall by regulation exempt from the requirements of this subchapter any class of electronic fund transfers within any State if the Bureau determines that under the law of that State that class of electronic fund transfers is subject to requirements substantially similar to those imposed by this subchapter, and that there is adequate provision for enforcement.

(Pub. L. 90–321, title IX, §922, formerly §920, as added Pub. L. 95–630, title XX, §2001, Nov. 10, 1978, 92 Stat. 3741; renumbered §921, Pub. L. 111–24, title IV, §401(1), May 22, 2009, 123 Stat. 1751; renumbered §922 and amended Pub. L. 111–203, title X, §§1073(a)(3), 1084(1), July 21, 2010, 124 Stat. 2060, 2081.)

EDITORIAL NOTES

CODIFICATION

Another section 922 of Pub. L. 90–321 is classified to section 1693q of this title.

Renumbering of section 920 of Pub. L. 90–321 as section 921 by section 401(1) of Pub. L. 111–24 was executed prior to the renumbering of section 921 of Pub. L. 90–321 as section 922 by section 1073(a)(3) of Pub. L. 111–203 as the probable intent of Congress, notwithstanding section 403 of Pub. L. 111–24, set out as an Effective Date note under section 1693l–1 of this title and section 4 of Pub. L. 111–203, set out as an Effective Date note under section 5301 of Title 12, Banks and Banking, which provided that the renumbering by Pub. L. 111–24 was effective 15 months after May 22, 2009, and the renumbering by Pub. L. 111–203 was effective 1 day after July 21, 2010.

PRIOR PROVISIONS

A prior section 922 of Pub. L. 90–321 was renumbered section 923 and is classified as an Effective Date note under section 1693 of this title.

AMENDMENTS

2010—Pub. L. 111–203, §1084(1), substituted "Bureau" for "Board" in two places.

STATUTORY NOTES AND RELATED SUBSIDIARIES

EFFECTIVE DATE OF 2010 AMENDMENT

Amendment by section 1084(1) of Pub. L. 111–203 effective on the designated transfer date, see section 1100H of Pub. L. 111–203, set out as a note under section 552a of Title 5, Government Organization and Employees.

This marks the end of the Electronic Fund Transfer Act
15 U.S.C. §§ 1693-1693r

This edition is revised and current as of January 2024

2024 | Applied Legal Publications

Made in the USA
Columbia, SC
15 August 2024

4237aba9-4cb2-4cf2-b49a-1292016be783R01